SAGE was founded in 1965 by Sara Miller McCune to support the dissemination of usable knowledge by publishing innovative and high-quality research and teaching content. Today, we publish over 900 journals, including those of more than 400 learned societies, more than 800 new books per year, and a growing range of library products including archives, data, case studies, reports, and video. SAGE remains majority-owned by our founder, and after Sara's lifetime will become owned by a charitable trust that secures our continued independence.

Los Angeles | London | New Delhi | Singapore | Washington DC | Melbourne

CRITICAL THEMES *in* ENVIRONMENTAL HISTORY OF INDIA

Thank you for choosing a SAGE product!
If you have any comment, observation or feedback,
I would like to personally hear from you.

Please write to me at **contactceo@sagepub.in**

Vivek Mehra, Managing Director and CEO, SAGE India.

Bulk Sales

SAGE India offers special discounts
for purchase of books in bulk.
We also make available special imprints
and excerpts from our books on demand.

For orders and enquiries, write to us at

Marketing Department
SAGE Publications India Pvt Ltd
B1/I-1, Mohan Cooperative Industrial Area
Mathura Road, Post Bag 7
New Delhi 110044, India

E-mail us at **marketing@sagepub.in**

Subscribe to our mailing list
Write to **marketing@sagepub.in**

This book is also available as an e-book.

CRITICAL THEMES *in* ENVIRONMENTAL HISTORY OF INDIA

EDITED BY

RANJAN CHAKRABARTI

Los Angeles | London | New Delhi
Singapore | Washington DC | Melbourne

First published in 2020 by

 SAGE Publications India Pvt Ltd
B1/I-1 Mohan Cooperative Industrial Area
Mathura Road, New Delhi 110 044, India
www.sagepub.in

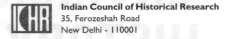 **Indian Council of Historical Research**
35, Ferozeshah Road
New Delhi - 110001

SAGE Publications Inc
2455 Teller Road
Thousand Oaks, California 91320, USA

SAGE Publications Ltd
1 Oliver's Yard, 55 City Road
London EC1Y 1SP, United Kingdom

SAGE Publications Asia-Pacific Pte Ltd
18 Cross Street #10-10/11/12
China Square Central
Singapore 048423

Published by Vivek Mehra for SAGE Publications India Pvt Ltd. Typeset in 10/12.5 pt ITC Stone Serif by AG Infographics, Delhi.

Library of Congress Cataloging-in-Publication Data

Names: Chakrabarti, Ranjan, editor. | Sage Publications.
Title: Critical themes in environmental history of India / edited by Ranjan Chakrabarti.
Description: Thousand Oaks, California : SAGE Publications India Pvt Ltd, 2020. | Includes bibliographical
    references and index.
Identifiers: LCCN 2020008930 (print) | LCCN 2020008931 (ebook) | ISBN 9789353883140 (Hardback) |
    ISBN 9789353883157 (ePub) | ISBN 9789353883164 (eBook)
Subjects: LCSH: Human ecology–India–History. | Environmental policy–India. | Geographical perception–India.
Classification: LCC GF661 .C75 2020 (print) | LCC GF661 (ebook) | DDC 333.70954–dc23
LC record available at https://lccn.loc.gov/2020008930
LC ebook record available at https://lccn.loc.gov/2020008931

ISBN: 978-93-5388-314-0 (HB)

SAGE Team: Rajesh Dey, Vandana Gupta and Rajinder Kaur

Contents

SECTION I: ENVIRONMENTAL HISTORY OF INDIA—METHODOLOGY AND SCOPE

SECTION II: RIVERS AND WATER

SECTION III: FORESTS, LAND USE, WILDLIFE AND ANIMALS

SECTION IV: CLIMATE AND DISASTER

Foreword

The research project titled 'Environmental History of India' was commenced by the Indian Council of Historical Research (ICHR) on the recommendations of a working group of historians in the year 2015, constituted by my predecessor Professor Y. Sudershan Rao. The project was planned in seven volumes with a separate editor for each volume. Dr Nanditha Krishna, being a member of the Council, was requested to take up the responsibility to monitor the project in the capacity as the Member Incharge. The commencement of the publication of the collection of essays under the project 'Environmental History of India', ends a long period of gestation and presents before us the first fruits of that enterprise.

As far as I understand, environmental history in India has generated a rich literature on forests, wildlife, human–animal conflict, tribal rights and commercial degradation, displacement and development, pastoralism and desertification, famine and disease, sedentarism and mobility, wildness and civility, and the ecology versus equity debate. Further, it is always about human interaction with the natural world, or to put it in another way, it studies the interaction between culture and nature. Here, the principal goal of environmental history is to deepen our understanding of how humans have been affected by the natural environment in the past, and also as to how they have affected that environment and with what results.

I am grateful to the editor of the volume, Professor Ranjan Chakrabarti, who has pointed out in an excellent introduction the highlights of the present collection of essays.

We look forward to the early publication of the subsequent volumes in this series. Along with Professor Ranjan Chakrabarti, I also thank the expert authors who have contributed chapters for the current volume and Dr Nanditha Krishna, Member Incharge of the project, for having successfully completed Volume 1 of the project.

Also, I compliment the ICHR officers—Dr Rajesh Kumar, Director (Journal, Publication & Library), Dr Md Naushad Ali, Deputy Director (Publication) and Dr Saurabh Kumar Mishra, Deputy Director (Journal)—for extending their services in bringing out this publication with care and attention. Last but not least, I thank Mr Rajesh Dey and his team at SAGE Publications for their help in bringing out the publication in a neat and presentable format.

Arvind P. Jamkhedkar
Chairman, ICHR

Preface

Fernand Braudel, a well-known French historian and a leader of the Annales school, made a laudable attempt to write a total history of the Mediterranean world, giving adequate importance to the role of geography and climate behind history in a *longue duree* context (*The Mediterranean and the Mediterranean World in the Age of Philip II*, New York: Harper Colophon Books, 1972). Unfortunately, there is no such Braudelian history of India yet. There may be a few notable exceptions at the regional level (Iftekhar Iqbal, *The Bengal Delta: Ecology, State and Social Change 1840–1943*, London: Palgrave, 2010; Richard Eaton, *The Rise of Islam and the Bengal Frontier, 1204–1760*, Los Angeles: University of California Press,1973). Historians who practised history of India or colonial Bengal mostly thought of history in ideological and political lines. They wrote hundreds of pages to understand the political forces that led to the Battles of Plassey and Buxer but did not care to historicize the riverscape, waterscape, landscape, climate and the natural world in the midst of which all these political events were unfolding (cf. Rajat Kanta Ray, *Palashir Sarajantra O Sekaler Samaj* (Bengali), Kolkata: Ananda Publishers, 1994; S. Chaudhary, *The Prelude to Empire: Plassey Revolution of 1757*, Delhi: Manohar Publishers, 2000; B. K. Gupta, *Sirajuddaulah and the East India Company, 1756–1757*, Lieden: E.J.Brill, 1966, etc.).

Alfred Crosby, the author of *The Columbian Exchange: Biological and Cultural Consequences of 1492* (Westport: Greenwood Publishing Group,1972), chronicles a parallel development that transformed global ecology forever—the trans-Atlantic movement of plants and animals in which Europe transported staple crops such as wheat, oats and fruits along with pigs, horses and goats to the Americas, where they were unknown and sent back to Europe the New World products like maize, potatoes and beans. As a result of the discovery of America, the continents on the opposite sides of the Atlantic, which were so different, began to become biologically and ecologically alike. Fernand Braudel and Alfred Crosby were able to raise new and fundamental questions because they conceived history, unlike many of us, in ecological, biological and cultural terms. The geographers and geologists have revealed how the Bengal Delta had been formed through the ages by the action of rivers. It was historians' turn to ascertain how much of Bengal's political economy, its production, crop pattern, inland and overseas trade, openness, demographic pattern, culture and economy were shaped by its river systems and hydrology. But it is surprising enough to note that historians remained by and large reluctant to be drawn into these important questions. As a result, there is a serious slippage and silence in India's history relating to the ecological and historical importance of rivers. The present volume and the ICHR series proposes to reverse the trend and encourage young researchers to write Indian history from a fresh perspective. In the context of Indian history, I would prefer to argue along with Donald Worster (*Nature's Economy: A History of Ecological Ideas*, Cambridge: Cambridge University Press, 1977; ed., *The Ends of the Earth*, Cambridge: Cambridge University Press, 1988) to make space in history books for the voice of nature to be heard distinctly.

From the early Indus Valley Civilization, named after the river system in which it was located, through invasions from Asia and Europe to the division of India and Pakistan in 1947, and finally the human tragedy caused by the tsunami of December 2004, the people of South Asia have influenced, and been influenced by, their ecological surroundings in many ways.

The historiography of environmental history of India or South Asia is fast expanding, and there seems to be no dearth of books in this field. However, a comprehensive account of the environmental history of India is missing. Christopher Hill (*South Asia: An Environmental History*, Santa Barbara: ABC-Cleo, 2008) made an attempt to present a total chronological history of India, Pakistan, Bangladesh, Nepal and Sri Lanka from the perspective of the mutual relationship between humankind and the environment. He reveals how the civilizations of this geographically diverse region came into existence through their interactions with the physical environment—a relationship with particularly strong social and spiritual dimensions because of the interdependence of the predominantly agrarian population and the land.

His focus swings from ancient irrigation techniques and adjustment of peasant societies to the environment and the forceful thrust of British imperialism on the natural world, the effect of post-colonial technology and the interaction of religion with ecological issues. But the scope of the work, although laudable, is too large and ambitious to handle in a single volume as attempted by the author.

Sometime in 2016, Professor Y. Sudershan Rao, the then Chairman of ICHR and Dr Nanditha Krishna, the then member of ICHR and a noted environmental historian, approached me and enquired if I can be associated with a project of compiling a multi-volume environmental history of India from the ICHR. I gladly accepted their proposal. Professor Rao was very quick to respond and initiated the ICHR Special Project on Environmental History of India with the objective of publishing a seven-volume series on the same subject. It was decided by the Advisory/Monitoring Committee that each volume will be edited by a senior scholar, and the present author will act as the General Editor or Series Editor. Accordingly, the following themes and titles for the seven volumes were proposed:

1. *Critical Themes in Environmental History of India*, ICHR Series, Volume 1
2. *Forests and Wildlife*, ICHR Series, Volume 2
3. *Environmental History of Water*, ICHR Series, Volume 3
4. *History of Environmental Disasters*, ICHR Series, Volume 4
5. *Urbanization and Environment*, ICHR Series, Volume 5
6. *Environment and Culture*, ICHR Series, Volume 6
7. Land Use, Agriculture and Environment, ICHR Series, Volume 7

The series opens with the present volume titled *Critical Themes in Environmental History of India*. This collection of essays addresses some of the fundamental questions or select critical themes most relevant and fundamental to the very discipline of environmental history.

As scholars from diverse disciplinary backgrounds have contributed to the field of environmental history, it has acquired an interdisciplinary character and remained an open-ended subject. Within the discipline of history, 'environmental history' remains universally acknowledged as a significant area of inquiry but without specific disciplinary canons or methodological guidelines. This is one major vacuum that this volume intends to fill in. Environmental history shares a very porous border with economic and social histories, history of science and technology and with various other sub-fields of history. Environmental historians, historical geographers and historical ecologists are usually engaged with similar sorts of questions, although their methodologies may vary.

The choice of the subject of research is the unique autonomy of historians. The present work brings under its purview a number of emerging critical themes in environmental history such as rivers, water bodies and water, forest, land use and wildlife, and the issue of the history of climate. Water is always a symbol of social, economic and political relationships—a barometer of the extent to which identity, power and resources are shared. In recent times, we are witnessing a growing concern over water. The current environmental agenda, including the questions associated with climate change, is related to the question of sustainable management of water. Forest, land use and wildlife has been a consistent theme in environmental history of India, and the present volume has incorporated four chapters on all the major issues related to this critical theme. The final section of the book throws light on climate and disaster and reveals how climatic changes exert a significant influence on the pattern of historical developments.

The volume brings together many leading scholars sharing a common interest in environmental history. It attempts to address the broad areas of environmental concern in the Indian context and to enquire into the complex patterns of the human–nature interaction.

Ranjan Chakrabarti

Acknowledgements

In the course of preparing this volume, I have accumulated a great many debts of gratitude. I would like to express my sincere thanks to Professor Y. Sudershan Rao and Dr Nanditha Krishna for their personal care and initiative to keep the project going. I am particularly grateful to Professor Arvind P. Jamkhedkar, the Chairman of ICHR, who has all along been a major source of encouragement. His personal interventions at different junctures have allowed this special project, the first of its kind, to continue. I would also like to thank the Member Secretary and all the officials of ICHR who were closely associated with this special project on environmental history. My special thanks are of course due to all the contributors who, despite their busy professional schedule, were quick to get back to me with their replies to all editorial queries. The members of the ICHR Advisory Committee have saved me from many errors during our lively discussions and debates in the meetings. My special thanks are due to all of them. I also convey my sense of gratitude to Dr Murugesan Amirthalingam, the Project Coordinator, and Ms Mili Ghose, the Project Assistant, ICHR, for their continuous help in all matters.

Finally, I would like to thank Mr Rajesh Dey, Managing Editor, SAGE Publications, India, for bearing with the delay on my part to comply with their editorial and other technical requirements. I sincerely thank SAGE for undertaking the publication of the book.

The responsibility of all lapses is mine alone.

Ranjan Chakrabarti

Environmental History of India: Methodology and Scope

Environmental History of India

An Introduction

Ranjan Chakrabarti

Within the discipline of history, environmental history remains universally acknowledged as a critically important area of inquiry, but without well-defined disciplinary standards and methodological strategies. It is felt that only professional historians with the requisite methodological training will be able to (a) develop and define the agenda and disciplinary canons of this field of inquiry and (b) historicize the present-day concerns and anxieties in the broad area of environmental history. Unfortunately, professional historians in India and abroad appear to be reluctant to come forward to undertake this task in a concerted and coordinated manner. This is the vacuum that the present book intends to fill in. It also marks the formal beginning of a special project funded by the Indian Council of Historical Research (ICHR), which proposes to write a comprehensive multi-volume environmental history of India, the first of its kind in the country. At least half a dozen publications are lined up as the outcome of this special project on environmental history of India.

It is critical for the historians to understand that environmental history is intimately connected with history of land use, water and climate in more than one way. Earth's hydrological cycle—the sun-powered movement of water between the sea, air and land—is an irreplaceable asset that human actions are now disrupting in dangerous ways. Although vast amount of water resides in oceans, glaciers, lakes and deep aquifers, only a very small share of Earth's water—less than 1/100th of 1 per cent—is fresh, renewed by the hydrological cycle and delivered to land. That precious supply of precipitation—some 110,000 cubic kilometres per year—is what sustains most terrestrial life. Like any valuable asset, the global water cycle delivers a steady stream of benefits to society. Rivers, lakes and other freshwater ecosystems work in concert with forests, grasslands and other landscapes to provide goods and services of great importance to human society. The nature and value of these services can remain grossly underappreciated, however, until they are all destroyed or depleted. Environmental history calls for an understanding of the interconnectivities between water resource on the one hand and deforestation, rainfall, river flows, soil erosion, climate change, global warming, drought, famine and various natural calamities on the other.[1]

The concern for environment in human society has always been there. Of all the decisions human society takes, perhaps the most crucial ones have always been related to the natural world. One of the flash points in the inner conflicts within the human societies of the past was fuelled by the continuous effort to resolve the question of the legitimate use of the natural world. As human settlements spread across the earth and technology advanced, the urge to resolve this fundamental question relating to the legitimate use of the natural world increased. South Asia is no exception in this line. In ancient India, forests were regarded as abodes of spiritual solace, and the concept of preserving forests and wildlife developed around the ashrams of the sages. These forest-based ashrams propagated *aranya sanskriti* or a forest culture and human understanding of the fundamental ecological utility of forest ecosystems and their economic importance, which led to trees and animals being treated with veneration.[2]

The present work on Environmental History of India will address some of the fundamental questions that are most relevant and fundamental to the very discipline of environmental history. The volume brings together many leading scholars sharing a common interest in environmental history. It makes an attempt to address the broad areas

---

[1] Ranjan Chakrabarti, ed., *Does Environmental History Matter? Introduction* (Kolkata: Readers Service, 2006).

[2] Ranjan Chakrabarti, ed., *Situating Environmental History* (Delhi: Manohar Publishers, 2007), 12–13.

of environmental concern in the Indian context and enquire into the complex patterns of the human–nature relationship.

One of the flash points in the inner conflicts within the human societies of the past was fuelled by the continuous effort to resolve the question of the legitimate use of the natural world. As human settlements spread across the earth and technology advanced, the urge to resolve this fundamental question relating to the legitimate use of the natural world increased. With the passage of time, the urgent need of resolving this unresolved question has been increasingly felt everywhere. It may be possible to explain many relations in the language of power. The human encounter with the natural world as well can be explained in the language of power. Environment is one of those spaces where we see the most intense form of demonstration of power. Nature may be seen as a parallel category with race, class, gender, ethnicity or nationalism, that is, as categories deployed to reveal power relationships in societies. The rapid unfolding of power relations, the random misuse of the natural world, the rise of new technology to exploit the nature and the growing resource crunch have now made this age-old debate very dense and intense as never before. It is a question most central and global to the entire human civilization. The more the human society progressed and prospered, the more became the longing to resolve the problem.

In ancient India, forests were regarded as abodes of spiritual solace, and the concept of preserving forests and wildlife developed around the ashrams of the sages. These forest-based *ashram*s propagated *aranya sanskriti* a (forest culture) and human understanding of the fundamental ecological utility of forest ecosystems and their economic importance, which led to trees and animals being treated with veneration.[3] The ancient texts like the Ramayana give clues to sensibilities. When Rama, the prince of Ayodhya, is about to set out on his long exile in the forests south of the Gangetic plains, his mother Kaushalya expresses fears about his safety, 'may the huge elephants not harm you, my dear son, she says, nor the lions, tigers, bears, boars or ferocious horned buffalo'. Rama himself, in a bid to dissuade his wife, Sita, from following him into the woods, paints a similar portrait of the forest as a place of hidden menace. Even the word *vana* (forest) was only given to lands where pleasure gave way to hardship, but it is also a place that is beautiful. The twin themes of the forest as a place of dangers to be confronted and of beauty to be enjoyed run like a thread through the epic. The protection of elephants became serious business by the time of the Mauryas.

---

[3] A. S. Rawat, *A History of Forestry in India* (Delhi: Indus Publishing House, 1991), 130.

The *Arthashastra* mentions the rules for protecting the elephant forests. Apart from elephant forests, there were other forests where the aim was to secure timber and tiger and lion skins. The protector of the forest worked to eliminate thieves, tigers and other predators from the woods to make them safe for cattle herders. The same tenor of concern for the wilderness runs through the medieval period. Babur gives much interesting information about wildlife in his memoir. He was a keen observer of wildlife.[4] Interestingly, everywhere the conservationist urge became more pronounced after the industrial revolution. The industrial revolution transformed the rural and urban landscape of Europe. The loss of woodlands and changing landscape created space for ideas of the romantic world of nature. The romantic writings, which were in some ways also a critique of the industrial revolution, celebrated lost nature. It encouraged a back to land movement. William Wordsworth, John Ruskin and William Morris were some of the leading literary figures who contributed to the back to land movement and the setting up of environmental societies in Europe. The rapid disappearance of forests in Europe and America also gave birth to the idea of wilderness, which combined elements of morality, science and aesthetics.[5]

Such direct concern for environment or its impact on human societies was, however, rare among the professional historians until the 1970s. Barring a few exceptions, until the mid-1970s, historians have, by and large, indirectly addressed various environmental or ecological issues while writing economic, social and cultural histories of various types. So, various environmental issues actually remain scattered in the history of peasant resistance or history from below, agrarian history, tribal history, social and cultural history, history of ideas, etc. It is true that such histories concentrated primarily on the arable parts of the landscape with some minor exceptions. This meant that non-arable forests—pastoral, mountain, marsh, etc.—were, on the whole, ignored by the practitioners of the discipline. Sir Jadunath Sarkar, who focused primarily on the political history of the Mughal Empire, writes in detail about the impact of Mughal military expedition to the Indian deep south on the environment. But here, as anywhere else, references to environmental degradation were made occasionally and rarely. Only in the history of medicine and public health have environmental issues acquired real prominence in

---

[4] Chakrabarti, *Situating Environmental History*, 12–13.

[5] Madhav Gadgil and Ramchandra Guha, *This Fissured Land: An Ecological History of India* (Delhi: Oxford University Press, 1992), passim; Madhav Gadgil and Ramchandra Guha, 'State Forestry and Social Conflict in British India', in *Peasant Resistance in India 1858–1914*, ed. David Hardiman (Delhi: Oxford University Press, 1993), 259–295.

historical scholarship before 1970. Some environmental issues do feature in themes such as history of crime, conflict over forest laws, movements for folk justice and microscopic studies of popular culture.[6]

Historiography

Ramchandra Guha, in his articles and subsequently in his books, asserted that in the pre-British period, there was little or no interference with the customary use of forest and forest produce. Thus, Guha views colonial forest policy and conservation as primarily driven by materialistic considerations, that of serving the strategic and revenue interest of the British Empire. In opposition to the argument propounded by Gadgil and Guha that imperial needs for timber and shipbuilding propelled scientific forestry with its associated bureaucracy, Richard Grove argues that colonial conservationism was based on humanist concerns motivated by growing deforestation and drought. He opines that it was desiccation that promoted the idea of forest conservancy in the colonies. Desiccation draws on the connection between deforestation and drought, shrinking water resources, soil erosion, productivity, etc.[7] The officials of the European trading companies were able to take note of them. These people systematically developed the desiccationist discourses and sought state intervention in the protection of forests. In the process, Grove plays down the importance of imperialist or capitalist greed behind the forest policy and focuses on other considerations, which were more humane.[8] Mahesh Rangarajan does not see simple polarities between the two sets of ideas and suggests that a convergence of ideas was indeed the case. He argues that the desiccationist fear had only a limited impact and was only one of the influences that shaped the course of the early 19th-century Indian forestry.[9] Ajay Skaria views

---

[6] Eric Hobsbawm, *Primitive Rebels* (Manchester: Manchester University Press, 1974); Eric Hobsbawm, *Bandits* (Harmondsworth: Penguin, 1985); E. P. Thomson, *Whigs and Hunters: The Origin of the Black Act* (New York: Pantheon Books, 1975; Douglas Hay et al., *Albion's Fatal Tree: Crime and Society in 18th century England* (1975); J. C. Scott, *The Moral Economy of the Peasant: Rebellion and Subsistence in Southeast Asia* (New Haven, CT: Yale University Press, 1976), etc.

[7] Richard Grove, op. cit.; see also Richard Grove, *Green Imperialism: Colonial Expansion, Tropical Edens and the Origins of Environmentalism* (Cambridge: Cambridge University Press, 1995); Richard Grove, *Ecology Climate and Empire* (Delhi: Oxford University Press, 1998).

[8] Ibid.

[9] Mahesh Rangarajan, *Fencing the Forest: Conservation and Ecological Change in India's Central Provinces* (Delhi: Oxford University Press, 1996).

forest conservancy that emerged out of the desiccationist discourses also as a part of the broader 'civilizing mission' of imperialism. Skaria disagrees with Grove and says that the agenda of forest conservancy was not 'innocent of colonial domination'.[10] In a recent article, D. D. Dangwal followed up the view of Skaria and shows how desiccationism was frequently used by the state to extend control over the central Himalayan forests (Uttaranchal).[11]

Grove rejects the Guha thesis as 'a golden age' approach to South Asian environmental history and questions the assumptions about the existence of pre-colonial common property and communal customary forest use. Recent research of Rangarajan, Skaria, Damodaran and others certainly took some of its cues from the early works of Tucker and the subalternists. But it has been also influenced by the globalist approach of Alfred Crosby and the revisionism of Christopher Bayly. Bayly has encouraged some of the environmental historians to treat colonial rule not as a watershed but as a period in which continuities with the pre-colonial period were to be regarded as important. Grove also sees the bias in South Asian environmental history caused by an overemphasis on the post-1857 period.[12] Both Mahesh Rangarajan and Grove rightly pointed to the significance of the forest policies pursued by the successor states to the Mughals. Grove, in particular, draws our attention to the need of a comprehensive history of drought, famine and climatic changes. In considering the impact of climatic change on the history of this region, we have advanced very little so far. It is perhaps in this area of research that we can expect to see most movement in the environmental history of South Asia in the coming years. This inclination has already surfaced in some of the essays in the volume edited by Grove and others.[13] South Asian environmental history sees the coming of colonialism as an environmental watershed and its legacy as the key agent of all environmental problems. There is a clear emphasis on the negative impact of the interventionist role of colonial

---

[10] Ajay Skaria, *Hybrid Histories: Forests, Frontiers and Wilderness in Western India* (Delhi: Oxford University Press, 1999).

[11] D. D. Dhangwal, 'Scientific Forestry and Forest Management in Colonial and Postcolonial India,' in *Contemporary India*, Vol. I (Delhi: Nehru Memorial Museum and Library, 2001).

[12] Alfred W. Crosby, *Ecological Imperialism: The Biological Expansion of Europe 900–1900* (Cambridge: Cambridge University Press, 2004) also Christopher and Susan Bayly, 'Eighteenth-century State Forms and the Economy', in *Arrested Development in India* (Delhi: Manohar Publishers, 1988).

[13] Richard Grove, ed., *Nature and the Orient: The Environmental History of South and South East Asia* (New Delhi: Oxford University Press, 1998).

and post-colonial states in the degradation of human ecologies. Fresh turns in this historiography will help to rejuvenate it. I will comment further on this point later.

Methodology

Knowledge is considered as knowledge only when it is methodologically obtained. History is a piece of knowledge as it is obtained through a definite methodology. The practitioners of the discipline are expected to practice the discipline according to certain methods. Like any other histories, here too, it is necessary for the historian to concentrate on the collection of primary and secondary sources and the selection and interpretation of such sources. As to the choice of subjects, historians are usually attracted by silences or slippages in the writing of history. Environmental history is a new area and here, such slippages and silences are understandably too many. They now await their historians. I will argue that environmental history does not call for any separate methodology; the basic tenets of the discipline remain very much valid in this sub-discipline of the history of environment. It might, however, require specific strategies, tactics and some preliminary knowledge of environmental sciences on the part of the historian to negotiate particular issues depending on the subject or the nature of his or her research.

Environmental history shares a very messy border with economic and social histories, history of science and technology, disease history and even with various other disciplines. It shares a lengthy border with historical geography and historical ecology. Roughly speaking, environmental historians, historical geographers and historical ecologists try to answer similar sorts of questions though their methodologies vary. For example, historical ecologists are usually trained in anthropology or archaeology and their work is collaborative in nature. Environmental historians, on the other hand, are expected to work alone. Climate history also shares a porous border with environmental history. Those climate historians who work on textual sources are very similar to environmental historians. In the United States, however, climate history relies heavily on the natural sciences due to poor textual documentation.[14]

---

[14] J. R. Mcneill, 'Observations on the Nature and Culture of Environmental History', *History and Theory* 42, no. 4 (Middletown, CT: Wesleyan University, 2003): 10. Climate history may be particularly useful in understanding draught, famine, bad harvest, price rise and mortality. See C. E. P. Brooks, *Climate Through the Ages* (London: Earnest Benn Ltd., 1926); Emmanuel Le Roy Ladurie, *Times of Feast, Times of Famine, A History of Climate Since the Year 1000*

The appellations of all the various branches of history are labels of convenience rather than names of essences. The phrase environmental history is no exception. Environment is a broad term, which encompasses all that surrounds us, both the natural world in which we live and the technology of production and things produced by us. In this sense, all histories can be viewed as environmental history. However, in fact, we make a distinction between environmental history and other histories. The historiography of the history of environment shows that in environmental history, there is an emphasis on various ecological factors and their impact on the history of a particular region. Historians might be of some help in mapping out the social, economic and cultural impacts of the changes in the ecosystem. An ecosystem can be defined as the grouping of various kinds of plants, animals and microorganisms interacting with each other and with their environment. Thus, an ecosystem consists of living organisms and the physical environment in which they live. Grassland, a forest, a pond or a lake may be considered an ecosystem. A historical study of an ecosystem is ecological history or environmental history. It is important for the environmental historian to remember that unlike other branches of history, it may not remain confined to a strictly guarded chronological framework; shorter periods may not be ideal for ecological histories, on the contrary, the emphasis here is on long *durée*. I have already said that in a sense all histories can be viewed as environmental history. Environment is a broad term, which encompasses all that surrounds us. Environmental history is pregnant with immense possibilities. There is a wonderful opportunity to undertake various social, economic, cultural and intellectual histories under the umbrella of environmental history and explore themes such as race, ethnicity, class, community, gender, power, knowledge, etc. One could see, for example, how the *jungle* (the Indian forest) became an important site for the interplay of various forces like racism, colonialism, nationalism and struggle for equality during British colonialism in India. It is understandable that the forest became one of the important social sites for the exercise of colonial power and for the domination and inferiorization of the 'Indian other'. I have argued elsewhere that it is possible to comprehend the implication of the exercise of power in various social and cultural sites or spaces when social construction of space is viewed historically. The historical transformation of space as container of power can only be identified when we study discourses in their dialectical interaction with the dynamic of human agency or

---

(New York: Doubleday, 1971); Neville Brown, *History and Climate Change: A Eurocentric Perspective* (London: Routledge, 2001), one of the most important areas that attracts historians now are El Nino episodes.

producers or architects of such discourses. I have shown in one of my articles how, in the course of the 19th century, the forest turned into an important venue where the Euro-American selves and the Indian Others started interacting.[15]

Editorial Notes

The present book is divided into four sections. Section I, including this editorial chapter, focuses on the methodological and historiographical aspects of environmental history.

Mayank Kumar, in Chapter 2 titled 'Invisible–Visible: Sources, Environment and Historians', argues that a careful reading of concerns of society in general and political dispensation of 17th–18th-century Rajasthan reveals a lot about the nature. Along with human negotiations with monsoon for agrarian production, these sources suggest that societies took special care of its pastoral wealth. Traditional knowledge, available in the folk tales and epigraphic evidence, forms an important tool to make invisible nature visible. The author reflects upon ways in which conventional sources are being reread by scholars to offer a very rich insight into the working of environment in past societies and human negotiations with nature.

Rivers, lakes and other freshwater ecosystems work in concert with forests, grasslands and other landscapes to provide goods and services of great importance to human society. The nature and value of these services can remain grossly underappreciated, however, until they are all destroyed or depleted. Environmental history is essentially a history of water and river and the entire hydrological cycle vis-à-vis its relation with human societies. Section II harps upon some aspects of river and water. Gopa Samanta, in Chapter 3 titled 'Environmental History of Water in Indian Cities', using secondary sources, explores the role of water history in understanding the present context of water in Indian cities. The arguments are built around three core issues: (a) the role of environmental history in solving the present-day problem of water in cities; (b) the colonial history and post-colonial legacy of centralized networked water supply and the death of traditional and diversified sources of water; and (c) the depletion of river and regional ecosystems, affecting long-term supply of water in cities.

---

[15] Ranjan Chakrabarti, ed., *Space and Power in History* (Kolkata: Penman, 2001).

In Chapter 4, 'History of Water Bodies in India', M. Amirthalingam explains the complex services rendered by various water bodies through Indian history.

Section III of the volume is on forests, land use, wildlife and animals and it includes four chapters. The section opens with, Nanditha Krishna's Chapter 5 titled 'Ancient Forests and Sacred Groves'. The author argues that forests once covered the entire subcontinent of India, as the seals of the Indus Valley Civilization indicate. In the Vedic period, forests were a spiritual retreat. But attitudes to the forest did not remain static. Later, in the Ramayana, there were different classifications of forest. But forests were also burnt down for urbanization, as the conflagration of the Khāndava forest suggests. Kautilya developed a system of forest management which lasted through most of the ancient period. In the south, forests were protected but kings were cutting down forests to build water tanks and towns. The ancient forests live on in the sacred groves which are found all over India. Each state and region has a separate name and management system, providing a window into the concerns of rural and tribal communities, the plant and animal species they protected and the elaborate mythologies they created to ensure that protection. Their existence is very important for a study of India's environmental and forest history. The deities of the groves also reflect the ecological concerns of local people. Their conservation was carried out in spite of the many threats of deforestation in the colonial and post-colonial periods. In many places, the sacred groves are the last remnants of local biodiversity. This was a method used by tribal and rural communities all over India to protect their forests. As a result of this protection, today we are able to have a glimpse of what the great forests of ancient India were like and their biological diversity.

In the following chapter (Chapter 6) titled 'Plant Domestication and Evolution of Agriculture in India', with special reference to Peninsular India, Anantanarayanan Raman shows that India's extraordinary landscape and geography have favoured natural evolution of plants, resulting in the exquisite diversification of a plethora of fruit trees. The monsoonal rains are another key factor that has enabled the rich biodiversification. With the establishment of the Mughal Empire, many Middle Eastern, Persian plant elements were deliberately introduced with the introduction and rise of new cultures and new medical practices. When the English (and other Europeans) arrived, they were astonished by the biological variety they saw in the Indian subcontinent. They nurtured experiments to improve the available plant germplasms, by introducing newly form elsewhere, *Cinchona*, ipecac, rubber and tea, to cite a few examples, which have indeed changed the complexion of Indian landscape to a large extent. Plant or animal domestication is not (and has not been) a single-stage, sudden, abrupt event, similar to a chromosomal mutation. It is an ongoing process, which in reality embodies and includes various levels of human experience and degrees of dependence between humans and plants and humans and animals. One daunting question in the domestication process that is coupled with a strong synergistic potential between the seeker, namely the humans and the giver, namely the plants, rests with the process of domestication and the preferential spread of some domestication alleles over others.

In Chapter 7 titled 'Environmental Change and Forest Conservancy in Southwest Bengal, 1890–1964', Nirmal Kumar Mahato explores the forest conservancy and environmental change in Southwest Bengal and the way the principles of Dietrich Brandis were introduced in a region of 'zone of anomaly' like Manbhum. The growing need for ship building, railway sleepers and charcoal for steam engine accelerated the hasty degradation of forests in North and South India. During the time, the desiccation theory was fundamental to the argument of climate change. It ultimately created the path for the formation of forest department. The zamindars of Bankura, Birbhum and Midnapur and Purulia held the forests under a special kind of tenure, known as the *ghatwali* tenure. In consideration of the environmental hazards, the Bengal government reviewed the role of zamindars as forest managers in the British Empire Forestry Conference held in South Africa in 1935. Subsequently, Bengal Private Forests Act came in 1945 and West Bengal Private Forest Act, 1946, came into force. Under the West Bengal State Acquisition Act, 1953, all forests became vested in government and transferred it to the forest department. In Independent India, forests were utilized in order to meet the demands of the industrial sector. Mahato opines that the state scientific forest management was questioned due to its hegemonic nature. As contestation came from different forest-dependent communities, a new policy was undertaken, which ushered people's participation in the management of forests.

Kakoli Sinha Roy, in Chapter 8 titled 'Hunting, Wildlife and Preservation in Colonial India, 1850–1947', concentrates on the massive slaughtering of wildlife in Colonial India and the ideological impetus behind the imperial hunt and the subsequent shift in their policy at a later period. She maintains that from the 1880s, it began to dawn on the colonial power that things had gone far enough. In the 19th century, the minds of those in power were opened to enclose the woodlands by enacting legislations in order to own this untapped treasure house. By the end of the 1860s, the pressures began for legislation. The first bit of wildlife or forest legislation concerned the protection of elephants. But the major objective of this protection was to carve out an exclusive domain of resource use, in which the native 'other' was excluded. India's woodlands and wildlife continued to be decimated and things did not change even after independence. It was only in the early 1970s that the woodlands and wildlife started to be considered seriously in the face of imminent destruction.

The theme in the final section is 'Climate and Disaster' and four chapters embark upon the subject with their specific case studies. Michel Danino opens the section with Chapter 9 titled 'Climate, Environment and the Harappan Civilization', wherein the author makes a brave attempt to revisit the much debated question of the disappearance of the Indus or the Harappan Civilization. Danino makes an endeavour to correlate archaeological evidence with sedimentological, palynological and other palaeoclimatic studies and suggests a few possible conclusions and lines of further explorations. Earlier theories based on invasions or man-made conflicts have been increasingly discarded; on the other hand, there has been growing evidence and acceptance that climatic and environmental factors played a significant role. While climatic studies from the 1970s to 1990s tended to support the view that a marked trend towards aridity had set in even before the urban or Mature Harappan phase (2600–1900 BCE), more recent studies have pushed this shift to the end of the third millennium BCE. This is also the time when, in the eastern domain of the Harappan civilization, the Sarasvati dwindled to a minor seasonal river, while floods appear to have been caused by a shifting Indus in the west. Other possible causes include the pressure put on remaining forests by intensive industrial activities. In any case, the archaeological evidence records the abandonment of Harappan sites in the Sarasvati's central basin and a migration of Late Harappan settlements: northeastward towards the foot of the Shivalik Hills, eastward across the Yamuna, possibly too westward towards the Indus plains and southward towards the Vindhyas.

In Chapter 10 titled 'Environmental History of Coastal India: Study Based on Archaeological and Historical Accounts', A. S. Gaur reveals that archaeological and historical records indicate that all along the Indian coast, several port cities and big and small settlements existed and their prosperity was supported by the overseas trade and commerce during its 5,000-year-old history. Ancient Indian literature is flooded with the information on the destruction of the settlements, situated along the coastal belt, by the sea in form of religious beliefs. However, in actual fact, due to changes in coastline and sea level fluctuations, several ancient ports and settlements have been submerged in the sea and many of them are situated far hinterland. These records clearly indicate fluctuations in coastal environment over a long *durée* of human history and beyond.

In Chapter 10, 'History of Earthquakes in India', M. Amirthalingam presents a graphic account of earthquakes through Indian history. He argues that earthquakes have been a common phenomenon recorded in history going back to the Harappan period. Even the Vedic people were fully aware of disasters like earthquakes (AV.19.1.10.8). In the *Brihat Samhita*, Chapter 32 discusses the earthquake cloud theory and the signs of earthquakes. The first well-recorded earthquake in the sub-continent dates back to 893 CE in the Delhi region. Later, the medieval chroniclers have described in detail the many earthquakes that took place in the Sultanate and Mughal periods. The numerous earthquakes that took place in Assam and Kashmir during the medieval period have been particularly well recorded.

In Chapter 11 titled 'Cyclones of East Coast of India', Mili Ghose maps out the complex pattern of cyclonic depressions in the Bay of Bengal and their massive environmental impact on the coastal socie-ties. The four states of India, namely West Bengal, Odisha, Andhra Pradesh and Tamil Nadu, face brutal cyclones every year, leading to high casualties. Agriculture and industries suffer heavily; both human and non-human forces are put to test every time a cyclone strikes. The author also gives a critical account of several vital steps taken by the government agencies to mitigate the impact of such cyclonic disasters.

In the concluding chapter (Chapter 12) titled 'Climatic Change and Its Impact on Northeast India', Sajal Nag details the indications cor-roborated by the findings of the climatologists and environmentalists to depict the environmental scenario in Northeast India. Nag speaks about the need to investigate the current environmental degradation in the region so that measures could be taken to prevent further dev-astation of the environment of the region. Northeast India has been experiencing environmental depletion which was a result of colonial policies, exploitation of its ecological and mineral resources, large-scale trans-border immigration and settlement of people, establishment of plantation industry through deforestation, dependence of dairy indus-try on grazing and so on. Invisible to public eye there are signs that would spell doom for the future of the region. The rainfall has seen a decline in Cherrapunji—world's wettest place; there have been regular massive dust storms in Guwahati, massive deforestation in all the states despite the ban by Supreme Court and monsoon seasons have changed; there have been massive floods due to melting of glaciers at the origins of the rivers, spells of drought despite the rains; climatologists predict more drought and desiccation of the region, unseasonal storms in Manipur, dying of rivers and water bodies and decline of river crops. All these have a massive impact on the crop production of the region affecting the food security.

Concluding Remarks

The present anthology raises new questions and opens up new windows leading to fresh research questions. The authors, by penetrating into diverse themes, disclose that environmental history would serve as one of the important gateways to knowledge in general, and the history of the human–nature relationship, in particular. There is no doubt that environmental history would help to guide the historians to areas hitherto unexplored, raise questions hitherto unasked, penetrate into the mysterious pathways of the mental world of the common people and disclose how the attitudes to environment change in keeping with the changing structure of culture and ideology. The author of this chapter would prefer to define environmental history in simple terms: it is the history of mutual relations between human beings and the rest of nature. Human beings have established their control over nature. Humans have exerted a marked influence on earthly ecosystems. Cutting of trees or destruction of wildlife may contribute to their happiness apparently, but the 'idea of progress' implies an interventionist and aggressive management of nature which may eventually turn out to be suicidal for the humans.

Invisible–Visible

Sources, Environment and Historians*

Mayank Kumar

From its very modest beginning, environmental history has come a long way and now occupies a place of prestige among ancillary sub-disciplines of history. Its evolution on the one hand challenged long-held view of historians that it is difficult to write environmental history, particularly because our sources are silent, and on the other hand, it paved the way for greater interactions with other disciplines as varied as geology, dendrochronology, oceanic science, metrology, international diplomacy, etc. Silences of historical sources were made vocal by drawing insights often from the natural sciences, and at times, from rereading the historical materials. For a volume like this, it is imperative on my part to deal with both the issues for a comprehensive treatment of the subject at hand. Therefore, this chapter is divided into two parts: the first part briefly traces the evolution of environmental history in India and the second part focuses on the issues related with questions of source material for writing environmental history. However, before venturing deeper into the subject matter, let me address the issue of definition and domain of environmental history by citing an attempt

---

* This chapter draws heavily from my previous works, and most of them have been cited at relevant places.

to define environmental history by the editor of the *Environment and History*, which clearly reflects the dilemma of the present-day historians working on environmental issues:

> The words 'environment' and 'ecology' have been subjected to extensive efforts at definition during the past twenty years or so. Already it has been found necessary to allow them space to breathe. So it is also with 'environmental history' or even 'Environment and History'. As with most commitments, it is possible to have 'hard' and 'soft' positions. The 'hard' might suggest that environmental history necessarily involves an examination of environmental dynamics through human agency in which the change is quantifiable in some shape or form. A softer approach would suggest, perhaps, that change could be inferred from even where data are not available. Interactions with environment may also be frozen in narrow time-scale where change is less significant. Relevant sections of legislation are all part of environmental history.[1]

It is difficult to deny that initial writings on environmental history emanated from the documentation of ill impacts of 'industrial society' across the globe in general and the documentation of the ecological changes/disruptions due to the introduction of colonialism in particular for developing societies like India. It will be erroneous not to point out that there have been very important and significant aberrations too, especially pertaining to study of environment of ancient societies. Generally, works on environmental history have focused on the analysis of the disruptions in the traditional way of living as a consequence of industrialization-led development and ultimately globalization and consumerism. In the case of most of the non-European societies, these disruptions were caused by colonialism which was subsequently replaced by neoliberalism and thus able to penetrate even the independent sovereign states. Soon environmental historians expanded their domain and started exploring issues related with the disruptions in the habitat of natural vegetation and creatures—tiny to mammoth—and explanations of the causes and effects have been the major concerns of the environmental historians across the globe. However, initially their focus remained confined to flora which was exploited extensively due to pressures of industrialization and colonization and on the megafauna only. Recently, 'keen to fend off charges of prioritizing charismatic mammalian megafauna, *Environment and History* flies the flag for avian

---

[1] John M. Mackenzie, 'Editorial', *Environment and History* VII, no. 3 (August 2002, 253–254).

and ectothermic critters in the last two papers here',[2] thus suggesting that the concerns of environmental historians have extended, from exploring the important disruptions in the nature and natural habitats, to map the impacts of climate variability on diverse species and process of adaptations since ancient times. Similarly, on the other hand, concerns of historians were greatly influenced by the debates related with the concerns initiated by the revisionist school of history writing and subaltern historians' conscious efforts to explore the agency of and response of the marginal sections of society. At present, thus, it can be safely suggested that environmental history has emerged as a 'fruitful endeavour of approaching historical questions with an environmental focus and vice-versa'.[3]

Before moving further, it is imperative on our part to point out the interdependence between science-based reconstructions of past societies and historical reconstruction carried out by relying more on conventional historical tools. In the recent past, there has been remarkable advance in our understanding of past climate mainly due to progress in the field of paleoclimatic studies,[4] but the construction of past climates is inconclusive. Most of the formulations lack unanimity among scientists.[5] This has necessitated intervention of the historian, as at times they can offer corroboratory evidence on the basis of a different set of data. Ladurie writes,

When meteorologists, geologists, and biologists wanted to find out about the climate of the eleventh and sixteenth centuries, they invited a dozen rural and economic historians to their meeting. And they entrusted to them the task of establishing most of the series for the periods concerned, the historians having brought along with them the continuous, annual, quantitative, homogenous lists of figures

---

[2] Karen Jones, 'Editorial', *Environment and History* 22, no. 2 (2016): 155–156.
[3] Jones, 'Editorial', 1–2.
[4] However, it is important to note that science/s which can map the historical process of changes in vegetation are still in nascent stages and it will take long to conclusively prove either the process of change or the change itself solely in terms of mathematical scientific evidences. Hannah M. David, Paul J. Wood, and Jonathan P. Sadler, 'Ecohydrology and Hydroecology: A "New Paradigm"?' *Hydrological Processes* 18 (2004): 3439–3445.
[5] Marco Madella and Dorian Q. Fuller, 'Palaeoecology and the Harappan Civilisation of South Asia: A Reconsideration', *Quaternary Science Reviews* 25 (2006): 1283–1301. One can also see limitations of new tools/disciplines in predicting the precipitation, Ulrich Von Rad, et al., 'A 5000-yr Record of Climate Change in Varved Sediments from the Oxygen Minimum Zone off Pakistan, Northeastern Arabian Sea', *Quaternary Research* 5 (1999): 39–53.

which the scientists had need of. So the relations between the history of climate and the related disciplines involve a fruitful exchange, a constant flow of information in both directions.[6]

Importance of corroboration by historians cannot be undermined as 'historical records have the advantage of delineating the social and economic impacts of extreme cleimatic events and passages, which physical and biological recorders of climate such as coral growth bands or tree ring series cannot do'.[7] However, the verification by the historians is not an easy task in the absence of coherent historical records of past societies. The task involves enormous efforts for pre-historic and/or proto-historic societies when historians, to a great extent, rely solely on archaeological evidence.[8]

I: Indian Environmental History—An overview

The beginning of environmental history has been very interesting where writings took note of environment and the significant role played by environmental factors without articulating it as environmental history. Richard Grove and Vinita Damodaran have very lucidly and comprehensively documented the evolution of environmental history in a two-piece article published in EPW in 2006. To offer an oversight of the historical evolution, introduction/abstract of both the parts is given below.

> The intellectual origins of environmental history as a self-conscious domain of enquiry can be traced to the encounter of 17th and 18th century western Europeans with the startlingly unfamiliar environments of the tropics and the damage inflicted on these environments in the course of resource extraction by European empires. For nearly a century from the mid-19th to the mid-20th century, the discipline developed primarily in the form of 'historical geography'. A new phase of global environment history began with European

---

[6] Emmanuel Le Roy Ladurie, *Times of Feast, Times of Famine: A History of Climate Since the Year 1000*, trans. Barbara Bray (New York, NY: Doubleday & Company, Inc, 1971), 21.

[7] Richard H. Grove and John Chappell, 'El Nino Chronology and the History of Global Crises During the Little Ice Age', in *El Nino: History and Crisis Studies from Asia-Pacific Region*, eds. Richard H. Grove and John Chappell (Cambridge, MA: The White Horse Press, 2000), 5.

[8] Nayanjot Lahiri, *Marshalling the Past: Ancient India and Its Modern Histories* (Ranikhet: Permanent Black, 2012).

decolonisation from the 1950s onwards. The imminence of a nuclear catastrophe and pesticide pollution stimulated the rise of a worldwide and populist environmental movement that reached full fruition in the 1970s.[9]

Furthermore, Richard Grove and Vinita Damodaran have rightly suggested:

[T]he developments in environmental history that in the 1950s had their roots in the nexus that had developed in the 1930s between world history, the 'Annales' school of history and aspects of local history as well. Scholars of environmental history in this period also came under the towering influence of the historian Arnold Toynbee, whose narratives and explanations of the global cyclical movements in world history stemmed from his understanding of the classical Greek and Roman periods of world history. Toynbee's later writings imparted a new ecological and internationalist direction to world history. The latter 1950s saw the spread of environmental history to scholars in other countries and an admixture of different disciplines and specializations gave a new thrust to the subject. Earlier histories of imperialism and colonialism now began to be looked at anew from their impact on the environment and the ecology.[10]

Evolution of environmental history has followed a very different trajectory in India. Impacts of colonial exploitation of natural resources in general and forest resources in particular can be easily termed as the driving force behind the initial writings of environmental history. However, soon after,

Studies discussing the current environmental crisis as well as environmental history of India have started appearing regularly. The dominant discourse in studies of both kinds has centred round a socio-biological perspective. It has meant a focus on the process of adaptation of, or otherwise, the societies to their surrounding environments as a key concern. This discourse has given rise to a proposition that holds that in pre-modern societies, by and large, the local communities had managed the environmental resources with such care as to

---

[9] Richard Grove, 'Imperialism, Intellectual Networks, and Environmental Change; Origins and Evolution of Global Environmental History, 1676–2000: Part-I', *Economic and Political Weekly* 41, no. 41 (October 14, 2006): 4345–4354.

[10] Grove, 'Imperialism, Intellectual Networks, and Environmental Change; Origins and Evolution of Global Environmental History, 1676–2000: Part II', *Economic and Political Weekly* (October 21, 2006): 4497–4505.

avoid many undesired consequences of such a use as that of a severe depletion of these resources. In other words, the communities lived a life of balance with nature basically satisfying those needs which did not greatly strain the environment. This proposition also holds that beginning with the colonial control over India policies of commercially exploiting these resources were unleashed in such a manner that within a short time the environmental resource base was undermined and a crisis began to loom large. This crisis assumed alarming proportions much sooner than anticipated. A discourse of this kind has been called the standard environmental narrative (SEN).[11]

The environmental histories have thus distinguished the pre-colonial stage of harmonious relationship with nature from the stage when India came under colonial control and policies conspicuously in support of abusive environmental practices that came into vogue. In some ways, the SEN has also constituted a nationalist critique of colonial policies where 'colonial' has also been intermingled with 'modern'.[12]

To a great extent, these concerns have characterized the trajectory of environmental history in India especially in its nascent stage when deforestation in various parts of India by colonial power was extensively examined. Desiccation, scientific forestry and creation of reserve forests, displacement and its social and ecological consequences proved to be a vibrant zone. Examination of these issues forced historians to examine the colonial powers/states negotiations with the classification of customary rights and claims of tribal. In their attempt to locate the traditional rights and claims, historians often ventured into pre-colonial pasts. The centrality of these issues in the environmental history can be easily measured by the following acceptance of the editors of *Nature & The Orient*:

> We make no apology for devoting so much of the book to the history of the relationship between forests, people and the state, and to the history of the discourse and ideology of colonial forestry in India, Burma and Malaysia. At the peak of its power the Indian Forest Department, for example, directly controlled over one-fifth of the land area of South Asia. Moreover, the forest history of the subcontinent and South Asia varies enormously from area to area, and we

---

[11] Stig Toft Madsen, ed., *State, Society and the Environment in South Asia* (Surrey, Great Britain: Curzon Press, 1999), 2–3.

[12] Ravindra Kumar, 'Course Introduction', 'Block-1 Studying Ecology & Environments: An Introduction', *History of Ecology and Environment: India* (New Delhi: IGNOU, 2005), 2.

feel it necessary to highlight these differences and make a start at producing a series of detailed and empirical environmental histories, concentrating quite deliberately on the forest sector.[13]

Although major departures can be located in the concerns of environmental historians who gradually moved beyond simplistic correlation between exploitation of environment and nature of colonial rule to document the human–nature interactions in the pre-colonial period, nevertheless, a recent collection of writings on environmental history of India by Mahesh Rangarajan and K. Sivaramkrishnan once again concedes that '[e]ven a cursory look at the wealth of writings on India's rich and varied past points to a pattern. Environmental historians have mostly been focused on the last two centuries, especially the period from 1858 when India came under rule of the crown.'[14]

Nevertheless, Mahesh Rangarajan and K. Sivaramkrishnan also document recent expansion in the concerns of environmental history which has gone well beyond mere documentation of environmental degradation under colonial rule in India. They point out:

> Yet, the long preceding eras were more than a mere benchmark against which the epochal changes of the late nineteenth centuries of the Common Era could be set. In recent years, the wealth of work by archaeologists and scholars of literary texts as also work that draw upon pictorial evidence especially from the Sultanate and Mughal periods (the thirteenth to the early eighteenth centuries CE), has provided the reason enough for a careful reassessment.... many insights into forest frictions and water disputes, the contests over urban or rural spaces between rival claimants to water or land, animal, plant, or mineral wealth have led to a re-interrogation of source materials on early and medieval India.[15]

Environmental History on Ancient Indian Past

Environmental history of ancient Indian past has borrowed on the one hand extensively from the archaeological evidence, paleoclimatic studies and on the other, it has resulted in re-examination of literary evidence.

---

[13] Richard H. Grove, Vinita Damodaran, and Satpal Sangwan, 'Introduction', in *Nature and The Orient* (Delhi: Oxford University Press, 1998), 1–17.

[14] Mahesh Rangarajan and K. Sivaramkrishnan, 'Introduction,' in *India's Environmental History, Part-I, From Ancient Times to the Colonial Period* (Ranikhet: Permanent Black, 2012), 1.

[15] Ibid.

The human impact on and wider interactions with the material and biotic environment in early India are now being pieced together afresh with careful interpretation of archaeological finds. Significant archaeological research shows a complex set of patterns that challenges any linear sequence of human-nature relationships.[16]

To begin with, historians have focused on the importance of climate as a factor in the emergence and decline of civilizations, especially Indus Valley Civilization.[17] The issue of forest clearance and urbanization in early historic times was examined by Makhan Lal to suggest that examination of the role and impact of environmental factors offers new insights to historical processes.[18] Integrating archaeological findings with the ecological context, M. K. L. Murthy has documented nuances of pastoral cultures of southern Deccan in ancient times and pointed out the gradual evolution in their relationship with the environmental conflict which vacillated often between contests and cooperation.[19]

Environmental history of ancient Indian past has benefitted to a great extent by ecological reading of texts. In the opinion of Francis Zimmermann, the term *jungle* of ancient Indian texts cannot be equated with the term forest. Zimmerman has argued that ancient societies classified animals broadly in two groups, *jungla* (those of the dry lands) and *anupa* (those of the marshy lands), and advocates that a closer examination of such texts may offer us insights into the functioning of ancient ecology.[20] Similar trends are visible in Ed Roger Jeffery's *The*

---

[16] Ibid., 8–9.

[17] F. R. Allchin, *The Archaeology of Early Historic South Asia: The Emergence of Cities and State* (Cambridge: Cambridge University Press, 1995); V. N. Misra, 'Climate, a Factor in the Rise and Fall of the Indus Civilization: Evidence from Rajasthan and Beyond', in *Frontiers of the Indus Civilizations*, eds. B. B. Lal and S. P. Gupta (New Delhi: Books and Books, 1984), 461–466, 473, 481–482; Gurdeep Singh, 'The Indus Valley Culture (Seen in the Context of Post-Glacial Climate and Ecological Studies in North-West India)', *Archaeology and Physical Anthropology in Oceania* 6, no. 2 (1971): 177–189; D. P. Agrawal, *The Copper Bronze Age in India* (New Delhi: Munshiram Manoharlal, 1971).

[18] Makhan Lal, 'Iron Tools, Forest Clearance, and Urbanisation in the Gangetic Plains', *Man and Environment* 10 (1986): 83–90.

[19] M. K. L. Murthy, 'Sheep/Goat Pastoral Cultures in the Southern Deccan: The Narrative as a Metaphor', in *Indian Archaeology in Retrospect: Archaeology and Historiography*, Vol. IV, eds. S. Settar and Ravi Korisettar (Delhi: Manohar, 2002): 297–307. Also see Shereen Ratnagar, 'Pastoralism as an Issue in Historical Research', *Studies in History* 7, no. 2 (1991): 181–193.

[20] Francis Zimmermann, *The Jungle & the Aroma of Meats: Ecological Themes in Hindu Medicine* (Berkeley, Los Angeles, CA; London: University of California Press, 1987).

Social Construction of Indian Forests.[21] Recently, Romila Thapar has very lucidly worked out the perceptions of forests in ancient times. Forests were integrated with the social life at multiple levels and thereby offer multiple readings of social perceptions of forests, which were captured by writers and poets.[22]

Inhabitants of forest have also attracted attention of historians. In a more conventional manner, Aloka Parashea-Sen has tried for the Mauryan period to 'understand how the state perceived the forest dwellers and sought to subordinate and assimilate them. Geography and the perceived existence of the hostile tribes defined the frontiers of the empire and both had to be mastered for the expansion and integration of the state.'[23]

In another work by Nandini Sinha[24] for the region of Mewar, similar themes have been explored. She asserts that forested and hill regions were integrated into wider imperial systems of South Asia. Moreover, the landscape of economic activities in any subregion was far more diverse than what is often realized. It is almost impossible to decipher clear-cut stages or phases like hunter-gatherer, herder, settled cultivators and artisan and city dweller. Extending the line of enquiry to megafauna, Thomas R. Trautmann has documented complexities of social negotiations with wildlife.[25] In the recent past, Shibani Bose has contributed a couple of articles on wildlife in ancient past. Her paper 'From Eminence to Near-Extinction: The Journey Of the Greater One-Horned Rhino' very lucidly documents history.[26] The role of hydraulic

---

[21] Roger Jeffery, ed., *The Social Construction of Indian Forests* (New Delhi: Manohar, 1998).

[22] Romila Thapar, 'Perceiving the Forest: Early India', *Studies in History* 17, no. 1 (2001): 1–16.

[23] Aloka Parasher-Sen, 'Of Tribes, Hunters and Barbarians: Forest Dwellers in the Mauryan Period', *Studies in History* 14, no. 2 (1998): 173–191.

[24] N. S. Kapoor, *State Formations in Rajasthan: Mewar During the Seventh–Fifteenth Centuries* (Delhi: Manohar, 2002).

[25] Thomas R. Trautmann, 'Elephants and the Maurya', in *India: History and Culture: Essays in Honour of A.L. Basham*, ed. S. N. Mukherjea (Calcutta: Firma L. Mukhopadhyay and Co., 1982): 54–73.

[26] Mahesh Rangarajan and K. Sivaramakrishnan, eds., *Shifting Ground: People, Animals, and Mobility in India's Environmental History* (New Delhi: Oxford University Press, 2014, 65–87); Shibani Bose, 'Human–Plant Interactions in the Middle Gangetic Plains (From the Mesolithic upto circa 3rd century BC): An Archaeobotanical Perspective', in *Ancient India: New Research*, eds. Upinder Singh and Nayanjot Lahiri (New Delhi: Oxford University Press, 2009, 91–107).

management in the process of settlement in ancient period as part of environmental history was explored by Ranabir Chakravarti.[27]

Environmental History of Medieval Indian Past

A decade back, there was a general dearth of scholars focusing on environment and on man–nature interactions in medieval Indian past; however, the recent past has seen several important contributions. What is also heartening to note is that the range of environmental factors explored for medieval Indian past is very diverse and intense. To begin with, it is undeniable that a serious influence on the man–environment studies in medieval India has been that of the *Annales*. Influences of environment on the social formations have been a major area of historical investigation for the *Annales*. Since the very beginning, we can trace the attempts made by *Annales* historians to explore the newer kinds of sources to analyse the role played by environment in historical processes. They have tried to place the role of environment in the wider settings of social formations. They also attempt to transcend the barrier of medieval and modern history, as they promoted study of *longue-durée* and have been more comfortable with the whole range of human activities in place of mainly the political history.[28]

Harbans Mukhia is credited with making *Annales* popular in India by translating the writings of French historians along with Maurice Aymard.[29] Borrowing extensively from the works of historians like Marck Bloch and other *Annales* historians, a study by Harbans Mukhia, titled 'Was There Feudalism in Indian History?' explores influences of environmental factors on human settlement and social formations as a sub-theme and not as the central subject.[30]

The influence of the *Annales* tradition is visible in an important contribution made by Chetan Singh and a series of subsequent scholars.

---

[27] Ranabir Chakravarti, 'The Creation and Expansion of Settlements and Management of Hydraulic Resources in Ancient India,' in *Nature and the Environment*, eds. Richard Grove, Vinita Damodaran, and Satpal Sangwan (Delhi: Oxford University Press, 1998), 87–105.

[28] Ravindra Kumar, Unit-3: 'Sources of Study', 'Block-1: Studying Ecology & Environments: An Introduction', *History of Ecology and Environment: India* (New Delhi: IGNOU, 2005).

[29] Harbans Mukhia and Maurice Aymard, *French Studies in History, Vol I: The Inheritance* (New Delhi, 1988) and *Vol II: The Departure* (New Delhi: SAGE, 1990).

[30] Harbans Mukhia, 'Presidential Address, Medieval India Section', *Indian History Congress*, Vol. 40 (1979), 229–280.

Chetan Singh examined the nature of connections between environment and society in Western Himalaya and argued that

> but my project rested on the belief that there were some long established and well understood relationships between society and its physical surroundings. ... Such fundamental relationships did, indeed exist: a society could hardly have survived for any length of time without them. It was, however, the clear-cut enunciation of these relationships that was missing. This required the deliberate elaboration both of socio-economic processes and specific ecological environment within which they operated.[31]

Role and influences of geographical factors on the historical process offered entry point to the historians working on environmental history. The beginning of this mode of investigation can be seen in the two initial chapters in the *Cambridge Economic History of India*, Volume I[32] by Irfan Habib and Burton Stein on 'The Geographical Background' especially of North India and 'South India: Some General consideration of the Region and its Early History', respectively, as studies located on the fringe of environmental history. In the same vein drawing upon the conventional sources, Shireen Moosvi has offered a useful study in the field of environmental history of medieval India.[33] One can also refer to an article by Md Afzal Khan published in 2002.[34]

Another path of investigation within the wider writings on the environmental history of medieval Indian past has been presented by Sumit Guha. He had very articulately argued that the historical investigation of the pre-colonial past in the Indian subcontinent should not borrow categories from the works dealing with colonial and post-colonial periods in Indian history. It is unfortunate to note that the seminal work on the ecological history of India by Madhav Gadgil and Ramchandra Guha had depicted the pre-colonial past as an era of 'prudent resource-use' in contrast to the exploitation of natural resources during colonial practices. Challenging such generalizations, Sumit Guha pointed out:

---

[31] Chetan Singh, *Natural Premises: Ecology and Peasant Life in the Western Himalaya 1800–1959* (Delhi: Oxford University Press, 1998).

[32] Tapan Ray Chaudhuri and Irfan Habib, eds., *Cambridge Economic History of India*, Vol. I (Cambridge: Cambridge University Press, 1982).

[33] Shireen Moosvi, 'Ecology, Population Distribution and Settlement Pattern in Mughal India in 1989', *Man and Environment* XIV, no. I (1989): 109–116.

[34] Md Afzal Khan, 'Environment and Pollution in Mughal India', *Islamic Culture* 76, no. 1 (2002): 101–116.

It must be evident that Gadgil's model breaks down at every point; small endogamous groups did not occupy the same location for long periods of time, and even when they did, they had lacked exclusive access to particular resources. The human species is too opportunistic and too versatile to be confined to particular niches for centuries on end.[35]

Further, he went on to examine the problematic understanding of different categories, designating relationships between particular sections of the society with the specific ecological setting in *Environment and Ethnicity*. He argued that one needs to revisit the categorization of different communities, which has unfortunately been done merely on the basis of resource-use practices, often ignoring the complex connection with the wider social and ecological settings. He also pointed out that modern categorization, primarily executed under the British colonial rule, has often reduced their identity in terms of resource-use practices and thereby negated possibilities of a wider social role to these communities.

Given the larger texture of concerns of writing on the pre-colonial past, it is not surprising to note that only a few writers have probed the significance of pre-colonial water systems,[36] and this is particularly true of North and Northwest India.[37] Kathleen Morrison, as part of a larger project to examine the water systems in and around Vijayanagara during 16th and 17th centuries, has documented the extension of agriculture in the marginal areas. Monsoon rains were being increasingly captured to develop the agrarian potential of even the areas on the fringes of agrarian landscape. Most of the times, it was the paucity of water that had restricted the agrarian production and with the channelization of monsoon rains, expansion of agrarian settlements became stable.[38] On the other hand, Devra has argued

---

[35] Sumit Guha, *Environment and Ethnicity in India, 1200–1991* (Cambridge: Cambridge University Press, 1999), 43.

[36] David Ludden, 'Ecological Zones and the Cultural Economy of Irrigation in Southern Tamilnadu', *South Asia* I, no. I (1978): 1–13; Burton Stein, *The New Cambridge History of India, Vol. 2, Vijayanagara* (Cambridge: Cambridge University Press, 1994); *Peasant State and Society in the Medieval South India* (Delhi: Oxford University Press, 1980).

[37] Tripta Wahi, 'Water Resources and Agricultural Landscape: Pre-colonial Punjab', in *Five Punjabi Centuries: Polity, Economy, Society and Culture, c.1500–1990*, ed. Indu Banga (Delhi: Manohar, 1997).

[38] Kathleen D. Morrison, 'Production and Landscape in the Vijayanagara Metropolitan Region: Contributions of the Vijayanagara Metropolitan Survey', in *Vijayanagara: Archaeological Exploration 1990–2000: Papers in Memory of*

that one can decipher a gradual extension of the desert in northern Rajasthan towards Punjab. He has suggested that a gradual shift in the river courses led to changes in the climatic landscape of the region.[39] At times, he challenges the findings of Dhavalikar who has argued that the Indian subcontinent witnessed climatic variability between the 7th and 11th centuries. Along with shifts in the river courses, Dhavalikar suggests that perhaps this era witnessed a change in the climatic patterns.[40]

There are scholars who have pointed out the role of traditional village community in construction and maintenance of irrigation systems. David Hardiman suggests that 'small-dam systems of irrigation existed in the past which were sustained over long periods of time ... by community based control'.[41] Extending this line of investigation Elizabeth Whitecombe has argued that irrigation 'works were financed by loan capital. Hence, in the sanctioning of constructions the emphasis was necessarily placed on the prospect of their remunerativeness.'[42] David Mosse has examined the interplay of 'developmental politics' to explain the intensity and character of interventions being made by the state. The role of community-based programmes to tackle contentious issues like management and allocation of 'common property resources' like

---

Channabasappa S. Patil, eds., J. M. Fritz, T. Raczek, and R. Brubaker, *Vijayanagara Research Project Monographs Volume 10* (Delhi: Manohar and AIIS, 2005), 423–434; *Fields of Victory: Vijayanagara and the Course of Intensification* (Delhi: Munshiram Manoharlal Publishers, Pvt Ltd, 2000).

[39] G. S. L. Devra, 'Problems in the Delimitation of the Rajputana Desert During the Medieval Period', in *Desert, Drought & Development: Studies in Resource Management and Sustainability*, eds. Rakesh Hooja and Rajendra Joshi (Jaipur: Rawat Publications, 1999), 371–382; 'Physiography and Environment of Thar Desert of Indian Sub-continent During Seventh and Eighth Century', Draft Paper presented at the 6th International Conference on 'Perspective on Rajasthan' organized by Institute of Rajasthan Studies, Jaipur, Rajasthan, India, 2–3 January 2010.

[40] M. K. Dhavalikar, 'Green Imperialism: Monsoon in Antiquity and Human Response', *Man And Environment* 26, no. 2 (2001): 17–28; 'The Golden Age and After: Perspectives in Historical Archaeology', in *Proceedings of Indian History Congress*, 60th Session, Calicut, 1999, pp. 1–18.

[41] David Hardiman, 'Small Dam Systems of the Sahyadris', in *Nature, Culture, Imperialism: Essays on the Environmental History of South Asia*, eds. David Arnold and Ramchandra Guha (Delhi: Oxford University Press, 1995), 185–209.

[42] Elizabeth Whitcombe, 'The Environmental Costs of Irrigation in British India: Waterlogging, Salinity, Malaria', in *Nature, Culture, Imperialism: Essays on the Environmental History of South Asia*, eds. David Arnold and Ramchandra Guha (Delhi: Oxford University Press, 1995), 237–259.

water bodies, etc., has also been examined.[43] R. J. Fisher has also tried to document social negotiations with water in the arid landscape of western Rajasthan.[44]

In an important contribution, Meena Bhargava has examined the processes of social negotiations to the changes in the river courses.[45] On a different trajectory, for the later period, Yogesh Sharma has documented the perceptions of European travellers with respect to artificial water bodies in India.[46] Similarly, Mayank Kumar has also attempted to examine the interaction between environment and society in medieval Rajasthan and argued that negotiations with climatic variability are a hallmark of human adaptation and there is greater need for documentation of local village-level negotiations.[47] He has investigated the notion that the communities in traditional societies always practised the methods aimed at a prudent use of natural resources and has pointed out several cases of 'exploitation' of natural resources by traditional societies in Rajasthan. He also cautions that the magnitude of exploitation of natural resources did multiply manifold under the impact of the Industrial Revolution[48] and further intensified after the discovery of oil.[49] Further, he examined the relationship between environmental features and the settlement patterns while giving primacy to the water resources.[50]

---

[43] David Mosse, *The Rule of Water: Statecraft, Ecology and Collective Action in South India* (New Delhi: Oxford University Press, 2003), 1–27.

[44] R. J. Fisher, *If Rain Doesn't Come: An Anthropological Study of Drought and Human Ecology in Western Rajasthan* (Delhi: Manohar, 1997).

[45] Meena Bhargava, 'Changing River Courses in North India: Calamities, Bounties, Strategies—Sixteenth to Early Nineteenth Centuries', *The Medieval History Journal* 10, no. 1&2 (2007): 183–208.

[46] Yogesh Sharma, 'The Circuit of Life: Water and Water Reservoirs in Pre-modern India', *Studies in History* 25, no. 1 (January–June 2009): 69–108.

[47] Mayank Kumar, *Monsoon Ecologies: Irrigation, Agriculture and Settlement Patterns in Rajasthan during the Pre-colonial Period* (Delhi: Manohar, 2013).

[48] Mayank Kumar, 'Claims on Natural Resources: Exploring the Role of Political Power in Pre-colonial Rajasthan, India', *Conservation and Society* 3, no. 1 (June 2005): 134–149.

[49] John Urry, *Societies Beyond Oil: Oil Gregs and Social Futures* (London and New York, NY: Zed Books, 2013).

[50] Mayank Kumar, 'Situating the Environment: Settlement, Irrigation, and Agriculture in Pre-colonial Rajasthan', *Studies in History* 24, no. 2 (2008): 211–233; 'Flexibility and Adaptability: Agrarian Expansion and Traditions of Water Management', *The ICFAI University Journal of History and Culture* III, no. 3 (2009): 31–55; Sugata Ray, *Climate Change and the Art of Devotion: Geoaesthetics in the land of Krishna 1550–1850* (Seattle: University of Washington Press, 2019).

The changing history of the encounters of humans and animals has emerged as another field of growing interest, largely in terms of changing elite taste and growing human–wildlife conflict. Gradual but regular expansion of agrarian landscape[51] has resulted in ground-level conflicts and has threatened their coexistence. In this context, *The End of Trail: The Cheetah in India*[52] stands out. The author traces the history of the cheetah in India, its origin, spatial distribution across the subcontinent, attitude towards the feline, gradual erosion of space for the big cats and finally the extinction of the species. Significance of the work lies in the fact that it offers insights to understand the complex relationships between fauna and the society, particularly the process of extinction of the animals. It is suggested that extinctions manifest as a side effect of the larger historical process and not as a direct process of elimination of the species as it was for other 'big game'. Another monograph by Divyabhanusinh on lions carries the quest further to explore the fauna in their own world.[53] Other interesting genre of writings has examined princely states' interactions with colonial power as mediated by the flora–fauna of their respective regions. Barbara Ramusack has explored the British hunting practices and its appropriation and reinterpretations by Indian Princes.[54] Locating the role of environmental settings in warfare and human negotiations with animals, recently, Pratyay Nath has suggested that Mughals reconsidered their reliance on cavalry as they moved towards wetlands of the Gangetic delta. In what ways this change from reliance on cavalry to elephants is reflected in the writings of Mughal court chronicles and Mughal paintings reflective of changing relations and perceptions towards environmental factors?[55]

---

[51] Neeladri Bhattacharya, *The Great Agrarian Conquest: The Colonial Reshaping of a Rural World* (Hyderabad: Orient Blackswan, 2018).

[52] Divyabhanusinh, *The End of a Trail: The Cheetah in India* (New Delhi: Oxford University Press, 1999).

[53] Divyabhanusinh, *The Story of Asia's Lion* (Mumbai: Marg Publications, 2005).

[54] Barbara N. Ramusak, *The Indian Princes and Their States*, 1st Asian ed. (New York, NY: Cambridge University Press, 2005); Anand S. Pandian, 'Predatory Care: The Imperial Hunt in the Mughal and British India', *Journal of Historical Sociology* 14, no. 1 (March 2001): 79–107; John M. MacKenzie, *The Empire of Nature: Hunting, Conservation and British Imperialism* (New York, NY: Manchester University Press, 1988).

[55] Pratyay Nath, *Climate of Conquest: War, Environment, and Empire in Mughal North India* (Delhi: Oxford University Press, 2019).

Environmental History on Colonial and Post-colonial Indian Past

It can be very safely suggested that environmental history on colonial and post-colonial Indian past that also set the tone for future writings is invariably associated with Ramchandra Guha and Madhav Gadgil's seminal monograph *This Fissured Land*[56] written in 1992. As suggested earlier,

> [A]uthors suggested that in pre-colonial India, resource utilization was in harmony with nature and resource sharing among various strata of the society was very cordial. The caste society with different claims on different resources led to a state of equilibrium in turn providing stability to the resource demand and supply. Caste was seen as consisting of endogamous groupings that were each marked by a particular economic activity and a particular ecological niche. However, perhaps unintentionally, the notion of self-sufficient villages was also justified by such arguments.[57]

Most of the environmental movements were explained in terms of disruptions caused by the British as it was argued elsewhere that in pre-British time, 'there was little or no interference with the customary use of forest and forest produce'.[58] A romanticized image of the human–environment interaction in the Indian context was thus portrayed by Guha and Gadgil, an imagery which was received with open hands by writers who doubled up as environmental activists also. Early writers were more concerned with the protection of environment as they had been actively supporting the cause of conservation of environment. Thus, they looked for evidence of popular protests against the exploitation and often neglected the contrary evidence. In the initial decades, works on environmental history of South Asia often focused on certain themes at the expense of others: the forest rather than agriculture, movements of adivasis and marginal peasants rather than changing responses of urban dwellers, histories of irrigation as opposed to conflict over water-rights, etc. Among the first few who focused on the impact of colonial forest policies on the Himalayan

---

[56] Madhav Gadgil and Ramchandra Guha, *This Fissured Land: An Ecological History of India* (Delhi: Oxford University Press, 1992).

[57] Mayank Kumar, Unit-3, 'Sources of Study', 'Block-: Studying Ecology & Environments: An Introduction,' *History of Ecology and Environment: India* (New Delhi: IGNOU, 2005), 39.

[58] Ramchandra Guha, 'Forestry in British and Post-British India: A Historical Analysis', *Economic and Political Weekly* 20 (1985), 1893.

region and Central Indian forests were Ramchandra Guha[59] and Mahesh Rangarajan,[60] respectively.

There have been a few exceptions to this general pattern of historical investigations. Sumit Guha has on the one hand tried to bridge the gap between pre-British and British period and on the other he has also avoided the illusionary divide between forest and agriculture and notions of ethnicity in the wider context of environment. His area of study has been the region dominated by Marathas and fortunately for this region we have rich repositories of documents. He has questioned the generally presumed isolation of tribals from the cradle of civilization.[61] Further, Sumit Guha has pointed out that the large areas of western plateau (Maharashtra) outside the rain-drenched Konkan coast were rendered treeless even during the heydays of Marathas.[62] Initially argued by him and later on seen in the writings of Kathleen Morrison, as mentioned earlier, the pattern of living has modified the environment of the region ever since. Sumit Guha pointed out that the use of fire and the keeping of cattle were practised here for at least 40 centuries, if not more. In the process, a thorny forest region was transformed into seasonal grassland: 'the ecology was re-shaped in major ways. The fluidity was more than matched in economic terms. Dry spells could lead to a resurgence of herding.'[63]

Setting the tone for future researchers exploring the environmental history of India, Sumit Guha argued that it is important to keep in mind that in South Asian past, a relatively small area was under permanent tillage and a much larger percentage of land was often in the state of transition, at least in the pre-modern period. He also offered a word of caution by suggesting historians to go beyond the state's perspective of land, forest, water bodies, etc., for a comprehensive understanding of human–nature interactions. Problems of statism were also highlighted by Ranajit Guha, who suggested that it is interesting to note that the basic effort of colonial historiography has been, and its later proponents have tried, to examine the historical progression in terms

---

[59] Ramchandra Guha, *The Unquiet Woods: Ecological Change and. Peasant Resistance in the Himalaya* (Delhi: Oxford University Press, 1989).

[60] Mahesh Rangarajan, *Fencing the Forest: Conservation and Ecological Change in India's Central Provinces: 1860–1914* (Delhi: Oxford University Press, 1996).

[61] Sumit Guha, *Environment and Ethnicity* (Cambridge: Cambridge University Press, 1999).

[62] Sumit Guha, 'Claims on the Commons: Political Power and Natural Resources in Pre-colonial India', *The Indian Economic and Social History Review* 39, no. 2&3 (2002): 181–196.

[63] Unit-3, 'Sources of Study', 'Block-: Studying Ecology & Environments'.

of 'evolutionary' time scale. For them, societies evolved in succession from primitive to tribal to chieftaincy to state, and this process is fundamentally unidirectional and mutually contradictory.[64] Ajay Skaria gave serious consideration to the question and explored the idea of wild and wilderness, which was usually located in opposition to civilized. The relationship between tribal people and ruling dispensation has also been located in terms of binary of civilized and primitive.[65]

Ajay Skaria questions the idea whereby tribals were equated with 'wild' and 'primitive' and settled agriculturalists under state polities with civilization. He has also highlighted the general disregard of issue at the margins and laments the importance given to issues related to economics of 'development'. As a response, he tries to locate the problems of marginalization in the context of contemporary character of developmental politics and finds that these narratives constitute the primary ingredient for the construction of ideas such as *jangali*/tribal/primitive.[66]

Subsequent writings on the environmental history of India during the colonial and post-colonial periods argued against the prevalent notion of a uniform British policy across the Indian subcontinent. Recent researches have highlighted the divergence of colonial administrative views and policies related with the forest resources, agricultural production and water resources.[67]

Similarly, Ravi Rajan points out the serious differences within the colonial administration. Contrary to conventional historiography, it is now evident that seeing the so-called colonial policy as a monolithic structure is nothing more than a myth. Exploring the deliberations at the Empire Forestry Conference on two crucial colonial agro-ecological policy concerns, shifting cultivation and soil erosion during 1920–1950, Ravi Rajan endorses the internal differences within the British colonial administration. Given the experience of 'Dust Bowl',[68]

---

[64] Ranajit Guha, *History at the Limit of World-History* (New Delhi: Oxford University Press, 2003).

[65] Ajay Skaria, 'Being Jangali: The Politics of Wildness', *Studies in History* 14, no. 2 (1998): 193–215.

[66] Ajai Skaria, *Hybrid Histories: Forests Frontiers and wildness* (Delhi: Oxford University Press, 1998).

[67] K. Sivaramakrishnan, 'Conservation and Production in Private Forests: Bengal, 1864–1914', *Studies in History* 14, no. 2 (1998): 237–264; *Modern Forests: Statemaking and Environmental Change in Colonial Eastern India* (Stanford, CA: Stanford University Press, 1999).

[68] S. Ravi Rajan, 'Foresters and the Politics of Colonial Agro Ecology: The Case of Shifting Cultivation and Soil Erosion, 1920–1950', *Studies in History* 14,

the regional diversity in the study of environmental histories of the Indian subcontinent received close attention by historians. Ajit Menon has pointed out that 'the forest-dependent communities view land in terms not so much of ownership but of use'. Thus, colonial administrators made necessary adjustments and thus due considerations were accorded to the concerns of local communities in the Kolli hills.[69]

It is interesting to note that there were attempts to legitimize the British Forest policies as initiators of forest conservation policies. It has been argued that, the original 'greens' in India were in fact colonial officials. Colonial forest policy … was rooted in an enlightened understanding of environmental issues developed in particular by a group of remarkable Scottish medicos serving in the colonies, who sought initially to understand the connection between climate and health, but very quickly became experts in botany and ecology. They argued that there was a close connection between deforestation and environmental desiccation and pressed strongly for state-led conservation of forests. Through their pressure, the earlier laissez-faire attitude towards forests was replaced from the mid-19th century onwards by active management and control.[70]

The state-initiated efforts of conservation of forests were justified on the pretext of imparting scientific knowledge or banishing the forest dwellers from their traditional habitat on the pretext of harming the forests. The primacy of agriculture was thus quite evident.[71] Over-exploitation of groundwater and associated concern for soil erosion were seen as important concerns. At times, forest growth was considered harmful for groundwater as it sustained itself on the groundwater only.[72]

Thus, it is evident that colonial concerns with regard to conservation of forests were principally guided by covert economic considerations. Emerging literary traditions of romanticism where nature in its pristine

---

no. 2 (1998), 217–236; *Modernizing Nature: Forestry and Imperial Eco-development 1800–1950* (Hyderabad: Orient Longman, 2006).

[69] Ajit Menon, 'Colonial Constructions of "Agrarian Fields" and "Forests" in the Kolli Hills', *The Indian Economic and History Review* 41, no. 3 (2004): 315–337; V. Sarvanan, 'Colonialism and Coffee Plantations: Decline of Environment and Tribal in Madras Presidency During the 19th Century', *Indian Economic and Social History Review* 41, no. 4 (2004): 464–488; V. Sarvanan, *Colonialism, Environment and Tribals in South India,1792–1947* (Delhi: Routledge, 2016).

[70] From David Hardiman, Review of *Nature & The Orient* in *Economic and Political Weekly*, issue dated 3–9 July 1999.

[71] Bhattacharya, *Great Agrarian Conquest.*

[72] Ravi, 'Foresters and the Politics of Colonial Agro Ecology', 217–236.

form was aspired also contributed to efforts of conservation. Forests were to conserve the environment in its natural conditions.[73] Further, such an orientation suggested that to conserve the primitive form of environment, there is need to protect the aboriginals of the forests.[74]

Vasant Saberwal relates changing orientation of colonial policies regarding forest, land and agriculture with the changes in scientific understandings. He writes:

> This essay examines the chronological progression of the desiccation debate, and I have located my analysis in the broader scientific context within which these ideas were articulated during the late 19th and early 20th century. I explore the connection between a scientific paradigm of a given era, and bureaucratic use of this discourse on Himalayan degradation, the institutional context within which the discourse has taken place, has in a sense, shaped or directed the discourse. Over-time, one observes a two-way process whereby bureaucracies may use science to inform a particular rhetoric; at the same time bureaucratic rhetoric comes to influence the scientific discourse itself, and thereby the very nature of science.[75]

The picture will be sharper if we simultaneously examine the work of Mahesh Rangarajan.[76] Rangarajan has analysed how and why certain types of animals were directly targeted and consequently became extinct. Apparently, the quest for agricultural expansion resulted in the gradual shrinking of space for big animals. The shrinkage of the forests culminated in human–wildlife conflicts. Improved capacity due to better technology enabled the colonial government to combat and at times eliminate the 'dangerous beast'. The reasons behind the conversion of wildlife as dangerous beats and the role of human action were not the concern of the contemporary society. Interestingly, he also brings out the possible political uses of colonial policies to combat the wild beast.

---

[73] Archana Prasad, *Against Ecological Romanticism: Verrier Elwin and the Making of Anti-modern Tribal Identity* (New Delhi: Oxford University Press, 2003).

[74] Thomas R. Metcalf, *Ideologies of the Raj*, Vol. III, Part 4: The New Cambridge History of India (New Delhi: Cambridge University Press, 1995).

[75] Vasant K. Saberwal, 'Science and the Desiccationist Discourse of the 20th Century', *Environment and History* 4, no. 3 (1997): 309–343.

[76] Mahesh Rangarajan, 'The Raj and the Natural World: The War Against "dangerous beasts" in Colonial India', *Studies in History* 14, no. 2 (1998): 265–299; Arupjyoti Saikia, 'Kaziranga, Dynamics of Social and Political History', *Conservation and Society* 7, no. 3 (2009): 113–129.

Understanding of environmental issues through in-depth regional histories has become the other area of exploration. The interplay of regional identity and ecological niche has come into sharper focus now than in the past. It is interesting that there have been a few detailed microhistories of a particular range of hills, a watershed or a valley system, a reserved forest or a princely reserve. The passage given below illustrates this process:

> With the fall of the Barabati Fort in Cuttack in October 1803 and the subsequent signing of the treaty of Deogan in December of that year, the East India Company formally extended its sway over deltaic Orissa. The task of consolidation, and establishing the finer mechanisms of administration, however, soon floundered upon the Company's ignorance of the delta's complex ecology and perplexing tenurial arrangements.[77]

There have been several useful works on pastures, fields and forests of colonial and contemporary western India.[78] The primary concern of N. S. Jodha has been to examine 'the changing status and usage pattern of natural resources ... and the possibilities of arresting their negative trends characterising these changes'.[79] Exploring the growing contestation over 'common property resources', P. S. Kavoori examined the conditions of the pastoralists in the contemporary era.[80] R. Thomas Rosin arrived at similar conclusions: he found a relative shortage of the 'common grazing land' and contemporary preference for the sedentary lifestyle culminated in the reduced opportunities for the pastoralists. Unfortunately, this also resulted in the loss of alternatives for the peasantry during times of drought and famine.[81]

It was not very different for the tribes; their nomadic character made the British uncomfortable. British policy was resisted by these tribes because the British could never comprehend the complex functioning

---

[77] Rohan D'Souza, 'Rigidity and the Affliction of Capitalist Property: Colonial Land Revenue and the Recasting of Nature', *Studies in History* 20, no. 2 (2004): 237–272; *Drowned and Dammed: Colonial Capitalism and Flood Control in Eastern India: 1803–1946* (Delhi: Oxford University Press, 2006).

[78] Ann Grodzins Gold and B. R. Gujjar, *In the Times of Trees and Sorrows: Nature, Power and Memory in Rajasthan* (Durham: Duke University Press, 2002).

[79] N. S. Jodha, *Life on the Edge: Sustaining Agriculture and Community Resources in Fragile Environments* (New Delhi: Oxford University Press, 2001).

[80] Purnendu S. Kavoori, *Pastoralism in Expansion: The Transhuming Herders of Western Rajasthan* (New Delhi: Oxford University Press, 1999).

[81] R. Thomas Rosin, *Land Reforms and Agrarian Change: Study of a Marwar Village from Raj to Swaraj* (Jaipur: Rawat Publications, 1987).

of nomadic lifestyle and their symbiotic relationship with the land-scape they inhabited. Amita Baviskar has pointed out great continuity between colonial forest policies and forest policies of Independent India. Maintaining a sharp focus on the politics of land in 'tribal areas', she has documented the struggle of local inhabitants against the ever-increasing exploitation of natural resources and thereby elimination of patterns of livelihood.[82]

II: Making Invisible-Visible

Past societies considered nature as 'given' and, therefore, we rarely find descriptions of environment. Most of the times, literary descriptions of nature followed normative prescriptive formulations, otherwise refer-ences were incidental. However, it was difficult to negate the agency of nature in influencing the course of human civilization. This section of the chapter, drawing extensively from the archival sources avail-able at Rajasthan State Archives, Bikaner Rajasthan, will argue that a careful reading of concerns of society for environment in general and social negotiations with immediate environment reveals a lot about nature. In the semi-arid and arid landscapes of Rajasthan, along with human negotiations with monsoon for agrarian production, these sources suggest that societies took special care of its pastoral wealth. Local negotiations, often based on traditional knowledge available in the form of folk tales and epigraphic evidence, form an important tool to make invisible nature visible. Thus, the following narrative on the one hand will reflect upon ways in which conventional sources are being reread by scholars, and on the other, how new sources are being deployed to offer a very rich insight into the working of environment in past societies and human negotiations with nature.

In any attempt to understand the interactions between humans and environment, it is imperative on our part to avoid the notions of geographical determinism. It has been a major cause of concern for the historians dealing with history of the Middle Ages. Lucien Febvre suggested that 'there were no necessities, only possibilities. A river might be treated by one society as a barrier, yet as a route by another.'[83]

---

[82] Baviskar, *In the Belly of the River* (Delhi: Oxford University Press, 1995); Amita Baviskar, 'Written on the Body, Written on the Land: Violence and Environmental Struggles in Central India', in *Violent Environments*, eds. Nancy Peluso and Michael Watts (Ithaca, NY: Cornell University Press, 2001), 354–379.

[83] Peter Burke, *The French Historical Revolution: The Annales School, 1929–89* (Cambridge: Polity Press, 1990).

Similarly, one should not overemphasize the power of human agency in modulating the functioning of environment. Ramchandra Guha and David Arnold have suggested:

> Moving more firmly within the parameters of environmental history *per se*, there is the study of human engagement over time with the physical environment, of the environment as context, agent, and influence in human history. Here, nature figures unabashedly as human habitat, but in a dual capacity. On the one hand are ranged those elements of nature-climate, topography, animal and insect life, vegetation and soils-which directly or indirectly shape human activity and productivity. In affecting land-use and subsistence, they help to promote or prohibit specific forms of social structure, economic organization and belief systems. They also extend the margins of historical analysis and bring centre-stage a 'cast of non-human characters' normally ignored, at least until recently. ...But the relationship is a reciprocal one, for man more than any other any other living organism also alters the landscape, fells tree, erodes soils, dams streams, kills off unwelcome plants and predatory animals, installing favoured species in their stead.[84]

This necessitates engagement with the interrelationship of cultures and nature in different settings and most of all in viewing both not as stationary[85] rather as dynamic entities. Such works would have to delve into a wider set of sources: folksongs and legends, music and lore, epigraphic and archaeological, etc., locating these against the changing backdrop of human–nature encounters. Thus, it means reflecting at both in new ways and revisiting established notions of both culture and nature, however defined.

Importance of sources for writing history cannot be overemphasized and this holds true for environmental history as well. The absence of detailed accounts on environment is a stark feature of the sources of the medieval period. The sources of the period are mostly 'elitist' in nature, imbued in the 'Persian traditions' of historical writings. We mostly get the sketches of the ruling classes and institutions, written with the objective of perpetuating their self-interests. The Persian accounts,

---

[84] David Arnold and Ramchandra Guha, 'Introduction: Themes and Issues in the Environmental History of South Asia', in *Nature, Culture, Imperialism: Essays on the Environmental History of South Asia* (Delhi: Oxford University Press, 1995), 2.

[85] P. C. D. Milly, et al., 'Stationarity is Dead: Whither Water Management', *Science* 319 (2008), 573–574.

which abound during this period, are moulded in the dynastic tradition and obviously have scanty references to the environmental features. The same is true of some of the traditional provincial sources. The environment and its perceptions, therefore, rarely find a place in such descriptions. Non-Persian and especially literature in regional languages provide good amount of evidence and information on environment.[86]

Fortunately for pre-colonial Rajasthan in general and 17th–18th century in particular, we have a variety of historical sources to make invisible nature visible. To begin with, let me introduce few categories of archival and literary documents available at various repositories. There are several genera of official documentation available for this period in the Rajasthan Archives. These are *Arzdasht, Arhsattas, Sanad Parwana Bahi, Kagad Bahi,* etc. These sources delineate the official response to the natural distress and at the same time by implication, these provide us glimpses of contemporary socio-political responses and concerns. Prachya Vidya Sansthan on the other hand has published several very important contemporary literary sources. Along with the publication of Munhot Nainsi's *Vigat,* a major portion of the sources published by Prachya Vidya Sansthan are *Khyats.* These sources have been very informative and later sections of the chapter substantiate the claims made above. Saraswati Bhandar in Lalgarh fort Bikaner, Pratap Shodh Pratishthan, Bhupal Nobles Sansthan, Udaipur, Man Singh Pustak Prakash, Chopasini, Kapat Dwara Records and Amber have been excellent repositories of a variety of literature/records and, not to forget, are the collection of material culture along with visual documentations. Documentation of rich oral tradition is another important hallmark of popular concerns for historical evidence and heritage in the region. Scholars like Vijaydan Detha and Komal Kothari devoted their life to scientifically collect and publish popular tales, proverbs, their origins, etc., which were/have been in circulation in oral world of society. Equally important is to mention the collection of Jain religious literature in the region and particularly, Jain Vishva Bharti, Ladnun.

As far as literary sources are concerned, Rajasthan is very rich. Rajasthani literature of the medieval period has flown into five major currents: Jain, Charan, Akhyan, Saint and Laukik. We need not go into the details of literary traditions; however, it is important to point out that these literary sources provide interesting insights on environment. The usage of various similes and imageries in describing plants, animal life as well as the physical features of the region throws light on

---

[86] Tanuja Kothiyal, *Nomadic Narratives: A History of Mobility and Identity in the Great Indian Desert* (Delhi: Cambridge University Press, 2016).

the contemporary perceptions of environment. The information thus gleaned is of great importance in exploring certain dark patches in our narrative and occasionally supplements the information obtained from various other sources.

Thus, it is certain that the regional literature abounds in references to the physical environment. However, these sources require careful scrutiny, as the biases of the contemporary concerns are part of any kind of documentation. Before we delve into the historical contextualization of such references, it is important to mention that the descriptions of landscape by official and literary sources differ; yet, they quite often complement each other. The traditional descriptions of environmental features of any region perpetuate certain stereotypes. The traditional images of environment that are constantly reinforced in the conventional sources focus on the physical features of the region. It is more so with the 'official sources', which were written to serve specific purposes. The major concerns have therefore been mainly to study the geographical features vis-à-vis the production possibilities. For the official sources, landscapes were the basis of production possibilities and the strategic significance of the region in the wider context. Their primary concern was to describe the kind of soil, possible crops, mineral availability, etc., whereas literature provides glimpses of the perceptions of the environment vis-à-vis society.

The perceptions of environment have been extensively and beautifully traced in the contemporary literature. The immediate manifestations of environment are climate, seasons, landscapes, etc. Seasons are important manifestations of environment. These have been represented in the contemporary literature.

Contemporary literary representations of the region include the following:

थली वर्णन
थली सिरदार वर्णन
दसे दिस चावउ भोलो देस । उंफडा जल पीवइ बुरि असेस ।।
कहइ जे बोल मिलई सुखकार । सहु सिरि देस थली सिरदार ।।
जिहां नहीं कूड़ कलेस बजार । गिणहीं नहिं किणसूँ द्रोह लिगार ।।
धन थोड़े धर करइ साधर । सहु सिरि देस थली सिरदार ।।
धरा जिण बालक धर्म सु धीर । आया जिण काज अखंड अभीर ।।
नियाहण टेक जिहां नर नार । सहु सिरि देस थली सिरदार ।।
करइ चउकस जे होवै काम । सदा परदेस बीह जू ठाम ।।
करइ जिहाँ लोग सदा उपगार। सहु सिरि देस थली सिरदार ।।
जिहां नहीं रोग संभावइ जोर । भुजगल महा बलवंत अभोर ।।

डोलाला डाकी नइ डोकार। सहूसिरि देस थली सिरदार ।।
जिसा थल जोर अजंग अजेय । भला जिहां लोक गंभीर अभेय ।।
नर नारी होइ रतन्न न बार । सहू सिरि देस थली सिरदार ।।
जिहं भय होइ न दंड न जोर । चिहुं दिसि चावउ कोइ न चोर।
गटका जिहां दूध दही उद्गार। सहु सिरि देस थली सिरदार।[87]

[It is the best country in the world. Water is available at great depth, but is very good for the mind. It is very famous, and everybody knows, that *Thali is the king* of the land. There is no trouble on this land. Nobody fights. Prosperity is limited, however people are religious. *Thali* is the king of the land. Nobody talks ill of anybody, people are soft spoken and they believe in truth. *Thali* is the king of the land. Even the children believe in *Dharma*—righteousness. People will help you in the path of religion. People are helpful. People will do work with perfection. People from other regions come and settle here. People help each other. *Thali is the king* of the land. Here epidemics will not take place. Young men play with swords and even the old ones are very agile. *Thali* is the king of the land. The *thal* has been unconquered because the public is brave. People are like gems. *Thali is the king* of the land. People believe in charity. Even a little donation is enough to make one famous. People worship their teachers. *Thali is the king* of the land. There is nothing to fear or any need to use force. Honesty is everywhere; there is no theft. The land is full of milk and curd. *Thali is the king* of the land.]

थली दोस वर्णन

उड़ई जिहां खेह न थंभि रहइ । वज्जई जिहां पवन न किउही सहइ ।।
जल खारउ सोइ पावेइ वली । पिफट देस कुदेस कुखंड थली ।।
पट मासे नीर निवाण लहइं । जिहां चउपद जीवति स्याइ रहइ ।।
जिहां त्रास जलइ नर आस पफली । पिफट देस कुदेस कुखंड थली ।।
जिहां सूरख लोग पिसाच जिसा । काला अति भूछ कि भूत जिसा ।।
भरी रीवड छाछि पिवंति रली । पिफट देस कुदेस कुखंड थली ।।
जिहां डाढी मूछ न सूढ किसी । मिली भूहन दीसइ मुख दिसी ।।
जम्मारउ जाबइ साथि हली । पिफट देस कुदेस कुखंड थली ।।
जिहां तरबर सांगर बोर तणा । तिणि पाखलि दीसई साप घणा ।।
मिलि तोड़इ क्राढ़ै लोक लली । पिफट देस कुदेस कुखंड थली ।।
उफघाड़इ माथई कूक करइ । चड़ि खेजड़ि सांगर भार भरइ ।।
दीसंता भूत कि दैत दली । पिफट देस कुदेस कुखंड थली ।।
नित नीर न लागइ नीर जिया । भलउ भख्य न देखइ जेथ तिया ।।
जिहां सुख न कोई भेद मिली । पिफट देस कुदेस कुखंड थली ।।

---

[87] Agarchand Nahata, 'Thali Varnan', *Maru Bharti* 2, no. 1 (1954), 81–83. Cited earlier in Kumar, *Monsoon Ecologies*.

जिहां कांटा क्रँपड़ वाडि करइं । गाडां धरि हांडल तेथ भरइ ।।
पसु जीवित जीवई कवण कली । पिफट देस कुदेस कुखंड थली ।।
जल जेध न पावई पक्षी जिहां । तरू छोह न दीसइ पंथि तिहां ।।
चढ़ि खेजड़ क्रपड़ि सार चली । पिफट देस कुदेस कुखंड थली ।।
धरा थल पंथी दुक्ख धरइ । भरि पाए लागि भुरट्ट भरइ ।।
जिहां बोलै बसती एह जली । पिफट देस कुदेस कुखंड थली ।।
जिहां पीवइ सांढां दूध सकोइ । मरि मोगा थामो ठामइ हाइ ।।
लागइ उठि पंथी लोक बली । पिफट देस कुदेस कुखंड थली ।।
जिहां पीवण सांप निसा विचरइ । मणिधर पन्नग पफोंकार करइं ।।
धरि धवल देह आनंद रली । पिफट देस कुदेस कुखंड थली ।।
जिहां छक्कड़ दुक्कड़ द्रव्य घणाँ । जिहां जउवाकेरी कांई नमणा ।।
जिहां पूफल न पान न तेल पफली। पिफट देस कुदेस कुखंड थली ।।
जिहां कांटा आगलि पंथ नहीं । कोइ मानव पंथि न दीसई जहीं ।।
दादउ तिहां पावइ नीर मिली । पिफट देस कुदेस कुखंड थली ।।
जहां ढोल दमक्कइं नीर भरइ । साठीका कोहर कृक करइं ।।
केई नारी उफपरी नारि ढलो । पिफट देस कुदेस कुखंड थली ।।
जिहां उफन उखेली वस्त्रा करइं । धण माडर छाली दूध धरइं ।।
उफधड़ै गाडै वास गली । पिफट देस कुदेस कुखंड थली ।।
जिहां काचर बोर घमंड करइ । बलि रांध मतीरा पेट भरइ ।।
मन मांहे आयो आप रली । पिफट देस कुदेस कुखंड थली ।।
जिहां उफठि चढी दिन राति बहइ । दस कोसां एको कोस कहइ ।।
जिहां आकां कयरा छांह छली । पिफट देस कुदेस कुखंड थली ।।
कहुं केता थली तणां बाखांण । ए माणस नांही छइ पाखांण ।।
कह्या गुण देखी किउं संभली । पिफट देस कुदेस कुखंड थली ।।[88]

[It is a place where sand blows without any restriction. Here wind
blows at great speed. The water is brackish, so it is not potable hence
thali is such a bad land to live in. Ponds retain water only for six
months, and livestock suffers due to limited availability of water.
Thali is such a bad land to live in. Here people are like *Pishach*—ghosts
and as black as ghosts. People drink a lot of *chhachh*. *Thali* is such a
bad land to live in. People keep beard and moustache and their face
is full of dust, which blows here continuously. It is as if *yamraj*, the
god of death, accompanies the peasants who work in these conditions. *Thali* is such a bad land to live in. Here *Sangri*—dominates the
vegetation, which is an abode of snakes … *Thali* is such a bad land
to live in. People speak very loudly. They fetch *Sangri* from the trees
of *Khejri*. People look like ghosts or demon. *Thali* is such a bad land
to live in. People cannot take bath daily, not much is available as
food and there is no pleasure. *Thali* is such a bad land to live in. Here

---

[88] Ibid.

vegetation is full of thorns. Here water is not available for birds, trees do not provide shade and *khejar* dominates the land. *Thali* is such a bad land to live in. It is very difficult for someone to travel in these conditions as *Buhrat* grass pierces the feet. Heat makes it difficult to live even in the villages. *Thali* is such a bad land to live in. One gets milk of camel to drink. People migrate to other places. *Thali* is such a bad land to live in. Here yellow snakes roam around in the night. *Manidhari*—snakes with gems on their forehead play in the night. There are plenty of cattle and carts, which help in trade. There are no flowers or greenery. *Thali* is such a bad land to live in. There is no road which is not full of thorns. Even on long stretches of road there is no traveller. *Thali* is such a bad land to live in. The wells are so deep that water can be fetched only with the help of camels/bullocks. Water being so deep the fetching rope has to be very long. A camel is used to draw the rope up. In the process the camel goes so far that when the bucket comes up, it is informed by the beating of a drum. Such wells are known as *Saathi Ka Kuwa*. *Thali* is such a bad land to live in. Here cloths are woven from the wool, although milk is available in plenty, it is mainly camel and goat milk, grass is produced in abundance. *Thali* is such a bad land to live in. We have only *Kachar*, *Ber*, they make vegetable of *Matira*. These are the staple diet of *thali*. *Thali* is such a bad land to live in. This is the place where a day reigns supreme and nights are short. Land is so destitute that people call ten *Kos* of distance as only one. During daytime whatever shade is available is from the bushes of *Aak*. *Thali* is such a bad land to live in. This is how *Thali* is and it is not an exaggeration. These are its qualities also. *Thali* is such a bad land to live in.]

An interesting feature of contemporary literature is the almost simultaneous mention of both the virtues and vices of the region. There are various reasons to settle in the region described as the best country in the world. The water is available at great depths but is very good for the mind. Prosperity is limited but people are religious. People are helpful and hard working. People from other regions come and settle in this epidemic-free region. Young men are playful and even the old ones are very agile. Similarly, the vices have also been described at great length. Sand blows unhindered in this region. Wind blows here at a great speed. The water is brackish, so it is not potable. Ponds retain water only for 6 months, and livestock suffers due to limited availability of water.[89]

Literature very aptly documents human adaptation to the given climate, and thereby offers glimpses of the environment. This is reflected

---

[89] Cited earlier in Kumar, *Monsoon Ecologies*.

in the conversation between peoples living in different regions, wherein every speaker highlights the beauty of one's own region while criticizing other regions' problems. It is very much evident from the description in the folktale of *Dhola Maru Ra Duha* where Malwani, being a resident of Malwa, points out the problems with the environment of Marwar, whereas Maruni defends Marwar[90]:

ततखण माळवाणी कहइ, साँभलि कंत सुरंग । सगळा देस सुहाँमणा, मारू–देस विरंग ।।
बाळउँ, बाबा, देसड़उ, पाँणी जिहाँ कुवाँह । आधीरात कुहक्कड़ा, ज्यउँ माणसाँ मुवाँव ।।
बाळउँ, बाबा, देसड़उ, पाँणी–संदी ताति । पाँणी–केरइ कारणइ प्री छंड़इ अधराति ।।
बाळूँ, ढोला, देसड़उ जइँ पाँणी कूँवेण। कूँ–कूँ–वरणा हथ्थड़ा नहीं सुँ घाढा जेंण ।।
बाबा, म देइस मारूवाँ, सूध एवाळाँह । कंधि कुहाड़उ, सिरि घड़उ, वासउ मंझि थळाँह ।।
बाबा, म देइस मारूवाँ, वर कूँआरि रहेसि । हाथि कचोळउ, सिरि घड़उ सीचंती य मरेसि ।।
मारू, थाँकइ देसड़इ एक न भाजइ रिडड । ऊचाळउ क असरसणउ, कई फाकउ, कइ तिडड ।।
जिण भुइ पन्नग पीयण, कयर–कँटाळा रूंख । आके–फोगे छाँहड़ी, हूँछाँ भाँजइ भूख ।।
पहिरण–ओढण कंबळा, साठे पुरिसे नीर । आपण लोक उभाँखरा, गाडर–छाळी खीर ।।
मारू–देस उपन्निया तिहाँका दंत सुसेत । कूझ–बची–गोरंगियाँ, खंजर जेहा नेत ।।
मारू–देस उपन्निया, सर ज्यउँ पध्धरियाह । कड़वा कदे न बोलही, मीठा बोलणियाह ।।
देस निवाणूँ, सजळ जळ, मीठा–बोला लोइ । मारू काँमिणि दिखणि धर हरि दीयइ तउ होइ ।।
देस सुरंगउ, भुइँ निजळ, न दियाँ दोस थळाँह । घरि–घरि चंद–वदन्नियाँ, नीर चढइ कमळाँह ।।[91]

[Malwani says that except Marwar, all other regions are good. She complains that in Marwar it is so tedious to fetch water from deep wells that people begin this chore from mid-night itself. She says I would not live in such a region where husbands leave home at midnight to fetch water while the wives cannot do so as the excessive depth of water in wells makes it a laborious process. I wish that my father would not marry me off in Marwar because it is a place of pastoralists; one has to carry a vessel to fetch water and an axe. They live in the desert. I would prefer to stay unmarried than to go to Marwar where hands are bruised trying to fetch water from the deep wells. She tells Maruni that Marwar is full of problems. There is either drought or rains are delayed or one has to migrate or a locust attack. In Marwar, snakes abound and in the name of vegetation one gets only grass of Kair and Katra are considered as tree and bushes of Fog and Akra is the source of shelter from the sun. It is a place where

[90] Ibid.
[91] Mahavir Singh Gahlot, ed., *Dhola Maru Ra Duha* (Jodhpur: Rajasthani Granthagar, 1985), 176–180. Cited earlier in Kumar, *Monsoon Ecologies*.

water is available in wells only at a depth of sixty arms' lengths. Due to limited agricultural production, people are nomadic and get milk of sheep and goat only.

To these criticisms Maruni answers that Malwa is not a good place to live and defends Marwar. She says that people of Marwar are fair coloured and their teeth are bright. People of Marwar are soft spoken and straightforward. Marwar is full of tanks and the water of the region is good for health. She says that a girl from Marwar and the state of Marwar is bestowed only on lucky persons.]

One of the most prominent literary traditions in Rajasthan has been the writing of *Khyat*. The term is self-explanatory, meaning glory. Along with details of political developments, *Khyats* are also very informative with respect to social perceptions and concerns. Generally, the *Khyats* were written to describe the deeds of the kings or patrons of the bards. Precisely for this reason, *Khyats* constitute an important source for analysing the contemporary attitudes, perceptions, concerns and reactions of the patron kings. It is pertinent to point out here that although these works are good examples of literary efforts, the authors seem to be more concerned with the politico-administrative needs of the kingdoms.

If literary evidence at times tends to generalize and/or borrow from the long-established characterization of a region, archival administrative documents offer very localized and specific information of nature. The archival administrative records are often in the nature of official correspondence between the rulers on the one hand and officials posted in different parts of the concerned kingdoms on the other hand. Some of these were part of the royal communication and some of these were official directives. Several historians working on Rajasthan have extensively examined these documents. However, they have primarily focused on the socio-politico-economic factors to explain the major characteristics of the period.

An important category of official document available in archival repositories is the *Arzdasht* (petition) written by the Amils, Faujdar or other pargana officials to the ruler at Amber. These officials regularly reported, to the ruling authorities, about various revenue and administrative details of the areas under their control. These documents were written in response to the problems faced by concerned officials or local inhabitants, and therefore provide useful insights into the various concerns of political apparatus and common man. Simultaneously, they also give us the responses/remedies evolved to solve the problem. The other important archival source used in study is the *Arhsattas* (ledgers of receipts and expenditure) maintained at the pargana level. The

Arshattas are known to have contained basically 68 (*arhsat*) categories of information and were thus called *Arshattas*. The measurements of cultivable land, that is, land under actual cultivation, the tax thereupon and other such taxes realized in a pargana as was deemed necessary by the revenue officials, are also provided in these documents.

As far as the northwestern region, that is, Marwar, is concerned, we have used a very informative document known as *Sanad Parwana Bahi*. The terms *sanad* and *parwana* explain the functions that the documents performed. These are primarily imperial directives issued to the pargana officials in response to various complaints and representations received by it. The subject matter of these documents ranges from routine complaints, of undue exaction of revenue, against the revenue and other officials, to the mutual disputes over share of water of a well. To maintain the regular supply of revenue, it was necessary to ensure continuous settlements and, therefore, availability of water. With the assistance of the administrative set-up, the state not only appropriated greater revenue but could also locate and promote water-harvesting methods and negotiate with climatic variability.

The *kagad bahi* of Bikaner is particularly significant for a better comprehension of the land revenue system. A good deal of light is thrown on the problems faced by the peasants and the methods of redress adopted by the administrative machinery of the realm. Various kinds of concession and help were offered by the king and landed intermediaries to the peasantry, as monsoon failures were frequent in this region. Along with directives issued to the traders not to hoard the grain, details of various concessions dispensed by the ruling elite in times of natural exigencies have also been recorded in the *kagad bahi*.

A closer examination of the content and concerns of the archival and literary sources offers immense insights into the social perceptions, sensibilities and ecological settings. These sources also carry immense suggestions to decipher the concerns, perceptions, socio-politico negotiations and make it amply clear that during pre-colonial times the region, regional and local were closely integrated through ecology, socio-politico-economic networks.

An *Arzdasht* written by Fateh Chand Ramji from pargana Malarna dated Paus Vadi 5, 1716 vs (1659 AD), informs Raja Sawai Jaisingh that water from wells was being used for irrigation purposes as directed by the state.[92] An *Arzdasht*, written by Mouji Ram dated Kati Sudi 15, 1831

---

[92] *Arzdasht, Paus Vadi* 5, 1716 vs (1659 AD), Historical Section, Jaipur Records, Rajasthan State Archives, Bikaner. Henceforth, HS, JR, RSAB.

VS (1774 AD) HS, JR, RSAB., informs the state about meagre rainfall leading to drought. This resulted in the migration of the peasantry. In his *Arzdasht*, dated Jeth Sudi 1, 1819 VS (1762 AD) HS, JR, RSAB., Lal Chand Dala Ram informs about the migration of peasantry due to drought and the resultant decline in revenue collection. Similarly, another *Arzdasht* by Ajit Das, Man Ram dated Chait Vadi 3, 1809 VS (1752 AD) HS, JR, RSAB, informs that villages were deserted. Although contents of the following two *Arzdashts* prima facie depict concerns of administration vis-à-vis rainfall, these very aptly capture the nature of monsoon, one of the most important environmental factors in the life of peasantry. Two documents of the same year for Jaipur state provide contrary images of the monsoon. An *Arzdasht* by Rup Ram, dated Asad Vadi 1, 1752 VS,[93] informs us about drought, whereas for the same year, Purohit Haras Ram writes in his *Arzdasht* dated Bhadva Sudi 6 about good rainfall.[94] The same concern is corroborated by following popular saying:

The timely arrival of rains was very important. The following saying represents the desperation for rains. It is suggested that people are prepared to sacrifice their wealth to ensure rains:

सौ सांढीया सौ करहलां, पूत निपूती होय।
मेवड़ला बूठा भला, होणी होय सो होय ।।[95]

[Hundred female camels can be sacrificed, sons may die, but we need rains.]

and,

मेह ने पावणां किताक दिनां रा ।
राजा मान्या सो मानवी, मेयां मानी धरती।[96]

[Rains occur for a very limited period and if the king is happy, everybody is happy; similarly land shall be happy only with the rains.]

Clearly, the state was aware of the ecological realities, and therefore almost always attempted to maximize the utilization of available water.

In the year 1744 AD, an *Arshatta* provides an incident from the village Dhamorki, pargana Khori, that the Patel had diverted water from

---

[93] *Arzdasht*, Asad Vadi 1, 1752 VS, HS, JR, RSAB.

[94] *Arzdasht*, Bhadva Sudi 6, 1752 VS, HS, JR, RSAB.

[95] Kanhiya Lal Sahal, 'Rajasthan ki Varsha Sambandhi Kahavaten', *Maru Bharati* 4 (1956), 18.

[96] Ibid., 17–18.

the river without permission. He was punished with a fine of ₹20.[97] In the year 1768 AD, another complaint recorded that Rupa Patel of village Raitoli breached the embankment of the river to divert water for his use.[98] In another incident, the state punished a Gujar for diversion of water from other person's field in Qasba Baswa, pargana Bahatri in 1717 AD.[99] A similar dispute is reported in the same year from village Neembla, pargana Bahatri where Goverdhan Brahman fought with Tulani Brahman over the issue of diversion of water and hit him with an axe. Subsequently, he had to pay ₹11 as fine.[100] The village pond was used not only for washing clothes and ancillary activities but also by cattle for drinking purposes. Thus, any irresponsible act of causing pollution was punishable. We have evidence from Qasba Malpura, pargana Malpura that in the year 1734 AD, Lona dyer was fined ₹5.50 for washing dyed cloth in the pond, thereby polluting the water.[101] A *Sanad Parwana Bahi* informs about the construction of wells in the regions with a relatively high water table.[102] At times, these water bodies were constructed at the directives of the state.[103] Recognizing the value of animal husbandry to the economy of the kingdoms, the rulers even intervened to regulate the usage of grass. It was mandatory for the cultivators to share one-fourth of the grass produced by them with the state.[104] Apparently, these incidents document the administrative functions but a closer examination reveals that nature is being documented and social negotiations with environment are being recorded.

Sensibilities of the times and broader outlook of the kings and his advisors are very aptly reflected in the Munhot Niansi's *Khyat*. When Rao Jodha (ruler of Marwar) defeated Rana Kumbha (ruler of Mewar), it was decided that land, which sustained trees of *Babool* (acacia tree), would be bestowed to Marwar, whereas the *Aanwla* (Indian gooseberry) land would go to Mewar.[105] It very clearly highlights the point that land was identified by the kind of vegetation it supported. The division of

---

[97] *Arshatta, Pargana* Khori, 1801 vs (1744 AD) HS, JR, RSAB.

[98] Ibid., *Pargana* Dausa, 1825 vs (1768 AD) HS, JR, RSAB.

[99] Ibid., *Pargana* Bahatri, 1774 vs (1717 AD) HS, JR, RSAB.

[100] Ibid.

[101] Ibid., *Pargana* Malpura, 1791 vs (1734 AD) HS, JR, RSAB.

[102] *Sanad Parwana Bahi*, no. 1, 1764 vs (1707 AD), Jodhpur Records, RSAB; Bhadani, *Peasants, Artisans and Entrepreneurs*, 49. Wherever wells occurred more frequently in c. 1660, the water table was nearer the surface.

[103] *Sanad Parwana Bahi*, No. 2, 1765 vs (1708 AD), Jodh. Rec. RSAB.

[104] Kagad Bahi, 1827 vs/1770 AD, RSAB.

[105] Nainsi Munhot, *Marwar ra Pargana ri Vigat*, ed. Narain Singh Bhati, Vol. I (Jodhpur: Rajasthan Oriental Research Institute, 1968), 36.

territory between regional polities on the basis of natural environmental features once again highlights the significance of environmental context. Although Rao Jodha was victorious, his acceptance of land dominated by the growth of *Babool*—low productivity and arid conditions—as his territory and acceptance of the claim of Rana Kumbha for the region with thick growth of *Aanwla*—more fertile region—substantiate the fact that regional polities stressed their identification on specific ecological settings.

Similarly, Nainsi informs that, once the territory between Hardas and Sekha was divided on the basis of grass it supported. Sekha took control of land, which produced *Karar* (Dichanthium annulatum), while the Hardas got the *Bhurat* (Cenchrus biflorus) land.[106] The above division very clearly points out that regions were identified by the kind of vegetation it supported. Even the kind of grass grown in any region became the basis of political identification of regions. Thus, political narrative makes invisible nature speak and we not only get descriptions of landscape but also the glimpses of social perceptions of nature.

Even a cursory look at the above-cited evidence and arguments in both the sections of the chapter make it clear that recent past has produced a very rich and diverse depiction of nature, social negotiations with nature, impact of human activities on nature, etc. These writings on the one hand establish the fact that historians have enlarged their area of investigation and now it is almost impossible for historians to ignore the environmental factor from their investigations. Recent works have also very forcefully demonstrated that lack of historical sources is no more an acceptable excuse to ignore the significance of ecological context. The above write-up has suggested numerous ways of making invisible environment visible, and it is expected that future researchers will make use of such a rich and important set of writings, highlighting the significance of ecological context in any historical investigation.

---

[106] Nainsi Munhot, *Munhot Nainsi Ri Khyat*, ed., Acharya Badri Prasad Sakaria, Vol. I (Jodhpur: Rajasthan Oriental Research Institute, 1984), 89.

Rivers and Water

Environmental History of Water in Indian Cities

Gopa Samanta

Introduction

Drinking water is most obviously a *physical resource*, one of the few truly essential requirements for life. Drinking water is also a *cultural resource*, of religious significance in many societies. A *social* resource, access to water reveals much about membership in society. A *political resource*, the provision of water to citizens can serve important communication purposes. And finally, when scarce, water can become an *economic resource*.

—James Salzman[1]

Water is not simply a material element in the production of cities but is also a critical dimension to the social production of space. Water implies a series of connectivity between the body and the city, between social and bio-physical systems, between the evolution of water networks and capital flows, and between the visible and invisible dimensions to urban space. But water is at the same

[1] James Salzman, *Thirst: A Short History of Drinking Water* (Duke Law School Legal Studies Research Paper Series, Research Paper No. 92, December 2005), 3, http://ssrn.com/abstract=869970.

time a brutal delineator of social power which has at various times worked to either foster greater urban cohesion or generate new forms of political conflict.

—Matthew Gandy[2]

In the 21st century, management of water resources is emerging as one of humanity's most significant challenges. Population growth, economic development, expansion of irrigated agriculture and the enormous growth of cities led to dramatic increases in water use during the 20th century. The seriousness of the water management challenge is underscored by the fact that signs of water scarcity are already appearing around the globe. It is estimated that 41 per cent of the world's population lives in river basins where the per capita water supply is so low that disruptive shortages could occur frequently.[3]

The story of water in each big city in India, especially Mumbai, Chennai, Delhi, Kolkata and Hyderabad, is almost the same. There is acute crisis of water during winter and summer months, and urban flooding during the rainy season. Like other flood situations in the country, the cities do not require incessant rainfall for days to be flooded; just a few hours of heavy downpour can cause flooding of streets, creating havoc for transport, livelihoods and access to safe drinking water. In the discussion on the crisis of water in the cities, the first reason cited is the size of the population and its steady increase over time. The second point raised includes the diminishing sources of water, unpredictability of rainfall and increasing demand of water per person for the rising middle class of those cities. Policymakers and engineers always try to find newer sources of water to cope with the increasing demand in the city.

The point we often miss in discussions is the environmental deterioration being caused to the water sources, either in the name of development or to mitigate the increasing demand of water. Over-exploitation of the river regime, destruction of surface water sources, reduction of the diversified sources in the name of safety and purity, and depletion of groundwater are all very common in the history of water in this country. Yet, we never try to look at the histories of the water supply system from which we can probably learn some lessons

---

[2] Matthew Gandy, 'Rethinking Urban Metabolism: Water, Space and the Modern City', *City* 8, no. 3 (2004): 373.

[3] T. W. Fitzhugh and B. D. Richter, 'Quenching Urban Thirst: Growing Cities and Their Impacts on Freshwater Ecosystems', *BioScience* 54, no. 8 (2004): 741.

and correct certain strategies to prevent a water-poor future for the cities. An in-depth analysis of environmental history reveals to us the right and wrong decisions humans have taken to mitigate the demand of water at different times. Although right and wrong are very subjective and time-specific terms, there is a need to look into the sustainable dimension of the environment over a longer period of time, taking the historical context into consideration.

This chapter, using secondary sources of material, tries to explore the role of water history in understanding the present context of water in Indian cities. The arguments are built around three core issues: (a) the role of environmental history in solving the present-day problem of water in cities; (b) the colonial history and post-colonial legacy of centralized networked water supply and the death of traditional and diversified sources of water; and (c) the depletion of river and regional ecosystems, affecting long-term supply of water in cities.

Environmental History of Cities: A Little Background

Recently urban environmental scholars have become increasingly pessimistic about the future of large cities and their ability to reach the levels of sustainability if current trends of resource use and economic development continue. As a historian I am in no position to provide models and technical solutions to these problems. History, however, can offer perspectives and analyses that provide scholars of the current environment and policy makers with a deeper understanding of the urban predicament. By so doing, historians can also help to clarify choices and options in the formulation of current policy.[4]

Although it started as a separate branch of study only in the 1990s in America and subsequently in Europe, urban environmental history has become a significant component of historical research, owing to the present-day environmental crisis, ranging from pollution, water, to sanitation and, finally, climate change. Initially, environmental historians did not consider the urban setting as an important aspect to consider for research, as they hardly found much nature within the cities. That is why they continued to consider cities as spaces produced by industrial activities, where nature did not have an important role to play, and instead engaged themselves in understanding the environmental

---

[4] Dieter Schott, 'Urban Environmental History: What Lessons are There to be Learnt?', *Boreal Environment Research* 9 (2004): 519.

history of naturalized spaces such as forests, agriculture and rivers. On the contrary, the urban historians used to study the

> infrastructure, public works, and engineering [which] emanates from the history of technology; the study of building technology from architectural history; interest in public health and disease from medical history; pollution regulation from law; urban reform from political history; and city growth and city services from urban history and city planning history.[5]

In the 1990s, Melosi[6] argued that

> cities are also major modifiers of the physical environment. Their existence can influence the course of basic physical processes, such as the hydraulic cycle. Urbanization removes much of the filtering capacity of soil and rapidly channels precipitation into available watercourses, thus encouraging flooding. City building affects the atmosphere by increasing air-borne pollutants and also creating heat islands where temperatures are greater than the surrounding area. Various urban activities produce huge volumes of waste products which require complex disposal mechanisms.

To understand those processes, we need to fall back on environmental history. These studies will inform the policymakers how much harm the city-building processes cause to nature in and around cities. The current policymakers can learn from historians, to decide future policy and to curtail the environmental cost.

Thus, urban environmental history, as a newer branch of environmental history, started to develop only in the 1990s as a reaction to the reduction of environmental history to natural spaces.[7] Since then, the situation started to change, and a number of studies were conducted on the environmental history of American cities. These studies covered a wide range of cities, from the industrial city of Chicago in the north to St. Petersburg, Florida in the south. In America, the environmental history studies were more focused on the city-building process, while their counterparts in Europe were more engaged with pollution, public health, water and sanitation. Since then, urban environmental history studies have gained momentum in other countries

---

[5] Martin V. Melosi, 'The Place of the City in Environmental History', *Environmental History Review* 17, no. 1 (1993): 11.

[6] Ibid., 7.

[7] Ibid.

too. Even in India, environmental historians started to engage themselves in studying the environmental history of metropolitan cities
such as Mumbai[8] and Delhi.[9]

Flanagan[10] proposed three premises for the field of environmental
studies to encompass more centrally the urban context:

> The first premise is that it is incorrect to view the built environment
> as only a recent industrial phenomenon. The second is that human
> beings have existed in a historical dialectic with the natural world
> for thousands of years. The third is that cities themselves are envi-
> ronmental spaces.

He further explained how cities were always intimately linked to the
environment and caused enormous damage to the environment.

> The founders of Rome altered the natural world to build their city;
> the Roman emperors reshaped the hills of the city to build their mag-
> nificent urban structures and exhausted the available land to keep
> building the city. The crush of inhabitants of ancient Rome or early
> modern London and Paris altered the land and the biosphere for waste
> disposal and for burials. The walls erected around medieval western
> cities disrupted the harmony of nature. The tons of stone quarried
> and cut out of mountains to erect the monumental Romanesque
> and Gothic cathedrals of European cities just as surely altered the
> biosphere as did agriculture.[11]

Today, cities throughout the world are suffering from enormous
environmental crisis, mostly in the fields of water, sanitation and
pollution. Among all these, the most significant issue is the future of
water in cities, which is the main lifeline for the survival of the city.
To understand the depth of these problems and to minimize the environmental risks in future, environmentalists and policymakers need
to learn from history. To minimize the future risk, we also need to
unearth the history of traditional sustainable practices of the original
inhabitants of each and every place, which does not currently exist in

---

[8] Mariam Dossal, *Imperial Designs and Indian Realities: The Planning of Bombay
City, 1845–1875* (Bombay: Oxford University Press, 1991).

[9] Ardhendu Sharan, *In the City, Out of Place: Nuisance, Pollution, and Dwelling
in Delhi, c. 1850–2000* (New Delhi: Oxford University Press, 2014).

[10] Maureen A. Flanagan, 'Environmental Justice in the City: A Theme for
Urban Environmental History', *Environmental History* 5, no. 2 (2000): 159,
http://www.jstor.org/stable/3985633, accessed 20 June 2016.

[11] Ibid., 159–160.

the mainstream knowledge domain. In a discussion on the mitigation of climate change and disaster, Ghosh[12] explains why the indigenous islanders of Asia were largely unaffected by the devastating Tsunami in 2004: 'It is because of their traditional historical knowledge about the behaviour of seas and that is why they used to live in the interiors. In contrary the people from mainland occupied the coastal location, the rich occupying the places more close to the city.' Following Flanagan,[13] it can be said, 'Finally cities themselves are environmental spaces. What goes on inside the city, whether of the walled ancient and medieval variety or the sprawling metropolis of today, involves a contestation over the realm of nature and the use, distribution, and preservation of its resources.' We need to explore these facets just to save the cities in future.

History of Water in Cities

The most significant problem each city is encountering throughout the world is of water, in terms of both quantity and quality. Though the urban environmental history has made tremendous efforts to bring the environmental issues of the cities to the fore, the history of water in cities is still not sufficiently explored and analysed, especially in India. However, from the above-mentioned discussion on environmental history, it is understood that it is significantly important. The future of the cities is entirely dependent on the sufficient supply of safe drinking water.

In dealing with the problem of the present condition of water and developing a model for the future, people have started rightly to fall back on history. In developing a six-staged water transition framework from 'water supply city' in the 1800s to 'water sensitive city' of the future and in identifying sustainable urban water management policies in major Australian cities, scholars[14] have relied on the history of water management policies in the country. Through a historical analysis of changing institutional and technological arrangements supporting

---

[12] A. Ghosh, *The Great Derangement: Climate Change and the Unthinkable* (New Delhi: Penguin Books, 2016), 46.

[13] Flanagan, 'Environmental Justice in the City', 160.

[14] R. Brown, N. Keath, and T. Wong, 'Transitioning to Water Sensitive Cities: Historical, Current and Future Transition States', Paper presented in 11th International Conference on Urban Drainage, 2008, Edinburgh, Scotland, UK, https://web.sbe.hw.ac.uk/staffprofiles/bdgsa/11th_International_Conference_on_Urban_Drainage_CD/ICUD08/pdfs/618.pdf

urban water management practices for the last 200 years, they have developed the water transition framework to provide a typology of the attributes of hydro-social contracts and proposed the potential future hydro-social contracts underpinned by the sustainable principle.

In India, the studies available on environmental history of water are more commonly located within the geographical spaces of forest, agriculture and rivers. The urban environmental history studies by Dossal[15] in Mumbai and Sharan[16] in Delhi accommodated one chapter each on the colonial history of metropolitan water supply. There might be a possibility that the history of urban water studies lies in documents in the vernacular languages of different states in India, which is hard to access for the mainstream English academia. Thus, there is an emergent need to explore the history of water in different cities of India located in different geographical locations and having different trajectories of development.

The water history of each city, to some extent, varies from each other. Even in India, all the metropolitan cities got their first centralized piped network of water during the British period and by British engineers. Yet, the history of Mumbai varied from the history of Chennai.

> Had the then Mumbai's British administrators not taken seriously an agitation by the island's natives over the drinking water problem in 1845 and subsequent search for water sources even 100 km deep into the mainland, Mumbai's citizens, perhaps, would have been as harassed for water as Chennai's people are now. Like Chennai, Mumbai also depended on wells and ponds/lakes for its water supply. Overdrawing of water by ever-increasing population caused depletion of groundwater sources and also ingress of seawater in Chennai. The same could have happened to Mumbai, as both these are coastal cities.[17]

We need to know the history of water to solve the present-day problems linked to it—whether it is water scarcity or urban flooding. To understand the frequent and severe urban flooding in the city of Mumbai and to search for a solution, Ghosh[18] recommends learning about the environmental history of the city-building process:

---

[15] Dossal, *Imperial Designs and Indian Realities*.

[16] Sharan, *In the City, Out of Place*.

[17] The Bombay Community Public Trust, *Understanding Our Civic Issues: Mumbai's Water Supply*, http://www.bcpt.org.in/articles/watersupply.pdf, accessed 1 September 2016.

[18] Ghosh, *Great Derangement: Climate Change and the Unthinkable*, 52.

The Islands of South Mumbai did not long remain as they were when they were handed over to the British: links between them, in the form of causeways, bridges, embankments and reclamation projects, began to rise in the eighteenth century. The reshaping of estuarine landscape proceeded at such as pace that by the 1860s a Marathi chronicler, Govind Narayan, was able to predict with confidence that soon it would never occur to anybody that Mumbai was an island once.

Colonial History of Centralized Water Supply in Indian Cities

The challenges of constructing large municipal water systems were quite formidable during the nineteenth century (indeed, they are not trivial today). A variety of complex decisions had to be made, each one involved extensive research and planning together with a precarious balancing act in volatile political environments. An appropriate water source had to be identified. For most cities, there were generally many candidates, including surface water (streams, rivers and lakes) and groundwater sources of various sorts. Survey work by geologists and engineers was a difficult and time-consuming task, and their findings were often controversial and subject to political pressure. Each potential source required estimates of supply volume and purity (particularly difficult before science elucidated what "purity" meant). Engineers would then attempt to estimate how water from each source could be delivered to city populations.[19]

The introduction of centralized water systems took place in Europe in the early 19th century—in 1802 in Paris, 1808 in London and 1856 in Berlin. Since then, the European model of a centralized network had been implemented as the universal model of water supply system in other parts of the world, especially in the cities of British colonies. India was no exception to this rule, being part of the then British empire. Although influenced by Western modernity through the British rulers, these cities have their own trajectories in history. Sharan[20] opined that Indian cities have different configuration of things and discourses that merit their own account, and this account is a historically situated one. Environmental quality, in the past and in the present, must be

---

[19] David Cutler and Grant Miller, 'Water, Water Everywhere: Municipal Finance and Water Supply in American Cities', in *Corruption and Reform: Lessons from America's Economic History*, eds. Edward L. Glaeser and Claudia Goldin (University of Chicago Press, 2006), 157. http://www.nber.org/chapters/c9982
[20] Sharan, *In the City, Out of Place*, 2.

simultaneously interrogated, to better apprehend the contemporariness of our distinctive urban modernity.

The history and the politics of this colonial initiative for metro cities of India have been scholarly analysed at length by Dossal,[21] Sharan[22] and Lahiri-dutt[23] in their respective studies on Mumbai, Delhi and Kolkata. All these studies indicate that the British were very suspicious about the use of river water—Ganga in Kolkata and Yamuna in Delhi—on the grounds of hygiene maintained by the river user community. The fear of epidemic and scarcity of water during summer months and consequent dependence on the Indian community for water were the major reasons for developing a centralized network of piped water supply. Before the advent of the British in these cities, the chief sources of water supply were ponds, tanks and wells constructed by rich households for individual use or for public use in memory of loved ones. For example, in Mumbai, the Cowasji Patel Tank was constructed in 1823 and the Framji Cowasji Tank in 1831.[24] In Kolkata, it was primarily the water from the River Ganga and the inland ponds and tanks which were major sources of water. Delhi, being the capital of the Mughal Empire, had developed some organized inflow of water from the Yamuna river through canals, and the rest of the city depended on wells. Sharan[25] narrates the situation of Delhi as follows:

> Before the British occupied Delhi in 1803, the city had diverse water sources. There were numerous well and tanks beside the canal bringing water from Yamuna built and maintained by the Mughal Emperors. By 1860s, there were reportedly 1000 wells in the city, with 600 being private and 400 public.

The British never thought of universal access to piped water supply. They wanted to arrange safe supply of drinking water first for their military and then for the citizens, especially to the European and elite Indian neighbourhoods. The primary purpose of a centralized water

---

[21] Mariam Dossal, 'Henry Conybeare and the Politics of Centralised Water Supply in Mid-nineteenth Century Bombay', *The Indian Economic and Social History Review* 25, no. 1 (1988): 79–96; Dossal, *Imperial Designs and Indian Realities*.

[22] Sharan, *In the City, Out of Place*.

[23] Kuntala Lahiri-Dutt, 'Researching World Class Watering in Metropolitan Calcutta', *ACME: An International E-Journal for Critical Geographies* 14, no. 3 (2015b): 700–720.

[24] Dossal, *Imperial Designs and Indian Realities*, 96.

[25] Sharan, *In the City, Out of Place*, 26.

network in India during the British period was the good health of imperial troops, as troop mortality in India owed far more to disease than to war casualties, and to protect the health of the troops, the good health of the residents of the native towns and villages that adjoined the cantonments was paramount.[26]

In Mumbai, following inadequate monsoon rain between 1845 and 1855, the British wanted to do something to deal with the scarcity of water in the city, especially to ensure supply to their troops stationed in Colaba. Faced with the fear of recurrent water crisis and cholera epidemics, the government requested British engineers to work on a long-term solution. The network's water from the Vihar Project reached primarily the colonial quarters as opposed to the native ones.[27] According to Lahiri-Dutt,[28] until about the 1920s, most households in Kolkata did not have piped water supply because only the richer, whiter parts of the city and the homes of a few aristocratic families were connected to the corporation pipeline. A similar situation is noted by Sharan[29] in Delhi. He mentioned that the system in Delhi was more an archipelago than a universal network that featured in contemporary European cities. Sharan[30] narrates: 'Delhi's piped water connection first came to the walled city, which housed the cantonment, followed by the western suburbs, and finally the Civil Lines. The richer natives were encouraged to connect their houses to the water supply.'

The centralized water supply was not only an essential service to the citizens in colonial India but also a symbol of power and control. It was required to centralize the control in government hands and to establish a more effective urban order. The efficient arrangement of sufficient water made the British Empire more powerful. Dossal[31] describes that the Vihar Project was an attempt to further extend the government's control over the everyday life of the town's inhabitants and over a vital economic resource for the sustenance of shipping and commercial activities. He further mentions that the availability of assured municipal piped water from Vihar substantially reduced Bombay island's dependence on its wells and tanks, which was politically advantageous to the

---

[26] Ibid., 23.
[27] Marie-Hélène Zérah, 'Splintering Urbanism in Mumbai: Contrasting Trends in a Multilayered Society', *Geoforum* 39 (2008): 1922–1932.
[28] Lahiri-Dutt, 'Researching World Class Watering'.
[29] Sharan, *In the City, Out of Place*.
[30] Ibid., 38
[31] Dossal, *Imperial Designs and Indian Realities*, 103.

government as it reduced the government's dependence on Bombay's inhabitants for water during the long summer months.[32]

From the very beginning, finance was always an important issue for the construction of big water work projects even in the colonial period. The British government in India had to make a lot of efforts to convince the British government in London to pass the funds necessary for centralized water works in Indian cities. Sharan[33] states that colonial efforts at urban environmental improvement were, however, only partially realized. In the absence of adequate financial support, several projects either made paper deaths or could only meet some of their targets. These big projects needed huge expenses as maintenance cost besides the large amount of capital cost for construction. The British India government wanted to divert the financial responsibility of maintenance cost through increase in the property tax of the Indian inhabitants. As for example, after the construction of Vihar Project in Mumbai, it was handed over to the municipal authority in 1863, and the then municipality ruled by the British decided to increase the property tax to meet the expense further needed to maintain the system. While balancing mechanisms were implemented early on to ensure coverage expansion, in Bombay the cost of a connection proved to be affordable only for Europeans and well-off Indians.[34] Putting financial responsibility on the citizens was not accepted by the merchant community in Mumbai, and with this apprehension in mind, they had protested against the Vihar Project even before its construction.

Dossal[35] lamented the history of this resistance from the merchant community as follows:

> The Vihar water works project met with the strong resistance from the merchants of Bombay. Many of them had in the past constructed tanks or opened their private wells and tanks to the general public in times of water scarcity. But this project was no one-time act of charity, no individual decision to allow the public the use of private wells. These works were planned on a scale and in a manner which would increase taxation on the Indian communities. No one recognized this sooner than the merchants.

---

[32] Ibid., 116.
[33] Sharan, *In the City, Out of Place*.
[34] Zérah, 'Splintering Urbanism in Mumbai'.
[35] Dossal, *Imperial Designs and Indian Realities*, 102.

The merchants wrote a letter to the Bombay government and proposed an alternate solution to meet the water shortage in the city. Dossal[36] explained:

> To solve the problem of water shortage the merchants recommended improvements in the supply and distribution of the existing resources of spring water. This could be done by pipes and siphons, by the construction of filtering wells, by covering Tanks and wells, by altering the shapes of the sides of the tanks to lessen evaporation. Special storage reservoirs of filtered water could be constructed when the tanks dried up and the water shortage grew severe. All this could be done 'at a comparatively small expense' and be much cheaper than the Vihar works.

The Vihar Project in Mumbai was experimental as a model of centralized water supply system in British India. The successful implementation of this project was followed by replication of the model in other important cities like Delhi and Kolkata. Since the British started to develop their own centralized water networks in different cities, they either ignored or destroyed the traditional systems and water sources in Indian cities in the name of public health. The existing wells in Delhi had been closed down on grounds of insanitation in the early part of the 20th century.[37] Many ponds were filled up in Kolkata following the same argument.[38] Thus, the diversified water sources of pre-British Indian cities were destroyed during the colonial period.

The same trends were continued in post-independence Indian cities but with a major diversion from surface to groundwater. Sharan[39] opined that the colonial legacy of material, technical and institutional arrangements continued in Indian cities in the post-colony even when much else changed regarding democratic citizenship and the possibilities of technological modernization. Groundwater is overemphasized for the sake of cheaper cost and purity. The traditional sources of water within the cities lie relatively ignored, while groundwater resources get depleted at a faster pace. As Sharan[40] points out, '[t]hese actions

---

[36] Ibid., 103.

[37] Sharan, *In the City, Out of Place*.

[38] Mohit Ray, *Kalikata Pukur Katha: Paribesh, Itihas, Samaj* [The Story of Kolkata Ponds: Environment, History and Society] (Kolkata: Ananda Publishers, 2013).

[39] Sharan, *In the City, Out of Place*, 5.

[40] Ibid., 5.

indicate deep impact that the colonial modern communities have on urban environmental thought and practice even today'.

History of Transition from Diversification to Centralization and from Surface to Groundwater

Starting from big metropolitan cities to the smaller cities of India, the historical trajectory of water is the same. The supply always runs from diversified sources to a centrally organized piped network. The metropolitan cities (Mumbai, Kolkata, Delhi and Chennai) of India experienced these trajectories during the colonial period following the model of centrally managed water supply and sewer system of British cities, especially of London. The same legacy is being carried forward in the post-independence period with overwhelming importance given to the centrally organized water network utilizing mostly groundwater and ignoring the other sources which helped the citizens to survive over generations.

This high dependence of groundwater has been continued and enhanced for several reasons. These sources of pure water are therefore free from the fear of contamination; they are cheaper at cost as they do not require big capital investment like building a tank or water treatment plant. At present, almost all cities of India are thus fully or partially dependent on groundwater, but in the process, the cities' groundwater is overexploited, and in most cases, their levels have reached an alarming low. Moreover, in the cities of coastal locations such as Chennai, the overexploitation of groundwater has led to the intrusion of seawater in many places, affecting the potability as indicated by a battery of indicators.[41]

The dependence on groundwater increases with the decrease in the size of the cities. The utilization of the surface water from rivers needs big projects and huge financial resources, which are often not available to the city governments. That is why the cheapest option available to them is the tapping of groundwater. This is more so in the case of smaller cities whose financial conditions are not good compared to the big cities.[42]

---

[41] S. Janakarajan, M. Llorente, and Marie-Hélène Zérah, 'Urban Water Conflicts in Indian Cities: Man-made Scarcity as a Critical Factor', in *Urban Water Conflicts: An Analysis of the Origins and Nature of Water-related Unrest and Conflicts in the Urban Context* (UNESCO Working Series SC-2006/WS/19, 2006), 91–112.

[42] D. Sengupta, P. Goswami, and K. Rudra, *Jwal* (*Water*) (Kolkata: Anvel Press, 2014).

However, if we try to trace the history of water supply of major cities in India, we will see that the dependence on groundwater has increased over time in each city. In most cases, the available groundwater is exploited in an unplanned and unregulated manner, resulting in ecological degradation.[43] Besides four water reservoirs located in the northern part of the city, which are filled by monsoon rainfalls, Chennai city is entirely dependent on its groundwater resources. Chennai's river basin mainly comprises three rivers, but these are not used as drinking water sources, as the rivers are highly polluted with sewage and waste.[44] The city of Kolkata has had five water treatment plants in use for a long time. There has been no addition to the list in the recent past to use the water from River Ganga. However, the city has 28 pumping stations with reservoirs to utilize the groundwater and six more are under construction. These data indicate that the story of water in the Indian city has become the story of groundwater, irrespective of the city's size.

In an in-depth empirical study on the city of Chandernagore in West Bengal, Ganguli[45] has shown how along with the provision of piped water supply, the water culture of the people in the city has changed over time and diversified sources have been abandoned by the people who have access to the centralized piped supply. The city is located on the banks of the River Hugli, but the city government withdraws groundwater from 43 deep tube wells to supply water. Although the water table rises during the rainy season and falls during the dry season, the overall trend of groundwater level has been observed to have declined in the area. The water is drawn from a depth of 100–135 m because of the good quantity and purity of water. There is a new water treatment plant that has been constructed using central government funding to utilize the river water, but the city government does not use it because of high maintenance cost, which needs to be met by the city government itself.

To cope with the increasing demand for water, the number of pump houses has increased, withdrawing groundwater without considering the standard norms of minimum distance between pump houses. Moreover, the municipal workers often install new pumps near older,

---

[43] Janakarajan, Llorente, and Zérah, 'Urban Water Conflicts in Indian Cities'.

[44] Mahesh Kumar S. T. 'With three rivers and five wetlands, why is Chennai staring at ecological collapse?' February 6, 2017. https://chennai.citizenmatters.in/chennai-rivers-wetlands-marsh-environment-heritage-1577

[45] Malay Ganguli, *Urban Water Management and the Question of Sustainability of Chandernagore and Chinsurah Cities* (Unpublished PhD thesis, University of Burdwan, 2014).

abandoned ones to use the established electricity set-up of the previous pump house. Because of this closer spacing of pump houses, ecological deterioration takes place in terms of aquifer yielding capacity.[46] Most of the pump houses supply water to the households directly, as they do not have enough storage tanks. Thus, the pumps need to be kept running during the entire supply hours. As a result, the system costs a huge amount of power and causes wastage of water flowing down the open taps.

Being located in the Ganga delta area, Chandernagore is also rich in both surface and sub-surface water sources. The rich sub-surface water could easily be tapped through dug wells. Before the augmentation of piped water supply by the municipal corporation, a large number of households in the city had dug wells. These wells accumulate water from the sub-surface and can be recharged easily by monsoon rain. Places where the clay layer dominates the surface get plenty of surface and sub-surface water. The clay layer helps to create artificial tanks such as ponds, dug wells, etc. This gives a great opportunity to store water, which can play an important role in saving groundwater for future use.

Ganguli's[47] calculation estimated an annual availability of water from dug wells in the year 2011 as 118.962 ham. The total water demand in the city in the same year was 822.6412 ham. Therefore, dug wells can supply 15 per cent of total annual water demand of the city and they can reduce the pressure on groundwater to a considerable extent, as dug well water is easily renewable from the surface water sources, which ensures the net availability of water. He also observed that newly added areas of the city are still dependent more on dug well water, as they do not get sufficient municipal supply. Thus, we see that with the centralization of water sources—which is groundwater in this city—the diversification of sources is getting reduced.

The physical set-up of the town gives the area a real opportunity to utilize a good amount of surface water. Many ponds of different sizes are present in the area. Around 8.30 sq. km area (37.7% of the total) of the city is under surface water bodies. These ponds, besides supplying direct water to the community, also recharge dug wells round the year. In the past, people used these ponds for bathing and washing before they had access to piped water supply. The water culture has undergone tremendous changes in the city from diversified sources to mono source of municipal supply.

---

[46] Ibid.
[47] Ibid.

The ponds are not special to Chandernagore alone; rather, most of the cities located in Bengal used to have enormous number of ponds as dominant water bodies. The soft alluvial soil of the Bengal delta area facilitated the digging of ponds through centuries to offer an easy source of water to the people of the city. The ponds in the cities were dug either by individuals or by communities. Digging a pond for community use was considered as pious work for quite a long time, since these were used for drinking purposes. It was also the responsibility of the local zamindars and rajas to dig ponds to facilitate the uninterrupted supply of water to the citizens.

Burdwan town in Bengal has four big ponds (locally called *sayar*), which were mainly dug by the family of Burdwan Raj in the 17th and 18th centuries.[48] Chakraborty also tried to trace the name and the history of hundreds of ponds in the city, which give us a fascinating cultural history of pond water in the city. Most of these ponds are now either in a bad condition or have lost their existence due to the real estate demand supported by political power in the city. *Pukur churi*, a Bengali term meaning theft of pond, has become a reality in today's cities in West Bengal, whether they are located in the metropolitan city of Kolkata or in other small towns.

In explaining the history of ponds and lakes in Kolkata city, Ray[49] states that the initial development of the city of Kolkata during the British period was intimately connected to the construction of ponds and lakes. It was a marshy lowland area frequently interspersed with wetlands. That is why the city-building process itself needed extra soil to raise the land higher, and in doing so, people usually dug ponds to get the additional supply of soil. It was the practice not only of individual households but also of the local government institutions such as Kolkata Improvement Trust. This Trust dug Dhakuria Lake, later named as Rabindra Sarobar, between 1920 and 1930, to enhance the city-building process in the watery parts of the south.[50]

During the British period, too many ponds in the city became a significant problem in terms of health and hygiene conditions, since the British found most of these ponds to be unclean and breeding grounds for mosquitoes and other insects affecting the public health of the city. The British administrators started to build big tanks such as Lal Dighi to supply safe drinking water to the city and simultaneously

---

[48] Sanjib Chakraborty, *Sahar Barddhamaner Jalabhumi* [Waterbodies of Barddhaman Town] (Natun Chithi Sharad Sankha, 2010b), 324–330.

[49] Ray, *Kalikata Pukur Katha*.

[50] Ibid., 23.

destroyed small ponds on the grounds of hygiene. After independence, Kolkata received an enormous flow of refugees from Bangladesh. To accommodate these people, the city was expanded towards the south and east at the cost of ponds and wetlands.

The ponds and wetlands were earlier used by the poor people not only for bathing and washing but also for their livelihood. In each city of Bengal, the death of ponds has been accentuated since the time the municipal governments started to supply piped water in sufficient quantities even to the poor. The poor could not afford to pay for private tube wells and would earlier use the ponds to fulfil their many different needs. The filling of ponds for real estate development also becomes easier when local communities lose interest in ponds, as they are no longer directly dependent on the ponds, and when no protest is seen from the communities living near those ponds.

The sheer negligence of urban surface and subsurface water in places like the Bengal delta, where such sources are naturally available, and too much dependence on groundwater make the future of water in cities unsustainable. At one point of time in history, people depended on diverse sources, but with the advent of technology, groundwater has become the only source being utilized, neglecting all other sources. Now the time has come when we need to turn the trend again to diverse sources for the sake of the future of the water vis-à-vis the future of the cities.

Indian Middle Class and Changing Water Culture

It is no wonder then that the middle-class in India is endeavouring to find new ways of being; hungrily consuming resources such as water and energy that were hitherto out of the reach of ordinary Indians.[51]

The rise of the middle class in the neoliberal regime and their changing consumption pattern has become an important subject matter of urban studies in India.[52] The new middle class constitutes the major water-consuming class in the cities after industrial houses. Access to uninterrupted and sufficient supply of water has become part of the citizen's demand in each and every city in India. The city government

---

[51] Lahiri-Dutt, 'Researching World Class Watering', 703.

[52] See for instance, M. Voyce, 'Shopping Malls in India: New Social "Dividing Practices"', *Economic and Political Weekly* (June 2, 2007): 2055–2062; C. Brosius, *India's Middle Class: New Forms of Urban Leisure, Consumption and Prosperity* (New Delhi: Routledge, 2010); Lahiri-Dutt, 'Researching World Class Watering', 703.

can deny that demand for the poor but cannot ignore the demands of the middle class, as this section represents the most powerful class in the city. Even an election can be won or lost on the grounds of sufficient supply of water in Indian cities.

Lahiri-Dutt[53] and Ganguli,[54] in their respective studies on water culture in Kolkata and Chandernagore cites, have found that a large variety of appliances such as flush toilets, washing machines, showers, bathtubs and geysers or water heaters are being used by the new Indian middle class. Enhanced use of water-intensive gadgets has increased the consumption of water to a large extent, thus increasing its demand. The severity of water use by the middle class is often not reflected in the per capita consumption, as each city has a large section of poor people who do not even consume the bare minimum amount necessary for survival.

The demand for water has increased, not only from the citizens but also from the city government in the name of beautification of the city. The beautification and maintenance of parks and lawns in a city like Delhi, which is located in a drier part of the country, poses enormous challenges to the city's supply. The total amount of water Delhi alone consumes for maintaining gardens and lawns is probably more than the total demand of the millions of poor living in the city. Thus, the city governments need to consider not only the demand imposed by the increasing urban population but also the ever-increasing demand from the citizens, especially from the middle class.

Traditional Community Managed Water System

The significance of traditional knowledge in water resource management of the country has been explained by many people like Anupam Mishra[55] and Rajendra Singh.[56] They are often appreciated and awarded by the governments at different levels, but enough initiative has not been taken to actually learn about the traditional knowledge of water management practised by various communities across India. According to Anupam Mishra (Gandhian and author), the governments need to rely more on people's traditional wisdom in matters concerning water harnessing. In the post-independence era, both the governments and the people of

---

[53] Lahiri-Dutt, 'Researching World Class Watering'.

[54] Ganguli, *Urban Water Management*.

[55] See https://en.wikipedia.org/wiki/Anupam_Mishra; 'Anupam Mishra and Traditional Indian Rainwater Harvesting', http://www.hydratelife.org/?p=181

[56] See https://en.wikipedia.org/wiki/Rajendra_Singh; 'Rajendra Singh—The "Waterman of India"', http://www.hydratelife.org/?page_id=935

this country started ignoring their traditional time-tested techniques of water conservation. What these people are trying to encourage today is an exploration of the history of water management at local levels by different community groups, utilizing their traditional knowledge.

Traditional knowledge has been defined as 'a cumulative body of knowledge, know-how, practices and representations maintained and developed by peoples with extended histories of interaction with the natural environment. These sophisticated sets of understandings, interpretations and meanings are part and parcel of a cultural complex.'[57] There was no dearth of traditional knowledge on water resource management in India among different community groups before the advent of technology took over human skill. Since the historic past, we have had indigenous methods of water harvesting and conservation, which are often limited within local areas and in smaller communities. Indian towns, cities and settlements have been around for thousands of years, surviving through droughts on dry and arid land, on the basis of these systems. Anupam Mishra alone has tried to revive several types of traditional water harvesting methods. One of those methods, known as the 'kuin' system, is used in areas that have saline water, to prevent the fresh water from becoming saline. Some of the kuins that are still in use in India are over 100 years old and can catch up to 100,000 litres of water per season (Note 55). Another system he detected was in the cities of Rajasthan. Jaisalmer town, built long before Mumbai and Delhi, had a traditional water harvesting system using water tanks and roofs, which never failed to supply water to the people of the city in the past. In this system, the rain falls onto the roof of the house, runs to a hole in the roof that is connected to a pipe, and the pipe runs to a storage tank. These types of systems can store up to 25,000 gallons of water per year. One of the largest examples of traditional rainwater harvesting is seen in the Jaigarh Fort near Jaipur. This 400-year-old building can store up to 6 million gallons of water in one season. It collects water from a little over 9 miles of canals that run out from the building. Step wells of the cities of Rajasthan are also significant traditional water management systems, using which people of those cities survived for generations in the desert (Note 55).

In another study on the traditional water conservation and management practices, Iyengar[58] identified 20 different kinds of traditional

---

[57] See https://en.wikipedia.org/wiki/Traditional_knowledge

[58] Vatsala Iyengar, *Waternama: A Collection of Traditional Practices for Water Conservation and Management in Karnataka* (Bangalore: Communication for Development and Learning, 2007).

sustainable water management practices in the state of Karnataka. These practices were scattered over spaces, starting from old forts to cities and villages, and from drought-prone areas to flood-prone areas. The traditional water systems were practised using different kinds of water sources such as ponds, tanks, water pools, wells and so on. The most common thread among all these different stories of traditional water conservation and management systems is that of community management and ground knowledge outside the mainstream organized models of water management. These systems survived for a long time in history, but the main condition for these to succeed was control over the demand.

Now the question arises, what made those traditional water harvesting systems defunct? Anupam Mishra told a story at the TEDIndia Talk in 2009[59] about how the government spent millions of dollars to build a number of large canals to bring in water from the Himalayas. While they were building the canals, advertisements were posted along the way, telling the people to abandon their traditional systems because these canals would bring them all the water that they needed. While the canals did work in some places, they were plugged up with water hyacinth (a type of vegetation) in some parts, while in other places sand blew into them, resulting in their eventual clogging. Anupam Mishra went on to explain why the traditional systems ran and served people with uninterrupted water supply over centuries. According to him, it was because of the respect the community had for nature, for everybody in the community and for the traditional knowledge of the elderly people.[5] Thus, it is very clear that because the new technology promised sufficient supply of water to the people, they left the traditional systems of water management. Presently, the new technology cannot solve our current problems and we need to fall back on the history of traditional water management systems to learn how to cope with the current crisis.

The cities are spaces where the sheer size of the population prevents the implementation of an easy solution for the water problem using the traditional management system. Moreover, the traditional management systems were based on the philosophy of minimizing consumption and wastage which are not practised by the citizens of consumerist societies in today's world. In spite of consistent negligence of traditional knowledge, we find that some such systems still exist in certain cities of India.

---

[59] 'Anupam Mishra: The ancient ingenuity of water harvesting', Video filmed in November 2009 at TED India. https://www.ted.com/talks/anupam_mishra_the_ancient_ingenuity_of_water_harvesting?language=en

Some of these systems are not even documented either by historians or by scholars of traditional knowledge of water management.

During my field work in November 2015, in the hill town of Kalimpong located in the Eastern Himalayan region, I detected a traditional water management system called *bagdhara*. To trace back its history, I tried to search online and saw that the search engines do not recognize the word. This means that there is no mention of this system in online resources. I spent a few days in that small city and to my utter surprise, I observed that many people of the city do not know anything about *bagdhara*. I also tried in vain to trace any material written on this system in the local library. Failing to get access to historical material sources, I tried to depend on exploring facts on *bagdhara* from the available oral history.

Kalimpong town faces endemic water scarcity because of its location on the hills. The city's built-up area has been expanded, destroying many water sources called *jhora* (natural spring) in and around the city. On the contrary, the water demand has increased due to the increases in population and the per capita demand. As a result, middle-class households, in most cases, buy water from public vendors to supplement the meagre municipal supply, while the poor who cannot afford the cost of private supply suffer the most. Poor people usually try to collect water from natural springs sometimes located at distant places and spend a long time just to collect and carry water. To cater to the needs of the poor, a local businessman developed a 'water point' at the beginning of the 20th century. After interviewing local elderly people, I retrieved the following information about this *bagdhara* system:

Bagdhara water management was established in 1922 by Sriram Moolchand Agarwala. This was probably considered by him as charity for poor people as per his religious beliefs. The system basically works to restore a natural spring by building a concrete structure around it so that people can use the water at the place itself. What is strictly maintained in the system is that nobody can take water from these public places for commercial purposes and/or in bulk like in big tanks. People are allowed to use the water for bathing and washing at that place and can also take away water for home use in buckets and other small water containers which they can carry along with them. No pipelines or pumping is allowed from this water point. As the source of the spring is natural, the intensity and volume of flow changes from season to season—high flow during rainy season and low in winter and summer months.

As for the management of this community water system, it is controlled by the local community through an organised institution called the All Star United Youth Club. There are 50 members in this club and the membership is open to anybody who would like to join. The management strategies are decided in open meetings where water users also have some say on management and can raise problems if any that they face in using the water. No decision is taken without a discussion on the issue in the open meetings. If anyone, either from the members list or from outside, would like to clean or maintain the area, they are always welcome, all that they need is an advance permission from the club. For repair and construction work, the local ward commissioner provides financial help from the municipality. The capacity of this water point is high, but is not used by many people except the poor, as most people who can afford it have got used to the piped water supply and to the water delivered at home by private vendors.

The lesson we can learn from understanding the history of this traditional community water management system, which has been functioning for over a century and from which people are still getting water, is that these modes can be more sustainable options in the long run. We are not sure how many other hill cities in India had developed such community-managed water systems which have been ignored as soon as the cities got centralized piped connections.

A similar history of small-scale traditional community water supply system developed in Nepal during 500–800 BC and lasted for generations—over 2,000 years. Its loss during the augmentation of centralized piped water supply and its revival again after the failure of piped water supply in Kathmandu has been narrated by Shrestha[60] as follows:

As early as 1875, Kathmandu has a rudimentary piped water supply system. The valley experienced an exponential population growth around 1950. To deal with growing water demands, government built modern water supply systems, by constructing dams and diverting river water to artificial reservoirs and distributing water through pipes. Many people including the traditional *guthi* (local community associations to maintain the network of springs, canals, stone spouts and

---

[60] Hari Krishna Shrestha, 'Small-Scale Community Water Supply System as an Alternative to Privatized Water Supply: An Experience from Kathmandu', in *Globalization of Water Governance in South Asia*, eds. Vishal Narain, Chandra Gurung Goodrich, Jayati Chourey, and Anjal Prakash (New Delhi: Routledge, 2014), 139–140.

dug wells) system, who depended on stone spouts, started to receive water in their houses through the new government-managed system which diminished the importance of these traditional sources of water. Most of the new users of the stone spouts were recent migrants who had no tradition, and hence no understanding and appreciation of the traditional water supply system.

This disconnection between the new users and the old caretakers of the stone spouts further deteriorated the system since the users had no idea whom to approach if and when the system malfunctioned. The descendants of the original *guthi* members felt less and less responsible for the maintenance of the old system, since they grew up with the piped water systems in their houses. The long neglect of the maintenance and cleaning of the water supply network resulted in either diminished water flow or a complete dry-up of the stone spouts.

Shrestha's study[61] also indicates that since the 1980s, the condition of piped water supply started to become inefficient and the water distribution system went on deteriorating because of lack of new available sources of water and the constantly increasing demand. With no improvement in the piped water supply system and no prospects of improvement in the near future, the local communities are coming together to form new users' groups and to revive the small-scale community-based water supply systems. Based on the overall performance of such small-scale traditional community water systems, Shrestha[62] states that such traditional systems can offer viable alternatives to the centralized water supply system at local level, but they cannot replace the centralized system due to the inherent nature of limited size and scope.

Thus, both the empirical study in Kalimpong and the study by Shrestha[63] in Kathmandu clearly point to the fact that the history of water in the form of traditional management needs to be well explored by environmental historians, who can inform the policymakers about the importance of the traditional water supply/distribution systems and how to preserve and maintain the diverse sources and systems for a healthy and sustainable water supply alternative for cities. However, in doing so, we have to keep in mind that beyond each traditional community-managed water conservation and management system was a system of control over the demand and use. Presently, the control over demand has become a very problematic issue in water management

---

[61] Ibid.
[62] Ibid.
[63] Ibid.

due to the high interference of political economic power in present-day Indian cities. Today's urban societies are no longer in the control of the traditional community like before. Consumerism and neoliberal economy have complicated the systems to a large extent, and that is why revival of traditional water systems alone cannot solve the problem, it can only supplement the total supply of water to some extent.

Rivers and the Cities of India

Rivers acted as the prime reason for locating and supporting great ancient civilizations of the world and nourished great cities alongside them.[64] Around 74 big cities[65] and many small towns of India are located near rivers. Besides, there are a number of small rivulets which also pass through the cities, the full list of which is very difficult to access. Across sizes, in the history of the growth of these cities, the rivers played a key role in the development of these cities by sustaining transportation, industries, water supply and recreation sectors of the city. This exploitation of river water has been taking place for generations, both by the city governments and dwellers, until these rivers have been reduced to a polluted stream of water with a very negligible flow within their shrinking channel, faced by immense encroachment.

Borthakur and Singh[66] have studied the history of six Indian rivers and rivulets: the Bharalu and Bahini (Guwahati), Varuna and Assi (Varanasi) and Mula and Mutha (Pune). According to them, these rivers have been reduced to mere *nallahs* (sewers) due to rapid, unplanned and haphazard developmental activities and urbanization processes ubiquitous in major Indian cities. They also explained the trajectories of the lost glory of Indian rivers as follows[67]:

> The river and rivulet ecosystems, which once provided the dwellers with water and food besides contributing significantly to sectors such as agriculture, pisciculture and transportation, are now at the verge of extinction at several places. The rapid and haphazard urbanization

---

[64] Kuntala Lahiri-Dutt, 'Towards a More Comprehensive Understanding of Rivers', in *Living Rivers, Dying Rivers*, ed. Ramaswamy R. Iyre (New Delhi: Oxford University Press, 2015a), 421–434.

[65] See https://en.wikipedia.org/wiki/List_of_Indian_cities_on_rivers

[66] A. Borthakur and P. Singh, 'India's Lost Rivers and Rivulets', *Energy, Ecology and Environment* (2016), http://link.springer.com/article/10.1007/s40974-016-0039-2

[67] Ibid., 4.

and industrial development are significant factors responsible for such depletion. Besides creating significant pollution, the riverbed is destroyed in the process of encroachment. Encroachment of river-banks is a major challenge for local authorities of most Indian cities. Moreover, some rivers have been core disposal bodies of sewage and effluent from the urban and industrial activities. River Varuna in the city of Varanasi is a live example.

Often we see government initiatives like the Ganga Action Plan for the major rivers, especially Ganga, because of its religious value in addition to its importance in the activities of sustaining civilization. The small rivers and rivulets, which had significant importance in sustaining cities for quite a long time, are utterly ignored for revival under government initiatives. Rudra[68] has analysed in depth the incidence and causes of death of a huge number of rivers and rivulets in the Bengal Delta area due to anthropogenic interventions. Changing the river regimes and too much control over and encroachment on their natural flow are the biggest threats to the future of water for the entire region. There were a large number of rivers such as Saraswati, Haor and Kanaganga in the Bengal Delta which do not exist now, and over time, the death of these small rivers is going to affect the flow of the big rivers, as these rivers function as feeders to the big rivers.[69] Therefore, the Ganga Action Plan cannot save the Ganga unless care is taken to revive its many other small tributaries.

Lahiri-Dutt and Samanta[70] analysed the environmental history of river control by the British and its consequent impacts on the river as well as on the riverine civilizations in the context of Damodar. Similar studies by Chakraborty,[71] on the River Damodar and its distributary network of rivulets located in and around Burdwan town of West Bengal, meticulously explain how the process of British river control in the form of embankment, and later the urban expansion of the town

[68] Kalyan Rudra, *Banglar Nadikatha* [The Story of Bengal Rivers] (Kolkata: Sahitya Sangsad, 2008).

[69] Jayanta Basu, 'The Future of The River: There is Reason to Worry', *Anandabazar Patrika*, 15 September 2016, 4.

[70] Kuntala Lahiri-Dutt and Gopa Samanta, *Dancing with the River: People and Life on the Chars of South Asia* (New Haven, CT: Yale University Press, 2013).

[71] Sanjib Chakraborty, *Damodar-Banka-Ballukar Sahar Barddhaman* [Barddhaman: The City of Damodar-Banka-Balluka] (Natun Chithi Sharad Sankha, 2009), 231–236; Sanjib Chakraborty, *Nadir Sahar Barddhaman* [Barddhaman: The City of Rivers], *Itihas Anwesha: Barddhaman Sahar* (Natun Chithi Prakasana, 2010a), 91–101.

destroyed many small distributary flood channels of River Damodar and caused considerable impact on the local environment. The initial location of the town was preferred by the active water-borne trade of the Damodar river, and the natural levee (higher land between Damodar and Banka) was the natural site selected for the town. Until the development of roadways during the Mughal period and thereafter railways during the British period, the town was located along the river. Later on, the town started to shift its location towards the railways and roadways, away from the river. They converted wetlands and ponds and left water channels disconnected from the River Damodar by the embankment into the built-up area. The process of slow conversion of the water channels went on for decades, to such an extent that today it is very hard to trace those channels in the midst of the town settlement. The Banka river, which used to flow through the middle of the town, lost its flow due to its disconnection from the River Damodar through embankment and was merely reduced to the main drain of the city.[72] However, during the rainy season, river flood and water logging have become a common phenomenon even with 2–3 hours of heavy rain, due to the encroachment of water channels and wetlands mainly located in the northern and eastern parts of the city.

The rivers and rivulets flowing through the cities of India have been in most cases converted into the main drainage channels carrying the sewage of the cities. Dumping sewage into the river not only destroys it but also impacts its entire ecosystem through pollution. The condition of the rivers flowing through cities is the same, whether in a small town like Burdwan in West Bengal or in a big city like Hyderabad in Andhra Pradesh. The Musi river flowing through the city of Hyderabad has been reduced to the main drain of the city, carrying liquid waste and creating foul smell. Seeing its present condition, it is difficult for people to understand that this river was once a beautiful aspect of the city. Many cities have been ruined in the past due to the alteration of riverbeds, and the history of India can be linked to the changing courses of rivers.[73] At present, rivers are under threat not only from natural and human activities but also from the effects of climate change. Engineers usually mange the rivers and see the rivers only as a source of water and nothing else. The immense social and cultural impacts the rivers have on the civilizations thriving on their banks are usually ignored by them. Environmental historians need to work on the history of the rivers and their relations with the cities in greater detail, so that engineers and

---

[72] Chakraborty, *Nadir Sahar Barddhaman*.

[73] Lahiri-Dutt, 'Towards a More Comprehensive Understanding of Rivers'.

other water policymakers can learn from them how important it is to protect our rivers from dying.

Neglecting and destroying rivers flowing along the cities not only affects the future water scenario of the cities but also has tremendous impact on the destruction of the regional ecosystem and hydrological system, thus creating a long-standing impact on the life and livelihoods of the greater community in and around the cities. Fitzhugh and Richter,[74] through case studies of water resource development in and around five large urban areas of the United States, demonstrate that providing freshwater ecosystems with water flow is necessary to sustain their health. While meeting the other challenges of urban water management, there is a need to take the ecosystem into account. According to them, ultimately, the water planners will also need to set limits on human alterations to river flows in many basins in order to spur greater water productivity and protect ecosystem water allocations before water supplies become overtaxed.

Regional Ecosystem and the Rising Conflicts between Urban and Peri-urban Areas

In the Quito declaration on cities by the UN Habitat III which was held in October 2016, the case for water was mentioned in three sections. It was mentioned under (a) ecosystem and cities; (b) sustainable consumption and production; and (c) urban basic services.

Under sustainable consumption and production, it says

We call for an integrated system of water planning and management that considers urban-rural linkages, minimises conflicts and ecological risks, maximises positive synergies and mutual benefits, at the local and regional scales. The sustainable use of water should be promoted through a holistic water cycle approach, rehabilitating water resources within the urban area, reducing and treating water waste, increasing water storage, and providing safe and healthy drinking water within short distance in cities and human settlements, emphasizing measures to avoid conflicts and minimize the impacts of climate-related disasters especially floods and droughts and sharing experiences among cities.[75]

---

[74] Fitzhugh and Richter, 'Quenching Urban Thirst', 741–754.
[75] UN Habitat III, 'Zero Draft of the New Urban Agenda, 6 May 2016', Habitat III Quito, United Nations Conference on Housing and Sustainable Development, October 2016, p. 11, declaration 74.

Under ecosystem and the cities, it further mentions:

> We will ensure that sources of critical resources which are part of a city's basic services and daily consumption (e.g. clean water, food, access to modern energy services) are secured and protected by policy at all levels of governance. We also commit to enact national and territorial policies that safeguard against environmental degradation and to mainstream ecology in the institutional setting, allocating responsibilities for environmental governance to appropriate institutions at all levels of government.[76]

Both these declarations indicate that the problem of urban water cannot be solved with the help of water management strategies which are being followed by the municipal governments within their territories, since urban water sources are essential components of the regional hydrological regime and of the local ecosystem. Since the colonial period, to ensure the supply of water in the cities, planners have always looked into sources of water far beyond the territorial limits of the city, and by doing so, they have exploited either regional surface or groundwater sources. As a result of this, enormous conflicts have occurred between the urban water users and the irrigation water users of the country.

The development of water resources to satisfy urban water needs has had serious impacts on freshwater ecosystem integrity and on valuable ecosystem services.[77] History tells us that whenever the cities—with their growth and increasing demand—exhausted the nearby sources of water, they looked into distant sources and transported the water from long distances. The earliest history of such water transport was found in Rome around 312 BCE, where the Romans routed water through nine aqueducts of different lengths, varying between 16 and 91 km.[78] In modern times, the Los Angeles aqueduct was completed in 1913, which was the biggest at that time. Afterwards, by the end of the 20th century, China transferred water from the rivers of the south to the drier northern parts through three parallel aqueducts, changing the entire river ecosystem of the southern and the northern regions.[79] In fact, in Beijing, the water source is more than 100 km away from the city.[80] Such cases are also not

---

[76] Ibid., p. 10, declaration 70.
[77] Fitzhugh and Richter, 'Quenching Urban Thirst'.
[78] Sengupta, Goswami, and Rudra, *Jwal.*
[79] Ibid.
[80] Marie-Hélène Zérah, *Water: Unreliable Supply in Delhi* (Delhi: Manohar, 2000).

unfamiliar in India. Zérah[81] noted that 'Chennai city has to bring water from a distance of more than 200 km, which leads to conflicts with the neighbouring states', and the condition since then has worsened. The recent unrest in Karnataka and Tamil Nadu over sharing Kaveri river water is an ideal example of such conflicts.

Janakarajan, Llorente and Zérah[82] identified three main categories of urban water conflicts in India:

1. *Conflicts linked to quantity:* Conflict arises between sectors or users, such as municipality versus industries, connected versus unconnected people, and urban versus peri-urban, present and future generations.
2. *Conflicts linked to quality:* Unsafe water reduces the availability of potable water and causes water-borne diseases; poor people are more affected, as they do not have any system to treat water; it is too expensive; domestic users complain to the municipality.
3. *Conflicts linked to water access:* Legal (water rights), economic (price) or physical barriers prevent access to water and their unfair settlements generate conflicts.

They also opined that in all the cases, the protagonists have unequal bargaining powers and there are winners and losers. It is rare that a conflict generates a win-win situation, mostly with regard to sustainable criteria.

These kinds of conflicts will be aggravated in future if India's river linking project, planned long before and revived recently, is implemented.[83] Consequently, it will change the river ecosystems of different regions of India. These water transfers are mainly targeted to serve the irrigation and urban sectors and require a huge investment. Such big investments are sometimes beyond the capacity of the governments, and that is why water, which remained for a long time a public sector resource, is turning into a consumer product in the private sector in different Indian cities.[84]

---

[81] Ibid.

[82] Janakarajan, Llorente, and Zérah, 'Urban Water Conflicts in Indian Cities', 94.

[83] Medha Patkar, ed., *River Lining: A Millennium Folly?* (NAPM & Initiative, 2004).

[84] Gopa Samanta and Kaberi Koner, 'Urban Ecology of Water in Darjeeling, India', *South Asian Water Studies* 5, no. 3 (2016): 42–57.

With the increasing demand for water, the cities of India also look further and further for their water sources, and the phenomenon of acquiring water from other uses, notably agriculture, has become common. Such water transfers may be private, unplanned and ad hoc, with individual well owners pumping water into tankers to be sold in the city, or public and planned, with water districts taking water from the villages for selling to the city, with or without compensation.[85] Janakarajan, Llorente and Zérah[86] analysed the complexity of water conflict between cities and peri-urban rural areas in the context of Chennai and Delhi. In another study, Narain[87] has explained how the rural–urban conflict developed between Delhi city and the villages located on the peripheries. The urban elite move to the peripheries for cheaper land and other avenues of investment and can afford costly water extraction technologies, depriving the locals of access to this resource. Narain[88] opined that this water crisis is an outcome of the short-sightedness of the government in issuing licenses for malls and residential areas for the urban elite without taking cognizance of the water availability. To supply water to the cities, water treatment plants are often built on land acquired from the peripheral areas. As a result, peri-urban people not only lose land but also lose water sources located on those lands. Sometimes, water is transported from longer distances through canals that pass through peripheral villages, but the people living in the periphery do not get access to that water.[89]

At present, most of the big cities of India such as Delhi, Chennai, Bangalore and Mumbai have exhausted their nearby water sources, as they never took care to sustain those systems for the long term. In fact, the water management of each city is in the hands of engineers who most often do not have any knowledge either of the area's history or of the environment. Now these big cities bring water from sources that are hundreds of kilometres distant to meet their ever-increasing demand. This distance will increase in future, along with the number of conflicts along their pathway either with the rural areas or with the other cities.

---

[85] Vishal Narain, 'Urbanization and Water: A Conundrum and Source of Conflict', in *Globalization of Water Governance in South Asia*, eds. Vishal Narain, Chandra Gurung Goodrich, Jayati Chourey, and Anjal Prakash (New Delhi: Routledge, 2014), 195–203.

[86] Janakarajan, Llorente, and Zérah, 'Urban Water Conflicts in Indian Cities'.

[87] Vishal Narain, 'Gone Land, Gone Water: Crossing Fluid Boundaries in Peri-Urban Gurgaon and Faridabad, India', *South Asian Water Studies* 1, no. 2 (2009): 143–158.

[88] Narain, 'Urbanization and Water', 199.

[89] Ibid., 200.

Conclusion

Scarcity of water in Indian cities is not a new phenomenon. What is new is the dimension of the problem and the impacts, which again are not limited within the territorial limits of the cities. Thus, the excessive resource use in the cities does not only create problems for the residents of these cities but also destroys the regional natural ecosystems, especially water bodies, rivers and soils within the vicinity of the cities. Water has become the core concern of everyday negotiation in all major cities of India—lack of water in summer and urban flooding vis-à-vis water logging in the rainy season. Water has become such an important issue for human lives in cities that even an election can be fought and won on promises made on sufficient supply of water in the city.

This study suggests that to find a durable solution, we need to look into history so that we can learn from the mistakes which we have made towards hydrological systems in the maintenance of our cities on a contingent basis. Contingent solutions in most cases cause a lot of harm to the environment, but those impacts are felt much later, when it is very difficult to rectify the system. Ghosh[90] reminds us, 'money flows towards short term gain and towards the over-exploitation of unregulated common resources. These tendencies are like the invisible land of fate, guiding the hero in a Greek tragedy toward his inevitable doom'. But it is never too late and there is always a time to start saving the future of cities and civilizations.

Finally, following Janakarajan, Llorente and Zérah,[91] it can be said that water is never a part of urban planning in India, and the peri-urban issues are also utterly neglected in the urban planning process. Therefore, the surface, groundwater and land use should be an integral part of the urban and peri-urban planning process to make the future of the cities sustainable and, for doing so, we need to learn from history.

---

[90] Ghosh, *Great Derangement*, 149.

[91] Janakarajan, Llorente, and Zérah, 'Urban Water Conflicts in Indian Cities'.

4

History of Water Bodies in India

M. Amirthalingam

Water is the elixir of life and is one of the essential substances without which life cannot exist. It has been the driving force of each civilization.[1] The history of civilizations reveals that great cities have developed solely on the banks of mighty rivers that provided a perennial source of water. As the population increased, settlements developed into cities and agriculture expanded. Hence, it became essential to develop techniques for collection and storage of these precious goods.[2] A water body may be defined as a smaller version of a large dam. The purpose of water body is to capture a body of water behind and embankment. Usually, these water bodies supply most of the drinkable water for a city or village.

The standing water percolates into the ground and recharges the water level. Therefore, the wells within the encompassing territory are furnished associate bumper stockpile of water.[3]

---

[1] K. Radha, 'Water in Ancient India', *Indian Journal of History of Science* 31, no. 4 (1996): 327–337.

[2] MoRD, 'Chapter II: Water Harvesting—Our Age Old Tradition', in *Rajiv Gandhi National Drinking Water Mission Department of Drinking Water Supply* (New Delhi, 2004), 3–11.

[3] Sunita Narain, *Real Pride of Ancient Indian Science* (2015), http://stage.downtoearth.org.in/blog/real-pride-of-ancient-indian-science-48219.

The green cover in the surrounding areas also increases. The water bodies also regulate the flow of rivers and filter pollutants. They form the natural habitat for wildlife and fish. Soil erosion is reduced; floods and run-off also get reduced. The silting of rivers is thus reduced. The water bodies also play an important role in the development of agriculture of the region. They also constitute an important element of the economy as a means of transportation. There are many types of water bodies, namely, natural lake, artificial lake or tank (*kund, yeri*) and constructed tank (*baoli,* stepwell, *vav, sarovar, kovilkulam, pushkarni*).

History of Man-made Water Storage Reservoirs

India is a country with a long and hoary past and rich cultural and religious tradition. In India, the first major urban civilization started in the Indus Valley (3000–1500 BCE). The origin of the practice of storing water in India can be dated back to the period of the 'great bath' of the Harappan civilization. There is archaeological evidence of sophisticated drinking water supply and wells with brick lining found in these settlements. Dholavira, which is an important site of this civilization, had several reservoirs to collect rainwater. In Lothal (Gujarat) and Inamgaon (Maharashtra), we have found evidence of small bunds to store rainwater for drinking and irrigation purposes.[4] The excavations at Harappa and Mohenjo-daro reveal that even people of that era placed much importance on proper water supply for domestic purposes, irrigation and public baths.[5] The Vedic religion regarded water as a symbol of spiritual purification. Its cleaning virtue stands a mystical representation of the cleansing power of religion. A number of myths and legends have grown up around the sublime power of water, all up lauding its divine virtue.[6] The Vedic seers, in their hymns, often invoked water as a purifying agent, which cleanses mankind and removes all kinds of physical ailments. The Rig Veda emphasizes the Vedic views on the origin of water and its sacrificial and practical importance, whereas the Atharva Veda highlights the therapeutic and emancipative strength of water, aqua-related spirits and their influence on human beings.[7] There

---

[4] A. Agrawal and S. Narain, *Dying Wisdom: Rise, Fall and Potential of India's Traditional Water Harvesting Systems* (State of India's Environment—A Citizens' Report, No. 4) (New Delhi: Centre for Science & Environment (CSE), 1997); M. Iravatham, *The Indus Fish Swam in the Great Bath: A New Solution to an Old Riddle* (Chennai, 2011), 14.

[5] Radha, 'Water in Ancient India', 327–337.

[6] Savitri V. Kumar, *The Puranic Lore of Holy Water Places* (New Delhi, 1983).

[7] R. Seneviratne, 'Divine, Panacean & Emancipative Water in Vedic Religion', in 37th Spalding Symposium, Merton College, University of Oxford, UK, 2012, p. 1.

is a wealth of geographical information available in the Vedas. Apart from rain, there are numerous references to major sources of water such as rivers, lakes and reservoirs, which are named according to their characteristics and location. In fact, the Rig Veda mentions no less than 30 names of rivers including the famous *sapta-sindhu* (seven rivers) and *panca-ap* (five waters) in the area now known as Punjab.[8] They also believed that water gave strength to men. Hence, they prayed, 'may the water be pleasant to our taste, be free from diseases, sin and sickness, be the remover of fear of death, be full of divine qualities and be the strength of eternal laws'. The Vedic hymns reveals that these prayers were addressed to Lord Varuna, the presiding deity of the waters. It is therefore evident that as early as the Vedic period people took precautions to use only unpolluted water. In the Vedic religion, water played an important role in religious rituals and ceremonies because it was believed that pure water was an offering to the gods.[9] Even in medical treatment, water having specific qualities was prescribed for different types of diseases. The sources reveal that a larger number of tanks, lakes and ponds were dug and river water was also used. Artisan or deep wells were also dug for the purposes of irrigation. Water was stored in larger reservoirs. There is no doubt that the science of hydrology was highly advanced in ancient India.[10]

According to the *Satapatha Brahmna*, the whole universe was born from water.[11] A passage from the *Chandogya Upanishads* says that water is more essential than food. If there is less rain, human beings get worried because they will get less food. However, if there is adequate rain, they become joyful as it would bring about surplus food. Thus, water assumes completely different forms and becomes the planet, sky, heaven, mountains, gods, men, cattle, birds, herbs, trees, worms, midges and ants.[12]

In the Valmiki Ramayana, there are references to three lakes, the Panchapsarotataka (the lake of five nymphs, associated with Mandkarni or Satkarni), the Pampasaras and Matanga Saras.[13]

A number of lakes are mentioned in the Mahabharata. These include lakes such as Bindusar, Brahmasar and Jyotisar, which Saraswati

---

8 Ibid, 3.
9 Radha, 'Water in Ancient India', 328.
10 Ibid.
11 Seneviratne, 'Divine, Panacean & Emancipative', 11.
12 Ibid., 4.
13 Valmiki Ramayana, 3-73-11; 73-12a, 13b; 3-73-14b, 15, 16a.

occupies. This is a clear indication that River Saraswati had become a small river by then and was only occupying lakes.[14] Another reference is found within the Vana Parva of Mahabharata. Bhima goes trying to find Kubera's lake, where wonderful lotuses bloom. Once he found the lake, he was required to battle with the devils in it. To heal his wounds and recover his strength, he plunged into the lake and felt revived and restored.[15]

In the Puranas, we locate the most intricate type of love of water. Water is viewed as extraordinary, sacred, heavenly and divine. They have various gods as their presiding deities who are blessed with many power and attributes. Many of them are said to have divine origin and are thus regarded as sacred and hence worshipped.[16]

In the Mauryan period, the *Arthasastra* of Kautilya gives an elaborate account of the dams and bunds that were built for the purposes of irrigation. Strict rules and regulations were laid down for the management of these water bodies. There were also privately owned water bodies, and the owners of these water bodies were free to sell or mortgage them.[17]

In the *Arthasastra*, there is a detailed description of the procedure to be followed for constructing irrigation works. Semicircular bunds were to be raised adjacent to small hillocks and water reservoirs. Kautilya further prescribes that the king should arrange for a permanent source of irrigation for agriculture such as tanks and *bandhas*. In case the people themselves come forward to construct these works, the king should provide them with necessary land, water and wood. However, the ownership of these sources would remain with the king.[18] The *Arthasastra* specifies that there were two kinds of dikes, to be specific the *sahodaka*, where there is regular progression of water, and *aharyodka*, which is a capacity tank, where water streams in through channels uncommonly burrowed for this reason.[19]

---

[14] J. A. B. Van Buitenen, trans., *Mahabharata: 2. The Book of the Assembly Hall; 3. The Book of the Forest* (Chicago, IL and London, 1975), 513 (MBH 3.80.118).

[15] MBH, *Vanaparva*, 3.152.20-50.

[16] R. Santosh Kumar, 'Concept and Origin of Sacred Tanks', *Orissa Historical Research Journal (OHRJ)* XLVII, no. 1 (2012): 100, orissa.gov.in/e-magazine/ Journal/jounalvol1/pdf/orhj-13.

[17] Government of India, *Water Harvesting and Artificial Recharge* (New Delhi: Rajiv Gandhi National Drinking Water Mission, 2004).

[18] N. Pant and R. K. Verma, *Tanks in Eastern India: A Study in Exploration* (Lucknow: IWMI-Tata Policy Research Program Hyderabad and Centre for Development Studies, 2010), 2.

[19] Agarwal and Narain, *Dying Wisdom*.

The famous Junagadh inscription of Rudradaman, the Saka ruler dating back to 150 CE, records the restoration of Lake Sudarshana by Mahakshtrapa Rudradaman. This lake was originally constructed by Chandragupta Maurya. Around 150 CE, severe floods caused a breach in the embankment. The restoration of the dam was carried out by Rudradaman's minister Suvisakha who was a Pahlava (Parthian). This engraving uncovers the way that the individuals of antiquated India realized how to develop dams, lakes and water system frameworks even in the 4th century BCE. Three hundred years later, the embankment of Sudharshana lake breached again due to floods in 455 CE. The repairs were carried out under the orders of Chakrapalika. This fact is recorded by a second inscription during the reign of Skandagupta (455–467 CE).

There are many common features found in the two inscriptions. Both mention the name of the lake as Sudarshana *tataka*. They also mentioned the term *sethubandhana* or embankment. Kautilya also mentions the term *sethu* for embankments. Other Sanskrit terms used in the inscription are *puranali* for waterway, *parivaha* for weir and *midhavidhana* for removal of residue from the lake. The inscription even contains the detailed measurements taken to repair the tank. It is possible that the Sudharshana lake fell into disuse around 8th or 9th century CE.[20]

It was the Sathavahana dynasty (1st century BCE to 2nd century CE) which introduced brick and ring wells. In the 4th century BCE, the Nanda dynasty (363–321 BCE) constructed irrigation canals to transport water from the rivers to the agricultural fields. Their successors, the Mauryan dynasty (321–185 BCE), were renowned for their irrigation works besides constructing wells for public use and rest houses for the use of travellers. In Kalinga (Odisha), the famous Hathigumpha inscription of 2nd century BCE describes the major irrigation works carried out by the kings of that area. During the Gupta period (300–500 CE), large-scale works relating to the development of water resources took place.[21]

Sringaverapura was the site of a 250 m long tank fed by the River Ganga. An 11-m wide and 5-m deep canal took the excess water from the Ganga into a silting chamber, where the dirt settled down. Thereafter, relatively clean water entered a brick tank and, after further

---

[20] Ibid., 14–15.

[21] A. Pandey, 'Society and Environment in Ancient India (Study of Hydrology)', *International Journal of Humanities and Social Science Invention* 5, no. 2 (2016): 27.

filtering, only clean water could reach the second tank. The water then went to the third circular tank with terracotta sculptures on the side. The excess water went back to the Ganga.[22]

In Madhya Pradesh, during the 1010–1055 CE, King Bhoja constructed a huge lake across two hills. This lake covered an area of over 65,000 ha. There is an interesting legend connected with the construction of this lake. According to the story, King Bhoja was suffered by a skin disease. A sage advised the king to build a lake fed by 365 streams and springs and then have a bath in it to wipe out the skin disease. Accordingly, the king sent his engineers to survey the Vindhyan range of mountains. The engineers found that only 356 streams fed the valley. However, a Gond chief named Kalia came up with a solution. He called attention to a missing stream with its tributaries which made up the imperative number. The waterway was named Kaliasot or Kalia's stream, a name which continues till today.[23]

In Rajasthan, some of the famous man-made lakes are the Ana Sagar Lake in Ajmer; the Ghadsisar Lake was located in Jaisalmer which was built in 1367 CE by the Bhatti ruler, Rawal Ghadsi; and different lakes in Udaipur. Another artificial lake is the Raj Samand Lake fabricated by Maharana Raj Singh of Mewar in 1676 CE. Thus, the Rajput dynasties in Rajasthan and the Pal and Sen Kings (760–1100 CE) in Eastern India promoted a large number of lakes and tanks in their kingdoms.[24]

The state of Jammu and Kashmir is also renowned for its technologically excellent and varied hydraulic tradition. Kalhana's *Rajatharangini* mentions vast and well-planned irrigation systems such as canals, irrigation channels, embankments, aqueducts, circular dykes, barrages, wells and water wheels. Among these were the vast embankment called Guddasetu built by lord Damodara II and a progression of Arghat or water wheels built by the 8th-century rulers, Lalitaditya Muktapida of the Karkota line. These works were fabricated in order to lift the waters of the Jhelum stream and disseminate them to the encompassing towns.[25] There is another reference in Kalhana's work to a famous engineer named Suyya, who is credited with 'depleting the water of the Vitasta waterway and controlling it by building a stone dam and clearing its beds'. Suyya is additionally credited with building the enormous

---

[22] Agrawal and Narain, *Dying Wisdom*, 16.

[23] W. Kincaid, 'Rambles Among Ruins in Central India', *The Indian Antiquary* XVII (1888): 348–352.

[24] Pandey, 'Society and Environment in Ancient India', 26–31.

[25] Ibid.

Mahapadma Lake, currently known as the Wular lake.[26] The Wular lake lies in the northeast of the valley and is the largest freshwater lake in India. It is 12.5 miles long and 5 miles wide. There are many popular legends about the submersion of the city under the Wular Lake, which are connected with stories of some of the lost kings.

Recent studies have indicated that during the Neolithic period (2600–200 BCE), Mahapadamsar (Wular) was not a lake but a low-lying plain of the valley. This fact is proved by the discovery of Neolithic settlements in Kashmir including the one near Mahapadamsar (Wular Lake), where megalithic settlements dating 1600–200 BCE have been discovered. This place may possibly be referring to Chandrapura of the King 'Visvagasva'. It may also be mentioned that there is a reference in Kalhana's *Rajatharangini* to a larger city named Chandrapura which was submerged under the lake.[27]

Recent excavations at Sanchi in Madhya Pradesh have revealed a group of 17 dams located close to the Buddhist site. The dams have earthen cores faced with stone slabs and are laid across valleys up to 1,400 m in length. Also discovered is a 350-m-long dam, which, together with a second dam in the west, would have created a reservoir about 3 km² in area. In addition, two smaller reservoirs at Karondih and Dargawan were also discovered. It appears that the dams built on the sloping terrain acted as inundation tanks for upstream irrigation, whereas dams built in the valleys were useful for downstream irrigation. Studies indicate that the earliest dam construction occurred between the 3rd and 2nd century BCE. It is possible that these dams were constructed due to increase in population.[28] The Satvahanas (1st century BCE to 2nd century CE) introduced the brick and ring wells. In 1958, excavations revealed an ancient canal built by brick and limestone mortar, datable to the 3rd or 4th century CE, during the rule of the Ikshavakus. The canal has a length of more than 800 yards, with an average width of 50 ft and depth of 6 ft.[29]

In South India, under the Cheras, Cholas, Pandyas and Pallavas, a vast network of tanks and canals was constructed. Natural depressions

---

[26] Rima Hooja, *Channeling Nature: Hydraulics, Traditional Knowledge Systems, and Water Resource Management in India—A Historical Perspective*, http://indian-science.org/projects/t_pr_hooja_book.shtml.

[27] P. N. K. Bamzai, *A History of Kashmir* (New Delhi: Metropolitan Book Co., 1962), 62, 198, 325.

[28] J. Shaw, 'Landscape, Water and Religion in Ancient India', *Archaeology International* 9 (2005): 46, doi: http://doi.org/10.5338/ai.0912.233.

[29] I. K. Sarma, 'Ancient Canals', *JIH* XL, Part I (1962), 309.

were converted into irrigation tanks. The Pallava dynasty expanded the irrigation systems during the 7th century CE. The Pallavas created several fine reservoirs, some of which are in a remarkable state of preservation even today. The greatest builder of irrigation tanks was Mahendravarma Pallava I (600–630 CE), including Mahendra *tatakam* at Mahendravadi and Perumpidugu *vaykal* (canal), which were enlarged by him.[30] Pallava king Nandhivarman's Kasgudi copper plates mention about the Thirayaneri tank situated to the east of Kancheepuram. An inscription near the tank contains a pertinent message 'whenever the bund is to be strengthened, earth for the purpose should be excavated from the tank bed well way from the bund'.[31] Another ruler by name Parameswaravarman (670–700 CE) was responsible for Parameswara tataka. His successor was Nandivarman II. From the Kasakudi plates of this king, it was found that he built a tank called Tirayan ery. His son Dantivarman (796–847 CE) was another great builder of irrigation systems. The Vairamegha tataka at Uthiramerur was built during his reign. Two other famous tanks built were Marpidugu *yeri* and Marpidugu-perunkinaru.[32] The next king Nandiverman III (846–869 CE) created the largest and most extensive tank in the northern part of Tamil Nadu. The tank was 4 miles long stretching from north to south. Other important tanks built were the Gudimallam tank near Renigunta, the twin tanks called Tumbaneri and Velleri at Gudimallam, the tank at Ukkal, the Kanakavalli tataka near Vellore. Thus, it is reasonable to conclude that during the Pallava period, irrigation was carried on with the help of tanks, canals and wells.

Irrigation tanks were constructed by kings, ministers, village communities, temple authorities and private individuals. Epigraphic records indicate that great attention was paid to the construction and maintenance of water bodies. During the Pallava period, there were engineers, known as *jala sutrada*, who specialized in the construction of tanks and dams. The Villavatti grant of Simhavarman mentions the collection of taxes from water diviners or kupadarsaka.[33] However, the construction of irrigation tanks soon led to social inequalities. The rich landowners obtained lands nearer the tanks and cut water channels to their lands.

---

[30] T. M. Srinivasan, *Irrigation and Water Supply—South India, 200 B.C.–1600 A.D.* (Madras, 1991), 21.

[31] *SII*, Vol. 3., Part iii, no.73, p. 351; Srinivasan, *Irrigation and Water Supply*, 21–22.

[32] Srinivasan, *Irrigation and Water Supply*, 84.

[33] N. Natarajan, 'Water Resources Development in Tamil Nadu—Cauvery River System', in *Water Resources: Development and Management in India Through the Ages, Presented Papers*, ed. G. Venkataraman (Madras, 2003), 52.

The famous Kaveri *anicut* was constructed during the period of Karikala Chola (2nd century CE). The Cholas were also great builders of irrigation systems. They perfected the system of chain tanks, which is a number of tanks with connecting channels.[34]

Agriculture, the main occupation of the Tamils, was in a rather primitive stage during the early Sangam period.[35] King Karikala Chola is said to have destroyed forest lands and brought more lands under cultivation (*kaadu konrru naadaaki kulamtottu valam perukki*—which means he destroyed forests to establish villages in the country and dug tanks to improve fertility). For irrigation purposes, he built a dam across the river Kaveri.

The socio-economic conditions prevalent in Tamil Nadu during the 1st millennium BCE are vividly captured in Sangam literature, belonging to the beginning of the Christian era. Another source is 'Periplus of the Erythrean Sea' (81–96 CE), which refers to the trade between the Roman Empire and Tamil kingdoms. The most notable feature of this period is the spread of rice cultivation adopting irrigation methods. Some of the irrigation structures outlined in Sangam literature are still in vogue and they are the historical evidences to indigenous irrigation technology.

A tank is to be located at a place where it can receive optimum inflow of water from its catchment areas. Selection of a place with good hydrologic potential to locate the tank should also ensure economy in construction cost. Sangam literature makes elaborate references to the location of tanks, tank construction and water lifting devices, sluices, gates and channels.

A poem from *Purananuru*, written by Kudapulavianar, exhorts the king to create tanks wherever there are land depressions conducive to storing rainwater. The tanks were generally not dug but created by forming bunds to hold water in a sloping terrain or encompassing a depression on plain grounds.

During the megalithic age, there was a practice of placing the dead in an urn and burying them near a water course, on the banks of a river or near a tank (either in the foreshore or out in the bund). If a sepulchral urn is found near a tank, we can presume, without fear of contradiction, that the tank belongs to the Sangam period (1650 BCE–200 CE). The systematic surveys on the megalithic sites had not

---

[34] Ibid.; Srinivasan, *Irrigation and Water Supply*, 84.
[35] T. K. Venkata Subramanian, *Environment and Urbanisation in Early Tamilakam* (Thanjavur, 1988), 26.

focused on tanks. Nonetheless, these surveys help us to identify the tanks and their antiquity. Around 60 of such tanks are known so far. There may be more tanks of megalithic period still in existence and yet to be identified. Several tanks are observed within the epigraphs and copper plate inscriptions found in several components of Tamil Nadu.

The best shape of a tank is described by a Sangam poet Kabilar who, while praising King Pari, asserts the tanks in King Pari's state resemble the shape of the moon on the 8th day after new moon, that is, it is in crescent shape. There are many tanks constructed in crescent shape in the gently sloping terrain.

The period between the Sangam age and the rise of two major powers, the Pallava and the Pandya rulers, saw many irrigation facilities being created, especially in the Kaveri basin. In the second quarter of the 9th century CE, the imperial Cholas came to power in the Kaveri basin. They built a vast network of canals and branch canals from the Kaveri as also a number of large reservoirs. They also built a large number of tanks. The Chola king Parantaka I was responsible for creating the Veeranarayana Caturvedimangalam as also the famous Veeranam *yeri*. He also built Chola varidhi near Sholingur, the Vinnamangalam tank at Ambur, the Kaliuaneri near Anaimalai (Madurai), the Sodiyambakkam tank near Ukkal and the Veeracholan *vadavaru* near Thanjavur and Madurantakam *avatar*. He also diverted the waters of the Kaveri along the Manna river. The big tank at Madurantakam and one at Tirubhuvani (Puducherry) was constructed by Uttama Chola (970–985 CE). Parantaka II (956–970 CE) dug two big tanks called Sundara Chola periya *yeri* and Kundavai periya *yeri*. Another successor Raja I (985–1014 CE) built three big tanks, namely Kavirkulam, Bahur (Puducheri) and Arikesarimangalam tank. He also constructed the Uyyakondan channel to irrigate the lands near Thiruchirappalli. Rajendra I (1012–1044 CE) was also responsible for constructing a large irrigation tank called Chola Gangam at his new capital Gangai Konda Cholapuram[36]

Rajendra I also constructed Lake Mekhalachampalle in Chittoor district of Andhra Pradesh. His successor Kulothunga Chola (1070–1120 CE) excavated several reservoirs. These include Rajendra Cholapperiya *yeri* in Kunganur (Punganur in Andhra Pradesh) and Madurantakapperiya *yeri* at Idaiyur. He also built Kulothungasolappereri at Muniyur and the Sindhuvalli tank at Mysore. Another ruler to realize the importance of irrigation was Raja Raja III (1216 CE). He built two reservoirs, Narayanapputteri and Veeranaasingadevapputteri, at Yogimallavaram

---

[36] Srinivasan, *Irrigation and Water Supply*, 27.

in Puttur of Andhra Pradesh.[37] He is also reputed to have constructed the famous Chembarambakkam tank.[38]

One epigraph details the construction of a sluice in Vaigai River by the Pandya king Chezhian Sendan in 620 CE.[39] The period, with other relevant particulars of construction about some of the tanks, has been identified from stone inscriptions or copper plates. But most of the stone inscriptions speak only about the improvement works done or maintenance works undertaken.

Irrigation tanks or reservoirs were made by constructing major embankments (an earthen bund) across the line of the slope that stops the rainwater run-off from its catchment area. Two-sided embankments, gradually falling in height, were added to this major embankment to create a three-sided storage. The fourth side was left open for water to enter. Basically, the irrigation reservoirs were three-sided storage structures above the surface, whereas temple tanks needed lifting of water. These reservoirs were not only used for irrigation system, but they also acted as an array for run-off water from the catchment area, source of silt to fertilize the lands and for making construction material like clay (mud house) and brick. It is a source of recharging the groundwater, source of drinking water for livestock and for irrigating the agricultural land.

Maintenance of reservoirs was essential for the health and economy of the state. In South India, on the other hand, most reservoirs were and continue to be desilted annually, thus ensuring sufficient water for irrigation.

The advantage of tank irrigation is its proximity to the command area so that the requirement of water for the agricultural crop can be assessed and supplied from the tank, which is the core issue of water management. An oversized portion of the tiny tanks serve one single city and its villas, empowering deconcentrated administration to achieve success.[40]

There are references to this form of irrigation system in Sangam literature (2nd century CE). The sacred tanks of South India were called

---

[37] S.I.I. Vol. XVII, Nos. 299 and 304.

[38] ARE 191, 194, 198 & 225 of 1929—30 CE.

[39] E I, Vol. 38, pt.1, pp. 27.

[40] C. R. Shanmugham, *Irrigation Tanks and Their Traditional Local Management: A Remarkable Ancient History of India*, in National Seminar on Water and Culture Hampi, Karnataka, 25–27 June 2007, pp. 1–11.

Chandra *kundam* (tank of the moon). Chandra, incidentally, was one of the treasures that came out of the *samudra manthana*.

In South India, the tradition of creating a tank aboard a temple still prevails. Each village incorporates a temple and a temple tank. These tanks are reservoirs, which were created to reap water and capture rain run-off. Sometimes, channels were created to bring water from a closeby stream or watercourse. The temple tanks are called *kovil kulam* in Tamil Nadu, *kulam* in Kerala, *kalyani* in Karnataka, *pushkarini* in Andhra Pradesh and *tataka* in Sanskrit language. Water was essential for maintaining the groundwater level.[41]

Many of the plains of Tamil Nadu are characterized by an average rainfall of less than 1,000 mm and a near absence of perennial rivers. Not surprisingly, this region was described as *vaanam paartha bhoomi* (land that is looking at the skies). In this context, creation of several kinds of water tanks made practical sense. The best-known water-holding structures were the specially excavated water tanks around the many temple sites.

In fact, the two entities, temple and the water tank, complemented each other, both serving an essential part of rural and urban life, of rituals and domestic use. 'In fact, the temple and the tank are linked in the term *kovil kulam*, meaning temple tank.' Sacred place, deity and sacred water, the temple and the tank all these fulfilled the requirements of pilgrimage.

The temple tank is also the location of the annual *teppotsavam* (float festival). The bronze image of the deity is taken in procession around the temple tank, on a palanquin by the devotees. Sometimes, as in Mylapore (Chennai), a *mandapa* may be built in the tank or a wooden *mandapa* floated in the tank, where the deity is placed to the chanting of *slokas* and *nadaswaram* music.

Several temples had two tanks, one of which served to cleanse the pilgrims while the other was the deity's ritual bath or *abhishekha* and the site of the float festival at some of the temples; also, these helped nurture the gardens which provided flowers for the many rituals. 'But these *kovil kulams* served more than just the ritual needs; these played an important in the prosperity of the area; these helped recharge and maintain the groundwater level and proved to be a boon for local ecology

---

[41] M. Amirthalingam, *Temple Tanks of Chennai* (Chennai: C.P.R. Environmental Education Centre, 2004).

as well.' According to the *Tamil Nadu Temple express* (17 October 2002), 'there are more than 70 temple tanks in and around Chennai city alone, and around 4,000 temples traditionally had water tanks that were used for various rituals. The tanks also served as natural aquifers and helped recharge groundwater, though most of these have fallen into a state of utter neglect in recent times.'

Made of brick or plain earth, most temple tanks are rectilinear in shape. The original structure was a beautifully planned affair, with appropriately situated inlets to gather rainwater from surrounding areas and outlets for excess water. Even surrounding architecture was made in sync with the objective of enhancing the rain-harvesting potential of these tanks. For instance, many of the older homes had sloping roofs that facilitated flow of rainwater into the tanks, some of which were even connected with one another through channels to enable optimum harvesting and use of water.

The temple tanks were good indicators of the aquifer level. But they were very different from the irrigation reservoirs which required arduous manual labour to lift water and were therefore replaced by easier means of irrigation, like canals.

The crucial issues of tank structure are its physical structure and the inlet and outlet channels. The most important part is the tank catchment, which is a part of the tank.

Whereas the sacred temple tank was typically set ahead of the temple, the irrigation reservoir was a lot larger and was made singly over an oversized space and used completely for irrigation. The reservoir had channels to direct freshwater into the tank and channels to require the surplus water to alternative close tanks, besides smaller channels that took the water to the fields to be irrigated. This method of irrigation can still be seen in the *yeris* and *kulams* and ponds of South India severally.

The Vijayanagara Empire covered the entire region south of the Tungabhadra and Krishna rivers. One of the main reasons for the prosperity of this empire was the construction of major irrigation works, bringing new areas under cultivation. This increased the revenue of the empire.[42] A prince of the Vijayanagara dynasty, Baskara, constructed a huge tank in Porumanilla in Badvel taluk of Kadappa district. The construction of this tank is recorded in one of the inscriptions of Bukkaraya I (1356–1377 CE). The artificial bund or dam was

---

[42] *Frontline*, 12–15 December 1987, 76.

500 *rekhadandas* long, 8 *rekhadandas* wide and 7 *rekhadandas* high. It is pertinent to point out that the tank supplies water to the district to this day. Another important tank was dug by Bukka I at Kaluchapalli (Cuddapah). It is evident that the Rayars of Vijayanagara and their ministers, nobles and officers were great builders of irrigational systems, which met the needs of the agriculturalists.[43] Another major work undertaken by the Rayas was the construction of the huge dam at the Tungabhadra river, with an aqueduct, which is 15 miles long, from the river into the city.[44] The Vijayanagara kingdom (1336–1546 CE) within the south took keen interest in building giant and tiny storage tanks. Anantraj Sagar tank was designed with a 1.37 km long earthen dam across the Maldevi watercourse. The tank stands till today with an improved form situated 2 miles to the east of the village of Porumamilla. The lake is 7 miles in length and two-and-a-half miles in breadth. It was built by Bhaskar, the son of Bukka I of the Vijayanagara dynasty, during the year 1369 CE.[45]

Part I: Traditional Water Harvesting Systems in India

India has a rich and varied tradition of water harvesting that dates back to the time of the Indus Valley Civilization. It would be no exaggeration to say that the ancient Indians were the world's greatest water harvesters. Based on centuries of experience, Indians developed a wide range of techniques to harvest rainwater, groundwater, river water and flood water. Traditionally, Indian culture and religion show great reverence to rivers.

India can be broadly divided into 15 ecological regions. These vary from the dry cold desert of Ladakh to the dry hot desert of Rajasthan; from the climatic zone of the Western Ghats mountain chain running parallel with India's West Coast; from the deposits of the Indo-Gangetic plains to the plateaus of Deccan and Chota Nagpur; from the dry slopes of the Aravallis to the wet forests of the north east.[46]

The technology and engineering of the traditional water harvesting systems varies from region to region. Different techniques were used to

[43] N. Venkataramanayya, *Studies in the Third Dynasty of Vijayanagara* (Madras, 1935), 88.

[44] R. Sewell, ed., *A Forgotton Empire* (1924), 245.

[45] K. K. Chakravary, G. L. Badam, and V. Paranjpye, *Traditional Water Management Systems of India* (Bhopal/Delhi, 2006), 26.

[46] Agarwal and Narain, *Dying Wisdom*, 25.

harvest drinking water or water to be used for irrigation purposes. The water bodies meant for drinking water like wells were usually covered with steps leading down to the water. Thus, the amount of water collected by the people was strictly rationed. On the other hand, irrigation systems to water the agricultural fields had a large and complex system of pipes and channels.

Trans-Himalayan Region

This region consists of Ladakh and Kargil of Jammu and Kashmir and the Lahaul and Spiti valleys of Himachal Pradesh. In Ladakh, the customary water harvesting system is known as *zings*. The *zings* are small tanks that collect melted glacier water through channels.

Kuls are water channels found in the Spiti valley of Himachal Pradesh. These channels carry water from the glaciers to the villages. They are also found in the Jammu region.

The central-western Himalayan region, comprising Kashmir valley, Jammu, Uttarakhand, Himachal Pradesh and Uttar Pradesh, developed varied methods of water harvesting. This is an area of wide geological and ecological diversities. This resulted in the development of various methods of water harvesting systems such as *naulas, baoris, nauns, dharas, panihars, chharedus, khals, chaals* and *ktuitris*. A unique feature of this region is the thousands of kilometres of hand-dug *kuhls* and *guhls* that tapped mountain streams. These were used to transport water for irrigation and powering thousands of *gharats* or watermills.

These irrigation systems not only served the utilitarian needs of transporting water to the agricultural fields but were also used for decoration and displaying architectural skills. The water-gathering frameworks of the district used all domestically accessible water. These included precipitation, surface runoff, snow-melt, lakes, ponds and groundwater, as springs and wells. The water to be used in the households was collected from springs, mountain streams and man-made rainwater harvesting structures. For the use of animals, open water bodies like ponds, masonry tanks, *chappris* or *chaak* were utilized.

For the purpose of human consumption, the local people harvested underground seepages in *baoris* or *khatris* as in Himachal Pradesh and *naulas* in Uttarakhand. They also used to tap springs through *dharas* as in Uttarakhand or *panihars/chharedus* as in Himachal Pradesh. There were a wide variety of water harvesting structures due to the wide ecological and geological diversities of the region. It is to be noted that all these water management systems were managed by the local communities themselves, and there was little or no state intervention.[47]

Chaals, Khals, Naulas, Baoris and Simars

The local communities have found ingenious ways of using the formations and the depressions in the mountain for the purposes of rainwater harvesting. These are known as *chaals* or *kiwis*. These are usually found along mountain ridge tops, in the saddle between two adjacent crests. Another means of storing rainwater are the *Khals* or lakes, which can store several thousand cubic metres of water. The water is used for domestic purposes as also for livestock. In Pauri district alone, there are 70 well-known *khals*. Other natural rainwater harvesting structures include *chuptyaulds* and *simars*. These water harvesting structures are used by wildlife too.

In Uttarakhand, *naulas* are sometimes known as *baoris*. These may be defined as shallow, four-sided stepped wells. Most *naulas* have a similar basic design. Water may seep in from fissures in the steps or the base. The structure of *naulas* can vary considerably. Elaborate drainage systems keep the source water clean. In Almora, the famous *naulas* include the *Kapina, Champa, Dhara, Hathi, Khazanehi, Dugalkhola, Malla* and *Baleshwar*. However, it should be noted that varied *naulas* on the old Kailash-Mansarovar pioneer course and the *naulas* of Pithoragarh space and Almora town area unit are unnoticed, silted up or cleared over and lost.[48]

Historic Naulas of Kumaon

Many of the ancient *naulas* of Kumaon district were built to serve the pilgrims on the Kailash-Mansarovar route. The foremost established *naula* in Kumaon seems to the Badrinathji-ka-naula in Gadser city of Bageshwar scene. Other famous *naulas* are the Bhannaula near Meldungari village in Pithoragarh district and the Haat-Boragaon *naula* near Balakot. Several *naulas* in villages near Gangolihat are well known for their sheer size.[49]

---

[47] R. Chopra, 'Water Harvesting Tradition', in *Survival Lessons: Himalayan Jal Sanskriti* (Delhi, 2003), 3.

[48] S. Krishan, 'Water Harvesting Traditions and the Social Milieu in India: A Second Look', *Economic & Political Weekly Supplement (EPW)* XLVI, nos. 26 & 27 (25 June 2011): 87–95.

[49] A. Upadhyay and P. Bisht, *Uttarakhand Mein Jal Prabandhan: Ek Sinhavlokan, Nainital*, 2001, 7 (in Hindi)

Baoris *and* Nauns *of Himachal Pradesh*

Baoris are usually covered structures, but *nauns* are uncovered. Very large *baoris* are called *nauns*. While water from the *baoris* is used for all domestic purposes, *nauns* are mainly used for bathing and washing clothes. A channel is typically provided outside *baoris* for animals to drink water from them.[50]

Himachal's Baoris

Mandi district abounds in *baoris*. The town of Mandi is especially famous for its temples, exquisite *baoris* and big *rutuns*. People use the water which flows out of the *baori* through a pipe. A fine example of *baori* is the one found in Jubhal town, which was built by Raja Karam Chand about 300 years ago. The majority of village *baoris* has been built by local communities and are very simple structures.[51]

Eastern Himalayas

The eastern Himalaya includes Sikkim, Arunachal Pradesh and, the Darjeeling region of West Bengal. The folks of eastern Himalaya apply the system of Apatani. Streams are the most trustworthy wellspring of water here. Bamboo channels are used to occupy the water for water system. The Apatani arrangement of Arunachal Pradesh was practised by the Apatani clans. They harvested both ground and surface water for irrigation.[52] The stream water was blocked by constructing a 2–4-m-high and 1-m-thick wall near forested hill slopes. This water was taken to the agricultural fields through channels.

Northeast Hill Ranges

The northeastern slope reaches include the slopes of Assam, Nagaland, Manipur, Mizoram, Tripura and Meghalaya, stretching out into Bangladesh and Myanmar. They likewise incorporate the southern slants of Brahmaputra natural depression and therefore the northern, eastern and southern slopes of the Barak valley. (http://environmentnman.

---

[50] Chopra, 'Water Harvesting Tradition', 9.

[51] Ibid, 36–63.

[52] S. C. Rai, 'Apatani Paddy-cum-fish Cultivation: An Indigenous Hill Farming System of North-east India', *Indian Journal of Traditional Knowledge* 4, no. 1 (2005): 65–71.

blogspot.com/2009/03/). Precipitation and groundwater are the elemental wellsprings of water in this district. In any case, the landscape makes it exhausting to collect the surface water. Traditional springs are used for potable functions. Zabo, signifying 'appropriating run-off', is trained in Nagaland. The run of water is collected in the ponds in the middle terrace. At times, it goes through inclines, wherever there are cow yards, and at last arrives at the paddy fields. This is known as drip irrigation. Bamboo pipes are used to regulate the flow of water (http://www.cpreec.org/pubbook-traditional.htm).

Brahmaputra Valley

This region of Assam, comprising the Brahmaputra and Barek valleys, contains many natural depressions. The flood water accumulates in this depression and the farmers utilize the same for the purposes of cultivation. The Bodo tribes of Assam are known to construct *dongs* or ponds, which are then used to harvest water for irrigation. Within the connecting condition of West Bengal, within the region of Jalpaiguri, very little water system channels known as fertilizers or *jampois* are worked to move water from the streams to their rice fields.

Indo-Gangetic Plains

The Indo-Gangetic plains are comprised of flat alluvial soil. Hence, the main sources of water are the mighty rivers that flow down from the Himalayas. In the region of South Bihar, the indigenous system of flood water harvesting is known as *Ahar Pyne*.

- The *Ahar Pyne* may be defined as a catchment basin embanked on three sides. The fourth side is the natural slopes. The *Pynes* commence from the river and run through the fields and end up in an *ahar*. This system of flood water harvesting is best suited to this region.
- Bengal's inundation channels: Bengal is known for its unique system of inundation channels. These channels are broad and shallow and carry the crest water of the river floods to the agricultural fields.
- A *dighi* may be defined as a square or circular reservoir of about 0.38 metres by 0.38 metres with steps to enter. Each *dighi* has its own sluice gate. A *dighi* is fed by canals from the rivers.
- The *baolis* of Delhi consist of shallow pits, with a sloping path leading down to the water. In the rocky regions, they have vertical walls and dented steps.

Thar Desert

The Thar desert is the region of scanty rainfall. Hence, it becomes necessary to capture the rainwater and store it in underground tanks. There are different types of storage ponds found in the Thar desert.

- A *tarai* could be a reservoir that is built within the natural depression between sand hills by building bunds at the two closures. The water is gathered within the reservoir. Nevertheless, the *tarais* evaporate during a few months, owing to the deeply leaky soil. The saving grace is that the region around it remains wet and moist. Wells are usually dug close to the *tarai*.
- The *tankas* are very little underground tanks found primarily within the Bikaner region. They have spherical openings created within the grounds and glued with fine cleansed lime, within which the monsoon water gathers. They were often beautifully decorated with tails, which help to keep the water cool. The water is employed unambiguously for drinking. In the years when the monsoon fails, water from nearby wells and tanks is used to fill the *tankas*.
- Step wells are India's most unique contribution to architecture and are mainly found in the states of Gujarat and Rajasthan. They are known as *vav* or *vavadi* in Gujarat, and *baolis* or *bavadis* in Rajasthan. The progression wells of Gujarat comprise a vertical shaft within the centre from which water is drawn. The well shaft is encompassed by hallways, chambers and steps that lead right down to the well. They are often profusely carved and serve as a cool resting place in summer.
- A Kund or kundi is essentially a circular underground well with a saucer-shaped catchment area that slopes gently towards the centre where the well is situated. The edges of the well are secured with disinfectant lime and dust. Most pits have a dome-shaped cover or at least a lid to protect the water. They are mainly used for the drinking water purposes.
- *Kuis* or *beris*, which are deep pits dug near the tanks to collect the seepage water, are mainly found in western Rajasthan. They can also be used to harvest rainwater. The mouth of the pit is usually very narrow. This is to prevent evaporation. The pits get wider or become deeper, so more water can seep in. The opening of this structure is usually covered or locked.
- The *Jhalaras* are water bodies found in Rajasthan and Gujarat. They are often rectangular in shape with steps on three or four sides. The steps are built on a series of levels. They are mainly used for communities and for religious purposes.

- *Nadis* are town lakes found in Jodhpur in Rajasthan. They are primarily utilized for storing water from a characteristic catchment region. The area of the *nadi* depends upon its stockpiling limit because of the related catchment and spillover qualities. The villagers select the site for the *nadi* based on the natural catchment and its water yield potential.[53]
- *Tobas* are situated in a patch of land with low porosity with the depression, and a natural catchment area is selected for the construction of *tobas*.[54]
- *Khadin* consists of a very long earthen embankment (100–300 m) built across the lower hill slopes. It is mainly designed to harvest surface runoff water for agricultural purposes.
- *Paar* system is a structure constructed through traditional masonry technology and is found mainly in western Rajasthan. The rainwater flows from the *agar* (catchment) and percolates into the sandy soil. They are usually 5–12 m deep.

Central Highlands

This region includes the Bundelkhand region and Jhabua district of Madhya Pradesh, Eastern Mewar, Mewar region in the Thar Desert and Alwar district of Rajasthan. These areas are dotted with innumerable natural and artificial lakes, tanks, ponds, wells and drainage canals. There are little (*talai*), medium (*talab*) and enormous (*sagar*) lakes. For instance, Pichola, Fatehsagar and Udaisagar are the genuine case of the lakes.

The Chandela kings (851–1545 CE) of Bundelkhand and Madhya Pradesh built up a system of a few hundred tanks that guaranteed an agreeable degree of groundwater. They were built by halting the progression of a *nullah* or a stream running between two slopes with an enormous earthen bank. The quartz reefs running under the slopes restricted the water between them (downtoearth.org.in).

- *Talab/Bandhis* are otherwise known as reservoirs. In Tikamgarh, in the Bundelkhand region, these may be natural ponds (*pokhariyan*). A *talai* is a reservoir with region of less than 5 bighas. A medium-sized lake is known as a *bandhi* or *talab* and some greater lakes are called *sagar*

[53] A. S. Jethoo and M. P. Poonia, 'Traditional Domestic Rain Water Harvesting System Suitable for Rajasthan State and Their Sizing: A Review', *International Journal of Modern Engineering Research* 1, no. 2 (2011): 715–718.

[54] R. Dande et al., 'Sustainable Rain Water Harvesting Techniques Prevailing in Ancient India', *International Journal on Theoretical and Applied Research in Mechanical Engineering* 5, no. 2 (2016): 16–24.

or *samand*. *Saza Kuva* is mostly found in the Aravalli hills in Mewar of eastern Rajasthan. It is an open well with multiple owners.

- *Johad* is otherwise known as earthen check dam which receives the rainwater. This improves percolation and recharging the groundwater.
- *Naadas* are found for the most part in the Mewar district of Rajasthan. This is the stone check dam built over the stream or ravine so as to catch the rainstorm downpour.
- *Pats* are found mainly in Jhabua district of Madhya Pradesh. This system diverts the water from the hill streams into irrigation channels called *pats*.
- Chandela tank is this system whereby the flow of water is stopped by constructing earthen embankment across rivulets. The embankments are supported on both sides by walls of stone. The tanks are made up of lime and mortar, and hence they can survive even after a thousand years.
- Bundela tanks are bigger in size than Chandela tanks. They are solidly built with steps leading down to the water.
- *Rapat* is a percolation tank with a bund to collect the rainwater and waste wear to dispose of the surplus water.

Eastern Highlands

The *katas*, *mundas* and *bandhas* were the fundamental water system sources in the antiquated inborn realm of the Gonds (presently in Odisha and Madhya Pradesh). A *kata* may be described as a strong earthen embankment, built across a drainage line to hold the water. The water is diverted by means of a cut in the embankment and led by a small channel into the agricultural fields.

Deccan Plateau

The Deccan plateau contains many and varied systems of irrigations such as wells, embankments across rivers and streams, reservoirs and tanks.

The tanks are built on the slopes of the Gaikhuri range in Maharshtra. A feature of these tanks is that the larger tanks are situated on the higher slopes, whereas the smaller ones are in the foothills.

In Maharashtra, check dams or diversion weirs called *bhandaras* are built by villagers across rivers (http://www.rainwaterharvesting.org/Rural/dec_plat_tradi.htm). This raises the water level of the rivers and makes it flow into channels.

The *phad* system of irrigation, prevalent in the northwestern part of Maharashtra, came into existence from 300 to 400 years ago. It is mainly found in the basins of the rivers such as Panjhra, Mosan and Aram in Dhule and Nasik district of Maharashtra. It consists of *bhandara* or check dam from which *kalvas* or canals carry water into the agricultural fields. The length of the canal varies from 2 to 12 km.

The Ramtek model, followed in Maharashtra, involves an intricate network of groundwater and surface water bodies connected through surface and underground canals.

In Andhra Pradesh, where the yearly precipitation is 1,000 mm, huge tanks called *cheruvu* are the fundamental water system source. They are sustained by streams. *Anicuts* are worked crosswise over numerous streams. Chain tanks are built in bumpy locales with wide valleys.

In Karnataka, the traditional method of irrigation by means of tanks called *kere* is prevalent. They are fed either by channels branching off from anicuts (check dams) built across streams or by streams in valleys. The tanks are built in a series, usually situated a few kilometres apart.

Western Ghats

Surangam is the unique water reaping structure found in Kasaragod locale in northern Kerala. A horizontal well is dug in hard laterite rock formations until water is found. The water leaks out of the hard shake and streams out of the passage where it is gathered in an open pit.

Western Coastal Plains

Virdas are dug in low depressions known as *jheels* (tanks). They are found mainly in the Great Rann of Kutch in Gujarat. They are built by the nomadic tribe of Maldharis. They are the source of sweet potable freshwater.

Eastern Ghats

A *Korambu* might be characterized as a brief dam built over the mouth of a channel and made of brushwood, mud and grass. The motivation behind building a *Korambu* is to bring the water level up in the trench and to redirect the water into the rural fields.

Eastern Coastal Plains

The coastal plains of Odisha are subject to water logging and floods. Hence, the villagers have built a community pond in each village, with huge bunds to stop saltwater ingress. Adjacent ponds were linked to form a chain of pond.

- *Yeri*: In the state of Tamil Nadu, about one-third of the irrigated area is watered by *yeris* or tanks. These tanks maintain the ecological balance, act as flood control systems and prevent soil erosion and run-off of rainwater besides recharging the groundwater level.
- *Ooranis* are found mainly in South Kerala and are useful only to irrigate a few acres of land. Due to the topography of the region, it is not possible to construct large tanks as in Tamil Nadu.

Part II: Sacred Water Bodies in India

The traditional beliefs are deeply embedded in every society; several lakes are sacred to local communities, and strict taboos and local rules shape the use of wetland resources. These traditional beliefs are still followed today and have helped maintain the ecological integrity of the water bodies. In this section, the sacred tanks are discussed region wise with their local names.

Northern Region

This region includes Delhi, Haryana, Himachal Pradesh, Punjab, Uttar Pradesh and Uttarakhand. The sacred water bodies of northern region are known by different names in each state and they are *baoli* in Delhi; *baoli*, holy water bodies, *sarover* in Haryana; *kund* in Himachal Pradesh; *Kund* or *sarovar* in Punjab; *kund* and *bowli* in Uttar Pradesh and Uttarakhand.

A *baoli* could also be outlined as a step well that contains a water supply and which may be accessed by a flight of stairs. These *baolis* were open to all communities to draw water. The *baolis* are known by completely different names such as *bawdi, barav, vav, bain* and *pushkarini*. A fine example for *baoli* is that of Red Fort *baoli*, New Delhi. This *baoli* was originally designed by the Firuz Shah Tughlaq and placed within the Red Fort complex; this *baoli* was restored and enlarged by the Emperor Shahjahan. It served as the resort area for the fort of Salimgarh. This massive *baoli* has two perpendicular staircases downhill, and therefore the circular pit holds the water. Throughout the recent summers, it was used as an area of retreat and additionally as an area wherever communities may gather all around the year. In contrast to different *baolis* that have steps leading to the water level, there are two perpendicular staircases downhill all the way down to the water. Today, it is a protected monument by the archaeological Survey of Asian country.[55]

Kunds/Kundis

A kund is a circular underground well. It looks like a saucer-shaped catchment area which gently slopes towards the centre where the well (*kund*) is situated. They have been built to harvest rain water and are found in the western part of the Thar Desert, some parts of Punjab, Himachal Pradesh, Uttarakhand and Uttar Pradesh. They need a saucer-formed geographical area that slopes towards the centre. They are usually covered by wire mesh to protect the water. Their depth and diameter depend upon the use to which they are put.

A good example is Suraj *kund*, which is an ancient reservoir located in Sunam, Faridabad district of Haryana. Suraj *kund* (literal meaning is 'Lake of the Sun') is an artificial *kund* (*kund* means 'lake' or reservoir) built in the backdrop of the Aravalli hills in a semicircular form. It is said to have been built by Tomar king Suraj Pal of Tomar dynasty in the 10th century. Suraj Kund is found close to the Suraj Kund village between the villages of Baharpur and Lakkarpur in Faridabad district of Haryana. The lake's geographic region is an element of the Aravalli hill ranges. According to bardic tradition (a tradition steeped in the history and traditions of clan and country), the Tomar kings who initially lived near the Aravalli hills shifted to the Suraj *kund* area near Lal Kot, which was built by the Tomars. Bound engraved stones were recently recovered from the reservoir. Throughout the Tughlaq kinfolk rule of Firuz Shah Tughlaq (1351–1388), the reservoir was refurbished by reconstruction of the steps and terraces with stones in lime mortar. On the western bank of the reservoir, a *garhi* (cave-like structure) was designed on the brink of the traditional website of the sun temple. The reservoir has been built in the form of the rising sun with associate eastward arc. Rainfall was intercepted here to form a reservoir of 130-m (427 ft) diameter to satisfy the water shortage in Delhi.

The ecological disaster that is causing the rapid depletion of ground water in the Aravalli hill ranges between Tughlaqabad and Gurugram

---

[55] S. Ahuja, *Red Fort Baoli*, 2013. https://indiaheritagehub.org/2013/03/10/delhi-gate/. Accessed 23 August 2016.

via Suraj *kund* due to indiscriminate mining has invited the attention of the Supreme Court of India through the efforts of environmental activist. This activity is also stated to be affecting the adjoining Asola Bhatti Wildlife Sanctuary. Consequent to a writ petition filed by the Delhi Ridge Management Board, the Supreme Court has asked the Haryana Government 'to stop all mining activities' and pumping of groundwater within a 5-kilometres (3 mi) radius of the Delhi–Haryana border in the Haryana Ridge and in the Aravalli hills.[56]

Sarovar

A *sarovar* could be a tank, pool or lake found at a sacred site or a holy shrine. It is chiefly used for ablutions and different non-secular ceremonies. In Indo-Aryan, a *sarovar* is additionally referred to as *sar, sarvar, tarag* and *vapl*. In Sikh sacred literature, *sarvar, sar, sarovar* and mansard are used in the sense of a lake or pool. These sorts of water body area units are found within the states of Haryana and Punjab.

According to Hindu mythology, there are five sacred lakes, which are called *panch sarovar* (*sarovar* means lake). The names of those lakes are Mansarovar, Bindu *sarovar*, Narayan *sarovar*, pampa *sarovar* and pushkar *sarovar*. Hence, it is no wonder that Pushkar is considered to be one of the most sacred *sarovars* in India. There is also a popular belief that taking a bath in one of the lakes on *Kartik Poornima* days is equivalent to performing *yagnas* (fire sacrifices) for several centuries. Another name for pushkar is *tirtha-raj* or the king of journey sites.

The foremost illustrious pushkar in Punjab is the one at the Golden temple in Amritsar. In fact, the town of Amritsar derives its name from the sacred tank. 'Amrit' which means 'nectar of immortality' and 'sarovar' which means a 'pool'. It is obligatory for the Sikhs to take a holy dip in its waters.[57]

Another *sarovar* of Punjab is the Muktsar *sarovar* at Shri Darbar European Gurudwara. Thousands of devotees take bath in the holy tank on the eve of Maghi Mela. It is aforementioned that Guru Govind Singh himself enlarged the tank and referred to it as Muktsar or the tank of salvation.[58]

---

[56] Y. D. Sharma, *Delhi and Its Neighborhood Surajkund and Anagpur Dam* (New Delhi: Archaeological Survey of India, 2001), 100.

[57] G. Gian Singh, *Twarikh Sri Amritsar* [Reprint] (Amritsar, 1977).

[58] A. Chaudhry, 'Muktsari Jutti Walks Again', *The Indian Express*, 5 August 2012. https://indianexpress.com/article/news-archive/print/muktsari-jutti-walks-again/

Northeast Region

Arunachal Pradesh (*Kund*)

Situated in the lower reaches of north Tezu of Lohit district of Arunachal Pradesh is a place of great religious importance. This is Parasuram *kund*, which is associated with the legend of Parasuram. There is also an interesting story connected with this *kund*. It is said that once Renuka, the mother of Parasuram, went to fetch water from the river. En route, she fell in love with king Chitranathan and dallied with him. On hearing this, her husband, the sage Jamadagani, became enraged and ordered his son to kill his mother. Obeying his father's instructions, Parasuram beheaded his mother. This was a great sin and the only way he could atone for it was to take a bath in the holy Brahma *kund*. Accordingly, Parasuram cut a passage from the Brahma *kund* for the water to come out and the place where his axe fell came to be known as Parasuram *kund*. Brahma *kund* is also situated near the place where Parasuram had cut open the passage through the hills for the Brahmaputra to flow.[59]

Assam (*Pukhuri*)

The practice of the construction of temple tanks in Assam can be dated back to the mediaeval period. The kings of Assam, especially the Ahoms, were adept at constructing/excavating these temple tanks for the benefit of their subjects. Among these, the four largest were the *Joysagar* tank (318 acres), *Sibsagar* tank (129 acres), *Gowrisagar* tank (150 acres) and *Rudrasagar* tank, which are still extant. In Assam, the sacred water bodies are known by different names such as *Pukhuri*, temple tank and pond. For example, the tank at Joysagar, the largest tank in India, stands on an area of 318 acres, half of which is under water. It was built by the Ahom King Rudra Singha (1697 CE) in memory of his mother Joymoti at Rangpur in Sibsagar district. There is evidence to show that it was built during a period of 45 days. Many temples are situated on the banks of the lake.[60]

Manipur (*Pukhri*/Ponds)

An important place of pilgrimage of Manipuris who live in Manipur, Assam, West Bengal, Uttar Pradesh, Bangladesh and Myanmar is Kangla.

---

[59] http://www.team-bhp.com/forum/travelogues/87309-guwahati-burma-stillwell-road-pangsau-pass-6.html

[60] P. Ganguli, S. Boruah, P. K. Dutta, S. Sharma, and A. P. Biswas, *Prospects of Ecotourism in Temple Tanks and Floodplain Lakes of Upper Assam.* Proceedings of Taal 2007 in 12th World Lake Conference, Jaipur, 2008, pp. 1329–1332.

Lord Pakhangba is the presiding deity of Kangla. The holy tank is situated here, which is believed to be the abode of Lord Pakhangba. There are also some sacred pools like *Chingkhei Nungjeng, Manung Nungjeng* and *Lai Pukhri.*

A temple is also constructed to Radha Kunja and Kali at Ningthem Pukhri, and daily worship according to the traditions of the Ramandi religion is performed here. A statue of Hanuman engraved from a big stone is kept in a temple at Mongbahanba. A big *pukhri* (pond), measuring 100 ft in length and 100 ft in breadth, is situated at Wangkhei Leikai.[61]

Meghalaya (Lake)

In Meghalaya, some of the lakes are considered to be sacred by the local communities. Nartiang is a place of some religious importance. There are two temples in Nartiang: one dedicated to Durga and the other to Shiva. There are also two lakes dug by Sajar Nangli, namely Umtisong and Myngkoi tok. Another protected lake is the Thadlaskein lake. For example, the Umhang lake is an artificial lake situated in the Wataw village and surrounded by thick forests on either side. This lake gained importance because the Jaintia chief Sajar Nangli drank water from a spring here. He was so enamoured of the place that he decided to create an artificial lake here. It took several months to create the lake. Since that time, the lake has become sacred to the people of Wataw. They perform annual sacrifice beside the lake.

Thadlaskein lake is an artificial lake situated in Jaintia Hills district and is fed by a perennial spring. This is one of the lakes dug by the Jaintia chief Sajar Nangli. According to the legend, the lake was dug within a day using bows. The lake is sacred to the local people and sacrifices are still offered here.[62]

Sikkim (Sacred Lakes)

Sikkim is home to natural sacred lakes, which are located mostly in northwest, northeast and extreme north. Many of them are sources of the River Tista and River Rangit. They are also considered to be the abode of local guardian spirits such as *Devas, Yakshas, Nagas,* nymphs and demons and also to various tantric deities. The government has

---

[61] Sairem Nilabir, *Laiyingthou Sanamahi Amasung Sanamahi Laining Hinggat Eehou* (Imphal: Thingbaijam Chanu Sairem Ongbi Ibemhal, 2002), 102.

[62] H. H. Mohrmen, 'Heritage Sites in Jaintia Hills', *The Shillong Times*, 30 July 2012. http://theshillongtimes.com/2012/07/30/heritage-sites-in-jaintia-hills/

identified many of the sacred lakes. However, many are situated in inaccessible places and are yet unknown. Some of the important holy lakes are Gurudongmar Lake and Tsho Lhamo Lake, North Sikkim, Tshomgo Lake, East Sikkim, Khachoedpalri Lake (Khechopalri Lake) and Kathok Lake, Yuksam.

Guru Dongmar Lake, North Sikkim

This lake is included as one of the 109 Tshochen or major lakes of Sikkim as per the text 'Nay-sol'. This lake was first recognized by Guru Padmasambhava, popularly known in Sikkim as Guru Rinpoche. This lake is the gateway to the northern territory otherwise known as the hidden land of Demojong. Today, the lake has become one of the important pilgrimage sites of Northern Sikkim. In Sikkim, the holy lakes are still revered as the abodes of the gods, nagas and *yakshas*. The local people believe that whoever worships there with devotion will definitely have their prayers answered. It is also popularly believed that Guru Nanak himself rested on the banks of this lake on his way to Tibet. At a nearby site called Lachen Gompha, the Guru's footprints, his robe and water utensil are preserved. The local people call Guru Nanak as Rimpoche Nanak Guru.[63]

Tsomgo Lake

Another sacred lake of Sikkim is the Tsomgo (Changu) lake, a glacial lake situated at a distance from 40 km from Gangtok. In the Bhutia language 'tsomgo' means source of the lake. The lake is about 1 km long and 15 m deep and is situated at an altitude of 3,780 m. It remains frozen during the winter months. It is an important pilgrimage site, where the deities are worshipped in small gumphas (caves) near the lake. Prayer flags are hoisted around the lake. A small temple of Lord Shiva is also built on the lakeside. During the olden times, lamas used to study the colour of the water of the lake and forecast the future. It was said that if the waters of the Tsomgo lake had a dark tinge, it foreshadowed a year of trouble and unrest in the state. The star-shaped gurudwara (Sri Hemkund sahib), located on the banks of the lake, is one of the most important pilgrimage sites for the Sikhs. Hemkund is also sacred for the Hindus. According to Hindu mythology, Hemkund is where Lakshman

---

[63] C. Acharya and A. S. Gyatso Dokham, 'Sikkim: The Hidden Holy Land and Its Sacred Lakes', in *Bulletin of Tibetology*, eds. Acharya Samten Gyatso, Rigzin Nyodup and Thupten Tenzing (Gangtok, Sikkim: Namgyal Institute of Tibetology, 1998), 10–15.

(Lord Rama's brother) did his penance. The mythological name for Hemkund is 'Lokpal'. There is a temple dedicated to Lakshman on the banks of the lake. The river flowing through this valley along the path from Gobindghat to Gobinddham is called Lakshman Ganga.

The lake is considered sacred and is worshipped by all Sikkimese. In the Bhutia language, the word *Changu* literally means 'above the lake'. The name is believed to have been given by yak herders in an earlier time, when the yak herders lived just above the lake. The lake is woven with rich legends and folklore. It is said the lake was earlier in a different location named Laten, several kilometres away from its present location. A story goes that an old herder woman at Tsomgo one night had a dream that the lake at Laten was to shift to Tsomgo. She and her herder friends were warned to leave the place. The lady told her friends about her dream and the warning, but no one listened. The old lady milked her yak and poured the milk on the ground as it was considered an auspicious gesture. She then left the place. As she was leaving, she saw an old lady with strikingly long white hair and fair complexion carrying yarn entering Tsomgo. It is believed that the lady with white hair was actually a water nymph. The coming of the lake to the region was considered a good omen. The local people of Sikkim worship the lake and consider it a pilgrim rather than a tourist destination. The lake is considered a deity. The local people visit the lake and pray to it for their well-being. Ceremonies are held especially during '*Guru Purnima*'.[64]

Khecheopalri Lake

This lake is situated at an altitude of 6,000 ft and is considered to be a lake that fulfils wishes. In the Sikkimese language, it is known as *Tsho-Tsho*. The water in this lake is crystal clear. It is surrounded by dense forests. There is a legend about the origin of the lake. It was once simply a grazing ground for the cattle. The local Lepchas used to collect nettles that abounded here to make various articles. According to the story, Lepcha couples were collecting the nettles as usual, when they saw a pair of conch shells flying towards them. The conch shells entered the ground and an enormous spring gushed out. This was the origin of the lake. The lake is considered to be sacred by both the Buddhists and the Hindus of Sikkim. From a higher vantage point, the lake resembles a footprint. Hence, the local people believe that it is Shiva's footprints.

---

[64] Government of Sikkim, *Draft Management Plan for Tsomgo Lake* (Department of Forest, Environment and Wildlife Management, August 2008).

There is a charming story connected with this lake. It is said that even if a leaf falls on the waters of the lake, it is immediately picked up by a bird. The lake is surrounded by prayer flags. The later Buddhist saints sanctified this lake and gave it the name 'Khachoedpalri'(*mKha-sPyod-dPal-ri*), which means 'mountain of blissful heaven' and recognized it as an abode of 'Tsho-sMan Pemachen' the protective nymph of Buddhism.[65]

Tripura (*Sagar*)

Tripura is a small state in Northeast India and is famous for its many temples and places of religious worship. Almost all the districts of the state contain important temples, where fairs and festivals are held, in which the local people take part in an enthusiastic manner. Especially in the capital city of Agartala, there are many temples dedicated to various gods and goddesses. These were constructed during the period when Tripura was ruled by kings.[66]

Kamalasagar Lake is one of the important water bodies, which is a huge artificial lake and is situated about 27 km from Agartala. It was constructed by Maharaja Dhanya Manikya Bahadur in the late 15th century. The lake enhances the serene beauty of the temple situated just beside the Bangladesh border. The sacred pond, which is situated to the west of the temple, is covered with lotus flowers. However, the name Kamalasagar (pond of lotus) does not denote this. In fact, it was named after Maharani Kamala Devi, wife of Maharaja Narendra Manikya.[67]

Dumboor Lake

A huge and breath-taking water body with an area of 41 km[2] with thick forest all around is one of the sacred water bodies of Tripura. The name derives from the fact that it looks like a *tabour*, a small drum of Lord Shiva. There are 48 islands situated in the midst of the lake. The lake attracts migratory birds from far and near. The lake originates from the River Gomati at a place called *Tirthamukh* and is the confluence of the rivers Raima and Sarma. The famous *pous Sankranti* is celebrated on 14 January every year. The lake also contains a rich reservoir of natural and cultured fish.[68]

---

[65] *State of Environment* (Sikkim, 2007), 56–57.

[66] W. W. Hunter, *The Statistical Account of Bengal* (New York, NY, 1876).

[67] G. K. Bera, 'Temples, Fairs and Festivals of Tripura', *TUI, Journal of Tribal Life and Culture* 16, no. 2 (2013): 108.

[68] Dhalai District Profiles, 2015, 4.

Western Region

Rajasthan (*Baori, Baoli, Baudi, Bawdi* or *Bavadi*)

Rajasthan is located in the northwestern region of India and once consisted of a number of princely states. The arid desert is situated in the far west of Rajasthan, but there is a habitable and fertile tract in the northeast. Cultivation is naturally very precarious in the arid region. However, there are some well-built towns like Jodhpur and Jaisalmer in this region. The Luni river originates in the Aravalli hills and flows from Ajmer to the Rann of Kutch, thus draining a large part of the arid zone. The region receives 1,525 mm to 1,780 mm rainfall annually. Thus irrigation is restricted to deep wells and rainwater harvesting systems.

Water harvesting is thus deeply rooted in the social fabric of Rajasthan. Since Rajasthan is a region where there are no perennial rivers, most water-related problems are related to the fluctuating weather and river systems. Nearly all the natural sources of water like the *jharnars* (springs) have some mythological origin. Bangangas emerged from places where the Pandavas are said to have lived. Bhimagoda is a place where Bhima pressed his knee to the earth to send the water gushing out. Water is so scarce in Rajasthan that sources of natural water have become places of pilgrimage.

Types of Water Bodies

In Rajasthan, there are various traditional water source systems, such as *nadi, talab, johad, bandha, sagar, sammand* and *sarovar*. Wells are another important source of water. Different types of wells are found in Rajasthan. *Kua* is usually a well owned by an individual. The large wells are known as *kohar* and are usually owned by the community. The step wells are known as *baoli*. They are usually constructed as a good deed performed to obtain *punya*. Another name for *baoli* is *jhalara*. The most primitive step wells might probably date back to 550 AD. However, the most illustrious step wells were constructed in the mediaeval period. It is roughly estimated that more than 3,000 step wells were constructed in two major northern states of India.

Step wells are known by different names, such as *baudi* (including *bawdi, bawri, baoli, bavadi* and *bavdi*). They were developed as a response to the huge variations in the availability of water supply. A step well makes it easier to reach the groundwater level and also to maintain the well. Another type of step well known as *johara* was developed with ramps so that cattle could reach the water easily.

Deep trenches were dug into the earth so that there would be water supply all around the year. The walls of the trenches were lined with blocks of stone. Steps were also built leading down to the water level. These step wells also served as a venue for social gatherings, especially popular among the women, who usually collected the water. They were also decorated with architectural and ornamental patterns.

These step wells had a unique system of water harvesting. The huge open surface of the well acted as the rain-catching conduit that collected the water and consigned it to the bottom of the well. The system of step wells was meant to ensure that the people had direct access to water throughout the year. They also served an architectural purpose.

Architecture of Step Wells

There are two common types of step wells. The first one is the step pond with a large-mouthed apex and modified sides that meet at a moderately low profundity. The next one would be the actual step well category that generally includes a tapered shaft, guarded from direct sunbeams by full or partial covering that ends with a curved, profound 'well-end'. Many step wells are painted with lime-based paint. Different types of primeval colours were used.

Chand Baori

The Chand baori in Abhaneri village is one of the primitive step wells in the state of Rajasthan and is thought to be one of the largest. It appears exactly like a well. There are 3,500 tapered steps in this step well. The green water at the base of the well indicates that the well is no longer used. The steps encircle the step well on three sides, while the fourth side has a group of pavilions that are constructed one on top of the other. The famous Chand *baori* at Abhaneri was featured in a movie called 'The Fall' and another called 'The dark knight rises'. At present, this step well is one of the vital assets of the country and is administered by the Archaeological Survey of India (ASI).

Bundi, Kota

Bundi is a beautiful town and important in the history of Rajasthan. It is surrounded by the Aravalli hills on three sides and a massive wall with four gateways, famous for their intricate carvings and murals. Bundi is known for its *baoris* or step wells. Constructed by royalty and affluent members of society, they served as water reservoirs whenever there was a scarcity of water. The finest example is the Raniji-ki, which was built by Rani Nathavati ji in 1699 AD during her son Budh Singh's time. It is adorned with finely sculpted pillars and arches. It is a multi-storied structure with places of worship on each floor. The steps built into the sides of the water-well made water accessible even when at a very low level. The *baori* is one of the largest examples of its kind in Rajasthan.[69]

In Bundi, there are about 86 *baoris*. After the monsoon, these *baoris* get filled up with water. The streets channel the run over of water from one tank to the other. The deepest step well is about 46 m deep.[70]

Karz *Kund* and Tulsi *Kund* at Eklingji Temple, Udaipur

These *kunds* are situated near the 15th century AD Jain temple, situated in the town of Eklingji. The water is utilized for the rituals in the temple, especially the *alankar* ritual of Lord Shiva. Two artificial pools have been created in the temple of Galtaji in Jaipur district. The water is collected in seven tanks, the holiest being the Galta *kund* which never becomes dry. Another temple complex in Jaipur is the Ram Gopalji temple, also known as the monkey temple. There is a cluster of sacred *kunds* near the temple complex.

Kaman in Bharatpur district of Rajasthan is an old sacred town of the Hindus and forms part of the Braj area where Lord Krishna spent his early life. Kaman also has 84 *kunds*, many of which have dried up. It was long ruled by the Maharajahs of Jaipur. During the rainy season, a fair is held called the Parikramma mela.

The Nawal Sagar lake is situated in Bundi and is an artificial lake built in the form of a square. It contains many tiny islets. The temple of Lord Varuna, the Vedic God of water, is situated in the middle of the lake. The Dabhai *kund*, also known as the jail *kund*, is the largest and most historical *kund* of Bundi district. There are many steps leading down to the water level.

Ancient surface water bodies have been in news for many hundreds of years. They are excellent examples of architectural and engineering design and were built on the principle of community sharing. An unwritten code maintained this water system for many centuries. However, with the introduction of public water supply, these ancient water bodies have gone into decline.

---

[69] A. Agarwal, S. Narain, and I. Khurana, ed., *Making Water Everybody's Business: Practice and Policy of Water Harvesting* (New Delhi, 2001).

[70] Agarwal and Narain, *Dying Wisdom*.

Nadis are village ponds constructed in valleys by strategically build-ing earthen embankments across natural depressions. These *nadis* are found in Jodhpur and Rajsamand districts of Rajasthan. They are used for storing water from an adjoining natural catchment during the rainy season. The site is selected by the villagers based on available natural catchments and their water yield potential. Water availability from the *nadi* ranges from 2 months to a year after the rains. In the dune areas, they range from 1.5 to 4.0 m and in sandy plains from 3 to 12 m. The location of the *nadi* depends on its storage capacity due to the related catchment and runoff. These *nadis* are mainly used for the water requirements of the livestock. However, one-third of these *nadis* have been badly polluted due to the absence of maintenance. Due to the large surface area of the *nadis*, there is heavy water loss from evaporation.

Talabs are otherwise known as lakes or large reservoirs constructed in natural depressions or valleys. They are traditionally constructed by villagers on community lands, using lime masonry walls on the sides, with soil as the filling material between the walls. Some *talabs* have wells in their beds. For example, the Kharasan *talab* was a historically important water harvesting structure. It was constructed by an earthen embankment on the downstream side and a curvature on the upstream side to give more strength to the structure. *Talabs* are famous in the Mewar region and the city of Udaipur has a large number of *talabs*. Hence, this was named Lake City. The reservoirs are in various sizes and named as variously: a small lake is called *talai*; a medium-sized lake is called *bandh* or *talab*; and a bigger one is called *sagar* or *samand*. Water from these reservoirs is used for drinking as well as irrigation purposes. A large number of *talabs* are lost due to urbanization and industrializa-tion. Earlier, they used to serve the drinking needs of the community, but of late, they are being increasingly used for cattle and irrigation purposes. When the water dries up, the beds are used for agriculture.

Tanks, in contrast to *talabs*, are constructed with huge masonry walls on four sides. They are either square or rectangular in shape and can hold massive amounts of water. They are invariably provided with a system of canals to bring in rainwater from the catchment areas. Most of the famous tanks are constructed in Jodhpur. Some of these have now been abandoned and receive sewage and polluted waters from the adjoining colonies. The feeder canals have fallen into disuse and are used as sewage lines and for dumping garbage.

Baoris are community wells, found in Rajasthan, that are used mainly for drinking purposes. Most of them are very old and were built by Banjaras (nomadic communities) for their drinking water needs. They can hold water for a long time because of almost negligible water evaporation. They do not have a catchment area of their own nor are they connected to any water course. They access the water from the seepage of *talab* or a lake situated nearby. They occupy minimum space in order to save money, time and energy. Jodhpur is especially famous for baoris. There is very little water evaporation from the *baoris* compared to other water bodies. The condition of half of the *baoris* is fairly good while the remaining require maintenance.

Jhalaras are man-made tanks, essentially used for community bathing and religious functions. They are rectangular in design and have steps on three or four sides. They collect subterranean seepage of a *talab* or a lake situated upstream. An outstanding example is the Maha Mandir *Jhalara* constructed in 1660 CE. They are excellent examples of architectural designs and need to be protected. Some of these *jhalaras* are now used for irrigation purposes. Some *jhalaras* are being destroyed by mining and industrial activities. There is an urgent need to protect them by controlling the activities in the catchment areas. Reforestation is also an effective method of regenerating these *jhalaras*. Desilting is essential if these *jhalaras* are to be used for their original purpose.

Tobas is the local name given to a ground depression with a natural catchment area. A hard plot of land with low porosity consisting of a depression and a natural catchment area was selected for the construction of *tobas*. It provides water for human and livestock consumption and the grass growing around it provides pasture for cattle. In order to preserve and enlarge the capacity of the *tobas*, the catchment areas were widened. No encroachment was allowed to damage the catchment. The *tobas* are also deepened to increase the storage capacity.

Kunds are rainwater harvesting structures found in the sandier tracts of the Thar Desert in western Rajasthan. They dot the region and are the main source of drinking water. A *kund* is a circular underground well. It looks like a saucer-shaped catchment area, which gently slopes towards the centre where the well (*kund*) is situated. The depth and diameter of *kunds* may depend on the requirement of water used for drinking and domestic purposes. The sides of the well pit are covered with lime and ash. Most pits are covered by a lid to protect the water. The *kunds* may be owned by rich businessmen and landlords. During the period of the Mahabharata, this place had 84 *kunds* associated with an equal number of *tirthas*. All have now disappeared due to encroachment. However, the *kunds* are very essential, in that the importance of *kunds* with respect to the recharge of the aquifers is recognized in the low-lying regions of Rajasthan. These *kunds* are owned by the community and sometimes built by community cooperation. Before the onset of the monsoon, the catchment area of the *kund* is regularly cleaned. Especially in the Thar Desert, these *kunds* serve the important purpose of providing the drinking water requirements of far-flung settlements. The *kunds* are by and large circular in shape, with a diameter ranging from 3 m to 4.5 m. Lime plaster or cement is used in the construction of the *kunds*. The catchment area varies from 20 m² to 2 ha. In times of deficient rainfall, the *kunds* can be used as water reservoirs by filling them by water tankers.

Kuis and *dakeriyan* are found in abundance in Bikaner district of western Rajasthan. These are 10–12-m-deep pits dug near tanks to collect the seepage. *Kuis* can also be used to harvest rainwater in areas of meagre rainfall. The mouth of the pit is usually made very narrow to prevent the collected water from evaporating. The pit gets wider as it burrows under the ground, so that water can seep in into a large surface area. The openings of these entirely *kuchcha* (earthen) structures are generally covered with planks of wood, or put under lock and key. The water is used sparingly as a last resource in crisis situations.

Tankas, also called small tanks, are traditionally found in the main house or in the courtyard of Bikaner houses. It is an underground tank with circular holes made in the ground, lined with fine polished lime, where the rainwater is collected. Often, *tankas* are beautifully decorated with tiles which helped to keep the water cool. This water is used only for drinking purposes. The *tanka* system is also found in pilgrim towns like Dwaraka in Gujarat, where they have been in existence for centuries.[71]

Western Region

Water wells have played a key role in the architecture of India since the dawn of history. Excavation has proved the existence of step wells in Mohenjo-daro and Harappa. Step wells can be defined as water sources such as wells or ponds, in which water may be accessed by descending a flight of steps. These wells may often be enclosed and protected and may contain many intriguing architectural designs. These wells were constructed with the main objective of ensuring water supply during periods of drought. They also reflected the deep faith in the water god, which is recounted even in the Vedas. They may often also

---

[71] M. Amirthalingam, 'Traditional Water Harvesting Systems of Rajasthan', in *Ecological Traditions of India*, eds. Nanditha Krishna and Aman Singh, Vol. X. (Rajasthan, 2014), 174–183.

be multi-storied. Step wells thus represent a unique combination of technology, architecture and art of the subcontinent.[72]

As many as 700 wells have been found in Mohenjo-daro and Harappa.[73] More recently, the construction of step wells can be dated to at least 600 CE, especially in the northwestern part of India, particularly Gujarat and Rajasthan.[74] The construction of these step wells reached its nadir between the 11th and 16th century CE. Most existing step wells can be dated to at least 800 years ago. This tradition of building step wells continued even during the Islamic and British rule.

Step Wells in Gujarat

The step wells or *vavs* were common in the semi-arid regions of Gujarat to cater to the drinking water needs of the people. These wells were also scene of colourful festivals and sacred rituals. Gujarat is famous as the land of *vavs* or step wells, since it is an area of scanty rainfall. These *vavs* go by different names in different parts of the country. In the Hindi-speaking belt, they are usually called *baudi*. In the Gujarat and Marwar region of the Rajasthan, they are known as *vav*. In Kannada, they are called kalyani or *pushkarani* and in Marathi, *barav*.

An interesting feature of the *vav* is that the direct sunlight cannot penetrate the well and the evaporation of water is thus reduced and also the water gets filtered from the earth, thus remaining pure and fresh. These step wells are so well constructed that they can withstand earth-quakes to the scale of 7.6 on the Richter scale.[75]

There are a number of step wells found in the state of Gujarat. These tanks are constructed in different forms, plans and structures and designs, with steps leading to the water level. In the modern wells, a brick parapet wall surrounds the well shaft. Water is drawn by a pulley system. These step wells not only fulfilled the need for water but also acted as cool retreats. The walls and pillars of the step wells were embellished with decorated sculptures.

---

[72] S. Takezawa, 'Stepwells—Comology of Subterranean Architecture as Seen in Adala (English text translated by Vasanti Menon), The Diverse Architectural World of the Indian Sub-continent: Special the World of Indian Architecture', *Journal of Applied Behavioral Science (JABS)* 117, no. 1492 (2002): 24.

[73] U. Singh, *A History of Ancient and Early Medieval India: From the Stone Age to the 12th Century* (New Delhi, 2008), 151–155.

[74] P. Davies, *The Penguin Guide to the Monuments of India* (London, 1989).

[75] A. Shekhawat, *Water Harvesting Through Some Remarkable Projects, Like Spreading Channels, Open Mines & Step Wells in the Gujarat State* (Gujarat, 2013).

The step wells can be divided into four categories. The first, called Nanda is the most common and least complicated type, with one flight of steps leading to the shaft. The second is *bhadra*—two flights of steps aligned in line with the shaft in the middle. The third is Jaya—three flights of steps perpendicular to the adjacent ones and arranged in three directions around the central shaft. The fourth is Vijaya—this type of *vav* is similar to those of the Jaya type.

Thus, the *vavs* are not only a fine example of Gujarati architecture, but they also seem to be designed to arrange the meeting of gods and men to quaff the elixir of life—water. These wells are usually surrounded by a circular walkway for easy circumambulation.

The *vavs* or *baolis* (step wells) consist of two parts: a vertical shaft from which water was drawn and the inclined subterranean passageways, chambers and steps which surrounded it, providing access to the well. The galleries and chambers surrounding these wells were profusely carved, which became cool retreats during summers. A few examples are given in this chapter.

Rani-Ki-*Vav* (Queen's Well) at Patan

One of the most famous of the Gujarati *vavs* is the Rani-Ki-*Vav* at Patan. It is reputed to have been built by Udaymati in memory of her husband Bhimdev I (1022–1063 CE) during the period of the Solanki dynasty.[76] *It is a fine case of the design of this period. It measures approximately 64m long, 20m wide and 27m deep. Interestingly, the Rani-ki-vav is multi-storied, with colonnades and retaining walls that link the stepped tank to a circular well.* Columns, brackets and beams are embellished with scrollwork and wall niches are richly carved depicting Lord Vishnu and his various *avatars*, alternating with maidens flanked on the walls surrounding the staircase. *The last advance of the well prompts a little entryway which is the passage to a 30-km long passage which is currently hindered by stones and mud. It is said that this passage was utilized as a break course by the lords during times of war. It is accepted that around 50 years back, this zone was well known for ayurvedic plants which were utilized in the treatment of viral infections like fever. Rani-ki-vav was included in the list of UNESCO world heritage sites in 2014.*[77]

---

[76] M. Jarzombek, V. Prakash, and D. K. Ching, *A Global History of Architecture* (New York, NY, 2011), 907.

[77] *Adlaj Vav: An Architectural Marvel.* https://maverickonthemove.wordpress.com/2017/01/02/adalaj-stepwell-an-architectural-marvel/. Accessed on 14 January 2016.

Adalaj *Vav*, Ahmedabad

Adalaj is a small village near Ahmadabad. *Over the centuries, it was a halting place for travellers. A fine example of Indo-Islamic architecture, it was built by Queen Rudabai in 1499* CE. *It contains five celebrated step wells joining Islamic, Hindu and Jain themes. A feature that attracts many visitors is the Ami Khumbor (a pot that contains the water of life) and the Kalpa vriksha (a tree of life) carved out of. There is also a small frieze of navagraha (nine-planets). The vav is octagonal in shape and is built out of sandstone and is richly ornamented. There is a three-dimensional lattice with stone floor slabs running across. This creates a rhythm of light and shade which is very pleasing to the eye.*[78] The temperature inside the well is reputed to be about five degrees lower than the outside ambient temperature. The women who came to fetch water were tempted to linger here and worship the gods and goddesses and to exchange notes with their friends.[79] It is even said that the rich sculptures that adorn the walls of the *vav* resemble those that are found in palaces.[80]

Champaner-Pavagadh *Vav*

The residents of modern Champaner-Pavagadh in Panchmahals district of Gujarat are probably unaware of the historical importance of their town. Champaner-Pavagadh was given the status of World Heritage Site by UNESCO in 2004. Champaner-Pavagadh *vav* was built in the year 1485 CE after a war between Khichi Chauhan Rajputs and Sultan Mohammad Begda. The Jama Masjid is one of the most important heritage structures that stand tall in Champaner.

Joshi, a tourist guide, states that this mosque is one of the few that has seven *mehrab* (sanctum sanctorum). The other masjids that are worth visiting are the Shahi Masjid, Kewada Masjid and Nagina Masjid. It got the Global Heritage Site status due to the stunningly decorative etchings on the mosques. The tourist trail takes one through Gebanshah's *vav* or step well that is 80 ft deep, Mehdi talao, Vada talao, water channels, various fortifications, including the Atak Fort, which till today, has 83 catapult structures. The palace has a few rooms and bathtubs complete with the ancient version of jacuzzi, according to

---

[78] Shuichi Takezawa, 'The Diverse Architectural World of the Indian Subcontinent: Special the World of Indian Architecture', Eng. Tr. Vasanti Menon Nii, *Journal of Applied Behavioral Science (JABS)* 117, no. 1492 (2002): 24.

[79] M. Livingston, *Steps to Water: The Ancient Stepwells of India* (Princeton, NJ, 2002), 211.

[80] *IANS*, 'Gujarat's Rani Ki Vav added to UNESCO World Heritage Site List'. *IANS*.news.biharprabha, 2014. Accessed 14 January 2016.

Joshi. The most stunning architectural structure is the Lakulisha temple of the 10th century, en route to the Kalika Mata Temple.[81]

Gebanshah's *Vav*, Champaner

Reputed to have been built in the 16th century CE by a fakir named Gebanshah, this stepwell comes under the category of the Nanda type. In general, steps alternate with lined landings in that area unit known as *kutas*. The well-lit well is totally hospitable, the sky revealing an exquisite read of the beams and pillars crossing each other at angles. This is like looking at the skeleton, the very bare bones of well construction.

Ornamentation is border line and might be seen in kumbhas below beams lining the well walls. It is calculated that the well is 20 m deep, with the shaft having a diameter of 6 m. The length of the well at ground level is 50 m. This well used to have water throughout the year[82]

Helical Step Well

It is set a bit outside the city of Champaner, towards Vadodara. It consists of a 1.2-m-wide way that spirals down the wall of the well shaft. The town of Champaner is additionally otherwise called 'the city of 1000 wells'. At the well of Gebanshah, the well is clearly visible with a protracted line of beams and also the flight of steps resulting in the shaft. There is also a brick parapet wall around the shaft and also a flight of steps leading into the well. These steps square measure narrower towards the centre and wider at the wall. The well wall is made of brick, whereas the steps square measure is fabricated from stone. There are many landings wherever individuals will take rest. This well is often dated to the 16th-century metallic element. This step well is exclusive, therein it is a circular staircase leading right down to the water. The Pavagadh hills that overlook the town of Champaner contain variety of pools and ponds and square measure, therefore called 'the hills of 100 pools'[83]

Dada Harir *Vav*, Ahmedabad

This octagonal step well is arranged in the Asarwa territory of Ahmedabad city in Gujarat. It was worked by the Muslim lord Sultan

---

[81] V. Latha, 'On a Heritage Trail', *Business Line*, 25 September 2005.

[82] http://www.indiasinvitation.com/stepwells_of_gujarat/

[83] Indian Journey, *Stepwells of Gujarat*, https://indianjourneys.wordpress.com/2009/12/31/stepwells-of-gujarat/. Accessed on 22 January 2016. 31 December 2009.

Bai Harir in 1485 CE, and along these lines, it got the name Dada Harir Vav. This progression well is of the Nanda type, with the staircase in the east-west direction. On the eastern side of the well, there is an open octagonal structure. This leads down westwards through numerous arrivals. There is likewise a rectangular tank for putting away water. The well is structured in five levels, the east level being octagonal fit as a fiddle. Each level is given finely moulded columns and volute capitals. The specialties are brimmed with finely moulded stonework and parapets of kumbha or geometric friezes. The developer has additionally given stone edges for individuals to take rest. Every stair likewise contains a square domed booth with an overhanging *chajja* (front of a rooftop). The columns and stages raise vertically one over the other. The means are available to the sky, though the *kutas* (arrivals) are shut with stone chunks. The well shaft is round. There are entry ways at all levels, which associate the pole to the octagonal space over the tank. The pole divider is secured with geometric plans.[84]

Adi-Kadi *Vav*

It is situated at the foot of the Girnar slopes close to Junagadh in Gujarat. Adi-Kadi *vav* is an old step well that can be dated to as far back as 319 BCE. Undiscovered for a long time, it was uncovered in 976 CE. It was modified by numerous lords throughout hundreds of years. The two significant advance wells are Adi-Kadi *vav* and Naugham *kuva*. A fascinating component of these wells is that they have a crisscross staircase which is abnormal. These two wells are special in that most advance wells are delved in the subsoil and shake layers and the sections, floors, stairs and dividers are built in the ordinary way; be that as it may, these two wells have been cut out of the first shake. This implies the well itself has been made with a solitary stone.

One of the vavs is named Adi-Kadi Vav, built in the 15th century CE. It has a place with the Nanda kind of well. It is presumed to be one of most established step wells in the nation. This well contains a straight way to deal with the round well shaft. The pole gives an impression of being apsidal (half circle) at the base. Unlike most advance wells in Gujarat, the Adi-Kadi *vav* does not contain any beautifying themes or even any shafts or columns. The steps are carved straight into the hard rock. A flight of 120 stairs leads down to the water. There is a fascinating legend associated with this well. It is said that when the

---

[84] Campbell James Macnabb, *Gazetteer of the Bombay Presidency* (Ahmedabad, 1879), 282.

labourers began exhuming the stone, they found no water. The regal cleric exhorted the lord that two unmarried young ladies ought to be yielded before water could be found. Subsequently, two young ladies by the name of Adi and Kadi were yielded, and it is said that water was found at the spot from there on. Another variant says that Adi and Kadi were the two young ladies who brought water from the well each day. Regardless, even today, individuals still hang material and bangles on a tree close by in their memory.

Navghan Kuvo, Junagadh

Cut incompletely out of delicate shake, Navghan kuvo is just about 1,000 years of age being developed in the year 1026 CE. It is a shining example of the early rock-cut architecture of the period hewn into the rock. This well sustained the town of *Uparkot* through many a long siege. A flight of spiral stairs lead down 52 metres to the water. The shaft itself is square-shaped. Openings in the side divider let in light. The well is encompassed by a huge forecourt. The well itself is a lot more established than the forecourt. The well is named after Ra'Navghon (1025–1044 CE). The forecourt can be dated to the rule of Ra'Navghon. It is conceivable that this progression well is one of the most established to be found in the nation.[85]

Adalaj Step Well

This progression well is situated in the town of Adalaj, close to Ahmedabad city in Gandhinagar locale of the western state. It was built in the year 1499 CE by the Muslim ruler Mohammed Begda for Queen Rani Roopba, spouse of the Vaghela chieftain, Veer Singh.[86] These *vavs* not only served the more mundane purpose of supplying drinking water but also were intricately and exquisitely carved, thus making them good examples of the architecture of the period. They also served the double purpose of being mini temples, as the statues of various gods and goddess were carved into them. They were also an example of blending of Hindu and Islamic architecture. The walls of these *vavs* are beautifully carved with various pastoral scenes, dancers and musicians as well as scenes from the Hindu epics.[87]

---

[85] D. P. Vala, *Historical Monuments of Junagadh District: History and Development* (Pune, 2012), 17.

[86] *Ancient Step-wells of India.*

[87] *Adlaj Vav: An Architectural Marvel.*

Maharashtra and Goa: Deccan

Sacred water bodies in Maharashtra are commonly called *kund* and tank. A few examples are quoted in this chapter.

Shri Godavari Ramkund, Nasik

The most significant spot in Panchavati is Ramkund, which is 1 km away from the Central Bus Stand. It is so called because Lord Rama is believed to have taken bath there. In Hindu culture, the body after death is committed to fire, the ashes are then submerged in the Godavari; Ramkund is where the remains are liberated in the water. A dip in this sacred *kund* is considered very religious.[88]

Located at the foot of Mandakini Mountains, Vajreshwari was formed by volcanic eruptions. The area is also known for its hot springs, the most famous of which are the seven hot springs at Akloli *kund*. The water that erupts from this spring is rich in sulphur and minerals. The water is channelized from the spring to the temple tanks, where thousands of devotees cleanse themselves. Several hot springs are located near this spot. In fact, within a 5-km radius of the temple, there are 21 hot springs. The Tansa river flows near here. There is a Shiva temple nearby where the water of the seven hot springs is channelized. The water is black in colour due to the presence of minerals. At a distance of 1 km from Vajeshwari, one can find the hot springs of Akloli village. According to a popular legend, the hot water is the blood of demons and giants who were killed by the goddess Vajeshwari.[89]

In Goa, the sacred water bodies are locally known as sacred pools or tanks. Unlike in the past, Goa today faces an acute shortage of clean, pure and potable water. The sacred tanks of Goa are located near the temples and were constructed to store holy water. In the past, religious tradition ensured that people maintained these tanks very well. A good example of a sacred tank is the one known as Mae de Agua or the 'mother of water' in the fortress of Aguada. Similarly, in Goa, many Hindu temples are associated with sacred tanks. An ancient percolation tank is situated on top of a hill in Betki of Ponda and is named after the folk deity Mandodari. During the monsoon season, the outlet of the tank

---

[88] S. Sumita, 'First Time in 139 Years, Nashik's Sacred Ramkund Dries Up', *Times of India*, 7 April 2016. https://timesofindia.indiatimes.com/india/First-time-in-139-years-Nashiks-sacred-Ramkund-dries-up/articleshow/51720282.cms

[89] http://www.ebdir.net/enlighten/vajreshwari_akloli.html

is kept open so that the rainwater collects in the tank. This helps to recharge the springs below the tanks and enable the villagers to grow paddy and kulagars (horticulture). Especially, during the festival of Mahashivarathri, the local people take bath in the tank.

Another famous tank of Goa is the one near the temple of Hatkeshwar in Narve of Divar Island. In the days gone by, this tank was considered to be very sacred and a large number of devotees used to come here to take a holy dip. The water of some of the sacred tanks of Goa is considered to possess medicinal properties. For example, the sacred grove of Coparde in Sattari contains a sacred tank. The water from this tank is collected in a sacred spot known as *kolos* and is used for the treatment of skin diseases.

In the past, the prevalence of religious traditions and customs meant that the whole community used to participate in the cleaning of the tank. However, in the present day, due to the decline of religious beliefs, this practice has been sadly neglected. In many tanks of Goa, fertilizer residues have started entering the tanks, leading to inorganic eutrophication. There is also a steep rise in the recycling of biomass of aquatic weeds such as water hyacinth, salvinia and reed grass. Also, due to irrigation by canal system and the pumping of groundwater, there has been a gradual degradation of these sacred tanks. Thus, there is an urgent need for the revival and rejuvenation of the sacred tanks of Goa.[90]

Central India Region

Madhya Pradesh (*Kund*)

The sacred water bodies of Madhya Pradesh are known locally as *kunds*. One of the most important of these is the Janaki *kund*, which is located at a beautiful stretch of the River Mandakini. This is a place of ethereal beauty and natural scenic splendour. According to a legend, Lord Ram and goddess Sita spent many years of their exile here. Janaki *kund* was Sita's famous bathing ghat. Indeed, it is said that the footprints of the goddess are still visible here. It is a place visited by many pilgrims, since it is believed that the waters of the *kund* contain restorative powers. A temple of Hanuman called Sankat Mochan is also located here.

---

[90] R. Kerkar, 'Ecological Traditions of Goa', in *Ecological Traditions of Goa*, eds. Nanditha Krishna (Chennai, 2010), 91–93.

Narmada *kund* or pond is located at a height of 1,048 m and is the origin of the River Narmada. This is place of some religious importance and it has a number of temples such as Narmada and Shiva temple, Kartikey, Shri Ram Janki, Annapurna, Guru Gorakhnath, Sri Shuryanarayan, Vangeshwar Mahadev, Durga, Shiv Pariwar, Siddheswar Mahadev and Sri Radha Krishna temples. It is a serene place, with the Vindhya Mountains forming a magnificent backdrop. The area is thickly forested with sal trees and is a bioreserve.

Markandeya *Kund*, Amarkantak, Madhya Pradesh

This *kund* situated in the Amarkantak region of Madhya Pradesh. There is a legend behind the Markandeya *kund*. Once, sage Markandeya was blessed by Paramatma to achieve immortality for seven Kalpas. He had to swim through the rough waters till he reached the Purushottama Kshetra, in which the divine tree 'akshay vat' was the lone survivor. Lord Vishnu in a miniature form was sitting on the top of the tree. He urged Markandeya to somehow reach the tree in order to receive his blessings. Markandeya did so and Lord Vishnu blessed him and materialized a *kund* by the use of his Sudarshana Chakra, which later came to be known as the 'Markandeya *kund*'.

Suraj *Kund*, Gwalior

It was constructed in the 15th century CE and is situated within the walls of the Gwalior fort. Legend has it that Suraj Sen, the founder of Gwalior city, was suffering from leprosy. He met a saint called Gwalipa near the fort, who advised him to drink some water from the *kund*. The king did so and was cured of leprosy. In gratitude, he named the city after the sage Gwalipa; this later came to be known as Gwalior. Suraj *kund* is named after the king and it commemorates the mythical story.

Chhattisgarh (Tanks, Ponds)

Historically, the temples in Chhattisgarh have played a crucial role in water harvesting. Every village has at least one temple and a sacred tank. The temples can be square, rectangular or circular in plan, based on which the shape and size of the tank are decided. Hence, the larger temples have larger tanks.

These tanks enable the growth of a wide range of plants as well as algal and other aquatic vegetation. These tanks are provided with inlets and outlets, which enable the control of the inflow and outflow of water. There are also canals which interconnected the tanks together. However, with the advent of the modern water distribution system, these tanks are no longer in use. There has also been a great degree of eutrophication and growth of microorganisms. This leads to reduction in quantity of water. For example, the Mahamaya temple located at Ratanpur has a pond belonging to the period of 12th or 13th century CE. The temple is built in the Nagara style of architecture, facing north with a huge temple tank. Recently, a study has been undertaken to assess the economic importance of the structures, duly taking into account various parameters such as hydrography, planktonology and biodiversity.[91]

Eastern Region

Bihar

In Bihar, particularly in Gaya, the practice of sun worship is common. During the long periods of Chaitra (March–April) and Karttika (October–November), a huge mass of aficionados pay respect at the hallowed tanks associated with the love of the sun. These are Surya *Kunda*, Uttar Manasa and the sun temple at Brahmani Ghat. The enthusiasts perform unique customs, clean up and offer consecrated things to the sun god. The greatest picture of the sun god (2.44 m high) is at the Brahmani Ghat, facing east towards the Phalgu stream. There is also a reference in the Vayu Purana (111.2,22; 111.6,8) to the two tanks associated with the sun god, namely, Uttar Manas and Surya *Kunda*.[92]

Jharkhand (*Sarovar*, Holy Water Bodies)

There is an interesting legend connected with the excavation of this sarobar. It is said that Vardhamana Mahavira, the last Jain Tirthankar, attained Nirvana here at Pawapuri in 490 BCE. His devotees started collecting ashes from the funeral fire; when there were no more ashes, they began to collect the soil. Hence, after a period of time, a tank was excavated at this spot. The tank is covered with lotus flowers, hence the name Kamal *sarovar* (lotus tank). This tank is situated at a place called Pawapuri, about 101 km from Patna. It is an important centre of Jain pilgrimage. There is a temple of white marble at the centre of the tank, which is called the Jala Mandir. The tank is also a refuge for many species of birds that flock here from near and far.

---

[91] S. Mene, 'Tanks: The Ancient Water Harvesting System of Chhattisgarh and Their Multifarious Roles', *International Journal of Science and Research* 4, no. 1 (2014): 218–220.

[92] F. M. Asher, 'Gaya: Monuments of the Pilgrimage Town', *Marg* (Bombay) 40, no. 1 (1989): 45–60.

West Bengal (*Kund*)

There are many sacred tanks located in West Bengal. One of these is located in Chhandar village of Bankura district. The name of the pond is Bodher pukur and seems to derive from the word 'Bouddha' or Buddhist and can be dated to the 12th or 13th century CE. There is a ban on the use of the pond, as the villagers believe that this would disturb the goddess and invite wrath. Hence, the tank is only used on the occasion of Manasa festival in mid-June.

The Thakurpukur sacred pond in Belboni village of Bankura district is the main source of drinking water for two neighbouring villages. Adjacent to it is a sacred grove dedicated to the goddess Manasa. The pond is protected by the villagers from any polluting activities like washing and bathing.[93]

The Gorakshabasi tank in eastern Calcutta (presently called Kolkata) can be dated back to 300 years. It is attached to a temple dedicated to a Jain monk, Gorakshanath. The tank is well stocked with fish, mainly Indian carp.

In Cooch Behar district, there is an old tank attached to the Baneshwar (Shiva) temple and can be dated back to the 16th century CE. There is a strict taboo on washing, bathing and fishing in this tank. The pond houses large populations of *Ophicephalus morilinus* and turtles (*Lissemys punctata* and *Chitra indica*), which receive complete protection from the community.

In a sacred grove inside the Jayanti forest in Jalpaiguri district, there is a large pond which is held sacred by the local Buddhists. There is strict ban on fishing, bathing, washing and even stepping into the pond. The pond is home to a large population of catfish (*Clarius batrachus* and *Heteropneustes fossilis*). The patch of forest surrounding the pond is also considered sacred and has remained undisturbed for centuries.

A tank which is situated at a high altitude of 3,108 m above the sea level is the Kali Pokhri sacred pond in Darjeeling district. The dark water of this pond does not freeze in winter, although a thin crust of ice forms on the surface.[94]

---

[93] D. Deb and K. C. Malhotra, 'Conservation Ethos in Local Traditions: The West Bengal Heritage', *Society and Natural Resources* 14 (2001): 711–724.

[94] D. Deb, 'Sacred Ecosystem of West Bengal', in *Status of Environment in West Bengal: A Citizens' Report*, ed. A. K. Ghosh (Kolkata, 2008), 122.

Temple Tanks of Odisha

Many hundred years ago, when great temples arose across the length and breadth of India, some of the greatest expressions of religious creativity, were built in the holy cities of Odisha. The developers of these grand sanctuaries made incredible works of engineering, yet additionally comprehended the importance of water: they raised it to extraordinary holiness. Tirtha implies a portage, an intersection where there is a well, lake, waterway or ocean, the waters of which are viewed as sacrosanct. Tirtha has now come to signify 'consecrated water', suggesting, by strict convention, any place of pilgrimage on the banks of a sacred stream of water. Water has always been considered sacred in India. The excavations of Mohenjo-daro and Harappa have revealed large tanks that were used for religious, domestic and agricultural purposes. Water was considered one of the five elements (*paanch tatva*).

In the *Arthasastra*, there is a description of a well-organized system of specially created water tanks.[95] The Padma Purana talks about the conservation of water tanks (*tirthas*) in detail. Manu takes water tanks seriously and suggests death penalty for anyone found damaging or destroying a water tank.[96]

Bhubaneswar, the capital of the state, has 500 temples located principally within the recent city space. Every temple contains one of the additional tanks. Many of them are quite tiny, whereas others have a large body of water.[97] They were originally excavated at the time of the building of the temples, when huge amounts of soil were removed to create ramps for the building of the temple towers. Later these huge depressions thus created were lined with the surplus stone available and converted into temple tanks. These were utilized for ceremonies and celebrations.

Sacred Tanks

It is a typical belief that taking a dip in a consecrated tank of a temple vindicates sins. In Bhubaneswar, there is a temple with a Sahasra Linga sara or tank of 1,000 lingas. It is interesting to wonder whether this was the inspiration for Phnom Kulen, the river of 1,000 lingas, situated in

---

[95] Kautilya was a political economist of ancient India who compiled *Arthashastra* in around 300 BCE (AS.3.9.33).

[96] Kumar, *Puranic Lore of Holy Water*, 11.

[97] *Draft Report on Environmental Resources* (Government of Orissa, 1985).

a pristine rainforest high above the plains of Angkor, the lingas carved on the bed of the river.

Another acclaimed temple is the Kotitirtheshwar temple, whose tank is believed to be at the juncture of 10 million sacrosanct pools. At the Bramha *kunda* and Mukteswar *kunda* also called *Mirchi kunda*, barren women come to take a bath in the temple tank, believing that they will give birth to a baby. There are other temple tanks which are credited with miraculous powers. These incorporate Gouri *kunda*, Dudha *kunda*, Kedar *kunda*, Ashok *jhara*, Gosahasreshwar, Papanashini *kunda*, Kapileshwar *kunda* and Bhima *kunda*. It is accepted that the waters of these sacred lakes have marvellous restorative properties and treat dyspepsia. Bindu sagar, which signifies 'drops of water making a sea', is a tank which is accepted to get water from all the blessed waterways of India. Various temples are situated around the tank.

Bindu Sagar

Bindu sagar is one of the most significant hallowed tanks of India arranged close to the Lingaraja temple at Bhubaneswar in Odhisha. It is a spring-sustained rectangular tank of 450 m length and 320 m breadth. The base is level and smooth with laterite, and free of any macrophytic vegetation. The term Bindu sagar actually signifies 'the water body with fine suspension of sediment' that sparkles splendidly in the sun beams, conferring dark shading to the wave of the water. It is accepted that this spot was once known as Ekamra vana. There is a fantasy associated with this temple tank: After destroying the evil presence, the goddess Parvati was parched. She appealed to Lord Shiva. Recognizing her supplication, Lord Shiva made this *sagar* to extinguish her thirst. It is accepted to be bolstered with waters from all the heavenly waterways of India. An entire host of sanctuaries is arranged around the *sarovar*. Numerous Hindu sacred texts, for example, the Padma Purana, the Shiva Purana, the Brahmanda Purana, the Kapila Samhita and the Ekamra Purana have applauded the strict value of the water in the sacrosanct Bindu sagar. A plunge in the lake before going into the temple is viewed as propitious. In any case, in recent times the *sagar* has been getting polluted through a little gulf at the north western end with sewage water running off from the close by paddy fields, entering the tank. The *sagar* likewise is a dumping site for left-over prepared and uncooked food from the nearby Ananta Vasudev temple. It is likewise utilized as a washing ghat, a spot for washing garments, other than being a strict tank for performing services. It is particularly sacrosanct in view of its relationship with Shri Kapil Muni—a heavenly manifestation and author of Sankhya theory. It was here that Shri Kapil Dev lectured the best approach to accomplish moksha to his mother.[98]

Kedar Gouri Tank

The temple of Kedar Gouri is dedicated to Lord Shiva and Goddess Gouri. It is situated next to the Mukteshwar Temple. It is believed that a single sip of water from this tank absolves the drinker from the repeated cycles of birth and death. It is also believed that the temple was built by king Lalatendu Kesari after a tragic episode relating to two lovers, Kedar and Gouri. There are two tanks situated in the temple: the Khira *kunda* and Marichi *kunda*. The water of Khira *kunda* is white and extremely hygienic. The water of Marichi *kunda* is sold on Ashokashtami day by auction and it is taken by barren women who want to conceive.

The Kedar Gouri tank is situated inside the premises of the temple of a similar name. It is around 1,000 years of age and incredible strict sacredness is related with it. The water body is fixed with stone revetments. The base is made of little stones. The water is fairly transparent and the bottom is visible. The tank is spring fed.

Towards the west of the Kedareshwar temple, there is an enduring spring called Dudha *kunda*, signifying 'milk tank'. Its water is prized for therapeutic properties. The Kedar *kunda* is situated in the sanctuary premises. According to legend, the tank has heavenly properties and a single sip of water is enough to emancipate the devotee from all future transmigrations.[99]

Indradyumna *Sarovar*

The Indradyumna *sarovar* at Puri is viewed as sacrosanct because of its relationship with the temple of Lord Krishna. Sri Chaitanya Mahaprabhu was believed to have been engaged in water sports (*jala krida*) with his partners in the tank. It covers a zone of four and a half sections of land. The tank has a little hallowed place committed to King Indradyumna. It is one of most consecrated tanks in Odhisha. There is a legend with respect to the origin of this tank. During the time of the Mahabharata, King Indradyumna had embraced 1,000 ashvemedhayajnyas, had constructed

---

[98] M. Praharaj, 'Historic Conservation and Sustainability: A Case of Bindusagar Lake, Old Bhubaneswar', *Elixir Sustainable Architecture* 51A (2012): 11090–11093.

[99] M. Amirthalingam, 'Temple Tanks of Odisha', in *Ecological Traditions of India*, ed. Nanditha Krishna, Vol. VII (Odisha, Chennai, 2011), 64.

1,000 yupa shafts and had given a great many cows to the penniless. A gigantic wretchedness was hence made by the development of steers and was topped off by water utilized during the yajna. Therefore, the lake bears the name Indradyumna *sarovar*. It is situated about 2.7 km from the Puri Jagannath temple and, as indicated by legend, its origin can be followed to the time of the Mahabharata.

It is accepted that the individuals who take a blessed plunge in this tank are exonerated of their wrongdoings. There is a story behind this conviction. It is said that once King Indradyumna was reviled by the holy man Agastya to turn into an elephant in his next birth. Agastya, likewise, made the condition that he would be eased of his revile just by Vishnu's touch. Indradyumna accepted his birth as an elephant. At some point, the elephant Gajendra went to drink water from a lake at Mount Trikuta. A Gandharva called Huhu, who had been reviled by the sage Devala to turn into a crocodile, likewise lived in this lake. As Gajendra (Indradyumna) stepped into the lake, the crocodile assaulted him. They battled for 1,000 years. At last, Gajendra was depleted and was going to surrender the battle. In distress, he started to implore Lord Vishnu. This petition later turned into the acclaimed Gajendra stuti. Lord Vishnu heard his petitions and slaughtered Huhu and, in this manner, eased Indradyumna from his revile.

Markandeshwar *Sarovar*

Markandeshwar tank is situated facing the north of the Jagannath Temple. This tank is likewise significant, as it is associated with a ton of customs related with Lord Jagannatha, the most significant being Chandan yatra. The temple bears antiquated stone engravings relating to the Ganga line.

Narendra *Sarovar*

The Narendra *sarovar* at Puri is one of the most sacrosanct tanks in Odisha. It covers a territory of 3.24 ha and is situated in a beautiful zone around 2 km northeast of the acclaimed Puri Jagannath temple. Inside this tank is a little temple on an island committed to Lord Jagannath, Balarama and Subhadra. During the Chandana yatra, the pontoon celebration is held in the tank. Ruler Madanamohana (the agent of Lord Jagannath) goes for a vessel ride on a finished buoy, privately known as 'chapa'.

This tank is additionally called the Chandana pushkarani after the popular yatra of a similar name. Numerous mediaeval Oriya writings have been shown on this tank. As indicated by one legend, Narendra Deva, the sibling of Gajapati Kapilendra Deva unearthed this tank and it was so named after him. It is said that Veer Narendra Deva, his more youthful sibling, yielded his life for his country. After his passing, his significant other Kalandi Mahadevi took up sanyas and started to live in a nursery. She was an enthusiast of Lord Shiva and Lord Krishna. Babaji Govinda Das was her Guru. One day the Guru gave a pumpkin seed to the queen. The growth of the plant was so luxurious that it spread out over a large area. Hundreds of pumpkins were produced. These pumpkins were used for preparing the maha prasada at the temple. The news spread far and wide. Gajapati Kapilendra Deva caught wind of it and visited the nursery joined by his Guru, Mahadev Brahma. At that time Babaji Govinda Das was engaged in the worship of Lord Gopinath. Govinda Das favoured the lord and mentioned him to uncover a tank named after her late spouse, Veer Narendra Deva. He likewise mentioned him to name two ghats after Narendra Deva and his sovereign Kalandi Devi. The lord additionally developed 14 ghats named after the 14 children of Narendra Dev. The Chandana bije ghat (Lamba chakada) was built to lead 'Chandan bije' of Lord Jagannath. This chakada is named after Narendra Deva. He likewise built a temple of Kalandishvara Shiva and Gopinath on the bank of the blessed tank. The Brahma jaga, named after the court artist Narahari Brahma, was additionally settled. The acclaimed Chandan yatra of Lord Jagannath is being celebrated with grandeur since those days.

There is additionally a legend that the formation of the chakada is because of a pumpkin seed. The story goes as follows: King Narendra Deva was an extraordinary enthusiast of Lord Jagannath. When he found a pumpkin seed in the patio of his royal residence, he gave the seed to his sarbarakara (income authority) to plant the seed for the sake of Lord Jagannath and to offer each of the pumpkins along these lines created to the Lord. The sabarakara did as trained. The pumpkin creeper developed to such a degree, that it secured a territory of 14 sections of land. This creeper delivered lakhs of pumpkins. The sabarakara sold the pumpkins and offered the cash to the lord. Ruler Narendra Deva, thus, offered the cash to the Gajapati lord of Puri. Accordingly, both the rulers chose to develop a tank at Shrikshetra out of this store. The pumpkin creeper grew to such an extent that it covered an area of 14 acres. This creeper produced lakhs of pumpkins. The sabarakara sold the pumpkins and deposited the money to the king. King Narendra Deva, in turn, offered the money to the Gajapati king of Puri. Subsequently, both the kings decided to construct a tank at Shrikshetra out of this fund.[100]

---

[100] S. K. Rath, 'Narendra Tank in Legend and History', *Orissa Review* (June Issue, 2004): 13–15.

This tank is the greatest one at Shrikshetra, built up in the 1400–1500 AD, during the Ganga time frame. Chara Ganesha is worshipped in the nearby temple. The tank covers a region of 14.533 sections of land. There are 16 ghats of the tank, of which, 14 ghats are named after the 14 children of Narendra Deva, one after the sovereign Kalandi Devi and one after Narendra Deva. There are three ghats on the east, three on the north, six on the south and four on the west. The tank has an island inside, in which there is a little temple called 'Chandana mandapa'. During the Chandana yatra, Madanamohana, the moving deity of Lord Jagannath is kept here for 21 days.

During the past, the tank was a fine sheet of water kept clean by flushing from the Madhupur stream (Mitiani waterway) during the downpours through a divert in the western corner. Presently, both the delta and outlet are totally broken down, with the outcome that the framework never again works. Thus, presently the water has turned dirty.

Parbati *Sarovar*

Parbati *sarovar* is the tank appended to the Loknath temple, which is situated around 3 km from the Jagannath temple. The main deity of the temple, Shri Loknathji is the guardian of Shri Jagannath Temple's treasure house. Loknathji (as a linga) consistently stays submerged in the water from the regular spring at Parbati *sarovar*. Loknathji is otherwise called Bhandar Lokanath.

Rohini *Kunda*

Rohini *kunda* is situated inside the sanctuary of Lord Jagannath. It is one of the 'Pancha tirthas' (five heavenly spots), the other four being Swethaganga, Indradyumna *sarovar*, Markandey *sarovar* and Tirtharaj Mahanadhi (Puri ocean).

Swetha Ganga

Swetha Ganga is a little tank situated towards the west of the Jagannath temple. On the banks of the tank are two little sanctuaries, one committed to Sweta Madhava and the other to Matsya Madhava, the two manifestations of Lord Vishnu.[101]

In Karnataka, a *kalyani* is an artificially constructed temple tank, and a *devara kalyani* was reserved for gods and goddesses. The *kalyani* is usually either rectangular or square in shape and has stone steps. Its water may

---

[101] Amirthalingam, 'Temple Tanks of Odisha', 61–69.

be used to bathe the deity or for drinking purposes. Bathing and washing were not permitted, while separate *kalyanis* were built for washing the hands and face, and strict rules were formulated to prevent pollution.

Kerala is a state with heavy rainfall, so the *kulams* and *Cheras* were built for drinking water, water for washing the hands and face and for bathing before entering the temple.

Pushkarani is the temple tank of Andhra Pradesh, the most famous being the Swami Pushkarani of the Tirumala temple. The *pushkaranis* are sacred, and were used to provide water for bathing the deity, for the annual *theppam* and for bathing. They also served to maintain the water levels.

Tamil Nadu, a rain-fed state, is very dependent on the *kulams* or temple tanks, which were used for providing drinking water, water for washing the hands and face, and maintaining the groundwater level. The paucity of water in the state required all homes to be built facing the tank, necessarily a square or a rectangle so that the water would run off the sloping roofs and into the tank.

Temple tanks are the spots of socio-religious and cultural activities. These are arranged in the extremely focus of the town and are the storehouse of age-old customs. Further, they are also used for float festivals every year on a full moon day, which is celebrated at the end of the monsoon. Individuals commend this celebration to thank the Almighty for giving adequate downpour. The festival creates awareness among people regarding the need to store rainwater.

'In fact, the temple and the tank are linked in the term *kovil kulam*, meaning temple tank.' Sacred place, deity and sacred water, the temple and the tank all fulfilled the requirements of a pilgrimage.

Several temples had two tanks, one of which served to cleanse the pilgrims while the other was for the deity's ritual bath or *abhishekham*; also, these helped nurture the gardens which provided flowers for many rituals. 'But these kovil *kulams* served more than just ritual needs; these played a crucial role in the prosperity of the area; these helped recharge and maintain the groundwater level and proved to be a boon for local ecology as well.'

Made of brick or plain earth, most temple tanks are rectilinear in shape. The original structure was beautifully planned with appropriately situated inlets to gather rainwater from surrounding areas and outlets for excess water. Even surrounding architecture was made in sync with the objective of enhancing the rain-harvesting potential of these tanks. For instance, many of the older homes had sloping roofs that facilitated flow of rainwater into the tanks, some of which were even connected with one another through channels to enable optimum harvesting and use of water. The water loss due to evaporation can be high in Tamil Nadu, owing to its hot weather and so, by introducing proper aquatic flora such as lotus and water lily, steps were taken to reduce water loss from evaporation.

Part III: Important Lakes in India

The purpose of a water body is to capture a large body of water behind an embankment, which can then be utilized for irrigating the agricultural fields. This is done through a system of sluices and canals. In India, this system of harvesting water has been in existence since very ancient times. It was considered the duty of the kings and rulers to improve the irrigation system. There is ample evidence to prove that this precept was followed by most of the kings and rulers. In India, there exist about 500,000 irrigation tanks out of which 150,000 are located in the semi-arid region of the Deccan upland.

Andhra Pradesh

Kolleru Lake is the largest freshwater lake situated in Andhra Pradesh. It acts as the natural flood balancing reservoir for the two rivers, namely the Budameru and Tammileru. It is additionally associated with the Krishna and Godavari frameworks by 68 inflowing channels.

The lake acts as a reservoir for a large number of fish. It also attracts a wide variety of migratory birds. Hence, it was notified as a wildlife sanctuary in November 1999 under the India's Wildlife (Protection) Act, 1972. It was also declared as a wetland of worldwide significance in November 2002 under the International Ramsar Convention.

The lake has been under severe threat from sewage inflow from the towns of Eluru, Gudivada and even Vijayawada and industrial effluents, pesticides and fertilizers from the Krishna–Godavari delta region. As a result, the Andhra Pradesh government set up the Kolleru lake development committee with a budget of ₹300 crores to clean up the lake. This involves checking encroachments, regulating and monitoring pollution, clearing the lake of weeds and using it as compost and raw material to produce biogas.[102]

---

[102] M. K. Durga Prasad and Y. Anjaneyulu, ed., *Lake Kolleru: Environmental Status (Past and Present)* (Hyderabad, 2003), 236.

The second largest brackish water lake in India is the Pulicat Lake located about 60 km north of Chennai. The lake is also home to the Pulicat Bird Sanctuary. The barrier island of Sriharikota separates the lake from the Bay of Bengal. The three rivers that feed this lake are the Arani, the Kalangi and Swernamukhi, in addition to some smaller streams. The lake is rich in flora and fauna and, hence, was declared as a site of international importance under the Ramsar agreement. However, the lake faces a severe threat from effluents such as sewage, pesticides and industrial wastes.[103]

Assam

In Assam, there are about 23 natural beels and nine man-made lakes. Of these, I propose to discuss only three water bodies.

Sone Beel

Sone beel or (wetland) of Assam is situated between two hill ranges, namely, the Badarpur-Saraspur range and the Chowkirmukh-Dohalia range. This wetland might have originated after the Dupitila sedimentation during the Mio-Pliocene period.[104] This lake is fed by the River Singla, which drains a total catchment area of 46,105 ha. This lake also receives water from 12 minor inlets and many of the canals, which together drain a total catchment area of 18,942 ha. During the monsoon, the wetland receives some humic as well as inorganic and organic nutrients from the hillocks and cultivable areas, particularly around the swollen tail end of the wetland.[105]

Chandubi lake is situated at a distance of 64 km from the city of Guwahati in Assam. The lake holds a rich floral system. It is home to a large number of aquatic plants. The lake also holds exotic wildlife. It is the breeding ground of both residential and migratory birds.[106]

---

[103] P. J. Sanjeeva Raj, 'Macro Fauna of Pulicat Lake', *NBA Bulletin*, Chennai, no. 6 (2006): 67.

[104] D. Kar et al., 'Fish Bioresources in Certain Rivers of Assam and Manipur with a Note on Their Assessment, Management and Conservation', *Proceedings of National Symposium Assessment and Management of Bioresources*, Calcutta, 28–30 May 2003, p. 56.

[105] D. Kar and S. C. Dey, 'An Account of Ichthyospecies of Lake Sone in Barak Valley of Assam', *Proceedings All-India Seminar Ichthyology* 2 (1986): 3.

[106] M. K. Devi, 'Ecotourism in Assam: A Promising Opportunity for Development', *South Asian Journal of Tourism & Heritage (SAJTH)* 5, no. 1 (2012): 187.

Dipor Bil is another lake situated near Guwahati (also spelt Deepor Beel (*Bil* or *Beel* means 'lake' in the local Assamese language). It is a permanent freshwater lake in a former channel of the Brahmaputra River, to the south of the main river. In November 2002, it was declared a wetland of international importance under the Ramsar Convention. Since it is one of the largest beels in the Brahmaputra valley, it can be classified under the Burma Monsoon Forest biogeographic region. Its resources provide a livelihood for 14 indigenous villages or 1,200 families.[107]

Bihar

Kanwar lake or Khabar tal, located about 22 km northwest of Begusarai town in the state of Bihar, is considered to be Asia's largest freshwater oxbow lake. It was formed due to the shifting of the course of the river Budhi Gandak. However, it is presently arranged in the flood plain of the Ganga waterway, and therefore the stream Budhi Gandak. It gets associated with these waterways during serious flooding circumstances. It is one of the most significant wetlands for waterfowl in the Gangetic plain, supporting a colossal number of different types of transitory and inhabitant avifauna. To check the wild poaching of these birds, Khabar tal has been declared as a protected zone by the Bihar state government in 1986, proposed for Ramsar site in 1987 due to its rich biodiversity followed by declaration as wildlife bird sanctuary in 1989 by the Government of India.

However, of late, a significant portion of this lake has been converted into agricultural land. This has resulted in the degradation of the eco-system and an alarming reduction in the number of migratory birds that visit this wetland. The significant shrinking of the wetland area clearly indicates an imperative need for restoration of the landscape.[108]

Chandigarh

Sukhna Lake was made in 1958 by damming the Sukhna Choe, an occasional stream descending from the Shivalik Hills. The absolute catchment zone of the lake is 4,207 ha, out of which 3,312 ha establish

---

[107] S. Roy and J. C. Kalita, 'Identification of Estrogenic Heavy Metals in Water Bodies Around Guwahati City, Assam, India', *International Journal of ChemTech Research* 3, no. 2 (2011): 700.

[108] S. Anand and P. K. Joshi, *Remote Sensing to Quantify Wetland Loss*, in 14th Esri India User Conference, 10–12 December, New Delhi, 2013.

the Shivalik slopes and the rest of the zone of 895 ha fall within the three towns of Kaimbwala (Chandigarh), Kansal (Punjab) and Suketri (Haryana). Sukhna is an asylum for some outlandish transient feathered creatures such as the Siberian ducks, storks and cranes, throughout the winter months. Around 30 species are inhabitants and the rest are migratory, mainly the winter migrants. Pisciculture is the main economic activity associated with the lake. It was also popular with the local people as a site for performing religious ceremonies and rituals. This has led to water pollution and resulted in an increase in the number of sick birds. Hence, the administration banned the performance of rituals in January 2008. Dead storage level and pollution level in the lake have been rising.[109]

Gujarat

In Gujarat, there are about 34,750 ha wetlands distributed all over the state. These wetlands can be classified into two categories, namely inland wetlands and coastal wetlands. There is also a third category consisting of a vast saline desert, the Rann of Kutch. Some representative lakes are described below.

Hamirsar Lake

Bhuj in Gujarat is known for its hot and dry summers. However, there is a water body, Hamirsar Lake, located in the heart of Bhuj town. This lake is a virtual oasis in the saline and arid district of Kutch. It was constructed during ancient times to meet the water needs of the people of Bhuj. Hamirsar Lake has a well-developed system of canals and tunnels that can carry the water from three rivers to fill the town's reservoirs. However, after the earthquake of 2001, this water system was badly disrupted. This man-made lake is named after Rao Hamir, a Jadega king who ruled here about 450 years ago. The Jadega community claims to be the descendants of Lord Krishna, a divine incarnation from the epic Mahabharata. The state was ruled by a combination of 12 landowning families and two Waghela families.

A unique festival, celebrated in Kutch district of Gujarat, is the Augun of Hamirsar. This festival is celebrated during the monsoon when the lake overflows with rains. In olden times, the king would perform a *puja* and distribute Megh *laddoos* (sweets) as prasad to the

---

[109] S. Yadvinder, *ENVIS Bulletin: Himalayan Ecology and Development* 10, no. 2 (2002): 18–31.

people. People from the surrounding villages also take part in the festival. There is an atmosphere of gaiety and joy during the festival (Jethwa, R.P. 2007, p. 63).[110]

Kankaria Lake

Ahmedabad city was founded in 1451 CE. Kankaria lake formed a part of it. The tank was included in the municipal limit of the city in 1884 CE. Architecture is represented in terms of public-related buildings and open spaces like temples, gardens, etc. The mediaeval art forms, consisting of rich carvings, have been gracefully preserved by the lake front redevelopment project. There are many examples of mediaeval architecture at the Kankaria lake front. These include Dutch tombs, summer palace in Naginawadi and historical Dadu Dayal Temple along with the sluice. The world's largest mural is under construction, of which 3,100 ft^2 is already built. Thus, the project aims to create an inclusive public space, which has the ability to be the image of the city. The project also fosters local cultural values and existing cultural patterns of food, festivals and making a space for them.[111]

Thol Lake

The Thol water body is situated in Mehasana district in Gujarat and it is a man-made inland wetland. It was constructed in the year 1912 CE by the Gayekwadi leaders of Baroda to avert disintegration and flooding and to store water for irrigation purposes.[112] It is spread over an area of 54.95 km^2 covering six villages. It has a well-developed canal base irrigation system. The catchment zone of the water body that covers 320 km^2 is situated to its north and northeast, so the spread is from Kadi taluka of Mehsana locale and Kalol taluka of Gandhinagar area. Notwithstanding the feeder trench, the water body gets run-off water legitimately from the catchment zone. There is additionally a feeder canal joined to the water body named Nalsarovar bird sanctuary found southwest of Thol bird sanctuary. Thol and Nalsarovar bird sanctuaries are thus connected with each other.[113]

---

[110] R. P. Jethwa, *Kutch Gurjar Kshatriyas: A Brief History & Glory* (Calcutta, 2007), 63.

[111] A. Desai, *India Guide Publications* (Gujarat, 2007), 95.

[112] D. K. Vaghela, *Fishes of Pond and Annual Survey* (M. Phil. dissertation, Department of Zoology, Gujarat University, Ahmedabad, 1993).

[113] N. R. Modi, N. R. Mulia, and S. N. Dudani, 'Ecological Investigations of Shahwadi Wetland', *International Journal of Pharmacy and Life Sciences* 4, no. 12 (2013): 3193–3199.

Haryana

Badkhal Lake

The Badkhal lake, occupying an area of 1,870,000 m², is surrounded by the Tilput range of hard quartzite. Notwithstanding, because of the unsettling influence of the watershed and the catchment, the lake has constricted to 510,000 m². The lake dries up during the summer season. It is fed by rainfall run-off from the northern, western and south-western sides of the Delhi ridge. An embankment has been built to control the water flow on the eastern side. The lake acts as a barrier to the flood water flow and also prevents soil erosion. The rapid phase of urbanization on the Delhi ridge has led to the reduction of water bodies. As a result, the water table has sunk very deep. Thus, the Badkhal lake has shrunk to about 25 per cent of its original size. A study of the watershed system was carried out of the Badkhal lake by Siddhiqui et al. in 2012.[114] It was commented in the report that the watershed is greatly disturbed due to the rapid process of urbanization, as a result of which sufficient amount of run-off does not reach the lake. Quarrying and mining activities near the lake have also resulted in an increase in the deposition of sediment in the lake. However, it is possible to regenerate the lake by a well-thought-out engineering design.[115]

Suraj Kund

Located in the Aravalli range, south of Delhi, this tremendous *kund* or water tank was developed by the Rajput ruler Surajpal in the 11th century CE. The name literally means 'lake of the sun'. It said to have been re-established during the rule of Firuz Shah Tughlaq (1351–1388). The supply has been worked in the state of the rising sun with an east-bound bend. It was intended to meet the water necessities of the city of Delhi. Be that as it may, generally, mining exercises close to the lake have prompted the exhaustion of the groundwater level.[116]

Brahma Sarovar

Located in the site sanctified by the Kurukshetra war is the holy tank known as Brahma *sarovar*. It is a support of human advancement. It

---

[114] R. Siddiqui, G. Mahmood, and S. R. Ali, 'Analysis of Revitalization of Badkhal Lake Using Innovative GIS Technique', *International Journal of Scientific & Engineering Research* 3, no. 11 (2012): 1–10.

[115] Ibid.

[116] http://en.wikipedia.org/wiki/Surajkund

is accepted that Lord Brahma, the maker of the universe, considered the earth here. The tank is mentioned in the well-known diaries of Al Beruni, the *Kitab-ul-Hind*, wherein he compares the tanks to an immense sea. Recently, the Brahma *sarovar* has been renovated. It now measures about 3,600 ft × 1,500 ft. It is also reputed to be the holy seat of Lord Mahadev. The lake is now lined by bathing steps and there are also arched enclosures for pilgrims. Wide platforms, stairs and a wide 'parikarma' have also been built. It is believed that a dip in the *sarovar* is equivalent to performing the *Ashvamedha Yagna*. Krishna, Balarama and Subhadra came here to bathe during a solar eclipse. Thus, the Brahma *sarovar* is one of the holiest *sarovars* in India.[117]

Himachal Pradesh

Prashar Lake

The state of Himachal Pradesh is blessed with as many as 52 lakes and ponds nestled at high elevation and providing spectacular views of the mighty Himalayas. One such lake is the Prashar Lake situated at an altitude of 2,630 m and located between 31°45′30″N and 77°6E. Its depth and water content still remain to be assessed. According to the legend, the great sage Parashar meditated here. The water of the lake is considered to be sacred and the people take it to their homes for worship. However, during the winter season, the valley remains totally inaccessible due to heavy snowfall. The lake is facing a threat from solid wastes, overgrazing and collection of herbs. Therefore, there is an urgent need for a comprehensive management plan for organizing festivals, creating roads, clearing the trekking route and creating facilities for the pilgrims.[118]

Renuka Lake

Another important lake of Himachal Pradesh is the Renuka lake located about 60 km from Nahan hill in the district of Sinnour at a longitude 77°27′E, latitude 300°36′N. It is situated at an altitude of

---

[117] A. V. Narad and P. V. Gupta, 'Tourism in Kshetra; A Substantial Sustainable Approach', *International Journal on Recent and Innovation Trends in Computing and Communication (IJRITCC)* 3, no. 2 (2015): 75–78.

[118] P. K. Attri and V. K. Santvan, 'Assessment of Socio-cultural and Ecological Consideration in Conserving Wetlands—A Case Study of Prashar Lake in Mandi District, Himachal Pradesh', *International Journal of Plant, Animal and Environmental Sciences* 2, no. 1 (2012): 131–137.

645 m above sea level. The lake is oblong in shape, with a small outlet leading to an adjoining pool, the Parashuram Tal. The catchment area includes about 250 ha of subtropical deciduous reserve forests. The wetland is home to 443 animal species. The water sources are from the southwest monsoon through various streams. The shape of the lake resembles a female figure, which is believed to be the body of the goddess Renuka, the mother of Lord Parashuram. The national committee on wetlands has designated this lake as a wetland of national importance.[119]

Pong Dam Lake

One of the largest man-made wetlands of northern India is the Pong Dam Lake situated in the Kangra district of Himachal Pradesh. It was formed by the construction of the Pong dam across the river Beas in 1974. The Pong wetland was selected as an international Ramsar site in 2002. Streams from the Dhauladhar Mountains feed water to the Pong Lake. The wetland acts as a nesting zone for migratory birds from the trans-Himalayan region in the winter season. The Pong wetlands also support more than 415 bird species belonging to more than 60 families. The wetland also supports a large number cattle breeder and is also a major tourist attraction. There is a lot of scope for the development of pisciculture.[120]

Jammu and Kashmir

Dal Lake

In Jammu and Kashmir, there are about 23 water bodies, of these, 10 are natural and 13 are man-made. One of the most beautiful and the second largest lake in Jammu and Kashmir is the Dal Lake situated at an elevation of 584 m above sea level. The catchment area is spread over 316 km^2. The lake gets its water from its catchment through a perennial inflow channel, the Telbal Nallah, which enters the Hazratbal basin on its northeast side. In addition, many springs arise from the lake bed itself. The lake is being polluted by a large quantity of sediments and nutrients with the run-off from its catchment

---

[119] Editor-Director, *Fauna of Renuka Wetland: Wetland Ecosystem Series 2: i–vi* (Calcutta, 2000), 1–187.

[120] M. Kohli, 'Wetlands of International Importance in Himachal Pradesh', *International Journal Economic Plants* 2, no. 1 (2015): 23–27.

through Telbal Bota Khul. Sewage from the settlements around the lake also adds to the pollution. The drains also carry sludge and solid wastes from the surrounding areas into the lake. Also, the channel connecting Dal with Nagin and the Pokhribal and Baba Demb basins are choked by solid wastes. There are floating gardens (*radh* in Kashmiri) spread over Hazratbal to Gagribal basins, which are used for cultivating vegetables. High nutrient loads in the lake have led to excessive growth of floating leaved plants. Steps have been taken for the rehabilitation of the lake by altering the agricultural practices in the catchment area and improving the water circulation within the lake. Further, encroachments have been controlled and the larger floating islands are being removed.[121]

Pangong Lake

Pangong Tso is an endorheic lake in the Himalayas situated at a height of about 4,350 m in the Leh district of Jammu and Kashmir. It is one of the largest brackish water lakes in Asia, straddling two countries, India and China. It is also known as the Hollow Lake and it is a good example of nature's craftsmanship. It is not part of the Indus River basin area and is geographically a separate land locked river basin. The lake is 5 km wide at its broadest point. The lake freezes completely during the winter, despite the water being saline. During winters, the lake freezes completely, despite being composed of saline water. The lake is in the process of being identified, under the Ramsar Convention, as a wetland of international importance.[122]

Karnataka

In Karnataka, tanks and lakes play an important role in irrigating agricultural lands and also recharging groundwater. There are a total of 36,568 inland water bodies in Karnataka. The Malnad region, in particular, is known for its large number of tanks. However, these tanks harvest only rainwater. The Bellandur lake in Bangalore city covers an area of 892 acres. It has a storage capacity of 17.66 million ft^3. It is also 3 km in length and 2.5 km in width. However, the lake has one of the highest water pollution indexes. Physical, chemical and biological parameters are

---

[121] NLCP, Ministry of Environment and Forests (New Delhi, 2001).

[122] B. Gujja et al., 'Wetlands and Lakes at the Top of the World', *Mountain Research and Development* 23, no. 3 (2003): 219–221.

used to assess the water quality of the lakes.[123] Three main streams join the tank, which form the entire watershed. The lake feeds the Varthur lake which, in turn, feeds the Pinakini River in Tamil Nadu. The storm water run-off finds its way to the lake. The tank is a receptor of three chains of tanks. A large portion of the Bellandur lake is now covered by weeds. Even the sewage treatment plant set up by the Bangalore Water Supply and Sewerage Board is non-functional. Untreated sewage gains entry into the lake. One of the solutions is to grow *Canna indica*, which will help in minimizing the impact of pollution in the lake.[124]

Rachenahalli Lake

The large Rachenahalli lake, located near Jakkur, caters to the irrigation needs of Rachenahalli, Dasarahalli and Jakkur. The lake covers an area of about 50 acres. However, the Jawaharlal Nehru Centre for Advanced Scientific Research (JNCASR) has encroached upon some portion of the lake. A study revealed that once the tank had supported agricultural activities, was a breeding ground for fish and even helped in the maintenance of livestock. Many educational institutions and private parties have encroached upon the lake. Since it is a large water body, it attracts a large number of migratory birds. Even now, one can notice a large number of waterfowl on the lake. A good portion of the lake has been covered by water hyacinth. There is also heavy flow of sewage into the main body of the lake.[125]

Kerala

Kerala is a nature lover's paradise. The lush and verdant landscape gladdens the eye and soothes the spirit. The state possesses vast stretches of seas, rivers, mountains, forests, lakes and waterfalls. The state has as many as 34 lakes, which can be divided into three broad categories. The first one is bordered by sandbanks and runs parallel to riverbanks. The second one has land on its front side, while the third one runs almost perpendicular to riverbanks.

---

[123] N. Ramesh and S. Krishnaiah, 'Scenario of Water Bodies (Lakes) in Urban Areas: A Case Study on Bellandur Lake of Bangalore Metropolitan City', *IOSR Journal of Mechanical and Civil Engineering* 7, no. 3 (2013): 6–14.

[124] H. Roselene, 'A Study on Remediation of Polluted Water Using Canna Indica', *International Journal of Research & Review* 1, no. 1 (2014): 3–4.

[125] Thippaiah, *Vanishing Lake: A Study of Bangalore City* (Bangalore: Institute for Social and Economic Change, 2009), 42.

Ashtamudi lake, which is located in Kollam district, is one of largest and deepest wetland ecosystems in Kerala. It has often been described as a palm tree or even likened to an octopus. The wetland has been included in the list of wetlands of international importance under the Ramsar Convention. It is also an important source of livelihood for the local population, as it supports fishing, coconut husking and inland navigation services. It supports 43 species of marshy and mangrove associate such as *Avicennia officinalis*, *Bruguiera gymnorrhiza* and *Sonneratia caseolaris*. It is also home to 57 species of avifauna, of which 6 are migratory and 51 resident species. Terns, plovers, cormorants and herons are most abundant birds in the lake.[126]

Another famous wetland of Kerala is the Vembanad Kol wetland, which receives drainage from 10 rivers, adding up to a total drainage area of 15,770 km² (40% of the area of Kerala), and an almost 30 per cent of the total surface water resource of Kerala. It is the largest and longest lake in Kerala, in which the famous Nehru Trophy boat race is conducted. The lake by itself is an ecosystem and covers an area of 2,033 km². The lake lies at sea level and is separated by the Arabian Sea just by a barrier Island. The lake is the most important source of freshwater in the state and helps to irrigate a major portion of the farm lands.[127]

Madhya Pradesh

Madhya Pradesh possesses a multitude of stunning lakes. Among these are the Bhojtal in Bhopal and Tawa reservoir situated in Hoshangabad district. Apart from these, there are many scenic reservoirs, namely Moti lake, Sharangpani lake, Tawa reservoir and Shahpura Lake. The Madhya Pradesh lakes have a nice combination of tamed wilderness and landscape architecture. In the introductory part of this chapter, I have discussed the Bhojtal lake. I will now discuss the Tawa reservoir under the heading of lakes.

Tawa Reservoir

Tawa reservoir is situated in Hoshangad district of Madhya Pradesh and measures about 1,815 m long and 58 m deep and covers an approximate area of 204 km². It supplies the water needs of Hoshangabad district. There are two canals supplying water to both right and left sides of the

---

[126] *Ramsar Sites in Kerala* (Kerala: ENVIS, 2015).
[127] South Asia Network on Dams, Rivers & People (2011): 10–11.

Tawa reservoir. Anthropogenic activities such as use of chemicals in agriculture and logging have adversely affected the biodiversity of the region. Thus, there is an urgent need for an effective management plan to be put in place to protect the environment as well as to conserve the avian diversity and vegetation.[128]

Maharashtra

Thane town in Maharashtra state is also popularly known as the city of lakes as it contains about 35 lakes. The lakes are fed by the run-off from the surrounding highlands. These lakes help in the overall recharge of the groundwater in the district. Rankala lake in Kolhapur district is the oldest of all lakes in Maharashtra. There is another lake, Ramkunk lake, in Nashik district, which is considered to be sacred, since it is believed that Lord Ram and goddess Sita used to take bath here. Other important lakes of Maharashtra include the Mushi lake near Lonavala, Venna lake in Mahabaleshwar, Khindsey and Ambazari lakes near Nagpur, Lonar lake in Buldhana district, Pashan and Pimpri lakes in Pune and the Tansa, Tulsi, Vihar and Powai lakes in Mumbai.

Thane, located about 35 km from downtown Mumbai, is also known as the City of Lakes. There are as many as 30 lakes located in the district of Thane. Of the 30 lakes, Talao Pali Lake (also called Masunda Talao) and Upvan Lake are better known. Other lakes are Kacharali Talao, Makhamali Talao, Siddheshwar Talao, Bramhala Talao, Ghosale Talao, Railadevi Talao, Kausa Talao, Kolbad Talao, Hariyali Talao, Rewale Talao, Kasar Vadawali Talao, Kidkaleshwar Talao and Nar Talao.

Talao Pali Lake

Masunda lake, also called as Talao Pali, is one of the prominent lakes in the heart of Thane city. It is famous for the Ganesha festival and also the temple of Kopineshwar, which is situated on its banks. However, the water in the lake is now highly polluted, turbid and greenish black in colour. The lakes are also infested with dense growth of aquatic plants such as water hyacinth, salvinia and algae. Thick deposits of organic sludge are common to all the lakes.

---

[128] P. Joshi and V. K. Krishna, 'Diversity of Avifauna and Effects of Human Activities on Birds at Tawa Reservoir Area of Hoshangabad District (Madhya Pradesh)', *Advance Research in Agriculture and Veterinary Science* 1, no. 2 (2014): 78–82.

Rankala Lake

Kolhapur is also known as the city of lakes. It houses about 24 lakes in and around the city. These lakes each have their own religious, cultural and medicinal importance. The oldest of these is the Rankala lake, created during the reign of Chhatrapati Shahu Maharaja. There are major streams which are the source of water to the lake, which flow from the southern side. As Rankala lake is located in the centre of the city, there are many sewage terminals pouring sewages into the Rankala lake water, and thus heavily polluting the lake. A lot of aquatic life and fish culture are recorded in Rankala lake, and thus 24 different types of fish have been recorded in the lake. However, due to uncontrolled urbanization and creation of infrastructure, the lake is facing a severe threat of pollution due to thousands of litres of sewage entering into its body as well as due to the solid waste dumping practices in the lake's catchment area. There is also profuse growth of water hyacinth and other submerged plants like Hydrilla. The lake water is polluted by pesticide residues entering through the irrigation of agricultural lands in the vicinity. Washing of animals, clothes, vehicles, bathing activities, immersion of Ganesh idols and Nirmalya, disposal of remains of fast foods at Chaupati in the lake, are also contributing to pollution in the lake.[129]

Manipur

Loktak lake is the largest freshwater lake in Northeast India and is situated in the central valley of Manipur, about 38 km from Imphal. It covers an area of 287 km². and is at an average height of 800 m–2,070 m above mean sea level. It has a direct catchment area of 1,040 km². It also has an indirect catchment area of 7,157 km² (which includes the catchment of five important rivers, namely Imphal, Iril, Thoubal, Sekmai and Khuga). It is also known as the floating lake due to the large number of floating 'phumdis', which are commonly known as floating mats in Manipur. It also plays a vital role in the local economy by providing employment to the people of the surrounding villages. The central valley of Manipur supports about 61 per cent of the population of the state. About 15 per cent of the valley population is concentrated around the Loktak lake area. This lake plays a significant role in terms of physical, ecological, economic and social benefits to the local

---

[129] A. S. Ghone and S. K. Singal, 'Study on Pollution Sources, Water Quality and Conservation of Rankala Lake, Kolhapur, India', *International Journal of Advanced Technology in Engineering and Science* 3, no. 1 (2015): 565–574.

communities. It also plays host to migratory birds, mammals, fish, amphibians, reptiles and many plant species.[130]

Meghalaya

Umiam lake, also known as Barapani or Big Water, is tucked away amidst the hills of Meghalaya about 15 km from Shillong. This lake owes its inception to the Umiam-Umtru Hydro Electric Power Project, which was inaugurated along with the state of Meghalaya in 1972. The main catchment area of the lake is spread over 220 km² and includes Shillong and its surrounding areas besides a portion of Ri Bhoi district. The lake serves many other purposes besides power generation. It is the scene of water sport and adventure facilities.

However, due to rapid urban growth, the lake has been used as a dumping ground for Shillong's wastes. Recent research by the Central Pollution Control Board (CPCB) confirms that the water in the rivers Umkrah and Umshyrpi is contaminated with sewage. There have also been many encroachments, deforestation activities, blockage of natural drainage systems and unscientific mining, which have resulted in the despoiling of the lake. Excessive silt load in the lake has also lowered the storage capacity.[131]

Mizoram

In Mizoram, the lakes are locally known as *dils*. Among the larger lakes found here are Palak *dil* and Tam *dil*, which have been included under the National Wetland Conservation Programme in 2005. Other smaller lakes include Rengdil (0.6 km²), Rungdil (0.75 km²), Diltlang (0.5 km²), Hmawngbu (0.7 km²). Tamdil is the only lake which has been developed for its economic potential. It lies between 23°44'20.4"N latitude and 92°57'10.8"E longitude. The circumference of the lake is 890 m, with a maximum depth of about 7 m; it has a catchment area of 13.5 km². It is situated about 110 km from Aizawl, the state capital. Tamdil is the only lake that has the potential for being fully developed for fish culture.[132]

---

[130] A. L. Singh and K. Moirangleima, 'Dying Wetlands: A Threat to Livelihoods of Loktak Lake Dwellers', *Greener Journal of Physical Science* 2, no. 4 (2012): 107–116.

[131] http://www.rainwaterharvesting.org/umiam_lake.htm

[132] C. Lalzahawmi and B. P. Mishra, 'Assessment of Seasonal Variation in Chemical Characteristics of Tamdil Lake, Mizoram, Northeast India',

Palak *dil* is a natural lake set in a natural depression in the hills. It may possibly be a combination of valley and tectonic lakes. It is situated within the Mara autonomous district council, which is a region inhabited by the Mara tribe. There is folklore on the origin of the Palak *dil* among the Mizo people. According to the legend, this area was originally a big urban area called Hnychao. The people of the village observed that the children playing around the rock frequently disappeared and thus, the lake was eventually called Pala Tipo (swallowing lake).[133] The shape of the lake is oval with a length of 870 m, width of 700 m and depth of 17–25 m. The lake is fed by two main streams from the nearby mountains. Its drainage is through a small river called Pala Lui. The lake is home to a number of resident and migratory animals and birds. It is unique for its variety of different species of fishes, prawns, snails, crabs, turtles and tortoises. Besides, aquatic birds and wild ducks are found only in this lake.[134]

Nagaland

There are three important lakes in Nagaland and they are Doyang lake, Chathe lake and Shilloi lake. Shilloi lake is situated in a valley surrounded by pine forests and beautiful landscape. The real name of the lake is *Lutsam* meaning 'the place where water is collected'. It was originally called *Shiloh* by the British, but today, it is officially known as *Shilloi*. It is also the largest natural lake in Phek district of Nagaland. An aerial view of the lake shows that it is in the shape of a human footprint. It plays host to migratory Siberian cranes during the months of March–June. It is well stocked with fish, and the best season for fishing is from June to September. There is a legend associated with this lake. Once upon a time, a baby girl from *Lunadvu* village was taken into the lake while her parents were working in the field near the lake. An intensive search was launched for the missing baby when a cry was heard from the middle of the lake. Two hands appeared from the lake holding the baby and went back into the water again. It is believed by the local people that the baby is now the reigning spirit of the lake. It is also said that after this incident, no one has drowned in the lake. Another story

International Journal of Scientific Engineering and Applied Science (IJSEAS) 2, no. 7 (2016): 157–165.

[133] Palak Lake, Department of Tourism, State Government of Mizoram. https://en.wikipedia.org/wiki/Palak_Dil

[134] Lalmuansangi and H. Lalramnghinglova, 'Preliminary Assessment on Water Quality and Biodiversity in and Around Palak Dil in Southern Mizoram, India', *Science Vision* 14, no. 1 (2014): 39–45.

says that such incidents stopped when a British army officer swam to the middle of the lake with a written note and dropped it into the water.[135]

Odisha

Kanjia Lake

It is situated on the northern outskirts of Bhubaneswar and is a natural lake. The wetland covers an area of 105 ha out of which 75 ha constitute the lake. It is area of rich biodiversity and helps to maintain the city's ecology. The ecosystem contains 37 species birds, 20 species of reptiles, 10 species of amphibians, 46 species of fishes and three species of prawn, 10 species of submerged microphytes, 14 species of floating macrophytes and 24 species of emergent macrophytes. However, of late, the lake is facing a serious threat from quarrying and dumping of solid waste and creation of infrastructure around the lake area.[136]

Ansupa Lake

It is the largest freshwater lake covering an area of 382 acres in Cuttack district in the state of Odisha. The lake is associated with the Mahanadi stream on the southern side by methods for a channel known as Kabula nana, through which the rising waters of the Mahanadi enter the lake. The length of the lake is around 3 km and the expansiveness changes from 250 to 500 m. A major portion of the lake remains submerged throughout the year. There is an urgent need to study the ecosystem of this lake in order to control the habitat destruction, exploitation of its wilderness, human interference and pollution.[137]

Puducherry

Puducherry, a union territory, is well known for its wetlands. It has a total of 82 major and small wetlands in and around the town. The most important of these are Outeri and Bahour lakes. These lakes are a source of livelihood for the local communities, as they help in irrigating the agricultural lands and produce fuel, fibre and fodder.

---

[135] European Bank for Reconstruction and Development ('EBRD' or the 'Bank'), *Environmental and Social Policy & Procedure* (Nagaland, 2015).

[136] *National Wetland Atlas of Odisha* (Bhubaneswar, 2010), 182.

[137] R. N. Pradhan et al., 'Checklist of Birds in and Around Ansupa Lake, Odisha, India', *International Research Journal of Environmental Sciences* 2, no. 11 (2013): 9–12.

Ousteri Lake

Located about 10 km to the west of the town, the Ousteri wetland was declared as a bird sanctuary. The Ousteri is Oussudu *yeri* in Tamil, which means freshwater lake. The lake acts as a major wintering ground for the large number of migratory birds which flock here during the cold season. This lake is also an Important Bird Area (IBA) identified by the Bombay Natural History Society (BNHS), Mumbai. Asian Wetland Bureau declared Ousteri as one of the 115 significant wetlands in Asia. The lake has been confronting genuine dangers from numerous fronts, for example, recovery, horticulture, siltation, weed attack and poaching. It is additionally swarmed with the weed *Ipomoea carnea* (water hyacinth), which is spread over the surface of the lake. Anthropogenic activities have resulted in drastic biological changes influencing the nature of the lake. The threats include rapid urbanization and infrastructure development in the immediate vicinity of the lake, agriculture, siltation, weed invasion and poaching, aquatic weeds, encroachment like agriculture, land reclamation, runoff from agricultural fields, illegal fishing and poaching, natural resource utilization such as gravel extraction, firewood and fisheries.[138]

Punjab

In Punjab, there are three significant wetlands, to be specific, Harike, Kanjli and Ropar. These have just been perceived as wetlands of significance under the Ramsar Convention. These wetlands are significant amphibian environments in nature and are the living space for waterfowl, fish and other widely varied vegetation. They are also home to the significant dangers confronting these wetlands such as the extreme issues of siltation in the supply, prompting shrinkage of wetland territory, the unsettling influence to occupant and transient flying creatures by illicit angling and poaching of untamed life, unintentional surges of poisons from businesses situated in the region, inflow of pesticides and manures from the farming fields and sewage from the town, invasion and growth of weeds in the wetland area and finally, the lack of public awareness due to ignorance about wetland values and functions.

The Ministry of Environment and Forests, Government of India, is giving monetary help to the execution of protection programmes. At

---

[138] B. A. K. Prusty et al., *Comprehensive Management Action Plan for Conservation of Ousteri Lake, Puducherry* (Puducherry, 2011).

Karike wetland, the conservation programme was initiated as far back as 1987–1988, at Kanjli in 1988–1989 and at Ropar in 1996–1997. Projects incorporate afforestation of local tree species, soil protection to avoid siltation, preservation of untamed life and fisheries, weed control, water quality checking and open mindfulness. The Ropar wetland came into existence in the year 1952 with the construction of headworks. The territory encompassing Ropar land is uneven within the north-west and plain within the south and southeast. The area within the wetland is highly cultivated with crops such as wheat, rice, sugarcane and sorghum. The nearby hills have been greatly denuded due to little streams that empty into Ropar ground area unit, which is important from an ecological point of view. A large amount of silt and nutrients from the Shivalik hills get deposited in the wetland. This has resulted in reducing the capacity of the lake to hold water. There are also 55 species of fish and 318 species of birds, which have been reported from these wetlands. Migratory birds also frequent these wetlands. Some of the rare plants available here are *Acacia, Dalbergia, Ipomea* and Salix.

Survey of wetland has been taken up. Out of the entire space of 1,365 ha, 800 ha is below watercourse and reservoir. And 30 ha is below biome and referred to as Sadabarat forest. Afforestation has occurred in about 30 ha. Heavy metals such as zinc, chromium and nickel have also been detected. There are nutrient contribution, agriculture, sewage from Anandpur Sahib and Kiratpur Sahib town and effluents from Nangal.[139]

Rajasthan

Rajasthan, with its long and ancient history, is the abode of many lakes. Especially, the city of Udaipur is endeavoured with many lakes, the most famous of which is the Pichola lake and island. Due to the presence of many water bodies, Udaipur is able to boast of a pleasant climate for most of the year. According to the wetland inventory report, there were as many as 29 lakes reported in Rajasthan. Some of these include Rajsamand Lake, Udai Sagar Lake, Nakki Lake, Kaylana Lake, Raj Bagh Talao, Malik Talao, Lake Fateh Sagar, Gadsisar Lake, Lake Pichola, Swaroop Sagar Lake, Udai Sagar Lake, Raj Bagh Talao, and many others. Here, I have discussed three representative water bodies, namely Pichola lake, which is the freshwater lake, Ana Sagar lake, and the other Sambhar lake, which is a saltwater lake.

---

[139] N. S. Tiwana et al., *Conservation of Ramsar Sites in Punjab*, in Proceedings of Taal 2007: The 12th World Lake Conference, eds. M. Sengupta and R. Dalwani, 2008, pp. 1463–1469.

Pichola Lake

One of the most beautiful and picturesque lakes in Rajasthan is the Pichola Lake situated in the heart of the city of Udaipur. The lake was built during the year 1362 CE by Pichhu Banjara during the reign of Maharana Lakha. The lake extends to 3 miles in length, 2 miles in width and has a depth of 30 ft. There are two islands, Jag Niwas and Jag Mandir, located in the lake. The lake is surrounded by lofty palaces, bathing ghats and elevated hills on all its sides. The beauty of the lake attracts people from all over the world.

Ana Sagar Lake

The Ana Sagar lake is an artificially created lake situated in the city of Ajmer in Rajasthan. It was built by Anaji Tomar in 1135–1150 CE and is named after him. The lake is spread over 13 km. In Ajmer, it is one of the biggest lakes, with an area of 5 km². The depth of the lake is 4.4 m, with a storage capacity of about 4.75 million m³. The catchment area of the Anasagar lake is 70.55 km² and its circumference is 12.88 km and it was originally a monsoon-fed shallow water lake. Later, the Mughal emperors made certain modifications to it. There are several factors which are degrading the Anasagar lake. The main cause of eutrophication is due to the discharge of sewage, municipal wastewater and industrial effluents. A large amount of heavy metals are also being bioaccumulated in the lake; the result is that the human food chain is getting affected with adverse implications for human health. The lake water is further polluted by the dumping of municipal solid wastes. There is also the effect of sewage discharge into the lake, which results in growth of algae. Discharge of sewage, municipal wastewater and agricultural run-off has increased the primary productivity and physico-chemical values of the lake.[140]

Sambhar Lake

It is India's largest inland saline wetland and is located in Nagaur, Jaipur and Ajmer districts of Rajasthan. It is spread over an area of 190 km² and has been the source of salt production for at least a 1,000 years.

The state government of Rajasthan took over the wetland in the year 1950. Sambhar Lake has a catchment area spread over 5,700 km². The climate of the lake is subtropical monsoon. Being an inland lake, it has

---

[140] D. N. Pandey, B. Gopal, and K. C. Sharma, *Evidence-Based Holistic Restoration of Lake Anasagar, Ajmer, Rajasthan, India* (Rajasthan, 2012).

a unique ecosystem and supports a highly specialized group including the algae. Flocks of flamingos use this as the nesting ground. However, the natural inflow of water has been drastically reduced and there is deposition of nutrients and sediments in the lake.[141]

Sikkim

Sikkim, a small state in the Eastern Himalayas, has only natural inland wetlands belonging to the category lakes/ponds. There are as many as 227 high-altitude lakes (wetlands) found in this state. These are locally known as *Chhokha* or *Tso* or *Chhona* in Bhutia; *Chho* in Lepcha and *Pokhari* or *Jheel* or *Tal* in Nepali. The most important lake is the Khecheopalri lake, which is located in the middle of a dense forest at an altitude of 1,700 m. The lake is sacred to both Buddhists and Hindus.[142] The watershed of the lake extends to an area of 12 km², which includes a 91 ha area specifically as the lake watershed. However, the lake has been subjected to degradation due to excessive land use and heavy deposition of sediments.

Another important lake of Sikkim is the Tsomgo Lake, which is oval in form, 1 km long, 22 ha in size and is considered as sacred by the native folks. It remains frozen throughout the winter. It contains varied biodiversity in terms of flora and fauna. The third lake is the Gurudongmar wetland. It is an amalgamation of three glacial water bodies at an altitude of 5,180 m and having an area of 40 ha. It is a pristine glacial ground, which but, has been subjected to pressures of encroachment, siltation, skinny vegetal cowl and unplanned tourism. However, it still remains a source of freshwater supply.[143]

Tamil Nadu

Tamil Nadu is richly endowed with 39,202 lakes. These lakes come under the management of the general Public Works Department, native bodies, such as firms, municipalities, panchayat unions and different departments. Chennai city is surrounded by many lakes such as Red

---

[141] H. S. Sangha, 'The Birds of Sambhar Lake and Its Environs', *Indian Birds* 4, no. 3 (2009): 82–97.

[142] A. Jain et al., 'Hydrology and Nutrient Dynamics of a Sacred Lake in Sikkim Himalaya'. *Hydrobiologia* 410 (1999): 13–22; A. Jain, S. C. Rai, and E. Sharma, 'Hydro-ecological Analysis of a Sacred Lake Watershed System in Relation to Landuse/cover Change from Sikkim Himalaya', *Catena* 40 (2000): 263–278.

[143] *State of Environment-Sikkim*, 2007, 55–60

hills, Poondi and Chembarambakkam. These lakes are used as a source of supply of water for Chennai city. However, recent studies have shown that irrigation through tanks is on the decreasing trend; however, irrigation though wells is increasing. The main source of drinking water in Tamil Nadu is from rivers, lakes and tanks. Due to anthropogenic pressure, the maintenance of the tanks has greatly deteriorated, which has resulted in the reduction of water supply.[144]

In the main towns of Coimbatore, Pudukkottai, Tiruvannamalai and Tirunelveli, the water bodies have been maintained in a good condition. Hence, there is ample availability of quality water in these towns. However, in the other district headquarters such as Dindigul, Madurai, Krishnagiri, Nagapattinam, Nagercoil, Namakkal, Ramanathapuram, Thanjavur, Tiruchirapalli, Tiruvarur and Villupuram, the situation is not satisfactory. This is due to dumping of garbage, sewage inflow and weed growth in the water bodies.

In Chennai city, there are 46 water bodies, of which only eight contained water before the monsoon. The quality of water of Ayapakkam and Velachery lakes was reasonably good. However, several arterial roads have been constructed on the water bodies.

The major threats faced by many of the water bodies are disposal of solid waste, sewage, weed growth, encroachment and siltation. Hutments and nomadic settlements around the water bodies pose a great threat. The inlet and outlet are totally blocked in many of the water bodies, which lead to eutrophication. In few water bodies, there is no water; hence, bore wells have been dug to draw water.

The Nilgiris is famous for its lake situated in the Nilgiris district at an altitude of 2,240 m. The lake was formed in the year 1823; its depth is 12 m and average depth is 6 m. Another famous lake of Tamil Nadu is the Kodaikanal lake in the Dindigul district of Tamil Nadu situated at an altitude 2,285 m. It was formed during the year 1863. The water unfold is 26.30 ha and its maximum depth is 11.50 m and a mean depth is 3 m. The third most important lake in Tamil Nadu is the Yercaud Lake located in the Servarayan hills at an altitude of 1,320–1,400 m. The lake has a water spread area of 11.5 ha. The outlet of the lake may be a little watercourse that runs dry throughout the season.[145]

---

[144] K. S. Neelakandan, *Conservation and Restoration of Lakes in Tamil Nadu*, in Proceedings of Taal: The 12th World Lake Conference, 2007, pp. 1669–1671.

[145] R. Rajamanickam and S. Nagan, 'A Study on Water Quality Status of Major Lakes in Tamil Nadu', *International Journal of Research in Environmental Science (IJRES)* 2, no. 2 (2016): 9–21.

Among the brackish water lakes is the Pulicat lake, which is the second largest brackish water lake in India. The lake is enclosed by the Pulicat lake bird sanctuary. The area of the lake is 250–450 km² (from tide to high tide), the average depth is 1 m and maximum depth is 10 m. The main source of supply of water to Chennai city is the Poondi reservoir built in 1944 across the Kosasthalaiyar River. It has a storage capacity of 91 million m³. Another source of supply to the city is the Red Hills lake in Thiruvallur district. It is one of the rain-fed lakes, along with Chembarambakkam lake and Porur lake. The storage capacity of the lake is 93 million m³. Porur lake is situated in the suburb of Porur in south-western Chennai and is the main source of supply of water to Chennai city.

Veeranam lake is located in Cuddalore district and supplies water to Chennai city. It was originally constructed during the time of the Chola dynasty. It receives water from Kollidam via Vadavar river. It has a storage capacity of 41.23 million m³.[146]

In the days gone by, Chennai city used to have about 150 small and big water bodies in and around it. However, the number has since been reduced to 27. Some of them include Adambakkam and Mugappair, Red Hills, Manali and Madhavaram *jheel*, Korattur lake, Ambattur lake, Pulicat lake, Pallikaranai, Velachery and Chembarambakkam lake, Rettai *yeri*, Porur lake, Sunnampu Kolathur lake, Chetpet lake, Vyasarpadi lake and Chitlapakkam lake.[147]

Telangana

Telangana is a newly formed state carved out of the erstwhile Andhra Pradesh. It contains many natural as well as man-made lakes. These include Hussain Sagar lake, Himayat Sagar, Pakhal lake, Palair lake, Pocharam lake, Durgam Cheruvu, Fox Sagar lake and Shamirpet lake. Some of the artificial water bodies can be dated to even to medieval times and the rule of the Nizams.

The most famous of these is the Himayat Sagar, situated 20 km away from Hyderabad city. It lies parallel to another large artificial lake called Osman Sagar lake. This lake plays an important role in the irrigation system and also helps to maintain the ecological balance.

---

[146] Ibid.

[147] M. Amirthalingam, 'Ecological Heritage Sites of Chennai—Wetlands', *Eco News* 9, no. 2 (2003): 20–22.

Hussain Sagar is a mediaeval artificial lake, built by Hazrat Hussain Shah Wali in the year 1562 CE, during the rule of Ibrahim Quli Qutb Shah of Iran. It is unfolded across a district of 5.7 km² and is fed by the Musi River, a tributary of the Krishna River. The maximum depth of the lake is about 32 ft.

Pakhal lake is also a man-made lake, located in Pakhal wildlife sanctuary in Warangal district of Telangana state. It was constructed around the year 1213 CE by the ruler of Kakatiya dynasty of Warangal named Ganapathideva. It is spread over an area of 30 km² and set within the Pakhal wild life sanctuary, which encompasses an area of 839 km².

The rainwater lake of Telangana is the Laknavaram Lake situated at a distance of 6 km from Govindaraopet. It is the scene of scenic splendour and a paradise for nature lovers. It sprawls over an area of 10,000 acres and it is surrounded by the Govindaraopet mountains. The nearest big town is Mulugu, located 30 km away.[148]

Tripura

It is a small state in the Northeast India bordered by Bangladesh to the north, south and west, and the Indian states of Assam and Mizoram to the east. It is to a great extent uneven and forested. There are many water bodies in and around Agartala, the capital town of Tripura. Durgabari Lake and Laxminarayanabari Lake are relatively large man-made lakes. Laxminarayanabari Lake is heavily infested with weeds. However, the quality of the water is good. The lake is additionally used for bathing, swimming, laundry, idol immersion and alternative rituals.

The Durgabari lake is about 3 ha in area and having a maximum depth of 2.5 metres. The lake is used for pisciculture, bathing and swimming. It receives waste water from the surrounding areas. The southern part of the lake is covered with weeds.[149]

---

[148] R. Datta, 'From Ruined Temples to Huge Manmade Lakes and from Dying Art to Long Hanging Bridges, the District of Warangal in Andhra Pradesh has Something to Offer to Every Tourist and Traveller', *One India One people* (2014): 23–36.

[149] B. Gopal et al., *Conservation and Management of Lakes: An Indian Perspectives* (New Delhi: MoEF, 2010), 73–74.

Uttarakhand

This hilly state was carved out of the erstwhile state of Uttar Pradesh. Ninety-three per cent of the state is mountainous territory. The mighty river Ganga and its major tributary, the Yamuna, originate here. There are about 22 lakes found in this state. One of the important lakes of this state is the Nainital lake, which is a natural lake of tectonic origin located in the Kumaon Himalayas at elevation at lake level is 1,938 m and encompassing hills rise from 2,139 to 2,611 m above the sea level. This excretory organ formed lake that is 1,432 m long and 42 m wide with water unfold of 48.76 ha. It is encircled by steep hills and the area unit is lined with mixed oak and evergreen forests. Earlier, the lake had very clear water and very little aquatic vegetation comprising chiefly of *Potamogeton* species. Excessive discharge of domestic wastes and the steady erosion in the hills due to deforestation and grazing have resulted in extreme eutrophication of the lake. Another lake, named Bhimtal Lake, is located about 22 km from Nainital at an altitude of 1,346 m. The 'C' shape lake has a surface area of 47.8 ha and a catchment area of 10.77 km^2 and an average width of 451 m and maximum depth of 18 m. The water is released through sluice gates for utilization in Haldwani. A significant drawback confronting the lake is that the extraordinary measure of residue that guarantees the development into the lake and gets stored on the bed. Hence, dredging is required.[150]

Uttar Pradesh

A large northern state, Uttar Pradesh, shares a fringe with Nepal. It includes the Ganga, Yamuna Doab, the Ghaghra, the Ganga fields and the Terai. In the south are included a part of the Vindhya hills and the plateau. There are many natural lakes, including oxbow lakes that occur in the flood plains of the Ganga system. There are a total of 106 lakes which are found in the state.

Ramgarh *taal* is a large natural lake situated to the southeast of Gorakhpur town in eastern Uttar Pradesh. The lake has the maximum water spread of 723 ha which has now shrunk to 678 ha. The maximum water depth has conjointly declined from 4.5 m to 3.5 m. It has a catchment area of more than 11,500 ha. The lake supports a significant fish population and many people depend upon it for their livelihood. The water is also used for irrigation and recreation. However, in recent

---

[150] Ibid., 75–78.

years, the lake has been degraded due to huge amounts of domestic waste water and solid waste from the urban catchment area. Also, massive amounts of sediment are carried with the storm run-off. This has resulted in large-scale fish kills. The growth of water hyacinth has also created serious problem in water quality. Manasi Ganga Lake is located in Govardhan, about 20 km west of Madura. It has a maximum spread of 3.74 ha with a depth of 9.3 m and a shoreline of 1,700 m. The lake is fed by groundwater. It is also supplied by some run-off during the rainy season. The lake is famous for the *parikrama* of the holy hill. It is also used for bathing, washing of clothes and religious offerings. This has deteriorated the quality of water. Also, large quantities of domestic sewage are discharged into the lake. Considerable siltation has also occurred.[151]

West Bengal

The state of West Bengal is situated on the eastern bottleneck of India, stretching from the Himalayas in the north, Bay of Bengal in the south, Bangladesh in the east, Assam, Sikkim and the country Bhutan in the northeast, Odisha in the southwest, Jharkhand and Bihar in the west and Nepal in the northwest. North Bengal plain begins from the south of Terai region and continues up to the vicinity of the Ganges River. Ganga stream flows from west to east and divides the plain into northern and southern parts. This plain is created primarily by the alluvial deposit of Ganga stream and its branches. Therefore, the state has many shallow flood plain lakes (oxbows), marshes and river courses. There are about eight famous lakes and they are Debar Lake, East Kolkata wetland, Jore Pokhri, Mirik Lake, Rabindra *sarovar*, Rasikbil, Santragachhi Lake and Senchal Lake. One of the important lakes is the Rabindra *sarovar*. This lake is spread over an area of 30 ha and was excavated in the 1920s. It is surrounded by a 50 ha area with parks, gardens and tree plantations and is used for sport, recreation and cultural activities. It is popularly referred to as the 'lungs of Kolkata'. However, anthropogenic activities have affected the water quality. Erosion of the shore is common and waste water from non-point sources additionally contributes to high nutrient loading that has resulted in protecting blooms. Thus, the lake is suffering from extensive environmental degradation. Water pollution is also on the rise, owing to encroachment. This famous lake of Kolkatta has now shrunk beyond recognition, as its water is heavily

---

[151] Ibid., 81–83.

polluted due to activities such as washing and bathing.[152] Set amidst hills at an altitude of 1,700 m in Kurseong division of Darjeeling district is a beautiful lake named the Mirik Lake. It is spread over an area of 110 ha and has a maximum depth of 8 m. It is fed by several springs in the surrounding hilly catchment area. There is a dense cone-bearing forest to the south-western of this lake. The lake was created in 1979 by damming the stream that feeds the stream Mechi. Outflow sewage from human settlements and tourists' activities and dumping of solid wastes have contributed to the degradation of the lake. Washing and bathing activities also impinge upon the quality of water. Appropriate measures have to be taken to control erosion from the hilly catchment area as well as the lake shore.[153]

Conclusion

The present chapter has attempted to focus on three major systems of water bodies that have seen the passage of times from the ancient period till the present across the Indian subcontinent, regions and states: the traditional water harvesting systems, sacred water bodies and lakes. The study reveals that India has a long and rich tradition of water harvesting systems that date back to the Indus Valley Civilization. Each region of the country developed its own unique system of water bodies suited to its climate and soil conditions.

Modern environmental history calls for an interdisciplinary approach to enable placing things in perspective. There is a felt need for a fuller and deeper understanding of current environmental issues that will lead to contemporary problem solving. The threats to water bodies in India are innumerable. Some of the well-known ones are encroachment, unauthorized mining, pollution, release of untreated and raw sewage into water bodies, gradual and dramatic decline of groundwater, leading to a fall in the level of lakes and absence of a proper administrative frame works and political will to manage water bodies. Added to these is public apathy towards the subject of water management in the country today. Funding by government departments and international agencies is restricted to only a small number of water bodies. Another aspect that needs to be borne in mind is that a proper balance needs to be achieved between development and conservation. The dynamics

---

[152] S. Bhattacharya, K. Mukherjee, and J. K. Garg, *Wetlands of West Bengal* (Institute of Wetland Management and Ecological Design, 1992), 134.

[153] Gopal, *Conservation and Management of Lakes*, 85–86.

of social and ecological changes call for a proper understanding that is based on contemporary knowledge and a strong appreciation of the past. An integrated approach to watershed management that is scaled down to conditions of individual tanks at the local level is required. This will essentially mean a decentralized management of water bodies and or wetlands, placing priority for ecosystem services over narrow sectorial economic values. It is only through such approaches that the contemporary conflicts between development and conservation can be resolved in an amicable manner.

Forests, Land Use, Wildlife and Animals

5

Ancient Forests and Sacred Groves

Nanditha Krishna

Once upon a time, forests covered most of the Indian subcontinent. The seals of the Indus Valley Civilization contain wild animals such as the elephant, water buffalo, rhinoceros, deer, gazelle, antelope, wild sheep, goat, ibex, rhinoceros and elephant, and carnivores such as the tiger and leopard,[1] which means that the area was once covered with thick forests. Rhino habitat ranges from open savannah to dense forests in tropical and subtropical regions. They spend the day wallowing in lakes, rivers, ponds and puddles to cool down. Tigers live in swamps, grasslands and rainforests, where there are trees, bushes and tall grass which protect animals from the sun and help them to camouflage with their surroundings and surprise their prey. They love the water and are very sensitive to heat. Elephants also require savannah and forests, with fresh water to cool their thick dark skins. The frequency of the rhino, tiger and elephant on the seals of the Indus Valley Civilization suggests that these animals existed in large numbers.

---

[1] J. M. Kenoyer, 'Master of Animals and Animal Masters in the Iconography of the Indus Tradition', in *The Master of Animals in Old World Iconography*, eds. Derek B. Counts and Bettina Arnold (Budapest: Archaeolingua Alapítvány, 2010), 39.

A few ceramic vessels painted with lions and terracotta figurines of the lion indicate that this animal also prevailed around some cities of the Indus region.[2] But lions prefer scrub jungle, grassland or open woodland. The frequency of seals of the tiger, elephant and rhinoceros, unlike the lion, suggests that the Indus Valley Civilization was once a thick subtropical rainforest.

The ancient Indus-Sarasvati Civilization included much of Pakistan, Western India and northeast Afghanistan, from Pakistani Balochistan in the west to Uttar Pradesh in the east, Afghanistan in the north to Maharashtra in the south, lasting from 7000 BCE in Mehrgarh to 1300 BCE in Harappa. More than 500 Harappan sites have been discovered along the dried-up river beds of the Ghaggar-Hakra River and its tributaries[3] and about 100 along the Indus and its tributaries. The Ghaggar-Hakra River has since been identified with the lost Sarasvati River,[4] converting the Indus Valley Culture into the Indus-Sarasvati Culture. The discovery of Mehrgarh, one of the earliest sites with evidence of farming and herding in South Asia, suggests that the modification of the environment—from forest to agriculture—had begun very early in northwest India (now Pakistan). Early residents of Mehrgarh lived in houses made of brick and mud, stored their grain in granaries, used tools made of copper ore and lined their basket containers with bitumen. They cultivated barley, wheat and dates and herded sheep, goats and cattle. Later residents of Mehrgarh (5500–2600 BCE) were craftsmen, working with flint, tanning, bead production and metal.[5] Mehrgarh is the earliest known centre of agriculture in South Asia.[6]

The Indus-Sarasvati Civilization was primarily urban. Domesticated animals included sheep, goats and bullocks (for drawing carts). Terracotta toy carts yoked to the Indian zebu suggest that this was the frequent form of transport. However, much of the Indus–Sarasvati region was marshland and thick jungle, as suggested by the frequent appearance of the tiger, rhinoceros and elephant. The spread of

---

[2] A. Ghosh, ed., *An Encyclopaedia of Indian Archaeology* (New Delhi: Munshiram Manoharlal Publishers, 1989), 338; R. R. S. Chauhan, *A Guide to the National Museum*, New Delhi, 1993, 6.

[3] S. P. Gupta, ed., *The Lost Sarasvati and the Indus Civilisation* (Jodhpur: Kusumanjali Prakashan, 1995), 183.

[4] Michel Danino, *The Lost River: On the Trail of the Sarasvati* (Penguin, 2010).

[5] Richard H. Meadow, 'The origins and spread of pastoralism in northwestern South Asia', in *The Origins and Spread of Agriculture and Pastoralism in Eurasia*, ed. David R. Harris (London, 1996), 393.

[6] U. Singh, *A History of Ancient and Early Medieval India: From the Stone Age to the 12th Century* (New Delhi: Pearson Education, 2008), 130.

agriculture in the region made it possible for the urbanization of the area, for cities live on the excess produce of villages.

Trees were obviously important in the Indus–Sarasvati Civilization, for so many trees appear on the seals. Many trees are placed on a pedestal and/or fenced in, like the *sthala vriksha* (sacred trees) of Indian temples. The most important is the pipal, associated with scenes of sacrifice and worship and even growing out of the head of a three-faced male figure, who has to be a proto-Shiva.[7] The *shami* or *khejri* (the desert plant of Rajasthan) is associated with a female figure associated with the tiger, maybe a proto-Durga. The importance of trees and forests thus goes back to India's earliest civilization.[8] While the pipal is found all over the subcontinent, the *khejri* is a desert plant, widely prevalent in the Thar Desert in Rajasthan, which is sacred to the Bishnois who live in the desert and graze cattle.[9] The presence of this tree on the Indus seals suggests that the desertification of the region had already set in. Interestingly, in the *aindu tinai* (five geographical classifications of land), the *pālai* (desert) is associated with Kotravai or Durga and the *kotrān* (a desert plant of doubtful identity). It could easily have been the *shami* of the Ṛig Veda, the *khejri* of the later Bishnois.[10]

The Vedas were composed in the Indus–Sarasvati region. In the Vedas, a fundamental sense of harmony with nature nurtured an ecological civilization. Forests are the primary source of life and inspiration, not a wilderness to be feared or conquered. The Vedas were written by sages living in the forest who were inspired by a philosophy of life, where the forest was not perceived as primitive or a primeval forest to be feared but a deliberate choice, the home and a source of inspiration for the great sages who composed some of the greatest verses of philosophy. The forest was regarded as the highest form of cultural evolution. Human ability to merge with nature was the measure of cultural evolution. People drew intellectual, emotional and spiritual sustenance from the twin concepts of *srishtī* (creation) and *prakritī* (nature).

'So may the mountains, the waters, the liberal (wives of the Gods), the plants, also heaven and earth, consentient with the Forest Lord (*Vanaspati*) and both the heaven and earth preserve for us those riches.'

---

[7] Nanditha Krishna, *Sacred Plants of India* (Haryana: Penguin Books, 2014), 6–8.

[8] Ibid, 8–10.

[9] The khejri is the sacred plant of the Bishnois who live in the deserts of Rajasthan. They were instructed to worship this tree, essential for desert ecology and their own survival, by their religious leader Shree Guru Jambeshwar Bhagwan, also known as Jamboji (1451–1536 CE), in the 16th century.

[10] Krishna, *Sacred Plants of India*, 6–10.

(Ṛig Veda, VII.34.23). Here the forest is regarded as the sovereign or ruler of the earth.

Atharva Veda (V.4.3) says that it is prohibited to cut the *vatavṛkṣa* (banyan tree) because Gods live on the tree and there is no disease where this tree is situated.

Another hymn from the Atharva Veda says:

Whatever I dig out from you, O Earth!
May that has quick regeneration again;
May we not damage the vital habitat and heart.

Āranya means forest. Early Vedic literature includes the *Āranyakas* that represent the earlier sections of Vedas, which are speculations of the philosophy behind many rituals. *Āranyaka* means 'produced by or relating to the forest' or 'belonging to the forest', because they were composed by sages living in the forest. Forests represented the feminine principle or *prakriti*.

One of the most beautiful hymns of the Ṛig Veda is dedicated to Aranyānī, a Goddess of the forests and the animals who dwells within them. Aranyānī is described as an elusive spirit, fond of solitude, and fearless. The author of the hymn asks her to explain how she can wander so far from civilization without fear or loneliness. He creates a beautiful image of the village at sunset, when the sounds of the grass-hopper and cicada and the cowherd calling his cattle pervade. She is never seen, but her presence is felt by the tinkling of the bells of her anklets. She can feed both man and animal, though she is no farmer. The hymn of Aranyānī evokes a mysterious forest spirit:

Aranyānī Aranyānī, who are, as it were, perishing there, why do you not ask of the village? Does not fear assail you?

When the chichchika (bird) replies to the crying grasshopper, Aranyānī is exalted, resonant, as with cymbals.

It is as if cows were grazing, and it looks like a dwelling, and Aranyānī, at eventide, as it were, dismissed the wagons.

This man calls his cow, another cuts down the timber, tarrying in the forest at eventide, one thinks there is a cry.

But Aranyānī injures no one unless some other assails him; feeding upon the sweet fruit, he penetrates at will.

I praise the musk-scented, fragrant, fertile, uncultivated Aranyānī, the mother of wild animals. (Ṛig Veda, X.146, 1-6)

Aranyānī never returns in later Sanskrit literature or modern Hinduism. Forests have been central to Indian civilization, representing the feminine principle. Yet, she lives on in future Goddess of Hinduism. We see shades of Aranyānī in Prakritī, who symbolizes nature; Bhū Devī, the Earth goddess; Annapūrnā, the giver of food; Vana Durgā, goddess of the forest. Much later in Bengal, she is Bonbibi, the lady of the forest; Bāminī in Comilla, Bangladesh; Rūpeshwarī in Assam; Amman (in many forms) in Tamil Nadu; and so on.

The Lord of the Forest Vanaspati is invoked to taste the sacrificial offering and take it to the gods (Rig Veda, X.70.10). Vanaspati is asked to sweeten the sacrificial oblation with honey and butter. Śāyana says Vanaspati is the deified *yupa* (sacrificial post) (Rig Veda, X. 110.10). Vanaspati is the protector of the traveller: 'May Vanaspati never desert us nor do us harm: may we travel prosperously home until the stopping (of the car) until the unharnessing (of the steeds)' (Rig Veda, III. 53.20). The tree is the 'Lord of the Forest (*Vanaspati*), the shedder of nectar, and rejoicing the generations of men (is present) in the midst of our sacred rites' (Rig Veda, IX.12.7).

The Rig Veda says that plants are 'those that grew in old times ... much earlier than even the Devas ... and are different from many different places' (X. 97). There is knowledge that plants have life. 'As (the tree) suffers pain from the axe, as the śimal flower is cut off ... so may my enemy perish' (Rig Veda, III.53.22), and Indra, hero of the Rig Veda, lives in the forest: 'He (Indra) is in the forest...' (Rig Veda, I.55.4). Nature was exploited very judiciously, and trees compared to gods and humans. Forests should be green with trees and plants. The *Oshadhi Sūkta* of the Rig Veda addresses plants and vegetables as 'O Mother! Hundreds are your birth places and thousands are your shoots'. Plants existed on earth before the creation of animals (Rig Veda, 10.97.1). The Atharva Veda mentions the names of some herbs with their values. A medicinal herb is a Goddess born on earth (Atharva Veda, VI.136). Later, this information became an important source of material for Ayurveda. The Rig Veda very specifically says that forests should not be destroyed (8.1.13). The Atharva Veda says that 'The earth is the keeper of creation, container of forests, trees and herbs' (12.1.57.61). Plants are live (Atharva Veda, 12.1.57 61). 'Plants and herbs destroy poisons (pollutants)' (Atharva Veda, 8.7.10); 'Purity of atmosphere checks poisoning' (pollution) (Atharva Veda, 8.2.25); 'Plants possess the qualities of all duties and they are saviours of humanity' (Atharva Veda, 8.7.4).

Vedic scriptures have a very clear idea about the earth's relationship with nature and the necessity for maintaining the ecological balance.

A verse from Ṛig Veda says, 'Thousands and hundreds of years if you want to enjoy the fruits and happiness of life, then take up systematic planting of trees'.[11] These verses carry a clear message not to inflict any injury to trees, which make up the forest, and emphasize the importance of afforestation for survival, or else the ecological balance of the earth would be jeopardized. Ṛig Veda has dwelt upon various components of the ecosystem and their importance. 'Rivers occasion widespread destruction if their coasts are damaged or destroyed and therefore trees standing on the coasts should not be cut off or uprooted.'[12] The Yajur Veda also speaks of the ill effects of deforestation.

> The earth provides surface for vegetation which controls the heat build up. Herbs and plants having union with sun rays provide a congenial atmosphere for life to survive (Atharva Veda, 5.28.5). *Brihadāranyaka Upanishad* (3.9.28) equates trees with human beings: 'Just like a tree, the prince of the forest...'

Plants are very important for locating a text. The Ṛig Veda lists about 16 plants, besides aquatic plants and grasses, all of which are found in the plains of India and Pakistan.[13] Trees, grasses and herbs were regarded as divine. Trees, says the Ṛig Veda, are the Lords of the Forest (Vanaspati), self-regenerating and eternal, the homes of the gods (X.97).

The *Bhūmi Sūkta* of the Atharva Veda celebrates the role of the earth, as the home of 'hills, snowy mountains, forests...on whom stand always the fixed the trees, the forest trees ... the mother of herbs ... What forest animals of yours, wild beasts set in the woods, lions, tigers go about man-eating—the jackal, the wolf, O earth ...' (Atharva Veda, XII.1). The mention of both lions and tigers is significant, because it suggests an area of grassy plains, savannah, open woodlands and scrub country for the lion and subtropical forests for tigers. The *Bhūmi Sūkta* is the best commitment to the environment in ancient Indian literature.

As per Vedic tradition, all villages came under three main categories: *tapovana*, *mahāvana* and *śrīvana*.[14] In Vedic literature, the term *āranya*

---

[11] C. Pathak, H. Mandalia, and Y. Rupala, 'Bio-cultural Importance of Indian Traditional Plants and Animals for Environment Protection', *Review of Research*, Vol. 1, no. VI, pp. 1–2 (March 2012).

[12] R. Renugadevi, 'Environmental Ethics in the Hindu Vedas and Puranas in India,' *African Journal of History and Culture* (*AJHC*) 4, no. 1 (January 2012): 1–3, http://www.academicjournals.org/AJHC.

[13] Krishna, *Sacred Trees*, 13–14.

[14] M. S. Umesh Babu and S. Nautiyal, 'Conservation and Management of Forest Resources in India: Ancient and Current Perspectives', *Natural Resources* 6 (2015): 256–272.

means forest, where the hermits lived and where the *Āranyakas* were produced. The *tapovana* was a special place in the forest used for meditation. Both *āranya* and *tapovana* are known as *abhayāranya* (sanctuaries), where kings and commoners visited to seek the wisdom and guidance of sages. They were probably the sacred groves of yore. The ancient Indian civilization was nurtured in the forests which were the abodes of saints and sages. The *mahāvana* was the great all-embracing forest in which all species could find refuge. The *śrīvana* was the forest which provided prosperity, also referred to as a grove. It was donated to and maintained by the temple. These forests were set aside exclusively for the practice of religion.

Parashara's *Vrikshāyurveda* is a treatise covering basic aspects of plants. The chapter on *Bijotpatti kānda* mentions *Vanavargasūtriyāni*, which deals with forest regions. Forests are connoted by different terms such as *atavi, bipina, gahana, kanana, vana* and *mahāranya*. Parashara has described forests where trees, shrubs, creepers and grasses grow naturally. *Caitraratha vana* was a beautiful sylvan tract frequented by the *Devas* and *Gandharvas*. The classification of *vana* varies according to the regions, and the vegetation in these forests is influenced by the characteristics of the soil and plant variations within the diversity of the season (verse 20).[15]

As literature moves east, we learn more about the forest, especially from the Rāmāyana. The forest is made up of four sentiments: *shānta* (calm), *madhura* (sweet), *raudra* (angry) and *vibhatsa* (fearful). There are two forest types: the principal forest or *mahāvana* represented by Chitrakuta and Dandakaranya, and the sub-forest of peace or *tapovana* represented by Panchavati. The forests described are generally deciduous, and water occupies an important place in them.[16] The *tapovana* was the sacred grove where *rishis* lived in their *āśramas*.

In the first phase of his exile, Rama stays at Chitrakuta hill, a deciduous forest filled with fruit-bearing trees such as the mango, jackfruit, jujube, beal and many more; flowering trees, hardwood trees, grass varieties like bamboo and herbal plants. His next stop is Dandakaranya, situated in modern Madhya Pradesh, Odisha and Andhra Pradesh, also a deciduous forest with the sal, badari and bilva trees, among others. Dandakaranya is named after the *danda-trina* grass. Dandakaranya is described as abounding in tall trees, sacred trees

---

[15] N. N. Sircar and R. Sarkar, *Vrksayurveda of Parasara* [A Treatise of Plant Science] (Delhi: Sri Satguru Publications, 1996), 13–18.

[16] M. Amirthalingam and P. Sudhakar, *Plant and Animals in the Valmiki Ramayana* (Chennai: CPR Environmental Education Centre, 2013), 13.

and secret fruit-bearing trees.[17] Panchavati, where Sita was abducted, is a tropical dry deciduous forest, again named after a plant, the five *vata* or banyan trees. Kishkinda, where he visits the Pampa Sarovar or lake situated between Rishyamukha hill and Matanga Hill, is a dry and moist deciduous forest. Beyond these forested hills lay another *vana*, where the climate is very pleasant, says the epic. The epic's description of Kishkinda is a thickly forested area, quite unlike the barren region we see today. The last forest on the subcontinent is situated in the trans-Himalayan region with Alpine plants, the Oshadhi mountains of Kailasha, Rishabha and Mahodaya. Between Rishabha and Kailasha were the Dronagiri hills, where grew plants with medicinal properties which Hanuman took back to Lanka. Finally, the author describes the evergreen forests of Lanka, situated off the Indian mainland.[18] It is amazing how little has changed in the type of forests that are found in each of these places, except the extent, density and wildlife. Rama also visited several *āśramas* in these forests, some of which may have formed the nucleus of future settlements.

The Rāmāyana also mentions various types of sacred trees: the *rathya vriksha* (roadside trees) (Rāmāyana, II.3.18.50; V.12.18.22-29); and the *devatānishthāna vriksha,* which were the abode of deities. The latter were divided into *yaksha chaitya* (the tree with the spirit within) and *vriksha chaitya* (the protector tree). There were also the *chaturpatha varti vriksha* (tree at the junction of crossroads with revetments around the trunk) and *smashāna vriksha* (trees grown in burning ghats).[19] The *yaksha chaitya* and *vriksha chaitya* became, in time, the *sthala vriksha* or sacred trees of temples, in memory of the trees that had once grown in plenty in that region.[20] The Rāmāyana is a botanist's delight, with detailed descriptions of forests types and the plants that grew therein. The forests were the home of many Rākshasas or demons, as unfamiliar tribes were described. There were strict injunctions against the felling of trees in Lanka. Ravana said that he had not cut down a fig tree in the month of *Vaiśakha* (April–May). Hence, he wondered why had this cruel fate befallen him? The Rāmāyana observes that even in the kingdom of Ravana, the planting of trees was considered a worthy objective. There was a popular belief that the cutting of trees would bring about the destruction of the wood cutter and his family.[21]

---

[17] *Ramayana* (2.1.5)—*āranyaisca mahāvriksaih punyaih sveduphalairvritam.*
[18] Amirthalingam and Sudhakar, *Plant and Animals*, 13–16.
[19] S. N. Vyas, *India in the Rāmāyana Age* (Delhi: Atmaram and Sons, 1967).
[20] Krishna, *Sacred Plants*, 44–45.
[21] N. Bhatla, T. Mukherjee, and G. Singh, 'Plants: Traditional Worshipping', *Indian Journal of the History of Science* 19, no. 1 (1984): 37–42.

Often, there were conflicts over the use and protection of the forest and forest rights, such as those between Rama and many Rākshasas. The forest was peopled by Rākshasas, Asuras, Daityas and Dānavas, many of whom were famous rulers of ancient India. Yayati, an ancestor of the Yadavas, married Sharmishtha, daughter of Vrishaparvan, a Dānava king; Bhima's wife Hidambaa; Ravana, king of Lanka; Bhagadatta, king of Pragjyotisha; and Kamsa, king of Mathura and Krishna's uncle, all came under this category. The word Rākshasa comes from the root *raksha*, which means to guard, protect, save, take care of and preserve. The word appears in the early books of the Ṛig Veda. They are enemies of the Devas in Vedic and epic literature. Rākshasa is an enemy of Indra. Among their many sins of commission, they disrupt the sacrifice (Ṛig Veda, VII.104.18), and several deities are invoked to kill them. There is a story that when Brahma created the waters, he created Rākshasas to guard them. It appears that the Rākshasas were the denizens and protectors—as their name suggests—of the forest, who opposed the expansion of settlements that were destroying the forests.[22]

With the advent of agrarian economies, people began to establish settlements everywhere. In this new type of livelihood and populations began to expand faster than before. A sedentary agricultural life made it possible to construct villages, cities and eventually states, which were constructed by destroying forests and were highly dependent on water.

Agni was the destroyer of forests. 'Agni, who of old thou burnt up Jaratha (a demon/tribe?)...' (Ṛig Veda, I.1.7), 'Agni... consumes the forest trees' (Ṛig Veda, I.140.2), 'The great devourer of plants' (Ṛig Veda, I.163.7) and so on. The forests could have been destroyed by deliberate or accidental burning. This was a tribal society that had learnt the use of fire and used it both for their rituals and for clearing the forest.

The best example of the burning of forests is to be seen in the story of the Khāndava *dahana* or the burning of the Khāndava forest, in order to build Indraprastha. Khāndava *vana* was an ancient forest situated west of River Yamuna in modern Delhi. This forest was inhabited by Takshaka and his tribe of Nāgas. Arjuna, with the help of Krishna, cleared this forest by setting it on fire, to construct the new capital city of the Pandavas, Indraprastha, named after Indra, who lived here. The epic describes the terrible massacre of animals and birds as Khāndava was burning.

Then those foremost of car-warriors (Krishna and Arjuna), riding in their cars and placing themselves on opposite sides of that forest, began a great slaughter, on all sides, of the creatures dwelling in

---

[22] N. Krishna, *Book of Demons* (Haryana: Penguin Books, 2007), 64–68.

Khāndava. At whatever points any of the creatures residing in Khāndava could be seen attempting to escape, thither rushed those mighty heroes (to prevent its flight). Indeed, those two excellent cars seemed to be but one and the two warriors also therein but one individual. And while the forest was burning, hundreds and thousands of living creatures, uttering frightful yells, began to run about in all directions. Some had particular limbs burnt, some were scorched with excessive heat, and some came out, and some ran about from fear. And some clasping their children and some their parents and brothers, died calmly without, from excess of affection, being able to abandon these that were dear to them. And many there were who biting their nether lips rose upwards and soon fell whirling into the blazing element below. And some were seen to roll on the ground with wings, eyes, and feet scorched and burnt. These creatures were all seen to perish there almost soon enough. The tanks and ponds within that forest, heated by the fire around, began to boil; the fishes and the tortoises in them were all seen to perish. During that great slaughter of living creatures in that forest, the burning bodies of various animals looked as if fire itself had assumed many forms. The birds that took wings to escape from that conflagration were pierced by Arjuna with his shafts, and cut into pieces; they fell down into the burning element below. Pierced all over with Arjuna's shafts, the birds dropped down into the burning forest, uttering loud cries.....

The mighty flames of the blazing fire reaching the firmament and caused great anxiety to the celestials themselves.....Then numerous birds of the Garuda tribe bearing excellent feathers, beholding that the forest was protected by Krishna and Arjuna, descended filled with pride, from the upper skies, desirous of striking those heroes with their thunder-like wings, beaks and claws. Innumerable Nagas also, with faces emitting fire descending from high, approached Arjuna, vomiting the most virulent poison all the while. Beholding them approach, Arjuna cut them into pieces by means of arrows steeped in the fire of his own wrath. Then those birds and snakes, deprived of life, fell into the burning element below. And there came also, desirous of battle, innumerable Asuras with Gandharvas and Yakshas and Rakshasas and Nagas sending forth terrific yells. Armed with machines vomiting from their throats iron balls and bullets, and catapults for propelling huge stones, and rockets, they approached to strike Krishna and Partha, their energy and strength increased by wrath. But though they rained a perfect shower of weapons, Vibhatsu, addressing them reproachfully, struck off their heads with his own sharp arrows. That slayer of foes, Krishna, also, endued with great energy, made a great slaughter of the Daitya and the Danava with his discus.... Then the inhabitants of the forest of Khāndava, the Danavas and Rakshasas and

Nāgas and wolves and bears and other wild animals, and elephants with rent temples, and tigers, and lions with manes and deer and buffaloes by hundreds, and birds, and various other creatures, frightened at the falling stones and extremely anxious, began to fly in all directions.... Beholding the forest burning in innumerable places and Krishna also ready to smite them down with his weapons, they all set up a frightful roar. With that terrible clamour as also with the roar of fire, the whole welkin resounded, as it were, with the voice of portentous clouds. Kesava of dark hue and mighty arms, in order to compass their destruction, hurled at them his large and fierce discus resplendent with its own energy. The forest-dwellers including the Dānavas and the Rākshasas, afflicted by that weapon, were cut in hundreds of pieces and fell unto the mouth of Agni. Mangled by Krishna's discus, the Asuras were besmeared with blood and fat and looked like evening clouds. And, O Bharata, he of the Vrishni race moved about like death itself, slaying Pisachas and birds and Nāgas and other creatures by thousands. The discus itself, repeatedly hurled from the hands of Krishna, that slayer of all foes, came back to his hands after slaughtering numberless creatures. The face and form of Krishna, that soul of every created thing, became fierce to behold while he was thus employed in the slaughter of the Pisachas, Nāgas and Rākshasas.[23]

In the end, only Takshaka's son Aśvasena, the Asura Maya and four Saranga birds escaped the fire. Out of gratitude for sparing his life, the Asura Maya built a grand palace for Pandavas. Takshaka, who was not in the forest when this incident took place and lost his wife in the massacre, swore bitter vengeance. He was banished from Khāndava and went away to Takshashila (modern Taxila), which is named after him. The burning of the Khāndava forest was the cause of the enmity of the forest tribes—Asuras, Gandharvas, Yakshas, Rakshasas and Nāgas—towards the Kurus and the Vrishnis, and the later death of Arjuna's descendant Parikshit, Arjuna's grandson, who was killed by Takshaka (Mahābhārata, I.50).

This story is a terrible indictment of Arjuna and Krishna, who show no compassion towards the inhabitants of the forest. It also indicates the bitterness of local tribes towards the destruction of their forest and the usurping of their land by the Kuru prince. This was a man-made environmental havoc that resulted in the migration of the remaining people, led by Takshaka, out of the Khāndava forest and the founding

---

[23] The *Mahabharata* of Krishna-Dwaipayana translated by Kisari Mohan Ganguly, 1883–1896, at the Internet Sacred Text Archive, I.228–230.

of the city of Takshashila (modern Taxila), which became a thorn in India's flesh ever since. Some tribals, like the Asura Maya, stayed and became allies of the Kurus.

The vivid description of the burning of the Khāndava forest makes it obvious that settlements, especially urban, were created by burning down forests. Although Arjuna and Krishna revel in the destruction of the Khāndava forest, the Pandavas treat the other forests that they visit during their years of exile with great respect, forming alliances that would stand them in good stead during the great war of Kurukshetra. Bhima, for example, marries the Rākshasī Hidimbā after killing her brother Hidimba. Their son Ghatotkaca takes part and is killed in the Kurukshetra war.

According to Karve,[24] Gadgil and Guha,[25] the introduction of iron in India around 1000 BCE resulted in the development of agriculture and pastoralism in the forested Gangetic Valley. The combined use of iron and fire made it possible to bring the middle Gangetic plains under intensive agricultural and pastoral colonization, especially wet paddy cultivation. The destruction of forests and wildlife weakened the resource base of the food gatherers who lived in those forests. The burning of the Khāndava *vana* on the banks of the Yamuna by Krishna and Arjuna was couched in the language of a great ritual sacrifice to please the fire god Agni, but its prime purpose was obviously to provide land for Arjuna's clan, for the building of the city of Indraprastha and for the expansion of agriculture and pastoral lands in the region.

Kings were permitted ferocity, even expected to show off their prowess, whether it was burning down the forest as in the Khāndava *dahana*, or during a hunt. When the Mahābhārata narrates the story of Śakuntalā, the poet starts with Dushyanta entering the forest to hunt, with his large battalion of soldiers, horses and elephants. He slaughters the animals—tigers, deer and elephants and their families—at random, leaving predator and prey hiding together (Mãhābhārata, I.62-69). The *āśrama* of Kanva was situated deep in the forest, and Dushyanta's foray may have also been an attempt to conquer more territory, since expansion was the goal of kings. Forests were never far away from habitations, and the Chinese Buddhist monk Hsuan Tsang writes, in the 7th century CE, of forests near Kapilavastu and Kushinagara

---

[24] I. Karve, *Yuganta: The End of an Epoch* (Poona & New Delhi: Sangam Books, 1974).

[25] M. Gadgil and R. Guha, *This Fissured Land: An Ecological History of India* (Delhi: Oxford University Press, 1992).

in north Bihar.[26] In the Mahābhārata, the Pandavas have to traverse several forests as they wander in the wilderness during their exile.

To offset the destruction of forests may be the reason why the *purānas* exhort the reader to plant trees. The *Varāha Purāna* (172.39) says that 'One who plants a pipal (*Ficus religiosa*), a neem (*Azadirachta indica*), a banyan (*Ficus benghalensis*), two pomegranates (*Punica granatum*), two orange (*Citrus reticulate*), five mango trees (*Mangifera indica*) and 10 flowering plants or creepers will never go the hell'. The practice of *vanamahotsava* (tree plantation ceremony) is an ancient tradition. *Matsya Purāna* speaks about it. *Agni Purāna* says that the plantation of trees and creations of gardens leads to the eradication of sin. In the *Padma Purāna* (56.40-41), the cutting of a green tree is an offence punishable in hell.

Buddhist traditions attribute Gautama's enlightenment to his meditation under the pipal tree, which was his tree of enlightenment. His first sermon was in the deer park at Sarnath, obviously a protected area. In the Buddhist period, patches of vegetation were preserved as *amara vana, venu vana, sālai vana, Ashoka vana, kadamba vana, vilva vana*, etc., named after the dominant tree species.[27]

Early Buddhist literature reflects the agrarian landscape of the period. Around the *gāma* (village) or suburban area lay the *khetta* (pasture), the woodland where the people collected their biomass requirements, and primeval uncleared forests like the *andha vana* of Kosala, *sita vana* of Magadha, etc., which were retreats haunted by wild beasts and woodland spirits.[28]

The forest was seen in several ways, and time and historical context changed the narrative. The forest was a place of retreat for agricultural and pastoral societies and vacillated from a haunt of demons (*Rākshasa*) who were obviously hunter-gatherers to a romantic paradise, as described in Kalidasa's *Abhijnāna Śākuntalam*. People visited *rishis* and thinkers, including the Buddha, in the forest for spiritual and moral guidance. Even Buddhist monks lived in monasteries in the forest, albeit along trade routes, as the Buddhist *chaityas* and *vihāras*, built into caves along the Western Ghats, indicate. Since the earliest Vedas, there was a desire to use the forest as a retreat. Indian

---

[26] Si-yu-ki, Vol. I (London: Routledge, 2013), 234; Vol. II (London: Routledge, 2014), 25, 43.

[27] B. S. Somashekar, 'Treasure House in Trouble', *Amruth* 2, no. 5 (1998): 3–7.

[28] E. J. Rapson, *The Cambridge History of India, Vol. I: Ancient India* (Cambridge, 1985).

philosophical discussions took place in the forest, rather than in villages, towns and cities.

While the Vedas hail the forest as a mystical and spiritual place of retreat, the Rāmāyana describes the types of forest and the Mahābhārata describes the burning of the forest. Kautilya's *Arthaśāstra* describes the management of the forest.

In the Mauryan Empire of Chandragupta, forest was state property and its use had to be undertaken by state officials. There was a separate department headed by a head *samāhartā*, a kind of collector, with several subordinate officers under a superintendent of the forest, whose duty was to look after every matter related to the forest (*Arthaśāstra*, II.6.1-2), collect and process forest produce such as timber, fruits, fibres, medicine, etc., fix the price and sell it at the proper time (*Arthaśāstra*, II.17.1-3). He was responsible for providing water and irrigation facilities to the forest during draught and other seasons. The superintendent of the forest could impose penalties on erring officers and anti-social persons misusing the forest produce or destroying the vegetation. The *samāhartā* had to collect the revenue derived from forest produce and trade and increase the economy of the state (*Arthaśāstra*, II.6.28). The *Akshatapāla* was the controller of accounts and audit, who maintained and checked the records of income and expenditure of the forest department (*Arthaśāstra*, II.1.20). The entire system was integrated in such a way that each one was a check for another. The result was the luxurious growth of the forests all over the subcontinent during Kautilyan times. The forest management system, like everything else in the *Arthaśāstra*, had an excellent set of checks and balances.

The *Arthaśāstra* describes four kinds of forests: forests of deer (*mṛigavana*), economic forests (*dravyavana*), elephant forests (*hastivana*), bird sanctuaries (*pakshivana*) and forests of wildlife, *paśuvana* and *vyālavata*, the last reserved for tigers and wild animals. The *dravyavana* is a source of forest produce, while the *hastivana* was a sanctuary for elephants. Kautilya also mentions the *brahmāranya* (forest where the Brahmins can continue their studies of the Vedas and other scriptures); *somāranya* (forest fit for carrying out religious sacrificial rites); and *tapovana* (forest of hermitages for ascetics). Deforestation and illicit tree felling were punished by a levy (*deya*) and a fine (*atyaya*). Ecological balance was maintained, as there was a state of environmental awareness.[29]

---

[29] S. Rath, 'Kautilya's Attitude Towards Fauna in the Arthasastra', in *Kautilya's Arthasastra and Social Welfare*, ed. V. N. Jha (New Delhi: Sahitya Akademi, 2006), 279–280.

Protection of different species of animals was the main duty of the state:

> with a single entrance, surrounded by ditches, planted with delicious fruit trees, bushes, bowers and thornless trees, with an expansive lake of water, full of harmless animals, and with tigers (*vyāla*), beasts of prey (*mārgāyuka*), male and female ... and young elephants and bison, all deprived of their claws and teeth shall be formed for the king's sports (hunt). On the other extreme limit of the country or in any other suitable locality, another forest with game beasts, open to all, shall also be made. In view of procuring all kinds of forest produce described elsewhere, one or several forests shall be reserved ... In the extreme limit of the country, elephant forests, separated from wild tracts, shall be formed....Whoever kills an elephant shall be put to death. (*Arthaśāstra*, II.2.50)[30]

> Of timber forests, whoever plants a forest which produces valuable articles, which expands into wild tracts, and which possesses a river on its border over-reaches the other; for a forest containing a river is self-dependant and can afford shelter in calamities. Of game forests, whoever plants a forest full of cruel beasts, close to an enemy's forest containing wild animals, causing therefore much harm to the enemy, and extending into an elephant at the country's border, over-reaches the other. (*Arthaśāstra*, VI.12.299)[31]

> Mines are the source of whatever is useful in battle. Timber forests are the source of such materials as are necessary for building forts, conveyances and chariots. Elephant forests are the source of elephants. Pasture lands are the source of cows, horses and camels to draw chariots. (*Arthaśāstra*, VI.14.307)[32]

Thus, the forest was 'managed', a source of resources to be exploited in the historical period, during the reign of Chandragupta Maurya, when Kautilya (or Chanakya) lived. Animals were a source of pleasure for the king who hunted, while the elephant was protected as an essential part of the war machine. Forests of wild carnivores were situated between the Mauryan state and its neighbours to ensure peace, for riding on a horse through a carnivore-infested forest would have required more than mere courage. In fact, from Kautilya's description, the forest was a buffer zone whose role was to dissuade neighbouring states from attacking.

---

[30] R. Shamasastry, R., trans., *Kautilya's Arthasastra* (Mysore, 1929), 48–49.
[31] Ibid., 327.
[32] Ibid., 335.

From a wilderness and a place of spiritual inspiration in ancient Vedic India, to different types of forests in the Rāmāyana, to the destruction of the forest in the urbanization process in the Mahābhārata and to the management of forests as a source of produce and elephants in Kautilya's *Arthaśāstra*, the forest has come a long way. Forests must have been burnt down for the construction of the cities of the Indus Valley Civilization, but forests were generally protected. While in the period of Kautilya, specific areas were set aside for forest produce (*shrivana, dravyavana*), elephants (*hastivana*), other forests were protected for spiritualism (*tapovana*), for the king's hunt and for wildlife (*mahāvana*). Thus, forest management goes back to the Mauryan period.

An important aspect of nature worship was the protection of patches of forest dedicated to local deities or ancestral spirits and manifested the spiritual and ecological ethos of local indigenous communities. The *Prithvi sūkta* hymns of the Atharva Veda (12.1.11) say: 'O Earth! Pleasant be thy hills, snow-clad mountains and forests; O numerous coloured, firm and protected Earth! On this earth I stand, undefeated, unslain and unhurt'. Another hymn from the Atharva Veda (12.1.35) says: 'Whatever I dig out from you, O Earth! May that have quick regeneration again; may we not damage the vital habitat and heart'.

In Kalidasa's *Abhijñāna Śākuntalam*, there is a reference to the importance of forests and preservation of wildlife and the symbiotic relationship between people and the forests through *āśrama* life. This was the *tapovana*, a peaceful and tranquil part of the forest, where all forms of life could live in complete harmony. Kalidasa's evocative description of prancing deer and singing birds, of flowers in bloom and leafy creepers evokes an image of an idyllic forest rich in plant and animal life, the sacred grove of India's ecological tradition.

Sacred Groves

Sacred groves are the home of local flora and fauna, a veritable gene pool of animal, insect, bird and plant species, a mini-biosphere reserve and the most important conservation tradition of India. The rich plant life helps to retain subsoil water and, during the hot summer months, the pond in the grove is often the only source of drinking water. The groves are a unique form of biodiversity conservation and are living examples of the Indian tradition of conserving the ecology as a natural heritage.

Sacred groves are an area of conservation as well as a spiritual retreat. They probably represent the single most important ecological heritage of the ancient culture of India. Sanskrit and Tamil literature are full of references to forests, where wise and holy men lived, but the tradition probably goes further back in time to food-gathering societies who venerated nature and the natural resources on which they depended for their existence. Sacred groves are the *tapovana* that once existed within the forests of ancient India, where the *āśramas* of the *rishis* were located. The *tapovana* were inviolate, unlike the *mahāvana* where man encountered and hunted powerful predators, or the *śrīvana*, which were exploited for their resources. Other sacred groves go back to pre-agricultural hunting and gathering societies, before human beings had settled down to till the land or raise livestock. At the dawn of civilization, primitive societies believed that deities resided in stones, trees, animals and woods, which was their expression of the gratitude to and respect for nature for providing food and services to human society. Images and temples came much later. Sacred groves are perhaps as old as civilization itself, born at a time when pristine religion was taking shape.[33] They exemplify the perceived interlink between man and his natural environment as well as his ecological prudence,[34] provide a cultural identity to each community, represent native vegetation in a natural or near-natural state, and thereby contribute to biodiversity and environmental conservation.[35]

Sacred groves have served as significant reservoirs of biodiversity, conserving unique species of plants, insects and animals. The sanctity attached to specific trees, mountains, rivers, animals, caves and sites continues to play an important role in the protection of local biodiversity. Plants are used by tribal healers and priests who take a strong interest in the preservation of such ecosystems. The belief that spirits inhabit remote areas has served to quickly regenerate abandoned and hidden plots into mature forests.[36]

Sacred groves are the remnants of India's ancient tradition of protecting nature and natural resources through culture and religious belief. The religious and cultural traditions of India have always respected

---

[33] H. Skolmowski, 'Sacred Groves in History', *Himalaya Man and Nature* XV, (1991), p. 5.

[34] M. Gadgil and V. D. Vartak, 'Sacred Groves of India: A Plea for Continued Conservation', *Journal of the Bombay Natural History, Society* 73 (1975): 623–647.

[35] S. A. Bhagwat and C. Rutte, 'Sacred Groves: Potential for Biodiversity Management', *Frontiers of Ecology and the Environment* 4, no. 10 (2006): 519–524.

[36] N. Krishna, 'Sacred Groves: An Indian Heritage', in *Sacred Groves of India—A Compendium*, eds. Nanditha Krishna and M. Amirthalingm (Chennai: CPR Environmental Education Centre, 2014), 71–79.

nature and protected it. Culture and environment have always been closely interlinked. The myths and traditions that venerate plants and animals, forests, rivers and mountains have played a key role in protecting and preserving India's biological diversity over the centuries. The close connection between nature and divinity has been an important part of the Indian religious ethos.

Sacred groves are patches of vegetation found across the country and have been preserved through millennia out of faith and tradition. This is one of the most remarkable aspects of India's traditional respect for nature and also unifies the faith systems of India, uniting the tribal and the philosopher, the cattle grazer and agriculturist. A sacred grove may be a patch of trees left on the outskirts of villages in the plains, or a part of a forested area, dedicated to local folk deities or ancestral spirits.[37] Sacred groves are protected by local people through ancient traditions and taboos, which incorporate spiritual and ecological values. Thousands of such groves have survived from ancient times, as repositories of rare and varied local biological diversity, with an important local ecological role.

Sacred groves are cultural markers of the people and their relationship with the environment. The existence of sacred groves gives a fresh insight on environmental, historical and socio-cultural information. Woods, forests, rivers, streams, rocks, mountains, peaks and trees belonging to ancestral spirits or deities are found throughout the world.

The ENVIS (Environmental Information System) Centre on the Ecological Heritage and Sacred Sites of India at CPR Environmental Education Centre has documented, till date, 13,270 sacred groves from across India (Andhra Pradesh 750, Arunachal Pradesh 101, Assam 40, Chhattisgarh 600, Gujarat 42, Haryana 248, Himachal Pradesh 5,000, Jharkhand 21, Karnataka 1,424, Kerala 2,000, Maharashtra 1,600, Manipur 365, Meghalaya 79, Odisha 322, Rajasthan 9, Sikkim 56, Tamil Nadu 448, Uttaranchal 1, West Bengal 670) (Figure 5.1). The sacred groves range in size from 0.01 to 900 ha, covering about 10,511 ha of vegetation. Of this, only 138 ha comprise undisturbed vegetation and 3,188 ha have an open canopy. Most of these groves (66 out of 79), covering an area of 10,251 ha, are located in the catchment areas of major rivers and rivulets; 58 (9,621 ha) are at the origin of perennial streams and 38 (6,454 ha) are on hillsides.[38]

---

[37] D. D. Kosambi, *Myth and Reality: Studies in the Formation of Indian Culture* (Bombay: Popular Prakashan, 1962).
[38] www.cpreecenvis.nic.in

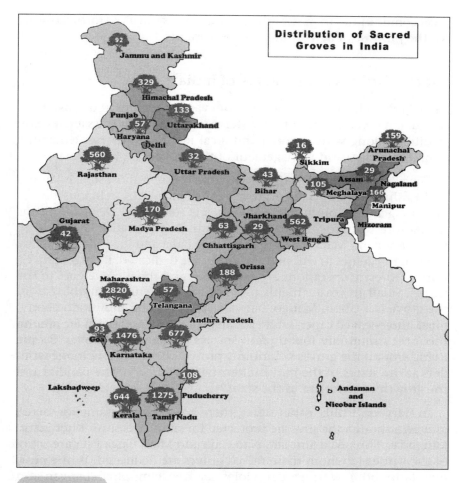

FIGURE 5.1 *Distribution of Sacred Groves in India*

Courtesy: cpreecenvis.nic.in, CPR Environmental Education Centre, Chennai.
Disclaimer: This figure is not to scale. It does not represent any authentic national or international boundaries and is used for illustrative purposes only.

Another estimate, however, suggests that the number of groves in the country may be as high as 100,000–150,000.[39]

Generally, each grove is attached to a village or a community or to a tribe, which preserves the grove as a repository of native plant, animal, insect and microorganism species. This is a testimony to the efforts of

---

[39] K. C. Malhotra et al., *Cultural and Ecological Dimensions of Sacred Groves in India* (New Delhi and Bhopal: Indian National Science Academy, 2001, p. 13).

local communities to protect their natural forests against forest clearing for the purpose of agriculture and settlements.

Sacred Groves in the States of India[40]

Sacred groves have been reported from various regions and ecosystems of India. A diverse range of ecosystems is preserved in the sacred grove tradition, along with regional and local identities represented in the names, practices and management of the groves.

Travelling first from north to south, the northernmost state is Jammu and Kashmir, where sacred groves are managed by religious bodies or management committees. *Bani* means forest and *Dev bani* means sacred forest or grove. Baba Roachi Ram, Bua Sjawati ji, Bua Dati ji, Lord Hanuman, Mata Vaishno Devi, Peer Baba and Raja Mandlik ji are some of the deities to whom these groves are dedicated. In larger groves, normal forestry operations are carried out and the income goes to the shrine. Small groves are highly protected and to remove anything from the grove is a taboo. Mango, banyan, Indian plum, mountain ebony, pipal, three-leaved caper, white fig, Bengal quince and neem are among the most commonly found plant species in the sacred groves. People living around the groves voluntarily protect them, although one wonders at the status of the groves after the migration of the pandits and the growth of terrorism in the state.

In Haryana, unlike other states, there is no generic name for sacred groves, although the sites are protected for similar reasons. Khetanath, Jairamdas, Shiv, Bala Sundari, Nao Gaja and Mani Goga Peer are some of the deities to whom these sacred groves are dedicated. White pear, mandarin, bruisewort, garden violet, lac tree, elm, pipal, banyan and flame of the forest are among the most commonly found plant species in the sacred groves. The groves act as a repository for medicinal plants and as a source of honey, fruits and water.

In Himachal Pradesh, the local myths and legends associated with sacred groves preserve the forests. There are several groves named *Dev van* or *Devta ka jungle* where one is not allowed to cut trees or even carry dry leaves outside the area. Bakhu Nag Devta, Ringarishi Devta (named after an ancient sage) and Devi are the deities to whom these sacred groves are dedicated. Deodar, kail and oak, with occasional

---

[40] The following information regarding the sacred groves in the individual states of India is taken from www.cpreecenvis.nic.in, which this author has been involved in collating.

spruce and silver fir are among the most commonly found plant species in the sacred groves. The thick forests provide a good habitat for leopards, barking deer, ghariyal, black bears, hares, wolves and many more animals. There are about 10,000 temples in the state with well-defined management committees and *birādari* panchayats (caste councils). The major deities in the state have their own groves.

The sacred groves in Uttarakhand are locally known as Deo *bhūmi* and *bugyal* (sacred alpine meadows). A *bugyal* is a high-altitude alpine grassland or meadow in Uttarakhand, locally referred to as 'nature's own gardens'. Chandrabadni Devi, Hariyali Devi, Kotgadi Ki Kokila Mata, Pravasi Pavasu Devata, Devrada and Saimyar are the deities to whom these groves are dedicated. The sacred groves of Uttarakhand serve as a gene pool and are a source of rich plant diversity. Turnip-root chervil, Himalayan cedar, Sanjeevani, Indian barberry, Himalayan firethorn and Indian valerian are among the most commonly found plant species in the sacred groves. Ritual and traditional practices in sacred groves play a crucial role in fostering threatened species like the Griffon vulture.

Sacred groves are known as *Dev van* or just *van* in Uttar Pradesh. Samaythan, Vansatti Devi, Bhairav Baba, Phoomati Mata, Shiv and Ram-Janaki are the deities to whom these groves are dedicated. The sacred groves of Uttar Pradesh hold special significance in improving the soil fertility through biomass build-up, efficient nutrient cycling, conserving soil moisture and providing a deeply penetrating root system with soil-binding properties. To achieve this end, neem, golden shower tree, bird lime tree, East Indian rosewood, banyan, cluster fig, pipal, Indian elm, Ceylon ironwood and Indian jalap are among the most commonly found plant species in the sacred groves.

The sacred groves in Bihar are locally known as *sarnas*. Raksel, Darha, Marang-Baru, Jaher-Buri, Chandi, Dharti, Satbahini and Jaherera are some of the deities to whom these groves are dedicated. Hatubongako, the village gods of the groves, are regarded as the guardians of the village and their help is invoked in agricultural and other economic operations. Bamboo and *sal* trees are among the most commonly found plant species in the sacred groves of Bihar.

The tribals of Jharkhand worship their sacred groves which are known as *sarnas*. A *sarna* is a cluster of trees where the Adivasis worship on festive occasions. Such a grove must have at least five *sal* (*Shorea robusta*) trees, held to be very sacred by the tribals. Non-tribal Hindus also worship in such *sarnas*, which they call *mandar*. The *sarhul* festival is celebrated in the *sarhul sarana* when the *sal* trees start flowering. The sacred groves celebrate the importance of the *sal* tree in their culture. Indian black plum, Indian plum, White marudah, tulasi, Indian gooseberry, neem, mango, Malabar nut, thorn apple, sal and champak are among the most commonly found plant species in the sacred groves.

Sarna means grove and is etymologically related to the name of the sacred *sal* tree, from which is derived the other name *sari dharam* ('a religion based on truth'). *Sari* means truth. The term *sarna* refers to a grove of *sal* trees, where the tribes of Chhotanagpur venerate their Gods and spirits.[41]

In West Bengal, sacred groves are known as *gram than*, Hari *than*, Sabitri *than*, Jahera *than* (shortened to Jahera), Santalburi *than*, Shitala *than*, Deo *tasara* and *mawmund* (meaning a grove or a group of trees). Sitala, Manasa, Devimani (lady of the grove) and Makali are the deities to whom these groves are dedicated. The sacred grove is associated with a range of oral narratives and belief systems. These make up a unique social means to prevent intra-group conflicts and violation of the sacred grove from infringement by outsiders. The sacred grove represents the unique fragments of the gene pool of respective species. Sal, bamboo, mango, Indian butter tree, neem, white mardah, wild date palm, narrow-leaved Indian mulberry and trumpet flower tree are among the most commonly found plant species in the sacred groves.

In Sikkim, *gompa* means monastery, which is managed by the *gompa* authority or Lamas, or by the village community.[42] Sacred groves in Sikkim are attached to Buddhist monasteries and are called Gompa Forest Areas. Cho Chuba, Loki Sharia, Guru Padmasambhava and Rolu Devi Than are the deities to whom these groves are dedicated. The highlands of Demojong below the Khangchendzonga peak are the most sacred site. Cypress, silver oak, *tooni*, *thotnay*, *aiselu*, *tusare* and *ruk saro* are among the most commonly found plant species in the sacred groves.

Forest dwelling tribes such as Bodo and Rabha, inhabiting the plains and foothills of Western Assam, have the tradition of maintaining sacred groves which are locally called *than*. Dimasa tribes of the North Cachar hills in Haflong district of Assam call sacred groves

---

[41] Chota Nagpur is a plateau in eastern India, which covers much of Jharkhand state as well as adjacent parts of Odisha, West Bengal, Bihar and Chhattisgarh.

[42] N. Jain, 'Community Conservation in the Sikkim Himalaya', in *Community Conserved Areas in India—A Directory*, ed. Neema Pathak (Pune/Delhi, 2009), 629–640.

'Madaico'.[43] Sibrai, Alu Raja, Naikhu Raja, Wa Raja, Ganiyang, Braiyung and Hamiadao are the various deities to whom these sacred groves are dedicated. Vaishnav temples called Shankara Deva *mathas* are distributed all over the state. Sacred groves are attached to these *mathas*. Giant bamboo, pear bamboo, pink banana, metico pepper, Indian smilax, areca nut, sandpaper tree and devil's cotton are among the most commonly found plant species in the sacred groves. The identity of an area/village is often associated with plant resources either available in the area/village or important locally. The identity of an area or village is often associated with plant resources either available in the area or important locally. There is a taboo in the groves on killing of deer during their mating season, and protection is extended to birds during the nesting period.

In Arunachal Pradesh, the *gompas* or sacred groves, managed by Lamas and the Mompa tribe, are attached to the Buddhist monasteries: they are called Gompa Forest Areas (GFAs). These sacred groves are dedicated to local deities such as Ubro or Ubram and Thouw-gew. The monasteries with sacred groves are mainly located in West Kameng and Tawang districts of the State. Fifty-eight GFAs were reported from these two districts and a few sacred groves from Lower Subansiri and Siang district of the State. Various ethnic groups have preserved and protected forest patches and even individual trees or animals due to their traditional beliefs and respect for nature. Banyan, pipal, ashoka, bela and harada are among the most commonly found plant species in the sacred groves.

The worship and protection of forests called *umanglai*, because of their associated deities, is still practised by Manipuris who preserve their ancient tradition. *Umanglai* in Manipuri comes from two words: *umang,* meaning forest and *lai,* meaning gods and goddesses. These groves are locally known as Gamkhap and Mauhak (sacred bamboo reserves). Some of the deities to whom these groves are dedicated are Umanglai, Ebudhou Pakhangba, Konthoujam Lairembi, Chabugbam and Chothe Thayai Pakhangba. Ecologically valuable species are found in several sacred groves of Manipur. Keystone species contribute to the maintenance. Siris, fig, cluster fig, marlea, chamomile, broken bones plant, konara oak, moner moton gaas, common walnut, common grey mango, tippera and bollygum are among the most commonly found plant species in the sacred groves.

---

[43] P. Medhi and S. K. Borthakur, 'Sacred Groves of the Dimasas of North Cachar Hills', in *Sacred Groves of India—A Compendium*, eds. Nanditha Krishna and M. Amirthalingam (Chennai, 2013), 71–79.

The local name for sacred groves in the Mizo language is *ngawpui,* meaning virgin or very old grove. *Ka niam* is characterized as *Ka niam tipbriew tipblei,* that is, the religion of knowing man and knowing the God. Man must behave well with his fellowmen so that he may do God's will.[44]

The sacred groves in Meghalaya are known as Law lyngdoh, Law niam and Law kyntang in the Khasi hills, depending on the places where they are located. *Khloo blai* in the Jaintia hills and *Asheng khosi* in the Garo hills are owned by individuals, clans or communities and are under the direct control of the clan councils or local village. *Law lum jingtep* is dedicated to ancestors and is the forest for graves.[45] Ryngkew, Basa, Labasa are some of the deities to whom these groves are dedicated. Bamboo, needle wood, Indian birch, white pear, royal robe, balsum of Peru, phurse champ, lac tree and plot's elm are among the most commonly found plant species in the sacred groves. A number of perennial streams originate from many of these groves. Ancestral worship is traditionally performed in the sacred groves. In forested areas, the focus of worship is on ancient monolithic stones erected in memory of departed elders.

Sacred groves are found all over western India. In Rajasthan, they are called by various names such as *vani* in Mewar, Kenkri in Ajmer, *oran* in Jodhpur, Bikaner and Jaisalmer, Shamlat *deh* and Dev *bani* in Alwar. Garva ji, Bharthariji, Naraini Mata, Peerbaba, Hanumanji and Naharsakti Mata are the deities to whom these groves are dedicated. Rajasthan provides an ideal example of the support of the tradition of service to the ecosystem. The resources in the groves are used in a controlled fashion or only in case of emergency. Cutch tree, Indian mesquite, mukul myrrh tree, salvia leaved cross berry, Indian tree of heaven, neem, Indian plum, banyan and pipal are among the most commonly found plant species in the sacred groves. The Gujjar people of Rajasthan have a unique practice of neem (*A. indica*) planting and worshipping it as the abode of God Devnarayan.

The word *oran* is derived from the Sanskrit word *āranya* which literally means forest or wilderness. *Orans* are sacred groves of trees set aside in Rajasthan for religious purposes. Considering the fact that the ancient River Sarasvati once flowed beneath the deserts of Rajasthan, and that

---

[44] Sib Charan J. Roy, *Ka jingiapyni ka kmie bad ki khun* (Shillong: Ri Khasi Press, 1911), p. 3.

[45] S. K. Barik, B. K. Tiwari, and R. S. Tripathi, *Sacred Groves of Meghalaya—A Scientific and Conservation Perspectives* (Shillong: NAEB, NEHU, 2006).

Vedic literature came into existence on the banks of the Sarasvati, it is likely that the *Āranyakas* are named after the *āranya* or *orans* of Rajasthan. In some *orans*, there are platforms covered with tiled roofs with *havan kunds* of different shapes, not unlike Vedic *homa kunds*. However, for the most part, *oran* today simply denotes common land with trees and some grass cover on it. In Rajasthan and Gujarat, these *orans* are known as *oran mata, oran*, Dev *bani* and *jogmaya*. The *orans* in western Rajasthan, filled with *khejarli* trees (*Prosopis spicigera*), deer, blackbuck and nilgai (Bluebull), are protected by the Bishnoi community, for whom they are sacred. In the year 1730, in the village of Khejadli in Jodhpur district, 363 Bishnoi women gave up their lives to protect the khejarli trees, giving rise to the Chipko or 'Hug a Tree' movement.

Sacred groves are seen throughout Gujarat. Khodiyar mata, Oran mata, Jhalai mata, Panch Krishna, Mahadev are some of the deities to whom the groves are dedicated. Cotton tree, Bengal quince, neem, mango, flame of the forest, sissoo, thorny staff tree, banyan and pipal are among the most commonly found plant species in the groves. Sacred groves play an important role in the conservation of biodiversity, recharge of aquifers and soil conservation in this partially desert state. The cutting and climbing of trees and removal of wood are strictly prohibited.

Tribals form 19.9 per cent of the population of Madhya Pradesh in Central India. Sacred groves, known as *deogudi* or *sarana*, conserve many plants and animals.[46] Bursung, Pat Khanda, Ganganamma, Mahadev, Bhandarin mata and Danteshwari mata are some of the deities to whom these groves are dedicated. The tribals believe that if the groves are not maintained properly or are destroyed, natural calamities will ruin their clan. Indian butter tree, banyan, pipal, calotrop, Indian mesquite, Bengal quince, flame of the forest, khakan and sal tree are among the most commonly found plant species in the sacred groves.

In Chhattisgarh, sacred groves are locally known as Matagudi, Devgudi and Gaondevi. Different tribes have their own Mata or Gaondevi (village goddess in the Devgudi. Some of the deities to whom these groves are dedicated are Andhari Pat, Chala Pachao, Sarna Burhia, Sarna Mata, Mahadania and Budhadev. *Sarana* or *jahera* (sacred groves) are predominantly found in the Chhotanagpur region.[47] Sal, Indian

---

[46] V. Choudhary and V. Gupta, 'Tradition of Sacred Groves in India—A Review', *Global Journal For Research Analysis (GJRA)* (September 2014): 185–187.

[47] S. Patnaik and A. Pandey, 'A Study of Indigenous Community Based Forest Management System: Sarna (Sacred Groves)', in *Conserving the Sacred for Biodiversity Management*, eds. P. S. Ramakrishnan, K. G. Saxena and U. M. Chandrasekara (Enfield, NH: Science Publishers, 1998), 315–322.

gooseberry, bedda nut, Indian laurel, Indian frankincense tree, black myrobalan, cuddapah almond, Indian butter tree and axile wood are among the most commonly found plant species in the sacred groves. Most of the groves are managed by the local communities and owned by a group of families or a clan. The community rituals are often synchronized with the blossoming of the flowers of the trees in the groves, and other agricultural operations, revealing the close harmony between nature and tribal communities.

In Maharashtra, sacred groves are found in tribal as well as non-tribal areas. The sacred groves in the western part are called Devrai or Devrahati whereas in the east, the Madiya tribals call them Devgudi. Some of the deities to whom these groves are dedicated are Maruti (Hanuman), Vaghoba (tiger god), Vira, Bhiroba, Khandoba, Vetal, Mhasha and Shirkai. Kosambi (1962) and Gadgil & Vartak (1976, 1981) state that most of the cults associated with sacred groves in Maharashtra are Mother Goddess cults—Kamaljai, Mariai, Bhavani, Bhagvati and Tathawade.[48] Sontheimer traces the origin of Khandoba to the worship of the anthill, the seat of snakes, of Goddess Shirkai in Poona district.[49] The felling of timber and the killing of animals in sacred groves is taboo. The most commonly found plant species in the sacred groves are portia tree, casuarina, silk cotton tree, Indian laurel, Indian elm, bead tree, Indian butter tree, turmeric and Japanese ginger. Sacred groves form an important landscape feature in the deforested hill ranges of the Western Ghats, sometimes being the last remnants of local forests.

In Goa, sacred groves are known by various names such as *devrai*, *devran* or *pann*. The sacred groves are dedicated to the deities Durga and Rashtroli. The tribes of Goa—Gavda, Kunbi, Velip and Dhangar-gouli—worship various forms of nature. Ceylon oak, red silk cotton tree and pipal tree are among the most commonly found plant species in the sacred groves. They still maintain the tradition of sacred goats, sacred banyan trees, sacred hills, sacred stones and sacred ponds, along with the sacred groves. A unique feature is the offering of terracotta animals in the groves.

---

[48] Kosambi, *Myth and Reality*; M. Gadgil and V. D. Vartak, 'Sacred Groves of Western Ghats of India', *Economic Botany* 30 (1976): 152–160; 'Sacred Groves in Maharashtra: An Inventory', in *Glimpses of Indian Ethnobotany*, ed. S. K. Jain (New Delhi: Oxford and IBH, 1981), 279–294.

[49] G. D. Sontheimer, 'Hinduism: The Five Components and Their Interaction', in *Hinduism Reconsidered*, eds. G. D. Sontheimer and H. Kulke (New Delhi: Manohar Publications, 1989).

Pavitra vana, the local name of sacred groves in Andhra Pradesh and Telangana, means a sacred forest. There are small groves attached to each village that have been protected over years by local people. Most of the groves are rich in flora and fauna and have a good water source, such as a spring, well, waterfall, pond, river or stream. People have protected them, attributing divinity or other supernatural qualities.[50]

Sacred groves in Odisha are recognized by names such as *jahera* and *thakurnam*. *Jahera*, places of worship in Odisha, are located in forests outside the village, where the deities Moreiko and Turuiko (god of fire) are located.[51] Some of the deities to whom these groves are dedicated are Jhakeri, Gram Siri, Gossa Pennu, Pitabaldi, Loha Penu, Gaisri and Pat Baram. Sal, mango, dumri, senha, Arabian jasmine, Bengal quince, billy goat-weed, axile wood, neem, pig weed and silk cotton tree are among the most commonly found plant species in the sacred groves. Unique biodiversity has been reflected in the groves, as they harbour many medicinal plants, roots, fruit trees, creepers and shrubs, along with many faunal types including various resident birds, reptiles and wild animals.

The most notable community conserved areas of Karnataka are its sacred groves. They vary in size, ownership patterns and vegetation. The groves come under two classes: smaller groves or *kans* that are entirely protected and larger groves or *devarakādu/devarkan*, which function as resource forests, offering both sustenance and ecological security. The presiding deities to whom these groves are dedicated are usually Hulideva (tiger deity), Naga (snake), Jatakappa, Bhutappa and Choudamma, Mailara, Bhairava and Govardhan. Crab's eye, sage leaved alangium, neem, pipal, pithraj tree and powder puff are among the most commonly found plant species in the sacred groves. The sacred groves are rich in biodiversity due to their unique ownership and management traditions. A unique feature is the offering of terracotta hounds in the groves of Kodagu.

Kovil thoppu or *kovil kādu* means 'forest of the temple' in Tamil. In Tamil Nadu, every village has a sacred grove. These groves range in size from 1 to 500 acres. The sacred groves in Tamil Nadu are known as *kovil kādu, swami thopu, swami solai*, Ayyappan *kāvu* (in Kanyakumari), *kātttu kovil* and *vanakkovil*, meaning forest temple. The deities associated

---

[50] R. Rajamani, 'Ecological Traditions of Andhra Pradesh', in *Ecological Traditions of Andhra Pradesh* (CPR Environmental Education Centre, 2005), 11.

[51] C. J. Sonowal and P. Praharaj, 'Tradition vs Transition: Acceptance of Health Care Systems Among the Santhals of Orissa', *Studies on Ethno-Medicine* 1, no. 2 (2007): 135–146.

with the groves are Ayyanār, Sastha, Muniswaran, Karuppuswami, Vedappar, Andavar and goddesses such as Selliyamman, Kali, Mari, Ellaikali, Ellaipidari, Sapta Kannis, Pechiyamman, Rakkachiyamman and so on. The groves are the repositories of medicinal plants. Crab's eye, white babool, siris, white cutch tree, Indian persimmon and ebony are among the most commonly found plant species in the sacred groves of the plains. Wild lime, iron wood tree, alangium, capper bush and indigo wodier are among the most commonly found plant species in the coastal sacred groves. Indian mesquite, East Indian walnut, poison nut, tamarind, ebony and persimmon are among the most commonly found plant species in the sacred groves of the Eastern Ghats. Kurinji, white marudah, cycas, rudraksha, Indian black plum, champak and rosewood are among the most commonly found plant species in the sacred groves of the Western Ghats.

Once a year, a festival is held in the grove. *Pongal*, a mixture of rice, lentils and *vellam* (unrefined brown sugar), is prepared as *prasādam* (food as a religious offering), cooked on dry twigs from the grove. Apart from this, twigs and branches of the groves cannot be plucked or used. It is mandatory that the grove is always kept clean: one is not allowed to urinate or defecate within the grove. The characteristic feature of sacred groves in Tamil Nadu is the offering of terracotta horses to Ayyanār, the village *kāval kāran* (watchman) at the shrine of the Mother Goddess. Horses are offered to him to circumambulate the boundary of the village at night and guard it.

The sacred groves in Puducherry are locally known as *kovil kādugal* and Ayyappan *kāvu*. Sacred groves varying in size from 0.2 to 5.0 ha in around temples have been documented in the state. Ayyanār, Poraiyatta Amman, Pachaivaḷi Amman, Selli Amman, Kaliamman and Maduraiveeran are some of the deities to whom these groves are dedicated. Lebbek, Indian atalantia, neem, caper bush, bush plum, Indian-laburnum, Indian black plum and jackal coffee are among the most commonly found plant species in the sacred groves. These sacred groves are often dedicated to local spirits or deities and the people attach sanctity to them. Religious practices and cultural traditions deter people from exploiting the biodiversity contained within them.

The sacred groves in Kerala are known locally as *kāvu* or *sarpa kāvu* (snake groves): there are Ayyappan *kāvu*, Sastan *kāvu*, Bhagavati or Amman *kāvu*, depending on the deities to whom these groves are dedicated. Serpent worship is an important feature of sacred groves in the state, as nearly all *kāvus* have images of snakes. Deities of tribal-managed *kāvus* are *Yekshi* and *Vanadevata*, the goddess of forests or spirits. White dammar, night-flowering jasmine, black varnish tree, niepa bark tree, Santa Maria tree, Ceylon ironwood and tamarind are among the most commonly found plant species in the sacred groves.

This is a summary of the sacred groves found in the various states of India, whose existence is very important for a study of India's environmental and forest history, for they indicate the species of plants and animals that local people believed were important and the methods used to preserve them. This conservation method was carried out in spite of the threat of development and deforestation in colonial and post-colonial India. Often, the sacred groves are the last remnants of local plant diversity.

The deities protecting the sacred groves vary from state to state. The deity may be male or female, animals or ancestors. At the dawn of religious thinking, deities were imagined by primitive societies to reside in stones, trees, animals and woods. The deities could be installed in a forest patch or even under a single tree.

Another common practice found in many states as far apart as West Bengal and Gujarat or Tamil Nadu and Bihar is that of offering terracotta animals, especially horses of differing sizes, to the deity, from the Bankuras horse of Bengal to the Ayyanār horses of Tamilnadu, the terracotta dogs of Coorg to the clay crocodiles of Goa. This is done in the belief that it will result in a good harvest. This tradition is suggestive of the *aśvamedha*. Although real horses are not sacrificed, probably because of their cost, the similarity between the Vedic and sacred grove traditions suggests a common origin for the two. The horse is considered next in importance only to man, according to local people. The speed and strength of the animal are necessary for the protection of the village. The horse is gifted for the use of local spirits. According to local belief, Ayyanār in Tamil Nadu rides the terracotta horses around the boundaries—*ellai*—of the village at night to safeguard the village. Perhaps its importance dates back to the *Ṛig* Vedic period and the *aśvamedha*, when the territory covered by the horse, as it roamed for a year, was claimed by the tribe. In fact, the tradition of dedicating horses to the sacred grove makes us wonder about the origins of the *aśvamedha* sacrifice itself. Although horses are not known to be sacrificed at groves, goats, fowls and buffalos are sacrificed in some groves, in fulfilment of a vow.

The terracotta tradition is linked to Mother Earth as a symbol of fertility, and the many offerings to her are in fulfilment of vows for good health, a bountiful harvest and for the gift of life. The wealth of the grove, the richness of the plant life within and the life- and health- giving properties of the plants (which are generally medicinal) are all gifts of the earth, who is venerated as the Mother Goddess, the Great Earth Mother to whom the *Bhumi sūkta* of the Atharva Veda is dedicated. During the spring or summer season, week-long celebrations are conducted during which ritual prayers are offered to the deity. On these occasions, food is usually cooked using twigs collected from the grove.

Social and cultural mechanisms have played an important role in preserving the sacred groves. Over the centuries, tribal communities evolved customs, rituals and ceremonies, which coalesced into their own unique culture. The conservation culture diversified into different forms of beliefs, rites, rituals, myths, taboos and folk tales. Festivals are generally organized by the whole community. Folktales and folklore strengthen the cultural bond between the people and the grove. One of the main reasons why the local people do not plunder the sacred groves is the widespread belief among them that those who do so will invite the wrath of the deity. Taboos are an important means of social control in primitive societies. People do not harm the sacred groves mainly for fear of the unknown, believing that those who cut a tree or use an axe in a sacred grove may be harmed by the presiding deity. Understandably, ancient cultures imposed restrictions and punitive actions primarily to stop the changing attitudes that would destroy the groves, which were preserved for various ecological reasons. The gods were invoked through rites, rituals and folk tales to create a fear of the consequences. The social divide is also reflected in the preservation of certain groves for specific caste groups or for specific tribes.

Resource extraction and alterations of land use have been generally discouraged. Agricultural activities, erection of unauthorized structures and the axing of trees are totally prohibited. However, in many groves, fallen branches/trees and the collection of firewood for ceremonial cooking is permitted; most people are not averse to use dead and fallen twigs for cooking within the groves during rituals and ceremonies. Carrying tools such as swords, axes, knives, sickles, etc., is generally banned. The only metallic structures found within the grove are tridents, spears, swords, bells, etc., associated with the deity or the ritual. Non-vegetarian food can only be the meat of sacrificed animals, which can be served only on ceremonial occasions when animals are sacrificially offered to the deities.

The protection enjoyed by plants is extended to animals living within the grove, who may not be harmed, nor can animals dedicated to the deity be harmed even when they stray into the village. Footwear, urination and defecation are all not permitted as a matter of custom.

Rituals and festivals are an important component of the belief system, aimed at pleasing supernatural forces to ward off dangers such as drought, illness, epidemics, etc., and for seeking rich harvests and good health. Offerings are made ritually during festivals and these include offerings of terracotta horses, bulls and elephants, the last one being characteristic of the coastal groves of Tamil Nadu,[52] where elephants are not known to have existed.

Terracotta represents the powers of renewal inherent in the earth. It represents the Hindu philosophy of birth, death and rebirth. This is also the cyclic role of the clay—it represents the votive offering for a certain period. As the clay slowly disintegrates and goes back to Mother Earth, it is time for the creation of a new figure. The figurines can only be worshipped for a limited period of time. In fact, the new figure is often made from a handful of clay from the old figure to which more clay is added.[53] The terracotta offerings of animals—generally horses, bulls, elephants and ram—are always made of clay and left in the open to go back to the mud they came from. It is interesting to note that only working animals are given as votive offerings. Wildlife, such as leopards or peacocks, which once visited and sometimes continue to visit the groves, are rarely given as a votive offering, although I have visited groves in Tamil Nadu where clay figures of leopards and other wildlife share the platform with elephants, horses, bulls and rams.

The relationship between human beings and clay is as old as civilization itself. Mud was used to construct homes to live in, pots to store food and water and much of Palaeolithic and Neolithic life depended on it. With the discovery of metal, new materials were used, but the dependence on clay has continued till the present day, particularly in rural and tribal India. The sacred groves are intimately connected with the potter and pottery. The clay figures of the deities and the animals are an inseparable part of the sacred grove.

Generally, the potter is the priest at the sacred grove. He makes the terracotta figurines of animals; he also sacrifices the living animals on behalf of his clients. His pots are broken at every birth and death, representing the renewal powers of the earth. In fact, a wedding cannot begin without the arrival of the pots. The potter performs both the ritual of making the terracotta figures and the ritual of worship at the temple, before the clay

---

[52] M. Amirthalingam, *Sacred Groves of Tamil Nadu—A Survey* (Chennai: CPR Environmental Education Centre, 1998).

[53] This is a similar practice during Ganesh Chaturthi, the festival of Ganesha.

figures are offered to the deity.[54] His tools are few—the potter's wheel and his own hand. For the figurines, he uses a mixture of sand, husk and clay, unlike the mixture of sand and clay used for pots.[55] But the offering must be installed in a grove, in the open, and under the skies.

There are important differences in the management of the sacred groves, their preservation, existence of rituals and festivals, conflict resolution and harvesting of biomass. Some belong to tribal communities, others to the grām panchayats. In central, eastern and northeastern India, management is by the tribal elders. In Maharashtra, many groves are managed by the forest department. In western Maharashtra, many groves are managed by the revenue department.[56] In the 1960s, in Maharashtra, the Paschim Maharashtra Deosthan Prabodhan Samiti was formed to manage the sacred groves.[57] Two hundred and twenty-three such groves were documented by Gadgil and Vartak.[58] In Kerala, the sacred groves may be owned by a joint family, a nuclear family, a caste group or a trust. In the Kanyakumari district of southern Tamil Nadu, the groves are owned by Nair and Namboodiri families. Usually, about one-seventh of the land holding is earmarked for the maintenance of the grove. In the case of large Hindu temples, the groves are managed by the Devaswom boards under the overall control of the state government.

Sacred groves, as patches of virgin forests venerated on religious grounds, have preserved many rare and endangered plant and animal species, which were beneficial in medicine and agriculture. Sacred groves represent the ancient Indian tradition of in situ conservation of genetic diversity, while Gadgil[59] observes that 'In many parts of India, sacred groves represent surviving examples of climax vegetation'.[60] These miniature forests within human settlements are sustained by tradition and faith and linked with rituals and festivals of the local community.

---

[54] N. Krishna, *Arts and Crafts of Tamil Nadu* (USA, 1992), 90.

[55] S. Inglis, *A Village Art of South India* (Madurai, 1980).

[56] A. Godbole et al., 'Role of Sacred Groves in Biodiversity Conservation with Local People's Participation: A Case Study from Ratnagiri District, Maharashtra', in *Conserving the Sacred for Biodiversity Management*, eds. P. S. Ramakrishnan, K. G. Saxena and U. M. Chandrashekara (New Delhi, 1998), 233–246.

[57] J. J. Roy Burman, 'A Comparison of Sacred Groves Among the Mahadeo Kolis and Kunbis of Maharashtra', *Indian Anthropologist* 26 (1996): 37–46.

[58] Gadgil and Vartak, 'Sacred Groves in Maharashtra', 279–294.

[59] M. Gadgil, 'Conserving Biodiversity as If People Matter: A Case Study from India', *Ambio* 21 (1992): 266–270.

[60] V. Sarojini Menon, *Sacred Groves: The Natural Resources of Kerala* (Trivandrum: WWF, Kerala Office, 1997).

The evolution and elaboration of the belief system attained its zenith with the Bishnois who live in the deserts of Rajasthan. The *orans* at Peepasar and Khejarli villages are revered by the Bishnois; the former is the birth place of Guru Jambeshwarji, founder of the Bishnoi cult and the latter symbolizes the supreme sacrifice of 363 Bishnois who protested the felling of the Khejarli tree (*Prosopis cineraria*) in Khejarli village in the year 1730 CE by the subjects of the Jodhpur King. If the *khejarli* plant, the deer, blackbuck and blue bull and other animals of the Thar Desert have survived today, it is because of the commitment of the Bishnois, for whom conservation is a religious precept. Traditional societies often use symbols and cosmologies to impart the knowledge of conservation to younger generations. This, in turn, helps them to conserve the existing resources intelligently.

Gadgil and Vartak[61] have pointed out the ecological wisdom found in taboos. Taboos are ancient strictures that have been handed down through generations. The taboos govern the thinking and actions of the tribe or clan.[62] Taboos have thus played a useful role in preventing the destruction of the groves. These restrictions govern the social life of the community or tribe and help in preserving local ecology. They have played a very important role in maintaining the balance of nature. The fact that there are no artificial boundaries or fences for the groves is a case in point; the belief system is the 'social fencing'.

In Meghalaya, it has been found from both primary and secondary sources that there are as many as 514 species representing 340 genera and 131 families; the groves are also home to many medicinal plants. Endangered species are also found here. Besides, trees and shrubs, various species such as lianas, orchid, ferns, bryophytes and microbes grow in the sacred forests. The plant and animal diversity can be compared to those found in biosphere reserves. This reiterates the fact that the traditional forest management systems are more efficient than the modern systems. Rightly, they can be called 'Mini Biosphere Reserves'.[63]

A grove (0.45 ha) owned by the Gawli family at Muradhpur village of Maharashtra contains old *samādhis*. This is the site for performing the

---

[61] Gadgil and Vartak, 'Sacred Groves in Maharashtra', 266–270.

[62] Bhagwat and Rutte, 'Sacred Groves', 519–524.

[63] R. S. Tripathi, B. K. Tiwari, and S, K. Barik, *Sacred Groves of Meghalaya: Status and Strategy for Their Conservation* (Shillong: NAEB, NEHU, 1995), 112–125; B. K. Tiwari, S. K. Barik, and R. S. Tripati, 'Biodiversity Value, Status, and Strategies for Conservation of Sacred Groves of Meghalaya, India', *Ecosystem Health* 4 (1998): 20–33.

obsequies and ceremonial rites for the deceased. It houses giant specimens of *Terminalia bellirica, Lagerstroemia lanceolata,* etc. There is a giant tree *Mangifera indica* (mango) tree in a sacred grove of Maharashtra in the Western Ghats, which is fully covered by the *Tinospora sinensis* (a twiner), with a hanging stem and looking like the trunk of an elephant (refer Footnote 64). In the groves of Virachilai, Kothamangalapatti, in Pudukottai district of Tamil Nadu, there are giant trees such as *Tamarindus indica* (325 cm gbh, 17.6 m height), *Ficus benghalensis* (210 cm gbh, 15.4 m height), *Albizia amara* (240 cm gbh, 14 m height), *Azadirachta indica* (130 cm gbh, 11.9 m height) and *Drypetes sepiaria* (130 cm gbh, 10.75 m height); all are impressively tall and robust, thereby justifying the claim that sacred groves are a museum of giant trees, a gene bank of economic species and a refuge for rare and relict taxa, besides serving as spiritual retreats.[64]

The natural heritage of sacred groves is a veritable treasure unsurpassed in any other land mass of comparable size in the world.[65] Sacred groves are patches of climax vegetation of the respective areas, except in the case of some memorial groves where the species are selectively introduced. The groves represent a variety of vegetation ranging from typically evergreen to dry deciduous forest types, of the Himalayan ranges and the Western Ghats, swamps of the coastal plains along the Western coast, oases of thorny scrub in the Aravalli ranges and scrub woodlands of the Coromandel coastal belt, corresponding to the different climatic zones.

Sacred Groves of Tamil Nadu

In Tamil Nadu, almost every village has a sacred grove ranging in size from 1 acre to 500 ha. The sacred groves of Tamil Nadu are known as *kovil kādu, swami thopu* or *swami solai*. The deities associated with the groves are Aiyanar, Sastha, Muneeswaran Karuppuswami, Vedappar, Andavar and Amman. The groves are the repositories of medicinal plants.

Many sacred groves are also important archaeological sites with evidences of Palaeolithic or Neolithic cultures. Sittannavasal in Pudukottai

---

[64] V. D. Vartak, 'Sacred Groved of Tribals for In-situ Conservation of Biodiversity', in *Ethnobiology in Human Welfare*, ed. S. K. Jain (1996), 300–302.

[65] Gadgil and Vartak, 'Sacred Groves of India', 314–320; M. P. Ramanujam, 'Conservation of Environment and Human Rights; Sacred Groves in Cultural Connections to Biodiversity PRP', *Journal of Human Rights* 4 (2000): 34–38.

district, for example, combines 3,000-year-old Neolithic dolmens, ancient sacred groves, an ancient water tank, 1,500-year-old residential caves of Jain monks and 1,300-year-old painted Jain caves.

One of the important reasons for the continued survival of the sacred groves has been the taboos, beliefs and rituals along with the folklore. In many places, women are forbidden to enter the grove during menstruation. In some sacred groves, the practice of tonsuring the head and placing stone statues of the snake god is prevalent.

Sangam literature describes the *aindu tinai*, which is the five-fold division of the geographical landscape, its ecological and traditional perspectives. These landscapes are *kurinji* (mountains), *mullai* (forests), *marutham* (agricultural lands), *neithal* (coastal regions) and *paalai* (wastelands/desert). Each *tinai* has its own characteristic flowers, trees, animals, birds, climate and other geographical features. Of these, the trees have played important roles in the social, cultural and religious aspects of ancient anthologies. Flowers are associated with gods and goddesses and the tradition of offering flowers to them finds mention in *Sangam* literature.[66] Each *tinai* has its groves and the offerings therein are as per the *aindu tinai* tradition.

In the *Silappadikaram*, we learn that the Chola port city of Poompuhar had a number of groves such as *ilavandigai solai, kavera vanam* and *sampāti vanam* named after Sampati, elder brother of Jatayu and so on. *Sampāti vanam* is now known as *pullirikku velur* or Vaitheeswaran Koil, which was once a suburb of Kaveripattinam.

However, in the *Sangam* period, there was also a celebration of rulers who cut down forests and replaced them with water bodies, town and agriculture. There is a description of Karikala Chola in a stanza from *Pattinappālai* (II.283-292) (190 CE):

He destroyed forests and made them habitable, dug ponds, moved his capital from Uranthai; Built towns with temples where people were settled, erected gates in forts and created places for soldiers to hide on its ramparts; Brave men who were ready to fight enemies and who did not run away, showing their backs. His prosperous tall forts glistened like lightening.

The early Cholas were followed by the Pallavas, whose large-scale deforestation won them titles such as *kāduvetti* (forest cutters) and

---

[66] N. Krishna, *Ecological Traditions of Tamil Nadu* (CPR Environmental Education Centre, 2005).

kādavarkon (chief of the forest people), among others. There are several inscriptions describing the Pallava kings as *kādavar* (forest people) or *kāduvetti* and their feudatories as *kāduvetti tamilapperaiyar* (Tamil chiefs under the forest cutters).[67] That the Pallavas were rulers of forest lands is established by the Talagunda inscription of Kakusthavarman, according to whom the Pallavas were rulers of inaccessible forests stretching to the gates of Sridarvata.[68]

Apparently, the attractions of urbanization and the need for water harvesting lakes had set into the Tamil country at a very early period, not unlike the destruction of the Khāndava forest for the creation of Indraprastha in the Mahabharata.

Sacred groves represent local folklore and religion. Every village has a grove, which is a protected area associated with local folk deities of uncertain origin. *Sangam* literature belonging to the period between 300 BCE and 400 CE describes a scenario where people were seen as one of the components of five different ecosystems.[69] Each ecosystem had its own unique habits of hunting, gathering, cultivating and worshipping deities. It appears that the ancient deities of Tamil Nadu are the same present deities worshipped in villages under different names. Although some of the deities may not be associated with extensive forest cover, most are found in intimate association with at least a small grove of plants or sacred groves.

The Kollimalai hills, situated in Namakkal and Perambalur districts of Tamil Nadu, is closely linked with ancient Tamil literature. In the Tamil epics *Silapadikāram* and *Maṇimekalai*, there is an interesting reference to Kollipāvai, the deity in the sacred grove, who is also the guardian of the forests. Apparently, the sages were looking for a peaceful place to undertake penance and chose Kollimalai. When they began their rituals, the demons invaded the hills to destroy their peace. The sages prayed to Kollipāvai who, according to the myth, chased away the demons with her enchanting smile. Kollipāvai is still worshipped by the people here and her smile is revered. The Kollipāvai temple is located in one of the 15 sacred groves here and can be approached only on foot.[70]

---

[67] C. Minakshi, *Administration and Social Life Under the Pallavas* (Chennai: University of Madras, 1977), 361–362. S.I.I., Vol. IV, No. 135.

[68] *Mysore Gazeteer*, II, C. Hayavadana Rao (ed.), (Bangalore: Government Press, 1930), 561–562.

[69] S. Xavier, Thaninayagam's tr. *Pattuppāṭṭu* (Bombay, 1966).

[70] P. Dayanandhan, 'Origin and Meaning of the Tinai Concept in Sangam Tamil Literature', in *Indological Essays, Commemorative Volume II for Gift*

There is an ancient temple in the Kolli Hills dedicated to Lord Arapalīśwarar on the Aiyaru stream. Many sacred groves, guarded by the local temple deities, are found in the forests near the Akashagangai falls even today, where the felling of trees is strictly prohibited. The area surrounding the temple of Arapalīśwarar and the sacred groves is still held in reverence. The groves are kaveri *vanam* and *sāya vanam*, where the temples were located.[71]

Nanda vanam or temple gardens were groves associated with ancient temples during the medieval period in South India. There are vivid descriptions of them in about 300 epigraphs belonging to the period between the 3rd and 15th centuries CE. Several inscriptions refer to the grant of land by rulers to maintain temple gardens called *Thirunanda vanam*. Many varieties of flowering plants were cultivated and flowers from these gardens were offered to the deity to perform *puja*. There is a 10th-century inscription belonging to Chola king Rajaraja I, which refers to a temple of Kalar, the leader of Aiyanar's army. Another reference relates to Pidariyamman in the village of Maganikkudi in Venkonkudikandam in Māranādu and mentions a '*nanda vanam* of coconut trees'. Even today, the temple of Sri Ranganathaswamy at Srirangam near Trichy has a floral garden called Madhura Kavi *nanda vanam*, which extends over an area of 10 acres. Apart from the garden, there is also an orchard, where every tree is named after a Vaishnava saint or *āchārya*.[72]

Rajaraja I donated lands and paddy for *pongal* and land for the maintenance of the Pidari and Ayyan *kovil kādugal* (SII, Vol. II, p. 56). A festival called *vanamahotsavam* or spring festival was conducted on the full-moon day in the sacred grove. The decorated idol was taken out in procession to the sacred grove, where it was kept for throughout the full moon night. The villagers were allowed to enter the grove and worship the deities on condition that they would not harm the animals and plants.

They are five types of groves in medieval Tamil Nadu, namely (a) exclusive floral gardens, (b) groves of fruit-bearing trees (orchards), (c) gardens having flower and fruit-bearing plants, (d) groves having

Sironmoney, ed. Michael Lockwood (Chennai: Department of Statistics, Madras Christian College, 1992), 27–44.

[71] G. Arunachalam et al., 'Ethno Medicines of Kolli Hills at Namakkal District in Tamil Nadu and Its Significance in Indian Systems of Medicine', *Journal of Pharmaceutical Sciences and Research* 1, no. 1 (2009): 1–15.

[72] M. Amirthalingam, 'Conservation as a Tamil Ethic', *Eco News* 12, no. 4 (2006): 22–25.

only one type of plant and (e) a typical forest patch. They were maintained by the priest(s) or village committees as evident from an epigraph of the Chola King, Kulothunga III. The epigraph records that a committee consisting of three representatives of the king along with the temple superintendent, the priest, organizer of festivals, the manager, the temple mason and the accountant were entrusted with the task of maintaining the temple.[73]

Maravarman alias Tribhuvana Kulasekharadeva in 1272 CE, gifted land for the lighting of a *nanda vilakku* and for food offerings to the goddess housed in the *Varantaruvan Padāran kādu* (Forest of the boon-giving Padaran) of Pattivasekaranallur in Poliyurnadu (A.R. No. 452 of 1909, No. 475, p. 311). Inscriptions belonging to Devaraya II dated 1424 CE, and found on the south wall of the central shrine in the Masilamaniśwarar temple at Tirumullaivoyil, Saidapet Taluk, Chengalpattu district of Tamil Nadu, mention that the King Orri Mannan alias Udaiyar Orri-Arasar and Arasuperumal alias Kadavaraya (Devaraya II) gifted 4,000 kuli of land for conducting certain special festivals in the Kadavarayar *tiruttoppu* (sacred grove) (A.R. No. 665 of 1904). The Vijayanagara kings organized festivals in the sacred groves, called *tiruttoppu,* to establish their reverence for the groves and the deity within.

According to an inscription which can be dated to 1521 CE, Kandadai Madhavayyangar gifted 80 lb of gold, the interest from which was to be spent for the god Ranganatha, when he halted at Madhavayyangar *tiruttoppu mandapa,* and on the fifth day of the Masi festival instituted in the name of Krishnadeva-Maharaya, when the god halts at the garden adjoining *pradhani* Timmarasar *toppu* (A.R. No. 42 of 1938).

An inscription belonging to the period of Maravarman Sundara Pandyan I (1229–1230 CE) refers to a gift of two pieces of land at Sikaranallur in Kunriyur *nādu,* as *tiruvettai tiruttoppu* to the temple of Tirunalakkunramudaiya Nayanār by Sankaran Kandan of Kulattur in *Malaimandalam* (hill region) after purchasing the same from some local residents, in order to provide a garden where the image of the god would be taken in procession and worshipped on festival occasions. It records a further gift made by the same donor Sankaran Kandan providing, by means of an agreement with the *nāttār,* for the supply of 10 *kalam* and 5 *kuruni* of paddy every year by the *nāttār* of Malai Nadu (probably by some investment with them), for the offering of

---

[73] N. Krishna, *Ecological Traditions of Tamil Nadu* (CPR Environmental Education Centre, 1997) 62–65.

Tiruppāvādai amudu to the deity after being taken in procession to the grove of the sacred hunt *(tiruvettaittoppu)* on the days of the festival in the months of Mārgali, Māsi and Paṅguni (A.R. 354 & 355 of 1906).

An inscription of the 6th year of Kopperum-singa-deva records the gift of a grove, called Alagiya pallavan *toppu*, in Urrukkuruchchi in Kudal *nādu*, by Alappirandan Alagiyasiyan Kopperum-singan of Kudal in Kil-Amur-*nādu*, for supplying arecanuts, flower garlands, etc., to the god at Tirumudukunram in Paruvur-kurram, a sub-division of Irungolappadi in Merka *nādu*, situated in Virudaraja-bhayankara *valanādu*. The village of Adanur may be identified with one of the two villages of the same name in Vriddhachalam taluk. Kudal, the native place of Kopperunjingadeva, is probably identical with Kudalur, that is, Cuddalore in South Arcot District. The garden of Alagiya pallavan *toppu* must have been named after the chief. Incidentally, Kopperunjinga II also bore this surname (A.R. No. 83 of 1918).

In several groves, certain species have grown dominant over others for various reasons. For example, Alexandrian laurel is highly dominant in the grove dedicated to Kili-āl-amman in Cuddalore district.[74] Poison nut tree (Tamil = *etti*) is the dominant species of the Velleripattu sacred grove in Viluppuram district.[75] Tamarind trees dominate in the Thennambakkam sacred grove (coastal grove) in Viluppuram district.[76] The Palm tree is the dominant species of the Santhikuppam sacred grove and Semmankuppam sacred grove in Cuddalore district.[77]

Although there are several species found in the sacred groves, only very few have a wide distribution. Sixteen species with the total count of 361 are found to be widely distributed in the sacred groves of Tamil Nadu. In general, the sacred groves in southern Tamil Nadu harbour many varieties of mango, jamun (*Eugenia jambolana*) and fig.[78] The Allinagaram grove in Theni district supports four wild varieties of

---

[74] K. V. Krishnamurthy, 'Nandavanas (sacred groves) in the Medieval South Indian Epigraphical Data', in *Sacred Groves of India—A Compendium*, eds. Nanditha Krishna and M. Amirthalingam (Chennai, 2015).

[75] M. P. Ramanujam and K. Praveen Kumar Cyril, 'Woody Species Diversity of Four Sacred Groves in the Pondicherry Region of South India', *Biodiversity and Conservation* 12 (2003): 289–299.

[76] P. Jayanthi, *Biodiversity of Aiyanar Sacred Grove at Vellarippattu, Villupuram District, Tamil Nadu* (M. Phil. dissertation, Chidambaram, 2008).

[77] V. Krishnan, *Plant Biodiversity and Biocultural Perspectives of Sacred Groves in Pondicherry and Its Environs* (Ph.D. thesis, Puducherry, 2004).

[78] N. Kavitha, *Conservation Values of Minor Sacred Groves in Cuddalore Area of Tamil Nadu, South India* (M.Phil. dissertation, University of Pondicherry, 2007).

mango. The *Terminalia arjuna* tree found in this sacred grove with a girth of about 10 m may be one of the oldest living trees.[79] Similarly, the Kandanur sacred grove in Sivagangai district supports a rare rattan species (*Calamus rotang*), which might otherwise have vanished from the local landscape. Sacred groves in Kanyakumari district support numerous rare endemic orchid species and harbour many of the rare endemic plants of the Western Ghats, such as *Antiaris toxicaria*, *Diospyros malabarica*, *Diospyros ebenum*, *Garcinia cambogia* and *Gnetum ula*.[80] A miniature sacred grove, measuring the size of a basketball court on the Passumari hill top, near Vedanthangal bird sanctuary in Chengalpattu district of Tamil Nadu, has 110 flowering plants in 40 families and is a refuge of rare species such as *Amorphophallus sylvaticus*, *Kedrosiis foetidissima*, a rare cucurbit, *Strychnos lenticellata* and the insectivorous plant, *Drosera burmannii*. A huge fig tree, about 200 years old, stands majestically in the centre. Below it, there are clumps of 1-m tall Amorphophallus plants, which flower in June–July and bear attractive red berries in August–September. The undisturbed atmosphere and the shade provided by these trees have provided an ideal ambience for their survival and proliferation.[81]

Flying foxes (*Pteropus giganteus* Brunnich), also known as the greater Indian fruit bat, play a significant role in forest ecosystems, especially the semi-orange fruit bats. They pollinate flowers, disperse seeds of trees, shrubs and climbers, all of which are a part of their functions in the ecosystem. Besides, bat droppings in caves support a delicate ecosystem composed of unusual organisms. These bats are believed to be protected by the deities associated with the sacred groves, also their roosting sites. Local people do not hunt or even allow anybody to hunt the bats, because they believe that if they disturb the bats, the deity will punish the hunters. During the celebrations of marriages and other festive occasions, local people never use loudspeakers or crackers near the grove where the bats are roosting, as the sounds may disturb the bats. There is a local belief that seeing a bat before setting out to work is a good omen and nothing is done to disturb the animal. The tree in which they roost, generally the banyan, is protected with

---

[79] P. S. Swamy, *Ecological and Sociological Relevance of Conservation of Sacred Groves in Tamil Nadu*. Report submitted to UNESCO, New Delhi, India, 1997.

[80] S. Sukumaran and A. D. S. Raj, 'Sacred Groves as a Symbol of Sustainable Environment—A Case Study', in *Sustainable Environment*, ed. N. Sukumaran (Tirunelveli: SPCES, M.S. University, 1999), 67–74.

[81] B. Maheswaran, P. Dayanandan, and D. Narasimhan, 'Miniature Sacred Grove Near Vedanthangal Bird Sanctuary', in *Traditional Science and Technology of India* (Madras: *Bio3*, December 26–31, 1995).

great care. Sacred groves protected for their bat populations, can be found in Cuddalore, Villupuram, Tanjore, Tiruchi, Pudukottai and Ramanathapuram districts.

The temple within the groves was a later development. Temple construction was encouraged by the Mauryan kings and intensified during the Gupta period. Thereafter, it spread very fast throughout the country. Brahmanical Hinduism spread vigorously in the Western Ghats from 400 CE and readily integrated primitive local cults; in turn, the locals were also attracted by the Hindu pantheon and adopted it,[82] especially as they came with a structured pantheon of gods and a distinct hierarchy. The deity passed through several evolutionary stages: from a stone fetish, suggesting a human or animal figure, to an unorganized clump of bricks/stones; a metal object, even a trident; a carved stone relief or a statue on the floor; till finally it became a figure in the round, on a platform and surrounded by an ornate temple. The mysterious eruption of a termite mound, with or without association with a tree, could be equated to Amman, the goddess. However, most groves have only one presiding deity: Ayyanār or Amman in Tamil Nadu; when it sheltered more, local deities, minions called Veeran, and occasionally gods such as Ganesha or Hanuman, were installed besides the presiding deity. An inevitable corollary of the importance given to temples and images was the gradual neglect of the vegetation; cult practices and cultural traditions gained precedence over conservation practices. The attitudes changed slowly shifting the primacy from plants to prayers, conservation to culture and groves to gods. And that started the nemesis of the sacred groves.[83]

There is a tradition of erecting a hero stone and worshipping it as a deity in the sacred grove, in memory of heroes who laid down their lives defending their territory, a man who died in a battle with a tiger or leopard or bear, or one who made some supreme sacrifice for the sake of the community or the region. Usually, these stones, now called *Veerakkal* or hero stones, show the figure of the hero, the battle, the king in whose time the battle took place and the person who erected the stone. Sometimes, the hero stone may be carved with inscriptions, giving details of the hero and the age, and sometimes no inscription or reference may be found. Either they stand alone or in groups and

---

[82] M. A. Kalam, *Sacred Groves in Kodagu District of Karnataka (South India): A Socio Historical Study* (Pondicherry: Institut Français de Pondichéry, 1996).

[83] M. D. S. Chandran and J. D. Hughes, 'The Sacred Groves of South India: Ecology, Traditional Communities and Religious Change', *Social Compass* 44 (1997): 413–427.

are usually found outside the village limits, near a tank or lake or in the groves.

Every grove has an elaborate *sthala purāna* or story to justify its status. The story of Kili-āl-amman at Periyakumatti village in Cuddalore district of Tamil Nadu is a good example of a small protected grove, a mere 3 acres in size. The main deity, Kili-āl-amman, is sheltered within a temple of brick and mortar. A perennial pond is situated in the forecourt of the temple. According to the local legend, a merchant was carrying a cartload of tamarind to be sold at Cuddalore. While the merchant was crossing the grove, he heard a call and looked around. He could not find anybody except a parrot sitting on a banyan tree. The merchant got scared, since the place was desolate, and drove his cart faster. After reaching the market, the merchant found charcoal instead of tamarind. He realized his mistake of not responding to the divine call. He returned to the grove and sought pardon for disregarding the anonymous call. Kili-āl-amman, the goddess of the grove, appeared before the merchant to console him. After that, the merchant visited the grove and worshipped the goddess regularly. Kili-āl-amman was satisfied with Periyakumatti's devotion and reconverted the cartload of charcoal into tamarind. The merchant was happy and, as a token of atonement, installed an idol of the goddess inside the grove and started worshipping the Goddess regularly. Since the Goddess was believed to have incarnated as a parrot on a banyan tree, she was named *kili* (parrot) + *āl* (banyan) + *amman* (Goddess)—Or 'Parrot Goddess of the Banyan'—and the grove is known as Kili-āl-amman *thoppu'* (Kiliālamman grove). In this grove, Kili-āl-amman is the main deity and Ayyanar the secondary deity. Terracotta horses line the pathway to the Ayyanar shrine. Images of Kili-āl-amman and terracotta horses, flowers, fruits and *pongal* are offered to Ayyanar on special occasions. After the harvest, the village people ritually offer paddy to make *pongal* and to perform *puja,* and ghee for lighting the temple lamp. Oil extracted from the *punnai* (Alexandrian laurel) seed is used to light the lamp. The people believe that Goddess Kili-āl-amman protects them from catastrophic events. Hunting and gathering of wood are strictly prohibited, but fallen twigs and wood may be used for temple purposes. The annual festival is celebrated in the month of *Ādi* (June–July) every year. There is a common belief that those who want progeny must offer *pongal* to the deity and tie a cradle on the Indian Cherry tree in the grove. The grove surrounding the temple is a conserved patch of tropical dry evergreen forest. Around 45 plant species belonging to 33 families are found in the grove. The grove is also populated by parakeets (*kili*), which live on the banyan tree. The birds are excellent seed dispersers and are essential for the local agronomy. The story of Kili-āl-amman protects the birds and the trees of the grove and grants them immunity from timber extraction and hunting.[84]

Conclusion

It is apparent that ancient Indians saw in spirituality a method to protect their forests and biodiversity, especially those plants and animals essential for their lives and existence. The fruit bats, parrots of Kili-āl-amman and thousands of plants and animals of the groves were held sacred in the *tapovanas*, especially as rulers and their insatiable appetites for timber and other forest produce, as well as their predilection for hunting, made unmanageable demands on the forest. The taboos against harming the groves would have frightened the kings, who were both religious and superstitious. To ensure the survival of important species and their forests, local people invoked the Gods, especially the Earth Goddess or Bhūmī Devī of the Atharva Veda, who is the reigning deity in most groves all over India. Sacred groves also provide a window into the concerns of rural and tribal communities, the plant and animal species they protected and the elaborate mythologies they created to ensure that protection. Their existence is very important for the study of India's environmental and forest history, for they indicate the species of plants and animals that local people believed were important, and the methods used to preserve them. The deities of the groves also reflect the ecological concerns of local people. The conservation was carried out in spite of the many threats of deforestation in the colonial period and in post-independence India. In many places, the sacred groves are the last remnants of local biodiversity. This was a method used by tribal and rural communities all over India to protect their forests. As a result, today we are able to have a glimpse of what the great forests—the *mahāvana*—of ancient India were like, and their biological diversity.

---

[84] See http://www.heritageonline.in/the-sacred-grove-of-kili-aal-amman/

6

Plant Domestication and Evolution of Agriculture in India*

Anantanarayanan Raman

Introduction

Between 10,000 and 15,000 years ago, humans in different parts of the world made varied efforts to domesticate plants that were perceived useful by them in some measure. Considering the timescale of human evolution spread over 2.5–3 million years, domestication of plants leading to organized agriculture occurring especially in the last 6,000–10,000 years was remarkably rapid. In compliance with this general

* With fondness and gratitude I dedicate this chapter to my teachers at the Madras Presidency College: Bangalore Gundappa Lakshminarayana Swamy and Kulithalai Viswanathan Krishnamurthy. They inspired me by their brilliance and invigorating teaching practice.

I am thankful to Anupama Krishnamurthy and Srinivasan Prasad (Ecology), and Venkatesan Prakash (Indology—Tamil Studies) of l'Institut Français de Pondichéry, Pondicherry, for their constructive criticisms on the pre-final text of this chapter. Anamika Sharma (Charles Sturt University, Orange, NSW, Australia) generously spared time to prepare the illustrations meeting my requirements. I thank her for the help.

pattern of evolution all over the world, Indians too resorted to farming by nurturing specific plants, mainly as items of food. Between 8000 and 7000 BCE, digging poles and tools, somewhat similar to modern pickaxe, were used in India indicating that some form of organized agriculture had occurred.[1] In the later millennia, say, between 4000 and 3000 BCE, we have evidence to recognize that the 'Tamils', who have a documented history of 2,000 years,[2] used a spear-like tool to scar the land and thus 'prepare' it for growing plants. Indians knew of the spear-like tool for use both as a weapon and one useful in digging. They used it for thousands of years.[3] Spear in Tamil is *vel* and the people who used the *vel* to scar the soil came to be known as *vel-āṭar*, who, over time, came to be known as *veḷḷālar*.[4] However, Satyendranath Sen (1999)[5] indicates that *veḷḷalar* are the people who indulged in farming but managed their enterprises by regulating and using riverine waters via irrigation, since *veḷḷam* in classical Tamil and its sister language Malayalam means water. An elegant commentary on the use of stone tools during the Neolithic, not only in agriculture but also in other aspects of early life of southern Indians, is available.[6]

One major human intervention of Nature was establishment of settlements, which involved the disturbance of soil and associated vegetation. Humans cleared vegetation to build residences, which included pits principally used for storing and cooking. As long as humans remained hunter–gatherers, the disturbance was minimal, given the vastness of time. Once they moved to other localities establishing newer settlements, the previously occupied sites regenerated back to near natural, original state. Such a recovery never eventuated—and could never happen—when humans settled permanently. Clearing vegetation for building residences had its own other forms of consequences: the cleared sites encouraged aggressive plants to colonize and occupy

---

[1] H. Fischer, 'The Stone Implements of India', *Proceedings of the American Antiquarian Society*, 4, (1884–1887): 178–204.

[2] K. S. R. Sastri, *The Tamils: The People, Their History and Culture, Vol. 1: An Introduction to Tamil History and Society* (New Delhi: Cosmo Publications, 2002).

[3] D. F. Draeger and R. W. Smith, *Comprehensive Asian Fighting Arts* (Tokyo: Kodansha International, 1980).

[4] K. V. Krishnamurthy, *Tamizharum Thavaramum* (in Tamil) (Tiruchirappalli: Bharathidasan University, 2007), 184.

[5] S. N. Sen, *Ancient Indian History and Civilization* (New Delhi: New-Age International, 1999), 205–207.

[6] A. R. Brumm, N. Boivin, and R. L. Fullagar, 'Signs of Life: Engraved Stone Artefacts from Neolithic South India', *Cambridge Archaeological Journal* 16 (2006): 165–190.

vacant spaces. Colonization by such plants could have been due to either deliberate introductions or natural migrations. When human populations moved from one place to another, they carried seeds of certain plants either deliberately or inadvertently and 'introduced' them into newer environments. One recent-time example would be the deliberate introduction of mango plants (*Mangifera indica*, Anacardiaceae) by humans into a new biogeographical locality, namely West Africa in 1824 from where this plant spread to other tropical regions of the world.[7] Rivers are one other critical source that distributed seeds and vegetative material enabling them to propagate in new environments. Thus, various reasons explain colonization of cleared areas by plants that do not usually occur in (or belong to) a particular region. The best examples for the natural colonization of the plant material into the Indian landmass are the plant species that were domesticated by early Holocene 'farmers' of the Fertile Crescent nearly 12,000 years ago. Those introduced plants, later, in 9,000–10,000 years ago, stimulated the beginnings of systematic agriculture in southern Asia.[8]

The two early plant elements that Indians domesticated for cultivation were flax (*Linum usitatissimum*, Linaceae, Figure 6.1) and hemp (*Cannabis sativa*, Cannabaceae, Figure 6.2) that were introduced into India from the Zagros of modern Iran. Indians seem to have used these plant materials intensely as sources of fibre and oil[9] in addition to using hemp as a narcotic.[10] The Indus Valley farmers domesticated pea (*Pisum sativum*, Fabaceae), sesame (*Sesamum indicum*, Pedaliaceae, Figure 6.3) and the date (*Phoenix dactylifera*, Arecaceae, Figure 6.4).[11] Although remnants of domesticated rye (*Secale cereale*, Poaceae) occur in the final Epi-Palaeolithic strata in Tell Abu Hureyra site of the Euphrates Valley (modern Syria), this grass was an insignificant element

---

[7] J. Y. Rey et al., 'The Mango in French-speaking West Africa', *Fruits* 61 (2004): 121–129.

[8] S. Singh et al., 'Dissecting the Influence of Neolithic Demic Diffusion on Indian γ-chromosome Pool Through J2–M172 Haplogroup', *Scientific Reports* 6 (2016): 19157, doi: 10.1038/srep19157.

[9] R. C. Clarke and M. D. Merlin, *Cannabis: Evolution and Ethnobotany* (Berkeley, CA: The University of California Press, 2013).

[10] W. A. Emboden Jr., 'Ritual Use of *Cannabis sativa* L.: A Historical Ethnographic Survey', in *Flesh of Gods: The Ritual Use of Hallucinogens,* ed. P. T. Furst (Springfield, IL: Praeger, 1972), 214–236.

[11] R. E. Krebs and C. A. Krebs, *Groundbreaking Scientific Experiments, Inventions, and Discoveries of the Ancient World* (Westport, CT: Greenwood Publishing Company, 2003).

FIGURE 6.1 *Linum usitatissimum*

Source: J. E. Sowerby et al., *English Botany, or Coloured Figures of British Plants.* Published by J E Sowerby (Author) in London, Vol. 2: fig. 292, 1864.

in India during the Neolithic Period and turned common in India only after the spread of agriculture in Northern Europe, several centuries later.[12] Whereas we know so much about the Fertile Crescent, where domestication began about 12,000 years ago, our knowledge of domestication and agriculture in Asia at the same time is relatively less known, although multiple evidences point to domestication

---

[12] E. Weiss and D. Zohary, 'The Neolithic Southwest Asian Founder Crops: Their Biology and Archaeobotany', *Current Anthropology* 52 (2011): S237–S254.

FIGURE 6.2   *Cannabis sativa*

Source: F. E. Köhler, *Medizinal Pflanzen*, Verlag von F. E. Köhler, Gera-Unternhaus, Germany Vol. 1: figure 13, 1887.

of root vegetables and their cultivation in these regions.[13] One early domestication in the Far East, South, and Southeast Asia involved yams (species of *Amorphophallus*, Araceae) that grew naturally in these regions.[14] The elephant yam (*Amorphophallus paeoniifolius*, Figure 6.5)

---

[13] B. D. Smith, *The Emergence of Agriculture* (New York, NY: Scientific American Library, distributed by W. H. Freeman, 1998).

[14] F. J. Simoons, *Food in China: A Cultural and Historical Inquiry* (Boca Raton, FL: CRC Press, 1991).

FIGURE 6.3 *Sesamum indicum*

Source: *Curtis's Botanical Magazine*, Vol. 41, 1814–1815.

FIGURE 6.4 *Phoenix dactylifera*

Source: Jean Theodore de Bry, *Indiae Orientalis*, Vol. 4, figure 82, 1601. Francofurti (Frankfurt): Typis Wolfgangi Richteri.
Note: The illustration also shows *Mangifera indica, Piper betle* and *Ananas.*

and voodoo lily (*Amorphophallus rivieri*, Figure 6.6) were the two yams that were intensely domesticated in the landscapes that form India, China, Malaysia and Indonesia today, mainly for their massive tuberous underground stems (corms) for use as food primarily, and as medicine in later years.[15]

---

[15] G. Watt, *A Dictionary of Economic Products of India*, Vol. 1 (Calcutta: Superintendent of Government Printing, 1885).

FIGURE 6.5 *Amorphophallus paeoniifolius (A. campanulatus) from Ceylon (Sri Lanka)*

Source: J. Commelin, P. & J. Blaeu and Abrahamum at Someren, Amsterdam, Vol. 1, figure 52, 1697.

While talking about early forms of plant domestication and intensified cultivation, Nikolai Vavilov of Moscow and Robert Braidwood of Chicago are two names that need to be remembered with gratitude. Vavilov was a pioneer plant explorer, who sought food plants in particular. He collected seeds, tubers and fruits from more than 60 countries from 1916 to the early 1940s. He was one of the few biologists who listened to practising farmers; he understood why they sought seed varieties. He was convinced that the variety refers to 'gene pool'. Vavilov (1992)[16] proposed that where a plant was first domesticated,

---

[16] N. I. Vavilov, *Origin and Geography of Cultivated Plants*, trans. Doris Löve (Cambridge: Cambridge University Press, 1992).

FIGURE 6.6 *Amorphophallus rivieri (Amorphaphallus konjac, Proteinophallus Riveri)*

Source: W. H. Fitch, *Curtis's Botanical Magazine*, vol. 101, figure 6196, 1875.

that would be the location where the greatest diversity of that plant would also occur. This has been unestablished, since today we know a plant can originate in one location and can diversify strongly in another location. Another problem with Vavilovian concept is the mechanism he proposed to determine the wild ancestor of a domesticated plant. Nevertheless, Vavilov's pioneering studies and his proposal indicate that with a cautious pairing of molecular tools to determine the genetic ancestor of a domesticated plant and the physical map of the distribution of domesticated plants will lead us positively to understanding domestication and agriculture. The other key pathway to understand domestication of plants is to follow Robert Braidwood.

Braidwood indicated that archaeological excavations of the supposed early farming settlements is the only viable means of directly understanding the economic and cultural contexts of plant domestication and their transition to agriculture. An answer to the question why and how certain human societies initiated new relationships with specific wild plant species could be sought, Braidwood argued, following an archaeological approach, which he has illustrated enchantingly in his monograph.[17] Vavilov's and Braidwood's divergent propositions on plant domestication in relation to their wild relatives stand as two major paradigms today.

Technological innovations in the later decades of the 20th century paved the way for serious and definitive determinations in this direction. Precise dating techniques using radioactive isotopes, sophisticated excavation methods and superior optical instruments have enabled progress of research in this context by leaps and bounds from the 1960s.

Dorian Fuller, a British palaeoanthropologist, remarks (2011)[18]:

In the past few years there have been arguments in favor of independent agricultural origins in India. This has arisen in part from increased attention to identifying the wild progenitors for many crops that are poorly known in the mainstream Western agricultural literature and that are underdocumented relative to crops from the near East, West Africa, or the Americas. It is only the past few years that Southern Neolithic sites have joined the growing body of archaeobotanical evidence from South Asia. The Middle Ganges Plain has also seen rapid growth in new archaeobotanical information.

Fuller's remark has a basis. It builds on the argument whether farming as a practice evolved from exploiting the introduced plants—either natural migration and colonization or deliberate human introduction. Alternatively, the same can occur by domesticating the locally occurring native plants. Vavilovian theory emphasizing on epicentres of plant origins has enabled investigations on specific plants and specific landscapes. Fuller (2011)[19] attributes that such an approach has created

---

[17] L. Braidwood et al., *Prehistoric Archaeology Along the Zagros Flanks* (# 105) (Chicago, IL: The Oriental Institute of the University of Chicago, 1983).

[18] D. Q. Fuller, 'Finding Plant Domestication in the Indian Subcontinent', *Current Anthropology* 52 (2011): S347–S362.

[19] Ibid.

gaps in explaining the evolution of Indian agriculture. Nevertheless, Fuller (2011)[20] further says:

> The past 25 years have seen the steady increase in archaeobotanical evidence in South Asia, especially by floatation[21], which now accounts for more than half of the reported evidence. Of particular note is the recent addition of a rich database from Southern India.

In such a complex, intricately intertwined biological and anthropological scenario—complexity being driven essentially by poor understanding—we need to tread cautiously in making sense of what we know based on the dependable set of fragmentary evidences we have. Against that caveat, I progress here to consolidate the bio-historical information in the wake of modern understanding aiming to provide as wholesome a picture as possible.

Prehistoric Times

During the Lower Palaeolithic period (the Early Stone Age, 2.7 million–200,000 years ago), the early Indian inhabitants used crude tools, not knowing how to make pottery and to light fire. They are indicated to have lived on animal meat and wild vegetables. During the Mesolithic Age (18,000–12,000 years ago), the Indian humans were essentially hunters and survived feeding on herbivorous animals. The Indian humans must have known of the dog (*Canis*, Canidae), and it was an integral part of their lives (domesticated?), since two nearly intact skeletal remains of the dog have been found in western India, occurring

---

[20] Ibid., 347.

[21] Floatation technique in archaeology involves the use of water to soil and other kinds of filling materials to recover tiny objects of interest. In this technique, we bubble water gently through the dry soil on a mesh screen. Seeds, charcoal and other lighter material (the 'light' fraction) float, whereas relatively heavy stony materials (the microliths), bone fragments and similar sort (the heavy fraction) are left behind (S. Streuver, 'Flotation Techniques for the Recovery of Small-scale Archaeological Remains', *American Antiquity* 33 (1968): 353–362.). Stuart Streuver developed this method working in the Illinois Valley based on a prompt by Hugh Carson Cutler, a botanist with the Missouri Botanical Gardens, in the early 1960s. The floatation technique has today grown substantially with various quantitative embellishments and is used as a reliable, cost-effective tactic in interpreting plant distributions and nativity to specific landscapes (K. J. Gremillion, 'Palaeoethnobotany', in *The Development of Southeastern Archaeology*, ed. J. K. Johnson (Tuscaloosa, AL: The University of Alabama Press, 1993), 132–159.).

proximally to human remains.[22] Only from the Neolithic Age, fragmentary evidences are available suggesting that the Indian humans knew of 'growing' plants for food, domesticate animals, sewed skins using bone 'needles', made pottery and generated fire exploiting friction.[23] Domestication of grasses (Poaceae) played a critical role in human evolution because most of the cereals we use are grasses. Of the modern cereals, maize (*Zea mays*, Poaceae), rice (*Oryza sativa*, Poaceae) and wheat (*Triticum*, Poaceae) were domesticated in different regions of the world between 7,000 and 10,000 years ago.[24] Barley (*Hordeum vulgare*, Poaceae), the fourth maximally used cereal by humans in various contexts, is one other early domesticated cereal. Sorghum (e.g., *Sorghum bicolor*, Poaceae) ranks next, followed by oats (*Avena sativa*, Poaceae), rye (*S. cereale*, Poaceae) and a few other millets.[25]

The remains of barley (*H. vulgare*) grains found in the Fertile Crescent indicate that about 10,000 years ago this was domesticated from its wild relative *Hordeum spontaneum*. In the barley landraces of the Himalaya, an allele of the homeobox gene (BKn-3) occurs indicating that an allelic substitution had taken place during the migration of barley from the Near East to South Asia (India), reinforcing that in the Himalaya, early diversification of domesticated barley occurred.[26] However, this proposal is challenged by Sang[27], who indicates, using molecular investigations, that barley cultivation sequel to domestication developed in India independently, based on the evidence that the gene essential for 'domestication' occurs only in *H. spontaneum*, the wild barley, which occurs naturally and widely distributed across from North Africa to the Himalaya. DNA studies of rice (*O. sativa*) show that rice cultivation evolved in Gangetic plains in India and in Southern China.[28] However,

---

[22] H. D. Sankalia, 'Paleolithic, Neolithic and Copper Ages', in *The History and Culture of the Indian People: The Vedic Age*, eds. R. C. Majumdar and A. D. Pusalkar (Mumbai: Bharatiya Vidya Bhavan, 1951), 134–168.

[23] F. E. Zeuner, 'Cultivation of Plants', in *A History of Technology*, eds. C. Singer, E. J. Holmyard and A. R. Hall (Oxford: Oxford University Press, 1954), 353–375.

[24] T. Sang, 'Genes and Mutations Underlying Domestication Transitions in Grasses', *Plant Physiology* 149 (2009): 63–70.

[25] FAOSTAT, 2014, http://faostat.fao.org/, accessed 27 July 2016.

[26] A. Badr et al., 'On the Origin and Domestication History of Barley (*Hordeum vulgare*)', *Molecular Biology and Evolution* 17 (2000): 499–510.

[27] Sang, 'Genes and Mutations'.

[28] P. Priyadarshi, *Recent Studies in Indian Archaeo-linguistics and Archaeogenetics Having Bearing on Indian Prehistory* (2010). http://demo.bsmbharat.org/Encyc/2015/2/17/334_02_15_41_Origin-of-Indo-European-languages-and-farming-Evidence-from-Human-Animal-and-plant-DNAs-and-from-linguistics_(1).pdf, accessed 28 July 2016.

Priyadarshi (2010)[29] contends that the Chinese rice race includes multiple wild features, which suggest that domestication of rice and its cultivation occurred in India earlier than China.

To recap, the global origin of domestication involved certain unplanned, unchartered, undesigned consequences of changes in plants and animals. Those consequences in turn modified human behaviour as well. Differences among the domesticated plants and their wild ancestors evolved as consequences in plants being 'selected', 'gathered' and 'used' primarily for their taste and satiation of hunger,[30] sometime in the interface period between the Pliocene and Holocene.

Humans 'chose' and 'moved' certain grasses from the wild, thus paving the way for agriculture.[31] Jared Diamond (2002)[32] remarks:

> the emerging agricultural lifestyle had to compete with the established hunter–gatherer lifestyle. Once domestication began to arise, the changes of plants and animals that followed automatically under domestication, and the competitive advantages that domestication conveyed upon the first farmers (despite their small stature and poor health), made the transition from the hunter—gatherer lifestyle to food production autocatalytic—but the speed of that transition varied considerably among regions.

He[33] concludes his commentary with the question, why did food production eventually outdo the hunter–gatherer lifestyle almost over the whole world, at particular times and places that it did, but not at earlier times and other places? This question remains valid, but unanswered, although we have several fragmentary evidences about the domestication of plants and early signs of organized farming. Another critical, but puzzling question is that how did the early humans move over enormous distances along with the natural materials, which they may have thought of being relevant and useful. Barker (2006)[34] illustrates this that the Indus Valley farmers acquired some of the millets and pulses they farmed from Oman (1,250 km), Mesopotamia (2,500 km),

---

[29] Ibid.

[30] D. Rindos, *The Origins of Agriculture: An Evolutionary Perspective* (San Diego, CA: Academic Press, 1984).

[31] Smith, *Emergence of Agriculture*.

[32] J. Diamond, 'Evolution, Consequences and Future of Plant and Animal Domestication', *Nature* 418 (2002): 700–707.

[33] Ibid.

[34] G. Barker, *The Agricultural Revolution in Prehistory: Why did Foragers Become Farmers?* (New York, NY: Oxford University Press, 2006).

East Africa (3,000 km) and central and southern India (1,000 km). The distance indicated here between two points is simply staggering given that most of the movements were by foot.

Plant Domestication Efforts: Illustrative Examples

Evidences of hominin (*Homo erectus*) existence in India in general and southern India in particular occur from 1.2 million years ago, whereas those of the Early Palaeolithic, especially of southern India, are more abundant.[35] Attirampakkam site (13°13'N, 79°53'E, Tamil Nadu) includes abundant examples of stone tools, indicating that the hominins in this region were adapting to their immediate environment.[36] Kathleen Morrison (2006)[37] considers that the development of agriculture in South Asia was a mosaic with several centres of domestication arising at different times influenced by local factors; agriculture coexisted with pastoralism. She further contends that permanent cultivation did not arise until about 3000 BCE. Based on evidences gathered from various Neolithic sites from modern Karnataka, Andhra Pradesh and Tamil Nadu, she indicates that the southern Neolithic Indians developed a complex agro-pastoral economy, which consisted of both large permanent settlements and extensive mobility. In this process, they domesticated several local plants. They selected and accepted several plants that they found one or more uses in them in one manner or another; they also selected those plants which they considered had a potential use. Morrison thinks that the southern agricultural tradition was not seriously modified until 1000–500 BCE (the Iron Age), when new plants were added, keeping food production in focus. In the following section, for reasons of brevity, I will refer to the origin(s) of the rice plant (*O. sativa*, Poaceae), banana (*Musa x paradisiaca*, Musaceae), coconut palm (*Cocos nucifera*, Arecaceae), sugarcane (*Saccharum* spp., Poaceae), mango tree (*M. indica*, Anacardiaceae) and cotton plant (*Gossypium* spp., Malvaceae) and their domestication as chosen examples. I have chosen these because of their extremely high human relevance. In the

---

[35] B. A. B. Blackwell et al., 'ESR Dating of an Acheulean Quarry Sites at Ismapur, India', *Journal of Human Evolution* 40 (2001): A3.

[36] S. Pappu, 'Changing Trends in the Study of a Palaeolithic Site in India: A Century of Research at Attirampakkam', in *The Evolution and History of Human Populations in South Asia*, eds. M. D. Petraglia and B. Allchin (Dordrecht: Springer, 2007), 121–135.

[37] K. D. Morrison, 'Historicizing Foraging in Asia: Power, History, and Ecology of Holocene Hunting and Gathering', in *An Archaeology of Asia*, ed. M. Stark (New York, NY: Wiley, 2006), 279–302.

following paragraphs, I will illustrate how these were domesticated and utilized in India in general and in southern India in particular. I fully recognize that the chosen examples are only illustrative, and they cannot be absolute examples by any stretch of imagination.

Rice (Oryza sativa, Poaceae)

Oryza sativa (Figure 6.7) was domesticated from the wild grass *Oryza rufipogon* 10,000–14,000 years ago. The two main subspecies of rice—*indica* (prevalent in the tropics of South and Southeast Asia) and *japonica* (prevalent in the subtropics and temperate regions of East Asia)—are not indicated to have been derived via independent domestication events. Another cultivated species, *Oryza glaberrima*, was domesticated

FIGURE 6.7 *Oryza sativa*

Source: Arthur Herbert Church, *Food-grains of India* (Committee of Council on Education, Oxford University, 1886).

later in West Africa. Recent genetic evidence shows that both *indica* and *japonica* came from a single domestication event that occurred 8,000–13,000 years ago in the Pearl River Valley of China. Movement of *O. sativa indica* southwards to Sri Lanka and to the west of India too occurred very early in time. Rice was a definite food crop in Sri Lanka as early as 1000 BCE. The crop may well have been introduced to Greece and the neighbouring areas of the Mediterranean by the returning members of Alexander the Great's army after visiting India in 4th century BCE. From Greece, rice spread gradually through Southern Europe and to a few locations in northern Africa. First used in English language in the mid-13th century, the term 'rice' derives from the Latin term *oriza*, which arises from the Greek term ὄρυζα (*oruza*). That the biological name *Oryza* arises from ὄρυζα is noteworthy. The origin of the Greek word is unclear. It is sometimes suggested to be arising from the Tamil term *arisi* (*ariçi*).[38] However, Krishnamurthy[39] disputes this explanation: *ariçi* being the root term for ὄρυζα. Krishnamurthy[40] indicates that *Oryza* has descended from the Proto-Dravidian *wariñçi* instead. A fascinating narration on the biological origin of *Oryza* (*Historia Oryzae Naturalis*) occurs in Philippo Tidyman's[41] 24-page dissertation entitled *Commentatio Inauguralis de O. sativa* dated 1800 CE, following a neat description of rice plant (*Descriptio Botanica Oryzae sativae*).

The rice is, in high possibility, the oldest domesticated plant in Southeast Asia.[42] Both in India and in China 5,000–6,500 varieties of rice have been cultivated over a long time; therefore, this plant should have originated in this segment of the world. Cultivation of rice in southern India should have been well developed and perfected at least 5,000 years ago.[43] Ghosh[44] tabulates the evidences collected from various parts of southern India with regard to rice cultivation (Table 6.1). Recent time excavations made at *Pôrunthal* (Tamil Nadu) need to be mentioned here

---

[38] J. Thorley, 'The Development of Trade Between the Roman Empire and the East Under Augustus', *Greece and Rome* 16 (1969): 209–223.

[39] Krishnamurthy, *Tamizharum Thavaramum*.

[40] Ibid.

[41] P. Tidyman, *Commentatio Inauguralis de Oryza sativa* (Göttingen: Dieterich'schen Verlagsbuchhandlung, 1800).

[42] B. G. L. Swamy, 'Sources for a History of Plant Sciences in India: I. Epigraphy', *Indian Journal of History of Science* 8 (1973): 61–98.

[43] G. Watt, *A Dictionary of Economic Products of India*, Vol. 5 (Calcutta: Superintendent of Government Printing, 1891–1892).

[44] S. S. Ghosh, 'Further Records of Rice (*Oryza* spp.) from Ancient India', *Indian Forester* 87 (1961): 295–301.

TABLE 6.1	Archaeological Evidences Rice in Southern India
Locality	**Approximate Time Frame**
Ādichanallur, Tamil Nadu	2000 BCE–200 CE
Kunrathur, Tamil Nadu	300 BCE
Periapuram, Kerala	100 CE–400 CE

Source: Modified from Ghosh (1961).

as it was the first time that a pot full of husk was recovered and physically dated using the radiocarbon decay technique as 410–520 BCE.[45] The long-grain *mahasāli* variety (today known as the Patna rice) is indicated to have been cultivated extensively in the Magadha kingdom in the 6th century BCE. In high likelihood, this variety entered southern India by the 13th century, since *Pôrunar-ātruppadai* (Tamil Poetry, 3rd century CE) includes references to '*sāli nél*' (= sāli rice) that were cultivated on the banks of Kaveri.

Southern India inscriptions of 9th and 12th centuries reinforce that rice yields were high even by elementary comparisons with modern yield statistics.[46] Epigraphical evidences of the later Çolā period (13th century) refer to the extended cultivation of *kār* rice variety in Tamil land.[47] *Paḻu* literature in Tamil language (13th–16th centuries) lists more than 150 varieties of rice, with specific names given to each of them based on their unique morphological features (Figure 6.8).[48] During this time, rice farmers grew two crops in a year: *sambā* variety in a single cultivation and *kuruvai* in another. Princep's report to the Government of Madras (1885)[49] and John Völcker's report on the improvement of Indian agriculture (1893)[50] are useful records of rice agriculture in the Madras Presidency 150–175 years ago.

---

[45] K. Rajan, *Early Writing System: A Journey from Graffiti to Brahmi* (Madurai, 2015a); 'Kodumanal: An Early Historic Site in South India', *Man and Environment* 40 (2015): 65–79.

[46] M. L. Smith, 'The Archaeology of Food Preference', *American Anthropologist* 108 (2006): 480–493.

[47] Swamy, 'Sources for a History of Plant'.

[48] A. Raman, 'Ecological Management of Rice Agriculture in Southern India', *International Journal of Ecology and Environmental Sciences* 39 (2013): 37–49.

[49] C. C. Princep, *Record of Services of the Honourable East India Company's Civil Servants in the Madras Presidency from 1741 to 1858* (London: Truebner & Company, 1885).

[50] J. A. Völcker, *Report on the Improvement of Indian Agriculture* (London: Eyre and Spottiswoode, 1893).

FIGURE 6.8 *Rediscovered Traditional Varieties of* Oryza sativa indica *of Southern India*

Courtesy: A. V. Balasubramanian, Centre for Indian Knowledge Systems, Madras.
(A) *Kouni nel* (grains nutritious to pregnant women and lactating mothers).
(B) *Māppilai sambā* (grains nutritious to prospective grooms).
(C) *Tanga sambā* (grains fine and long, appearing like gold).
(D) *Tuyamalli* (grain clusters resemble jasmine flower clusters; when cooked generate a pleasant flavour).

Banana (Musa x paradisiaca, Musaceae)

India includes hundreds of varieties of banana. For a reasonable explanation on most extensively used varieties of Indian bananas, see http://agropedia.iitk.ac.in/content/banana-varieties-its-characteristics. However, banana farming, today, supports only 12 'selected' indigenous and 30 exotic varieties. The origins of the banana are complex and convoluted. Kuk valley of New Guinea is the widely suspected location where the humans must have first domesticated banana. From New Guinea, the domesticated variety appears to have spread to the Philippines and then radiated widely across the tropics. Tracing the diffusion of banana after its arrival in the Philippines has been extremely difficult, and in many instances, it appears that the banana was introduced into newer areas only to be rediscovered, hundreds of years later. Adding to the confusing tangle of banana proliferation is the parallel development of hybrid fruits. Human ingenuity manipulated the seedless and thus asexual forms of domesticated bananas into hybrids by cautious culling and planting that fused and refined different domesticated varieties. Thus, the origins of the banana have been difficult to pinpoint. In general, however, it can be said that bananas originated in the Southeast Asia–South Pacific biogeographical realm between 8000 and 5000 BCE. Foreign invaders of India were fascinated by the banana: it is said that Alexander the Great tasted the bananas and captivated by them he sent bananas to Greece with his returning troops.[51]

From New Guinea and the Philippines, the bananas (Figure 6.9) dispersed into India, Indonesia, Australia and Malaysia, within the first two millennia after domestication. Banana production and consumption in the ancient and early modern world was mostly geared towards small-scale operations. Although individual 'fingers', 'hands' and 'bunches' were more than likely available for sale through commercial exchanges, most banana production occurred as a small-scale operation for local consumption. Banana's importance as a staple crop would have been well established, and its major use was likely either as the main starch consumed or, given its non-seasonal nature, as an important buffer crop between other staple harvests.

The parents of the cultivated varieties are *Musa acuminata* and *Musa balbisiana*, two wild progenitors, which are usually seedy. *Musa acuminata* evolved primarily in tropical rainforests in Southeast Asia, whereas *M. balbisiana* originated in monsoon areas in northern Southeast Asia, and Southern Asia. Thus, pure *M. acuminata* varieties developed first in Southeast Asia, and its hybrids with *M. balbisiana* arose where distributions of the two species overlapped. Because the binomial Latin nomenclature for edible varieties, for example, *Musa cavendishii* (cv.) Williams, proved unsatisfactory, the varieties are presently referred to as, for example, *Musa* spp. (AAA Group, Cavendish Subgroup) cv. Williams. Out of the approximately 500 varieties of bananas (including starchy, non-sweet plantains), about 150 of these are primary clones, while the rest are somatic mutants. Banana cultivars are complex diploid, triploid and tetraploid hybrids among *M. acuminata* and *M. balbisiana*. In general, those with a high proportion of *M. acuminata* produce sweet fruit, whereas those with a high

---

[51] S. Garson and M. Antonisse *Veggiana: The Dharma of Cooking with 108 Deliciously Easy Vegetarian Recipes* (Boston, MA: Wisdom Publications, 2011).

FIGURE 6.9 *Musa*

Source: Unknown artist, 1751.

proportion of *M. balbisiana* produce starchy fruit. Conventionally, the relative contribution of *M. acuminata* and *M. balbisiana* to the cultivar is indicated with As and Bs, respectively. They are further classified as to the presence of one or more sets of chromosomes (the ploidy level). For example, an AB is diploid, an AAB, triploid and ABBB, tetraploid. Most familiar, seedless, cultivated varieties (cultivars) of banana are triploid hybrids (AAA, AAB, ABB). Diploids (AA, AB, BB) and tetraploids (AAAA, AAAB, AABB, ABBB) are rare.

Both non-sweet and sweet varieties of banana occur commonly in the South Asian landscapes. Large-scale production of bananas occurs in Peninsular India, eastern India, Gujarat and in Sind (Pakistan). The varieties *Rastāli, Poovan, Nei Poovan, Sev-vāzhai* (the red banana), *Môntan, Karpuravalli, Virupakśi, Udayan, Sarkara-kéli* and *Pachanādan* are a few examples that are selectively grown in southern India. Among the southern-Indian banana varieties, the shortest fruit variety *Kadali* and the longest and largest fruit variety *Nendran* are unique to Kerala. In recent times (say the 1960s), one unique south-Indian variety *Malai-vazhai* was nearly completely lost to the then epidemic of bunchy-top virus. *Sirumalai-vazhai*, a variant of the *Malai-vazhai* banana, is cultivated in small measures in the Sirumalai Hills in Dindigul District (10°45′N, 77°52′E), and the delicious fruits of these varieties will hardly be 8 cm long and 1.5 cm thick, with characteristic triangular outline in cross-sectional views, and with a relatively thick, leathery skin, which grows dark-black spots on the yellow skin with ageing.

Pure germplasms of *M. balbisiana* are maintained, protected and cultivated in southern India, where the leaves are used as eating plates. Wild Musaceae have a patchy distribution in South Asia. They are restricted to a few vegetation zones that are endowed with adequate water and locally suitable microhabitats. First, it must be noted that there are few wild species, of which *Ensete superbum* is a key taxon that occurs almost throughout India. In Peninsular India, *E. superbum* occurs throughout the hills of the Western Ghats in evergreen and moist deciduous forests, usually growing on steep slopes and rocky cliffs. *E. superbum* has apparent relict distributions through some of the central Indian hill ranges up to the southern sides of the Narmada valley. *E. superbum* is claimed to be edible; its inflorescence is used as a vegetable and its young fruits are pickled. In Sri Lanka, *M. acuminata* occurs is found. Wild *E. superbum* are restricted to the west-facing Western Ghats, where rainfall is high, and they are not reported from the eastern side in central Tamil Nadu or in the wetter hill ranges of the Andhra Pradesh. In western India, the Himalaya and Gangetic plains, no wild Musaceae is found.[52]

The East-Asian *Musa* includes 20 chromosomes. Most edible bananas belong to the *Eumusa* section and are diploid or triploid hybrids from *M. acuminata* alone or through hybridization with *M. balbisiana*. The evolution from wild, non-edible to edible bananas involved seed suppression and parthenocarpic development. The earliest domestication of banana is claimed to have occurred in Papua

---

[52] D. Q. Fuller and M. Madella, 'Banana Cultivation in South Asia and East Asia: A Review of the Evidence from Archaeology and Linguistics', *Ethnobotany Research & Applications* 7 (2009): 333–351.

New Guinea (8000 BCE). Kurian (n.d.)[53] comments that spontaneous evolution of domesticated banana occurred in the Eastern segments of the Himalaya, the Eastern Ghats and Western Ghats along with other regions of Southeast Asia. He further comments that the natural evolution of domesticated *Musa* occurred due to mutation and parthenocarpic development. *M. balbisiana* var. *elavazhai* of southern India is one example of an early domesticated species. Wild banana is one of these distributed in the Malayan bioregion. Certain *Musa* species, the progenitor of domesticated banana, occurred in the Western Ghats. The ethnobotanical knowledge of the species and development of certain local varieties of bananas lead to a speculation that the region witnessed early domestication of banana. Two rock arts in Anamalai valley (10°10′N, 77°03′E) carry depictions of two wild bananas (*E. superbum* and *M. acuminata*). It indicates that the ancient people of Western Ghats knew of wild banana, which points to the fact that its domestication started here at least from the Neolithic period.

Coconut Palm (Cocos nucifera, Arecaceae)

Cocos nucifera (Figure 6.10) played a key role on human dispersal, particularly in the humid tropics. As a highly viable source of nutrition, *C. nucifera* gained importance and value in enabling humans to travel, establish trade routes and colonize lands along the Pacific Rim and throughout the Old World tropics—which incidentally enabled its wide distribution historically. This species is highly useful to humans as a source of food, drink, fibre, construction material, charcoal and oil. The coconut oil is highly prized and is useful in cooking, pharmaceuticals including the manufacture of cosmetic items, industrial applications and biofuels. More than 12 million ha of coconut are currently planted in nearly 100 tropical countries.[54] Several saturated fatty acids such as lauric, myristic, caprylic, capric, caproic, palmitic and palmitoleic essentially make up coconut oil with the lauric and myristic constituting the bulk of percentage. Nowadays, controversy prevails as to the validity of coconut oil as a promoter of low-density lipoproteins in terms of human health.

The long-term interaction between humans and coconuts shaped both the geographical distribution of *C. nucifera* and its phenotypic

---

[53] B. Kurian, *Walk Through Ages* (n.d.). http://keralaarchaeology.blogspot.com.au. Accessed 23 August 2016.

[54] B. F. Gunn, L. Baudouin, and K. M. Olsen, 'Independent Origins of Cultivated Coconut (*Cocos nucifera* L.) in the Old World Tropics', *PLoS One* 6 (2011): e21143, doi:10.1371/journal.pone.0021143.

FIGURE 6.10   *Cocos Nucifera*

Source: *Hortus Malabaricus*, 1753.

diversification. While the nut of the coconut plant is naturally adapted for dispersal by sea currents, its Pantropical dissemination was achieved because of human activity. As a native of the Old World tropics, coconut spread to eastern Polynesia and subsequently was introduced to the Pacific Coast of Latin America, most likely by pre-Columbian Austronesian seafarers from the Philippines.[55] Anywhere between 2,500 and 3,000 years ago, *C. nucifera* populations were influenced by Austronesian expansions westward towards Madagascar via Peninsular India, which, later, by 1500 CE were introduced by Europeans into the Atlantic coasts of Africa and South America and to the Caribbean from India.

The *niu vai* form of *C. nucifera*, whose fruits are nearly spherical and often brightly coloured, with a large proportion of liquid endosperm,

---

[55] L. Baudouin and P. Lebrun, 'Coconut (*Cocos nucifera* L.) DNA Studies Support the Hypothesis of an Ancient Austronesian Migration from Southeast Asia to America', *Genetic Resources & Crop Evolution* 56 (2009): 257–262.

was preferentially selected against the *niu kafa* form of *C. nucifera* with oblong, triangular fruits with a large proportion of fibrous husk. Coconuts have also been traditionally grouped into 'dwarf' and 'tall' varieties based on the tree habit. The dwarfs represent about 5 per cent of coconut palms and are cultivated extensively worldwide; they are usually grown close to human habitations and show traits closely associated with human selection, such as slow trunk growth, self-pollination and the production of *niu vai* fruits. The more common 'tall' varieties generally outcross and grow faster than the 'dwarfs', resulting in greater height at reproductive maturity. Curiously, a majority of the tall varieties are restricted to the Peninsular India, whereas the 'dwarfs' are confined to Malesian archipelago. The 'talls' are usually preferred for the production of *copra* used for oil extraction and fibrous coir. While actively cultivated, these varieties tend to lose many of the obvious domestication traits of the self-pollinating dwarfs. The lack of universal domestication traits among coconut varieties, combined with the long history of human interaction with this species, has made it difficult to trace the origins of coconut cultivation practices.[56] With modern molecular tools such as restriction fragment length polymorphism (RFLP), microsatellites and amplified fragment length polymorphism (AFLP) markers, we today know of the occurrence of two genetically distinct groups, corresponding broadly to the Pacific Ocean Basin on one side and the Indian and Atlantic Oceans on the other. Importantly, this worldwide collection has not been used previously to examine the coconut's cultivation history.

In southern India, coconut grows naturally and is cultivated mainly along the coastal tracts, namely the saline sandy soils of Kerala, Tamil Nadu, Pondicherry, Karnataka, Andhra Pradesh, although other states and territories such as Odisha, West Bengal, Maharashtra and the islands of Lakshadweep, Andaman and Nicobar too include them. In this context, a supplementary useful information would be that *C. nucifera* pollen have been found and used as a key marker in marine-sediment core studies to understand monsoon variations through time: three contrasting periods, namely the Holocene, 26,000–24,000 years ago, and 73,000 years ago.[57] The relevance of this is that other evidences indicate a mainly continental—coastal origin for these sediments. If I am not mistaken, this also adds to the conclusions of the genetic

---

[56] Gunn, Baudouin, and Olsen, 'Independent Origins of Cultivated Coconut'.

[57] C. Zorzi, 'Indian Monsoon Variations During Three Contrasting Climatic Periods: The Holocene, Heinrich Stadial 2 and the Last Interglacial–glacial Transition', *Quaternary Science Reviews* 125 (2015): 50–60.

studies regarding the origins of coconut palm. From a biological perspective, the intimacy of association between the terrestrial hermit crab (also known as the robber crab, *Birgus latro*, Decapoda: Coenobitidae) with populations of coconut palms in the Andamans and several Indonesian islands, extending up to the Polynesian islands further east is stunning.[58] Kerala is the main coconut growing state with an area of 102,000 ha and production of 5,911 million nuts, followed by Tamil Nadu (320,000 ha and 3,716 million nuts), Karnataka (287,000 ha and 1,493 million nuts) and Andhra Pradesh (95,000 ha and 780 million nuts). These southern states collectively account for approximately 90 per cent of the total production in India. In productivity too, India ranks first among the coconut growing countries in the world. The average productivity of coconut is 7,000 nuts/ha. Among the four major coconut growing states, Tamil Nadu has the highest productivity (11,620 nuts/ha), Andhra Pradesh has a productivity of 8,296 nuts/ha, followed by Kerala (5,793 nuts/ha) and Karnataka (5,204 nuts/ha). For detailed notes on the uses of coconut palms, the reader is referred to http://factsand details.com/world/cat54/sub343/item1575.html.

One theory explaining the etymology of the coconut-abundant Kerala is that the name Kerala derives from *C. nucifera*'s Sankrit name *nālikéra* (*najikéra*—Pāli, Rhys Davids and Stede 1905)[59]. This does not appear right, because of the introduced nature of *C. nucifera*. The term Kerala could have arisen from the Tamil term *Çéra*. The point to be noted here is that the ancient western segment of Tamil land—the modern Kerala—was ruled by the *Çéra* dynasty.[60] Alternatively, the term *kéra* broadly means free-flowing water and naturally occurring water bodies in Tulu and Konkani languages spoken in South Canara (northern Kerala districts adjoining Karnataka). It is highly likely that the name Kerala is derived either from *Çéra* or *kéra* (Tulu, Konkani).

Sugarcane (Saccharum, Poaceae)

Commercial sugarcanes have arisen through intensive selective breeding of species within the botanical taxon *Saccharum* (Figure 6.11) that principally involved crosses between *S. officinarum* and *S. spontaneum*

---

[58] I. W. Brown, et al., *The Coconut Crab: Aspects of the Biology and Ecology of Birgus latro in the Republic of Vanuatu*, ACIAR Monograph # 8 (Canberra, 1992).

[59] T. W. Rhys Davids and W. Stede, eds., *Pali: English Dictionary* (London: Pali Text Society, 1905), 351. (reprinted edition 1994, 2004).

[60] P. S. Menon, *A History of Travancore from the Earliest Times* (Madras: Higginbotham and Company, 1878).

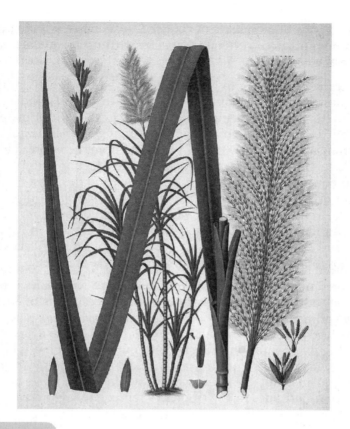

FIGURE 6.11 *Saccharum officinarum*

Source: Köhler, F. E., *Medizinal Pflanzen*, Vol. 2, Verlag von F. E. Köhler, Gera-Unternhaus, Germany, figure 169, 1890.

over hundreds of years.[61] *Saccharum officinarum*, also referred in popular language as 'noble cane', stores high levels of sweet sugar (sucrose) in their stems but generally have a low resistance capability to fungal and bacterial diseases. *Saccharum officinarum* is indicated to be the product of complex introgression among *S. spontaneum*, *Erianthus arundinaceus* and *Miscanthus sinensis*.[62] The origins of *S. officinarum* are intimately

---

[61] M. Cox, M. Hogarth, and G. Smith, 'Cane Breeding and Improvement', in *Manual of Cane Growing*, eds. M. Hogarth and P. Allsopp (Indooroopilly, Australia: Bureau of Sugar Experiment Stations, 2000), 91–108.

[62] J. Daniels and B. T. Roach, 'Taxonomy and Evolution', in *Sugarcane Improvement Through Breeding*, ed. D. J. Heinz, Vol. 11 (Amsterdam: Elsevier, 1987), 7–84.

associated with human activities, since *S. officinarum* is a cent-percent human-manipulated (cultivated) species with no members known to occur in the wild.[63]

Sugarcane was known in New Guinea since 6000 BCE. Its cultivation spread along human migration routes to Southeast Asia, India and the Pacific, naturally hybridizing with wild sugarcanes to ultimately produce 'thin' canes. Such hybrids and the parent germplasms reached the Mediterranean between 600 and 1400 CE and from there spread to Egypt, Syria, Crete, Greece and Spain followed by introduction into West Africa and subsequently Central and South America and the West Indies. The centre of origin of the original parent of *S. officinarum* is implicated as Polynesia. The species was probably transported throughout Southeast Asia by humans, leading to a modern centre of diversity in Papua New Guinea and Irian Jaya (Indonesia). A majority of canes collected in the late 1800s for curating purposes come from these areas.[64]

The presently valid theories on the origin of *S. officinarum* reinforce on the selection and domestication of the sweet forms of *Saccharum robustum* primarily for use in food.[65] *Saccharum spontaneum* is believed to have evolved in Southern Asia. It accumulates no sweet sugars (sucrose) but is a highly polymorphic species with much greater levels of disease resistance, adaptability and stress tolerance.[66] *Saccharum spontaneum* is a flexible and an adaptable species and grows in a wide range of habitats from various altitudes in the tropics to temperate regions from 8°S to 40°N latitude extending across several geographical zones.[67]

Sugarcane is an established agricultural field crop with a long history of use. It is believed to have become established as a domestic garden crop possibly as early as 2500 BCE.[68] In terms of use, sugar from sugarcane was better known in northern India than in southern India. Although the southern Indians knew of sugar cane and its sweetness,

---

[63] T. V. Sreenivasan, B. S. Ahloowalia, and D. J. Heinz, 'Cytogenetics', in *Sugarcane Improvement Through Breeding*, ed. D. J. Heinz (Amsterdam: Elsevier, 1987), 211–253.

[64] Daniels and Roach, 'Taxonomy and Evolution'.

[65] Ibid.

[66] R. Maheshwari and A. Raman, 'The Knight of Sugar Industry: T. S. Venkataraman (1884–1963)', *Current Science* 106 (2014): 1146–1149.

[67] L. Grivet, et al., 'A Review of Recent Molecular Genetics Evidence for Sugarcane Evolution and Domestication', *Ethnobotany Research & Applications* 2 (2004): 9–17.

[68] Daniels and Roach, 'Taxonomy and Evolution'.

for a long time, they did not know to extract sugar either as jaggery or as unbleached sugar. Until the 13th–14th centuries, sugarcane was chewed for its sweetness. Later in time, they developed simple presses to extract the juice. During the *Sangam* period of Tamil land, sweetening of food was mainly achieved by using honey. Nevertheless, by 1000 AD, northern Indians knew of extraction of the sugary juice (the syrup) from the wild *S. spontaneum* and domesticated *Saccharum barberi* and *S. officinarum*, and their hybrids, particularly in the context of medical procedures as suggested by *Çaraka* and *Śuśruta*.[69] Moreover, the Sanskrit terms *guda* and *šarkara* exemplify that the northern Indians knew of the extraction of sugar, although the technique of bleaching the sugar and making it white and crystalline was a technology that arrived from China in the 16th century. Asia's first sugar factory at Aska (Odisha) produced bleached sugar at an industrial scale in 1948 bringing in the Chinese method of producing white, crystalline sugar using bone meal. In southern India, the bleached crystalline sugar is popularly known as either *cheeni* (because of Chinese technology) or *aska* (because of the name Aska Sugar Factory). It is notable that in some of the Hindu temples in southern India, such as Sri Krishna Temple (Guruvayur, Kerala), even today, the bleached, crystal sugar is never used, but only the raw, unbleached sugar (*guda, vellam*) for preparing sweet delicacies as a part of temple rituals.

To meet the sugar demand in colonial India and in Britain, the British established the Sugarcane Breeding Station at Coimbatore in 1912 with Charles Barber, a South African, as its first superintendent, who recruited T. S. Venkataraman as his deputy. Venkataraman noted that in the warm climate, some close relatives of sugarcane would flower, enabling the production of hybrid canes by crossing, a physical process by which the pollen (the male reproductive cell) is transferred to the receptive surface of the female reproductive organ. Venkataraman collected plants with the cane phenotype that suited the prevailing hot (summer, April–June) and cold (winter, November–January) conditions in the Indo-Gangetic Plains (27°15′–27°25′N, 80°30′–80°5′E). Several varieties which did not flower in the northern states because of large variations in temperature, and/or diurnal variations in the photoperiod, flowered in Coimbatore (11°N, 77°E). The climate and geographical location of Coimbatore enabled many varieties of sugarcane to flower and produce seeds. Venkataraman succeeded in generating interspecific

---

[69] J. H. Galloway, *The Sugarcane Industry: A Historical Geography from Its Origins to 1914* (Cambridge: Cambridge University Press, 1989).

hybrids by crossing selected parents and developed high-yielding varieties (e.g., Co 205, Co 255, Co 299, Co 312, Co 313, Co 513, Co 527), as a result of which India changed from the status of holding a begging bowl for sugar to that of being a sugar exporter. It is to the credit of Venkataraman, who had known that pollen viability, stigma receptivity and the time of the day for cross-pollination were critical for fertilization and fertile seed formation. These varieties are used even now as stocks for breeding in Australia, Bangladesh, Indonesia and Pakistan. Today, sugarcane is even more valuable. It is a fuel crop, being the source of fibrous cellulosic and hemicellulosic biomass for its conversion into commercial alcohol via the conversion of its glucose contents using fungus-derived cellulase and subsequent anaerobic conversion into alcohol by yeast fermentation as a transport fuel.

Mango Tree (Mangifera indica, *Anacardiaceae*)

Anacardiaceae, to which *Mangifera* belongs, includes approximately 850 species in 73 genera.[70] Most species of Anacardiaceae are confined to the tropics and their species diversity is particularly high in Malesia—the phytogeographic region between the southern Malay Peninsula and eastern New Guinea.[71] Anacardiaceae is estimated to have originated in the Palaeocene (65–55 mya)[72] in Gondwana.[73] Among the extant Anacardiaceae, a variety of perennial plant forms exist, and all species include a characteristic endowment of latex and resins, besides a range of simple and complex phenols and esters.[74] Mangiferin, a phenolic glucoside, is a key compound in *M. indica*.[75] *M. indica* (Figure 6.12) is the most basic species from which every other edible variety has been developed.

---

[70] S. K. Pell, *Molecular Systematics of the Cashew Family (Anacardiaceae)* (Ph.D. dissertation, Louisiana State University (A&M College), Baton Rouge, LA, 2004).

[71] S. K. Mukherjee, 'Introduction: Botany and Importance', in *The Mango—Botany, Production and Uses*, ed. R. E. Litz (Oxfordshire, 1997), 1–20.

[72] J. Muller, 'Significance of Fossil Pollen for Angiosperm History', *Annals of the Missouri Botanical Garden* 71 (1984): 419–443.

[73] A. H. Gentry, 'Neotropical Floristic Diversity: Phytogeographical Connections Between Central and South America, Pleistocene Climatic Functions, or An Accident of the Andean Orogeny?' *Annals of the Missouri Botanical Garden* 69 (1982): 557–593.

[74] J. Corthout et al., 'Antiviral Caffeoyl Esters from *Spondias mombin*', *Phytochemistry* 31 (1992): 1979–1981.

[75] P. E. Nott and J. C. Roberts, 'The Structure of Mangiferin', *Phytochemistry* 6 (1967): 741–747.

FIGURE 6.12 *Mangifera indica*

Source: N. J. von Jacquin, *Icones Plantarum Rariorum*, C. F. Wappler, Vindabonae (Vindabona, Roman Army Camp, in Modern Austria). Vol. 2, figure 337, 1786–1793.

Almost 70 valid species exist within *Mangifera* in tropical Asia—its native range—and these species occur up to 30° North of the Equator and from 80° to 160° East.[76] *Mangifera sylvatica, M. caloneura, M. zeylanica* and *M. pentandra* are some of the examples of other species of *Mangifera*. Leaf impressions (Upper Palaeocene Period) from Assam (northeastern India; 26°09′–26°15′ N; 91°46′–91°77′E) indicate that an ancestor of *M. indica* (*Eomangiferophyllum damalgiriensis*) existed and subsequently spread to south-eastern Asia in the Eocene.[77] Modern *Mangifera* includes *M. andamanica, M. khasiana* and *M. sylvatica*, which are endemic to

---

[76] J. M. Bompard and R. J. Schnell, 'Taxonomy and Systematics', in *The Mango—Botany, Production and Uses*, eds. R. E. Litz (Oxfordshire, 1997), 21–48.

[77] R. C. Mehrotra, D. L. Dilcher, and N. Awasthi, 'A Palaeocene *Mangifera*-like Fossil from India', *Phytomorphology* 48 (1998): 91–100.

northeastern India and the Andaman Islands (6–14°N, 92–94°E), in addition to the ubiquitous and extensively cultivated *M. indica*.[78] The land bordered by Assam, Myanmar (Burma) and Bangladesh (Chittagong Hill tract) is considered the epicentre of *M. indica*, although currently this taxon has extended to the tip of the Malay Peninsula.[79] Within the Indian subcontinent, more than 1,000 established varieties exist,[80] and a majority of these varieties have evolved through natural hybridization between *M. indica* and *M. sylvatica*, with at least 350 of them being propagated for fruits.[81] The fossil material of *M. indica* found in Assam and the primitive species such as *M. duperreana* and *M. lagenifera* in Laos, Cambodia and Vietnam indicate that the original centre could be elsewhere as well. Therefore, it would be 'safe' to indicate that this taxon originated in South Asia. Its spread and maximum diversification occurred in India–Myanmar–Thailand stretch on the one side, and Indonesia–Borneo–Philippines stretch on the other.

Domestication of mango tree seems to have occurred in India certainly from 2000 BCE, although some biological historians indicate it as 4000 BCE. Mango fruit referred as *amrā* (Sanskrit) is referred to in *Bhāgavata Puranā* as occurring on the mythical Mount Mandara. The mango tree is considered sacred by both Hindus and Buddhists. Buddhist scriptures indicate that Buddha was once presented with a grove of mango trees enabling him to relax. Buddhists consider this plant sacred and the *Vedas* refer to mango as a heavenly fruit. The early domestication of this fruit tree in India aimed at larger fruits and pleasantly flavoured ones with lesser resin and fibrous material. This was a significant accomplishment given that these trees are highly heterozygous, and consequently the seedlings were highly variable in their capacities and performance. From here, the cultivation of mango tree spread to southern India wherein it diversified further as it spread to Sri Lanka. Abu'l-Fath Jalal-ud-din Muhammad Akbar (1542–1605) saw to it that large mango orchards were established throughout his empire.

[78] S. K. Mukherjee and D. Chandra, 'An Outline of the Revision of Indian Anacardiaceae', *Bulletin of the Botanical Survey of India* 25 (1993): 52–61.

[79] C. P. A. Iyer and M. D. Subramanyam, 'Improvement of Mango', in *Advances in Horticulture,* eds. K. L. Chadha and O. P. Pareek (New Delhi: Malhotra Publishing House, 1993), 267–278.

[80] S. S. Pandit et al., 'Genetic Diversity Analysis of Mango Cultivars Using Inter Simple Sequence Repeat Markers', *Current Science* 93 (2007): 1135–1141.

[81] J. F. Morton, *Fruits of Warm Climates* (Miami, FL: Echo Point Books & Media, 1987).

The recombination efforts made essentially by grafting of various varieties across India resulted in hundreds of preferred varieties of *M. indica* of varied sizes, colours, flavours and, most importantly, varied tastes. Some of the popular southern Indian varieties include *Bangalorã, Banganapalli, Mulgôa, Neelum, Rumãni* and *Swanarékha*. Further to these, many other hybrids achieved by crossing between varieties are popular today.

Cotton (Gossypium, Malvaceae)

Cotton plant (Figure 6.13) provides an amazing source of plant fibres. The Indian subcontinent includes a native cotton plant, *Gossypium arboreum*, popularly known as the 'tree cotton'. Fibres of cotton—obviously from *G. arboreum*—were extracted by Indians from ancient times. The extracted fibres were spun, woven and 'dyed' and used to weave fabrics. The most stunning aspect of cotton fibre is that it rules

FIGURE 6.13 *Gossypium*

Source: Robert Wight, J. B. Pharoah & Company, Madras, Vol. III, figure 269, 1840.

FIGURE 6.14 *Indus Valley Edifice Showing the Use of Ornate Cotton Fabric*

Source: https://commons.wikimedia.org/wiki/File:Mohenjo-daro_Priesterk%C3%B6nig.jpeg (accessed on 10 July 2016)

over the fabric industry even today, nearly all over the world, in spite of markets being flooded by synthetic fibres developed from cellulose. The Indians of the Mohanja-daro–Harappan region definitely knew of the use of cotton, which they used for draping themselves (Figure 6.14).[82] The earliest reference to cotton occurs in a hymn of the Rigveda (1500 BCE). Another early reference to cotton occurs in the *Śrauta Śutra* of *Aśvalayanā*, estimated 8th century BCE, in which the cotton fibre is compared with other fibrous materials, such as silk and hemp.[83] Herodotus (approximately 450 BCE) indicated that cotton material is

---

[82] N. Kumar and T. Jain, 'Rise and Decline of Indus Valley Civilization', *International Journal of Business and Administration Research Review* 3 (2015): 87–91.

[83] G. Watt, *The Commercial Products of India Being an Abridgement of the Dictionary of Economic Products of India* (London: J. Murray, 1908).

the customary wear of Indians: 'India has wild trees that bear fleeces as their fruits ... of this the Indians make their clothes'.[84]

During the reign of Chandragupta Maurya (321–297 BCE), high-quality *cotton* fabric was produced in Magadha kingdom. The *Periplus* (estimated 1st century CE) mentions cotton fibres and fabric exported from *Ariāké* and *Barygāzā* (the Rann of Kutch) to Arabia and Greece. For more details on the historical references and details to cotton use in ancient India, the reader is referred to Raman (2015).[85] Floatation samples from 12 sites in modern Karnataka and Andhra Pradesh[86] indicate that the domestication of *G. arboreum* occurred in India in the Neolithic period (2800–1200 BCE). From the time of Emperor Akbar (1542–1605), cotton fabric production prospered in India, especially in Bengal; spinning and weaving were done manually.

Throughout the world, three species of *Gossypium*, namely *G. barbadense*, *G. hirsutum* and *G. herbaceum*, were independently domesticated. Polyploidy is common in *Gossypium*. Five allotetra-ploids and 46 diploids are known today.[87] That the progenitors of the tetraploid cottons are *G. raimondii* of Ecuadorian and *G. herba-ceum* of southern African–Arabian Peninsula distribution is widely accepted today, although how these taxa hybridized in spite of vast spatial separation is unclear. Fibre quality of *G. arboreum* is inferior to those fibres extracted from other world taxa that have been intensely domesticated elsewhere. However, *G. arboreum* is innately hardy having evolved in the Indian soil and Indian climate conditions. John Forbes Royle (1839)[88] catalogued 11 cotton species from the Indian soil, although today many of them have been lumped into four

---

[84] W. H. Schoff, *The Periplus of the Erythraean Sea: Travel and Trade in the Indian Ocean, by a Merchant of the First Century* (New York, NY: Longmans, Green & Company, 1912).

[85] A. Raman, 'Cotton Heritage of India and Improvements Trialled on Cotton Germplasm in the Madras Presidency During the 19th Century', *Current Science* 109 (2015): 1347–1352.

[86] D. Q. Fuller et al., 'Early Plant Domestications in Southern India: Some Preliminary Archaeobotanical Results', *Vegetation History & Archaeobotany* 13 (2004): 115–129.

[87] B. M. Khadi, V. Santhy, and M. S. Yadav, 'Cotton: An Introduction', in *Cotton, Biotechnology in Agriculture and Forestry*, ed. U. B. Zehr (Heidelberg: Springer, 2010).

[88] J. F. Royle, *On the Culture and Commerce of Cotton in India, and Elsewhere, with an Account of the Experiments Made by The Honourable East India Company, up to the Present Time* (London: Smith, Elder & Company, 1839).

established species: *arboreum, hirsutum, barbadense* and *herbaceum*.[89] Extensive efforts were made in the Madras Presidency (Coimbatore and Tirunelveli) in the 19th century to grow cotton by Robert Wight by particularly importing American cotton germplasms. For further details, see Raman (2015).[90]

Neolithic Domestication and Cultivation in Southern India

Grain and other food item samples collected from deposits of habitation sites in northern Karnataka and western Andhra Pradesh[91] indicate the extensive use of the native millets such as *Brachiaria ramosa, Setaria verticillata* (*tinai*, Tamil), *Panicum sumatrense* (*sāmai*, Tamil) and *Paspalum scrobiculatum* (*varagu*, Tamil) (all Poaceae); *Vigna radiata* (*payaru, pacchai-p-payaru*, Tamil), *Vigna mungo* (*ulundu, uzhundu*, Tamil) and *Macrotyloma uniflorum* (*kôɬu*, Tamil) (all Fabaceae); and *G. arboreum* (*panju maram*, Tamil) (Malvaceae) by the then residing Indians (for the veracity of Tamil names, see Kimata 2016).[92] The same searches have also revealed the utilization of non-native taxa *Triticum, H. vulgare, Pennisetum glaucum, Eleusine coracana* and *O. sativa* (all Poaceae), *L. usitatissimum* (Linaceae), and *Lablab purpureus* and *Cajanus cajan* (both Fabaceae) by them. Fuller and Korisettar[93] indicate that these sites, mostly located on hill tops, suggest cultivation and year-round habitation. They attribute the natural vegetation (e.g., moist deciduous forests) of the upper and lower Deccan plateau as the principal source for many of the native taxa that were domesticated and brought under cultivation. For example, the *Terminalia–Anogeissus–Tectona*-dominant moist deciduous vegetation of the Deccan coupled with the grassy landscapes supplied *Vigna sublobata* (Fabaceae) the wild progenitor for two crucially cultivated pulses: *V. radiata* and *V. mungo*.

The dry deciduous forest landscape that keeps spreading on the interiors of the Deccan would have encouraged the evolution of several

---

[89] Raman, 'Cotton Heritage of India and Improvements', Table 1, 1349.

[90] Ibid.

[91] D. Q. Fuller and R. Korisettar, 'The Vegetational Context of Early Agriculture in South India', *Man & Environment* 29 (2004): 7–27.

[92] M. Kimata, 'Domestication Process and Linguistic Differentiation of Millets in the Indian Subcontinent', *Ethnobotanical Notes* 9 (2016): 12–24.

[93] Fuller and Korisettar, 'Vegetational Context of Early Agriculture'.

millet grasses over time, which would have been domesticated later in time by the inhabiting southern Indians. The preference pattern of millet grasses to more damp soil is one key factor that dictates the above conclusion. For example, *B. ramosa* (Poaceae) is rare along rocky slopes and in forest undergrowth of dry eastern Karnataka but occurs more plentifully in the dry deciduous areas of Kurnool and also along riparian regions therein. Populations of *B. ramosa*, therefore, are regulated by wetter conditions of the soil. From arid to very arid conditions prevailing in southern India do not allow preservation of organic evidences, such as seeds and grains, which makes the discovery of grains such as rice and millets rare. Findings of grains contained in earthenware by Rajan and Yatheeskumar (2013, 2014)[94] during excavations conducted at burial sites in *Pôrunthal* support the above. In contrast to the hilltop sites documented in Karnataka, *Pôrunthal* occurs at the foothills of the southern segments of the Western Ghats.

Domestication and independent origin of agriculture in India have been matters of intense debate in recent years.[95] The debate has evolved out of the determinations of wild progenitors for those plants domesticated as useful and economically important plants. Fuller[96] argues for the Deccan being a strongly potential candidate site for distinctive, indigenous early agriculture in India. According to him[97]:

> The crops that recur and dominate Southern Deccan Neolithic archaeobotanical samples (which he collectively refers as the 'Southern Neolithic Crop Package') include *Vigna radiata, Macrotyloma uniflorum, Bachiaria ramosa*, and *Setaria verticillata*[98] have wild ancestors to be found in the hills of scrub woodlands of the region.

---

[94] K. Rajan and V. P. Yatheeskumar, 'New Evidences on Scientific Dates for Brahmi Script as Revealed from Porunthal and Kodumanal Excavations', *Pragdhara*. 21–22 (2013): 279–295; *Archaeology of Amaravathi River Valley: Porunthal Excavation*, Vol. I–II (Delhi: Sharadha Publishing House, 2014).

[95] K. S. Saraswat, 'Agricultural Background of the Early Farming Communities in the Middle Ganga Plain', *Pragdhara* 15 (2005): 145–1477; R. Tewari et al., 'Early Farming at Lahuradewa', *Pragdhara* 18 (2008): 347–373.

[96] Fuller, 'Finding Plant Domestication'.

[97] Ibid., S348.

[98] Illustrations of *Vigna radiata* (*Phaseolus mungo*, Fabaceae), *Macrotyloma biflorus* (*Dolichos biflorus*, Fabaceae), *Setaria verticillata* (*Pennisetum italicum*, Poaceae) and *Bachiaria ramosa* (*Panicum milliaceum*, Poaceae) are supplied as Figures 6.15, 6.16, 6.17 and 6.18, respectively, from A. H. Church, *Food-Grains of India* (London, 1886).

FIGURE 6.15 *Vigna radiata (Phaseolus mungo,* Fabaceae)

Source: A. H. Church, *Food-grains of India*, 1886, p. 149.

The current pattern of use of *S. verticillata* throughout southern India and in adjacent stretches in the state of Maharashtra proves his point. He further argues that an ally of *S. verticillata*, namely *Setaria glauca* is being cultivated here today.[99] Most of these taxa in the crop package could have been more widely available in the drier grasslands of the Deccan. These do not form extensive populations as many other plants do, but they may have formed dense, disjunct patches. Therefore, their abundance alone stands as a viable factor in pointing to that they were the wild progenitors for encouraging the Neolithic period residents of the Deccan to domesticate them. The evolution of *V. mungo* could have been facilitated by the intergrading of dry grasslands into deciduous forests in the Eastern Ghats along River Krishna.

---

[99] M. Kimata, E. G. Ashok, and A. Seetharam, 'Domestication, Cultivation and Utilization of Two Small Millets, *Bachiaria ramosa* and *Setaria glauca* (Poaceae) in South India', *Economic Botany* 54 (2000): 217–227.

FIGURE 6.16   *Macrotyloma biflorus (Dolichos biflorus,* **Fabaceae)**

Source: A. H. Church, Food-grains of India, 1886, p. 165.

Loads of archaeobotanical evidences reconstructed by Fuller[100] point to the fact that many tropical, agriculturally important plants were domesticated in South Asia during Prehistoric Period[101]:

> It is now clear that different trajectories into the Neolithic took place in different parts of the subcontinent, and this suggests that different world regions may provide the most useful comparisons for assessing convergent processes in the various Indian regions.

---

[100] Fuller, 'Finding Plant Domestication'.
[101] Ibid., S359.

FIGURE 6.17 *Setaria verticillata (Pennisetum italicum,* **Poaceae)**

Source: A. H. Church, Food-grains of India, 1886, p. 54.

Fuller concludes that cultivation may have commenced in southern India, Odisha, Middle Ganges, Saurashtra and the Himalayan foothills of Punjab region before the introduction of exogenous crops and cultivation systems. Identification of these sites is based on the availability of wild progenitors and a growing archaeobotanical database. Nevertheless, the gap in the transition from hunter–gatherer behaviour to cultivators remains unbridged.

Agricultural Practices as Evident in Tamil Sangam Poetry

The Tamil land (*Tamizhagam*) during the Sangam Age (3rd century BCE to 4th century CE) spread from the Arabian Sea in the west to the Bay of Bengal in the east and from Tirumalai (Thirupathi) in the north to Kanyakumari in the south with the rivers *Pālār, Pénnar, Kaveri,* and *Vaigai* flowing within. The *Ādichanallur* and *Porunthal* findings of

FIGURE 6.18 *Bachiaria ramosa (Panicum milliaceum,* Poaceae*)*

Source: A. H. Church, Food-grains of India, 1886, p. 41.

rice reinforce that organized agricultural operations existed in Tamil land.[102] Two verses (1037 and 1038) of *Tirukkural* (estimated 200 CE) highlight the importance of tillage and minimization of the use of manure. The most illustrative description of rice agriculture occurs in *Pérumpān-ātrupadai* (estimated 200–300 CE, II, verses 226–233, 245–246), which emphasizes the importance of tilling and sowing and the relevance of transplantation in rice agriculture. The harvest produce of rice to be safely stored is described graphically in *Pérumpān-ātrupadai* (II, verses 282–285) and *Pôrunar-ātrupadai* (estimated 200–300 CE, II, verses 282–285).

Verse 306, *Ahanānuru* (estimated, 100–200 CE) refers extensively to sugarcane cultivation and describes the furrow and trench methods to grow sugarcane crop and also to the wet cultivation. Curiously,

---

[102] T. M. Srinivasan, 'Agricultural Practices as Gleaned from the Tamil Literature of the Sangam Age', *Indian Journal of History of Science* 51 (2016): 167–189.

sugarcane was raised as an accompanying crop along with rice. In some instances, the sugarcane cultivated along the edges of rice paddies served as a fence and protecting facility to the rice paddies (*Purananuru*, estimated 200 BCE to 150 CE, verse 322). Cultivation of dry crops such as *varagu* (*P. scrobiculatum*, Poaceae), *tinai* (*Setaria italica*, Poaceae), sesame (*S. indicum*, Pedaliaceae) and bean (*avarai, L. purpureus*, Fabaceae) is described in the Sangam poetry, namely *Puranānuru* and *Malaipadukadām* (*Sangam* Literature, estimated 100 CE). *Natrinai* (verse 93, *Sangam* Literature, estimated 100 BCE to 200 CE) refers to many of the cheaper food grains, which were generally referred in Tamil as *koolam*. This verse refers to the cultivation of green gram (*V. radiata*, Fabaceae), black gram (*Vigna munga*, Fabaceae) and horse gram (*M. uniflorum*, Fabaceae). For further extensive details, the reader is referred to pages 181–183 in Srinivasan.[103] Incidentally, wages paid to less-skilled workers of the society in those days were handed down as measures of *koolam* grains, which gave rise to the term *kooli*, whereas the skilled workers earned salary, which was handed down as measures of one of the dearer varieties of rice, namely *samba*, which over time came to be referred as *sambałam*. In later *f* years, the measures of grains offered either as wages or salary changed using either gold coins or paper money.

Conclusion

Obviously, two phases of domestication of plants and agricultural development occurred in the landscape that later came to be referred as the Indian subcontinent. In the first phase (9500–7500 BCE), agriculture was established in Mehrgarh (29°23′N, 67°37′E, Pakistan today). Barley (*H. vulgare*, Poaceae) was the earliest domesticated plant and, possibly, it was supplemented by growing of wheat (*Triticum*, Poaceae). The early grains of barley and wheat in Mehrgarh site were somewhat spherical, indicating that these were varieties 'selected' locally. During the second phase, from 7000 BCE, evidences of domestication of cotton arise, which, in high likelihood, was a local domesticate of *Gossypium arboreum* (Malvaceae). Other important crops with histories in the Indian subcontinent are mung beans (*V. radiata*), black gram (*V. mungo*), horse gram (*M. uniflorum*) and pigeon pea (*C. cajan*) (all Fabaceae), since evidences of their use appear after 5000 BCE. Evidences of rice (*O. sativa*, Poaceae) appear from about 7000 BCE; rice, fully domesticated, and that of the little millet (*P. sumatrense*, Poaceae) appear in archaeological records

---

[103] Srinivasan, 'Agricultural Practices as Gleaned'.

around 4500 BCE. Their appearance coincides with significant socio-economic changes in the subcontinent.

Agriculture was well established throughout most of the Indian subcontinent by 6000–5000 BCE. During the fifth millennium, the Indus River plains experienced an apparent explosion of an organized, sophisticated human society, better known as the Indus Valley Civilization, which flourished until shortly after 2000 BCE. Barley and wheat, supplemented by date-palm (*P. dactylifera*, Arecaceae), sesame (*S. indicum*), different peas and lentils (all Fabaceae) were the principally raised crops. Members of the Indus Valley Civilization also domesticated several mammals including elephants at this stage. Significantly they knew of cotton, wove fabric from cotton fibres and fascinatingly knew to colour them using plant dyes.

Southern India, the key centre of the distinctive Tamil culture, constituted a second, independent agricultural region. Crops were being raised there during the first half of the fourth millennium BCE. At least we have clear evidences of the farming of two lentils, namely *V. radiata* and *Macrotyloma biflorum* (both Fabaceae) and two millets *S. verticillata* and *B. ramosa* (both Poaceae). In the northern segments of the Deccan plateau, another early South Asian evidence of rice cultivation occurs. Subsequently, knowledge and use of wheat, cotton, flax and lentils spread into this region from the Indus Valley, and pulses and millets from the south.

India's extraordinary landscape and geography have favoured natural evolution of plants, resulting in the exquisite diversification of a plethora of fruit trees. The monsoonal rains are another critical key factor that enabled the rich biodiversification. With the establishment of the Moghul Empire, many Middle-eastern Persian plant elements were deliberately introduced with the introduction and rise of new cultures and new medical practices (e.g., *Unani-Tibbe*). When the English and other Europeans arrived, they were astonished by the biological variety they saw in the Indian subcontinent.[104] They searched for plant materials that were useful in medicine.[105] They nurtured

---

[104] A. Raman and S. Prasad, 'Two-hundred Year Changes in Plant-species Composition: A Case Study of Madras City in the Coromandel Coast, Peninsular India', *International Journal of Ecology and Environmental Sciences* 36 (2010): 205–214.

[105] R. Raman and A. Raman, 'A Western Science-based Materia Medica by Whitelaw Ainslie of the Madras-Medical Establishment Published in 1810', *Current Science* 107 (2014): 909–913.

experiments to improve the available plant germplasms, by introducing new form elsewhere[106]: for example, cinchona (*Cinchona*),[107] the ipecac (*Carapichea ipecacuanha*)[108] (both Rubiaceae), rubber (*Hevea brasiliensis*, Euphorbiaceae)[109] and tea (*Camellia sinensis*, Theaceae),[110] to cite a few examples, which have indeed changed the complexion of Indian landscape to a large extent.

Plant or animal domestication is not, and has never been, a single-stage, sudden, abrupt event, similar to a chromosomal mutation. It has been, and continues to be, an ongoing dynamic process, which in reality embodies and includes various levels of human experience and degrees of dependence between humans and plants, and humans and animals. The rice plant, *O. sativa*, for instance, demonstrates how gradually it moved and transcended along this dynamic process and has thus become a vital source of food for humans through umpteen modifications and improvements for certain preferred traits, although some of the finer and more noble traits have been lost over time. For example, preferring a white rice grain, in the 1940s and 1950s, we learnt to machine polish rice grains as against the hand-pounded grains of earlier days so as to separate the edible grain from the inedible husk. In that process, we lost much of the favoured and good nutrients, which is presently coming back into Indian culture in the name of paleo food. That apart, in such a continuously evolving process, the germplasm of *O. sativa* too has undergone several natural changes and human-induced changes. Consequently, it presents itself so differently, and strangely even, that it differs drastically from its nearest relative in the wild, both in appearance and function. Recent intense archaeobotanical and genetic investigations reveal exciting dimensions, which we have been unaware of until this point. Yet, we are struggling to know the precise steps, for example, in the evolution of *indica* and *japonica*

[106] A. Raman, 'Economic Biology and James Anderson in Eighteenth Century Coromandel', *Current Science* 100 (2011): 1092–1096.

[107] A. Raman, 'Malaria Management in the 18th and 19th Century India: Role Played by Madras Presidency', *Current Science* 102 (2012): 1717–1120.

[108] R. Raman and A. Raman, 'Amoebic Dysentery and Introduction of Emetine Source *Carapichea ipecacuanha* into Indian Subcontinent'. *Indian Journal of History of Science* 2017, vol. 52, pp. 54–65.

[109] A. Raman and C. Narayanan, 'Search for Rubber in Pre-*Hevea brasiliensis* days and Establishment of *H. brasiliensis* in India'. *Indian Journal of Natural Products and Resources*, 2017, vol. 8, pp. 9–17.

[110] A. Raman, 'Georges Guerrard-Samuel Perrottet, A Forgotten Swiss–French Plant Collector, Experimental Botanist and Biologist in India', *Current Science* 107 (2014): 1607–1612.

subspecies of *O. sativa*. How, where and when the diversification commenced and how human domestication efforts influenced across the range of *O. sativa* complex? Similar questions daunt us with every other plant material, such as sugarcane, cotton, mango, banana and coconut, which have been forced and stressed to perform better in the interest of humans; the new scientific breakthrough is the concept of genetically modified crops and what is worrisome is what would be their biological consequences when consumed, in large quantities and over long spans of time,[111] although several equally strong rebuttals to this worry and fear from America do exist.

One daunting question in the domestication process that is coupled with a strong synergistic potential between the seekers, namely the humans and the givers, that is the plants, rests with the process of domestication and the preferential spread of some domestication alleles over others. For example, while the most common allele resulting in white rice grains originated in *japonica* and spread to *indica*, there are independent mutations resulting in an identical phenotype found in both the *aus* subspecies of *O. sativa* and a close relative of the *O. sativa indica* and the African domesticate *O. glaberrima*.[112] This pattern may indicate the incipient development of domestication traits in some populations, with further spread or development stopped by the arrival of certain varieties with favourable—to humans—characteristics. Although genetic surveys of extant lineages can offer some insights into the frequency of this phenomenon, archaeological evidence of the presence of domestication traits (e.g., shattering and grain shape) is required to complete our understanding of the history of plant domestication, for example, *O. sativa*.[113]

[111] S. Bonny, 'Why are Most Europeans Opposed to GMOs? Factors Explaining Rejection in France and Europe', *Electronic Journal of Biotechnology* 6 (2003), doi: 10.2225/vol6-issue1-fulltext-4.

[112] M. T. Sweeney et al., 'Global Dissemination of a Single Mutation Conferring White Pericarp in Rice', *PLoS Genetics* 3 (2007), doi: 10.1371/journal.pgen.0030133; B. L. Gross, F. T. Steffen, and K. M. Olsen, 'The Molecular Basis of White Pericarps in African Domesticated Rice: Novel Mutations at the *Rc* Gene', *Journal of Evolutionary Biology* 23 (2010): 2747–2753.

[113] B. L. Gross and Z. Zhao, 'Archaeological and Genetic Insights into the Origins of Domesticated Rice', *Proceedings of the National Academy of Sciences USA* 111 (2014): 6190–6197.

Environmental Change and Forest Conservancy in Southwest Bengal, 1890–1964[*]

Nirmal Kumar Mahato

Introduction

India's forests were the products of anthropogenic interference and ingrained in agricultural landscapes. From the early 19th century, the commercial travellers, naturalists and surveyors started to document the forested landscape of central and eastern India. In their landscape descriptions, the forests, farms and grasslands were described as hybrid landscape. Recent scholars tended to describe the Indian forests from an

[*] I express my sincere gratitude to Professor Ranjan Chakrabarti, Hon'ble Vice Chancellor Vidyasagar University, West Bengal, for his valuable comments on the earlier draft of this chapter. I am also thankful to Professor Suchibrata Sen, Dr Archan Bhattacharya, Dr Ngurliana Sailo, Dr Hmingthanzuali, Dr Krishna Singh, Mrs Kunti Mahato, Mrs Sima Ghosh Das, Librarian, Directorate of Forests, West Bengal and Chief Conservator of Forests, Directorate of Forest, West Bengal for their sustained help and encouragement. Lastly, I acknowledge the financial support of ICHR for the presentation of my paper in the Workshop on Environmental History.

'agro-forest' perspective like the scholars of the United States, Africa and Southeast Asia.[1] Environmental scholarship of South Asia has focused on the relationship between the growth and development of scientific ideas and technologies of natural resource management during the time of modern empires in South Asia. The scientific ideas were very much associated with the forest management and conservation and its effects on the origin of different types of environmentalism.[2] This chapter seeks to shed light on the environmental change and forest conservancy in Southwest Bengal and in what way principles of Deitrich Brandis were introduced in a region of 'zone of anomaly' like Manbhum.[3] This aspect is least discussed in the historical research on forests, forestry and imperialism.

With the implementation of 'science', the colonial authority intended to conserve forest through the creation of forest management practices and by appointing technical bureaucratic experts. Recent studies questioned whether this 'scientific' forestry was at all a scientific policy. These studies also argue that colonial forest policy was shaped and guided by local factors. 'Hence, a complex picture of environmental impacts emerges', as S. Abdul Thaha argues, 'rather than a one-way narrative about exploitation, extraction, and commanding control over the forests'.[4] There is a debate on the nature of scientific forestry in India. Ravi Kumar argues that, considering it as a device of growth and development in India, scientific forestry was introduced in the countryside. He comments on: 'Initially forestry was perceived as science mainly to deal with timber trees and its preview was focused on

---

[1] K. Sivaramakrishnan, 'Transition Zones: Changing Landscapes and Local Authorities in Southwest Bengal, 1880s–1920s', in *India's Environmental History: Colonialism, Modernity and the Nation*, eds. Mahesh Rangarajan and K. Sivaramakrishnan (Ranikhet: Permanent Black, 2012), 197–245.

[2] K. Sivaramakrishnan, 'Science, Environment and Empire History: Comparative Perspectives from Forests in Colonial India', *Environment and History* 14, no. 1 (2008): 42.

[3] The district was bordered to the north by Hazaribagh and Santhal Parganas, to the east by Burdwan, Bankura and Midnapur, to the south by Singhbhum and to the west by Ranchi and Hazaribagh. This Bengal district was emerged as a part of South-West Frontier Agency in 1833 but it was part of Bihar and Odisha during the period of 1912–1956. In 1956 it was divided into two parts, one part became Purulia district of West Bengal and the other part became Dhanbad district of Jharkhand, India.

[4] Abdul S. Thaha, 'Forest Policy and Ecological Change: The Hydrabad State (1867–1948)', in *The British Empire and the Natural World: Environmental Encounters in South Asia*, eds. Deepak Kumar, Vinita Damodaran and Rohan D'Souza (Delhi: Oxford University Press, 2011), 262.

supply of timber to government departments. But from 1880 onward forestry became a part of the empire discourse of progress'. Colonial science was, thus, regarded as an important agency of progress for the development of colonial society.[5] Vinita Damodaran argues that the scientific forestry has been seen as 'a mechanistic science where nature, the human body, and animals could be described repaired and control—as could the parts of a machine, by separate human mind acting according to rational laws'.[6] The debate of scientific forestry was embedded within the scientific world view which is described by Carolyn Merchant as the

> world as dead and inert, manipulability from outside and exploitable for profit ... living animate nature died ... increasingly capital and the market assumed the organic attributes of growth ... nature, women and wage labourers were set on a path as human resources for the modern world system.[7]

In view of this domination over nature, it was inherent in the market economy's use of the both as resources. This domination became a natural trend in colonial Chotanagpur. In the interest of production and profit, the colonial rulers sought to dominate forest, mineral and water resources. That is why, on the one hand, there occurred large-scale deforestation in order to expand agricultural land, and on the other hand, forests were protected in the interest of colonial rulers. Thus, the scientific forestry has recently been described as 'masculine discourse'.[8] This process of domination dangerously threatened the life pattern of the Adivasis,[9] and as a result, dreadful ecological hazards

---

[5] V. M. Ravi Kumar, 'Colonialism and Green Science: History of Colonial Scientific Forestry in South India, 1820–1920', *Indian Journal of History of Science* 47, no. 2 (2012): 253.

[6] Vinita Damodaran, 'Indigenous Forests: Rights, Discourses, and Resistance in Chotanagpur, 1860–2002', in *Ecological Nationalism: Nature, Livelihoods, and Identities in South Asia*, eds. K. Sivaramakrishnan and Gunnel Cederöf (New Delhi: Permanent Black, 2005), 118.

[7] Carolyn Merchant, *Radical Ecology* (New York, NY: Routledge, 1992), 41–60. She observed that the mechanistic worldview is a product of the scientific revolution of the seventeenth century.

[8] Vinita Damodaran, 'Gender, Forests and Famine in 19th-Century Chotanagpur', *Indian Journal of Gender Studies* 9, no. 2 (2002): 142–144.

[9] The word 'Adivasi' means original inhabitant. Recently scholars like Rycroft do not italicize the word in order to normalize its use. See D. J. Rycroft, 'Looking Beyond the Present: The Historical Dynamics of Adivasi (Indigenous and Tribal) Assertions in India', *Journal of Adivasi and Indigenous Studies* 1, no. 1 (2014), 1–2.

appeared. The discourse of scientific forestry was totally different from the Adivasi (literally 'original inhabitant', an umbrella term designating the indigenous tribal people of India) concept of landscape management.[10] Paul Sutter observed that it 'has been concentrated more on the social consequences than the ecological consequences (to the extent that they can be separated) of that change'.[11] Similarly, Mahesh Rangarajan noticed that 'one crucial aspect of historical change often neglected, is the ecological part of the story: when, why and how particular human intervention led to major transformation in the natural world'.[12] Furthermore, the colonial rulers considered the land and natural resources as state property, as it primarily satisfied their revenue needs. However, colonial environmental agendas were often marked by internal conflicts because there were no clear-cut policies. In order to maintain ecological balance and continuous supply of timber, conservation measures were taken after the 1860s. But due to Adivasi revolts, the colonial environmental policies could not remain uniform. Moreover, both the colonial government and the Adivasis sought to follow a shared environmental ideology.[13]

Ecological Hazards

'The growth of a forest policy in India', as E. P. Stebbing notes, 'was extraordinarily slow'. In the late 18th and the first half of the 19th century, the forests were considered as an obstacle to agriculture so that 'the whole policy was to extend agriculture'.[14] The colonial policy

---

[10] The Adivasi people managed the landscape with their own indigenous knowledge system. Different sacred institutions were created in order to facilitate biological resource management, linked to religious myth and belief system. For details see N. K. Mahato, 'Adivasi (Indigenous People) Perception of Landscape: The Case of Manbhum', *Journal of Adivasi and Indigenous Studies* 2, no. 1 (2015): 1.

[11] P. Sutter, 'What Can US Environmental Historians Learn from Non-US Environmental Historiography', *Environmental History* 8, no. 1 (2003): 4.

[12] Mahesh Rangarajan, *Fencing the Forest: Conservation and Ecological Change in India's Central Provinces, 1860–1914* (New Delhi: Oxford University Press, 1996), 8.

[13] Asoka Kumar Sen, 'Collaboration and Conflict: Environmental Legacies and the Ho of Kolhan (1700–1918)', in *The British Empire and the Natural World: Environmental Encounters in South Asia*, eds. Deepak Kumar, Vinita Damodaran and Rohon D' Souza (New Delhi: Oxford University Press, 2011), 208.

[14] E. P. Stebbing, *The Forests of India*, vols. 1, 2, 3 (London: The Bodley Head, 1922–1927), vol. 1, 62–63.

of extending cultivable land at the expense of forest resulted in large-scale deforestation. They also exterminated the dangerous predators.[15] H. Coupland mentions the paying of 'rewards … for the destruction of three tigers and seventy-nine leopards'.[16] Due to the growing demand of the railway system, which required immense quantities of logs of sal (*Shorea robusta* Gaertn. f. [Dipterocarpacea]) to make sleepers for the railway, pressure was placed on the forest of Jungle Mahals.[17] By the first decade of 20th century, Purulia was connected with Asansol, Sini, Chakradharpur, Kharagpur, Gomo, Jharia and Katras. In 1908, a narrow-gauge rail line of 2'–6' was constructed linking Purulia with Ranchi. Coupland reported: 'this line affords an outlet for the grain and jungle products of the western portion of the district'.[18] Timbers were also required for ship building.[19] The opening of the main line of Bengal Nagpur Railway through Kharagpur and Jhargram (1898) had a profound impact on the forests of the region. The introduction of railways made areas in the interior more accessible. As the forest products could be transported to distant places by the railway, there was a sudden increase in the supply of these products.[20] Pallavi Das rightly notes, 'As railway construction and operation expanded to facilitate increased trade, the railways' timber demand on the forests increased causing deforestation. The railways depended directly on the forests for their sleeper and fuel supply.'[21]

Deforestation was carried out by two groups of people: (a) *indigenous*: the zamindar (landowner) recruited indigenous people on different forms of contract, notably *nayabadi* (new tillage) and *junglebary* (land tenures).[22] (b) *Foreigners*: the colonial ruler employed European

---

[15] Damodaran, 'Gender, Forests and Famine', 142–144.

[16] H. Coupland, *Bengal District Gazetteers: Manbhum* (Calcutta: Bengal Secretariat Press, 1911), 21.

[17] Mark Proffenburger, 'The Struggle for Forest Control in Jungle Mahals of West Bengal 1750–1990', in *Village Voices, Forest Choices: Joint Forest Management in India*, eds. Mark Proffenburger and Besty McGean (New Delhi: Oxford University Press, 1998), 137.

[18] Coupland, *Bengal District Gazetteers*, 185.

[19] West Bengal State Archives, Revenue Dept., File No. 95/7/19, Govt. of Bengal, Forest Branch, May 1919, paras 7–9.

[20] K. C. Roychowdhury, 'The Forests of the Southern Circle: Its History and Management', in *West Bengal Forests: Centenary Commemoration Volume*, Forest Directorate (Calcutta, 1966), 133.

[21] Pallavi Das, 'Hugh Cleghorn and Forest Conservancy in India', *Environment and History* 11, no. 1 (2005), 56.

[22] For *jungleburi*, W.W. Hunter, *A Statistical Account of Bengal*, Vol. 17 (Calcutta, 1887), 332 and for *nayabadi* see Manbhum District Records (MDR),

companies to collect wood, such as Midnapur Zamindari Company. Deforestation opened up crop fields for cultivation as well as valuable timber. From 1883 onwards, the Midnapur Zamindari Company took forest land on lease from the zamindars and sold the timber for ship building and the production of railway sleepers.[23]

In the wake of agrarian intervention and forest destruction came environmental deterioration.

In 1855, Henry Ricketts reported the total absence of trees in Purulia town.[24] In 1863, Major J. Sherwill and Captain Donald Mcdonald described the landscape as 'hilly, stony and broken' and added: 'The soil is poor.'[25] In 1863, as G. E. Gastrell observed the environmental degradation of Bankura district

> What, about a half century ago, was thick jungle and waving plains of grass, is now almost a sterile and barren waste. Whenever the land was fit for cultivation, it was ploughed up. The successive rains have washed away the soil of uplands, and had left only a half layer of kunkury earth on which nothing will grow.[26]

Vinita Damodaran argues, 'in the case of Chotanagpur the story of environmental degradation cannot be so easily challenged'.[27]

There was a dramatic change in the land use pattern as a result of agrarian intervention and forest clearance in the districts of Southwest Bengal. In Manbhum, agrarian expansion was extended up to the far remote and hilly region of Bagmundi.[28] In 1907–1908, 58 per cent and 22 per cent of the area of Birbhum district were net crop area and

---

Circle Note of Attestation Camp No. II, Barabhum, Session—1904–1910 by Mr. Radhakanta Ghosh, Assistant Settlement Officer, p. 51.

[23] MDR, Circle Note of Attestation Camp No. II, 51.

[24] H. Ricketts, 'Reports on the Agency Administration', *Selection from the Records of Bengal Government*, Vol. 20 (Calcutta: Bengal Secretariat Press, 1855), 2–3.

[25] Major J. L. Sherwill and Captain Donald McDonald, *Map of Pargana Pandra, Sherghor, Mahesh and Chatna*, Main Circuit No. 5 & 9, 1862–1863. The Survey was conducted by Major J. L. Sherwill and Captain Donald McDonald.

[26] Lt. Col. G. E. Gastrell, 'Report on the District of Bankura', Quoted in L. S. S. O'Malley, *Bengal District Gazetteers: Birbhum* (Calcutta: Bengal Secretariat Press, 1910), 5.

[27] Damodaran, 'Gender, Forests and Famine', 143.

[28] For Manbhum, see N. K. Mahato, 'Environmental Change and Chronic Famine in Manbhum, Bengal District, 1860–1910', *Global Environment (A Journal of Transdisciplinary History)* 6 (2010), 74.

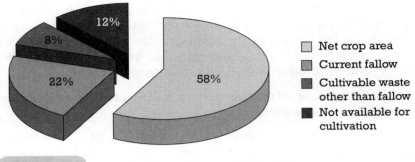

FIGURE 7.1 *Land Use in Birbhum, 1907–1908*

Source: O'Malley, L. S. S. *Bengal District Gazetteers: Birbhum.* Calcutta: Bengal Secretariat Press, 1910, p. 56.

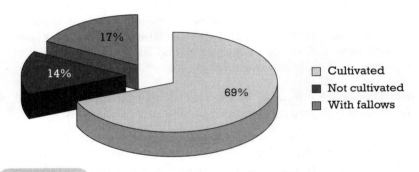

FIGURE 7.2 *Land Use in Birbhum, 1924–1932*

Source: Sarkar, Nandan. 'Birbhum Forests', in *West Bengal Forests: Centenary Commemoration Volume*, Forest Directorate. Calcutta: Divisional Forest Officer, Planning and Statistical Cell, 1966.

current fallow, respectively, while 12 per cent area was not available for cultivation (Figure 7.1).[29] In 1924–1932, 65 per cent area was under cultivated area and 17 per cent area was with fallows. But 14 per cent area was not available for cultivation (Figure 7.2). In 1946–1947, 65 per cent land and 25 per cent land were under cultivation and with fallow category, respectively, while 10 per cent area consisted of non-cultivated land (Figure 7.3). In 1958–1959, 74 per cent area and 6 per cent area were cultivated and with fallow category while 4 per cent area and 16 per cent area belonged to the category of other cultivated land including forest and non-cultivated land, respectively

---

[29] O'Malley, *Bengal District Gazetteers: Birbhum*, 56.

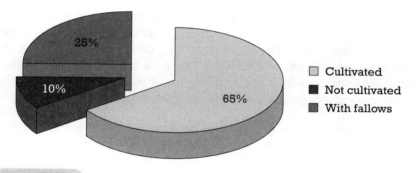

FIGURE 7.3 *Land Use in Birbhum, 1946–47*

Source: Sarkar, Nandan. 'Birbhum Forests', in *West Bengal Forests: Centenary Commemoration Volume*, Forest Directorate, Calcutta: Divisional Forest Officer, Planning and Statistical Cell, 1966.

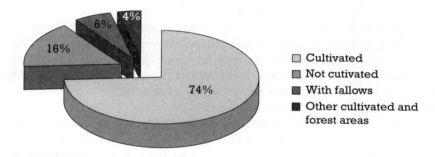

FIGURE 7.4 *Land Use in Birbhum during 1958–1959*

Source: Sarkar, Nandan. 'Birbhum Forests', in *West Bengal Forests: Centenary Commemoration Volume*, Forest Directorate. Calcutta: Divisional Forest Officer, Planning and Statistical Cell, 1966.

(Figure 7.4). The district Birbhum consisted of only 3 per cent land area under forest cover in 1964.[30]

This process can be viewed from different perspectives. Deforestation caused huge amounts of soil to be eroded by rainwater and deposited onto the bed of the river, reducing its depth.[31] The shallowness of the river increased the turbidity of its waters, making them contaminated. This, in turn, affected the health of the hunting and gathering Adivasis,

---

[30] Nandan Sarkar, 'Birbhum Forests', in *West Bengal Forests: Centenary Commemoration Volume* (Calcutta, 1966), 155–159.

[31] Coupland, *Bengal District Gazetteers*, 5.

Environmental Change and Forest Conservancy in Southwest Bengal 261

in particular the Savars and Birhors.[32] The colonial authority used *bandhs* (ponds) in total disregard of the Adivasi perception of water. They only employed them for irrigation, taking no account of the land–water–vegetation relationship. The agrarian invasion thus accelerated both soil erosion and the filling up of ponds. In 1910, Assistant Settlement Officer Radhakanta Ghosh reported:

> I found that the beds of some bandhs have been encroached upon by unscrupulous pradhan (village headman) and Bengali settlers who have recently settled in those villages. The beds of those bandhs are very fertile and yield rich crop. It is for this reason that the encroachment is made without any regard to the future injuries.[33]

As a result, the ponds silted up quickly and were reduced in size and, accordingly, water-holding capacity was also reduced. The clearing of the vegetation surrounding a pond and/or upstream of it accelerated soil erosion. The resulting siltation of the pond[34] started a chain of ecological havoc decrease in water volume, an increase in nutrient concentration, an increase in the productivity of the pond ecosystem and, ultimately, decreasing oxygen levels in the water. This led to a decrease in green plants and their replacement by blue-green algae, which generated toxins and a foul smell, causing the death of the water fauna, a dreadful process known as 'eutrophication'. After the denudation of the soil, evaporation increased, rapidly leading to dryness.[35] This reduced organic matter in the soil, affecting soil texture. The change in the soil microhabitat resulted in a harsh microclimate. The soil regeneration cycle in the area was thus altered and the seed bank jeopardized. Denudation reduced rainfall as well as soil moisture. Temperatures increased and a process of desertification ultimately set in over the whole region. Deforestation combined with monoculture has a devastating impact on tropical environments. In the tropics, a much larger portion of organic matter and available nutrients is contained in the biomass. This organic matter is recycled within the organic structure of the system, partly through the agency of a number of nutrient-conserving biological adaptations, which include mutualistic symbiosis between microorganism and plant remains. With the collapse of this elaborate and well-organized biotic structure, nutrients are rapidly lost

---

[32] Oral History collected from Sri Kalipada Savar, Savar Old Man, Vill-Sidhatarn, Dist. Purulia, 27 March 2003.

[33] MDR, Circle Note of Attestation Camp No. II, 45.

[34] Ibid.

[35] Coupland, *Bengal District Gazetteers*, 113.

to leaching under conditions of high temperatures and heavy rainfall, especially on sites that were poor in nutrients to begin with. E. P. Odum writes: 'For this reason, agricultural strategies of the temperate zones, involving the monoculture of short-lived annual plants, are quite inappropriate for tropical regions.'[36]

Forest Conservancy

In 1862, both the Government of India and Secretary of State at Home realized the systematic forest conservancy on immediate basis. As the Secretary of State notes, 'to remove the forests from the category of waste lands, their boundaries should be established and set apart in some strict and formal manner'.[37] The scientific forestry in colonial India was developed, as Ramachandra Guha argues, in response to the revenue and strategic needs of the empire.[38] He further notes that 'the large scale destruction of accessible forest in the early years of railway expansion led to the hasty creation of a forest department, set up with the help of German experts in 1864'.[39] Due to increase of prices of both timber and fuel, the British authority felt that forest conservancy measures would be taken with a view to mitigate over-exploitation of forests. In 1862, Dr Deitrich Brandis was invited to visit and prepare a report on forests of Bengal. He made a tour to some parts of the forests and he talked about the future forest policy with Dr T.

---

[36] E. P. Odum, *Basic Ecology* (New York: Holt-Saunders, 1983), 211–212.

[37] Stebbing, *The Forests of India*, Vol. 1, 532.

[38] Ramachandra Guha, *The Unquiet Woods: Ecological Change and Peasant Resistance in the Himalaya* (New Delhi: Oxford University Press, 1999), New Expanded Edition. He argues that colonialism 'constituted an ecological watershed in the history of India'. See also Madhav Gadgil and Ramachandra Guha, *This Fissured Land: An Ecological History of India*, Chap. V–VIII (New Delhi: Oxford University Press, 1992). However, Richarad H. Grove in his work *Green Imperialism* contested this thesis (Richarad H. Grove, *Green Imperialism: Colonial Expansion, Tropical Island Edens, and the Origins of Environmentalism* [Cambridge: Cambridge University Press, 1995]). He argues that the ideological commitment of a section of colonial officials to conservation was much more significant than narrow materialist concerns. Rangarajan, *Fencing the Forest*, 7, has commented on this controversy that 'many of the differences between Guha and Grove are due to the difference in the chronological focus of their research. Grove is concerned with the early colonial period; Guha focuses on the late 19th century. There is also a marked contrast in their central concerns. Guha examines the broad unity of imperial interests while Grove brings out the divisions among colonial officials'.

[39] Guha, *Unquiet Woods* (new expanded edition), 37.

Anderson, the Superintendent, Botanic Garden in Kolkata. Dr Brandis submitted his proposal on 18 December 1862. The Government of India asked the Bengal Government to undertake forest conservancy in 1863 and the Bengal Government assigned the responsibility to Dr T. Anderson to examine the forests.[40] Forest service emerged in India with the appointment of Dr Deitrich Brandis (1824–1907) as an Inspector General of Forest of India in October 1864. He tried to organize forestry in India and Burma on the basis of three principles of German forestry—'minimum diversity', the 'balance-sheet' and 'sustained yield'. In the concept of 'minimum diversity', Brandis tried to emphasize on producing appropriation to the extent of teak, the predominant commercial woods. It levelled across the inherent diversity of forest. Therefore, the forests were eventually transformed into 'commercially marketable monocultures'. Brandis formulated guidelines for the management of forest and enunciated ground rules on felling. Thus, his approach was to regularize repair, tending and pruning. He advocated diffuse replacement of felled trees by dibbling seed or planting seedling in the gaps, landing and other forest openings. To prevent either under- or overutilization of wood, Brandis provided guidelines. In his guidelines, the 'annual yield' would be based on the amount they put on. The useful species gained special attention for conservation and plantation. Thus, the attitude to nature adopted by the Indian forester in the second half of 19th century was 'clearly conservationist in character'. Ravi Rajan writes 'by the end of the nineteenth century this utilitarian conservation sentiment became a developmental ideology in its own right'.[41]

In various parts of an ecologically and socially heterogeneous subcontinent, the imposition of the new regime of control had different consequences. Mahesh Rangarajan writes that 'the specific ecological milieu both in terms of forest types and agrarian regimes (land ownership patterns and production system) will build up a better understanding of contrasts between and within different regions'.[42] This chapter also explores Rangarajan's point in case of the forest management of Manbhum district.

---

[40] Stebbing, *Forests of India*, Vol. 1, 514.

[41] Ravi Rajan, 'Imperial Environmentalism or Environmental Imperialism? European Forestry, Colonial Foresters and the Agendas of Forest Management in British India, 1800–1900', in *Nature and the Orient: The Environmental History of South and Southeast Asia*, eds. Richard H. Grove, Vinita Damodaran and Satpal Sangwan (New Delhi: Oxford University Press, 1999), 343–351.

[42] Rangarajan, *Fencing the Forest*, 202–203.

In his book, 'Forestry in British India' (1900), Ribentrop categorized the Indian forests into seven forest zones, and the forests of Southwest Bengal belonged to the Central India Deciduous Region.[43] Forest conservancy was started in India in August 1864, and the forests of Bengal were managed by 10 divisions which included Bhagalpur, Santhal Parganas, Patna, Rajshahye, Burdwan, Nuddea (Sunderban and 24 Parganas), Cuttack, Chotanagpur, Dacca and Cachar.[44] Among the Southwest Bengal districts, Bankura, Birbhum, Burdwan and Midnapur were included in the Burdwan Division and the District Manbhum was integrated with the Chotanagpur division.

Burdwan division: During the period of 1865–1870, as E. P. Stebbing notes, most of the parts of Bankura district were covered with young sal trees and all of the area belonged to the zamindars. But the district Birbhum comprised of 11 zones of forests each containing 2,000 or 3,000 bighas, which were private property. In the case of Midnapur district, areas covering a distance of 1,200 mi^2 were known as 'Jungle Mahals' distributed in privately owned pergunnahs, and out of it, 700 mi^2 was timber-producing forest land. There was no conservancy measure undertaken in the Division. The growing trees were the sal, mohwa (*Basssia latifolia*), asan (*Termonalia monemtosa*) and jam (*Schima wallichii*). The government had not extracted any revenue from the forests.

In Midnapur, the owners cut down trees for selling timber in different towns and weekly hats and licences were given to owners of forests to prepare cocoons, dhuna and charcoal. But in Birbhum, no licence was granted to cut woods from the forest of the district. In order to float out woods and forest products, rivers were used. Most of these came from outside the division. Timbers were transported from Raipore, Simlapal and Manbhum through 'Jungle Mahals', and rifts were floated down through the Cossye River during rainy season.[45]

Chotanagpur division: Manbhum, Singhbhum, Lohardaga and Hazaribagh districts belonged to the Chotanagpur division. In order to meet the demands of railway sleepers and Public Works Department, woods were extracted from the forests near the highway and rivers. Damodar River, an important waterway, was utilized for floating timber.[46]

---

[43] The Seven Forests zones were (a) evergreen forests zone, (b) deciduous forests zone, (c) dry forest zone, (d) alpine forest zone, (e) riparian forest zone, (f) tidal forest zone and (g) zone without forests. For details see Stebbing, *The Forests of India*, Vol. 1, 39–45.

[44] Ibid, Vol. 2, 375.

[45] Stebbing, *The Forests of India*, Vol. 2, 385–386.

[46] Ibid., 391–395.

Private forests: With the commercialization of forests,[47] new form of land use came into existence. Forests could bring larger return per acre than tenanted lands that could be cultivated. The big *zamindars* (landlords) took steps for preserving forests. As K. C. Raychoudhury wrote:

> The zemindars of most parts, of Bankura, Birbhum and Midnapur and particularly Purulia held the forests under a peculiar lease and undefined form of tenure, known as the *ghatwali* tenure originally granted in lieu of watch and ward duties of the ghats, that is, the hilly tracts.

Also E. P. Stebbing comments on: 'The forests in the Manbhum District all belong to the 'zemindars' under the perpetual settlements...'[48] In Midnapur, the big landowners such as British-held Midnapur Zamindary Company, the Rajas of Jhargram, the Raja of Mayurbhanj absorbed most of the estates managed by small landowners.[49] The zamindars managed their forest with the very easy method of coppice system without giving adequate time for the mother trees for regeneration.[50] With the opening of new markets, felling went on with an increased tempo and sal (*S. robusta* Gaertn. f. [Dipterocarpacea]) being easy to regenerate by coppice. This method was followed by all owners. The rotation varied according to the need of forest owner, that is, for bigger parties, the rotation became necessarily smaller. The small holders brought down the rotation to 5 years or even less and hastened disappearance of forests.[51] As 70 per cent owners followed the 6 years rotation for the coppice crop, small amounts of stools died. It accelerated soil erosion and disturbed the natural regeneration capacity. Also, the private owner permitted grazing in the coppiced area, which endangered the new crops. The cultivators practised forest fire with a view to feed their nearby agricultural field with mineral ashes and silt during the rain. Adivasis also practised forest fire during their *lo bir sendra* (annual hunting festival). Due to lack of adequate capacity of power and lack of staff, the private owners failed to deal with the forest offences. They were neither interested to invest money with a view to fill the blanks in the forests or in the periphery nor undertook soil conservative actions. It resulted in gulley formation

---

[47] Ranabir Samaddar, *Memory, Identity, Power: Politics in the Jungle Mahals (WestBengal) 1890–1950* (Hydrabad: Orient Longman, 1998), 66.

[48] Stebbing, *The Forests of India*, Vol. 2, 91.

[49] Proffenburger, 'The Struggle for Forest Control', 138.

[50] S. N. Mishra, 'Forests of Midnapur', in *West Bengal Forests: Centenary Commemoration Volume* (Calcutta: Divisional Forest Officer, Planning and Statistical Cell, 1966), 152.

[51] Roychowdhury, 'Forests of the Southern Circle', 133.

and sheet erosion and ultimately, it affected the water regime of the region.[52] Though the zamindars maintained the forests as shooting reserves, they ruthlessly destroyed the woods by engaging agents to earn quick profit.[53]

In order to protect the original peasantry and their community leadership, new types of administrative set-ups like South-western Frontier Agency or Encumbered Estates/Court of Wards were introduced in many areas of Chotanagpur. But by the 20th century, general kind of administration was implemented in these regions of 'zone of anomaly' and the 'zamindars gained at the expense of headmen'.[54] When the forests were under the managements of managers, wards and encumbered estates, the forests gradually 'begun to disappear as a result of wanton destruction by tenants'.[55] In 1935, considering the environmental hazards, the government reviewed the role of zamindars as forest managers in the British Empire Forestry conference held in South Africa.[56] In the wake of forest destruction and environmental change, the Government of Bengal appointed a Forest Committee in 1936, with a view to understand the phenomenon and make recommendations for forest conservancy.[57] The Committee reported about Bhirbhum forests, 'The forests which the committee saw is in miserable condition ...' and it further notes 'As regards its forests, Birbhum may be said to be in a complete decadence'.[58] According to the recommendations of the Committee, the Bengal Private Forests Act 1945 was passed, and West Bengal division was created with its headquarters in Midnapur extending its jurisdiction in the districts of Midnapur and Bankura. With a view to manage the waste land of Nadia, another division, the Central Division was formed in 1946.[59] In the year 1945–1946, the first nursery was established in Contai and its aim was to distribute seedling to the general people and create public consciousness. In the following year, a forestation programme was started in the sandy waste land of Digha coast and Junput.[60]

---

[52] Ibid.; Mishra, 'Forests of Midnapur', 152–153.

[53] *West Bengal District Gazetteers, Puruliya* (Calcutta, 1985), 53–54.

[54] Sivaramakrishnan, 'Transition Zones', 217.

[55] MDR, Notes recorded by D. P. Sharma, Esq. I. C. S. Deputy Commissioner, Manbhum, 12 November 1940 on the working of the Barabum Wards Estate Forests, para 2.

[56] Sivaramakrishnan, 'Transition Zones', 227.

[57] T. K. Mitra, 'History of Forests: Bankura District', in *West Bengal Forests: Centenary Commemoration Volume* (Calcutta: Divisional Forest Officer, Planning and Statistical Cell, 1966), 144.

[58] Quoted Sarkar, 'Birbhum Forests', 157.

[59] Roychowdhury, 'Forests of the Southern Circle', 134.

[60] Mishra, 'Forests of Midnapur', 152.

Protected Forests in Manbhum: Matha and Kuilapal

The government and forest department took a wholesale programme of forest management to combat extensive deforestation.[61] In India, the growth of a forest policy was extraordinarily slow. Throughout the 18th century, the whole policy of the government was to extend agriculture and to destroy the forests. In the early 19th century, demands of forests increased. Colonial government attempted to conserve them. Though a forest conservancy system was introduced in some provinces, it was not raised above the level of revenue administration. Though in 1865 a Forest Act was passed, it took three more decades to implement the terms. 'Social complexity', as Sivaramkrishnan notes, 'was also a factor shaping managerial alternatives.' Here the social structure was not merely dual character like sovereigns and subalterns, but it was complex in nature.[62]

In Manbhum, following the suggestion of Dr John Augustus Voelker, a German expert, areas of jungle covering 8.90 and 4.32 mi^2 were notified as government protected forest in the two temporary settled estates of Matha and Koilapal in 1894. Those were the only government forest sites in the district. All the waste lands and forests in these two estates were originally declared to be 'protected forest'. However, some portions of the forests sufficient for the requirement of the villagers were subsequently assigned to them. The boundaries of these blocks had been demarcated with stone cairns.[63] It is noted that those forests which had not yet been surveyed were 'protected', and it was hoped that it would be reserved for future.[64] Towards the end of December, 1901, a forest officer was deputed by the Deputy Conservator of Forest, Singhbum district to hold the charge of these forests.[65]

With the formation of the province of Bihar and Odisha on 1 April 1912, the Forest Division of Santal Parganas, Palamu, Singhbhum, Chaibasa, Sambalpur, Angul and Puri were taken away from the lower province of Bengal and constituted into Bihar and Odisha Forest Circle and Mr H. A. Forteath held charge of this new circle with effect

[61] Damodaran, 'Indigenous Forests', 119.

[62] Sivaramakrishnan, 'Transition Zones', 199.

[63] MDR, Land Revenue Administration Report for 1903/1904. Revenue Dept. File No. XV(C), Issue no.135(R), Date of Issue: 27.04.1904, Item No.11.

[64] For protected and reserve forests see, John Augustus Voelker, *Report on the Improvement of Indian Agriculture* (London, 1893), 142–144.

[65] MDR, Land Revenue Administration Report for 1903/1904. Revenue Dept. File No. XV(C), Issue no.135(R), Date of Issue: 27.04.1904. Item No. 11.

from 1 April 1912. At the time, the following districts were under the Chaibasa Division.[66]

Name of the District	R.F. in sq. Miles	P.F. Area in sq. Miles	Total sq. Miles
Singhbhum		182	
Manbhum	182	14	196
Santal Parganas		292	292

Source: B. N. Prasad, *Bihar Forest Souvenir* (1965), 18–20.

Reserve forests: In India, some forest lands became 'reserved' with the emergence of Forest Act of 1865. In these forests, the government had the full right of ownership and thus banned all sorts of agriculture. By the Forest Act of 1878, the rules were tightened. In these forests, the peasants who lived in the reserved areas had no right to the forest.[67] Though the 'protected forest' concept came in force in 1894, it took nearly three decades to create a 'reserved' forest in Manbhum district.

The Government of Bihar and Odisha in Council (under the notification No. 7673 III F 67-R and in exercise of the powers conferred by the Sec.19 of the Indian Forest Act of 1878) declared the forests belonging to the Taralal encumbered estates situated in the Purulia police station in the district of Manbhum as 'reserve forest' with effect from 1 September 1925.[68] According to the order of Governor-in-Council, J. R. Dain Secretary to Government, in Jaipur Block I, the cart track was allowed from Jaipur village towards Hoyanda as a public right of way. In Block II, the cart track from Pirorgoria towards Popo, which passed through this block, was allowed as a public right of way. In Block V, the cart track from Popo to Bali onwards and towards Hazaribagh was allowed as a public right of way. In Block VII, Popo to Pirargoria, cart track was allowed as a public right of way.[69]

The government of Bihar and Odisha in Council declared the forest belonging to Kalimati encumbered estates situated in the Bagmundi

---

[66] Bihar Forest Souvenir (Bihar: Forest Department, 1965), 18–20.

[67] David Hardiman, 'Farming in the Forest: The Dangs 1830–1992', in *Village Voices, Forest Choices: Joint Forest Management in India*, eds. Mark Profenburger and B. MacGean (New Delhi, 1996), 112.

[68] MDR, No. 259. Forest Dept., Guard File of Inspection Note, By order of the Govt. in Council, J. R. Dain, Secretary to Government, 30 June 1925.

[69] Ibid.

police station of the district of Manbhum as 'reserve forests' with effect from 1 August 1925.

Description of Kalimati Reserve Forests

Village	Area in Acres
Pearitorang	258.06
Perorgoria	431.29
Kalimati	214.17
Banddi	720.70
Bagti	517.94

In Kalimati reserved forest, Dolgobinda Singh of Kalimati was allowed to cultivate plot no. 15 and 16 in Kalimati and 14, 15 and 16 in Perorgoria. Balai Mahato, son of Ratin Mahato of Pirorgoria, was allowed to cultivate plot no. 82–86 and 88–92 in Kalimati and 20–22 in Perorgoria. Brajraj Singh, son of Ganga Narain Singh of Kalimati was allowed to cultivate plot no. 2–13 in Kalimati and plot no. 2–14 in Perorgoroia. Kujla Bhumij, son of Rasaraj Bhumij of Bagti, was allowed to cultivate in plot no. 1340 in Bagti.[70]

Again, the Government of Bihar and Odisha in council declared the forest belonging to the Mudali encumbered estates situated in Purulia police station in the district of Manbhum as 'reserved forest' from 1 August 1925.

Description of Mudali Reserve Forest

Village	Area in Acres
Rajpur	1,312.11
Dumabera	284.31
Midali	499.61

In this forest, the villagers of the Dhanchatani and Lukuichatani were given the rights of way to the routes used by them for coming down to the plains from the top of the hills.[71]

---

[70] Ibid. (under the notification no. 70008 III F 67R and in exercise of the powers conferred by section 19 of the Indian Forest Act, 1878, Act of VII of 1878).

[71] Ibid. (under the notification no. 7010 III F- 67 -R and in exercise of the powers conferred by Sec. 19 of the Indian Forest Act, 1878, Act of 1878)

In another notification, the Government of Bihar and Odisha in Council declared the forest belonging to the Barabhum encumbered estates of district of Manbhum as 'reserved forest' with from 29 May 1925. The Governor in Council appointed the Sadr Sub-Divisional Officer of Manbhum to discharge within the limits of reserved forests of the Jaipur, Taralal, Kalimati, Mudali and Barabhum Encumbered Estates in the district of Manbum. The power of Forest Officer was vested to him.[72] All the rangers, deputy rangers, foresters and forest guards who might be appointed to the forests of these estates would also discharge the functions, which were similar to the officials of the forest department.[73]

The British Government considered the forest from the utilitarian outlook. In 1932, Forest Officer Rai Sahib P. N. Mukherjee reported that there were two reserved forests under the management such as Barabhum Reserve Forest and Taralal Reserve Forest.[74] Revenue orientation became more marked under the state management like Uttarakhand.[75] It has been reflected in the following table:

Revenue of Reserve Forests					
Reserve Forest	**Periods**				
Taralal	1929–30	1930–1931	1931–1932	1932–1933	1933–1934
	38-15-9	31-15-0	26-0-0	nil	
Barabhum	448-8-0	1062-14-0	36-2-0	100	577-0-0
Barabhum	1934–1935	1935	1936	1937–1939	1940
	608-0-0	433-0-6	1260-0-0	725-0-0	100-0-0
	(as against revenue expenditure 698-14-9)		(average)		

Source: Inspection note of the Forest Department made by Forest Officer, 1932–1940.
Note: The values are given in the following format: rupees-anna-paise.

---

[72] Ibid.

[73] MDR, By order, J. R. Dain, the 29 May1925 and 30 June 1925 (under the notification no. 7013 III F- 67 -R and in exercise of the powers conferred by Sec. 19 of the Indian Forest Act, 1878, Act of 1878).

[74] MDR, Inspection Note of Forest Dept. made by Forest Officer, Rai Sahib P. N. Mukherjee, 31 March 1932.

[75] Guha, *Unquiet Woods*, 37.

The income was mainly derived from compensation for Forest Act cesses and sale of minor forest produce. The figures for 1930–1931 included sales of firewood and brushwood in Block I. The firewood and brushwood in Block II would be sold in auction at Barabazar on 10 April 1932. The slight decrease in other income was due to the fact that there was a decrease in the price of lac. Therefore, settlement of the few lac trees could not be made.[76]

Forest Officer I. A. Habbuck reported that one reason for the big drop between 1930–1931 and 1931–1932 in Barabhum Reserve Forest was that firewood and brushwood in the coupe under clearance that year were not actually put up for the auction till 10 April 1932. In 1930–1931, a sum of ₹1,250 was obtained from the settlement of brushwood and firewood in Block I. The forest officer could not collect revenues from lac settlement in the forest in this session, but he collected it in the previous years.[77]

Taralal figures in 1932–1933 show no revenue at all, although three foresters were employed on this forest and there was also a deputy ranger for other two forests.[78] So the government decided to sell the reserve forests.

In Barabhum Reserve Forest, the income was derived from dried sal, (*S. robusta* Gaertn. f. [Dipterocarpacea]) straw, arrears of lac rent and kul [*Ziziphus mauritiana* Lamk. (Rhamnaceae)] trees for the year 1931–1932. In the year 1932, the miscellaneous receipts so far were ₹46, which had been derived from cattle grazing and catching of fish. S. U. Majumdar, Deputy Commissioner, reported that 'the former should not have been allowed as it was deadly to regeneration of forest'.[79]

Taralal Reserve Forest was given to a further lease to the proprietor of the Taralal Encumbered Estate. The forest staffs were discharged on 20 March 1933. Thus, there remained only Barabum Reserve Forest under management. In the year 1932–1933, ₹111 was derived as compensation from Forest Act cases and sale of minor forest products. As the price of lac had declined very heavily, it hardly covered manufacture cost, and there were no applications for lac settlement.[80]

---

[76] MDR, Inspection Note of Forest Dept. made by Forest Officer, Rai Sahib P. N. Mukherjee, 31 March 1932.

[77] MDR, Inspection Note of Forest Dept. made by Forest Officer, I. A. Habbuck, para 2.

[78] Ibid., para 3.

[79] MDR, Inspection Note of Forest Dept. made by Forest Officer, S. N. Mukherjee, February 1933, paras 2–3.

[80] MDR, Inspection Note of Forest Dept. made by Forest Officer, Rai Sahib P. N. Mukherjee, 29 and 30 March 1933, paras 2 and 6.

Rai Sahib P. N. Mukherjee reported that from Barabhum Reserve Forest, a sum of ₹500 had been received during the year 1933–1934 on account of sale of brushwood of Block I and ₹77 had been received on account of compensation levied on forest offence cases and settlement of minor products such as fishery in a *jor* (channel) and sale of thatching grass.[81] In the year 1935–1936, ₹608/1/ was derived from the settlement of palas (*Butea monosperma*) trees, straw and sale of sal trees. But the expenditure (i.e., ₹698-14-9) was more than the income.[82] In 1935, ₹433 was derived from settlement of sal trees (₹425-0-6) and compensation realized from forest offenses cases (₹8-0-0).[83] In 1936, the income of ₹1260-0-6 was derived from settlement of sal trees (₹1192-8-0), miscellaneous sources (₹33-8-6) and compensation realized from forest offenses (₹14-0-0).[84] For the period of 1937–1939, average revenue of ₹725 was derived from the sale of minor produce such as grass, firewood, etc. In the year 1940, the expected revenue was estimated as ₹1,000.[85]

Several recent studies on forest reservation recognized its territorial basis (Ramachandra Guha 1989, 1990, Mahesh Rangarajan 1992, Ajay Skaria 1999). In his study, Sivaramakrishnan has shown that 'the making of reserved and protected areas displays a regional pattern in Bengal'. He treated Southwest Bengal as a 'zone of anomaly to forest reservation'.[86] This section examines to what extent Brandis' three basic principles of forest reservation—'minimum diversity', the 'balance sheet' and 'sustained yield'—were implemented in Manbhum. He first of all applied this method in Northeast Province and Oudh from where it spread to various parts of equatorial tropics.[87]

Minimum diversity: The Barabhum Reserve Forest became a forest of 'commercially marketable monoculture'. In his inspection note written in 1933, Forest Officer Hardayal Singh recorded that 'these forests are good type especially those in block no. I just near Barabazar. On one side of a channel running in block no. I, the crop consists of only young sal (Shorea robusta) poles up to 12'''-18''', mix with a

---

[81] Ibid., 27 March 1934, para 6.

[82] MDR, Inspection Note of Forest Dept. made by Forest Officer, N. L. Bhagat, 17 March 1935, para 6.

[83] Ibid., 29 March 1935, para 6.

[84] MDR, Inspection Note of Forest Dept. made by Forest Officer, S. N. Majumdar, 31 March 1936, para 4.

[85] MDR, Inspection Note of Forest Dept. made by Forest Officer, D. P. Sharma, 1940, paras 2–3.

[86] K. Sivaramakrishnan, *Modern Forests: State Making and Environmental Change in Colonial Eastern India* (New Delhi: Oxford University Press, 1999), 76–78.

[87] Rajan, 'Imperial Environmentalism or Environmental Imperialism', 346.

small percentage of miscellaneous species i.e., of girth of the log varying from 2" to 6"'.[88] Sal was the most commercially valuable timber. Though of little importance, other species such as neem (*Azadirachta indica*), mahanim (*Melia dubia*), karanja (*Pongamia pinnata*), arjun (*Terminalia arjuna*), piasal (*Pterospermum marsupium*), etc., were also grown.[89] The research officer strongly recommended sabai grass planting as there was high demand for fuel.[90]

The forest of Block II of Barabazar Reserve Forest was of much uniform type than that in Block I. It contained nothing except small poles and saplings of sal, the maximum girth hardly exceeding 12–18 inches. There were other patches containing species such as dhadhki (*Woodfordia fruticosa*), siuli (*Nyctanthes arbor-tristis*), sihuri (*Cleistanthus collinus*), etc., all growing in a mass and quite up to the firewood size.[91] Forest Officer P. N. Mukherjee suggested to sow simul (*Bambax malabaricum*), tetul (*Tamarindus indica*) and Asan (*Terminalia tomentosa*) trees in this area.[92] Many other valuable wood species such as teak, bamboo, gamar, mohua (*Madhuca indica*, Gmelin [Combretaceae]) had been introduced later.[93]

Balance sheet: The scientific forestry was introduced in India in the form of silviculture plantation. It was introduced in South India in order to generate resources, and in this way the forest department tried to test its viability. 'Sylviculture plantations', as Ravi Kumar argues, 'became laboratories of experiments of scientific forestry to test the ability of objective science in manipulating the nature'.[94] The principle of balance sheet was reflected in the sylvicultural method followed by the foresters of Barabhum Reserve Forest. After visiting the forest in 1933, Forest Officer Haradayal Singh reported that the young sal poles up to 12"–18" girth would be felled provided suitable offers of price were available. The patches were to be vigorously

---

[88] MDR, D.O. No.151, From Hardyal Singh, Divisional Forest Officer, To, Sahib P. N. Mukherjee, Forest Officer, Manbhum, dated 26 January 1933, para 2.

[89] MDR, Inspection Note of Forest Dept. made by Forest Officer, S. U. Majumdar, 23 February1933, para 5.

[90] MDR, D.O. No. 2846/22(12), From Hardyal Singh, Divisional Forest Officer, To, Sahib P. N. Mukherjee, Forest Officer, Manbhum, dated 29 February 1934, para 4.

[91] Ibid., para 6.

[92] MDR, Inspection Note of Forest Dept. made by Forest Officer, Rai Sahib P. N. Mukherjee, 26 March 1934, para 2.

[93] MDR, Inspection Note of Forest Dept. made by Forest Officer, N. L. Bhagat, 29 March 1935, para 7. See also, PDRRC, Inspection Note of Forest Dept. made by Forest Officer, D. P. Sharma, 1940, para 4.

[94] Kumar, 'Colonialism and Green Science', 246.

protected from grazing after completion of felling. Removal of dead leaves and sal seeds would not be allowed. It would ensure getting coppice regeneration on the cut stumps with enriched surfaced soil to feed them. There were differences of opinion regarding the sylvicultural method between Rai Sahib P. N. Mukherjee, Sadar Sub Divisional Officer, Manbhum and Haradyal Singh, Divisional Forest Officer, Chaibasa Division. Deputy Commissioner's idea was 'to fill up these patches with *sasbai* (*Ischaemum angustifolium*) grass'. The divisional forest officer suggested that 'it would be better of teak root and shoot-cutting are planting instead'. Accordingly, teak is one of first growing species and it is not very much damaged by cattle grazing. Haradayal Singh made an important observation that

> in certain places [it] will improve the crop considerably. But it should be done only by skilled hands and no dishonest contractor should be allowed to enter the area. It is much better to let the crop stand as it is than to ruin it in the name of thinning.[95]

Forester of Barabazar Reserve Forest derived some revenues from cattle grazing. The Divisional Forest Officer Chaibasa Division, who inspected the forest at the end of January 1933, had remarked that cattle grazing 'is deadly to the regeneration of forest'. He found that the ground was swept of even dead leaves and had suggested that the area should be vigorously protected from grazing. He also mentioned that the deputy ranger who was appointed in 1926 had received no training in forest work. So, it would not be possible for him to develop the forest on scientific line.[96]

There was also difference of opinions among the forest officials. While Mr B. P. Basu, IFS, the Forest Research Officer strongly recommended sabai grass planting, Haradayal Singh suggested that a few patches in the forest would better be filled up with tree species.[97] Sabai was the most valuable grass at that time. It had been brought from Singhbhum district. D. P. Sharma, Deputy Commissioner, Manbhum writes that its cultivation was extended for the last 4 years, 1936–1939.[98] In 1940, he reported that most valuable wood species, Sandal, was planted with the

---

[95] MDR, A letter From Hardyal Singh, Divisional Forest Officer, To, Sahib P. N. Mukherjee, Forest Officer, Manbhum, dated 26 January 1933, para 3.

[96] MDR, Inspection Note of Forest Dept. made by Forest Officer, S. U. Majumdar, 23 February 1933, paras 7–8.

[97] MDR, D.O. No. 2846/22(12), From Hardyal Singh, Divisional Forest Officer, To, Sahib P. N. Mukherjee, Forest Officer, Manbhum, dated 29 February 1934, para 4.

[98] MDR, Inspection Note of Forest Dept. made by Forest Officer, D. P. Sharma, 1940, para 4.

assistance of Forest Research Institute, Dehradun and Mysore. Another important wood called tung (*Aleurites fordii* [Euphorbiaceae]), which was a cling tree, was brought from Mysore in the same year. Its oil was very extensively used for paint and varnish during the time.[99]

Sustained yield: Now we are to examine the main German principle of 'sustained yield', which was adopted by the Indian foresters of Manbhum. The forest officials tried to desist themselves from overutilization of wood. But the district authority tried to extract revenues from forests without taking consideration of over utilization. In 1933, Rai Sahib P. N. Mukherjee, Sadar Sub Divisional Officer of Manbhum reported: 'the brushwood of Block I of the forest will be fit for the sale next year'. Sal tree in Nilmohanpur was numbered, but no action was taken for the sale of the large trees due to economic depression. In 1934, Haradayal Singh, Divisional Forest Officer, Chaibasa reported that the district authority sought to overutilize the forest. In his note, it is found that Block I was marked and advertised for sale in spite of the fact that there was absolutely no regeneration on the ground. He felt pity seeing the ruthless felling of all the so-called species by a contractor getting a lease of 2 years. While the primary aim should be to fill up the blanks, instead through the above process, more blanks were created. Thus, more and more of the surface became exposed and lost more and more of the potential value of the soil.[100]

The Divisional Forest officials were more careful to preserve the forest on Brandis line than the district authorities. The district officials always sought to collect more revenue than the previous year. For this, they were even ready to give permission for grazing. Sivaramakrishnan rightly observes that 'with forest becoming a state resource, control over their disposition, and control over all manner of revenues derived from them, become central to the conflict that arose between foresters and the district administration'.[101] This type of conflict prevailed in the third and fourth decades of 20th century also.

During the rule of East India Company, demarcation of external boundaries of the empire was the main concern. With the growing knowledge of the landscape and natural resources of the empire, the British Raj sought to concentrate, after 1858, on internal or managerial

---

[99] Ibid.

[100] MDR, D.O. No. 2846/22(12), From Hardyal Singh, Divisional Forest Officer, To, Sahib P. N. Mukherjee, Forest Officer, Manbhum, dated 29 February 1934, para 2.

[101] K. Sivaramakrishnan, 'A Limited Forest Conservancy in Southwest Bengal, 1864–1912', *Journal of Asian Studies* 56, no. 1 (1997): 87.

territorialization. It obviously demanded forest conservancy.[102] As in Manbhum district 'administrative exceptionalism' existed, it took three more decades to create protected forests. As most of the forest were under the possession of zamindars (landlords) and *ghatwals* (guardian of passes, sometime headman), there were constant conflicts over the jungle rights between them and the *raiyats* (peasants). In spite of that, in 1928, the Britishers hesitated to dissolve *ghatwali* rights. During the time, A. F. A. Hamid, Superintendent of Police, Manbhum wrote

> as this institution is very old one and more or less deeply rooted and as some of the ghatwals are probably under khuntkatti and stithiban rights, the abolition of the system may lead to unrest specially when lands etc., would be snatched from them and resettled.[103]

To meet the demands of II World War (1939–1945), recourse was taken under certain provisions of the Indian Forest Act. Colonial officials started negotiation with the *ghatwals* who held government forest under permanent service of *jagir* and also with the general manager of Wards and Encumbered Estates. As a result, the forest of Bagmundi Estate came under government management, with lease of 20 years in 1942. In 1943, the *ghatwali* or private forest of Kaira, Dadha, Bonta, Makuliah, Baroda, Gunda and Ramnagar came similarly under control and management of the Forest department of Bihar through a lease of 40 years. The forests of Palkia, Popo and Kenda were taken over by the government in 1944, and the forests of Tundi met the same fate in 1945. In the same year, Barabhum Reserved Forest was transferred from the Civil Department to Forest Department. During this period, the demand for timber and poles was increased, as timber prices were so high and the colonial government had given the priority of transportation of war materials. The government started to harvest good timber from remote areas of the forests to meet the war situation.[104] However, there were some exceptions. The Midnapur Zamindary Company protected the forests of villages of Asanboni, Khukro and Bandhdih in the Dalma hill region. The Jharia Water Board also undertook forest

---

[102] Ibid, 78.

[103] Bihar State Archives, Board of Revenue, File no. S-5 of November 1930, Nos 24–29, Board of Revenue, Bihar and Orissa. E- Enclosed(s) to Progs. no. 24. No. 5983, Purulia, dated 10 October 1928, From A. F. A Hamid, Esq. I.P.S. To the Deputy Commissioner of Manbhum, Manbhum, Sub: Abolition of Ghatwals, para 11.

[104] A. B. Rudra, 'Forests of Purulia District', in *West Bengal Forests: Centenary Commemoration Volume*, Forest Directorate (Calcutta: Divisional Forest Officer, Planning and Statistical Cell, 1966), 163.

conservancy measures in order to protect lake from siltation. Some zamindars conserved their forests by profiting people to cut trees in their forests. With the implementation of Bihar Private Forests Act in 1946, a broad and immediate programme of forest conservancy was started, as it implemented its control over the private forests.[105]

Post-colonial Times

In Independent India, commercial industrial zone extracted the chief yield of state forest resources,[106] and commercial utilization of forests was enlarged partially due to nationalization of private forests. As Mark Profenburger and Chhatrapati Singh note, 'Strengthen ties between politicians, business people, and some foresters which were based on remunerative industrial extraction, also drove deforestation, while further eroding the rights of forests communities'.[107] Gadgil and Guha categorized the industry-oriented Indian forestry into four phases. The first phase is the traditional 'sustained yield' selection method, whereas the second (1960–1965) is the 'programmes of clear-felling ad the plantation of quick growing, chiefly exotic, species'. In the third stage (1975), farm forestry was introduced and import and captive plantation was implemented in the fourth stage (1985).[108] For the first phase, selection felling was done in the natural forest in order to meet the demands of timber-based industry.

With the passing of the West Bengal Private Forests Act 1948, the scientific forestry was introduced in Southwest Bengal. According to the provision of this act, all the forest owners submitted their working plans for the area of 431.64 mi^2. Cutting cycle was extended up to 10 years, and preservation of standards was also fixed at the rate of 15 to 20 acres. It controlled the grazing and fire as well. In the case of experimental afforestation, the North Bengal model such as ploughing the soil, constructing small ridges and sowing the seed was implemented.[109] Due to dry weather, the seedling could not survive, so that cattle proof (6' × 4' × 4') and contour trenches (18" × 18" or 24" × 24", to provide adequate soil moisture) were constructed. Saddling was planted at the

---

[105] Ibid., 163–164.

[106] Gadgil and Guha, *This Fissured Land*, 193.

[107] Mark Proffenburger and Chhatrapati Singh, 'Communities and the State: Re-establishing the Balance in the Indian Forest Policy', in *Village Voices, Forest Choices: Joint Forest Management in India*, eds. Mark Proffenburger and Besty McGean (New Delhi: Oxford University Press, 1998), 60.

[108] Gadgil and Guha, *This Fissured Land*, 186–193.

[109] Roychowdhury, 'Forests of the Southern Circle', 134.

interval of 8' × 8' thalis[110] and along with it, box trenches were created for water conservation. Generally, transplants were put in thalis and pregerminated stumps were kept in polythene bags. The species such as Eucalyptus, teak (*Tectona grandis* L.f.), peasal (*Peterocarpus marsupium, Linn.*), simul (*B. malabaricum, Syn. Salmalia malabarica, Linn*) and sissoo (*Dalbergia sissoo*) were kept in pot plants and teak and peasal were raised by stumps. Fruitful results came from planting the species of gamar (*Gmelina arborea, Linn.*), asan (*T. tomentosa, Linn.*), bahera (*Terminalia belerica, Linn.*) and mango (*Mangifera indica, Linn.*). In the cattle-proof trench, gamar as well as mahanimb (*Ailanthus excelsa* Roxb) were generally planted. In order to make plantation a success, fire was strictly controlled in the tract.[111] Establishing a nursery at Arabari of Midnapur district afforestation work was started in the centre of Laterite zone and different species such as *S. robusta, Melia azedarach, Cassia siamea, T. grandis, Acacia arabica, Pongamia glabra, Albizzia* spp. were planted over 395 acres tract. The private forest owners neglected the aspects of afforestation of blanks, soil conservation and control of fire and grazing, but they concentrated only on felling restriction prescribed by the working plan.

In Independent India, Indian Forestry programme was formulated with the passing of Indian National Forest Policy in 1952. As Madhab Gadgil and Ramachandra Guha note,

in the National Forest Policy of 1952, the exclusion of local communities from the benefits of forest management is legitimized as being in the 'national interest', namely that the 'country as a whole' is not deprived of a 'national asset' by the mere accident [sic] of a village being situated close to a forest.[112]

In 1953, the West Bengal State Acquisition Act came into force and all forests became vested in government and transferred to the forest department for its management on 1 April in 1953. However, the ex-owners persuaded their ex-tenants to cut woods. Though by 1957, the government handled all the difficulties, 10,000 acres of forests in the Burdwan division and another 10,000–15,000 acres of forests had been transferred to Hindustan Steel Projects, Durgapur Group of Industries and Kangsabati canal system (Purulia, Bankura and Midnapur),

---

[110] In the case of timber species *thalis* are used and here a mixture containing tank silt, farm yard manure and application of balance nitrogen, phosphorus and potassium (N. P. K.) fertilizer was provided.

[111] Roychowdhury, 'Forests of the Southern Circle', 139.

[112] Gadgil and Guha, *This Fissured Land*, 194.

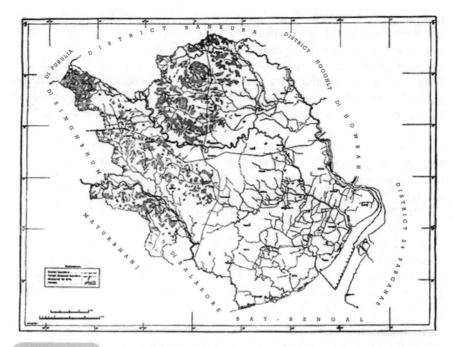

FIGURE 7.5 *Forests of Midnapur District, 1964, West Bengal Forests*

Disclaimer: The figure is for representation purpose only.
Source: Forests' Survey of India, 2011.

respectively.[113] Thus, at the cost of huge forests, big industries were created 'as the "national interest" has virtually been equated with industrial sector'.[114] The forest department acquired a large amount of forest land, so that the Midnapur division (see Figure 7.5) was divided into two parts, that is, East Midnapur division and West Midnapur division. The Burdwan division was divided into Birbhum and Burdwan divisions. After inclusion of Purulia into West Bengal, a new Purulia division was integrated with the Southern Circle (Table 7.1). West Bengal Estates Acquisition Act was also implemented in Purulia since April 1964. With a view to implement soil conservation measures, a new Soil Conservation Division was set up with its headquarters at Purulia.[115]

In the 1960s, wild animals such as leopards (*Panthera pardus*), bears (*Melursus ursinus*), wolves (*Canis lupus*), hyaenas (*Hyaena hyaena*),

---

[113] Roychowdhury, 'Forests of the Southern Circle', 135–136.
[114] Gadgil and Guha, *This Fissured Land*, 194.
[115] Ibid., Roychowdhury, 'Forests of the Southern Circle', 135–136.

TABLE 7.1 *Forests in the Southern Circle in 1964*

Division	Reserved Forests (sq miles)	Protected Forests (sq miles)	Un-classed State Forests (sq miles)	Total Forests (sq miles)
Burdwan	2.18	76.00	22.92	101.10
Birbhum	9.52	10.30	29.16	46.98
Bankura	–	537.60	3.68	541.28
East Midnapur	.007	204.74	96.00	300.474
West Midnapur	–	347.09	6.55	353.64
Purulia	39.87	398.41	–	338.38

Source: West Bengal Forests, p.136.

jackals (*Canis aureus*), civet cat (*Viverricula indica*), wild cats (*Felis chaus*), mongoose (*Herpestes edwardsi*), hares (*Lepus nigricollis*), squirrels (*Funambulus palmarum*), porcupines (*Hystrix indica*) and rats (*Bandicota bengalensis*) were found in protected forests of Bankura (see Figure 7.6). Sometimes tigers came from the forests of Bihar. Among the birds, quail (*Perdicula asiatica*), pigeons (*Columba livia*), peafowls (*Pavo cristatus*), jungle fowls (*Gallus gallus*), ducks (*Aythya ferina*), water fowl and grey and black partridges were very common. Among the snakes and reptiles, cobras (*Naja naja*), rat snakes (*Ptyas mucosus*), kraits (*Bungarus caeruleus*) and even pythons (*Python molurus*) survived in the forests. In Ranibandh, waterholes had been constructed with a view to attack the wildlife. Two aviaries were created for game birds, one in Joypur and another in Sonamuki.[116] As K. C. Roychowdhury notes, 'In Purulia-Bankura-Midnapur corner, there is an almost continuous block of 200 square miles of forests that could be ideal for development as a wild like sanctuary.'[117]

After Independence, only 3 per cent of the total land was forest cover in Birbhum. The district lost its fertility, which indicates chronic occurrences of crop yield failure. In the forest areas, successive coppice rotation was in very short duration, and there were occurrences of loss of soil and its nutrients and moisture in the adjoining forest areas. The Forest Department of Birbhum adopted a broad programme of afforestation on the banks of Mor Project Canal during the period from 1953–1954

---

[116] Mitra, 'History of Forests', 146.
[117] Roychowdhury, 'Forests of the Southern Circle', 140.

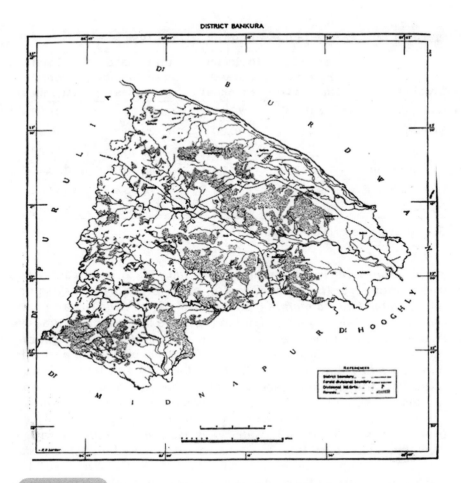

FIGURE 7.6 *Forests of Bankura District, 1964, West Bengal Forests*

Disclaimer: The figure is for representation purpose only.
Source: Forests' Survey of India, 2011.

to 1955–1956.[118] Under the old working plan of 10 years duration, the forests department followed its past policy of felling. The duration of coppice rotations was extended up to 15–20 years, and further it extended up to 20–25 years. The Forest Department allowed 32 acre of felling per annum in one square mile of forests for a period of 20 years coppice rotation. The forest department continued its role as a revenue-extracting organ, but it tried to cut short its felling as well (Table 7.2).[119]

---

[118] Sarkar, 'Birbhum Forests', 158–159.
[119] Roychowdhury, 'Forests of the Southern Circle', 136.

TABLE 7.2 *Revenues from Forests*

Year	Midnapore (in ₹)	East Midnapore (in ₹)	West Midnapur (in ₹)	Divisions Bankura (in ₹)	Burdwan (in ₹)	Birbhum (in ₹)	Purulia (in ₹)
1953–54	11,736	–	–	1,270	4,280	–	–
1954–55	–	6,196	11,284	6,425	1,798	2,132	–
1959–60	–	1,303,175	719,153	52,193	39,177	21,155	118,609
1964–65	–	2,005,954	1,228,682	2,394,465	318,966	63,777	135,128

Source: West Bengal Forests, p.137.

Conclusion

The forest policy adopted during colonial and post-colonial times ensured commercially valuable trees. Considering the environmental degradations, the colonial authorities adopted a broad programme of forest management. In Manbhum, we observed two contradictory views regarding forest conservation and utilization of forest resources. Forest officials were concerned with forest conservation following Brandis' line, while the districts officials were interested in extracting revenues. As the forest became an important resource for generating revenues, the colonial authorities sought to follow a pragmatic approach for forest conservancy. In 1932–1933, Taralal Reserve Forest was given to lease when no revenue was derived from it. In order to earn revenues, grazing was also allowed in some patches; revenue was also earned from selling minor forest produce like fishes caught from small channels.

The 'scientific forest policy' brought about significant changes in the landscape of Southwest Bengal (see Figure 7.7). Due to degradation of

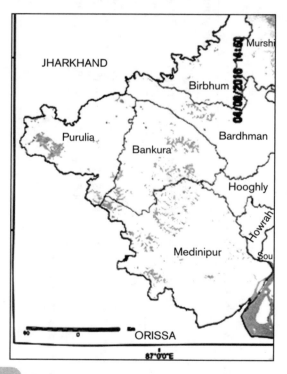

FIGURE 7.7 *Forests of South-Western Bengal*

Source: Forests' Survey of India, 2011.

forests, the sustainable economy of the region was permanently desta-bilized and the region became drought prone. The region faced severe chronic famine due to the environmental change. The villagers were deprived of any usage of forest resources they needed, whereas the lease felling of timbers and bamboos were continued following the provi-sions of the working plan. The fuel scarcity hardly hit the blacksmith and porters. This situation ultimately created an antagonistic attitude towards the forest department. Against this backdrop, the Naxalites CPIML (Communist Party of India(Marxist-Lelinist) Liberation) estab-lished a stronghold in the region in the 1970s. In the villages of Arabari forest of Midnapur, the first Forest Protection Committee (FPC) was appointed in 1972. The villagers were involved in the plantation pro-gramme, where they controlled grazing and collection of firewoods.[120] Community members became conscious about environmental degrada-tion and forest protection.

---

[120] Profenburger and McGean, eds., *Village Voices, Forest Choices*, 324–332.

8

Hunting, Wildlife and Preservation in Colonial India, 1850–1947

Kakoli Sinha Ray

Introduction

The study of the wild had largely been a neglected area of Indian history before the 1980s, and it entered into the realm of serious scholarship only from the 1990s as environmental history as a different historical genre began to be accepted by scholars. The worldwide concern for the environment made scholars delve deeper into the subject and search for the causes which had brought the world to the brink of disaster. In India, scholars and activists embarked on a mission to locate the causes of the spiralling environmental crisis, and this led to a surge of writing on issues of the environment in which the subject of the country's forests and wildlife predominated.

The world woke up to the reality of an impending crisis when Rachel Carson wrote *Silent Spring*,[1] a book which essentially dealt with the disastrous effect of the use of DDT, a chemical used to eliminate pests

---

[1] Rachel Carson, *Silent Spring* (Boston, MA: Houghton Miflin Co., 1962).

but which resulted in the decimation of wildlife to such an extent that by the 1960s, spring came to the United States without the beauty of birdsong. Probably no other book on the environment had such an impact on the consciousness of man as this. It helped in establishing a cardinal truth that 'in nature nothing exists alone'. This interconnectedness of life called for a modest, gentle and cautious attitude towards nature, rather than the arrogant, aggressive and intrepid route taken by synthetic chemistry and its products. Otherwise, the web of life could very easily become the web of death.[2] In India, 'synthetic chemistry' did wreak havoc on the environment, but that happened much later, that is, in the second half of the 20th century. The depletion of forests and wild animals began much earlier when an unbridled assault on nature and wildlife was perpetrated by the colonial power and its collaborators.

When the English first encountered India, they realized that this country defied any pre-conceived notion regarding it. It was far bigger and varied to be typified or classified under any one category such as the 'tropics' as could the West Indies or Haiti or even Burma, Siam or Sumatra. The great diversity of India's natural world, its diverse landscape, its different zones of climate and vegetation made it difficult to understand the country at first, so the first reaction was one of bewilderment. In fact, the Indian subcontinent evoked contradictory responses from the English; on the one hand, they were enthralled by its idyllic beauty, places of Edenic plenitude and fecundity enlivened and elevated to the heights of wonder and enchantment[3] by the brilliant variety of its flora, fauna and wide-ranging natural sites and the exotic people, and on the other, they were appalled by the intolerable heat and enervating humidity, the insects and pests, diseases, violent storms, savage nature, menacing crocodiles in rivers and prowling tigers in jungles and the 'superstitious and savage'[4] people. As they discovered the country, they realized that this land was indeed incredible—dreary landscapes gave way to a 'perfect paradise',[5] a land with 'rich variegated foliage', 'groves of towering cocoa-palms' waving their 'feathery plumes in the breeze', 'richly scented air and brilliant

---

[2] Ramchandra Guha, *Environmentalism: A Global History* (New Delhi: Longman, 2000), 71–72.

[3] David Arnold, *The Tropics and the Traveling Gaze: India, Landscape and Science 1800–1856* (New Delhi: Permanent Black, 2005), 111.

[4] In the European perception.

[5] W. Hoffmeister, *Travels in Ceylon and Continental India* (Edinburgh: William P. Kennedy, 1848), 196.

sunshine', which aroused 'pleasurable sensations'.[6] By 1818, the task of carving out an Indian empire was nearly complete, so now, the colonial state turned its attention to the conquering and controlling of India's woodlands. Thus began a new chapter in the history of wild India. In its endeavour to convert the woodlands into 'managed'[7] landscapes, the colonial state conjured up the regime of soil and tree manipulation, hence initiating a regime of intense man-animal conflict. The intervention was primarily intended to maximize resource use and thus increase profit.

The Pre-colonial Woodlands

In pre-colonial India, man's interaction with the natural world was varied; on the one hand, he had to confront the wilderness, overcome threats from fearsome beasts, clear forests, practise agriculture and settle down, and on the other, the woodlands provided him with innumerable resources—food, fuel and a plethora of minor forest products. Thus, the forests from the earliest of times evoked conflicting responses, one of fascination and the other of consternation, and the twin themes of the forest as a place of danger that needed to be resisted and a land of beauty to be admired and enjoyed is a theme found since the ancient times. In one of the earliest documents on wild India, the Ramayana, Kaushalya warns her son Rama about the wild animals that abounded in the jungles before he set out on his long exile in the forests south of the Gangetic plains. On the other hand, when Sita, in spite of her husband's best efforts to dissuade her, joined him in exile, the forests were depicted as regions of plenitude and beauty. This perception of the forests has continued through the ages.

Early man hunted animals for food, fought and killed them for protection and kept vigil to ward off 'marauders' that destroyed crops and attacked livestock, so there was a constant battle between man and beast for survival. With time, the domains of man and beast became distinctly different but overlapped, each encroaching into the territory of the other, so the struggle continued. As more and more land was brought under the plough as civilization progressed, man's dependence on wild animals for food decreased; only a few who lived in the

---

[6] Alexander Duff, *India and India Missions* (Edinburgh: John Johnstone, 1839), 205.

[7] K. Sivaramakrishnan, *Modern Forests: Statemaking and Environmental Change in Colonial Eastern India* (New Delhi: Oxford University Press, 1999), 76.

periphery or within the forests killed animals for food, but they were the marginalized. Hunting continued as a mainstream activity but in its transformed form, from an act indispensable for survival into a 'sport' which became a favourite leisure activity of the elite—the princes, royalty and their accomplices. *Mrigayas* were undertaken; the hunt became a means of pleasure and relaxation as is evident from the repositories of information on ancient India, the Puranas, the Indian epics, poems and plays of the times. The *Manasollasa*, written in the 12th century in the Chalukyan period, is perhaps one of the best manuals of the hunt in Sanskrit. It records in detail the technique of deer and antelope hunting including coursing with cheetahs or trapping a wild male blackbuck by using a tame decoy animal.[8] Hunting was pursued as a leisure activity by those that lived near forests also, but theirs was a lifestyle less worthy and hence not found in the records of court poets and writers who were more intent on recording the kingly conquests.[9] With the coming of the iron tools, more and more land was cleared for agriculture, and with the emergence of a settled agricultural life, animals like the rooster, water buffalo, zebu and the elephant were tamed and domesticated, but this did not greatly alter the character of woodland India. Ashoka, after embracing Buddhism, protected many birds and animals and even gave up the royal hunt. This does not necessarily mean that others followed suit, but there was effort even in those early times to protect certain animals. Moreover, since the population density was very low, India remained in the ancient times densely forested. The Chinese traveller Hieun Tsang, in his travel accounts of the 7th century AD, refers repeatedly to the immensity of the forests, which made travel perilous and difficult.

With the coming of the Mughals to India, hunting or shikar entered another phase; the imperial hunt acquired a new dimension. Mughal emperors and their accomplices used a range of weapons from the bow and the arrow to muskets for shikar. In addition to being a pleasure sport, shikar became a means to tone the body, test one's nerves and learn the fine art of stalking for a militarized, horse-borne nobility.[10] Abul Fazl, the biographer of Akbar, claimed that the hunt

---

[8] Ebba Koch, *Dara Shikoh Shooting Nilgais: Hunt and Landscape in Mughal Painting*, Occasional Papers Vol. I (Washington, DC: Freer Gallery of Art, Arthur M. Sakhler Gallery, Smithsonian Institution, 1998), 23–24.

[9] Romila Thapar, 'Forests and Settlements', in *Danger: Habitats, Species, Peoples*, ed. P. Manfredi (Delhi: Local Colour Private in association with Ranthambore Foundation, 1997), 112–119.

[10] Mahesh Rangarajan, *India's Wildlife History: An Introduction* (New Delhi: Permanent Black, 2001), 12.

was a means of gathering intelligence about the state of the realm.[11] The Mughals adopted the older traditions of the hunt but added to it significant new features. What is remarkable about the period is that they kept a record, both written and in the form of portraiture, of their hunts and escapades in the wild, for posterity, documents which are invaluable sources of the contemporary woodlands. Hunting was forbidden on certain days and killing not allowed on sacred sites of the Jains. Falconry was practised; capturing cheetahs in pitfall traps, tapping of francolins and the use of the musket were the innovative techniques of the Mughals. For Babur, a tribal warrior who had spent most of his life in Afghanistan, the new terrain he conquered offered great wonders and adventures. His memoir, the Baburnama, is replete with the mention of the birds and beasts of the new country. He hunted the Indian one-horned rhinoceros and wild ass, among other animals, from horseback with regular gusto.[12] This tradition was carried on by Humayun, but he was not fortunate enough to enjoy the court pleasures as he was driven out by the Afghan Sher Shah and took refuge at the Court of the Shah of Persia. Akbar appears to have taken great pleasure in the hunt as is evident from the records. In a painting titled, 'Akbar Hunts with Trained Cheetahs', Akbar is seen enjoying the hunt. The incident is also recorded by Abul Fazl who calls it 'a joyful occurrence' that had taken place in 1572 in Sanganer. Akbar was leading the hunt with his *cheetah-i-khas* or royal cheetah, Chitr Najan, and chasing a herd of blackbucks. One blackbuck leapt over a river of 25 yards, and the cheetah followed and ran it down, giving Akbar great happiness.[13] It was the accepted norm in India that cheetahs were trained to only hunt black coloured buck.[14] They (cheetahs) were trapped and caught from the jungle. Their training usually lasted for three months. Jahangir recorded that Akbar kept no fewer than 1,000 cheetahs (*yuz*) which, however, never mated.[15] The favourite style of hunting of the Mughals was the *qamargah* or enclosure, which involved the use of a large army.[16] Jahangir was also

---

[11] Ibid., 12.

[12] Divyabhanusinh, 'Hunting in Mughal Painting', in *Flora and Fauna in Mughal Art*, ed. Som Prakash Varma (New Delhi: Abhinav Publication, Vol. 50, no. 3, March 1999), 94.

[13] Ibid., 98.

[14] Ibid.

[15] Annemarie Schimmel, *The Empire of the Great Mughals: History, Art and Culture*, trans. Corinne Attwood, ed. K. Waghmar Burzine (London: Reaktion Books, 2004), 220.

[16] Bamber Gascoigne, *The Great Mughals* (New Delhi: Times Books International, 1987), 86.

an avid lover of shikar. He ordered a count of all the animals killed from his 12th regnal year to his 50th, and the number was 28,532, of which 17,167 had been shot by Jahangir himself. It included 1,672 antelope, deer and mountain goats, 889 *nilgais*, 86 lions, 64 rhinos, 13,964 birds and 10 crocodiles. Jahangir also built a hunting palace, the Hiran Minar, in Sheikhupura near Lahore.

After the death of Akbar, the interest in large-scale hunting like *qamargah* ceased and effortless methods evolved. The use of the cheetah continued. Bernier noted how the cheetah hunted down an animal from a herd.[17] It is known that Shah Jahan pressed peasants into service to corner a pride of lions in the Deccan. Dara Shikoh used decoy animals in hunting.[18] The Mughals used green clothes for hunting for effective camouflage. The low-caste hunters too pursued hunting by using bows and arrows, knives and spears, laying traps and digging pitfalls. In spite of the passion for shikar and its pursuance by the royalty and their accomplices, as well as hunting by the subaltern classes, hunting did not result in any drastic depletion of wildlife so as to cause alarm during the Mughal period, and there was still enough forest cover to sustain wild animals. An English traveller and merchant, Edward Terry, wrote: 'The whole kingdom as it were a forest, for a man can travel in no direction but see them, and except it be a small distance of the king, they may be every man's game.'[19]

The English Offensive Against Wild India

With the coming of the English, there was a major shift in the man–forest relationship. The Indian tradition of venerating the forest in the form of Aranyani, the goddess of the forest, as the primary source of life and fertility, was replaced by the commercial economy of British colonialism.[20] Their first reaction was one of bewilderment at encountering the remarkable variety of wildlife as also a dread and fear of the unknown, typical to the folklore of temperate zones wherein forests were regarded as places of danger.[21] Writes Fytte:

---

[17] Vincent Smith, ed., *Travels in the Mughal Empire 1656–1668 by Francois Bernier,* trans. Archibald Constable (New Delhi: Oriental Books Reprint Co., 1983), 376.

[18] Arthur M. Sackler Gallery, Washington DC.

[19] Rangarajan, *India's Wildlife History,* 17.

[20] Vandana Shiva, *Staying Alive: Women, Ecology and Survival in India* (New Delhi: Kali for Women, 1988), 55.

[21] Norman Meyers, *The Primary Source* (New York: W.W. Norton and Co., 1984), 13.

I would tell you of beasts that roam,
A tale of fear and wonder;
The shrieking elephant lure has home,
Here wakes the tiger's thunder.
The lordly bison here retreats,
His choicest grass-hills leaving:
The shapely deer, 'mid the summer heats,
Is seen his pathways cleaving.
The lovely peacock streams its note,
But scarce has the sound departed,
When bulbul tunes its fullest throat,
To heal the discord started.[22]

The poem draws a perfect picture of woodland India, an Edenic land but beset with danger, a mysterious site with incomprehensible facets. Hence, the imperial power decided to unravel the mystery of this land as only by knowing and understanding it could one extend one's power over this domain, so intervention was absolutely necessary. Moreover, this site was chaotic and unruly and needed to be controlled and ordered, and in this endeavour, the casualties were the animals, especially those that were perceived to be 'pests' and 'vermin'. The English assault on wild animals was unlike any that was experienced by India before. No other regime attempted to exterminate species, but the English declared a war against 'dangerous beasts and poisonous snakes.' Bounties were given out in various provinces to eliminate errant species. Reward hunting was effectively used to eradicate those beasts that were perceived to disrupt 'order'. The destruction of life and property could not be tolerated, so began the process of systematic annihilation. The more the deaths of men were recorded on account of predatory animals, the greater was the resolve to destroy problem animals. Tables 8.1–8.4 amply prove the same. The threat to life and property from wild animals was as potent in the period from 1913 to 1917 as it was in the earlier period between 1876 and 1880, so the war continued. The only exception was that some animals like the elephants were better alive than dead, and this saved them from the carnage that other 'vermin' were subjected to. Tables 8.1–8.4 testify to the same.

The threat factor helped justify sport hunting. The jungles teeming with wildlife was also the perfect getaway from the grind of the workplace. India was never the first choice of posting for the *sahibs*.

---

[22] Fytte, 'A Junglewallah's Letter, November 20, 1873', *In the Indian Forester*, ed. J. S. Gamble, Vol. 4 (July 1878 to April 1879), 400.

TABLE 8.1 Loss of Human Lives and Cattle due to Attacks of Wild Animals in the Period 1876–1880

Province	Number of Persons Killed					Number of Cattle Killed				
	1876	1877	1878	1879	1880	1876	1877	1878	1879	1880
Madras	981	885	852	1,336	1,405	10,322	7,255	6,350	6,455	8,894
Bombay	1,048	1,019	911	1,014	1,108	3,428	3,172	3,957	4,110	4,626
Bengal	9,989	10,135	11,318	10,779	11,359	11,932	10,329	11,444	12,046	15,815
Northwestern Frontier Province	4,692	4,593	4,219	4,494	5,284	12,122	10,513	7,214	8,391	8,361
Punjab	666	726	802	650	723	6,606	5,297	7,688	9,291	8,064
Central Provinces	1,098	1,461	1,233	1,099	1,280	4,366	3,062	2,299	2,795	3,750
British Burma	114	203	183	206	181	825	1,223	589	842	1,172
Mysore and Coorg	–	98	84	156	3a	–	5,508	4,280	6,001	219[a]
Assam	483	417	488	421	445	2,541	3,303	2,053	2,493	3,326
Hyderabad	165	126	154	130	149	2,220	3,621	2,684	3,196	3,943
Ajmere and Merwara	37	32	12	27	53	468	232	143	291	216
Total	19,273	19,695	20,256	20,312	21,990	54,830	53,197	48,701	55,911	58,386

Source: NAI, Home Department, Public Branch, Proceeding No. 104–17, dated October 1881.

Note: [a]Exclusive of Mysore figures.

TABLE 8.2 *Wild Animals and Snakes Killed and Rewards Given in the Period 1876–1880*

Province	Total Number of Wild Animals Destroyed					Total Number of Snakes Destroyed					Total Amount of Rewards Given[b]				
	1876	1877	1878	1879	1880	1876	1877	1878	1879	1880	1876 ₹	1877 ₹	1878 ₹	1879 ₹	1880 ₹
Madras	6,336	6,997	7,016	4,008	1,284	532	–	–	–	–	29,884	18,402	17,854	16,401	16,579
Bombay	1,019	1,237	941	1,875	1,717	153,090	93,154	86,796	102,232	177,078	11,197	9,249	7,791	8,105	11,697
Bengal	4,022	4,138	4,650	5,543	4,783	35,585	15,761	24,276	21,102	23,201	26,888	20,304	23,583	28,371	28,576
N.W.P and Oudh	6,382	3,910	4,495	3,032	2,924	816	414	1,697	952	1,029	13,711	9,578	10,938	8,176	7,305
Punjab	2,458	1,489	1,320	1,503	1,389	21,285	13,566	1,783	2,420	9,126	6,843	6,689	4,172	5,395	5,350
Central Provinces	1,801	1,608	1,197	1,030	1,408	30	61	410	924	866	18,699	17,359	14,277	12,569	18,223
British Burma	461	761	657	694	639	658	2,810	2,214	4,104	997	5,102	4,666	5,100	3,502	3,470
Mysore and Coorg	–	1,684	1,200	179	(a)26	–	1336	691	1,034	58a	–	3,983	3,541	4,016	(a)40
Assam	800	772	815	640	541	325	135	25	33	202	10,396	10,640	10,210	8,385	7,022
Hyderabad	187	238	173	124	167	–	–	–	88	158	1,882	2,110	1,676	1,043	1,613
Ajmere and Merwara	13	17	23	13	8	50	58	66	72	61	9	32	44	19	13
TOTAL	23,459	22,851	22,487	18,641	14,886	21,2371	127,295	117,958	132,961	212,776	124,574	103,017	99,189	95,985	99,990

Source: NAI, Home Department, Public Branch, Proceeding No. 104–17, dated October 1881.

Notes: [a]Exclusive of Mysore figures.

[b]The annas and pies have been omitted in these figures.

TABLE 8.3 *Number of Wild Animals and Snakes Destroyed*

	Year	Elephants	Tigers	Leopards	Bears	Wolves	Hyenas	Other	Total no. of Animals Destroyed	Snakes
Burma	1913	39	455	2,588	1,562	–	–	667	5,311	16,222
	1914	33	506	2,399	1,760	–	–	319	5,017	44,299
	1915	21	532	2,828	1,712	–	–	1,259	6,352	34,757
	1916	30	536	2,737	1,537	–	–	985	5,825	11,905
	1917	58	484	2,974	1,520	–	–	837	5,873	16,398
Bihar and Odisha	1913	–	96	345	157	206	234	512	1,550	16,784
	1914	4	100	415	199	659	249	1,134	2,760	17,204
	1915	1	105	386	192	156	247	265	1,352	16,566
	1916	–	71	334	157	139	157	140	998	5,740
	1917	–	76	258	119	273	99	281	1,046	9,171
Central Provinces and Berar	1913	–	192	870	344	77	–	419	1,902	1,265
	1914	–	164	852	275	122	–	419	1,832	1,350
	1915	–	131	791	251	92	–	466	1,731	1,508
	1916	–	139	691	182	61	–	344	1,417	849
	1917	–	158	651	180	240	–	335	1,564	728

(Table 8.3 Continued)

(Table 8.3 Continued)

	Year	Elephants	Tigers	Leopards	Bears	Wolves	Hyenas	Other	Total no. of Animals Destroyed	Snakes
Assam	1913	4	256	523	295	3	10	897	1,988	1,981
	1914	9	285	558	305	5	2	1,447	2,611	2,168
	1915	9	327	533	253	–	3	1,935	3,060	2,952
	1916	5	373	555	460	4	1	164	1,562	1,409
	1917	5	248	580	498	–	1	158	1,490	332
North-western Frontier Province	1913	–	–	14	–	76	–	–	90	595
	1914	–	–	25	–	62	5	–	92	540
	1915	–	–	9	–	49	–	–	58	478
	1916	–	–	11	–	57	–	–	68	436
	1917	–	–	5	–	39	–	–	44	396

Source: NAI, Home Department, Public Branch, Proceeding No. 1100, dated 15 August 1918.

TABLE 8.4 *Number of Reward (in ₹) Paid for Their Destruction in Each Calendar Year from 1913 to 1917*

	Year										
Burma	1913	100	16,810	39,951	13,495	–	–	760	71,116	1,373	72,489
	1914	200	18,850	36,975	15,132	–	–	935	72,092	5,680	77,772
	1915	–	19,540	44,084	15,173	–	–	1,277	80,074	12,641	92,715
	1916	530	19,250	43,545	13,392	–	–	1,110	77,827	–	77,827
	1917	356	17,390	45,990	12,933	–	–	870	76,339	–	76,339
Bihar and Odisha	1913	–	5,572	1,874	361	3,477	460	92	11,836	56	11,892
	1914	–	2,963	1,760	341	9,715	372	250	15,401	92	15,493
	1915	–	4,087	1,760	396	2,615	372	87	9,317	63	9,380
	1916	–	2,447	1,530	384	575	277	44	5,257	41	5,298
	1917	–	3,487	1,145	245	820	158	66	5,921	278	6,199
Central Province and Berar	1913	–	2,802	12,220	2,083	487	–	5,538	23,130	403	23,533
	1914	–	2,345	12,477	1,659	645	–	5,823	22,940	531	23,480
	1915	–	1,855	11,072	1,596	506	–	6,232	21,261	463	21,724
	1916	–	1,995	10,081	1,050	353	–	6,224	19,703	289	19,992
	1917	–	2,555	9,535	1,025	894	–	4,309	18,318	301	18,619

(Table 8.4 Continued)

(Table 8.4 Continued)

Assam	1913	69	4,528	4,280	1,135	10	7	555	10,584	122	10,706
	1914	100	5,385	4,703	1,058	47	5	7,000	11,998	71	12,069
	1915	275	6,788	4,520	1,078	–	–	959	13,620	212	13,832
	1916	275	8,012	4,805	2,068	10	1	802	15,973	202	16,175
	1917	350	5,463	4,740	2,005	–	2	728	13,288	131	13,419
North-western Frontier Province	1913	–	–	92	–	352	–	–	444	91	535
	1914	–	–	38	–	249	–	–	287	106	393
	1915	–	–	62	–	242	–	–	304	92	396
	1916	–	–	68	–	275	–	–	343	91	434
	1917	–	–	40	–	193	–	–	233	125	358

Source: NAI, Home Department, Public Branch, Proceeding No. 1100, dated 15 August 1918.

However, the opportunity this land provided to the aficionados of sport hunting was almost unparalleled. Hunting was pursued as a leisure activity. Leisure and recreation acquired a new meaning in industrial Europe. The upper classes cultivated leisure activities, and even the ordinary people got more free time to pursue recreational activities. Leisure became part and parcel of social institutions, social relations and socio-political discourses and regimes.[23] Shikar was passionately pursued as a leisure activity by the English in colonial India, and their passion for the sport is amply revealed in the diaries, memoirs, travelogues, etc., left behind by them. Comments Col. Richard Burton:

Not much to do (in the military station) with plenty of leisure for shikar. Weekend during the cold weather was frequently spent out of the station. Those chilly, starlit rides gave an exhilarating and adventurous feeling.[24]

The jungles had an irrepressible lure; its savageness, both real and imaginary, had a raw appeal that compelled the uninitiated English 'sahibs' and 'memsahibs' to savour its unique flavour. Writes Emma Roberts:

For a short period, a sojourn amidst the untamed wilderness of Hindostan is very desirable, all persons visiting India must have more or less experience of the savage life in their passage through those un-reclaimed tracts which continually occur during a long march ... in constant movements through wilds, however monotonous, the incidents of the march and the change of scene afford a salutary relief to the ennui, which is not to be found in fixed residence.[25]

The British civil, military and forest officials indulged in various forms of hunting as it was a standard means of recreation for them. In the military, almost everyone from high-ranking officers to white troopers participated in some form of the hunt or another. It helped them remain war-worthy in times of peace and also helped the colonial agenda of constructing a virile and manly image of the 'self'. The civil officers took short leaves to pursue the sport. The officers went on shikar not only for recreation but also to acquaint themselves with

---

[23] Peter Burke, *Viewpoint: The Invention of Leisure in Early Modern Europe in Past and Present*, Vol. 146 (Oxford: Oxford Academic, 1995), 136–150.

[24] Jacqueline Toovey, ed., *The Tigers of the Raj—The Shikar Diaries 1894–49 of Col. Burton, Sportsman and Conservationist* (London: Allan Sutton Publisher, 1987), 10.

[25] Emma Roberts, *Scenes and Characteristics of Hindustan With Sketches of Anglo Indian Society*, Vol. 2 (London: W.H. Allen and Co., 1835), 46–47.

their districts and their people. In many parts of India, they developed a patriarchal approach to hunting. Col. Richard Burton played saviour to villagers threatened by a tiger at Mudkhol in the Deccan. He states: 'An official of the railway staff saw the tiger and sent news to me, adding that the villagers were loud in their complaints against the beast.'[26]

He sat on a tree, and the tiger was brought out of its hiding place by the beaters and Burton killed it with his .005 Express rifle much to the joy and relief of the villagers. Here was the patriarch always ready to protect the 'helpless' natives from the clutches of an evil beast. The European forest officers had the best opportunities of hunting and regarded it almost as a professional requirement.

In India, the English adopted and fused two hunting traditions—the grand and opulent hunting practices of the Mughals and their successor states as well as the humble methods of the low-caste Indian hunters.

> Even Anglo-Indians are sometimes compelled to adopt native arts and when the assistance of elephants cannot be procured, they will condescend to lay bait for a tiger, and sit patiently in a tree until the fierce animal shall repair to his evening repast, and they can shoot him while in fancied security, he is indulging his appetite.[27]

But this was not much fancied as it was 'unwarlike',[28] something antithetical to the machismo of the Englishman. The weapons they used ranged from the spear and knife to firearms, culminating in the high velocity cordite rifle at the end of the 19th century. They also participated in various forms of shikar to stalk and hunt wild animals. The 'howdah' shikar borrowed from the Mughals involved the least risks, but it was expensive and meant only for the glitterati and high-ranking officials. Reginald Gilbert alludes to the advantage of howdah shikar:

> I know nothing grander than following up a wounded tiger on a good staunch elephant. From a position of perfect safety you are able to hold all the grandeur of the charge of an infuriated tiger, and to have all the fun of the sport without the danger of it[29]

This form of shikar could be best used to project the difference between the 'self' and the native 'other'. It was a mechanism to overawe the

---

[26] Toovey, *Tigers of the Raj*, 27–28.

[27] Roberts, *Scenes and Characteristics of Hindustan*, 67.

[28] Ibid.

[29] Reginald Gilbert, 'Wounded Tigers—How Should They Be Killed?' *Journal of the Bombay Natural History Society (JBNHS)* 9 (1894): 61.

onlookers and a covert ploy to establish supremacy. Another form of shikar was hunting from a *machan,* that is, a platform on a treetop or a perch on a tree. But this form of sport was risky and meant only for the seasoned shikari. Recounts Col. Burton:

> An hour passed, then I heard a shot fired by the head shikari as a signal for the beat to begin. A renewal of shouts and rattling of sticks set everything in the forest on the move; first to appear were the peafowl and the jungle fowl... several jackals came slinking by ... small birds fluttered from trees.... Soon the form of the tiger is viewed through the vista of bamboos and tree trunks.... He looks huge; his ruff stands out white on either side of his neck. The placing of the first shot is everything. With a grunt the great brute bounced forward, but then comes the welcome call from Abdul, 'Girgaya, margaya'—He is fallen he is dead.[30]

Stalking animals was also common, done mostly in the sub-montane forests of the North West Frontier Province, in the Himalayas of the outer Kumaon, in the spurs of the Kaimur and Vindhya ranges, and in the Sivalik hills east of the Ganges. The sahibs did not hesitate to negotiate very difficult terrain in pursuit of quarry. They would be led by shikaris who, being locals, had a good knowledge of the locality and also *khabbar* (information) about game. The most warlike of all shikar was to encounter a tiger singly on horseback.

> This is of course a very difficult and dangerous enterprise; few steeds, however noble, can be brought to face an enemy of which they entertain an instinctive dread.... Such enterprises must be of rare occurrence, and can only be contemplated by adventurous spirits, delighting in the excitement produced by the wild and dangerous sports of India.[31]

Native methods of using nets and spears were also adopted and the indigenous sport of falconry also pursued. The *shaheen* falcons were trained in the art of catching quarry, and this sport offered great pleasure and excitement. The whole exercise of falcons stooping repeatedly to catch quarry, the attacked bird trying its best to escape the talons of the peregrines, the shouts and yells of the falconers and shrieks of local boys all added to the excitement. It was indeed a sport of the kings.

Wild animals were also hunted with impunity, not only for leisure but also with the motive to 'civilize' a wild landscape, an imperial tool

---

[30] Toovey, *Tigers of the Raj,* 14–15.
[31] Roberts, *Scenes and Characteristics of Hindustan,* 288.

used to remove all impediments to settled agriculture. This is evident from the fact that the animals which were perceived as 'pests' were those from which the challenge to peaceful, settled life was the greatest. Tigers, snakes, elephants, pigs and even birds like sparrows and parrots were specially sought to be exterminated as they threatened life or crops. The wild landscape was the last 'frontier' that needed to be penetrated and conquered, and killing obnoxious beasts that roamed this site was imperative to achieve this. In fact, it was 'reward hunting' more than sports hunting which brought greater doom to the country's wild animals.

The three animals with which the English had a special relationship were the tiger, the elephant and the pig. The tiger evoked contradictory responses. It was a magnificent beast that inspired awe, but it was also dreaded. It possessed a compelling fascination, inspiring a great range of both negative and positive responses. Travellers' accounts and memoirs abound in tales of European deaths when tigers seized people on journeys, on picnics or out hunting, as many graves in European cemeteries testify. The most famous such incident was the death of the son of Sir Hector Munro on Saugor Island, near Kolkata, in 1792. Blake's, *Tiger! Tiger! Burning Bright in the Forests of the Night*, with its repeated use of the word 'dread', was known to most 19th century school children, so the primary objective of a shikar expedition was to get a tiger. E. Gouldsbury of the Indian Police Force states:

> This may seem incredible, for it must be borne in mind that a tiger, seen for the first time at large in its own jungles, is a sight few sportsmen ... can look on without experiencing a feeling of intense excitement, coupled with an almost uncontrollable desire to possess its head and skin ... it is (an) insatiable longing.[32]

News of the appearance of a man-eater had a powerful impact on any district. Stories developed into myths and legends of startling proportions. Superstitions were rife among Indians and Europeans alike, and the man-eating tiger was the brute that attracted the greatest attention. 'All the tigers of this Jeypore country are potential man-eaters and readily take a man if they meet him after dark,' opined Col. Richard Burton.[33] Often, man-eaters were created if not found. This helped in legitimizing their annihilation on the one hand, and on the other helped magnify

---

[32] C. E. Gouldsbury, *Tigerland: Reminiscences of Forty Years Sport and Adventure in Bengal* (London: Chapman and Hall Ltd., 1913), 261.
[33] Toovey, *Tigers of the Raj*, 42.

the achievements of the sahibs as killing a dreaded beast surely needed great courage and grit. It also helped the colonial endeavour to project itself as the 'protector'. The hunting books, like T. Williamson's *Oriental Field Sports*, are full of stories of beasts with over a hundred human victims to their credit, some of which were never destroyed, while others inspired startling deeds of avenging heroism on the part of the bereaved relatives.[34] Whereas in the past, threatened villagers would have turned to the professional shikari with his muzzle-loader, traps or spring poisoned arrows, now, they increasingly looked to the British officials for protection. The latter were ever ready to help as that suited their objective of emerging as the patriarch and protector. Every ICS man, army officer or policeman was executed to be a tiger-slayer (though in reality many, of course, spent their entire career in India without ever encountering a tiger). In many parts of India, they developed a patriarchal approach to hunting. This protective function was even more significant in the case of the tigers that took to killing domestic stock. Percy Wyndham, Collector of Mirzapur in Uttar Pradesh (1905–1915), a first-rate shikar district, was called the 'Bagmaroo sahib' as he killed quite a few tigers in the district.[35] This protection service was normally performed from the *machan* over tethered live bait (goat or young buffalo, usually) or the tiger's recent kill, even if it were human remains (though the relatives often protested). The more intrepid tiger hunters shot on foot, having the tigers beaten to them by the massed forces of the local villagers known as *hunqahs*. It was alleged that great celebrations could break out after the killing of a man-eater, and thousands of villagers would congregate to exult over the carcass. The noblest of the shikaris would divide the reward among his followers, though the rewards doled out were often very measly. Here too the difference between 'self' and 'other' was very pronounced, as here was the superior giving *bakshis* (tips) to the subservient.

Tiger shikar for sport rather than protection was normally conducted from elephant-back, again with the aid of a large army of beaters, but this was pursued by the most senior officials, and women could participate either as spectators or as shots. The 'state' version saw the hunters seated in howdahs on the backs of elephants, and the tigers were always driven towards them. There were rules about the order in which the guns on a line of elephants were permitted to fire, about the

---

[34] Charles Allen, *Plain Tales from the Raj: Images of British India in the Twentieth Century* (London: BBC Books, 1975), 135.

[35] Y. D. Gundevia, *In the Districts of the Raj* (Bombay: Orient Blackswan, 1992), 166.

positioning of the elephants according to the status of the occupants and the right of the 'first shot' to acquire the skin. Each viceroy had to indulge in the obligatory tiger shoot and often secured 'record' tigers because the method of measuring them was more favourable in the case of the viceroy.[36]

The sahibs took great care to click photographs with their kill. The way they posed with the hunted animal—gun in hand, one leg on the carcass, the pride of having overcome a formidable challenge writ all over the faces—testifies to the fact that they wanted to prove to the onlookers their masculine prowess and invincibility, though very often the job of finding the animal or even killing it was accomplished by the native shikaris. The whole exercise of measuring the animal after it was felled by bullets and revelling in having got a huge beast was also done with the same goal in mind, that is, to show how courageous and powerful they were.

The elephant was hunted for only a few decades of the 19th century, then its usefulness was discerned; it proved to be indispensable in plantations, for timber hauling and for use in the army, and this saved it. Only those elephants which were declared to be 'rogues' could be killed. With the imposition of the Elephant Preservation Acts of 1873 and 1879, strict controls on the shikar of elephants were enforced. Elephants were caught in *kheddahs*. A *kheddah* is a large enclosure surrounded by a ditch and a paling of timbers, with a long funnel leading to its entrance. The drive itself could last several days and, according to Williamson, often involved 6,000–8,000 persons using firearms, *drums*, trumpets and fireworks to force the herd towards the *kheddah*.[37] The ditch is then filled up by means of billets of wood being thrown in, and as the animal rises near the surface of the ground, the two ropes fastening him are pulled tighter around the trees. Eventually, he gets out of the pit somewhat fatigued; the ropes which secure him are fastened to two tame elephants, and the animals are marched in single file to the kraal and all the ropes are removed. He is watered three times a day and soon made tame by kindness, given sugarcane, etc. The work of capturing elephants is an exceedingly interesting one and only needs care and constant supervision to render it successful. Certainly, the more one has to do with these animals, the more one is

---

[36] Nigel Woodyatt, *My Sporting Memories: Forty Years with Note-Book and Gun* (London: H. Jenkins, 1923), 12.

[37] W. O. Horne, *Work and Sport in the Old I.C.S* (Edinburg: William Blackwood and Son, 1928), 125.

bound to recognize what intelligent, useful beasts they are.[38] Catching elephants in *kheddahs* was a specialized activity and required a lot of skills; it may not have been as fascinating as hunting tigers but it had an appeal of its own. States Isabel Savory:

> I had always been anxious to see an elephant khedder and when we were in Madras some of our party were able to avail themselves of an opportunity which afforded itself. One of the most exciting scenes witnessed (by me)—was the entrapping of these wild monarchs of the jungle.[39]

Pig-sticking and hog hunting were an extension of the wild boar chase pursued in England. The sport was one of the most loved by the English as it offered great opportunities for adventure and unbridled excitement. Major Henry Shakespeare described hog hunting as the best sport in the world, particularly in the hilly regions of the Deccan and Nagpur.[40] By the 1850s, three types of pig-sticking had emerged, in Bengal, in the Deccan, and in the Bombay Presidency. In Bengal, a short spear not more than 7 ft long was used, not as a lance but in such a way that a charging boar ran against it. The Bombay Pig-sticker Association operating in the area of Poona and Ahmednagar used a longer and lighter spear, from 8 to 9 ft long, while in the Deccan, a middle-sized spear of 9 ft was the norm. Each spear was supposedly appropriate to the terrain. At a later date, the united provinces became a celebrated pig-sticking country and Meerut one of its important centres. For Shakespeare, the hog was 'the most courageous animal in the jungle', and its pursuit offered the opportunity for Europeans and 'native officers' to come together.[41] At least this was the case till the Revolt of 1857; in the post-1857 period Indian participation was restricted to doing menial jobs or acting as beaters to facilitate the sporting activities of the white masters. Isabel Savory relates one of her experiences, which is an explicit account of the game and a wonderful testimony to the challenges faced in hog hunting and the sheer joy of overpowering that challenge.

---

[38] Elephant Capturing Operations on the Anaimalai Hills. From the Forester, 1895, H.B. Bryant in *JBNHS* 10 (1896): 135.

[39] Isabel Savory, A *Sportswoman in India: Personal Adventures and Experiences of Travel in Known and Unknown India* (London: Hutchinson and Co., 1903), 355.

[40] Henry Shakespear, *The Wild Sports of India* (London: Smith Elder and Co., 1862 [first edition 1859]), 41–50.

[41] George P. Sanderson, *Thirteen Years Among the Wild Beasts of India* (London: W.H. Allen and Co., 1879), 133.

It was a lengthy minute before S, leaning forward in his saddle called out 'Ride'. Everything was forgotten but the maddening, all engrossing present: the wind in the horses' faces; the rattle of their hoofs; and eyes only for one grey object fast disappearing. It was indeed Ride.

Over the valley, over the level,
Through the thick jungle, ride like the—
Hark forward! A boar! Away we go!
Sit down a ride straight!—tally ho!
He's a true bred one—none of your jinking;
Straight across country—no time for thinking.
There's water in front!—There's a boar as WELL;
Harden your heart, and ride pell-mell.[42]

The Prince of Wales gave the sport royal respectability in 1875. Beaters and elephants had to be withdrawn from elephant catching operations in Bengal to assist in the flushing of pig coverts for him.[43] The notion that pig-sticking was valuable to the peasant population in keeping down crop destroyers was somewhat subverted by the development of preservation policies. The pig had made the same transition as the fox in England, from vermin to protected species for sport. Coverts were preserved in the Central Provinces, and action was taken to discourage poaching by 'professional hunters of the criminal tribes'. Therefore, the transition to 'criminals' from being sons of the soil who had the first rights to resources helps to clearly reveal the real character of colonialism; self-interest was their sole driving force. In this period, pig-sticking was organized into hunts or tent clubs. The Nagpur Hunt, for example, was founded in 1863.[44] It had two cups—one presented by Colonel McMaster in 1869, the other subscribed by members in 1893—to be awarded to the member who obtained the largest number of 'first spears' (i.e., the first, but not necessary fatal, spear driven into the pig) in the course of the year. Tent clubs were also founded at Saugor, Delhi, Agra, Meerut and many other places. The hunt and tent clubs lay down the rules, and, in contrast to the free arrangements of the first half of the century, no one could hunt in their areas without the permission of the captain or secretary. By 1911 and 1912, they were recording bags of 257 and 385 boar respectively. Muttra returned a record bag of 400 in 1911, and the sport seems to have been pursued with greater assiduity than at any other time.

---

[42] I. Savory, op.cit., 18–19.

[43] J. W. Best, *Indian Shikar Notes* (Allahabad: Pioneer Press, 1931 [first edition 1920]), 186–187.

[44] Ibid., 198, 202–203.

The English love affair with hunting was not confined to just these three animals. All animals, birds and even reptiles, which were either perceived to disrupt order or whose novelty or exoticness attracted the sahibs, were sought to be killed. The cheetah was an animal which was largely harmless but, not being a very prestigious sporting trophy, was condemned as a vermin and extensively hunted. It was this indiscriminate slaughter that made the cheetah's sprint a thing of the past. The Indian lion preyed on livestock and was a threat to human life and property, and hence was sought to be exterminated. The animal came to be confined to a small pocket of western India alone. Bison, leopards, rhinos, bears, wolves, foxes, *dhols* or wild dogs, deer, *ghorals*, *makhors*, birds, snakes, crocodiles, everything was quarry. The innumerable freshwater tanks, lakes, *khals*, *bils*, *baors* and rivers and streams, all afforded excellent opportunities for angling.

> My first introduction to the Indian Bison was in the pages of 'The Old Forest Ranger,' when I was a very small boy. My youthful imagination was so excited by the account of the bull ... that I there and then was determined that when I grow up I should do little else than shoot bison ... I have spent several hot weather vacations in pursuit of that animal.[45]

The bison not only excited the 'youthful imagination' of the child but was equally sought after by shikaris for its regal horns, which had a great trophy value, as well as for the gastronomic delight it offered. 'Cold bison tongue is juicy and good ...'[46] The panther or leopard was found abundantly everywhere in India, and in the sahib's perception, it was a *'ruthless and wanton slayer'* and *'indomitable antagonist'*,[47] so killing it was legitimate. The Indian rhinoceros too was a prized quarry but difficult to hunt. General A. A. A. Kinloch observed:

> To hunt it most elaborate arrangements have to be made and no one but a millioner (sic) could afford to organize an expedition without assistance. Inhabiting as it does, immense expanses of giant grasses and reeds, it is generally impossible to obtain a view of it much less to shoot it, except from the back of an elephant.[48]

---

[45] The Indian Bison, 'With Some Notes On Stalking Him, J.D. Inverarity', *Journal of the Bombay Natural History Society (JBNHS)* 4 (1889): 294.

[46] Ibid., 303.

[47] Toovey, *Tigers of the Raj*, 50.

[48] F. G. A. Aflalo, ed., *Sportsman's Book for India* (London: J. Marshall and Son, 1904), 59.

The rhino was valued as a trophy animal and also had a number of other uses. 'I advise anyone who shoots a rhino to preserve the head, feet and whole of the hide. Most interesting trophies and a variety of useful articles such as tables, cigar boxes, lamp, pedestals, trays etc. may be made from them.'[49] Sloth bears were considered a danger by the local people as woodcutters and other jungle frequenters were mauled by them, but they were not adjudged as 'harmful' by the sahibs. 'I think this (mauling people) is rather to their being stupid, heavy sleepers, than to malice propense.'[50] However, the fact that they were feared by the natives induced the white shikari to kill them. The wild dog or *dhol* was 'wicked' and destructive, hence killing it was justified. 'Recently a pack of wild dogs attacked a herd of cattle here, devoured four calves and half killed a cow. These cases prove the increasing boldness of these dogs.'[51] Exotic animals like the Nilgiri *tahr* and the Himalayan *ghoral* were also much sought-after sport. Stalking them was extremely exciting as both these animals were very difficult to spot and generally lived in treacherous terrain; killing them gave a lot of satisfaction and they had great trophy value as well. These trophies mounted on the walls of the living rooms 'back home' would take the sahibs back to the good old days spent in the hills and mountains of India. The ibex was another animal that was worth courting hardships for. Its regal head with upstanding horns was a coveted trophy.

The variety of deer that the country possessed was also remarkable. The *cinkaras, nilgai, sambhars, cheetal*, barking deer, hog deer, four-horned antelope offered magnificent trophies and were hunted with great vigour. They also were a nuisance to crops, and therefore needed to be exterminated. 'Blackbuck, nylgae and cinkara harry crops'.[52] Sambhar stalking was a very popular sport, and the size of its horns was a much-talked-about subject; the longer the horns, the more prized was the kill. Blackbuck were also valued for their horns as were antelopes. Venomous snakes were despised for they caused harm to life and the scourge was sought to be wiped out. Just as in the case of other dangerous beasts and errant species, a veritable war ensued, and the help of native shikaris was taken to eliminate snakes.

---

[49] Ibid., 64.

[50] M. Gilbert Gerald, in Aflalo, *Sportsman's Book*, 55.

[51] Miscellaneous Notes, IV Wild Dogs Attacking Cattle, Randolph C. Morris, *JBNHS* 32 (1927): 211.

[52] Lt. Col. C. H. Stockley, *Shikar: Being Tales Told by a Sportsman in India* (London: Constable and Co., 1928), 111.

Birds constituted a valuable asset because of their plumage and were also favoured for their meat. The shooting of birds was taken up with great enthusiasm. Comments a member of the Bombay Natural History Society (BNHS):

> The black-tailed Godwit is common in the cold weather; its ally the Avoset Sandpiper, rather rare. The Stints are numerous, small as they are; they are well worth powder and shot, being for the table, barely inferior even to snipes. Totanus calidris, in a few places occurs in immense flocks. On one occasion, finding out their path to bed, I shot in a few minutes enough to supply a large camp and might have killed many more.[53]

Some birds like parrots and sparrows were considered destructive to agriculture and sought to be exterminated. The enormity in the trade for plumage can be discerned from the following:

> In March 1908, six cases described as containing 'cow hair' were shipped from India, and were found on their arrival in London to consist of the skins of 6,400 green paraquets. So lucrative was the trade that single districts, such as Lucknow in the United Provinces, and Amritsar in the Punjab, contributed between them nearly 16000lbs. of plumage annually.[54]

The senseless destruction resulted in the alarming depletion of species. Shooting of birds was normally indulged in by the sportsmen, but snares were used in areas which were not frequented by sportsmen and others and female birds were snared wholesale, resulting in the irreparable loss of the bird species.

Angling was a favourite pastime, and the rivers, streams, lakes and other water bodies were teeming with a wide variety of fish. Even alligators were sought to be shot though by the English sportsmen's own admission, they were 'not of much use when you have got them' because 'the bleached skull makes a ghastly trophy, and the skin is a very ugly one'.[55]

---

[53] The Waters of Western India, Part IV: Gujarat by a Member of the Society, *JBNHS* 2 (1887): 159–164.

[54] Protection of Wild Birds in India and Traffic in Plummage by P.T.L. Dodsworth, *JBNHS* 20 (1910–11), 1104–1107.

[55] A Sind Lake by Capt. E.F. Becher, *JBNHS* 1 (1886), 94.

Even though shikar or hunting was the best leisure activity that was pursued by the Englishmen during the colonial period, it went on to have various other uses and implications and was not confined to being a means of leisure alone. It fitted into the imperial agenda and also served as a field of war. It embodied an imperial world in microcosm, an elite ritual with its insistence on similar virtues of manliness, courage endurance and fortitude.[56] Hence, killing predators like tigers was upheld as a greatly courageous deed. Moreover, reward hunting was adopted to eradicate animals conceived as vermin. The hunt resulted in a veritable war against errant species. The practice of wiping out scourge was not new to India, but no previous ruler had attempted to exterminate any species; now, the war between man and nature became a fight to the finish.[57]

By the late 1870s, the average number of wild animals destroyed was more than 20,000.[58] Added to this was the mayhem unleashed by sports hunters. So, the enormity of loss can be easily understood. Animals were targeted after taking into consideration economic and cultural factors. Carnivores, unless valued by sports hunters, continued to be listed as vermin. Elephants once condemned because of their depredations that caused destruction of crops and loss of property began to be protected as early as in the 1870s because of their importance in warfare and in hauling timber, but the cheetah had no such use nor was it a trophy-worthy animal, so the assault on it went on unabated. Some animals were lucky to get protection because of local practices. But in general, the blow to the population of wild animals was unprecedented; the cheetah became extinct, the lion was confined to Saurashtra alone and the tiger battled for survival. The extension of agriculture had always taken its toll on animals but in colonial India they faced a state-sponsored assault. The situation was further aggravated by trophy hunting. However, by the late-19th century, the voice of the conservationist also began to be heard.

From Jungle to Forest: Enforcing a Regime of Preservation

The irresolute resolve of the colonial state to convert the wild—a storehouse of economic opportunities—into their exclusive domain is evident in view of the unflinching perusal of forest management from the

---

[56] Edward Said, *Culture and Imperialism* (London: Chatto and Windus, 1993), 226.

[57] Rangarajan, *India's Wildlife History*, 188.

[58] Data collected from NAI cited above in Table 8.2.

second half of the 19th century. The creation of a governmental forest service in India in the mid-19th century set in motion a programme to change systems of forest management and recast them in the continental mould. Over the next five decades, the Indian forest department erected a framework of resource use modelled along European lines. Laws restricting resource use were passed, silviculture systems inaugurated and new approaches to forest utilization launched.[59] The Forest Charter of 1855 was the first attempt by the colonial government in the direction of forest governance. It made teak timber state property, and its trade was strictly regulated. In 1856, Dietrich Brandis, a German botanist, was appointed the first Inspector General of Forests, and the Imperial Forest Department was set up in 1864 under his guidance. The first Indian Forest Act came into effect in 1865 and was followed by the Elephant Preservation Act of 1873, the Indian Forest Act, 1878, which gave greater power to the government, the Wild Birds and Game Protection Act, 1887 and the Act relating to fisheries in British India, 1897. It was all these laws that carried India into the 20th century, and they came about because a need must have been felt to preserve the forests, keep them alive and of course control them. Controlling them meant controlling the wealth of India.[60] The Act of 1887 was later replaced by the Wild Birds and Wild Animals Protection Act, 1912, and this, along with the Indian Forest Act, 1927 became the basis of preservation laws in the country. The anxiety about the supply of timber was the primary factor that led to the eventual annexation of what added up to one-fifth of the land area of British India. However, it was not timber alone over which sole control was sought to be established. Animals too were extremely valuable for sports hunting as well for products like hides, tusks, horns and meat, which had an economic value, so restrictions were imposed on them; they could now be removed from the reserved forests only with the permission of the foresters. The indigenous people whose sustenance had been dependent on these forests from time immemorial now became outsiders in their own lands. The use of the woodlands was regulated to suit the interest of the colonial power.

The first attempt at asserting state monopoly was through the Indian Forest Act of 1865,[61] and it empowered the government to appropri-

---

[59] S. Ravi Rajan, *Modernizing Nature: Forestry and Imperial Eco-development 1800–1950* (New Delhi: Oxford University Press, 2006), 79.

[60] Valmik Thapar, ed., *Battling for Survival: India's Wilderness Over Two Centuries* (New Delhi: Oxford University Press), 1.

[61] Madhav Gadgil and Ramchandra Guha, *The Use and Abuse of Nature* (New Delhi: Oxford University Press, 2004), 123.

ate any land covered with trees. However, notification could only be affected if the existing rights of individuals and communities were not impinged upon. It is, of course, quite another story how many of these people had the awareness and the wherewithal to come forward and have their rights acknowledged and recognized. Act VII of 1865, which inaugurated the 'scientific era' of forest management in India, went thus—extracts from the Forest Act of 1865:

2. The Governor-General of India in Council ... may, by notification in the Official Gazette, render subject to the provisions of this Act, such land covered with trees, brushwood, or jungle, as they may define for the purpose by such notification: Provided that such notification shall not abridge or affect any existing rights of individuals or communities.

3. For the management and preservation of any Government Forests or any part thereof in the Territories under their control, the Local Governments may, subject to the confirmation hereinafter mentioned, make rules in respect of the matters hereinafter declared, and from time to time may, subject to the like confirmation, repeal, alter and amend the same. Such Rules shall not be repugnant to any law in force.

4. Rules made in pursuance of this Act may provide for the following matters:

First: The preservation of all growing trees, shrubs and plants, within Government Forests or of certain kinds only - by prohibiting the marking, girdling, felling and lopping thereof, and all kinds of injury thereto; by prohibiting the kindling of fires so as to endanger such trees, shrubs and plants; by prohibiting the collecting and removing of leaves, fruits, grass, wood-oil, resin, wax, honey, elephants' tusks, horns, skins and hides, stones, lime or any natural produce of such Forests; by prohibiting the ingress into and the passage through such Forests, except on authorized roads and paths; by prohibiting cultivation and the burning of lime and charcoal, and the grazing of cattle within such Forests.

Second: The regulation of the use of streams and canals passing through or coming from Government Forests or used for the transport of timber or other the produce of such Forests - by prohibiting closing or the blocking up for any purposes whatsoever of streams of canals used or required for the transport of timber or Forest produce; by prohibiting the poisoning of or otherwise interfering with streams and waters in Government Forests in such a manner as to render the water unfit for use; by regulating and restricting the mode by which timber shall be permitted to be floated down rivers flowing through or from Government Forests and removed from the same; by authorising the stoppage of all floating timber at certain Stations on such rivers within or without the limits of Government Forests for the purpose of levying the dues or revenues lawfully payable thereon; by authorising the collecting of all timber adrift on such rivers, and the disposal of the same belonging to the Government.

Third: The safe custody of timber, the produce of Government Forests - by regulating the manner in which timber, being the produce of Government Forests, shall be felled or converted; by prohibiting the converting or cutting into pieces or burning of any timber, or the disposal of such timber by sale or otherwise, by any person not the lawful owner of such timber, or not acting on behalf of the owner.

7. All implements used in infringing any of the Rules made in pursuance of this Act, and all timber or other Forest produce, removed or attempted to be removed, or marked, converted, or cut up contrary to such Rules shall be confiscated.

8. Any Police Officer or person employed as an Officer of Government to prevent infringement of the Rules made in pursuance of this Act may arrest any person infringing any of such Rules, and may seize any implements used in such infringement, and any timber liable to confiscation under this Act.[62]

Almost immediately after the legislation of 1865, a search commenced for a more stringent and inclusive piece of legislation,[63] and after much debate and discussion the Act of 1865 was superseded by the Indian Forest Act of 1878, which was designed to facilitate strict state control over forest resources and was distinctly 'annexationist' in nature.[64] This Act sought to do away with all privileges and rights that were not explicitly granted by the state. Through a single piece of legislation, a centuries-old system of rights and privileges for forest-inhabiting and forest-dependent communities was terminated. The Act of 1878 went thus:

Chapter II: Of Reserved Forests

3. The Local Government may from time to time constitute any forest-land or waste-land, which is the property of Government or over which the Government has proprietary rights or to whole or

---

[62] E. P. Stebbing, *The Forests of India*, Vol. II (London, 1923), 8–10.
[63] Gadgil and Guha, *Use and Abuse of Nature*, 123.
[64] Ibid., 133.

any part of the forest-produce of which the Government is entitled, a reserved forest in the manner hereinafter provided.

4. Whenever it is proposed to constitute any land a reserved forest, the Local Government may publish a notification in the local official Gazette:

a) declaring that it is propose[65] to constitute such land a reserved forest;
b) specifying, as nearly as possible, the situation and limits of such land; and
c) appointing an officer (hereinafter called 'the Forest-Settlement Officer') to inquire into and determine the existence, nature and extent of any rights alleged to exist in favour of any person in or over any land comprised within such limits or in or over any Forest-produce and to deal with the same as provided in this Chapter.

8. For the purpose of such inquiry, the Forest-Settlement Officer may exercise the following powers, that is to say:

a) power to enter, by himself or through any officer authorised by him for the purpose, upon any land, and to survey, demarcate and make a map of the same; and
b) the powers of a Civil court in the trial of suits.

9A. (1) In the case of a claim relating to the practice of shifting culti-vation, the Forest-Settlement-Officer shall record a statement setting forth the particulars of the claim and of any local rule or order under which the practice is allowed or regulated, and submit the statement to the Local Government, together with his opinion as to whether the practice should be permitted or prohibited wholly or in part[66]
(2) On receipt of the statement and opinion the Local Government may make an order permitting or prohibiting the practice wholly or in part.
(4) The practice of shifting cultivation shall in all cases be deemed a privilege subject to control, restriction and abolition by the local Government.

25. Any person who

a) makes any fresh clearing prohibited by section 5, or,
b) sets fire to reserved forest, or, in contravention of any rules made by the Local Government, kindles any fire or leaves any fire burning, in such manner as to endanger such a forest; or who, in a reserved forest[67]

---

[65] Indian Forest Act 1927, substitutes 'it is proposed' with 'it has been decided'.
[66] Inserted by Act V of 1890.
[67] Ibid.

c) kindles, keeps or carries any fire except at such seasons, as the Forest Officer may from time to time notify in this behalf;

d) trespasses or pastures cattle, or permits cattle to trespass;

e) causes any damage by negligence in felling any tree or cutting or dragging any timber;

f) fells, girdles, lops, taps or burns any tree, or strips off the bark or leaves from, or otherwise damages the same;

g) quarries stone, burns lime or charcoal, or collects, subjects to any manufacturing process, or removes any forest-produce;

h) clears or breaks up any land for cultivation or any other purpose; or,

i) in contravention of any rules which the Local Government may from time to time prescribe kills or catches elephants,[68] hunts, shoots, fishes, poisons water or sets traps or snares; shall be punished with imprisonment for a term which may extend to six months, or with a fine not exceeding five hundred rupees, or with both, in addition to such compensation for damage done to the forest as the convicting Court may direct to be paid.

Chapter III: Of Village Forests

27. The Local Government may from time to time assign to any village-community the rights of Government to or over any land which has been constituted a reserved forest, and may cancel such assignment. All forests so assigned shall be called village-forests.

The Local Government may from time to time make rules for regulating the management of village forests, prescribing the conditions under which the community to which any such assignment is made may be provided with timber or other forest-produce or pasture, and their duties for the protection and improvement of such forest.

All provisions of this Act relating to reserved forest shall (so far as they are consistent with the rules so made) apply to village forests.

Chapter X: Penalties and Procedure

52. When there is reason to believe that a forest offence has been committed in respect of any forest-produce, such produce together with all tools, boats, carts and cattle used in committing any such offence, may be seized by any Forest-Officer or Police-Officer.

63. Any Forest-Officer or Police-Officer may, without orders from a Magistrate and without a warrant, arrest any person against whom a reasonable suspicion exists of his having been concerned in any forest offence punishable with imprisonment for one month or upwards.

---

[68] A separate clause was inserted later for this.

Chapter XI: Cattle-Trespass

69. Cattle trespassing in a reserved forest or in any portion of a protected forest which has been lawfully closed to grazing shall be deemed to be cattle doing damage to a public plantation within the meaning of the 11th section of the Cattle Trespass Act, 1871, and may be seized and impounded as such by any Forest-Officer or Police-Officer.

Chapter XII: Of Forest Officers

72. All Forest-Officers shall be deemed to be public servants with the meaning of the Indian Penal Code.

73. No suit shall lie against any public servant for anything done by him in good faith under this Act.

Most of the provincial governments were quite satisfied with the 1878 Act. But, as with the 1865 Act, the Madras government was unhappy with the various provisions of the new Act. So, in British India, central legislations did not find unquestioned acceptance by the provinces; the micro areas had strong opinions and they could choose to differ. However, both the centre and the provinces were driven by the same motives of the greatest benefit to the colonial state. The Indian Forest Act of 1878 radically changed the nature of common property and made it state property. The rights of people over forest lands and produce were later regarded as concessions. According to this Act, forests were categorized into three types: reserved, protected and village forests. Reserved forests were deemed the most commercially valuable and amenable to sustained exploitation. Overall, state control of reserved forests was sought, involving either the relinquishing or transfer of other claims and rights. Very occasionally, limited access to these forests was granted. Legally, the process of reservation of forests could be challenged though rural communities had little experience with legal procedures, and illiterate villagers were often unaware that a survey and demarcation was in progress. Protected forests were similarly state-controlled, but some concessions were granted conditional to the reservation of commercial tree species when they became valuable. Protected forests could also be closed to fuel wood collection and grazing whenever it was deemed necessary to do so. As the demand for timber increased, many protected forests were re-designated reserved forests so that the state could exercise complete control over them. The Act also provided for the classification of forests as village forests, apparently to meet the needs of people residing in villages so that they could be kept away from commercially valuable reserved and protected forests. However, this was not exercised by the colonial government over most of India. The new legislation greatly enlarged the punitive sanctions available to the forest administration, closely regulating the extraction and transit of forest produce and prescribing a detailed set of penalties for transgressions of the Act.[69] People were, by and large, disenfranchised from accessing their traditional forests, and no alternative was provided to them. The mapping of forests allowed the implementation of scientific management. There is no denying that the British introduced the concept of scientific management of forests in India, but its dominant paradigm very evidently was to pursue maximum sustainable yields, and management practices were organized around this principle. This is evident from the debates that ensued among the various functionaries of the colonial state before the passing of the Act. An important conference of forest officers was held in Allahabad in 1874 to discuss the limitations of Act VII of 1865. The conference was organized by Baden Powell, who was then officiating as the Inspector General of Forests. The following extract is from a paper entitled 'On the Defects of the Existing Forest Law', presented at the conference by Baden Powell.

The former rulers of these lands, of course had no idea of what forests were worth in any sense of the word; they only looked on them as immense jungles that were infested with tigers and wild beasts, and were far larger than was necessary for their sport; consequently they cared nothing for them. In the course of time ... without any distinct grant of license, and without any idea of asserting a right as against the ruling power, or against other individuals or communities, everybody got accustomed to graze and cut in the nearest jungle lands, because nobody cared whether he did or not. Now it is hardly necessary to point out that this does not constitute a legal or prescriptive right properly so called.... Hence, while the forests were, and are still, overrun with people cutting and doing what they like, they are nevertheless in theory, the absolute and unrestricted property of the state.

Now this settlement of forest privileges and this regulation and limited interference with private rights being conceded, how does our Forest Law, Act VII of 1865, deal with the question? Why, it quietly ignores the first subject altogether; and as regards the second, it deliberately declines to allow any interference with any private right whatever. I am aware that this would be enough of itself to condemn the Act without another word.... But besides these cardinal defects, there are, as I have already intimated, numerous others.... The section 8 [of the 1865 Act] gives the one satisfactory power in Act, and must be maintained in a law; arrest without warrant is absolutely essential.[70]

[69] Gadgil and Guha, *Use and Abuse of Nature*, 134.
[70] B. H. Baden Powell and J. Sykes Gamble, ed., *Report of the Proceedings of the Forest Conference at Allahabad 1874* (Calcutta, 1874), 3–30.

Another paper by C. F. Amery sought to establish that the rights of the local population were actually privileges, concessions granted by the state. In a later forest conference held at Shimla in October 1875, Amery openly declared: 'The right of conquest is the strongest of all rights-it is a right against which there is no appeal'[71] Dietrich Brandis, who wrote the first draft of the revised Act in 1869, set forth his views on the above issues in his *Memorandum on Forest Legislation,* written in 1875. On the question of the rights of the local population over forests, Brandis writes:

> The view of the case merits careful consideration, and doubtless in many cases what are sometimes called forest rights are not rights at all, but merely privileges which are exercised by permission and at the pleasure of Government and not as of right. A large class of cases will, however, remain and must be provided for by Forest Law, in which the custom to graze the village cattle and to cut wood for the requirements of the village have grown up in a manner in every respect similar to the growth of rights of Common or of forest rights in Europe.[72]

The above debates and speeches establish beyond doubt the mentality and objectives of the colonial power. In the name of scientific forestry, natives were denied their legitimate access to the forests. Their rights ceased to be rights and were termed privileges, which would be doled out by the colonial masters at their own will. The last unconquered frontier was being penetrated and controlled aggressively and its resources brought under the sole control of the white colonizer. That the era of scientific forestry was inaugurated to serve the interest of the colonial state is established beyond doubt when one looks at the following statistics.

Growth in Forest Revenue

Table 8.5 clearly establishes the phenomenal growth achieved in forest revenue with the inception of scientific forestry for quinquennial periods, from 1864 to 1939. The revenue for India (excluding Burma) was ₹30.19 million in 1937–1938 and ₹124.37 million at the end of the war

---

[71] C. F. Amery, *On Forest Rights in India*, in Report of the Proceedings of the Forest Conference Held at Shimla, October 1875, eds. D. Brandis and A. Symthies (Calcutta, 1876), 27.

[72] D. Brandis, *Memorandum on Forest Legislation Proposed for British India other than the Presidencies of Madras and Bombay* (Shimla, 1875), 13.

	Average Annual	Average Annual
Period	Revenue (Million ₹)	Expenditure (Million ₹)
1864–1869	3.74	2.38
1869–1874	5.63	3.93
1874–1879	6.66	4.58
1879–1884	8.82	5.61
1884–1889	11.67	7.43
1889–1894	15.95	8.60
1894–1899	17.72	9.80
1899–1904	19.66	11.27
1904–1909	25.70	14.11
1909–1914	29.60	16.37
1914–1919	37.14	21.12
1919–1924	55.17	36.71
1924–1929	59.54	35.11
1929–1934	44.15	32.51
1934–1939	43.94	28.29

TABLE 8.5 *Average Quinquennial Growth in Forest Revenue and Expenditure*[77]

Source: Based on the data in E. P.Stebbing, *The Forests of India*, Vol. II, p.530; Vol. III, p. 620.

in 1944–1945. On the eve of Independence in 1946–1947, the revenue from forests in India excluding those of Pakistan was ₹104.80 million.

Table 8.6 gives the increase in the area of forests under the control of the Forest Department and especially the progress achieved in the demarcation of reserved forests from 1878 till 1935. The total area classed as forests including private and other forests and waste lands, etc., was over 450,000 mi^2 in 1897–1898. After 40 years, in 1935–1936, this figure had come down to 319,286 mi^2, of which around 58,000 mi^2 constituted private forests and only 854 mi^2 constituted forests under the proprietorship of corporate bodies.

Reservation of forests went hand in hand with the 'protection' movement, which began in the1860s. Protection of the wealth of the forest was indispensable to the designs of the colonial state, and the regime of 'protection' culminated in the Wild Birds and Game Protection Act

TABLE 8.6	Growth in Area of Forests under the Forest Department (in sq. miles)			
Year	Reserved	Protected	Unclassed	Total
1878	–	–	–	14,000
1881–82	46,213	8,612		
1884–85	4,921	13,103		
1889–90	56,000	30,000		
1897–98	81,414	8,845	27,679	117,648
1913–14	96,297	8,390	140,925	245,612
1917–18	101,233	8,752	141,527	251,512
1922–23	100,922	7,238	115,544	223,704
1930–31	107,753	6,263	135,694	249,710
1934–35	106,240	6,938	168,333	281,511

Source: NHAI.

of 1887. Years of senseless slaughter of wild animals raised concerns of extinction, which would jeopardize the interest of the 'self'. Protection in effect meant the sole rights of consumption, and this is borne out by the fact that the objective of the pioneers of preservation like the Nilgiri Game Association, set up in 1879, was 'the preservation of existing game in the Nilgiri district and the adjoining areas included under Madras Act II of 1879 and the introduction and preservation of other game birds and animals'. With the introduction of license fees and 'open' and 'close' seasons, the right to enter the reserved forest was in effect confined to the colonizer and their native accomplices. There were certain genuine concerns about the depletion of species from individuals interested in natural history, like those gentlemen who went on to form the BNHS in 1883, but they too could not transcend their colonial identity, and even when they tried to influence the government on decision making, the interests of the colonizer were not compromised. The various hunt clubs and planters' associations also raised concerns about the depletion of wild animals, but the reason for their apprehensions is easily recognizable; decline of species meant decline of sports, and hence trophies. It was the concern being raised by sport hunters all across India that led to the Act of 1887. The Act protected game for the hunting season and attempted to prevent the slaughter of wildlife indiscriminately, and it also sought to protect insectivorous birds in the interest of agriculture. Preservation marked the extension of restrictions imposed for centuries by the British Empire in their mother country in one form or another.[73] Though the demand for preservation stemmed partly from a desire to save species on the brink of extinction, its primary purpose was to cater to the needs of the colonial power, that is, keep sufficient supplies of game for the white shikari, and thus ensure the steady supply of trophies. The imperial authorities held the natives solely responsible for the depletion of species, thus exonerating themselves of the crime. The whole exercise of systematic denial of access to the forests and the right to use its resources to the indigenous people was justified in the context of the above assumption. The Act of 1887 was confined to municipal areas and cantonments only because of:

a. The predominant claims of agriculture, to which all other considerations must be subservient.
b. The undesirability of interfering with the livelihood of forest and other wild tribes, who largely depend upon the capture of game for their subsistence.
c. The general objection to the creation of new penal offences.
d. The unjustifiability of legislation in the interest of the sportsmen.
e. The absence of evidence that the destruction of birds for the sake of their plumage was carried out on an extensive scale, and that there was any serious diminutions of their numbers.[74]

The imperial power was pragmatic enough to embrace caution in all their policies, and the policies regarding the forests of India were no exceptions. The Act of 1887 was limited to those areas over which imperial control was unquestionable. Moreover, the traditional rights of the tribes who resided in the forest and its vicinity were not interfered with. For the time being, it was cautious, sustained aggression, a case of realizing the objective slowly but surely. The next step towards control and domination was manifested by the adoption of the Forest Policy of 1894, which gave agriculture predominance in relation to forests; the path was thus paved to extend arable at the cost of forests. The sole motive of the colonial power was profit maximization; if conversion of forests to agricultural lands served this purpose, then it was resorted to by all means. The Act of 1887 gave way to the Wild Birds and Wild Animals Protection Act, 1912, and it put the interests of wildlife on the agenda of the country for the first time ever. The perusal of the Act of 1912 reveals

---

[73] John Mackenzie, *The Empire of Nature: Hunting Conservation and British Imperialism* (New York: Manchester University Press, 1988), 305.

[74] Elephant Capturing Operations on the Anaimalai Hills from the Forester, 1895 by H.B. Bryant, *JBNHS* 10 (1910–1911), 1105–1106.

the intent of the government to save the country's wildlife, but the tiger remained outside the schedule of the animals that were to be protected; it was still perceived as a 'vermin' whose extermination was justified. The imperial power's power struggle with the animal continued unabated till the closing years of the Raj. The Wild Birds and Wild Animals Protection Act, 1912 was an Act to make better provisions for the protection and preservation of certain wild birds and animals. It was enacted as follows:

'1. Short title and extent.

(1) This Act may be called the Wild Birds and Animals Protection Act, 1912; and
(2) It extends to the whole of India.

2. Application of Act.

(1) This Act applies, in the first instance, to the birds and animals specified in the Schedule, (given below) when in their wild state.
(2) The Provincial Government may, by notification in the Official Gazette, apply the provisions of this Act to any kind of wild bird or animal, other than those specified in the Schedule, which, in its opinion, it is desirable to protect or preserve.

3. Close time.

The Provincial Government may, by notification in the Official Gazette, declare the whole year or any part thereof to be a close time throughout the whole or any part of its territories for any kind of wild bird or animal to which this Act applies, or for female or immature wild birds or animals of such kind; and, subject to the provisions hereinafter contained, during such close time, and within the areas specified in such notification, it shall be unlawful-

(a) to capture any such bird or animal, or to kill any such bird or animal which has not been captured before the commencement of such close time;
(b) to sell or buy, or offer to sell or buy, or to possess, any such bird or animal which has not been captured or killed before the commencement of such close time, or the flesh thereof;
(c) if any plumage has been taken from any such bird captured or killed during such close time, to sell or buy, or to offer to sell or buy, or to possess, such plumage.

4. Penalties.

(1) Whoever does, or attempts to do, any act in contravention of Section 3, shall be punishable with fine which may extend to fifty rupees.

(2) Whoever, having already been convicted of an offence under this section, is again convicted thereunder shall, on every subsequent conviction, be punishable with imprisonment for a term which may extend to one month, or with fine which may extend to one hundred rupees, or with both.

5. Confiscation.

(1) When any person is convicted of an offence punishable under this Act, the convicting Magistrate may direct that any bird or animal in respect of which such offence has been committed, or the flesh or any other part of such bird or animal, shall be confiscated.
(2) Such confiscation may be in addition to the other punishment provided by Section 4 for such offence.

6. Cognizance of offences.

No Court inferior to that of a Presidency Magistrate or a Magistrate of the second class shall try any offence against this Act.

7. Power to grant exemption.

Where the Local Government is of opinion that, in the interests of scientific research, such a course is desirable, it may grant to any person a license, subject to such restrictions and conditions as it may impose, entitling the holder thereof to do any act which is by Section 3 declared to be unlawful.

8. Nothing in this Act shall be deemed to apply to the capture or killing of a wild animal by any person in defense of himself or any other person, or to the capture or killing of any wild bird or animal in bona fide defense of property.

9. XX of 1887 Repeal. The Wild Birds Protection Act, 1887, is hereby repealed.

THE SCHEDULE

i. Bustards, ducks, florican, jungle fowl, partridges, peafowl, pheasants, pigeons, quail, sand-grouse, painted snipe, spur fowl, wood-cock, herons, egrets, rollers, and king-fishers.
ii. Antelopes, asses, bison, buffaloes, deer, gazelles, goats, hares, oxen, rhinoceroses and sheep.[75]

As the tiger was not included in the above-mentioned Schedule it continued to be hunted indiscriminately. The bounty system was thoroughly abused, and the crisis was exacerbated with the improvement in guns and

---

[75] W. S. Burke, *The Indian Field Shikar Book* (Calcutta: Thacker Spink and Co., 1928), 340–343.

firepower. The hunting records of the sahibs and their native accomplices give a clear picture of the mayhem unleashed. George Yule had killed 400 tigers and M. Gerrard 227. The local rulers of Udaipur and Gauripur shot more than 500 tigers each. The Nawab of Tonk killed more than 600 tigers.[76] Wild dogs, wolves and leopards too did not make it to the list of animals given in the schedule. They were also subjected to incessant slaughter. Over 80,000 tigers, more than 150,000 leopards and 200,000 wolves were slaughtered in the 50 years from 1875 to 1925,[77] and this was only the recorded number of animals killed for rewards. If the unrewarded and unrecorded numbers are added to this, then the enormity of the destruction perpetrated by the imperial power becomes evident.

At the turn of the century, India had spiralled into a wildlife crisis. The First World War had taken a toll on India's timber supply. The guns were more advanced. Motor cars had entered India. The assault on wildlife increased further. With the deepening of the crisis, there were strident calls for conservation, and thus started a phase of 'battling' to save the wilds.[78] The 1920s were the crucial years. The horrors of hunting over the last decades must have given rise to a sense of hopelessness, but this was also the decade that witnessed great bursts in human populations. The pressure on the forests had increased sharply as forests were cleared to make way for settlements. By 1926, there was much discussion, dialogue and debate on 'game' preservation in India.[79] Organizations like the BNHS played a significant part in furthering the cause of preservation. In an article published in its journal, issues regarding preservation were discussed.

It is as a poacher that man is the great destroyer.

In considering how to deal with the problem of the native who kills game, the first thing to be considered is his reason for doing it, and three reasons immediately appear. These are first for profit, in order that he may sell the meat, hide and horns, and this would appear by far, the most common one.

The second is, for the meat only, and this is not so common.

The third reason is, to protect his crops, and no one can possibly complain of an agriculturist in any part of the world protecting his property in such a way.

---

[76] Thapar, *Battling for Survival*, 71.
[77] Mahesh Rangarajan, *Indian Wildlife History: An Introduction* (New Delhi: Permanent, 2001), 32.
[78] Thapar, *Battling for Survival*, 31.
[79] Ibid, 67.

The increase in number of gun licences issued has had a most fatal influence on the existence of game in many districts. It is not that the licences themselves have done the maximum damage, but they have a habit of lending or hiring out their weapons to others.

To summarize the impression gained from the letters read it appears that what is principally needed is a law forbidding the sale of any part of a big game (carnivore excepted) save by a Forest Officer in public interest. An adequate penalty to be enforced.

Secondly that the use of a gun except by the licence holder in person be strictly forbidden and penalties exacted.[80]

The most important point that emerges out of the above extract is singling out the poacher, almost always a native, as the chief culprit responsible for the destruction of animals. The Indian landed gentry too were held partly responsible as they loaned their guns to their retainers who destroyed animals, but the sahib was never held responsible for the decline of wildlife.

The closing years of the 1920s saw a spurt in the demand for conservation as nearly two centuries of assault on wild animals had spiralled into a wildlife crisis. The crisis was accentuated by the rapid rise in population, which led to a greater demand for arable land and also residential areas. The steady development of the railway network also took a toll on forests because it led to an endless demand for wooden sleepers. Deforestation was a natural fallout of the above. Wildlife had very little chance of survival under these circumstances. New legislations were enacted to bring the situation under control, and this led to the Indian Forest Act of 1927 which replaced the earlier Act of 1878. The Act embodied all the major provisions of the earlier one, extending them to include those relating to the duty on timber. Discussions were held on shooting rules, open and close seasons, the role to be played by game preservation societies and the need to save animals for the sake of posterity. However, on closer analysis, it becomes evident that the Act attempted only minor modifications of Act VII of 1878. One important change the Act brought forth was the replacement of all reference to 'rights of communities' by 'rights and privileges of persons'. Thus, age-old rights of the forest communities over the forest were legally prohibited. Many suggestions were made as to what possibly was the best policy that could be adopted to protect and preserve wild animals. There was an ongoing debate on whether sanctuaries were the best bet

---

[80] Editorial - Game Preservation, ed. by R.A. Spence, S.H. Pratter and Salim A. Ali, *JBNHS* 31 (1926), 803–804.

against extermination of animals. The annual report of the *Journal of the Bombay Natural History Society*, Vol. 34, 1929, gives us an idea about the prevailing state of affairs.

> The subject (of Game Preservation) is one of growing importance and is attracting attention in all parts of the Empire. The general consensus of opinion in India is that game sanctuaries, if by such are meant areas within which no shooting is to be allowed, are not the remedy. They will be paradise for poachers. What are wanted are Game Preserve in which shooting under regulation is allowed, and the alienation of forest land, which is the home of interesting species of Forest Game which would be exterminated were the land put under cultivation, should be prohibited. Our present difficulties are mainly due to the increasing number of officials with no interest in sport or natural history.[81]

The debate went on unabated, even before reserves came up to save endangered species. A rhino refuge was set up as early as in 1908 on the banks of the Brahmaputra in Assam. This was followed by the conversion of closed shooting blocks of Patli Dun in the United Provinces, the Duars forest in Jalpaiguri in Bengal and the Banjar Valley in Central India into wildlife sanctuaries,[82] and eventually, the first national park, the Hailey National Park, came up in the United Provinces in 1935. As the situation threatened to spiral out of control, new avenues were sought after to protect species. Issues like different regions creating new laws specific to those areas to protect species were mooted, as it was felt that every region had its local problems and so area-specific solutions were needed. It was in 1935 that forests became entirely the concern of the provinces.

However, the woodlands continued to bleed, the concern for wild animals did not result in prohibition of hunting and the two world wars saw large-scale tree felling to meet the wartime demands.[83] In fact, till their departure, the English continued their assault on this site. A few voices were raised against vanishing species, and these men genuinely espoused the cause of preservation; they were the avid hunters such as Jim Corbett, F. W. Champion, Dunbar Brander, S. H. Prater, Stanley Jepson, etc. Corbett's hunting tales have enthralled readers through

---

[81] The Annual Report of the Committee of the BNHS for the year ending, Dec. 31, 1929, ed. by R.A. Spence and S.H. Prater, *JBNHS* 34 (1929), 605.

[82] Vasant Saberwal, Mahesh Rangarajan, and Ashish Kothari, *People, Parks & Wildlife: Towards Co-existence* (New Delhi: Orient Longman, 2001), 21.

[83] Ibid, 23.

generations. Though he never gave up the gun, he did play a significant part in furthering the cause of preservation. He was instrumental in influencing the provincial government to set up the first national park in India in 1935, the Hailey National Park. The park was carved out of a reserved forest where hunting was forbidden but timber cutting not disallowed. There was the expectation that the number of tigers would increase in the protected area and move to the adjacent shooting block where hunting was legally permitted. The concern for preservation thus grew out of the ethos of the hunt.[84] In fact, the 1920s also saw a different Corbett, smitten by the beauty of wild India; he went to shoot in the woodlands not with the gun but with his newly acquired camera. Mahesh Rangarajan is of the opinion that this new Corbett personified the shift in the aesthetic sensibilities of the imperial authorities.[85] But such sensibilities were not the norm; it was evident only in exceptional cases. One of the earliest advocates of shooting animals with the camera rather than the gun was F. W. Champion; he was the pioneer of wildlife photography in India and a sharp critic of sportsmen. He was convinced that the invention of the motor car had aided the cause of the hunters and spelled doom for wild animals. Although he was one of the greatest defenders of wildlife, his identity as a colonial official was of greater importance. He was a forester, his departmental loyalties ran deep and one did see him coming out in support of the foresters held responsible for overkill; however, he himself abjured hunting.

The realization slowly began to dawn that men were more destructive than animals. Even the tiger, which was held with great dread and was perceived to be the greatest impediment to the colonial design of converting the woodlands into their exclusive domain, began to be considered 'a large hearted gentleman with boundless courage'[86] in some instances. Stanley Jepson in his 'Big Game Encounters' suggested measures that could help in the preservation of wildlife. Not only did he argue in favour of big game sanctuaries, he also stressed on other measures to save the faunal wealth of India and emphasized on arousing public awareness about the value of fauna. A Conference on Wildlife was inaugurated in 1935, and it resulted in the birth of the journal entitled *Indian Wildlife,* which was dedicated to the act of preservation of wildlife.

Voices began to be raised to save wildlife, yet the paternalistic tendencies of the imperial power were evident. It was conservation

---

[84] Rangarajan, *Indian Wildlife History*, 72.

[85] Ibid, 73.

[86] Jim Corbett, 'The Man-eaters of Kumaon', in *The Jim Corbett Omnibus*, ed. Jim Corbett (New Delhi: Oxford University Press, 1991), 11.

imposed from above, and it excluded the native inhabitants. The decline of game was attributed by most Englishmen to the destruction wrought against them by natives.[87] Hunting without firearms was labelled as cruel; stalking blackbuck with a cart was 'rather a poaching way of shikar'.[88] The tribals and peasant hunters were seen to be competitors and thus sought to be locked out of the forests. The colonial forest policy rendered them aliens in their own homeland; their practice of shifting cultivation was declared unscientific and banned wherever possible, the produce of their own forests was declared the property of the state and their culture, religion and lifestyles were dubbed primitive.

India's Legacy of Co-existence

Scientific forestry has never claimed to be non-oppressive; its main claim is that without ruthless means the forests would have entirely disappeared in India, but this contention is grossly incorrect. The luxuriant forest cover the English encountered can be attributed largely to the association between the original inhabitants of the woodlands and nature, which existed since time immemorial. W. W. Hunter commented that the jungle was their unfailing friend; it supplied them with their means of subsistence—timber, charcoals, fruits, honey, lac, resin, hides and horns, fur and bones. Their religion, recreation, social life and even medicinal needs were sustained by the forests, and this dependence on nature made them devise indigenous methods of protection. The sacred groves and the various taboos regarding wild animals that existed in this country could be taken as the precursor to the policies of conservation. W. G. Archer very lucidly portrayed the importance of the forest in the life of the Santals. It was their place of recreation where they could indulge in the hunt, seek privacy as well as celebrate the annual festival of the hunt. Santal songs are replete with their association with the jungle and their communion with the woodlands. A love-sick girl's song goes thus:

The osprey's voice is heard on the mountain
Then the people feel pity
Oh, mother at midnight, the peacock's tail,
Can be seen on the top of the hills
and in the valley.
My brother observes the white flower

[87] Lord Hardinge, *Bullet and Shot in Indian Forest, Plain and Hill* (London: Thacker and Co., 1900), 6.
[88] Shakespeare, *Wild Sports of India*, 205.

Upon the dried up tree,
The parrot has her young ones
Oh, aunt, when will you
Dandle my children,
When will you my aunt?
From the steep sides of the mountains
I hear a pair of flutes
And below in the valley
The beating of a drum.[89]

Taboos and totems used by the tribes represent the most important ecological heritage of our ancient culture. Mrs Collin Mackenzie, visiting India in the mid-19th century, recounts:

We entered the Parvati Jungle, about 24 miles in length, which abounds in tigers.... We asked if the gentlemen near did not go into the jungles to shoot tigers? They said, No; the forest was under the protection of the Goddess Parwatti and she has given no 'hukum' (order) that the tigers should be destroyed.[90]

The natives also knew how to recycle forests as is evident from the following song:

Let us plant mango and
Palm trees my brother,
Let us enclose a tank
my brother that we may be remembered
And on top of the embankment
May the sasung bird sing.[91]

The voice is of preservation, the call is for afforestation and the fervent prayer is to let the birds and even the beasts live unhindered in the forests. However, the native customs were not integrated with the colonial state's initiatives to protect and preserve the forest and wildlife; so, preservation failed to prevent the steady decline of both trees and wildlife.

---

[89] S. C. Roy, The Oraons of Chotta Nagpur: Their History, Economic Life and Social Organization (Calcutta: S.C. Roy, 1915), 108.

[90] W. G. Archer, *The Hill of Flutes: Life, Love and Poetry in Tribal India, A Portrait of the Santhals* (London: Allen and Unwin, 1974), 26.

[91] Shasanka Sekhar Sinha, *Restless Mothers and Turbulent Daughters: Situating Tribes in Gender Studies* (Kolkata: Bhatkal and Sen, 2005), 85.

In fact, in colonial India, the exclusionary logic of conservation was adopted in which the native voice went unheard. Preservation was need-based and not based on the altruistic mission of saving the fast declining plant and animal species. The priorities of colonial forestry were essentially commercial in nature,[92] hence the depletion of trees and wild animals went on unabated. The colonial state faced a strange dilemma because of the inner contradictions of its forest policy; the question was not about whether or not to consume—it was about how much to consume. The fine line between measured exploitation and excessive use often got blurred, and India's woodlands continued to be decimated.

Independence did not change the fate of India's woodlands, neither did it bring any relief for its wildlife. In the turmoil of Independence, no one had the time to worry about either the forests or wildlife. Post-Independence India was a horror for wildlife. Now, and with a vengeance, every forest officer's training commenced with 'shooting a tiger'. Travel agencies seduced hunters of the world. Forests were rapidly cleared using the magic word 'development'. The maharajas went out to fulfil their wildest dreams of hunting and creating records.[93] The Nehruvian years spelled doom for the forests and wildlife as the importance of the country's natural wealth was forgotten in the quest for development. It was left to Indira Gandhi to stem the rot, and she took up the case of forests and wildlife in right earnest. There was a change of priorities; the Indian Board for Wildlife acquired importance and Dr Karan Singh was made its chairman in 1968. From 1969 onwards there was a ban on shooting tigers, in 1970 was set up a tiger task force, in 1972 was promulgated the Wildlife Protection Act and, finally, Project Tiger was launched in 1973. The message was clear: save the forests and wildlife and save them now. The denudation of forests and depredations of wildlife did not stop, but the political will was there to save the natural world. Efforts were made to make the preservation of the environment the joint responsibility of both the centre and the states. It was realized that the maintenance of ecological balance had to be made a part of the development process; otherwise, the country would be pushed to the brink of disaster.

---

[92] Harish Chandra Das, 'Man's Relationship with Forest—Deification of Trees and Plants', in Man in the Forest, no.1, eds. K. Seeland and F. Schmithusen (New Delhi: D.K. Printworld Pvt. Ltd., 2000), 229.

[93] Thapar, Battling for Survival, 169.

Climate and Disaster

SECTION IV

Climate and Disease

9

Climate, Environment and the Harappan Civilization

Michel Danino

Introduction

Although archaeologists have warned against the pitfall of a simplistic 'environmental determinism' in explaining disruptions in the course of ancient civilizations and cultures, accumulating data has confirmed the impact of environment and climate on human societies. It is now a truism that our planet's climate has undergone numerous gradual as well as sudden changes, even if the mechanisms behind them remain partly understood. Although picturing direct cause-to-effect relations may be simplistic, in the last few millennia such changes have indisputably had a measure of impact on the rise and fall of civilizations. As Vivien Gornitz puts it:

> A growing body of evidence lends support to the idea of a relationship between rapid alterations in settlement patterns, growth or abandonment of cities, with cultural discontinuities on the one hand and climate fluctuations on the other. Climate change by itself may not have been enough to initiate major population shifts or topple an otherwise stable civilization; however, it could have provided the

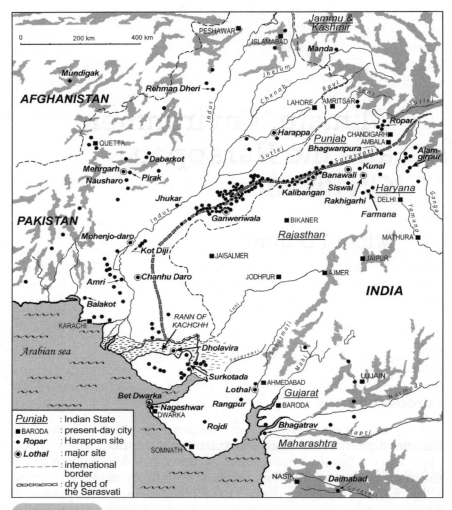

FIGURE 9.1 *Map of the Harappan Civilization's Mature Phase*

final straw in environmentally marginal regions or in conjunction with one of the other destabilizing influences listed above.[1]

The reasons behind the decline and disappearance of the Indus (also known as Harappan or Indus–Sarasvati) civilization in its urban form (2600–1900 BCE; Figure 9.1) have long been an object of debate: Why

---

[1] V. Gornitz, 'Ancient Cultures and Climate Change', in *Encyclopedia of Paleoclimatology and Ancient Environments*, ed. V. Gornitz (Dordrecht, 2009), 7.

should a brilliant and apparently prosperous Bronze Age civilization of the third millennium BCE disintegrate towards the start of the second? Initial answers to the question took the easy way out, basing themselves on the archetype of the Roman Empire crumbling under barbarian onslaughts; the barbarians here were the 'Aryans', an ethnically ill-defined group of Indo-Aryan speakers. However, the thesis of destructive invasions has in recent decades been ruled out for two reasons: there is no archaeological evidence of warfare or man-made destruction at any of the excavated Harappan sites, and no clear sign of an intrusive material culture in the second millennium BCE, despite persistent but archaeo-logically unsound and mutually incompatible claims to the contrary.[2]

Alternative scenarios include political, socio-economic or environ-mental factors, the first two of which are barely testable in the present state of our knowledge. As regards the last, the environmental and climatic conditions of the Indian subcontinent's northwest region before, during and after the Harappan age have suggested increased aridity, floods, diversion or loss of rivers and dwindling of natural resources; they could hardly have been of no consequence to the Harappans' modes of subsistence, from agricultural production to urban sustainability.

This chapter will survey a number of generally recent palaeoclimatic palaeoenvironment studies relevant to the Harappan region (i.e., the Indian subcontinent's northwest) and period and will attempt to draw a few general conclusions.

Palaeoclimatic and Palaeoenvironment Studies

Before we turn to the northwest of the Indian subcontinent, let us briefly stand back. In our times of rapid global climatic change, the wider public has become sensitized to climate studies, little realizing that without the inputs of palaeoclimatological and palaeoenviron-mental studies it would be impossible to understand where we stand

---

[2] E. Bryant, *The Quest for the Origins of Vedic Culture: The Indo-Aryan Migration Debate* (New York, NY: Oxford University Press, 2001); M. Danino, 'Aryans and the Indus Civilization: Archaeological, Skeletal, and Molecular Evidence', in *A Companion to South Asia in the Past*, eds. G. Robbins Schug and S. R. Walimbe (Chichester: Wiley-Blackwell, 2016), 205–224; B. B. Lal, *The Homeland of the Aryans: Evidence of Rigvedic Flora and Fauna* (New Delhi: Aryan Books International, 2005); B. B. Lal, *The Rigvedic People: 'Invaders'?/'Immigrants'? or Indigenous? Evidence of Archaeology and Literature* (New Delhi: Aryan Books International, 2015).

today in terms of atmospheric temperature, sea levels, forest density or wildlife diversity. An understanding of the complex factors that have driven climatic variability over millions of years is indispensable to an assessment of impending changes. Palaeoclimatology has therefore seen rapid progress in recent decades, while increasingly sophisticated scientific methods and instruments have made it possible to reach conclusions that are more precise.

Dating techniques, for instance, include measurements of certain important markers (including the notorious CO_2), of various radioactive isotopes, which decay in time and thus provide a time scale (such as Carbon 14 for recent epochs), of annual tree rings or varve deposits (alternately finer and coarser silt or clay, reflecting yearly variations in sedimentation), ice cores and much more. Ratios between stable isotopes are also used (most commonly between Oxygen 16 and the heavier Oxygen 18, the latter being therefore less prone to evaporation and precipitation) to work out mechanisms of climatic change, variations in sea levels or in the building of ice sheets.

The proxies used by climate researchers are therefore extremely diverse: sediments (from lakes, bogs, the ocean floor, ice sheets, caves), fossil records of flora and fauna, tree rings, pollens (a discipline known as palynology), phytoliths (silica bodies produced by many plants, which retain the shape of their cell structures and can therefore be used to identify the plant long after it has decayed), corals, stalagmites, records of salinity fluctuations in lakes, etc.[3] All of them have left an important testimony on the past evolution of the 'Earth System', as climatologists call our planet's climatic clockwork. In particular, that testimony is essential to the reconstruction of alternations between colder glacial and warmer interglacial episodes, some 50 of which are estimated to have occurred in the last 2.6 million years (the span of the Quaternary Period).[4]

The factors driving such changes are, expectedly, very complex; they include solar variability, periodical variations in the earth's axis and orbit, volcanic and tectonic activity, and of course, the concentration of greenhouse gases in the atmosphere, the current phase of which is undoubtedly anthropogenic in nature. The last major ice age that concerns us (the 'Younger Dryas', as it is called in the northern hemisphere) ended some 11,600 years ago (Figure 9.2) and was followed

---

[3] For an overview of both dating techniques and proxies used by climatologists, see A. K. Singhvi and V. S. Kale, *Paleoclimate Studies in India: Last Ice Age to the Present* (New Delhi: Indian National Science Academy, n.d.).

[4] Singhvi and Kale, *Paleoclimate Studies in India*, 2.

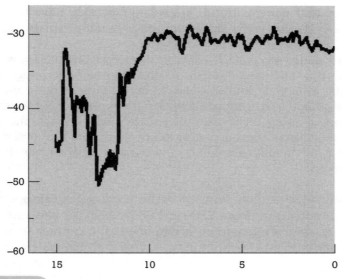

FIGURE 9.2 *World Temperature Over the Last 17,000 Years*

Source: Adapted and simplified from *Abrupt Climate Change: Inevitable Surprises*, National Academy of Sciences, Committee on Abrupt Climate Change, 2002.

by a sharp rise in temperature (as much as '7°C over no more than 50 years'[5] in Greenland). This climatic transition coincided in many parts of the world with the transition from hunter-gatherer nomadism to a settled, agricultural lifestyle—or, in terms of archaeological ages, from the Palaeolithic and Mesolithic to the Neolithic.

In the epoch that followed, known as the Holocene, global sea levels rose sharply; they were some 120 m lower 22,000 years ago, which means that a considerable landmass was swallowed by the rising oceans, probably the origin of humanity's widespread flood myths. Besides, the regions affected by the annual climatic cycle known as the Indian Ocean monsoon (which include much of central Africa's and Asia's southern belts) initially received sharply increased precipitation. By 4000 BCE, however, the monsoon had reduced considerably, ushering in a period of increased aridity which saw the spread of the Saharan, Arabian and Thar deserts, regions that were earlier rich in lakes and vegetation.[6]

---

[5] N. Roberts, 'Holocene Climates', in *Encyclopedia of Paleoclimatology and Ancient Environments*, ed. V. Gornitz (Dordrecht, Netherlands: Springer, 2009), 439.

[6] Roberts, 'Holocene Climates', 440. See also N. Brooks, 'Cultural Responses to Aridity in the Middle Holocene and Increased Social Complexity', *Quaternary International* 151 (2006): 29–49 and references therein.

Within that general trend, a few drier periods have been documented. As Harvey Weiss and Raymond S. Bradley explain:

> Climate during the past 11,000 years was long believed to have been uneventful, but paleoclimatic records increasingly demonstrate climatic instability. Multidecadal- to multicentury-length droughts started abruptly, were unprecedented in the experience of the existing societies, and were highly disruptive to their agricultural foundations because social and technological innovations were not available to counter the rapidity, amplitude, and duration of changing climatic conditions.[7]

Carrie Morrill et al., compiling 36 earlier studies, find abrupt climatic changes occurring at about 9500 BCE, 3000–2500 BCE and 1300 CE; the second one, of relevance to us, is described as 'widespread weakening in monsoon strength'.[8] Gornitz adds: 'Lengthy droughts in western Asia at around 8,200, 5,200, and 4,200 yBP [years Before Present[9]] may have triggered demographic shifts that resulted in depopulation of early settlements, relocation to more favorable areas, and re-colonization upon climatic amelioration.'[10]

In other words, those climatic events appear to have played a part in changing agricultural practices, migrations and social reorganization across large parts of Africa, Arabia, the Middle East and Asia, contributing in particular to the rise of the first Bronze Age riverine civilizations in Mesopotamia and Egypt. Other factors (including improved agricultural techniques capable of generating surplus food for the cities, the emergence of metallurgy and other technologies, the consolidation of long-distance trade networks, etc.) no doubt played a crucial part too.

The last mentioned date of 4200 yBP refers to a prolonged drought that affected, during about 2200–1900 BCE, large parts of Africa (as

---

[7] H. Weiss and R. S. Bradley, 'What Drives Societal Collapse?' *Science* 291, no. 5504 (2001): 610.

[8] C. Morrill, J. T. Overpeck, and J. E. Cole, 'A Synthesis of Abrupt Changes in the Asian Summer Monsoon Since the Last Deglaciation', *The Holocene* 13 (2003): 465.

[9] By convention, 'Before Present' refers to 'before 1950 CE'; on the time scales this chapter deals with, it will make little difference if, for the sake of convenience, we take it to mean 'before 2000 CE'. Another time unit common in the literature is 'ka' or kilo-annum, that is, a thousand years (Before Present being often implied).

[10] Gornitz, 'Ancient Cultures and Climate Change', 7.

evidenced by a study of ice cores from Kilimanjaro[11]), China (from a study of various plant remains in the western Chinese Loess Plateau[12]), North America (multiple studies[13]) and the Near and Middle East.[14] In the last region, it has been proposed that this drought triggered the collapse of the Akkadian Empire,[15] although some scholars have disputed this thesis. In the words of Peter D. Clift and R. Alan Plumb:

> Some of the earliest civilizations are known from the Indus (Harappan) and Yellow River (Qijia and Longshan) valleys, developing along with those in Mesopotamia and Egypt. These cultures collapsed around 4200 y BP at a time of rapid monsoon weakening, owing to direct negative impact on regional agriculture and more indirectly through changes in the river systems.[16]

The Indian Subcontinent

Numerous studies in the last few decades have contributed to a better understanding of the Indian subcontinent's palaeoclimatic changes. Some have focused on marine sediments (discharges from rivers being dependent on precipitation), others on river sediments (weaker monsoons leading to increased sediment deposits, or river aggradation, while fluvial erosion increases with higher rainfall regimes), lacustrine sediments (dependent both on fluvial contributions and on precipitation), palaeobotanical remains or fossils.

---

[11] L. G. Thompson et al., 'Kilimanjaro Ice Core Records: Evidence of Holocene Climate Change in Tropical Africa', *Science* 298 (2002): 589–593.

[12] Cheng-Bang An et al., 'Climate Change and Cultural Response around 4000 Cal Yr B. P. in the Western Part of Chinese Loess Plateau', *Quaternary Research* 63 (2005): 347–352.

[13] R. K. Booth et al., 'A Severe Centennial-scale Drought in Midcontinental North America 4200 Years Ago and Apparent Global Linkages', *The Holocene* 15 (2005): 321–328 (also for more references on the event's occurrences in other parts of the world).

[14] M. Staubwasser and H. Weiss, 'Holocene Climate and Cultural Evolution in Late Prehistoric–Early Historic West Asia', *Quaternary Research* 66 (2006): 372–387 (also for more references on worldwide Holocene climatic changes); A. K. Gupta et al., 'Adaptation and Human Migration, and Evidence of Agriculture Coincident with Changes in the Indian Summer Monsoon During the Holocene', *Current Science* 90, no. 8 (2006): 1082–1090.

[15] H. Weiss et al., 'The Genesis and Collapse of Third Millennium North Mesopotamian Civilization', *Science* 261, no. 5124 (1993): 995–1004; R. A. Kerr, 'Sea-floor Dust Shows Drought Felled Akkadian Empire', *Science* 279, no. 5349 (1998): 325–326.

[16] P. D. Clift and R. A. Plumb. *The Asian Monsoon: Causes, History and Effects* (Cambridge: Cambridge University Press, 2008), 231.

This review will focus on the climate and environment in the sub-continent's northwest during the Holocene, and more particularly the mid-Holocene from about 5000 BCE (or 7000 yBP). It is now well established that the Indian monsoon was weaker during glacial periods, growing strong again during interglacial warmer periods; as a result, the monsoon's steep increase after 11500 yBP (9500 BCE) revived the subcontinent's fluvial activity, which caused the Bay of Bengal to experience high sediment influx for a few millennia. However, as in many parts of the world, this was punctuated by phases of weaker monsoon lasting a few centuries, about 8200, 6000 and 5000 yBP for the period preceding the rise of the Harappan Civilization.[17]

Two caveats are in order at this point. The first is that such changes can only be taken as macro-trends; they are not applicable to the sub-continent's diverse ecological zones ranging from tropical to semi-arid and arid. Even within a region, studies have come up with varying dates for the shift to aridity, as we will see. The second illustrates a peril of palaeoclimatology dating in the particular case of the Harappan civilization; its urban or Mature phase being relatively short-lived—about seven centuries from 2600 to 1900 BCE—sizable margins of error on radiocarbon dates are apt to lead to very different conclusions. Moreover, because the production rate of the Carbon-14 isotope in the earth's atmosphere is not constant, radiocarbon dating requires calibration; while older publications generally used uncalibrated dates, newer ones have introduced a correction based on one of several calibration curves—for dates around 2000 or 3000 BCE, calibration pushes them back by 300–700 years. There is no calibration curve specific to the Indian subcontinent; most available curves have been painstakingly plotted in Europe or North America. In this chapter, I have calibrated the uncalibrated dates with the convenient online CalPal tool of University of Cologne[18]; other calibration programmes yield similar results.[19]

Finally, let us keep in mind that terms such as 'wet', 'dry', 'arid', etc., are relative; today's conditions are generally taken to be the standard for comparison.

Climate and the Harappan Civilization

Soon after its discovery in the 1920s, there were suggestions that the Indus or Harappan Civilization was influenced by the climate and environment

---

[17] Singhvi and Kale, *Paleoclimate Studies in India*, 14.

[18] www.calpal-online.de, accessed 13 May 2020.

[19] For instance, https://c14.arch.ox.ac.uk/oxcal.html or http://calib.org/calib/, both accessed 13 May 2020.

in Sindh and Punjab. John Marshall, who directed the Archaeological Survey of India as well as the early excavations at Mohenjo-daro, remarked in 1931 that the extensive use of fired bricks at Mohenjo-daro, rather than plain mud or sun-dried bricks, pointed to a wetter environment.[20] Mortimer Wheeler, who headed the Archaeological Survey of India in the 1940s, opined that the said fired bricks were more likely a flood-mitigating device.[21] Writing in the 1960s, he also adopted a more nuanced position, which, as we will see, holds good today:

> For a Civilization so widely distributed, no uniform ending need be postulated. Circumstances which affected it in the sub-montane lands of the central Indus may well have differed widely from those which it encountered south or east of the Indian Desert and in the watery coastlands of the Rann of Kutch. Later archaeologists often disagreed, finding little or no evidence for a climate significantly different in Harappan times from today's. And the evidence at present available indicates that such indeed was the case.[22]

About the same time, the US archaeologist George Dales was categorical:

> Convincing evidence, collected from both archaeological and natural science investigations, refutes the popular theories of appreciable climatic change in the South Asian area during the past four to five thousand years ... Climate has thus been practically eliminated as a major factor in the environmental fortunes of the Harappan civilization.[23]

More recently, the US archaeologist Gregory Possehl supported this assessment: 'The climate of this region [Greater Indus Valley] was not markedly different in the third millennium BC from the one we have today.'[24] The Indian archaeologist Dilip K. Chakrabarti also argues that 'there can be no question of aridity = decline of civilization correlation' and complains that 'there seem to be too many [environmental determinists] today'.[25]

---

[20] J. Marshall, *Mohenjo-daro and the Indus Civilization*, Vol. 1 (London: Arthur Probsthain, 1931), p. 2.

[21] R.E. Mortimer Wheeler, *The Indus Civilization*, 3rd ed. (Cambridge: Cambridge University Press, 1968), 8.

[22] M. Wheeler, *Civilizations of the Indus Valley and Beyond*, 3rd ed. (London: Thames and Hudson, 1966), 72.

[23] G. F. Dales, 'Recent Trends in the Pre- and Protohistoric Archaeology of South Asia', *Proceedings of the American Philosophical Society* 110, no. 2 (1966): 131.

[24] G. L. Possehl, *The Indus Civilization: A Contemporary Perspective* (Oxford: Altamira Press, 2002), 13.

[25] D. K. Chakrabarti and S. Saini, *The Problem of the Sarasvati River and Notes on the Archaeological Geography of Haryana and Indian Panjab* (New Delhi: Aryan Books International, 2009), 37.

What evidence, then, do we have to reconstruct the climate and environment prevailing in the Mature or urban Harappan phase? Taking our cue from Wheeler, let us examine some of the principal studies region-wise, moving broadly from east to west.

Sarasvati Basin

Let us begin with the Ghaggar–Hakra basin, the Harappan civilization's eastern domain, which was home to some 360 sites of the Mature Harappan period,[26] the best known of which include (from east to west) Farmana, Rakhigarhi, Banawali, Bhirrana, Kalibangan and Ganweriwala. Since the mid-19th century, this now seasonal, mostly dry but wide-bed river had been identified with the Sarasvati River, which the Vedic and Late Vedic literature of India located between the Yamuna and the Satluj (or Sutlej) and whose desiccation and disappearance it recorded. Generations of geographers, geologists, Indologists and archaeologists have accepted this identification.[27] Most of them have proposed that this river system received contributions from the Satluj or the Yamuna, or both. As the late Indian archaeologist V. N. Misra put it: 'The large number of protohistoric settlements, dating from *c.* 4000 BC to 1500 BC, could have flourished along this river only if it was flowing perennially.'[28] Or, as Amalananda Ghosh stated in 1952 after he discovered Harappan sites along the bed of the Ghaggar, those settlements 'on the bank of the Sarasvati' could not have been established there 'had the river been dead during the lifetime of the culture'.[29]

In the 19th century itself, the presence of freshwater wells along the river's dry bed was recorded by British officials.[30] Various studies have pointed to the existence of large groundwater reserves in the region.

---

[26] M. Danino, *The Lost River: On the Trail of the Sarasvati*, Chap. 6 (New Delhi: Penguin Books, 2010).

[27] M. Danino, 'Discovering the Sarasvati River: From 1855 to 2014', in *Indus-Sarasvati (Harappan) Civilization vis-à-vis Rigveda*, ed. B. R. Mani (New Delhi: B. R. Publishing Corporation and Draupadi Trust, 2016), 15–28.

[28] V. N. Misra, 'Indus Civilization and the Rigvedic Sarasvati', in *South Asian Archaeology 1993*, eds. Asko Parpola and Petteri Koskikallio, Vol. II (Helsinki: Suomalainen Tiedeakatemia, 1994), 515.

[29] A. Ghosh, 'The Rajputana Desert: Its Archaeological Aspect', *Bulletin of the National Institute of Sciences in India* I (1952): 37–42, reproduced in S. P. Gupta, ed., *An Archaeological Tour Along the Ghaggar–Hakra River* (Meerut: Kusumanjali Prakashan, 1989), 105.

[30] Danino, *Lost River*, Chap. 1.

In 1995, M. A. Geyh and D. Ploethner[31] carried out an isotopic study of palaeowaters in a 100-km-long section of the Hakra's floodplain in Cholistan, close to the Indian border. Their survey revealed a huge body of fresh groundwater, some 14 km wide, 100 km long and 100 m thick; it was unexpectedly shallow, at a depth of less than 50 m on average. A tritium-based isotope study established that 'the present recharge of groundwater in Cholistan is negligible',[32] pointing to 'a range of the actual water age from 12900 to 4700 years BP'.[33]

This suggests that shortly before the Mature phase, the Hakra stopped flowing in this section, a conclusion the Pakistani archaeologist M. Rafique Mughal had independently reached: 'On the Pakistan side [of the international border], archaeological evidence now available overwhelmingly affirms that the Hakra was a perennial river through all its course in Bahawalpur during the fourth millennium B.C. (Hakra Period) and the early third millennium B.C. (Early Harappan Period).'[34] Thus, about 2700 or 2600 BCE, the Ghaggar–Hakra lost some of its waters to the Yamuna's and the Satluj's systems, according to Mughal, causing a 100 km stretch from the international border to Fort Abbas, Marot and a little beyond, to be empty of Mature Harappan sites, while Early Harappan sites had thrived there.[35] The Mature Harappan sites found further downstream were watered through channels connecting the Satluj and the Hakra (several of which have been mapped by topographic and remote sensing).

In 1997, M. Rao and K. M. Kulkarni conducted isotope studies of water drawn from various tube wells and shallow wells in Jalore, Barmer and Jaisalmer districts of western Rajasthan, deep in the arid zone. They found that the 'groundwater samples exhibit negligible tritium content, indicating absence of modern recharge. Radiocarbon data suggest the groundwater is a few thousand years old'.[36] This suggested

---

[31] M. A. Geyh and D. Ploethner, 'An Applied Palaeohydrological Study of Cholistan, Thar Desert, Pakistan', in *Applications of Tracers in Arid Zone Hydrology*, eds. E. M. Adar and C. Leibundgut (Vienna: International Association of Hydrological Sciences, 1995), 119–127.

[32] M. A. Geyh and D. Ploethner, 'Origins of a Freshwater Body in Cholistan, Thar Desert, Pakistan', in *Climate Change and Groundwater*, eds. W. Dragoni and B. S. Sukhija, Vol. 288 (London: Geological Society Special Publication, 2008), 102.

[33] Ibid, 104.

[34] M. R. Mughal, 'Recent Archaeological Research in the Cholistan Desert', in *Harappan Civilization: A Recent Perspective*, ed. Gregory L. Possehl, 2nd ed. (New Delhi: Oxford and IBH, 1993), 94.

[35] For a more detailed analysis, see Danino, *Lost River*, 145 ff.

[36] S. M. Rao and K. M. Kulkarni, 'Isotope Hydrology Studies on Water Resources in Western Rajasthan', *Current Science* 72, no. 1 (1997): 55–61.

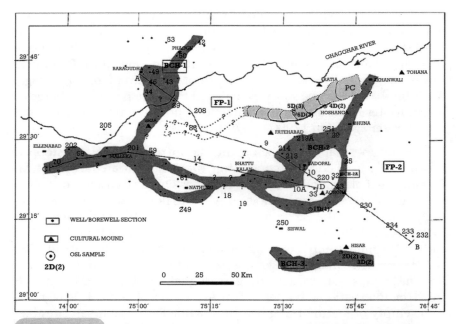

FIGURE 9.3 *Palaeochannels, in Dark Grey, Mapped in Haryana*

Source: Saini et al., 'Reconstruction of Buried Channel-Floodplain' (2009).
Note: The channel marked 'PC', in light grey, was mapped in an early remote sensing study.

the presence of abundant palaeowater reserves in the region and, therefore, a phase of river activity before a turn to aridity, although without a precise dateline. The study also proposed the presence of a 'Saraswati buried channel' in Jaisalmer District, which is part of the basin of the Ghaggar–Hakra.

Among recent geological studies, let us mention H. S. Saini et al. who in 2009 studied buried channels in the northwestern Haryana Plains and documented 'the existence of channel activity during the mid-Holocene ... in a part of the Haryana plains'; the mid-Holocene saw a 'second fluvial phase ... represented by a palaeochannel segment whose signatures are dated between ~6.0 and ~2.9 Ka'[37] (Figure 9.3). The dates, obtained by OSL dating of sands from wells or bore holes at depths between 8 and 25 m, bracket the Harappan Civilization

---

[37] H. S. Saini et al., 'Reconstruction of Buried Channel-Floodplain Systems of the Northwestern Haryana Plains and Their Relation to the "Vedic" Saraswati', *Current Science* 97, no. 11 (2009): 1642–1643.

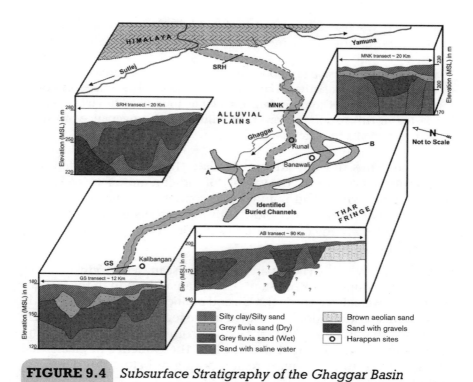

FIGURE 9.4 *Subsurface Stratigraphy of the Ghaggar Basin*

Source: Sinha et al., 'Geo-electric Resistivity Evidence' (2013).
Note: The four cross-sections correspond to transects in Punjab, Haryana and Rajasthan; the thin grey line shows the Ghaggar's bed.

and confirm that some channels, at least, were active in Haryana at the time.

The existence of such palaeochannels was confirmed by a 2013 study led by Rajiv Sinha, which mapped palaeoriver sedimentary bodies in the subsurface of Haryana, Punjab and northern Rajasthan by measuring their electrical resistivity, taking advantage of the lower resistivity of water-bearing sediments compared to that of dry ones (Figure 9.4). The study offered

> the first stratigraphic evidence that a palaeochannel exists in the sub-surface alluvium in the Ghaggar valley. The fact that the major urban sites of Kalibangan and Kunal lie adjacent to the newly discovered subsurface fluvial channel body ... suggests that there may be a spatial relationship between the Ghaggar-Hakra palaeochannel and Harappan site distribution.

The buried water-bearing sand bodies identified were measured at depths varying from a few metres to 50 m. Sinha et al. concluded:

> A thick and extensive sand body is present in the subsurface in parts of northwestern Rajasthan, Haryana and Punjab. ... The dimensions of the palaeochannel complex suggest a large, long-lived fluvial system existed in this region, however, the timing and provenance of this system remains to be resolved.[38]

This study thus did not attempt to date the palaeowater deposits. Importantly, it confirmed the validity of earlier remote sensing studies of the region, which had pointed to a complex of palaeochannels.[39] The above two studies also show shifting patterns for the channels, which is generally the case of Indo-Gangetic rivers, given the flatness of their alluvial plains.

A 2012 study of the Harappan fluvial landscape led by Liviu Giosan focused on sediments in Pakistan's Cholistan and Sindh in the Hakra's basin; they were dated through OSL and radiocarbon dating. The study showed that 'aridification intensified in the region after approximately 5,000 BP', that is, about 3000 BCE, which coincided with a weakening of the summer monsoon. It did not find the evidence of glacier-fed rivers flowing in the Ghaggar region during or before the Harappan period:

> Only monsoonal-fed rivers were active there during the Holocene. As the monsoon weakened, monsoonal rivers gradually dried or became seasonal, affecting habitability along their courses.... The most spectacular case of climate-controlled landscape transformation [towards the end of the Mature phase] is the Ghaggar-Hakra system, which became ephemeral and was largely abandoned.... Yet rivers were undoubtedly active in this region during the Urban Harappan Phase. We recovered sandy fluvial deposits approximately 5,400 y old at Fort Abbas in Pakistan.... This widespread fluvial redistribution of sediment suggests that reliable monsoon rains were able to sustain perennial rivers earlier during the Holocene.[40]

---

[38] R. Sinha et al., 'Geo-electric Resistivity Evidence for Subsurface Palaeochannel Systems Adjacent to Harappan Sites in Northwest India', *Quaternary International* 308–309 (2013): 66–75.

[39] For a summary of remote sensing studies, see Danino, *Lost River*, Chapter 3.

[40] L. Giosan et al., 'Fluvial Landscapes of the Harappan Civilization', *Proceedings of the National Academy of Sciences* 109, no. 26 (29 May 2012): E1688–E1694.

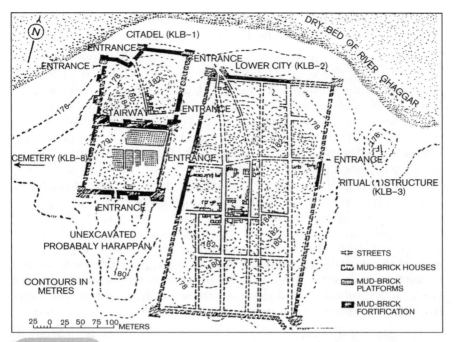

FIGURE 9.5 Plan of Kalibangan, With Entrances to the Upper City (left) and Lower Town (right) Facing the River Bed

Source: ASI.

In a later comment on their paper, Giosan et al. clarified: 'Our research points to a perennial monsoonal-fed Sarasvati River system with benign floods along its course.'[41]

There is thus a broad consensus on the flow of the Ghaggar–Hakra in Harappan times, at least down to today's international border, a point categorically established by features of sites in its central basin. For instance, both Banawali (in Haryana, on a palaeobed of the Ghaggar) and Kalibangan (northern Rajasthan; Figure 9.5) were built with the main entrances into their fortified areas facing the Sarasvati. Why build such cities a few metres from the riverbed if no water flowed in it? Moreover, unlike Mohenjo-daro with an estimated 700 wells, or Dholavira with its elaborate network of huge reservoirs, Kalibangan had only two or three wells and no known reservoir; the city must have drawn its water supply from the river, perhaps through a few channels. It was continuously occupied during the Mature phase, which would have

---

[41] L. Giosan et al., 'Sarasvati II', *Current Science* 105, no. 7 (2013): 888–890.

been impossible without a perennial river. Radiocarbon dating shows its abandonment (i.e., with no Late Harappan phase) about 1900 BCE.[42]

While geologists such as V. M. K. Puri[43] or K. S. Valdiya[44] had supported the existence of glacial sources for the Sarasvati in Mature Harappan times, Giosan et al.'s study characterized it as rain-fed: 'The lack of large-scale incision on the interfluve demonstrates that large, glacier-fed rivers did not flow across the Ghaggar-Hakra region during the Holocene.'[45] In 2013, Valdiya answered Giosan et al.'s arguments,[46] which the latter then articulated afresh.[47] More recent sedimentological investigations (in 2016) by Wout M. van Dijk et al. in the region have shown that 'The Ghaggar-Hakra paleochannel represents a filled, abandoned incised valley,'[48] contradicting Giosan et al. on the matter of incision. Lastly, preliminary results by geoscientists A. Chatterjee and J. S. Ray point to a 'paleo channel present beneath the modern Ghaggar-alluvium along a 120 km trail' which was active before 4000 BCE and whose sand deposits are 'akin to those of the sediment carried by higher Himalayan born Sutlej River and very different from the Siwalik derived Ghaggar sediments'.[49] If confirmed, these findings would contradict the view that the river was purely rain-fed throughout the Holocene.

As regards the cause of the river's desiccation, those who argue in favour of glacial sources, as does Valdiya's latest work on the Sarasvati,[50]

[42] B. B. Lal et al., *Excavations at Kalibangan: The Harappans (1960–69), Part I* (New Delhi: Archaeological Survey of India, 2015), 25.

[43] V. M. K. Puri, 'Vedic Sarasvati: Scientific Signatures on Its Origin from the Himalaya', in *Vedic River Sarasvati and Hindu Civilization*, ed. S. Kalyanaraman (New Delhi; Chennai: Aryan Books International; Sarasvati Research and Education Trust, 2008), 14–35.

[44] K. S. Valdiya, *Saraswati, the River that Disappeared* (Hyderabad: Indian Space Research Organization and Universities Press, 2002).

[45] Giosan et al., 'Fluvial Landscapes of the Harappan Civilization', E1689.

[46] K. S. Valdiya, 'The River Saraswati was a Himalayan-born River', *Current Science* 104, no. 1 (2013): 42–54.

[47] Giosan et al., 'Sarasvati II'.

[48] W. M. Van Dijk et al., 'Linking the Morphology of Fluvial Fan Systems to Aquifer Stratigraphy in the Sutlej-Yamuna Plain of Northwest India', *Journal of Geophysical Research: Earth Surface* 121 (2016): 218.

[49] A. Chatterjee and J. S. Ray, 'Evidence for a Mid-Holocene Buried Himalayan River Beneath the Ghaggar Plains, NW India: A Geochemical Provenance Study', Abstract submitted to the Goldschmidt Conference, Yokohama, 2016, Online, https://goldschmidtabstracts.info/abstracts/abstractView?id=2016002333, accessed 14 February 2017.

[50] K. S. Valdiya, *Prehistoric River Saraswati, Western India: Geological Appraisal and Social Aspects* (Society of Earth Scientists; Cham, Switzerland: Springer International, 2017).

generally attribute their loss to tectonics- or seismic-induced diversion of contributions to it from either the Yamuna or the Satluj, or both.

We will not go deeper into this debate here; the above-mentioned consensus on a perennial river flowing in the Ghaggar–Hakra basin in Mature Harappan times is enough for our purpose, even if it bears a few exceptions, notably Cameron A. Petrie et al., who in a 2017 study have sought to cast doubts on the perenniality of the Ghaggar–Hakra in Harappan times.[51] However, they offer no data to establish that the Ghaggar was non-perennial (only a 'likelihood' to that effect), counter Giosan et al.'s argument for perenniality only by proposing that the monsoon is 'unlikely' to have sufficed for the purpose, do not explain how a site like Kalibangan, which depended on the Ghaggar not only for water supply but also for trade and communication, would have coped with a non-perennial river and do not point out the flaws in the argument of archaeologists, such as the above-cited Misra, Ghosh or Mughal (to which those of Lal,[52] Kenoyer,[53] Possehl,[54] the Allchins[55] and several more could be added), that a perennial river was necessary to sustain the hundreds of settlements in its basin.

This archaeological argument is strengthened by J. P. Joshi et al.'s 1984 study of settlement patterns,[56] which showed that Harappan settlements in the river's central basin were abandoned about the beginning of the second millennium BCE (as we saw in the case of Kalibangan). The most parsimonious explanation for this phenomenon is the river's desiccation. The Late Harappan settlements of the early second millennium BCE crowded further north and east, along the Shivalik Hills' foothills, from where many streams continued to flow down, if seasonally; new settlements were also established across the Yamuna (Figure 9.6). Because a major stage in the river's desiccation coincided with the transition from

---

[51] C. A. Petrie et al., 'Adaptation to Variable Environments, Resilience to Climate Change: Investigating Land, Water and Settlement in Indus Northwest India', *Current Anthropology* 58, no. 1 (2017): 1–30, section 'The Role of the Paleo-Ghaggar/Hakra River in Northwest India'.

[52] B. B. Lal, *The Sarasvati Flows On: The Continuity of Indian Culture* (New Delhi: Aryan Books International, 2002), 77 ff.

[53] J. M. Kenoyer, *Ancient Cities of the Indus Valley Civilization* (Karachi and Islamabad: Oxford University Press and American Institute of Pakistan Studies, 1998), 27–29, 173.

[54] Possehl, *Indus Civilization*, 8–9, 239–240.

[55] R. Allchin and B. Allchin, *Origins of a Civilization: The Prehistory and Early Archaeology of South Asia* (New Delhi: Viking, 1997), 213 ff.

[56] J. P. Joshi, M. Bala, and J. Ram, 'The Indus Civilization: A Reconsideration on the Basis of Distribution Maps', in *Frontiers of the Indus Civilization*, eds. B. B. Lal and S. P. Gupta (New Delhi: Books and Books, 1984): 511–530.

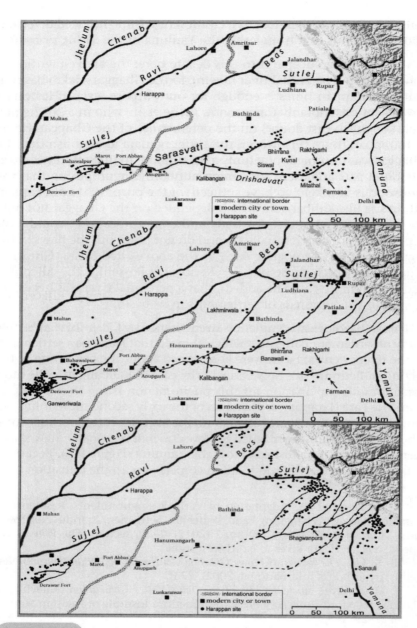

FIGURE 9.6

Settlement Patterns of Early Harappan (top), Mature Harappan (centre) and Late Harappan (bottom) Sites, With Proposed Reconstruction of the Region's Hydrology

Source: Maps from Danino, *The Lost River* (2010).

Mature to Late Harappan, there is a consensus in the archaeological community that it must have significantly contributed to the decline of the urban phase.[57]

Changes in settlement patterns were also conspicuous in Cholistan's Hakra basin, where M. Rafique Mughal surveyed 174 Mature Harappan and 50 Late Harappan sites. The latter's much reduced numbers, higher proportion of camp sites and, on average, smaller sizes caused Mughal to reflect: 'This change ... is strongly suggestive of the dispersal of inhabitants, if not depopulation, of the Hakra flood plain during the Late Harappan.... It seems almost certain that changing environmental conditions were profoundly affecting the long-established cultural pattern in Cholistan.'[58]

An independent corroboration of the turn to aridity in the region comes from a 2014 study by Yama Dixit, David A. Hodell and Cameron A. Petrie of the sediments of Kotla Dahar palaeolake in southern Haryana. The lake lies in the drainage of the now dry Chautang or Chitrang River, often associated with the Drishadvati of Vedic lore, and is adjacent to a few Harappan sites. Radiocarbon dating the gastropod shells in its sediments, they found 'relatively deep fresh-water lake existed at the site from 6.5 to 5.8 ka' (Figure 9.7). Then,

ca. 4.1 ka marking a peak in the evaporation/precipitation ratio in the lake catchment related to weakening of the ISM [Indian Summer

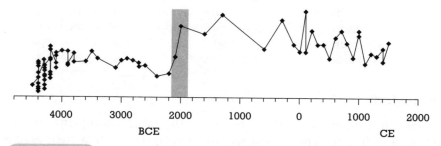

4000   3000   2000   1000   0   1000   2000

BCE   CE

FIGURE 9.7   *Variation of the Oxygen 18 Ratio at Kotla Dahar Palaeolake*

Source: Adapted and simplified from Dixit et al., 'Abrupt Weakening of the Summer Monsoon'.
Note: The sharp rise about 2100 bce corresponds to a sharp drop in monsoon precipitation.

---

[57] For instance, Kenoyer, *Ancient Cities of the Indus*; Possehl, *Indus Civilization*; Lal, *Sarasvati Flows On*; Chakrabarti and Saini, *Problem of the Sarasvati River*.

[58] M. R. Mughal, *Ancient Cholistan: Archaeology and Architecture* (Lahore: Ferozsons, 1997), 52.

Monsoon] ..., suggesting that climate may have played a role in the Indus cultural transformation.... Taken together, the records from Kotla Dahar, Mawmuluh [in northeast India], and the Arabian Sea provide strong evidence for a widespread weakening of the ISM across large parts of India at ca. 4.2–4.0 ka. The monsoon recovered to the modern-day conditions after 4.0 k.y. ago, and the event lasted for ~200 yr (ca. 4.2–4.0 ka) in this region.[59]

As Figure 9.7 makes it clear, precipitation in southern Haryana during the Mature phase was relatively high, though moving towards aridity in its second half.

Punjab

In 2008, Rita Wright et al. used models of archaeoclimatology to plot the intensity of the monsoon and river flow in the region of Harappa. They found that 'around 3500 BC the volume of water in the rivers increases, and the rivers flood', and 'from around 2100 BC the river flow [in the Beas] begins to fall'. Around Harappa, 'a 600-year period of reduced rainfall [sets in] after 2100 BC', leading to 'an unexpected agricultural crisis'. Those two dates roughly bracket the Early and much of the Mature phases. However, Wright et al. observe:

> During the Mature/Urban Harappan period there is an inverse, co-varying trend in rainfall seasonality, as yearly monsoon precipitation diminishes while winter rainfall increases almost proportionately. ... The two-season (winter/summer) multi-cropping system noted above may have been a conscious strategy [of the Harappans in Harappa's region] considering these fluctuations.[60]

Rajasthan

Rajasthan presents us with a number of dry lakes, prompting studies of their sediments and pollen record so as to reconstruct their active phases. (The density of pollen is in direct relation with the water level.) Gurdip Singh's oft-cited pioneering palynological study of 1971 focused on three salt lakes of Rajasthan—Sambhar, Didwana and Lunkaransar—the first two in a semi-arid belt. The pollen record showed the last lake, located in an arid belt, experiencing a wet phase from 3000 to 1800 BCE

---

[59] Y. Dixit, D. A. Hodell, and C. A. Petrie, 'Abrupt Weakening of the Summer Monsoon in Northwest India ~ 4100 yr Ago', *Geology* 42, no. 4 (2014): 339–342.

[60] R. P. Wright, R. A. Bryson, and J. Schuldenrein, 'Water Supply and History: Harappa and the Beas Regional Survey', *Antiquity* 82 (2008): 37–48.

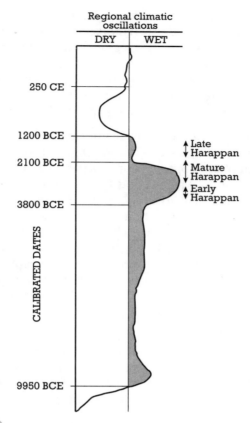

Regional climatic
oscillations

DRY	WET

250 CE

1200 BCE

2100 BCE

3800 BCE

9950 BCE

CALIBRATED DATES

↑ Late
↓ Harappan

↑ Mature
↓ Harappan

↑ Early
↓ Harappan

FIGURE 9.8 *Curve of Precipitation in Rajasthan*

Source: Adapted and simplified from Gurdip Singh, 'The Indus Valley Culture Seen' (1971).

(with a dry one setting in from 1000 BCE onward),[61] which brackets the Mature phase. This was marked by grasslands and freshwater swamps: 'Precipitation over Rajasthan, in terms of annual average rainfall, was probably 50 cm greater than at the present time in the arid belt.... A grassy steppe-savannah type of vegetation appears to have dominated the scene in most areas'[62] (see Figure 9.8).

[61] G. Singh, 'The Indus Valley Culture Seen in the Context of Post-glacial Climate and Ecological Studies in North-West India', *Archaeology and Physical Anthropology in Oceania* 6, no. 2 (1971): 183.

[62] G. Singh et al., 'Late Quaternary History of Vegetation and Climate of the Rajasthan Desert, India', *Philosophical Transactions of the Royal Society of London, Series B, Biological Sciences* 267, no. 889 (1974): 495.

The above conclusions were endorsed a decade later by A. Bryson and A. M. Swain, who revisited the pollen profiles of Didwana and Lunkaransar lakes. Their reconstruction of the region's palaeoclimate showed that between 3000 and 1500 BCE, there was 'at least double the present summer rainfall ... [and] the winter rains appear to have been maximum during Indus time, decreasing the winter desiccation now characterizing the region, and increasing the overall precipitation efficiency'.[63]

But Singh's and Bryson's dates were uncalibrated. Once calibrated by Shaffer and Lichtenstein, Singh's chronology seemed to show that the Mature Harappan phase 'appeared during a period of increasing aridity'.[64] And after calibration by Madella and Fuller, Bryson's wetter phase was also said to be pushed back 'to a pre-Mature Harappan period',[65] that is, to the Early Harappan phase that preceded the Mature phase. However, the author considers this point debatable; while Singh's transition date of about 1800 BCE rested mainly on two dates for the now dry Lunkaransar Lake's wet phase[66] and, on an 'extrapolation', for the transition to its dry phase—clearly a fragile foundation—Singh's and Bryson's wet phases continue to bracket the Mature phase after calibration by current curves (see Table 9.1).

A 1983 study by R. J. Wasson et al. of Didwana Lake's sediments, and the concentrations of its various minerals in particular, found deep-water conditions from about 6000 yBP to 4000 yBP, when the lake dried briefly; afterwards, the lake became ephemeral, with salinity comparable to today's.[67] After calibration, this points to a

---

[63] R. A. Bryson and A. M. Swain, 'Holocene Variations of Monsoon Rainfall in Rajasthan', *Quaternary Research* 16 (1981): 144.

[64] J. G. Shaffer and D. A. Lichtenstein, 'Ethnicity and Change in the Indus Valley Cultural Tradition', in *Old Problems and New Perspectives in the Archaeology of South Asia*, ed. Jonathan Mark Kenoyer (Wisconsin: University of Wisconsin, 1989), 120–121.

[65] M. Madella and D. Q. Fuller, 'Palaeoecology and the Harappan Civilisation of South Asia: A Reconsideration', *Quaternary Science Reviews* 25 (2006): 1297.

[66] Singh's two relevant dates for Lunkaransar Lake's wet phase are BP 5060 ± 70 and 5420 ± 70; calibrated with the online CalPal tool of University of Cologne, they become 3854 ± 82 and 4239 ± 92 BCE respectively.

[67] R. J. Wasson et al., 'Geomorphology, Late Quaternary Stratigraphy and Palaeoclimatology of the Thar Dune Field', in *Zeitschrift für Geomorphologie*, N.F. Supplementband 45 (1983): 117–151, partly reproduced in B. P. Radhakrishnan and S. S. Merh, eds, *Vedic Sarasvati: Evolutionary History of a Lost River of Northwestern India* (Bangalore: Geological Society of India, 1999), 219–223. See also R. J. Wasson, G. I. Smith, and D. P. Agrawal, 'Late Quaternary Sediments, Minerals, and Inferred Geochemical History of Didwana Lake, Thar Desert, India', *Palaeogeography, Palaeoclimatology, Palaeoecology* 46 (1984): 345–372.

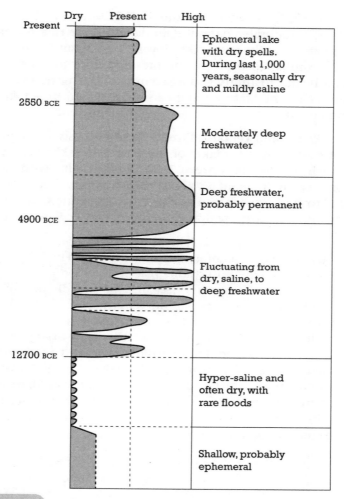

Dry   Present   High

Present ─

Ephemeral lake
with dry spells.
During last 1,000
years, seasonally dry
and mildly saline

2550 BCE ─

Moderately deep
freshwater

Deep freshwater,
probably permanent

4900 BCE ─

Fluctuating from
dry, saline, to
deep freshwater

12700 BCE ─

Hyper-saline and
often dry, with
rare floods

Shallow, probably
ephemeral

FIGURE 9.9 *A Graph of the Water Level of Didwana Lake, Rajasthan*

Source: Adapted and simplified from Wasson et al., 'Geomorphology, Late Quaternary Stratigraphy' (1983).

wet phase from about 4900 to 2550 BCE, with a marked drop afterwards. However, while the general curve (Figure 9.9) seems broadly in agreement with other studies, the chronology is based on just a few radiocarbon dates.

In 1999, the same Lunkaransar Lake's sediments were collected by Y. Enzel et al. down to the current water table, 2.4 m below the dry lake's bed; fifteen radiocarbon dates established that the lake held water in 8000 BCE, began to decline around 4000 BCE and 'dried completely' by 3500 BCE, in calibrated dates.[68] 'Our data indicate that the environment and climate of the past 5000 C^{14} years [i.e., about 5,800 calibrated years] were similar to those of the present', note the authors, who attribute this shift to aridity to a weakening of the monsoon, with the implication that the Mature Harappan phase would have taken place in an arid period.

Sushma Prasad and Yehouda Enzel's 2006 synthesis of palynological studies of now mostly dry lakes of the Thar Desert showed that they reached their peak levels between 7200 and 6000 yBP, with more arid conditions setting in about 5300 yBP.[69] This points to a wetter phase from 5200 to 4000 BCE, with an arid phase from about 3300 BCE, which coincides with the Early Harappan phase.

Evidence from the Rajasthan lakes thus broadly point to a mid-Holocene period of high precipitation and inflow followed by a weakening of the monsoon. Although most studies place the subsequent turn to aridity before the Mature Harappan phase, it remains a divided verdict. As M. D. Kajale and B. C. Deotare cautioned in their own palaeobotanical study of the same lakes, 'It is not possible to invoke a single cause, such as climate, for explaining intralake and interlake variations'.[70] More complex mechanisms—tectonics, erosion, river and aeolian activity, among others—were also at work. Besides, lakes such as Didwana and Lunkaransar are not in the Ghaggar–Hakra (or Sarasvati) basin proper, where numerous Harappan sites have been located, but on its margins; variations in their water levels may or may not be directly relevant to conditions prevailing in Harappan cities.

Sindh

Few palaeoclimatic studies of Sindh and surrounding regions are available. In the Lasbela district of southern Baluchistan, close to the border with Sindh, M. B. McKean studied in 1983 pollen and sediments in the region of Balakot and found nothing suggesting that

---

[68] Y. Enzel et al., 'High-resolution Holocene Environmental Changes in the Thar Desert, Northwestern India', *Science* 284 (1999): 125–128.

[69] S. Prasad and Y. Enzel, 'Holocene Paleoclimates of India', *Quaternary Research* 66 (2006): 442–453.

[70] M. D. Kajale and B. C. Deotare, 'Late Quaternary Environmental Studies on Salt Lakes in Western Rajasthan, India: A Summarised View', *Journal of Quaternary Science* 12, no. 5 (1997): 409.

'the climate during the protohistoric period in Las Bela was decidedly wetter than at present'.[71]

Returning to the issue of the Sarasvati's desiccation, the overall balance of evidence is in favour of a two-stage loss for the river: a first break-up upstream of Cholistan about 2700–2600 BCE and a drying-up of the river's central basin about 1900 BCE. Both events would imply the loss of contributions from the Satluj through several channels connecting it to the Ghaggar–Hakra system and, correspondingly, additional inflow into the Beas and therefore the lower Indus. 'As a result', write the Allchins, 'the Indus floods would have become greater in volume and more erratic'.[72] Kenoyer makes the same point, linking an eastward 'swing' of the Indus to the capture of part of the Sarasvati's waters by the Indus system.[73] Flam is more specific: 'The Sutlej River has the highest average annual discharge of all the main Indus tributaries of the Punjab as they exit their mountain catchments and enter the plains', and therefore 'an increase in water and sediment discharge of that magnitude [provoked by the westward shift of the Satluj] would have had dramatic effects downstream in the Lower Indus Basin'.[74] The German archaeologist Michael Jansen agrees that 'within at least 500 years of existence of the city [Mohenjo-daro], the river [Indus] must have changed its course several times'.[75]

In the 1960s, the US archaeologist-cum-hydrologist Robert Raikes and George Dales had proposed an ingenious theory of massive flooding of Mohenjo-daro caused by the tectonic uplift of a natural dam downstream of the city, which would have impounded the Indus waters.[76] H. T. Lambrick, a British official who served in pre-Partition Sindh for two decades, rejected such a possibility and proposed instead that the Indus shifted 'away' from Mohenjo-daro (in a process known as 'avulsion'): 'The surrounding country, starved of water, immediately

---

[71] M. B. McKean, *The Palynology of Balakot, a Pre-Harappan and Harappan Age Site in Las Bela, Pakistan* (PhD thesis, Southern Methodist University, Dallas, TX, 1983), quoted in Madella and Fuller, 'Palaeoecology and the Harappan Civilisation', 1292.

[72] Allchin and Allchin, *Origins of a Civilization*, 211.

[73] Kenoyer, *Ancient Cities of the Indus*, 173.

[74] L. Flam, 'The Prehistoric Indus River System and the Indus Civilization in Sindh', *Man and Environment* 24, no. 2 (1999): 55.

[75] M. R. N. Jansen, 'Mohenjo Daro and the River Indus', in *The Indus River: Biodiversity, Resources, Humankind*, eds. A. Meadows and P. S. Meadows (Karachi: Oxford University Press, 1999), 379, note 58.

[76] See Possehl, *Indus Civilization*, 238, for a brief discussion and references.

began to deteriorate.'[77] The deterioration would have stemmed not just from the loss of the river but also from that of its yearly floods that watered the soil in time for the winter crop and fertilized it with rich alluvium. It would also imply a complete disruption of the river-based communication network that Mohenjo-daro vitally depended on, in Jansen's opinion.[78] According to Flam: 'A major change ... in the main river channel would have brought widespread abandonment of many sites and a movement of population out of the Lower Indus basin into adjacent and more "stable" areas.'[79]

Lambrick's thesis, supplemented by Flam's studies (and compatible with the suggestion of diversion of Ghaggar–Hakra waters into the Indus system), seems more plausible than Raikes and Dales' theory, but it remains to be confirmed through precise sedimentological studies of the lower Indus's course.

Gujarat

Multi-proxy analyses by Sushma Prasad et al. at Gujarat's Nal Sarovar, a bird sanctuary west of Ahmedabad, showed in 1997 that the lake was almost dry from about 6600 yBP, when the Rajasthan lakes were at their highest, and was replenished between 4800 and 3000 yBP, with increased aridity afterwards.[80] After calibration, the lake's wet phase shifts from 2800–1000 to 3500–1200 BCE. Here, the Mature Harappan phase is common to both windows (and therefore assumed to be wet).

A decade later, Vandana Prasad et al. investigated the estuary of the Mahi River, which flows from the Aravalli Hills into the Gulf of

---

[77] H. T. Lambrick, 'The Indus Flood Plain and the 'Indus' Civilization', *Geographical Journal* 133, no. 4 (1967): 493.

[78] M. Jansen, 'Settlement Networks of the Indus Civilization', in *Indian Archaeology in Retrospect, Vol. 2: Protohistory, Archaeology of the Harappan Civilization*, eds. S. Settar and R. Korisettar (New Delhi: Manohar and Indian Council of Historical Research, 2000), 118.

[79] L. Flam, 'Ecology and Population Mobility in the Prehistoric Settlement of the Lower Indus Valley, Sindh, Pakistan', in *The Indus River: Biodiversity, Resources, Humankind*, eds. A. Meadows and P. S. Meadows (Karachi: Oxford University Press, 1999), 317. In the same volume, M. D. Harvey and S. A. Schumm also endorse Lambrick's theory of avulsion of the Indus: 'Indus River Dynamics and the Abandonment of Mohenjo-daro', 333–348.

[80] S. Prasad, S. Kusumgar, and S. K. Gupta, 'A Mid to Late Holocene Record of Palaeoclimatic Changes from Nal Sarovar: A Palaeodesert Margin Lake in Western India', *Journal of Quaternary Science* 12, no. 2 (1997): 153–159.

Khambat, a little to the north of the Narmada's estuary. Their main proxies were pollen and phytoliths, and their findings confirmed 'the well established weakening phase of the SW monsoon that commenced from 5500 yr BP'. During the period 3660–3400 yBP, their palaeoclimatic records showed a gradual decline of the southwest or summer monsoon activity, which 'almost ceased around 3400 yr BP'. On the other hand, 'winter precipitation, because of more active western disturbances, during 3660–3400 yr BP was much more pronounced and extended over larger parts of western India, though this too declined ~3400 yr BP. This was the time when the Indus Valley Civilization declined drastically in this region'.[81] In other words, the Harappan civilization flourished at a time of declining monsoon, though with the compensation of intense winter precipitation. However, this chronology appears to derive from a stratigraphy dated by earlier workers and does not seem to be calibrated. Once calibrated, the above dates would take us to about 2050–1750 BCE.

Further inland, Vandana Prasad led another multi-proxy study at the Wadhwana Lake, some 40 km southeast of Vadodara (Baroda), and obtained three calibrated radiocarbon dates from the sediments. The lake went through several phases: a high-water phase from 5500 to 3565 BCE, pointing to higher precipitation, followed by a dry phase with low water level from about 3565 to 2255 BCE, and a moderate increase in the lake's level from 2000 to 1240 BCE, with indications of a more humid and warmer climate.[82] This would place most of the Harappan Mature phase in an arid period, with a partial revival towards the end of the third millennium.

In 2013, Anjum Farooqui, A. S. Gaur and Vandana Prasad focused on the palaeoenvironment at two sites of coastal southern Saurashtra. They found 'low precipitation and arid climatic conditions ~ 2000 BC'. The previous two millennia, from about 4000 BCE, saw a shift from a moist to a dry environment but overall a wetter environment and the 'dominance of evergreen and moist deciduous arboreals'. In the authors' opinion, 'the moister climatic conditions and comparatively

    [81] V. Prasad, B. Phartiyal, and A. Sharma, 'Evidence of Enhanced Winter Precipitation and the Prevalence of a Cool and Dry Climate During the Mid to Late Holocene in Mainland Gujarat, India', *The Holocene* 17, no. 7 (2007): 895.
    [82] V. Prasad et al., 'Mid–late Holocene Monsoonal Variations from Mainland Gujarat, India: A Multi-proxy Study for Evaluating Climate Culture Relationship', *Palaeogeography, Palaeoclimatology, Palaeoecology* 397 (2014): 38–51.

rich forest cover around the Saurashtra coast was one of the main attractive reasons for the expansion and settlement of Harappans as they largely sustained on agriculture and domestication along with the maritime activity'.[83]

Northwest Coastline, Rann of Kutch and Saurashtra

Variations in sea levels along India's continental shelf have considerable impact not only on settlements in the coastal belts, in the opening or closing of sea channels, but also in the incision and aggradation of sea-flowing rivers, although in the case of low-gradient rivers like the Ganges, this impact may have been overemphasized.[84] Of relevance to our study are sea level changes along the subcontinent's northwest coastline. A 1996 study by N. H. Hashimi et al. plotted radiocarbon dates of sediments, shells, calcareous and carbonized wood, taken from a few metres above the present mean sea level (MSL) on the coast to varying depths on the shelf (Figure 9.10). 'The curve shows a gradient between 11,000–7,000 years BP' during which the sea level rose at an estimated 20 metres per millennium. 'After 7000 years BP it fluctuated more or less at the present level.'[85]

The above curve is a broad average, again concealing important local variations. For instance, archaeological investigations by A. S. Gaur, K. H. Vora and Sundaresh at Bet Dwarka, Saurashtra's northwest tip, revealed

that the oldest habitation was situated below the present high water line. This is an indication of a lower sea level during that period of settlement. 14C ages and archaeological data suggest a time bracket for these habitations between 2050 and 1650 yrs BP (calibrated)…. During that time a large area on the northern part of the [Bet Dwarka] island was exposed and the island was probably connected with the mainland towards its eastern side during low tide. Sea level rose up

---

[83] A. Farooqui, A. S. Gaur, and V. Prasad, 'Climate, Vegetation and Ecology During Harappan Period: Excavations at Kanjetar and Kaj, Mid-Saurashtra Coast, Gujarat', *Journal of Archaeological Science* 40, no. 6 (2013): 2631, 2646.

[84] S. K. Tandon et al., 'Late Quaternary Evolution of the Ganga Plains: Myths and Misconceptions, Recent Developments and Future Directions', *Golden Jubilee Memoir of the Geological Society of India* 66 (2008): 259–299.

[85] N. H. Hashimi et al., 'Holocene Sea Level Fluctuations on Western Indian Continental Margin: An Update', *Journal of the Geological Society of India* 46 (1995): 160–161.

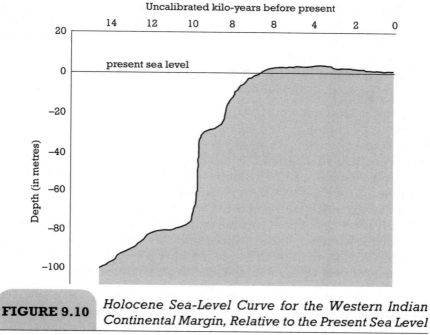

Uncalibrated kilo-years before present

FIGURE 9.10 *Holocene Sea-Level Curve for the Western Indian Continental Margin, Relative to the Present Sea Level*

Source: Adapted and simplified from Hashimi et al., 'Holocene Sea Level Fluctuations' (1995).

to its present state around 1000 yrs BP when most of the coastal sites of early historical period got submerged in the sea.[86]

At the same time, apart from geological evidence based on sediment analysis,[87] there is historical evidence that the sea receded from what is today the Rann of Kutch, since it was navigable during the time of Alexander the Great and of the *Periplus of the Erythraean Sea*.[88] The

---

[86] A. S. Gaur, K. H. Vora, and Sundaresh, 'Shoreline Changes During the Last 2000 Years on the Saurashtra Coast of India: Study Based on Archaeological Evidences', *Current Science* 92, no. 1 (2007): 103. See also A. S. Gaur and Sundaresh, 'Palaeo-coastline of Saurashtra, Gujarat: A Study Based on Archaeolgical Proxies', *Indian Journal of Geo-Marine Sciences* 43, no. 7 (2014): 1224–1229.

[87] N. Khonde et al., 'Environmental Significance of Raised Rann Sediments Along the Margins of Khadir, Bhanjada and Kuar Bet Islands in Great Rann of Kachchh, Western India', *Current Science* 101, no. 11 (2011): 1434.

[88] For a detailed analysis, see R. N. Iyengar and B. P. Radhakrishna, 'Geographical Location of Vedic Irina in Southern Rajasthan', *Journal Geological Society of India* 70 (2007): 701–702.

resolution of this apparent contradiction lies partly in massive sedimentation of the Rann caused by the eastern mouths of the Indus,[89] and partly in tectonics, with geological evidence for the uplift of Pakistan's nearby Makran Coast[90] corroborated by coastal Harappan sites such as Balakot, Sutkagen Dor and Sokhta Koh bearing evidence of sea trade but now located several kilometres inland.[91]

That the Rann was a navigable gulf in prehistoric and early historical times has been proposed since the 19th century. The US archaeologist Louis Flam summed up those studies thus: 'Terrestrial Kachchh would have consisted of an island, or islands, completely surrounded by a tidal and seasonal sea.'[92] The Rann was, according to U. B. Mathur, a 'shallow arm of the sea'.[93] More recent work by Gaur et al. suggests that it was 'an extended Gulf and must have been navigable at least up to the early centuries of the Christian era, [while] the Little Rann of Kutch was navigable even as late as 16th century AD'.[94] Figure 9.11 shows the reconstructed Rann in the third millennium BCE, with Harappan settlements, most of them now inland, dotting the conjectured coastline.

In this perspective, not only were today's two Ranns connected and navigable, but they appear to have been 'connected to the Gulf of Khambhat via Little Rann and Nal-Bhal region (that separates Saurashtra from mainland Gujarat)'.[95] This important conjecture, proposed earlier by a few geologists like S. S. Merh,[96] still needs to be geologically and archaeologically attested. It is broadly accepted that in Harappan times, a river and sea route existed between Sindh (where Mohenjo-daro is located) and Dholavira (a major Harappan city on the Khadir Island of

[89] A. K. Tyagi et al., 'Mid-Holocene Sedimentation and Landscape Evolution in the Western Great Rann of Kachchh, India', *Geomorphology* 151–152 (2012): 89–98.

[90] R. E. Snead, 'Recent Morphological Changes Along the Coast of West Pakistan', *Annals of the Association of American Geographers* 57, no. 3 (1967): 550–565.

[91] H. P. Ray, *The Archaeology of Seafaring in Ancient South Asia* (Cambridge: Cambridge University Press, 2003), 95.

[92] Flam, 'Prehistoric Indus River System', 61.

[93] U. B. Mathur, 'Chronology of Harappan Port Towns of Gujarat in the Light of Sea Level Changes During the Holocene', *Man and Environment* 27, no. 2 (2002): 64.

[94] A. S. Gaur et al., 'Was the Rann of Kachchh Navigable During the Harappan Times (Mid-Holocene)? An Archaeological Perspective', *Current Science* 105, no. 11 (2013): 1490.

[95] Ibid, 1488–1489.

[96] S. S. Merh and L. S. Chamyal, 'The Quaternary Sediments in Gujarat', *Current Science* 64, nos. 11 and 12 (1993): 823–827.

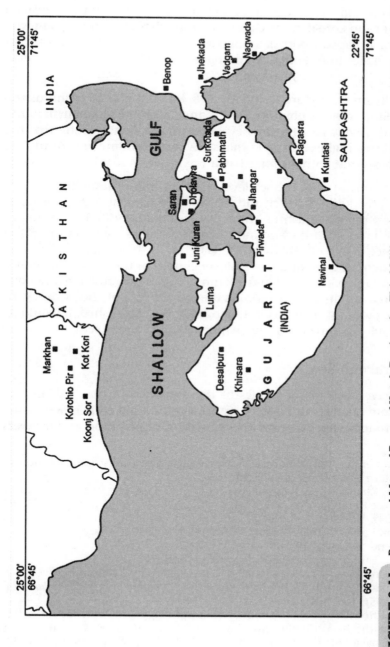

FIGURE 9.11 *Proposed Map of Rann of Kutch During the Third Millennium BC, with Harappan Settlements Plotted*

Source: Gaur et al., 'Was the Rann of Kachchh Navigable' (2013).

the Great Rann of Kutch) through the Indus's eastern branches, since 'the western Great Rann was under the dominance of a marginally high sea between 5.5 and 2 ka'.[97] If, in addition, a sea route existed between Dholavira and Lothal in the Gulf of Khambhat, that would explain why no major Harappan port has emerged on the Saurashtra coast—boats carrying wares from Lothal would have sailed this northward channel to today's Rann, rather than southward and around Saurashtra.

Equally important are studies by A. S. Khadkikar et al. of multispectral satellite imagery combined with an analysis of sediments around Lothal; the evidence of former estuaries inland demonstrates that the sea level was higher during Lothal's heyday,[98] lending weight to S. R. Rao's thesis that Lothal's huge basin was a dockyard.[99]

In Harappan times, the sea level was thus higher along the Makran Coast, in the Rann of Kutch and the Gulf of Khambat, but lower at the northwest tip of Saurashtra, where Bet Dwarka is located; a northeast-southwest tectonic tilt seems indicated, and studies have confirmed the occurrence of tectonic tilts and uplifts in this unstable region.[100] Indeed, one of them notes a 'mid-late Holocene uplift of the [Bela, Khadir and Bhanjada] islands [located in the Rann of Kutch] in a tilted manner due to tectonic activity'.[101] However, in the present state of knowledge, with absolute dates for such tilts not being securely established, it would be premature to assume that they happened as a single event.

The Arabian Sea

There have been many studies of the dynamics of the Arabian Sea, apart from changes in its level, as briefly discussed earlier. Sediments on its floor having recorded the formation of plankton and deposits

---

[97] Tyagi et al., 'Mid-Holocene Sedimentation and Landscape Evolution in the Western Great Rann of Kachchh', 95.

[98] A. S. Khadkikar, C. Rajshekhar, and K. P. N. Kumaran, 'Palaeogeography Around the Harappan Port of Lothal, Gujarat, Western India', *Antiquity* 78, no. 302 (2004): 896–903; A. S. Khadkikar et al., 'Palaeoenvironments Around the Harappan Port of Lothal, Gujarat, Western India', *Journal of Indian Geophysical Union* 8, no. 1 (2004): 49–53.

[99] For a discussion, see Danino, *Lost River*, 163–164.

[100] For instance, D. M. Maurya et al., 'Late Quaternary Geomorphic Evolution of the Coastal Zone of Kachchh, Western India', *Journal of Coastal Research* 24, no. 3 (2008): 746–758.

[101] V. Chowksey et al., 'Tectonic Geomorphology and Evidence for Active Tilting of the Bela, Khadir and Bhanjada Islands in the Seismically Active Kachchh palaeorift graben, Western India', *Zeitschrift für Geomorphologie* 54, no. 4 (2010): 467.

from rivers, among other proxies, they testify to changes in the intensity of the southwest monsoon and are thus relevant to the Harappan landscape, especially its Sindh heartland.

In 1996, Pothuri Diwakar Naidu, studying the remains of planktonic foraminifers from a core drilled in the sea bed off Oman in the Arabian peninsula (about 100 km offshore and at a sea floor depth of over 800 m), found that the upwelling, and therefore the southwest monsoon, declined sharply at 3.5 ka, which decline 'can be interpreted as a result of the onset of arid climate in general throughout the tropics and in particular in the Asian tropics'.[102] Once calibrated, the date for this transition to aridity becomes about 1850 BCE. Naidu also sought to establish a link with the drying up of the Sarasvati River and the decline of the Harappan Civilization as a whole.

A few years later, Ulrich von Rad et al. studied laminated (or varved) sediments in the Arabian Sea off Karachi and observed that 'precipitation decreased in the river watershed (indicated by thinning varves) ... after 4000-3500 yr BP',[103] that is, after 2000 BCE.

In 2003, Michael Staubwasser et al. analysed oxygen isotope ratios in plankton from a core drilled at 316 m water depth off the formerly active Indus delta. Their findings revealed climate changes during the last 6,000 years, 'with the most prominent change recorded at 4.2 ka BP' (or 2200 BCE), along with 'a reduction in Indus river discharge'. They observed: 'The 4.2 ka event is coherent with the termination of urban Harappan civilization in the Indus valley.'[104]

While the above dates are in broad agreement, Prasad and Enzel's study of Rajasthan lakes mentioned earlier compiled several other analyses of Arabian Sea sediment cores, with a broad agreement regarding the weakening of the southwest monsoon in protohistoric times, but some divergence as to the precise epoch when this happened.[105]

One of them, led in 2003 by Anil K. Gupta, examined shell remains in sediments from the same core used by Naidu above, but with a higher

---

[102] P. D. Naidu, 'Onset of an Arid Climate at 3.5 ka in the Tropics: Evidence from Monsoon Upwelling Record', *Current Science* 71, no. 9 (1996): 715–718.

[103] U. Von Rad et al., 'A 5000-yr Record of Climate Change in Varved Sediments from the Oxygen Minimum Zone off Pakistan, Northeastern Arabian Sea', *Quaternary Research* 51 (1999): 39–53.

[104] M. Staubwasser et al., 'Climate Change at the 4.2 ka BP Termination of the Indus Valley Civilization and Holocene South Asian Monsoon Variability', *Geophysical Research Letters* 30, no. 8 (2003): 7-1–7-4.

[105] Prasad and Enzel, 'Holocene Paleoclimates of India', 448–449.

resolution and calibrated dating. Their 11,000-year record showed 'several intervals of weak summer monsoon' at about 3900–3600, 2400–2200 and 1400 BCE (the last lasting for a few decades), with the first and third being more severe.[106] Interestingly, Gupta et al. find that these periods of weaker monsoon 'coincide with cold periods documented in the North Atlantic region'; in other words, 'the link between North Atlantic climate and the Asian monsoon is a persistent aspect of global climate'.

Further Afield

Although not necessarily relevant to the Harappan environment, it is instructive to briefly list a few studies beyond its geographical sphere.

We may begin with a general statement of the subcontinent's palaeoclimate. In 2006, Anil K. Gupta et al. synthesized research on the monsoon and other climatic inputs from many sources including their own. 'It appears to us', they concluded

> that the arid phase in the Indian subcontinent started ca 5000-4000 cal yrs BP coinciding with a stepwise weakening of the SW monsoon ... The arid phase might have intensified ca 4000-3500 cal yrs BP as has been in the Himalayas, western peninsula and northwestern India, and ended ca 1700 cal yrs BP, when the SW monsoon was the driest.[107]

In 2000, Netajirao Phadtare examined pollen and peat in the Garhwal Himalayas and found evidence of 'a warm, humid climate, with highest monsoon intensity' from about 4000 to 2500 BCE; after 2000 BCE, there was 'a sharp decrease in temperature and rainfall'. Phadtare cited five independent studies from other regions that support 'a decrease in the strength of the Southwest monsoon about 4000 cal yr BP'.[108]

Christian Leipe et al. in 2014 investigated pollen from a high-altitude lake in Ladakh. The record indicated 'low lake productivity with high influx of freshwater between ca. 11.5 and 4.5 cal ka BP which is in agreement with the regional monsoon dynamics and published

---

[106] A. K. Gupta, D. M. Anderson, and J. T. Overpeck, 'Abrupt Changes in the Asian Southwest Monsoon During the Holocene and Their Links to the North Atlantic Ocean', *Nature* 421 (2003): 354–57, dates read from Figure 2, p. 354.

[107] Gupta et al., 'Adaptation and Human Migration', 1086.

[108] Netajirao R. Phadtare, 'Sharp Decrease in Summer Monsoon Strength 4000–3500 cal yr B.P. in the Central Higher Himalaya of India Based on Pollen Evidence from Alpine Peat', *Quaternary Research* 53 (2000): 122–129.

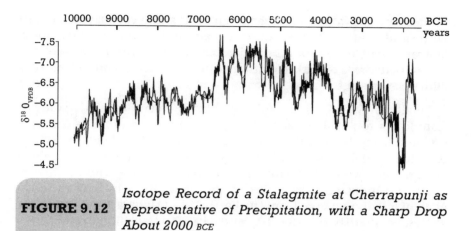

FIGURE 9.12   *Isotope Record of a Stalagmite at Cherrapunji as Representative of Precipitation, with a Sharp Drop About 2000 BCE*

Source: Adapted and simplified from Berkelhammer et al., 'An Abrupt Shift in the Indian Monsoon' (2012).

climate reconstructions' and suggested that during that period, 'the lake had a regular outflow and contributed large amounts of water to the Sutlej River, the lower reaches of which were integral part of the Indus Valley Civilisation area',[109] an outflow which dwindled or stopped afterwards.

M. Berkelhammer led an international team to a cave in Cherrapunji, Meghalaya, 'among the wettest locations on Earth with an annual average precipitation in excess of 11,000 mm', and studied the isotopic variations in a stalagmite—Oxygen-18 isotope—as an index of precipitation, and the Uranium–Thorium method for absolute dating of the stalagmite, which went back almost 12,000 years for a growth of nearly 2 m. The results highlighted a 'dramatic event ... ~4000 years ago when, over the course of approximately a decade, isotopic values abruptly rose above any seen during the early to mid-Holocene and remained at this anomalous state for almost two centuries' (Figure 9.12). This suggested either 'a shift toward an earlier Indian Summer Monsoon withdrawal or a general decline in the total amount of monsoon precipitation'. The study's 'tight age constraints of the record show with a high degree of certainty that much of the documented de-urbanization of the Indus Valley at 3.9 kyr BP occurred after multiple decades of a shift in the

---

[109] C. Leipe et al., 'Potential of Pollen and Non-pollen Palynomorph Records from Tso Moriri (Trans-Himalaya, NW India) for Reconstructing Holocene Limnology and Human–environmental Interactions', *Quaternary International* 348 (2014): 113.

monsoon's character'.[110] Interestingly, the study correlated the date with similar events in the Gulf of Oman, in the northern Red Sea (at Shaban Deep), at Mount Kilimanjaro and in the central United States. It was therefore 'a remarkable instance of a large-scale, abrupt Holocene climate event'.

Finally, moving further south, let us briefly mention a 2012 study by Camilo Ponton et al. of planktonic foraminifer in sediments collected offshore from the mouth of Godavari River (Andhra Pradesh), which detected several phases of aridification, the most acute occurring about 2000 BCE and 300 CE[111]; the former, of course, is in tune with findings in northwest India. Likewise, a 2015 multi-proxy study by Saswati Sarkar et al. of a sediment core from the Lonar Lake (Maharashtra) found the wettest period to be between 10.1 and 6 ka BP, a transition to arid conditions from 4.8 to 4 cal ka BP and a slight improvement afterwards, with a permanent saline lake. The peak aridity here is therefore 2800–2000 BCE, earlier than in the previous studies.[112]

Circumstantial Evidence

As we saw earlier, according to John Marshall, the extensive use of baked bricks at Mohenjo-daro, Chanhudaro and Harappa was a clue that the climate was wetter when those cities were built. Additionally, the depictions on Indus seals of animals like the elephant, the rhinoceros or the water buffalo, all of which thrive in humid conditions, were said to point to a moister and greener environment. It was objected in reply that the depiction of a particular animal did not prove its existence at the site and that the above-mentioned animals were still seen in parts of the Indus valley till recent decades or centuries.

The counterargument would have validity in the absence of positive evidence, but such evidence emerged at Kalibangan in the form of bone remains of the elephant, the one-horned rhinoceros, the water buffalo and the river turtle. In Bhola Nath's oft-quoted opinion, 'The remains

---

[110] M. Berkelhammer et al., 'An Abrupt Shift in the Indian Monsoon 4000 Years Ago', in *Climates, Landscapes, and Civilizations*. Geophysical Monograph Series 198, eds. Liviu Giosan (Washington: American Geophysical Union, 2012), 75–87.

[111] C. Ponton et al., 'Holocene Aridification of India', *Geophysical Research Letters* 39 (2012): L03704.

[112] S. Sarkar et al., 'Monsoon Source Shifts During the Drying Mid-Holocene: Biomarker Isotope Based Evidence from the Core 'Monsoon Zone' (CMZ) of India', *Quaternary Science Reviews* 123 (2015): 144–157.

of these animals show that the climate at that time was more humid than the arid climate of present day'.[113] The presence of the rhinoceros, in particular, 'strengthens the geological evidence that the desert conditions of this area are of recent origin'.[114] The animal's remains were confirmed by V. N. Prabhakar at the Harappan site of Karanpura, also in Rajasthan, in the form of four complete bones.[115]

Similar evidence came from Gujarat, where the late archaeozoologist P. K. Thomas observed:

The rhinoceros is identified from a large number of Harappan and Chalcolithic sites of Gujarat ... [and] inhabited a major part of the Gujarat plains in the protohistoric period.... The identification of large herbivores like rhinoceros, wild buffalo and probably wild cattle at many of the Gujarat Harappan sites suggests that the ecological conditions were more congenial for animal life during the protohistoric period in Gujarat.[116]

These observations do point to a greener environment during the Harappan urban phase, of course, without a dateline for its degradation to the present condition. Palaeobotanical studies, which are beyond the scope of this chapter,[117] broadly endorse this conclusion. Could human activities have played a part in the environmental degradation? Wheeler was among the first to suggest that the Harappans were 'wear-

---

[113] Bhola Nath, 'The Role of Animal Remains in the Early Prehistoric Cultures of India', *Indian Museum Bulletin*, Calcutta, 1969; quoted by Jagat Pati Joshi in B. B. Lal et al., *Excavations at Kalibangan: The Early Harappans (1961–1969)* (New Delhi: Archaeological Survey of India, 2003), 107.

[114] S. Banerjee and S. Chakraborty, 'Remains of the Great One-horned Rhinoceros, *Rhinoceros unicornis*, Linnacus from Rajasthan', *Science and Culture* 39 (1973), 430–431; quoted by Jagat Pati Joshi in B. B. Lal et al., *Excavations at Kalibangan: The Early Harappans (1961–1969)* (New Delhi: Archaeological Survey of India, 2003), 18.

[115] V. N. Prabhakar, 'Excavation at Karanpura, District Hanumangarh', *Indian Archaeology 2013–14—A Review* (New Delhi: Archaeological Survey of India, 2016), 126.

[116] P. K. Thomas, 'Investigations into the Archaeofauna of Harappan Sites in Western India', in *Indian Archaeology in Retrospect, Vol. 2: Protohistory, Archaeology of the Harappan Civilization*, eds. S. Settar and Ravi Korisettar (New Delhi: Manohar and Indian Council of Historical Research, 2000), 414, 417.

[117] For a general survey of Harappan archaeobotany, with numerous references, see D. Q. Fuller and M. Madella, 'Issues in Harappan Archaeobotany: Retrospect and Prospect', in *Indian Archaeology in Retrospect, Vol. 2: Protohistory, Archaeology of the Harappan Civilization*, eds. S. Settar and Ravi Korisettar (New Delhi: Manohar and Indian Council of Historical Research, 2000), 317–390.

ing out [the] landscape'[118] by overexploiting their natural resources, particularly forests, for their brick, pottery, bronze and seal-making industries. Intensive agriculture for the consumption of city dwellers combined with overgrazing by herds of cattle and goats would have added to the pressure on an already strained ecosystem. A year before Wheeler's statement, the US archaeologist Walter Fairservis attempted a calculation of the amount of fodder consumed by the cattle used by Mohenjo-daro both as a source of food (dairy products and meat) and for ploughing. His conclusion was:

> The inhabitants of the mature period at Mohenjodaro would have grown only about one-fourth of their fodder needs. It follows that the remaining three-quarters had to be obtained by foraging in the surrounding forests and grasslands. This formidable assault on the indigenous flora most certainly affected the ecology and had an adverse effect on the land and aided the spread of the active floodplain.[119]

If, as many of the palaeoclimatic studies we have surveyed point to, there was a general trend to aridity in Mature Harappan times, this intense exploitation of natural resources may well have compounded it and accelerated the process of degradation, although a precise climate-to-environment correlation remains to be quantified in the Harappan case.

More circumstantial evidence emerges from bioanthropological studies of Harappan skeletons by Gwen Robbins Schug et al., which have shown at Harappa that 'the prevalence of infection and infectious disease increased through time',[120] along with levels of interpersonal violence. Although the latter may be explained in a variety of ways, the former seems to be related to environmental changes; at Harappa, for instance, an increase of leprosy, tuberculosis and scurvy is noticeable during the deurbanized phase, which Schug et al. partly relate to reduced access to food resources.[121]

---

[118] Wheeler, *Indus Civilization*, 127.

[119] W. A. Fairservis, 'The Origin, Character and Decline of an Early Civilization', *Novitates*, no. 2302 (1967): 1–48, partly reproduced in Nayanjot Lahiri, ed., *The Decline and Fall of the Indus* (New Delhi: Permanent Black, 2000), 261.

[120] G. Robbins Schug et al., 'Infection, Disease, and Biosocial Processes at the End of the Indus Civilization', *PLoS One* 8, no. 12 (2013): e84814, and references therein.

[121] G. Robbins Schug and K. E. Blevins, 'The Center Cannot Hold: A Bioarchaeological Perspective on Environmental Crisis in the Second Millennium BCE, South Asia', in *A Companion to South Asia in the Past*, eds. G. Robbins Schug and S. R. Walimbe (Chichester: Wiley-Blackwell, 2016), 255–273, and references therein.

Conclusions

More studies and surveys of the Harappan environment and climate have been published.[122] Wheeler's warning of 1968 bears some repetition: 'For a civilization so widely distributed as that of the Indus no uniform ending need be postulated.' More recently, Yama Dixit et al. echoed him: 'The Indus settlements spanned a diverse range of environmental and ecological zones; therefore, correlation of evidence for climate change and the decline of Indus urbanism requires a comprehensive assessment of the relationship between settlement and climate across a substantial area.'[123] Dorian Q. Fuller, while cautioning against hasty conclusions,[124] pointed to a series of 'marked events of sudden aridity',[125] with the last one taking place around 2200 BCE, as many of the studies surveyed here have indicated. He concluded: 'A climatic event cannot be blamed simplistically for [Harappan] collapse and de-urbanisation, but Quaternary science data make it clear that we cannot accept a view of climatic and environmental stability since the mid-Holocene in the region (as promoted by Possehl).'[126]

Such is indeed our first conclusion. It seems no longer possible to hold that the Harappan climate and environment were more or less like today's and played no part in the disintegration (a better word than 'collapse') of the Indus-Sarasvati civilization. This does not imply 'environmental determinism' in the sense that this disintegration can be wholly accounted for by climatic and environmental changes; all that the evidence surveyed here implies is that they played some part—how much, and in what manner, clearly depends on the region.

Let us therefore sum up the evidence region-wise, to be read together with the summarized data presented in Table 9.1.

---

[122] For recent reviews and further references, see Prasad and Enzel, 'Holocene Paleoclimates of India'; Madella and Fuller, 'Palaeoecology and the Harappan Civilisation'; Fuller and Madella, 'Issues in Harappan Archaeobotany'; R. Korisettar and R. Ramesh, 'The Indian Monsoon: Roots, Relations and Relevance', in *Indian Archaeology in Retrospect, Vol. 3: Archaeology and Interactive Disciplines*, eds. S. Settar and R. Korisettar (New Delhi: Manohar and Indian Council of Historical Research, 2002): 23–59; G. MacDonald, 'Potential Influence of the Pacific Ocean on the Indian Summer Monsoon and Harappan Decline', *Quaternary International* 229 (2011): 140–148; Petrie et al., 'Adaptation to Variable Environments'.

[123] Dixit et al., 'Abrupt Weakening of the Summer Monsoon in Northwest India ~ 4100 yr Ago', 342.

[124] Fuller and Madella, 'Issues in Harappan Archaeobotany', 363, 366.

[125] D. Q. Fuller, 'Neolithic Cultures', in *Encyclopedia of Archaeology*, ed. D. M. Pearsall (New York, NY: Academic Press, 2008), 756.

[126] Madella and Fuller, 'Palaeoecology and the Harappan Civilisation', 1283.

TABLE 9.1 Summary of Some of the Studies Presented in This Chapter

Region	Study	Localities / Main Proxies	Wet Phase (BCE years)	Arid Phase (BCE years)	During Mature Harappan Period
Haryana	Saini et al. (2009)	Channel activity/OSL dating of buried sands	~4000 to 900	–	–
	Dixit et al. (2014)	Kotla Dahar palaeolake/ gastropods	Before 2200	2200–2000	Wet, moving towards aridity
Punjab (Pakistan)	Wright et al. (2008)	Harappa's region/climate modelling	–	Increasing aridity from c. 3000, with sharply reduced rainfall and river flow from 2100	Good river flow, decline of summer monsoon, increase of winter monsoon
Rajasthan	Singh (1971)	Sambhar, Didwana and Lunkaransar Lakes/pollen	3800–2200*	From 1600*	Wet
	Bryson & Swain, 1981	Didwana and Lunkaransar Lakes/pollen	3800–1800*	–	Wet
	Wasson et al. (1983)	Didwana Lake/sediments	4900–2550*	From 2550*	Dry
	Enzel et al. (1999)	Lunkaransar Lake/ sediments	8000–4000	From 3800*	Dry
	Prasad and Enzel (2006)	Rajasthan lakes/ multi-proxy	5200–4000	From 3200	Dry

Region	Reference	Proxy/method			Condition
Cholistan	Geyh and Ploethner (1995)	Isotope dating of Hakra waters	10,900–2700	–	–
Cholistan and Sindh	Giosan et al. (2012)	Sediments	Before 3000	After 3000	Dry
Sindh/Indus	Naidu (1996)	Off Oman/plankton	Before 1850*	After 1850*	Wet
	Von Rad et al. (1999)	Off Makran coast/varved sediments	Before 2000	After 2000 or 1500	Wet
	Staubwasser et al. (2003)	Off Indus delta/plankton	Before 2200	After 2200	Wet or normal
Gujarat	Prasad et al. (1997)	Nal Sarovar Lake/multi-proxy	3500–1200*	From 1200*	Wet
	Prasad et al. (2007)	Mahi estuary/multi-proxy (pollens, phytoliths, clays)	2050–1750* for winter rains	From 2100* for summer monsoon	Growing aridity compensated by higher winter precipitation
	Farooqui et al. (2013)	Coastal Saurashtra/multi-proxy (pollens, phytoliths, sediments)	4000–2000	From 2000	Wet
	Prasad et al. (2014)	Wadhwana Lake/multi-proxy (pollens, phytoliths, clays)	5500–3565	3565–2255	Dry, with partial revival after 2200
Himalayas	Phadtare (2000)	Gahrwal/pollen and peat	4000–2500	From 2000	–

(Table 9.1 Continued)

(Table 9.1 Continued)

Region	Study	Localities / Main Proxies	Wet Phase (BCE years)	Arid Phase (BCE years)	During Mature Harappan Period
Ladakh	Leipe et al. (2014)	Tso Moriri Lake/pollen	9500–2500	2500–200 ce	–
Meghalaya	Berkelhammer (2012)	Cherrapunji/stalagmite	–	Shortly before to shortly after 2000	–
Andhra Pradesh	Ponton et al. (2012)	Godavari estuary/plankton	–	2000–300 ce	–
Maharashtra	Sarkar et al. (2015)	Lonar Lake/multi-proxy	8100–4000	2800–2000	–
All India	Gupta et al. (2006)	–	–	5000–2000: stepwise weakening of monsoon, with intensification of the dry phase in 2000–1500	–

Note: All dates are calibrated; asterisks refer to dates calibrated for the purpose of this chapter.[127]

[127] Uncalibrated dates have been calibrated with the online CalPal tool of University of Cologne (www.calpal-online.de), verified with http://calib.org/calib/.

In the eastern region, the Sarasvati appears to have stopped flowing beyond today's international border shortly before 2600 BCE; in any case, it was lost in its central basin by about 1900 BCE, leading to its almost complete abandonment and a concentration of Late Harappan sites at the foot of the Shivalik Hills and in the Ganga-Yamuna Doab, at the least. (We saw also how Cholistan's Late Harappan sites were now fewer and smaller than their preceding Mature Harappan sites.) This loss of one of the two major lifelines of this civilization must have been a major factor in its de-urbanization. As Dilip Chakrabarti puts it: 'To a considerable extent the process [of weakening of the political fabric of the Harappan Civilization] must have been linked to the hydrographic changes in the Sarasvati-Drishadvati system.'[128] The fact that the river's desiccation followed the severe turn to aridity observed by many studies about 2200–2000 BCE may or may not indicate a causal link; the loss of glacial contributions through the Satluj or the Yamuna cannot be ruled out at this stage but is not directly relevant to our present concern.

Studies of Rajasthan's palaeolakes cited here agree on a wet phase in the mid-Holocene, during which the lakes were alive, but reach divergent conclusions as to the period of the transition to aridity. In any case, since the lakes lay on the margins of the Harappan Civilization, we have little to go by as regards Harappan sites in Rajasthan except that they (e.g., Kalibangan) appear to have thrived during the Mature phase as much as settlements in other regions.

In the Indus region, data from the upper basin is scanty, apart from evidence for reduced rainfall in the region of Harappa from about 2100 BCE. The studies of Sindh's palaeoclimate we have surveyed broadly agree on a wetter climate before 2200 BCE and a turn to aridity after 2200 or 2000 BCE. Possible, though as yet unproven, floods caused by the diversion of part of the Satluj waters from the Sarasvati to the Beas system would help explain the near complete absence of Late Harappan sites in this region; they may have been either washed away or buried under sediments. As regards the Indus's likely desertion of Mohenjo-daro, whose consequences would have been momentous, a securely dated chronology is yet to be worked out.

On the Makran coast, we saw how Harappan coastal sites like Sutkagen Dor and Balakot are now kilometres inland. Dales, who excavated Balakot, suggested that

---

[128] D. K. Chakrabarti, *The Archaeology of Ancient Indian Cities* (New Delhi: Oxford University Press, 1997), 140.

a sudden rise in the Arabian Sea coastline of West Pakistan apparently took place sometime around the middle of the second millennium. This resulted in a disastrous increase in the already serious floods in the major river valleys.... The Harappans were forced to migrate gradually to more fertile territory. There is now incontrovertible archaeological evidence that the major population shift was to the southeast into the area of the Kathiawar [= Saurashtra] peninsula.[129]

While Dales' migration theory seems broadly correct (and should include, as we now know, Kutch and its gulf on the way to Saurashtra), the precise date of the 'sudden rise' remains to be established.

The Rann of Kutch has an environmental history of its own, and we discussed its loss of navigability, probably owing to a tectonic uplift; whether it is the same event as the one affecting the Makran coast cannot be ascertained at the moment. Be that as it may, if at some point the 'metropolis' and major trading centre that was Dholavira found itself cut off from the sea route, its very survival as a city and major trade and manufacturing centre must have been challenged. Similarly, the Gulf of Khambhat's receding shoreline may have spelt doom for Lothal's trading activities.

The rest of the Gujarat domain, judging from two of our studies, felt the impact of the 2200 BCE turn to aridity, but this seems to have been mitigated by still abundant winter rainfall. This may explain the presence of nearly 200 Late Harappan sites (though with a strong regional cultural element); the region was not threatened with desertification as parts of the Sarasvati basin were, but urbanism must have become unsustainable owing to the break-up of long-distance networks.

*

Discussions on the disintegration of the Harappan Civilization have speculated on possible socio-political factors, disruptions in commercial exchanges with the Iranian plateau, Magan, Dilmun, Mesopotamia and BMAC, sheer geographical overstretch and a falling apart of the various Harappan regions.[130] To this list must be now added the near-certainty

---

[129] G. F. Dales, 'The Mythical Massacre at Mohenjodaro', *Expedition* 6, no. 3 (1964): 43.

[130] Useful discussions can be found in B. B. Lal, *The Earliest Civilization of South Asia*, chap. 14 (New Delhi: Aryan Books International, 1997); Possehl, *Indus Civilization*, Chap. 13; D. K. Chakrabarti, *The Oxford Companion to Indian Archaeology: The Archaeological Foundations of Ancient India* (New Delhi: Oxford University Press, 2006), chap. 11; N. Lahiri, ed., *The Decline and Fall of the Indus* (New Delhi: Permanent Black, 2000).

of a general trend towards aridity (admitting the likelihood that some regions still remained wetter than today during the third millennium BCE), with an acceleration in that trend between 2200 and 2100 BCE, and the probability of excessive grazing and consumption of wood.

While this event must have strained the Harappans' monsoon- and flood-dependent agricultural production, we should guard against picturing widespread famines; there are, on the contrary, enough signs that the Harappans showed considerable adaptability to changing conditions,[131] exploiting for instance the increasing winter rains to grow new crops. (A review of Harappan agricultural practices is beyond the scope of this chapter.)

The above should be warning enough against proposing a single environmental mechanism—for example, reduction of the monsoon, prolonged drought or the loss of the Sarasvati—for the final break-up of the Harappan urban order. Nevertheless, it still offers a useful reminder that human societies are ultimately dependent on the climate and environment they live in. Climate change and environmental degradation very likely contributed to the decline of the Harappan Civilization from the 21st century BCE, that is a lesson which, in the 21st century CE, we ought to ponder on.

---

[131] For a recent review, Petrie et al., 'Adaptation to Variable Environments', and references therein.

History of Earthquakes in India

M. Amirthalingam

Introduction

Earthquakes have been a common phenomenon recorded in history going back to the Harappan period. Even the Vedic people were fully aware of disasters like earthquakes (AV.19.1.10.8). In the *Brihat Samhita*, the 32nd chapter discusses the earthquake cloud theory and the signs of earthquakes. The first well-recorded earthquake in the subcontinent dates back to 893 CE in the Delhi region. Later, the mediaeval chroniclers have described in detail the many earthquakes that took place in the Sultanate and Mughal periods. The numerous earthquakes that took place in Assam and Kashmir during the mediaeval period have been particularly well recorded. During the period 1800–2008 CE, about 250 earthquakes have been recorded in the region. During the post-independence period, six major earthquakes have been recorded in the country. These are the Chamoli, Killari, Jabalpur, Latur, Koynanagar and Bhuj earthquakes, which have taken a heavy toll of life and property. In this chapter, we have catalogued the earthquakes region wise. In the introductory part, we have discussed the earthquakes which occurred from 3000 BCE to 2000 CE with the source of archaeological, Sanskrit literature and historical records. With the advent of British rule began the era of the scientific study of earthquakes. For the purpose of this study, the country has been conveniently divided into five regions, namely north, east, west, central and south, based on the availability of source material. Although there were innumerable earthquakes recorded, we have taken only a few major events which are discussed in this chapter.

A disaster is an occurrence that happens with no warning and causes serious disruption of life and even death or injury to large numbers of people. It requires large-scale emergency services. Disasters are of three types:

- frequently occurring natural phenomena such as earthquakes, volcanic eruptions, hurricanes and floods;
- accidents of anthropogenic origin like nuclear explosions or the Bhopal gas tragedy. This will affect the succeeding generations; and
- droughts, floods, landslides, wildfires and epidemics.

The destruction and loss of life associated with an earthquake are on a much larger scale than that due to any other disaster. Besides, an earthquake can also induce other phenomena like volcanoes and floods as it causes serious destruction of life, collapse of buildings, eruption of volcanoes and floods. In this chapter, a brief history of earthquakes and their effects on nature and human life has been traced.

The Indian subcontinent is prone to a variety of natural hazards such as droughts, floods, cyclones, landslides, earthquakes and tsunamis. The slew of earthquakes in the past decades has underlined the need to take proactive steps to contain the extensive damage that these earthquakes cause. This is especially seen in the densely populated Indian cities. Nevertheless, India has been witness to a number of earthquakes from ancient times to the present day.

Recent examples of earthquakes in India are the Khillari (30 September 1993), Jabalpur (22 May 1997), Chamoli (29 March 1999) and Bhuj (26 January 2001) earthquakes. It is not possible to entirely eliminate the seismic hazard due to an earthquake. It is possible, however, to lessen the damage to man-made structures by making them more robust. The increasing population has put a strain on the existing resources, and hence there is a felt need to increase infrastructure such as buildings, dams, roads, power plants and so on. Therefore, while building this infrastructure, care should be taken to build them in such a way that they can withstand severe shocks.

What Is an Earthquake?

An earthquake may be defined as the shaking of the earth's surface as a result of the sudden release of the stresses built up in the earth's crust.[1] It is a violent shaking, moving and vibrating of the earth's surface. Earthquakes are caused by the sudden release of pressures exerted from within the earth's crust due to tectonic movement of seismic plates. It may range from a mild tremor to a large-scale earth movement, causing extensive damage over a wide area. The place at which the earthquake originates is called the seismic focus and the point on the surface of the earth directly above the focus of an earthquake is known as its epicentre. Another cause of earthquakes could be the sudden movement of rocks in the vertical, horizontal or inclined plane. In the earth's crust, there are thin zones of fresh rocks with blocks of crust. These are known as faults. When one block suddenly slips and moves relative to the other, tremendous energy is released creating vibrations called seismic waves. The waves radiate up through the crust to the earth's surface, thus causing the ground to tremble.[2]

Why Do Earthquakes Occur?

Earthquakes occur due to the stress built up when the opposite sides of fault become greater than the two fault surfaces. One of the theories advanced as a cause of earthquake is plate tectonics. This theory states that there are huge rafts on the surface of the earth, which are 110 kilometres thick, always drifting over a semi-molten surface. When the stresses are released by fracturing of rocks, earthquakes are caused. The majority of earthquake epicentres are located along the plate boundaries.[3]

Natural Earthquakes

Natural earthquakes occur due to these faults at the natural points at which the pressure strives to be released. The fault slips and the energy is released. It does not occur below the upper mantle and crust because the elevated temperatures and pressures allow the rocks to deform

---

[1] S. Mahanti, 'Earthquakes', *Dream* 3, no. 5 (2001).

[2] K. Ramachandran, 'Waves of Shock', *Frontline* 12, no. 13 (1995): 78–84.

[3] A. K. R. Hemmady, *Earthquakes* (New Delhi: National Book Trust, 1996), 2–3.

plastically without accumulation of stress.[4] The material composing the crust is elastic and yields to stresses by slow creep spread over long periods. When the limit of elasticity at any point is exhausted or there is friction along a fault, an earthquake occurs suddenly.

Induced Earthquakes

Earthquakes can also occur as a result of manmade activities, which exert immense pressure or stress:

- The enormous weight of a huge manmade reservoir may release the energy stored in underground rocks and cause an earthquake.
- Atomic blasts could also trigger earthquakes.[5]
- The energy generated by a volcanic eruption or manmade explosion can cause an earthquake.
- Pumping water into the sub-surface in an area of nuclear waste disposal, mining and oil production can set up points of increased pressure.
- Construction of dams or blasting rock quarries[6] can send seismic waves or shocks across the earth's crust.

An earthquake is measured by the Richter magnitude scale, also known as the Richter scale, which assigns a magnitude number to quantify the size of an earthquake. The most severe earthquakes have had a magnitude of 8–9. In the 1970s, the Richter scale has been replaced by the moment magnitude[7] scale in the United States. This is the scale currently being used by the United States Geological Survey (USGS). Before the invention of the ground motion recording instrument, earthquakes were studied by recording the description of shaking intensity. Now the effects of earthquake motion can be studied in qualitative terms due to the development of intensity scale. Nowadays, the Modified Mercalli (MM) intensity scale and the Medvedev–Sponhener–Karnik (MSK)[8] Intensity Scale are widely used. The MSK scale is more specific in its recording of the earthquake effects.

---

[4] R. Mahapatra, 'Republic Quacked', *Down to Earth* 9, no. 19 (2001): 42–48.

[5] N. K. Jain, 'Disasters and Environment', in *Source Book on Environmental Education for Elementary Teacher Educators*, eds. K. K. Premi, Sheel C. Nuna, and Pramila Menon (New Delhi, 1994), 94.

[6] R. M. Hallon, 'Earthquakes', *Science Reporter* 38, no. 3 (2001): 20–23.

[7] C. F. Richter, *Elementary Seismology* (San Francisco, CA: AW.H.Freeman and Company, and London: Bailey Bros. & Swinfen Ltd, 1958).

[8] 'The European Macroseismic Scale EMS-98', Centre Européen de Géodynamique et de Séismologie (ECGS). Accessed 24 October 2016.

Causes of Earthquake

Below the earth's crust can be found a rocky layer of thickness varying from a depth of 10 km under the sea to 65 km under the continents. The crust consists of not one piece but of several portions. These portions are called 'plates' and can vary in size from a few hundred to thousands of kilometres. These plates ride on the more mobile mantle and are driven by thermal convection currents. When these plates rub against each other, stress is created in the crust. These stresses can be classified according to the type of movement along the plate's boundaries. These stresses can be categorized as: (a) pulling away from each other, (b) pushing against one another and (c) sliding sideways relative to each other.

Slipping or rupturing leads to release of accumulated energy and are known as faults. The crust is being continuously stressed by the movement of tectonic plates. When it reaches the point of maximum strain, a fissure occurs along the fault. This fissure generates vibrations which are called seismic waves, which radiate in all directions. The exact place of rupture is called 'focus' and may be located near the surface or even deep down. The place on the surface of the earth directly above the focus is called the 'epicentre' of the earthquake (www.imd.gov.in).

Effects of an Earthquake

Earthquakes cause violent motions of the earth's surface. When they occur on the sea bed, huge sea waves swell up, causing ships to capsize and sweeping onto the land with great force, drowning anything in there. Such waves often originate in the Pacific Ocean because of which many earthquakes and are known as *tsunami* or destructive waves. Earthquakes commonly trigger mass movements such as mudflows, avalanches and landslides. Floods and fires also occur during an earthquake due to explosions, burst water pipes and collapse of bunds and dams. Among the other effects of earthquakes are surface faulting, tectonic uplift, subsidence, soil liquefactions, ground resonance, landslides and ground failure.[9] These leave permanent impacts on the environment and also can destroy human structures. These are the common events observed during an earthquake and are vividly recorded in historical

---

[9] A. M. Michetti et al., 'Intensity Scale ESI 2007', in *Memorie Descrittive Carta Geologica d'Italia*, eds. L. Guerrieri and E. Vittori (Roma, Italy: APAT, Servizio Geologico d'Italia-Dipartmento Difesa del Suolo, 2007), 74, 53.

accounts and preserved in stratigraphical record (palaeo-earthquakes). Soil liquefaction and landslide are the other factors as also surface deformation and faulting and shaking-related geological effects, which leave a permanent imprint not only on the topology of the earth's surface but also on human settlements.[10]

Description	Magnitude	Average Per Year (Richter)
Great	≥8	1
Major	7–7.9	18
Strong	6–6.9	120
Moderate	5–5.9	800
Light	4–4.9	6,200 (estimate)
Minor	3–3.9	49,000 (estimate)
Very minor	<3.0	
	2–3	About 1,000/day
	1–2	About 8,000/day

Source: www.imd.gov.in.

Fifty-six per cent of the total land area of India is seismic. The table below gives five different seismic zones classified on the basis of the severity of the earthquakes.

Zone	Mag. (Richter)	Intensity	Land Area
I	4.5	V	<5%
II	5.0	VI	<8%
III	5.7	VII	<26%
IV	6.3	VIII	<18%
V	7.0	IX	≥12%

Source: ASC image, Indian Seismic Zones.

Among the five zones, Zone V is the most vulnerable to earthquakes, where historically the most powerful shocks have occurred. This region includes the Andaman and Nicobar Islands, all of Northeast India, parts of northwestern Bihar, eastern sections of Uttaranchal, the Kangra Valley in Himachal Pradesh, Srinagar area in Jammu and Kashmir and the Rann of Kutch in Gujarat. Major metropolitan areas lying in Zone IV include New Delhi, Mumbai and Kolkata. Much of India lies in Zone III. Only Chennai lies in Zone II. A large section of south-central India

---

[10] L. Serva, 'Ground Effects in Intensity Scales', *Terra Nova* 6: 414–416. doi:10.1111/j.1365-3121.1994.tb00515.x

lies in Zone I along with a section stretching from eastern Rajasthan into northern Madhya Pradesh. Some areas of Odisha, Jharkhand and Chhattisgarh also lie in Zone I. Even Latur, the site of a previous major earthquake, lies in Zone I.[11]

History of Earthquakes in India

India is considered to be one of the earthquake-prone regions of the world. More than 50 per cent of the country is classified as falling within the seismic zone. The Himalayan region is especially susceptible to damaging earthquakes of more than 8.0 on the Richter scale. The main cause of earthquakes has been ascribed to the fact that the Indian plate is moving towards the Eurasian plates at the rate of about 50 mm per year. Even peninsular India is not free from earthquakes as shown by the Koynanagar, Latur and Jabalpur earthquakes.[12]

Earthquakes had occurred in India even in very ancient times. Recent excavations at Kalibangan in Rajasthan have revealed evidence of faulting in the form of horizon displacements and tilted brick walls. This event can be roughly dated to 2700 BCE. Thus, there is evidence to show that earthquakes may have been one of the causes for the destruction of several Harappan sites. Besides, there is evidence that some of the buildings in the second layer of ruins near Taxila may have been destroyed during an earthquake around 30 CE.[13]

The next incidence relates to the drying up of the Sarasvati River. There are two streams of thought that try to explain this major event of the ancient period. One school of thought is that the Sarasvati River ceased to be a sea-flowing river about 3000 BCE. This explains why the Sarasvati River ends up in the sands of Bahawalpur region of the Punjab and does not flow into the sea. It is possible that there was a further drying up of the river in about 1900 BCE due to an earthquake. There is a theory that the two main tributaries of the river were absorbed into the Sindhu and Ganga river systems. According to the second school of thought, the Sarasvati River flowed into the sea until about 1900 BCE and then dried up. However, the first theory seems to be more plausible when viewed in relation to the evidence found in the Harappan sites.

---

[11] S. M. Mathur, *Physical Geology of India* (Roorkee: Earthquake Engineering Research Institute, 2000).

[12] S. K. Jain, 'Indian Earthquakes: An Overview', *The Indian Concrete Journal* 72, no. 11 (1998): 555–561.

[13] R. Chander and P. Singh, 'The Antiquity of Earthquakes', *Resonance* 5, no. 6 (2000): 30–39.

It is also plausible that after this earthquake, large numbers of Indic people moved to the west, namely Iran.[14]

Historically, the end of the Indus Valley Civilization is a matter of much debate and controversy. Various theories have been put forth as to what caused the destruction of this advanced civilization. These include the encroachment of the Thar Desert, regular floods and the invasion of the Aryans around 1700 BCE. It is also possible that changing river patterns also caused the destruction of the cities. These included the drying up of the Ghagger-Hakra river and changes in the course of the Indus river. These vast changes would have caused a total dislocation of the economy of the region. It is also possible that earthquakes and epidemics caused the end of this civilization. It is also postulated that the Indus Valley Civilization broke up into smaller cultures around 1700 BCE. According to Allchin (1995),[15] the deterioration of climate may well have been part of a wider phenomenon and this may have been the factor which led the population of these regions to move southward or eastward in search of better living conditions.[16]

A noted historian H. D. Sankalia has done extensive research on the end of Harappan settlements at Kalibangan. He is of the view that the first settlement of the Saraswati River must have taken place when the Yamuna or one of its tributaries turned towards the west around 2600 BCE. Later, around 1700 BCE, it turned eastward due to similar reasons. He, therefore, postulates that this resulted in the destruction of the site in the Saraswati valley. However, it is relevant to note that these events are related to the prehistoric period. Hence, we have to allow for a timeframe of several centuries.[17]

There is evidence of two older events that have been obtained from palaeoseismological studies in the Kutch basin. A study conducted in the Dholka area in Ahmadabad in the Cambay basin indicates the occurrence of an earthquake at 3000 BCE. However, its source remains uncertain. Another major event occurred at Dholavira between 2600 and 1600 BCE.[18]

---

[14] S. Kak, *The Wishing Tree: The Presence and Promise of India* (New Delhi: Manoharlal Publishers Pvt Ltd, 2001).

[15] F. R. Allchin, *The Archaeology of Early Historic South Asia* (Cambridge: Cambridge University Press, 1995), 38.

[16] Devendra Sharma Iyengar and J. M. Siddiqui, 'Earthquake History of India in Medieval Times', *Indian Journal of History of Science* 34, no. 3 (1999): 181–237.

[17] H. D. Sankalia, *Pre-history and Proto-history of India and Pakistan* (Poona: Deccan College Postgraduate and Research Institute, 1974), 390.

[18] J. P. Joshi and R. S. Bisht, *India and the Indus Civilization* (New Delhi: National Museums Institute (deemed university), 1994).

The Vedic people were fully aware of disasters like earthquakes (AV.19.1.10.8). In the Ramayana, there is a mention of the legend of Karthikeya in *Bala Kanda* (Ch. 36.16-19). In *Ayodhya Kanda* (Ch. 71), there is a reference to the rivers Sarasvati and Ganga as flowing next to each other. In *Yuddha Kanda* (Ch. 22), the desertification of the land of the *Abhiras* in the northwestern part of India is attributed to Rama's anger against the southern sea.[19]

According to an ancient Indian belief that is recounted in the Valmiki Ramayana (VR. 1.40.15), the universe was supposed to be supported by eight giant elephants stationed in the eight quarters. According to the legend, whenever the elephants became tired, they shook their heads and this resulted in earthquakes.[20]

There are two views regarding the date of the Mahabharata war. One viewpoint suggests that the pre-urban core events of the epic would clearly indicate that 3137 BCE was the date of the war. However, contrarily, it has also been suggested that the later Puranic tradition conflated the earlier events with the major earthquake of 1924 BCE. Naturally, there was greater accuracy in remembering the later event due to the use of the centennial *Saptarishi* calendar. The noted scholar Iyengar (1994) has also pointed out the early earthquakes described in mythical terms in the Mahabharata. It has also been pointed out by some scholars that the Puranic king lists indicate 1924 BCE as the date of the Mahabharata war.[21] Since this date roughly coincides with 1900 BCE for the drying up of the Sarasvati River, it is reasonable to assume that the two might be linked, if not the same event. The destruction brought about by the earthquake may have been a contributing factor to the war, or the war may be seen as a metaphor for the geological disaster.[22]

According to Pir Hasan Shah, the author of *Tarikh-i-Hassan*, there was an earthquake during the reign of Sundersena of the Pandu dynasty in 1250 BCE. The whole area from Sindmatnagar to Bijbhera, including the mount of Khadaniyar, was inundated. Another modern authority on the history of Kashmir, G. M. D. Sufi (1974), has stated that during the reign of Sundersena, 22nd in the line of the Pandu dynasty, there was

[19] R. N. Iyengar, 'Profiles of a Natural Disaster in Ancient Sanskrit Literature', *Indian Journal of History of Science* 39, no. 1 (2004): 11–49.

[20] S. N. Vyas, *India in the Ramayana Age* (Delhi: Atma Ram and Sons, 1967), 151.

[21] R. Bilham, 'Historical Studies of Earthquakes in India', *Annals of Geophysics* 47, no. 2 (2004): 839–858.

[22] F. E. Pargiter (rpt.), *The Purana Text of the Dynasties of the Kali Age* (New Delhi: Munshiram Manoharal, 1975).

a great earthquake (*Kashmir, Being a History of Kashmir from the Earliest Times to Our Own*, New Delhi: Light and Life Publishers, p. 696). The earth opened up and the whole city was submerged along with its king and inhabitants. This site is now occupied by the Wular lake. According to a legend, the Naga Mahapadma lives in the lake and is said to have converted the town of Chandrapur into a lake to make it his home. The ancient name of the Wular lake was Mahapadmasana.[23]

In the story of Buddha's life, it is said that soon after Buddha attained Nirvana at Kushinagara in 483 BCE, the earth trembled, stars fell down and celestial music was heard. It is also said that 3 months prior to this, when Buddha was camping in a grove near the village of Upabhoga, there was an earthquake. This was taken as a sign by the Buddha himself that he would soon pass away into Nirvana.[24]

There is a reference to an earthquake during the period of Alexander's invasion of India in 326 BCE. It is stated that during his journey through Iran and Afghanistan, a major earthquake occurred between Quetta and Kalat. This event occurred sometime in November 326 BCE and it was of a magnitude of 8.0 on the Richter scale. This massive earthquake altered the topography of the area and forced Alexander to alter his plans.[25]

Rajendran et al.[26] reported a historical event of magnitude Mw > 7 around 325 BC in the Kutch region. It may be remarked here that the first of the above palaeo-event matches closely with the 3rd millennium earthquake that is said to have damaged the flourishing city of Dholavira.

A famous scientist, Varahamihira, who lived in the Gupta period 587 CE (6th century CE) of ancient India, made appreciable contributions in various fields such as hydrology, geology and ecology. In the *Brihat Samhita*, the 32nd chapter discusses the earthquake cloud theory and the signs of earthquakes. Varahamihira correlates the influence of planets, undersea activities, underground water, unusual cloud formation and abnormal behaviour of animals to the occurrence of earthquakes.[27]

---

[23] Iyengar and Siddiqui, 'Earthquake History of India'.

[24] Bu-ston, *History of Buddhism in India and Tibet*, trans. E. Obermiller's (New Delhi: Sri Satguru Publications, 1986).

[25] A. Bapat, 'Beneath the Surface', *Frontline* 19, no. 2 (2002).

[26] C. P. Rajendran et al., 'Assessing the Previous Activity at the Source Zone of the 2001 Bhuj Earthquake Based on the Near Source and Distant Paleo-seismological Indicators', *Journal of Geophysical Research* 113, no. B05311 (2008): 1–17.

[27] Varahamihira, *Brihat Samhita*, 2 Vols, trans. M. R. Bhat (New Delhi: Motilal Banarsidas Publishing House, 1981).

Earthquakes in the Northern Region

In the year 883 CE, at Sopor (old Suyyapura), Bijbehra, there was an earthquake of great destructive magnitude. On the Baramula side, big boulders rolled down into the bed of the river Behat. As a result, the flow of the river was stopped. The entire area near Bijbehra was flooded and the nearby villages and the agricultural fields were destroyed. The modern town of Sopor (old name Suyyapura), which is located in Baramula district of Kashmir, is now named in memory of the able engineer, Suyya, who restored the flow of the river. Similarly, the memory of the king is commemorated in the place name of Avantipur (old name Vantipore).[28]

The first well-documented earthquake in the subcontinent dates back to 893 CE, since the Delhi region is considered to be an earthquake-prone region. Several earthquakes had occurred since historical times.[29]

The noted Kashmiri historian, Kalhana, who is the author of the famous work *Rajatharangini* or *History of Kashmir*, was the contemporary of king Sussala, who ruled Kashmir during the period between 1121 and 1126 CE. He has described a massive earthquake which stuck Srinagar in 1123 CE. Kalhana describes it thus: 'Fiercely burned the Sun earthquakes occurred repeatedly; and there blew sudden storms of great violence which broke down trees and rocks.'[30]

In 1255 CE, there was a massive earthquake in the Kathmandu valley[31]; this was followed by three years of aftershocks. The emergence and disappearance of coastal tracts have sometimes been ascribed to earthquakes. Another storm near Cochin in 1341 CE created an island, but inspection suggests this to be a common accretion feature of storms along the Malabar Coast.[32] There was an earthquake during the period of 1495 CE in the Avadhi-speaking region of Uttar Pradesh.[33] Similarly,

---

[28] Iyengar and Siddiqui, 'Earthquake History of India'.

[29] T. Oldham, 'A Catalogue of Indian Earthquakes from the Earliest Times to the End of AD 1869', *Memoirs—Geological Society of India* 19 (1883): 163–215.

[30] Kalhana, *Rajatharangini*, VIII, verse No.1167, p. 92.

[31] D. Wright, *History of Nepal* (reproduced with permission by Ranjan Gupta), (Calcutta, 1877), reprinted in 1966, 271.

[32] R. Bendick and R. Bilham, 'Search for Buckling of the Southwest Indian Coast Related to Himalayan Collision', in *Himalaya and Tibet: Mountain Roots to Mountain Tops*, eds. A. Macfarlane, R. Sorkhabi and J. Quade, Geological Society of America Special Paper 328, 1999, pp. 313–323.

[33] V. Singh, 'An Avadhi Language Account of an Earthquake in Medieval North India Circa CE 1500', *Current Science* 96, no. 12 (2009): 1648–1649.

the arrival of Vasco de Gama's fleet in 1524 CE was followed by a violent seaquake and tsunami at Dabul.

On 24 September 1501, there was a major earthquake in Srinagar. This is stated in *Tarik-e-Hasan*, which quotes *Rajatharangini* as the original source.

On 6 July 1505 CE, there was a terrible earthquake which took place at Agra and it was so severe that mountains shook and lofty buildings tumbled down. That day tremors were felt in Delhi and Agra and the villages of north India (Babur's memoirs indicate that this was probably the earthquake felt in Agra, India on the same day).[34] Agra was the capital of the Lodi dynasty. The last Lodi ruler Ibrahim Lodi and his brother Jalal came into conflict over the succession. Ibrahim captured the Raja of Gwalior, who had given shelter to Jalal and brought him into Agra. On 10 May 1526 CE, the famous first battle of Panipat was fought between Ibrahim Lodi and Babur. Ibrahim was defeated and killed and Babur captured Agra and made it his capital.[35]

In the year 1555 CE, Srinagar and other places were rocked by an earthquake. Many villages and towns were destroyed. On this occasion, the hamlet of Nilu and Adampur situated on this side of the river Bihat with their buildings and trees were being transported and appeared on the other side of the river and the village of Mawar which is situated below the mountain. Due to the falling of the mountain over it, about 60,000 people lost their lives.[36]

Another event was during the reign of king Shamsha Shah (1537–1539 CE). Another historian, Suka, has also mentioned this event. A 19th-century historian J. C. Dutt (1887) has also corroborated it. Another source, Nizamuddin Ahmad who was the Bakshi of the kingdom, has also described it in *Tabaqat-i-Akbari*. In *Tabaqat-i-Akbari Tarikh-i-Firishtah* by Ferishta, this major event is also recorded. Another source is Muhammad Qasim Hindu Shah Astarabadi. It is further confirmed by Haider Malik Chandma Raisul Mulk in *Tarikh-i-Kashmir*.

According to Haider Malik, the event occurred in the year 960 AH, which corresponds to 1553 CE. But this date seems to be incorrect as the original source *Rajatharangini* gives the year as 1555 CE. Narayan Kaul

---

[34] C. M. Agrawala, *Natural Calamities and the Great Mughals* (New Delhi, 1987), 22.

[35] E. B. Joshi, *Uttar Pradesh District Gazetteers* (Agra: Uttar Pradesh (India) Revenue Department, Government of Uttar Pradesh), 41.

[36] Kalhana, *Rajatarangini*, English translation by R. S. Pandit, The Saga of the Kings of Kashmir, Eighth Taranga, III (New Delhi, 1935), 74–77.

Aziz in *Tarikh-i-Kashmir* also records it as 960 AH. Khaja Muhammed Azam Deedamar states in *Nagiat-e-Kashmiri* that the date is 960 AH, which is not acceptable. Another source, Pir-Hasan Shah in *Tarik-e-Hasan*, also quotes 960 AH as the year of the earthquake. However, it is better to rely upon the earlier Sanskrit source, namely *Rajatharangini* rather than the Persian. A British source Newall (1854 CE), records that the river Jhelum changed its course after the earthquake. This is incorrect. Actually, it was the River Vesha (Vasav) that changed its course.[37] Vasav is the tributary of the river Jhelum.[38]

The 19th-century scholar Dutt (1887) has written about an earthquake that shook the capital city of Srinagar during the reign of Ghazi Shah.[39] Another earthquake occurred during the reign of Ali Shah during 1569–1577 CE.[40]

In 1665 CE, an earthquake occurred at various places located on the banks of the Ganga River.[41]

From 1669 to 1785 CE, a series of earthquakes occurred in Srinagar and its environment as attested by Kalhana. On 23 June 1669, there was an earthquake and the buildings rocked like cradles. However, there was no loss of life. Another severe earthquake took place in Srinagar in 1678–1679CE as recorded in *Tarikh-i-Hassan* by Pir Hasan Shah. Houses were destroyed and many people lost their lives. This date of 1678–1679 CE, is agreed upon by Newall (1854 CE) and Parmu (1969 CE).

On 30 May 1680 CE, a terrible earthquake occurred in Kashmir and it devastated an area of about 130,000 mi^2. Over 20,000 houses, 30,000 head of cattle and 3,000 people were destroyed. The centre of destruction was near Baramula, where the fort, traveller's bungalow and three-fourths of the town were totally wrecked.[42]

In 1684 CE, a destructive earthquake took place in Kashmir during the reign of Ibrahim Khan. Many houses were destroyed and a large number of people were killed. The destruction wrought by the earthquake was tremendous.[43]

---

[37] R. K. Parmu, *A History of Muslim Rule in Kashmir* (New Delhi: Peoples Publications House Private Limited, 1969), 325.

[38] Agrawala, *Natural Calamities*, 81–83.

[39] Kings of Kashmir, Vol. III, p. 387, Extracts from *Rajatharangini* of Srivara and Suka.

[40] Ibid., p. 394.

[41] Oldham, *A Catalogue of Indian Earthquakes*, 5.

[42] Agrawala, *Natural Calamities*, 83.

[43] Parmu, *History of Muslim Rule*.

Delhi and its surrounding areas have experienced earthquakes since ancient times. One such event took place on 15 July 1720 CE, causing enormous destruction to life and property. The impact was so severe that the fortification wall and builds collapsed. The Kabuli gates in the north up to the Lal Darwaza in the south were destroyed and many buildings were reduced to rubble. Even the battlements of fortification wall near the entrance gate of the Shaharpanah city wall were badly damaged.[44]

A major earthquake occurred in Srinagar and its neighbourhood on 24 March 1736 CE as recorded by Pir Hasan Shah in *Tarikh-i-Hassan*. It is said that many buildings in the city of Srinagar and its hamlets were razed to the ground. The earthquake persisted for 3 months. Again, during the rule of Kaimdad Khan, an earthquake occurred in 1779 CE and continued for half a month (*Tarkih-e Hasan*, 170, extract from *Tarkih-e Hasan* by Pir Hasan Shah).

During the reign of Azad Khan in 1784–1785 CE, an earthquake hit the city of Srinagar. Tremors continued for a period of 6 months. Many houses and lives were lost.[45] The largest historic earthquake was reported in the Chamoli region of Uttarakhand. It occurred on 1 September 1803. Several villages were reported to have been buried by rock falls and landslides caused by this earthquake. The Badrinath temple, located 40 km north of Chamoli, was severely damaged in this earthquake. The epicentre based on the maximum intensities is located 100 km west of Chamoli.[46]

The state of Himachal Pradesh lies in the seismically sensitive zone of the Alpine Himalayan belt. Hence, it is periodically subjected to damaging earthquakes. This vulnerability to earthquakes is due to the northern movement of the Indian plate and to the major dislocation tectonic features such as MBF, MBT, Punjab thrust and MCT. There are also a large number of transverse fractures. In addition, there are also many mild earthquakes. One of most famous earthquakes to have struck this region is called the Kangra earthquake of 1905 CE. Another important earthquake to have shaken the region is the Kinnar earthquake of 1975 CE, which was associated with the transverse Kauirik fault. During the period 1800–2008 CE, about 250 earthquakes have been recorded in the region. Out of these, the Chamba district recorded

---

[44] S. K. Agrawal and J. Chawla, 'Seismic Hazard Assessment for Delhi Region', *Current Science* 91, no. 12 (2006): 1718.

[45] *Tarkih-e Hasan*; Parmu, *History of Muslim Rule*.

[46] K. Rajendran, C. P. Rajendran, S. K. Jain, C. V. R. Murty, and J. N. Arlekar, 'The Chamoli Earthquake, Garhwal Himalaya: Field Observations and Implications for Seismic Hazards', *Current Science* 78, no. 1 (2000): 45–51.

186 earthquakes, Lahaul and Spiti (99) and Kinnaur (93) (nidm.gov.in/pdf/dp/himachal.pdf).

The earthquake on the early morning of 1st September 1803 was felt over a large area of north and eastern India from Punjab to Kolkata. In Kolkata, it was strong enough to throw water with fish from a water tank in the Botanic Garden. The earthquake damaged the upper part of Qutub Minar in Delhi and Imaumbarah in Lucknow. Almost exactly 30 years later (1833), another earthquake shook the Nepal valley, causing widespread damage in both Nepal and India. About 500 people were killed during this quake.[47]

In Kashmir, in 1827, there was a severe earthquake, which was followed by an outbreak of cholera. To compound these troubles, a frightful famine decimated three-fourths of the population. To make matters worse, the famine was followed by disastrous floods. In neighbouring Punjab, the ruler Ranjit Singh died in 1839. The Sikhs lost their unity and weakened their power by internecine squabbles. They finally fell a prey to the rising British power.[48]

An earthquake, having a magnitude of 8 on the Richter scale, shook the Kangra valley on 4 April 1905 CE. The impact was felt over an area of 416,000 mi^2 and it took a toll of 20,000 lives. It was one of deadliest earthquakes in the history of India. It was caused by a displacement taking place along a low angle fault at a depth of 34–64 km. Many buildings were destroyed including the Golden Temple, the municipal dispensary and Thana and the Treasury buildings. Even the Devi temple and the Mission Church were not spared. After Kangra, the impact was most felt in the towns of Dharamshala and Palampur. In Dharamshala, many buildings were destroyed and levelled to the ground. Even as far away as the plains of Punjab, there was considerable damage in Bijnor, Khangi, Haridwar and Roorkee. Buildings were damaged in Amirtsar, Lahore, Jallandhar, Sialkot, Jammu, Rawalpindi and Ambala. Light to moderate tremors were felt as far as Ahmadabad, Surat, Quetta and Jalalabad.[49]

From 1803 to 1994 CE, 29 major earthquakes were recorded in the northern region of the country. In 1828 CE, in the Kashmir valley, a severe quake jolted the area and caused the death of about 1,000 people.

---

[47] R. Bilham, 'Earthquakes in India and the Himalaya: Tectonics, Geodesy and History', *Annals of Geophysics* 47, no. 2/3 (2004): 839–858.

[48] M. C. Morison, *A Lonely Summer in Kashmir* (London: Duckworth and Co., 1904), 57.

[49] Hemmady, *Earthquakes*, 61–63.

The next major event was at Jammu in 1885 CE, when the shocks continued from the end of May till the middle of August. Fissures opened up in the earth and landslips took place. The casualties were 3,500. Another earthquake took place on the intervening night of 29 and 30 May 1885 CE, mainly in the towns of Sopore and Baramulla in Kashmir. The post shocks continued for a period of 3 months. The destruction was spread over an area of 800 mi^2 and the casualties amounted to 2,000 dead. All houses in the towns of Sopore and Baramulla were levelled.[50]

An earthquake of 8.4 magnitude occurred in northern Bihar and Nepal on 15 January 1934 CE. There was extensive damage over an area of about 300 km mean radius. The death toll was 7,253 in India and 3,400 in Nepal. The intensity was 10. Many buildings tilted and slumped into the ground in an area of about 300 km long and 65 km wide. There was also extensive liquefaction. At places, 6-feet high embankments became level with the surrounding space. On the other hand, the depth of lakes, ponds, borrows areas, and alternative depressions became lower. The area of slump belt was related to fissuring and emission of sand and water caused by liquefaction and formation of sand boils.[51]

On 20 October 1991 CE, an earthquake of magnitude 6.6 shook the districts of Uttarkashi, Tehri and Chamoli in the state of Uttarakhand. The death toll was estimated to be 768 persons. The maximum intensity was 9 on the MM scale. Houses collapsed and even an important bridge on the strategically important Uttarkashi–Harsil route was destroyed.[52]

The next major earthquake in this region occurred on 29 March 1999 CE. It was a moderate event. The earthquake triggered landslides, blocked several roads and disrupted electric and water supply. The intensity was 8. There was considerable damage in the district of Chamoli. Nearly, 2,600 houses collapsed, 10,800 were damaged and about 100 people were left dead and 400 injured. The intensity of the quake was such that it was felt as far away as Kanpur, Shimla and Delhi. Ground cracks developed at several places as part of slope failure, thus causing threats to the settlements. There was disturbance to groundwater discharge and the water in many springs turned muddy. There was an apprehension that the quake could cause damage to the Teri dam. The Chamoli

---

[50] J. Milne, *Catalogue of Destructive Earthquake*. Report of the 18th Meeting of the British Association for the Advancement of Science, London, 1911, pp. 649–740.

[51] Jain, 'Indian Earthquakes'.

[52] Ibid.

quake demonstrates that the area is seismically dynamic and there is a probability for more tremors in this region.[53]

Earthquakes in the Eastern Region

During the reign of Mahendrapala I (883 CE) in Bengal, the capital is said to have been destroyed by a severe earthquake and 180,000 people perished. The number of dead bodies dug out from the ruins was 15,000.[54]

There are many sources for the history of Assam. Information on earthquakes can be found in some Buranjis, which are the unique sources of the history of Assam written in Ahom, Sanskrit and Assamese languages. In the Buranjis, the cycle of years is counted every 60 years based on the Jovian calendar. Another important secondary source is the history of Assam by Edward Gait (1905)[55]. The first recorded earthquake was in Garhgaon in 1548 CE during the reign of King Suklemung. Gait (1905 CE) has also mentioned this earthquake. In 1596 CE, a terrible earthquake took place at Gajala. Water, sand, ashes and pebbles burst from the interior of the earth.[56] This earthquake occurred during the reign of Sukhampha (1552 CE–1603 CE). Several earthquakes shook upper Assam in 1642 CE. Gait (1905) has recorded that there was a heavy flood in 1642 CE, in which many cattle were washed away. Several earthquakes occurred in the same year. In 1649 CE, three earthquakes were recorded during the reign of Jayadhwaj Singha (1648–1663 CE). Similarly, there were several mild earthquakes at Kajali near Gauhati in 1663 CE. An eye witness to this event, Shihabuddin Ahmad Bin Muhammad Wali Talish, the author of *Fathiya-E Ibriya*, has recorded that on the evening of 7 February 1663 CE, there was tremendous lightning and thunderous storm and a strong earthquake shook the earth. The shock continued for half an hour. This event occurred during the last days of king Jayadhhwaj Singh alias Sutamala.

1664 Bangla

The French writer Berryat in 1664 CE has mentioned an earthquake that occurred sometime between 1663 and 1664 CE. It damaged the

---

[53] Rajendran et al. 'Chamoli Earthquake, Garhwal Himalaya'.

[54] R. C. Majumdar, ed., *The History of Bengal*, Vol. I (Patna: G. Bharadwaj, 1971), 367.

[55] E. Gait, *A History of Assam*, (1905, 1933), 3rd ed. (Calcutta: Sanskrit Pustak Bhandar, 1963).

[56] N. K. Basu, *Assam in Ahom Age* (Calcutta, 1970).

settlements in Bangla (West Bengal). The aftershocks of this earthquake lasted for 32 days. It was triggered from the bottom of a lake at a place at a distance of 140 km from Bangladesh. As a result, the lake dried up.[57]

In 1676 CE at about 5 O'clock in the morning, there was an earthquake off the port of Balasore in Odisha. The houses in the town were badly shaken. Its earlier name was Balesvara (also Balesar), with reference to Lord Krishna.[58]

The next earthquake occurred at Sadiya in February–August in 1697 CE from Phagu to Saon. This event was during the reign of king Swargdeo Rudra Singh alias Sukhrangpha, who ruled during 1696–1714 CE. Another earthquake took place at Tingkhang and Charaideo hill in 1714 CE. The domes of the temple at Tingkhang were broken as also those of the subsidiary temple at Charaideo hills (*Tungkhungia-Buranji*, Ch. IV, p. 26). Gait, 1905 CE, has also referred to this event. In 1759 CE, in the month of *Baisakh*, an earthquake occurred at Rangpur. This was preceded by a solar eclipse in 1758 CE, during the reign of King Rajesar Singh alias Surampha (The *Ahom-Buranji*).

A major earthquake occurred towards the end of August 1697 CE in Bengal and Assam Phagun from Phagu to Saon. The aftershocks continued in a desultory fashion for a period of 6 months. The earth was rendered asunder and *Sadiya, magur* and *kawai* fish appeared in the breaches. Sand and water also surfaced and the sides of the hills came tumbling down.[59]

About 67 earthquakes have been recorded in and around the area of Kolkata from 1737 to 1993 CE. One of the most severe events that affected Kolkata was between 11 and 12 October 1737 CE. There was a severe earthquake and hurricane that destroyed 200 houses near the river and killed about 300,000 people. There was a report that appeared in a London magazine that a tsunami also affected the coast of greater Bengal.[60] In a major earthquake in Kolkata on 11 October 1773 CE, about 300,000 people perished and there was great loss of property.[61]

---

[57] N. N. Ambraseys, 'Three Little Known Early Earthquakes in India', *Current Science* 86, no. 4 (2004): 506.

[58] S. Martin and W. Szeliga, 'A Catalog of Felt Intensity Data for 570 Earthquakes in India from 1636 to 2009', *Bulletin of the Seismological Society of America* 100, no. 2 (2010): 562–569.

[59] Iyengar and Siddiqui, 'Earthquake History of India'.

[60] D. R. Nandy, *Need for Seismic Microzonation of Kolkata Megacity* (Bangalore, 2007), 140.c.

[61] H. Myer, ed., *Reference Encyclopedia India 2000* (Karnataka, 1999), A2, 23.

At about 5.15 PM on the afternoon of 12 June 1897 CE, the entire northeast region of India, Bangladesh, West Bengal, Bihar and parts of Myanmar and Nepal were shaken by a great earthquake. The earthquake destroyed the famous Kamakhya temple at Guwahati. The quake lasted for about a minute. The damage was extensive; lowlands were turned into high land and vice versa. The paddy fields were covered with sand. Even concrete houses from Guwahati, Shillong and Cooch Bihar were not spared. Many people lost their lives. In Guwahati, the Shiva and Mangalsandi temples were completely destroyed. The Nabagrah temple was also destroyed at Guwahati. The stone bridge on the River Bomadi near Guwahati was completely destroyed during this earthquake. The earthquake even damaged the secretariat building at Shillong. Geologists and scientists were not able to determine the cause of the earthquake. However, the astrologers pointed out that the earthquake was caused by the position of the stars.[62]

On 12 June 1897 CE, an earthquake occurred and was severely felt in Kolkata; the steeple of the Cathedral was destroyed and about 1,300 people lost their lives.[63]

The secretary to the chief commissioner of Assam, E. A. Gait, prepared a detailed report and sent it to the home secretary, Government of Assam. The report stated that about 1542 persons lost their lives during the 1897 earthquake. Many aftershocks continued from 12 June 1897 to 14 August 1897 CE and damaged many buildings.[64] A two-storey building at Phatik Barua collapsed and the Assamese town hall was completely destroyed. The church at Guwahati was completely destroyed and the government buildings were partially damaged.[65]

Northeast India falls in one of the six seismically most active regions of the world. During the period between 1869 and 1988 CE, there were at least 17 major earthquakes in the region. It is expected that there will be a major earthquake in the Shillong area in the near future. While earthquakes cannot be prevented, steps can be taken to reduce the impact by building earthquake-resistant buildings. One of the important steps

---

[62] ASDMA, *Earthquake Catalogue in and Around Northeastern Regions of India* (Jorhat: Assam Disaster Management Authority, Government of Assam, 2012).

[63] W. W. Hunter, *Imperial Gazetteer of India*, Vol. IX (Oxford: Clarendon Press, 1908), 262.

[64] P. C. Dutta, 'Bhumikampar Buranji, Natun Asomi', *Assamese Daily*, October 1, 1950. https://www.academia.edu/9559319/Earth_List_of_NE_India

[65] R. Bilham and P. England, 'Plateau Pop-up During the Great 1897 Assam Earthquake', *Nature* 410 (2001): 806–809.

to be taken is retrofitting, which can mitigate the disaster, as most of the damages are caused by collapse of structure.[66]

A big earthquake struck parts of lower Assam on 10 January 1869 CE. The shock was so severe that it was felt from Patna in the west to northern Burma in the east. In the south, it was felt up to south Kolkata and Chittagong. In the north, the shocks were felt from Darjeeling to Dibrugarh in Assam. The damage occurred in the region from Dhubri in Assam to Imphal in Manipur and covered the area between Nowgong and Silchar. The affected area covered 250,000 mi^2.[67]

During the period between 1881 and 2000 CE, about 25 major earthquakes were recorded in the region. Out of these, we propose to discuss about five earthquakes that were major. On the 31 December 1881 CE, there was an earthquake which caused minor damage in the Andaman Island Penal colony and generated a tsunami that was observed throughout the Bay of Bengal but not along the Burmese coast. There was no damage around the Bay of Bengal, where tide gauges recorded the maximum amplitude of 0.8m.[68]

The great Assam earthquake of 12 June 1897 CE caused extensive damage in an area of about 500-km radius, comprising of 4.5 million mi^2. About 1,600 people were left dead after this earthquake. It resulted in extensive surface distortion and the area has also extensive liquefaction in the alluvial plains of Brahmaputra. Rail tracks and bridges were destroyed. The earthquake was believed to have been caused by a thrust fault dipping gently to the north, which is also known as a Himalayan basal thrust. The earthquake raised the northern edge of the plateau roughly by 10m.[69]

The northeast region of India, especially the Brahmaputra valley, is prone to many incidences of seismic activity. This is clearly evidenced by the number of earthquakes that took place in this region in the 1890s. Prominent among these events were the 12 June 1885 CE earthquake in the Shillong plateau, which caused widespread destruction. In 1895 CE, the valley was shaken by an earthquake, which was still the highest intensity tremor recorded in the world with 8.7 on the Richter scale.[70]

---

[66] T. K. Devi, 'Seismic Hazard and Its Mitigation in Northeast India', *International Journal of Engineering Science* (IJSEA) 1, no. 1 (2012): 79–84.

[67] Hemmady, *Earthquakes*.

[68] R. D. Oldham, 'Note on the Earthquake of 31 December 1881', *Records Geological Survey of India* 17, no. 2 (1884): 47–53.

[69] R. Bilham, 'Earthquakes in India and the Himalaya: Tectonics, Geodesy and History', *Annals of Geophysics* 47, no. 2/3 (2004), 839–858.

[70] A. Bapat, 'Shaken, But Not Stirred', *Down to Earth* 7, no. 15 (1998): 58.

Similarly, in 1897 CE, the Assam–Bengal alluvial area and river channels were affected by an earthquake. The impact was so severe that the
railway lines were bent into sharp curves and bridges were compressed.
Fissures and sand-vents were opened up. The earthquake resulted in the
loss of 5,000 lives. Again on 12 June 1897 CE, an earthquake affected
Kolkata and the steeple of the Cathedral was destroyed. The death toll
was 1,300.[71]

On 15 August 1950 CE, an earthquake shook the Patkai range in
Arunachal Pradesh. It measured 7.0 on the Richter scale. However, there
was no loss of life, but there was damage to property. At the same time,
this earthquake affected the region of upper Assam and about 1,520
people died.[72]

Earthquakes in the Western Region

In the Rann of Kutch, around the year 1000 CE, some tributaries of the
River Indus dried up or changed their course. As a result, some parts
of the Rann rose up and some parts subsided. This is why some of the
Harappan sites are now at a level with the Rann and some are situated
on the raised banks.[73]

Of 3 January 1519 CE, there was a violent earthquake in the valley of
Chandawal in the Pali district of Rajasthan. The tremors lasted for nearly
half an hour. However, the extent of damage could not be fully assessed.[74]

In 1605 CE, there was an earthquake in Gujarat which inflicted heavy
mortality. This earthquake damaged many industries and thus many
artisans and craftsmen were affected. As a consequence, it damaged
the industries located in that area. Due to this earthquake, the export
and import trade was held back and the port of Surat was also closed
for the time being.[75]

In the western regions of India, earthquakes occurred in Bombay,
Gujarat, Surat and the Rann of Kutch region. An earthquake occurred

---

[71] *Imperial Gazetteer of India*, Vol. I, p. 99; Vol. IX, p. 262 (Oxford: The
Clarendon Press, 1908).

[72] Devi, 'Seismic Hazard and Its Mitigation'.

[73] H. D. Sankalia, B. Chatterjee, R. D. Choudhury, M. Bhattacharyya, and S.
B. Singh, *History and archaeology: Prof. H.D. Sankalia felicitation volume* (Delhi:
Ramanand Vidya Bhawan, 1989), 405.

[74] C. M. Agrawal, *Great Natural Calamities* (Delhi: Satish Garg, Publishers
Distributors, 2000), 22.

[75] Ibid., 184.

at Bombay on 26 May 1618 CE.[76] A severe hurricane lashed the city as a result of which 2,000 lives and 60 vessels were lost. In 1664 CE, another earthquake occurred in Bombay. However, the exact date is not known. The aftershocks continued for a period of 32 days.[77] The next major earthquake, which occurred in Bombay, was on 16 June 1819 CE and it affected only the northern portion of Bombay.[78]

In 1636 CE, the President of the Surat factory, Methwold's diary narrates that the earthquake was felt at Surat and everyone felt that the shock lasted for a duration, in which counting up to 60 was possible. Thus, the time interval was about 30s.[79]

In Gujarat, there was another earthquake which occurred on 4 January 1699 CE. The earth shook and a number of houses tumbled down and many people were buried.[80]

The Italian traveller, Manucci, has referred to an earthquake in Gujarat, which occurred on 4 January 1699 CE. The earth was rocked and a large number of houses came crashing down, with the result that many people were buried in the ruins. The tremors persisted for a month. This event was so severe that the canals which supplied water to the town ran dry. The poorer inhabitants were forced to live in the open without food and water.[81]

In 1702 CE, there was a severe earthquake in Gujarat. The result was that rivers lost all their sweet water and the little water that remained started tasting of sulphur. Even the fish that lived in the rivers died in large numbers.[82]

In February 1705 CE, there was a severe earthquake which occurred in Goga district of Gujarat province. The earth was rifted over a length of five leagues and, in some places; the fissures were 10 and 20 to 30 cubits wide. After a few days, peculiar rains followed the quake. There were drops of blood in this rain and the earth became red. At the same time, a comet appeared which remained visible for 15 days. The astrologers

---

[76] B. K. Bansal and S. Gupta, 'A Glance Through the Seismicity of Peninsular India', *Journal of the Geological Society* 52 (1998): 67–80.

[77] Agrawal, *Great Natural Calamities*, 82.

[78] H. M. Chaudbury, *Seismology in India* (Tokyo, Japan: Institute of Seismology and Earthquake Engineering, 1965).

[79] Iyengar and Siddiqui, 'Earthquake History of India'.

[80] Agrawal, *Great Natural Calamities*, 84.

[81] N. *Manucci, Storia do Mogor*, 1656–1712, trans. *W. Irvine*, Vol. 4 (London, 1907), 248.

[82] Agrawal, *Great Natural Calamities*, 172.

predicted that the appearance of comet indicated that Aurangzeb's death was imminent and devastation in many parts of the Empire and the loss of the port of Surat.[83]

An earthquake occurred on 16 June 1819 CE and the shocks were felt over a large area of northern India and even as far as Kolkata. About 2,000 people in Bhuj and 500 in Ahmadabad were killed, and there was heavy loss of property in Kutch, Bhuj and Ahmadabad. It is said that the Indus River changed its course near the western end of Kutch and flowed through the low ground north of Lakhpat. There was a large-scale crustal deformation caused by the earthquake. It created a low ridge about 24 km wide and 80 km long from east to west. The land to the north of the bund rose to a maximum height of about 5–6 m and subsided to the south to a maximum depth of 3 m to 5 m. In the Rann of Kutch, blackish muddy water issued from the fissures, and cones of sands 2 m to 3 m high rose from the depths.[84]

On 3 January 1519 CE, there was a terrible earthquake in the lower part of the valley of Chandawal situated in the Pali district of Rajasthan. The extent of devastation caused by the earthquake is not exactly verifiable.[85]

At Mount Abu on the border between Gujarat and Rajasthan, a severe earthquake occurred on 26 April 1848 CE. The epicentre was in the Aravalli range in Sirohi district of Rajasthan. The earthquake was accompanied by a rumbling noise. It was also felt in the regions of Deesa of Banaskantha district; Ahmadabad, Cambay in the state of Gujarat; Mundlaisir in the state of Andhra Pradesh; and Sehore, Bhopal and Pahunpur which are in the state of Madhya Pradesh. The impact of this earthquake was such that cracks developed in buildings and the temple of Dilwara suffered some damage.[86]

On 15 August 1906 CE, in the neighbourhood of Janpalia, Rajasthan, an earthquake occurred. This is situated northwest of Bakhasar. The tremors were felt along the Indo-Pakistan border, Sindh and Gujarat. The aftershocks were felt in Rajasthan, Jodhpur and Ahmadabad and near the Gulf of Khambat.[87]

The west coast of India represents a fault scarp, probably of the Pliocene age. The fault is characterized by a strong positive Bouguer

---

[83] Ibid, 85.

[84] U. Chandra, 'Earthquakes of Peninsular India—A Seismotectonic Study', *Bulletin of the Seismological Society of America* 67, no. 5 (1977): 1387–1413.

[85] R. K. Mukherjee, *Hindu Civilization* (Calcutta, 1950), 74.

[86] Chandra, 'Earthquakes of Peninsular India'.

[87] Ambraseys, 'Three Little Known Early Earthquakes in India', 506.

anomaly with the steep gradient. During the last century, some 28 small to moderate earthquakes have occurred along the west coast. Significant among these are the Mahabaleshwar earthquake of August 1764 CE with an intensity of 7 and the Koynanagar earthquake of 10 December 1967 CE with an intensity of 7, in which 177 people lost their lives.[88]

In 1967 CE, due to a severe quake, Koynanagar collapsed; the nearby dam was affected and old arched roads and bridges collapsed. The shock was felt as far as Surat, Nagpur, Hyderabad and Bangalore. This quake belonged to the category of 'interaplate' which means 'within a plate'. There were about 177 human lives lost, 2,272 injured and 50,000 affected by this earthquake.[89]

In the period between 1864 and 2001 CE, about 17 major earthquakes were recorded in the region. Out of these, we proposed to discuss about five earthquakes that had a major impact. In 1919 CE, tremors were felt at Bhav nagar, Wadhwan, Sougandh, Chok Jhana and Bhoika. The intensity was 7. In 1970 CE, a quake affected Broach in Gujarat. Twenty-six people were killed and 2,500 houses damaged during this earthquake. The shocks were felt in south Gujarat and Bombay. In 1980 CE, a quake of 4.9 on the Richter scale affected the Koyna region of Maharashtra. The Killari earthquake in Maharashtra occurred on 18 October 1992 CE. Eighty villages were affected. The shocks continued to be felt even after a period of a week. Another major earthquake to hit the Maharashtra region was the Latur earthquake of 23 September 1993 CE, with an intensity of 7.8 on the Richter scale. In this major event, about 11, 000 people were killed and there was enormous destruction caused to 80 villages. The focal depth of the earthquake is estimated to be between 5 and 15 km. In the weeks to follow, there are about 25 reports of felt earthquakes. Even the aftershocks exceeded the magnitude of 4. There are reports of smoke and gas emanating from an area at a distance of 200 km from the epicentre.[90]

On the northwestern edge of the Indian plate, on 26 January 2001 CE, there was a massive earthquake, with its epicentre in the Bhuj district of Gujarat. The quake measured 8.1 on the Richter scale and lasted for 2 minutes. It left 50,000–100,000 people dead and five million people affected. The aftershocks continued for some time after the main

---

[88] B. K. Rastogi, 'Seismicity of Indian Stable Continental Region', *Journal of Earthquake Science and Engineering* 3, no. 1 (2016): 29–64.

[89] A. Bapat, 'Dams and Earthquakes', *Frontline* 16, no. 27 (25 December 1999 to 7 January 2000).

[90] G. H. Gupta et al., 'A Quick Look at the Latur Earthquake of 30th September 1993', *Current Science* 65, no. 7 (1993): 517–520.

earthquake. About 50 per cent houses in Ahmadabad, 90 per cent in Bhuj and 60 per cent in Rajkot were damaged. It should be noted even on 24 December 2000, there was a 4.2 magnitude quake which rocked the Rann of Kutch. This should have been a wake-up call for the Indian seismologists. Unfortunately, however, this signal was not heeded and the damage caused by the 2001 quake was tremendous.[91]

Earthquakes in the Central Region

The largest instrumented earthquake in Madhya Pradesh took place on 2 June 1927 CE at Umaria. It was a deep-seated event and the effects were felt as far as Allahabad in Uttar Pradesh and Dehri on Sone in Bihar as well as in many parts of central and eastern India. Umaria falls under the seismic Zone III, which indicates that earthquakes may occur in the future also.[92]

In 1927 CE, in the Sone valley regions of Madhya Pradesh, a quake of magnitude of 6.7 on the Richter scale shook the valley. The shocks were so severe that they were felt as far as Ranchi, Delhi and Allahabad.[93]

A well-documented earthquake was the one that occurred in 1938 CE in the Satpura region of Madhya Pradesh to the south of SONATA. It caused moderate damage and appears to have occurred in the deeper crust. The effects of this earthquake were felt over a huge area of about 100,000 mi^2 and the radius of about 500 km. The tremors were felt as far as Delhi in the north and Belgaum in Karnataka in the south. A peculiar feature was that a hot spring near Chopda disappeared after the shocks.[94]

In 1957 CE, there was an earthquake felt at Nagpur, Mandla, Gondia and Jabalpur. Also affected were the districts of Balaghat in Madhya Pradesh and Bhandara in Maharashtra. About 25 people lost their lives during this incident. The epicentre of this earthquake was north of the town of Waraseoni in Madhya Pradesh and the town of Gondia in Maharashtra.[95]

Another earthquake took place in Paunar-Amarwara area of Madhya Pradesh on 18 April 1987 CE. On 31 August 1994 CE, the earth shook at Gwalior–Gohad (Bhind) area, Madhya Pradesh. The effects were felt in many northern districts of Madhya Pradesh and adjoining areas of Uttar

---

[91] R. Mahapatra, 'Republic Quaked', *Down To Earth* 9, no. 19 (2001): 42–47.
[92] District Disaster Management Plan [DDMP], Umaria, 2016.
[93] Chandra, 'Earthquakes of Peninsular India'.
[94] Ibid.
[95] Ibid.

Pradesh and Rajasthan. It is known by the name of the Bhind earthquake. On 22 May 1997 CE, there were tremors in the Barela–Jabalpur area of Madhya Pradesh. About 38 people were killed and about a 1,000 injured in the city of Jabalpur and its environs. This was reported to be the first major earthquake in a densely populated urban area since 1947 CE. A moderate earthquake struck Jabalpur and its adjacent areas on 16 October 2000. It caused only minor damage (http://asc-india. org/seismi/seis-madhya-pradesh.htm).

Another major earthquake occurred at Jabalpur in Madhya Pradesh during the year 1997 CE. There was significant damage to structures in Jabalpur, Mandla, Sivni and Chhindwara districts in Madhya Pradesh. Of these, Jabalpur and Mandla were the worst affected districts. As many as 8,546 houses were destroyed and 52,690 houses were partially damaged in 887 villages. The earthquake also killed 43 people and injured about a 1,000 and left another 1,000 homeless.[96]

In September 1998 CE in Pandhana town of Madhya Pradesh and nearby 24 villages, there were microearthquake activities during a period of 3 months accompanied by a rumbling sound. The majority of the tremors occurred between 11 December 1998 CE and 5 April 1999 CE. The administration took necessary measures to minimize the loss due to the quake (http://khandwa.nic.in/activities.htm).

Earthquakes in the Southern Region

The Indian shield is considered to be part of the Indian Craton and occupies two-thirds of the Indian peninsula. The shield was found about 3,500 million years ago and has remained fairly stable since its formation. It is bounded on the west, south and east by the present-day coastline and Phanerozoic sediment cover. Towards the north, it is bordered by the Proterozoic Province. In the North East, it is bounded by the Godavari graben which preserves the Precambrian pakhal rocks and Gondwana sediments.

The shield can be divided into the following regions. The first is the Dharwar craton with its typical Archaean volcanic-plutonic belts surrounded by the vast gneissic terrain. The second is the southern granulite-gneiss terrain of Tamil Nadu–Kerala. The third is the eastern ghat mobile belt along the east coast, and finally, the intra cratonic

---

[96] C. K. Saikia, 'A Method for Calibration Using Regional and the Seismic Broad Band Seismograms: Application to the 21 May 1997 Jabalpur, India Earthquake (Mw. 5.8)', *Current Science* 79, no. 9 (2000): 1301–1315.

Purana basins with thick sequences of platform facies rocks and/or rift-related sediments.[97] The Peninsular shield has been considered to be a seismically stable shield area for a long time, with the potential of generating only low-level seismicity at isolated places.

South India is especially subject to multiple hazards which differ in nature and intensity. This was vividly illustrated during the tsunami of December 2004 CE. Besides tsunamis, the coastal regions face natural disasters like cyclones and floods. The plains and hilly regions are also subject to landslides, earthquakes and floods. Another added threat has been urban flooding as witnessed by the Chennai floods of December 2015 CE. Besides these events, this chapter illustrates only the earthquakes which occurred in south India.

A stone inscription in Kannada script found in the village of Billankote in Nelamangala taluka near Bangalore states that in the year of Kali 4608 (1507 CE), the earth shook four times. No other details are given. It is possible that it was a mild earthquake.[98]

The author of *Basatin-us-Salatin*, Muhammad Ibrahim Zuberi, has stated in the history of Bijapur that in the year 1064 AH (1653–1654 CE), water was brought inside the fort from Begam Talab by the efforts of Afzal Khan. In the same year, a severe tremor occurred. The record does not speak of any other damage.[99]

In Madras, on the night of 20 January 1679 CE, there is a record of an earthquake which continued for half a quarter of an hour. This has been noted in Streynsham Master's diary at the port of Fort St. George, Madras. It has also been noted that this earthquake was felt all along the Coromandel Coast and even in Burma and Bengal. However, this earthquake did not cause much damage.[100]

Padmanabha Menon, in his *History of Kerala*, has recorded that in the month of December 1784 CE, that there was a general agitation of the earth in the night. This continued for about 2 seconds. This phenomenon was called *Bhumikulukkam* in the Malabar language and *Bhoochalana* in Sanskrit.[101]

---

[97] R. S. Sharma, *Cratons and Fold Belts of India* (Berlin; Heidelberg: Springer, 2009), 304.

[98] Iyengar and Siddiqui, 'Earthquake History of India', 198.

[99] Basatin-us-Salatin, *History of Bijapur* (Hyderabad: Deccan, 1982), 346.

[100] Iyengar and Siddiqui, 'Earthquake History of India', 201.

[101] Padmanabha Menon, *A History of Kerala*, ed. T. K. Krishna Menon, Vol. I. (New Delhi, 1989), 121–122.

During the period between 1800 and 1975 CE, over 57 earthquakes took place in the state of Andhra Pradesh. One such occasion was on 29 October 1800, when incessant thunder and lightning were especially prevalent. Another significant earthquake occurred in 1843 in Bellary in Andhra Pradesh on 1 April 1843 CE (M = 6.0).[102]

It could appear, therefore, that the phenomena of earthquakes were sometimes accompanied by electric phenomena. However, it would be reasonable to assume that such phenomena were connected to earthquakes; however, there is not sufficient evidence to definitely conclude that the two are interlinked.[103]

The southern metropolis of Chennai has been witness to earthquakes of magnitude ≥5.0 in 1807 CE, 1816 CE and 1823 CE.[104] For example, on 10 and 11 December 1807 CE, a violent storm tore the roof off the grain store, thus leading to food riots. Another earthquake took place on December 9–10 in 1807 CE in the Poonamallee–Avadi area near Chennai. There was some confusion in reporting the event as two separate incidents. However, there is every possibility that the two events reported referred to one and the same. Additionally, Chennai falls under Zone III (moderate seismic activity). Therefore, it would appear that built-up areas like Chennai would require special attention during any assessment of seismic hazard and vulnerability. There is a possibility that even moderate earthquake events in a city like Chennai would result in lasting damage. Hence, it would be necessary to assess the seismic hazard and vulnerability as an important step in reducing the earthquake risk. A study on quantification of seismic hazards and vulnerability of the built-up environment, critical facilities and lifeline utilities of Chennai city would go a long way in meeting this need.[105]

During the period between 1807 and 1900 CE, there were about 28 earthquakes recorded in Tamil Nadu. The intensity varied from 3.0 to 6.0 on the MM scale. Some of the places which felt the shocks were Madras, Salem, Dharmapuri, Coimbatore, Pondicherry, Shevaroys, Tirupattur and Villupuram. According to *Rajarathnam*, Tamil Nadu has been experiencing many quakes up to a maximum of 6 on the

---

[102] Bansal and Gupta, 'A Glance Through the Seismicity'.

[103] The *Journal of the Asiatic Society of Bengal* 13, part 2 (1844): 979, edited by The Secretary and Sub-Secretary. Calcutta: Bishop's College Press.

[104] G. P. Ganapathy, 'Seismic Hazard Assessment for Tamil Nadu State and A Specific Study on Local Ground Motion Response for Part of Chennai City' (Ph.D. thesis, Anna University, India, 2005), 167 (Unpublished).

[105] G. P. Ganapathy, 'First Level Seismic Microzonation Map of Chennai City—A GIS Approach', *Natural Hazards and Earth System Sciences* 11 (2011): 549–559.

Richter scale. The reason for this was reactivation of faults under the earth surface. Though southern India seemed to be a stable land mass of 'craton rocks, there were several faults and shearing zones running under the tectonic plates.[106] Another earthquake struck at Coimbatore on 8 February 1900 CE. The intensity was 7 and this earthquake was felt throughout the southern part of India south of 14°N latitude over an area of about 250,000 mi^2. In the epicentral region, many houses suffered damage. There were cracks in the walls and the tiled roofs had their tiles displaced.[107]

In the southern shear zone, about 25 earthquakes occurred with an intensity of more or less 4 in Richter scale. The Idukki earthquake of 1988 indicates right-lateral slip parallel to the NW-SE trending Achankovil lineament. The Bangalore earthquake of 1984 CE showed right-lateral slip along a NW-SE trending shear.[108] In the past years, Chennai felt some seismic activity. Since, there is lack of sufficient information about earthquake details of the faults. Hence, it has been considered necessary to classify all the faults as active. The characteristic site period contours for the city range from 0.25 to 0.80 s. It was observed that higher amplification (greater than 3) occurs mostly in the central and southern parts of the city. The reason for this is the presence of deep soil site with clayey or sandy deposits.[109] On 12 December 2000 CE, a moderate earthquake with a magnitude of 5 was recorded with its epicentre in Idukki district of Kerala. However, its impact was felt even in Madurai, Theni, Coimbatore and the Nilgiris. This earthquake was said to be first of its magnitude in South India in three decades. Coimbatore city and parts of the district experienced tremors. In the Nilgiris too, the quake was felt in Coonoor, Kunda and some parts of Udhagamandalam. The tremors lasted for 2 seconds. Dharmapuri and Salem recorded mild earthquakes in 1998 CE in August and November. In Virudhunagar district, mild tremors occurred. The quake was also felt at Thenkasi town and surrounding areas for a few seconds. The previous earthquake of magnitude was recorded in Bhadrachalam in April 1969 CE (5.9M) and in Ongole in March 1967 CE (5.2M). However, no damage was reported.[110]

---

[106] K. Ramachandran, 'The Quakes in South', *The Hindu*, 27 September 2001.

[107] Chandra, 'Earthquakes of Peninsular India'.

[108] Rastogi, 'Seismicity of Indian Stable Continental Region'.

[109] A. Boominathan, G. R. Dodagoudar, A. Suganthi, and R. Uma Maheswari, 'Seismic Hazard Assessment Considering Local Site Effects for Microzonation Studies of Chennai City', *Journal of Earth System Science* 117 (2008): 853–863.

[110] Staff Reporter, 'Earthquake Hits Some Tamil Nadu Districts', *The Hindu*, 13 December 2000.

India is situated at the northwestern edge of the Indo-Australian plates. This includes India, Australia, the major portion of the Indian Ocean and other smaller countries. This plate is constantly colliding with the huge Eurasian plate and going under the Eurasian plate. This process is called subduction. Long ago, a sea called the Tethys separated these plates before they collided. A part of the lithosphere or the earth's crust is covered by the oceans and the rest by continent. When the ocean converges against another plate, subduction occurs. However, the continents are buoyant and hence tend to remain close to the surface. While the continents converge, large amounts of shortening and thickening takes place as in the Himalayas and Tibet.

The three chief tectonic subregions of India are the mighty Himalayas in the north, the plains of the Ganga and its tributaries, and finally the peninsula. The Himalayas primarily consist of sediments accumulated over a long period of time in the Tethys. On the other hand, the Indo-Gangetic basin with alluvial soil consists of a great depression caused by the load of the Himalayas. The peninsular portion of the subcontinent consists of ancient rocks, which were deformed in the past. In the Himalayas, erosion has removed the roots of the old mountains and altered the topography. The rocks are very hard but have been softened by weathering. Before the Himalayan collision, lava flowed across peninsular India leaving large areas of basalt rock. On the other hand, the coastal areas like Kutch show evidence of marine deposits. This proves that they emerged from under the sea millions of years ago.

An earthquake occurs most frequently at the plate boundaries. This is because the stresses are concentrated at this point and staining of the crust occurs. When there is intense seismic activity at the boundary between the Indian and Eurasian plates, compression occurs which results in intense thrusting. Thus, the Eurasian plates override the Indian plate and consequently the Himalayan ranges are uplifted. Therefore, it is obvious that northern India which is in the position of the collisional plate boundary is more susceptible to shallow and deadly earthquakes. On the contrary, South India is situated in the stable seismic cratonic part of the Indian plate. Hence, it is spared devastating earthquakes.[111]

---

[111] C. V. R. Murthy, *Earthquake Tips: Learning Earthquake Design and Construction* (New Delhi: National Information Center of Earthquake Engineering, Government of India, 2015), 7–8.

Conclusion

The Indian subcontinent, especially the Himalayan belt, falls under the seismically active zone. A study of the ancient archaeological and literary evidences shows that earthquakes were common phenomena even in the prehistoric, Vedic, Buddhist, Puranic and Mughal periods. However, prior to the British era, there was no scientific study of this event. It is very essential to collect the necessary data for forming reliable seismic hazard estimation. This is now being done on a scientific basis by various agencies. The recent earthquakes in Uttarkashi, Killari, Jabalpur, Chamoli and Bhuj have underlined the need to collect adequate information about these seismic events, in order to arrive at a scientific understanding of this phenomenon. The present work attempts to fill up the gap in this particular field of scientific endeavour. The author has carried out intensive research of primary sources in order to collect the relevant information. The major earthquake events that had not been properly classified so far are now been properly catalogued. It is to be hoped that the present work, will to some extent, fill up the lacunae in this regard.

Cyclones of East Coast of India

Mili Ghose

The sun was formed about 4.5 billion years ago. The solar system or the solar cycle is a primeval phenomenon. When humans were yet to arrive, that is, *Homo sapiens* were yet to conquer earth, cyclones and other calamities were still prevalent. Nobody knows when the first cyclone occurred in the world. Henry Piddington, one of the earliest meteorologists, coined the word 'cyclone' in his book, *The Sailor's Horn-book for the Law of Storms* (1848). The word 'cyclone' is derived from Greek word *kuklōma*, which means 'coiling of a snake'.[1] It refers to several types of storms, but they are known by different names. Some storms occur over land while others occur over water. When the storm occurs over the Atlantic Ocean and Northeast Pacific, it is popularly known as a hurricane. If this same storm occurs in the Northwest Pacific, then it goes by the moniker of a typhoon, and it is known as a tropical cyclone in the South Pacific and Indian Ocean. Tropical cyclones mean cyclones that occur over tropical or subtropical ocean regions. Most storms originate between the Tropic of Cancer and Tropic of Capricorn. Storms follow anti-clockwise rotation in the northern hemisphere and

---

[1] Ranjan Chakrabarti, 'The Kolkata Cyclone/Earthquake of 1737: Random Scribbles', *Vidyasagar University, Journal of History* 1 (2012–2013): 15.

clockwise rotation in the southern hemisphere. If there is a sudden rise in temperature at any place, then the wind pressure decreases and depression occurs at the place. The depression or drop in air pressure prompts cold winds from high-pressure regions to gush in with great velocity. This occurrence is popularly known as cyclone. The incident of tropical cyclones is a usual characteristic of the months of May (pre-monsoon) and October (post-monsoon) over the Bay of Bengal.

Tropical cyclone brings in heavy rain. Too much rainfall destroys life, property and crop through flooding—especially on densely populated valleys. The rotting of crops and saline incursion can also result in famine that can kill more people than the actual cyclonic event. The naming of tropical cyclones is a recent occurrence. The World Meteorological Organization maintains the lists. For the Indian Ocean region, planning for naming cyclones commenced in 2000. Eight countries, namely Bangladesh, India, Maldives, Myanmar, Oman, Pakistan, Sri Lanka and Thailand, contributed to the nomenclature. Cyclones began to be named in accordance to the name of the place where it first originated.

Usually, cyclones occur in oceanic regions, but due to climatic upheavals and global warming, all the environments or climatic zones on earth have significantly changed and cyclones occur frequently even in non-oceanic areas. In India, in particular, the climate has been central to the growth or prosperity of human civilizations. It has always been the most crucial determinant of rice production or of settled agriculture. The eastern parts of India have more cyclone-prone areas compared to the western part of the country. Tropical cyclonic pressures that are formed over the Arabian Sea generally affect Gujarat, Maharashtra and Karnataka. Tropical cyclones which originate from the Bay of Bengal can affect the west coast of India, though they usually weaken by the time they reach the coastline. *El Niño* and *La Niña* events also intensify the series of cyclones in the tropical Pacific region. Approximately two million people have died globally owing to tropical cyclones. The intensity of a tropical cyclone mainly depends on its size and location. A tropical cyclone consists of heavy storm surge, strong winds and very heavy rains, causing floods and landslides. Particularly in the coastal areas, cyclonic effects are more devastating, ravaging many places and damaging agriculture, farms and crops sprawled over large areas. Cyclones also immobilize the industrial sectors, which has a direct impact on the country's economic sector. For the past many years, tropical cyclones have compelled human settlements and settled economies to resettle in foreign lands.

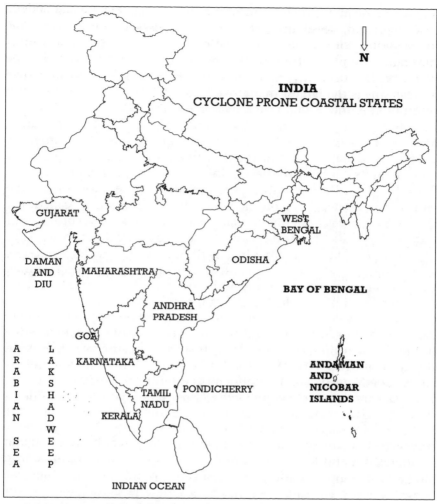

Cyclone-prone Coastal States in India

Disclaimer: This figure is not to scale. It does not represent any authentic national or international boundaries and is used for illustrative purposes only.

The Cyclone of 1737

The Sundarbans has a unique landscape and distinct climatic features. The marshy region presents a healthy combination of land and water. The Bengal deltaic region serves as an excellent example of *char* land in South Asia. It is not just a flood-prone area but also a cyclone-prone one. In this deltaic region, rivers are constantly eating into the existing land,

and the place, interestingly, had once been uninhabited. But along with land depletion, simultaneously and almost paradoxically, fresh land keeps getting formed due to deposition of silt. It is this phenomenon that had prompted settlers in the bygone days to settle down at this place and to turn into its permanent inhabitants. Interestingly, the Sundarbans is the largest mangrove forest. It enjoys a total land area of 4,143 km^2 and a total water area of a healthy 1,874 km^2.[2] Rivers— namely Muriganga, Harinbhahga, Raimangal, Saptamukhi, Thakuran, Matla and Gosaba—flow through the Sundarbans. The Sundarbans is a Gangetic delta that lies in the 24 Parganas District of West Bengal and shares its border with the adjoining country of Bangladesh. In the Bengal delta, a large quantity of fertile silt is carried down from the Himalayas and deposited on the riverbeds, which is locally called *char* land. *Char* land is a highly vulnerable area because of occurrences of sudden floods and frequent cyclones. *Char* people are usually very poor. They live amidst uncertainties in a fragile environment. Due to climate change, floods, cyclones, riverbank erosion and shifting river channel, the *chars* are physically, socially and economically susceptible and are occasionally displaced. In Bangladesh, rural people are displaced due to tornados, cyclones, floods and droughts. Crop production is heavily damaged due to shortage of water and occurrence of natural hazards.[3] In the deltaic region, the economy gets shifted because settlements are shifted. Throughout the 18th, 19th and even the 20th century, new *char* lands were formed. The Bengal delta is essentially a history of rivers. The *chars* are extremely vulnerable to floods and bank erosion due to shifting river courses. According to James Rennell's map, between 1793 and 1827, 82 *chars* were formed in Comilla district alone.[4] Agriculture on the lower valley and the delta is governed by rainfall and flood. The fertility of soil of the delta depends on the deposit of silt. The crops and methods of cropping have hardly changed at this place. The climate of Bengal is very favourable for agriculture. Crops, farming practices and irrigation on this place are dominated by wet climate, moist soil, floods and cyclones. The Gangetic delta is an immensely densely populated

---

[2] Ranjan Chakrabarti, 'Local People and the Global Tiger: An Environmental History of the Sundarbans', *Global Environment* 3 (2009): 76.

[3] Mohammed Rahman Zillur and Kuntala Lahiri-Dutt, 'Ensuring Water Security in Rural Area of Bangladesh Under Climate Change', in *Coping with Global Environmental Change, Disasters and Security: Threats, Challenges, Vulnerabilities and Risks*, eds. Hans Günter Brauch et al., (Berlin Heidelberg: Springer-Verlag, 2011), 974.

[4] Ranjan Chakrabarti, 'Introduction', in *Dictionary of Historical Places: Bengal, 1757–1947*, ed. Ranjan Chakrabarti (Delhi: Primus Books, 2013), xix.

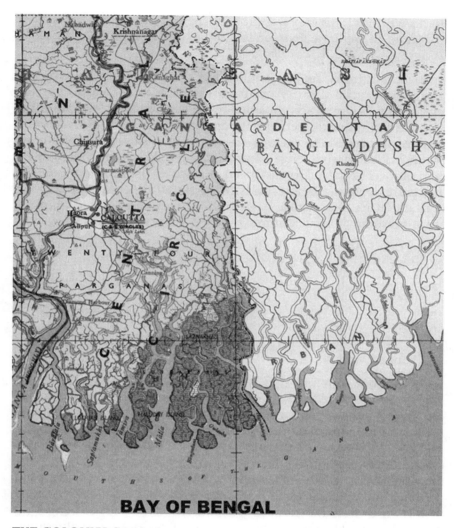

BAY OF BENGAL

THE COLONIAL Sundarbans

Source: http://pahar.in/indian-subcontinent-after-1900, 1976 Atlas of Forest Resources of India, Plate 9, Forest Calcutta.
Disclaimer: The figure is for representation purpose only.

area in the world.[5] There are countless references of the Sundarbans in the Ramayana, Mahabharata and the Puranas. Hiuen Tsang, a Chinese traveller who visited India in the 7th century AD, spoke of Sundarbans

---

[5] Radhakamal Mukherjee, *The Changing Face of Bengal: A Study in Riverine Economy* (Kolkata: University of Calcutta, 2009), 32.

in his writings. This area was probably part of the land of Samatata at that time. In medieval texts, oral traditions and folk songs, lower Bengal is normally called *Bati* or *Bhati*.

In British India, on 11 October 1737, Kolkata Calamity, the first recorded natural disaster occurred in the Indian Ocean rim. The cyclone of 1737 was accompanied by an earthquake.[6] This was called 'Calcutta Earthquake'. Perhaps, it was also the first recorded tsunami of the British period. The cyclone of 1737 possibly affected 300,000 lives in undivided coastal Bengal. Twenty thousand ships anchored in the harbour were believed to have been crushed by the super cyclone. The epicentre could not be precisely traced at that time when seismology was still at its infant stage.[7] The October cyclones are said to be the most powerful tropical storms.

Kolkata is located on the banks of the Ganges, Brahmaputra and Meghna delta. It is at a distance of almost 300 km from the principal faults of the Indo-Asian Plate boundaries in Burma and the Himalayas.[8] The number of deaths suggested that the earthquake that occurred in 1737 was a severe one, and the accompanying cyclone in Hooghly River was one of the deadliest cyclones in the world. The storm surge caused by the cyclone measured 30–40 ft and recorded 381 mm of rainfall.

The author contends that an earthquake accompanied by cyclone and flood did occur in Kolkata on 11 October 1737 even though in the East India Company reports there is no mention of an earthquake. Oldham has mentioned that St. Anne's Church shook and sunk into the ground without destroying anything. It points to the occurrence of an intense earthquake. The damage to straw houses and the sinking of people and animals is a testimony to the debatable fact that a major cyclone and a major earthquake occurred simultaneously. Possibly, it was an earthquake-induced tsunami. The entire lower Bengal was affected by the earthquake/tsunami. Further, the death casualties numbering 300,000 indicate that the entire coastal India was affected by the cyclone or the earthquake. This was the earliest recorded cyclone in the Indian Ocean rim. This super cyclone ruined many lives, caused high tide in the sea, affected the fertility of the land and paved the way for a catastrophic famine.

---

[6] Anuradha Banerjee, *Environment, Population, and Human Settlements of Sundarban Delta* (Delhi: Concept Publishing Company, 1998), 358.

[7] Lee Allyn Devis, *Natural Disasters,* Checkmark Books, 2008, p. 241.

[8] Roger Bilham, 'Calcutta Earthquake and Cyclone Evaluated', *Bulletin of the Seismological Society of America,* 84, no. 5 (October 1994): 1.

The Cyclone of 1864

On 5 October 1864, most of the city of Kolkata was flooded and destroyed by a cyclone. As many as 50,000 people were killed at once, and thousands perished later from the sicknesses and diseases that followed. It was a natural disaster of an unparalleled magnitude for a city to have more than 50,000 people killed, over 100 brick homes and thousands of straw huts were either razed or washed away and several ports at Khejuri and Hijli simply vanished. These were the direct consequences of the most severe tropical cyclones faced by Kolkata on 5 October 1864. The entire city was flooded by more than 30-foot high tidal waves in the Hooghly River. This 1864 cyclone has been rightly dubbed as a super cyclone. Raging over the Bay of Bengal, it ruined countless lives, projected sky-high tide at sea, prompted the land to lose its fertility and set the stage for a deadly famine. The entire coastal Bengal, and particularly the city of Kolkata, was severely affected by the cyclone. This was one of the earliest recorded cyclones in the Indian Ocean rim. Storms can affect human society, the economy, culture, polities and maritime activities in various ways. The storm can be observed for scholarly purposes from land as well as from the sea. The cyclone of 1864 was singlehandedly responsible for the destruction of the ports at Khejuri and Hijli.

Report of Kolkata Cyclone of 1864

James Eardley Gastrell and Henry Francis Blanford traced the progress of the cyclonic vortex from 2 October 1864. On that day, their ship *Moneka* gave the first indications of its existence to the west of northern Andaman up until the midnight of the 4 October, when the centre was in about the latitude 20°20′ and moving northward at an average rate of 10–11 miles an hour.

In the famous *Report on the Calcutta Cyclone of the 5th October 1864* by James Eardley Gastrell and Henry Francis Blanford, clearly an attempt has been made to sketch an account of the principal meteorological phenomena that preceded and accompanied the great Kolkata Cyclone of 5 October 1864. Hardly anybody could be more aware than Gastrell and Blanford of that phenomenon, and despite the imperfection of their account, it continues to serve as a great and largely reliable primeval source. It is unquestionably clear, however, that the fullest and more extensive information would have been of great value not only to scientific meteorologists but also to the general public. Their account, therefore, is unavoidably treated as being cursory and incomplete.

Special mention should be made of H. F. Blanford and authors such as Henry Piddington and I. R. Tanehill of the colonial era who had discussed the previous cyclones, like that of 1737. Blanford, a meteorologist working in India in the 1870s, all along had a hunch that the casualty figure was inflated, as he observed by judging from the character of Indian statistical estimates. Even in the present day, one might perhaps justifiably entertain a suspicion that these figures are somewhat excessive.[9] Blanford's source of information was Henry Piddington's book.

There were people who were familiar with the accurate and minute observations of European observatories and who knew how much the value of meteorological observations depended on the careful comparison of instruments, elimination of instrumental errors and the training and experience of observers. It might seem almost wasted labour to attempt to deduce any result from observations made in many cases by unpractised observers with excellent instruments and from such guesses at the direction and force of wind currents as can be made by persons in their own houses, unconscious of eddies and judging from a general knowledge of the compass bearings of the place.

The Kolkata-based observations of the Cyclone of 1864, moreover, were observed and recorded continuously at 10-minute intervals only during the earlier part of the storm but were thereafter intermitted. This owed partly to the destruction of the self-registering instruments and partly to the observers having left the observatory building under the assumption that it would not be able to withstand the storm whose catastrophic intensity, at one time, appeared much imminent.[10]

Both James Eardley Gastrell and Henry Francis Blanford, the authors of the *Report on the Calcutta Cyclone of the 5th October 1864*, therefore endeavoured to utilize all available data within such limits as their local knowledge led them to believe. The data thereof may be adopted without risk of serious error. Probable thermometric errors, for example, of two or three degrees, even barometric errors of a few hundredths and, in the case of marine barometers, probably tenths of inches and compass errors of three or four points must in many cases be allowed for, and

---

[9] Henry Francis Blanford, *On the Origin of a Cyclone* (London: The Royal Society, 1868). Also read, Henry Francis Blanford, *A Practical Guide to the Climates and Weather of India, Ceylon and Burmah and the Storms of Indian Seas* (London: McMillan, 1889).

[10] David Longshore, *Encyclopedia of Hurricanes, Typhoons, and Cyclones* (New York, NY: FoF, 2008), 39–40.

it would in general be futile to attempt to elicit residual phenomena from such slight anomalies, as may be evident.

Though this caveat to readers seems a necessary preface to a report prepared, partly at least, for the information of a scientific readership, the authors were far from intending thereby to disparage the assistance they had received freely and cordially from all quarters. Whatever record had been kept, to the best of their knowledge, had been frankly and readily communicated to them, and their warmest thanks were tendered to all who had thus assisted them. As the names of the different correspondents and observers to whom the authors were thus indebted were mentioned in every case in the body of the report, it is unnecessary to enumerate them here; but they could not delete, in this place, to record their indebtedness to other gentlemen whose names would not appear in the above category.

To the cordial and enlightened encouragement of the Lieutenant-Governor, Mr Cecil Beadon, at whose desire the report, which was originally intended to be prepared for the Asiatic Society, was published under the auspices of the government of Bengal, the authors were primarily indebted. They had thus had the advantage of all such assistance as could be afforded by government departments and officers at outstations, assistance that had not only added much to their scientific data, especially with respect to the height and extent of the storm wave, but had enabled them also to complete the record, by a more trustworthy account than would otherwise have been possible, of the destruction caused thereby.

To Captain Howe, late Officiating Master Attendant of the Port, Dr Partridge, Mr Obbard and Mr Heeley they owed the collection from ships and private correspondents of much information that they would not otherwise have obtained, and without which the deficiencies of the report would have been much greater than they actually are. The publication of the report had been delayed much beyond what the authors had wished and anticipated, mainly owing to the demands of other duties on their time. Although this delay would doubtless diminish the interest of the report to the general public, it had been so far an advantage in that it had enabled the authors to avail greatly increased materials. The more important deductions in the report had long been available to the authors in their duties in connection with the meteorological system established during the past year.[11]

---

[11] James Eardley Gastrell and Henry Francis Blanford, *Report on the Calcutta Cyclone of the 5th October 1864* (Calcutta: Military Orphan Press, 1866), iii–v.

Description of the 1864 Cyclone

According to the report prepared by James Eardley Gastrell and Henry Francis Blanford, one of the most intense Bay of Bengal cyclones on record, the Great Kolkata Cyclone, powered by central barometric pressure of 28.02 in. at landfall, delivered sustained 204 km/hr winds, torrential rains and an astounding 40-foot storm surge to the northeast coast of India in the month of October in the year 1864. The greatest pressure of the wind registered is 50 lb/ft^2. During the storms of 1864 and 1867, the anemometer was blown away. A great loss of life and property was caused along the river Hooghly by the storm of 5 October 1864.

James Eardley Gastrell and Henry Francis Blanford presented a good description of the cyclone in their report.[12] From barometric observations, they saw that southerly winds prevailed over the Bay of Bengal and the country of Bengal to the north, the only exceptions being Cachar in the valley between the Khasia Hills and the mountains of Tipperah, and the station of Comillah or Tipperah in eastern Bengal. Meanwhile, in the neighbourhood of the Andamans, a stormy current was setting in from the southwest. This had been felt at Port Blair as early as on the 27 September. The storm steadily increased, veering to the south, south-eastern and south-eastern on the 29 and 30 of the same month, and resuming its previous direction on the 1 October, in squalls accompanied by heavy rain.

One hundred fifty miles to the westward, the place experienced dark, rainy, squally weather, and west to west southwest winds with a low Barometer and with a heavy swell from the south to south-western. This lasted till midnight, the ship's course being west and northwest, when the wind turned milder and constant from the northwest but was unaccompanied by any rise in the barometer. On the second day, the ship's course being the same, the wind continued to stay light and unsteady from the same quarter; the sky presented an overcast visage though it did not rain, and the barometer kept sliding down gradually.

To the north and north–northeast, in the afternoon, the sky looked very black and low, and a high-rolling sea came down from that quarter, its waves rising very sharply. By midnight, the winds began increasing gradually from the west; the sky to north–northeast was still gloomy and the sea still very heavy from the same quarter. From the above, it was evident that the cyclonic vortex had formed by the noon of 2 October, and based on the observations of the *Moneka* and Port Blair, it seemed to have originated on the morning of that day.

---

[12] Ibid.

On 3 October, a great transition had taken place in the meteorology of Bengal and the northern part of the Bay. The northerly current hitherto felt only in eastern Bengal now prevailed over nearly the whole of the above area and extended far down the western part of the Bay. From 3 October, Blanford, with some confidence, traced the progress of the storm advancing at an average rate of 10 miles an hour towards the mouth of the Hooghly.[13] Thus, it was on 5 October that the cyclone, which had already originated somewhere around the Andaman Islands, advanced towards the northwest and struck the coastal areas of Balasore and Medinipur. In Medinipur, Tamluk had to endure the climatic impact of the cyclone, but the experience of the people in the south-eastern part of Kanthi subdivision was no less bitter. The Eden Gardens turned into a wilderness. In Tank Square, the trees and shrubs were blown away and, in several parts, the iron railings got torn up and overthrown. In Garden Reach, the roads got blocked and were rendered impassable owing to the trees that had fallen across them. The splendid avenue of trees in the compound of the school opposite St. James' Church, some of which must have been 4–5 ft in circumference, was entirely destroyed, the trees being snapped off above the level of the wall that had protected them but which now no longer stood there. The damage done to buildings was considerable. Among these, we notice that the roof of the Free School was blown away, the upper part of the Roman Catholic Church at the upper end of the Bow Bazaar road was entirely destroyed and the steeple of the Free Church of Scotland had caved in.

Even the minarets of the mosque in Dharmatala were all blown away. St. James' Theatre was unroofed and nearly destroyed, the roof of the Cathedral was heavily damaged, the sheds of the East India Railway Company had caved in, and Messrs. Thacker, Spink & Co.'s premises underwent serious damage. In fact, scarcely a *pucca* house in Kolkata escaped without injury, while the native huts, especially in the suburbs, were almost all blown down. The telegraph lines lay interrupted in all directions. All these losses seem sufficiently vexatious and lamentable.

Relief and Rehabilitation

In his memoir titled *Romanthan*, Mr Prasanta Pramanik, an illustrious denizen of Kanthi, alludes to the 'Bengal Administration Report of 1864–65' prepared by the then Superintendent of Kaukhali Light House.

---

[13] Ibid., 7–11.

A part of the report quoted in the book lends a picture of the fateful day of 5 October. It was the local officers who took measures at once, so far as lay in their power, to alleviate the distress caused by the gale. As soon as reliable information was obtained by the Magistrate of the 24 Parganas of the state of the southern portion of his district, he lost no time in sending out food for the starving population, providing for the burial of the dead and the removal of the carcasses of animals and other substances likely to cause injury to public health. He at once obtained an advance of ₹5,000 from the government and ordered copious supplies of rice to be discharged down to Diamond Harbour, Euttehpore, Atcheepore and Dabeepore, irrespective of the proceedings of the Relief Committee.

Overall, 11,864 persons were reported to have been relieved by these means in his district. Steps were at the same time taken for the clearance of tanks and drains and for the baling out of tanks filled with salt water. On these measures being reported to the government, the lieutenant governor directed that they should be persevered in until the entire portion of the area affected by the hurricane was cleared and the people were furnished with means of subsistence for themselves. Orders were also given for the set-up of a systematic plan for the regular supply of food and water to the distressed villages, and it was suggested that if the deficiency of good water should be found likely to be permanent, a scheme should be organized, if possible, for digging good freshwater tanks, with a view to overcoming the problem of want of water and for providing employment to the people. The Lieutenant Governor also authorized the employment of such extra police as might be required for the maintenance of order and protection of property and for executing relief measures expediently.

Similar steps were also adopted by the local officers of Midnapore and Howrah for the relief of distress in their respective districts. The Lieutenant Governor further directed that measures should be taken for immediately employing the whole of the population, which might be in want of work and food, in repairing the embankments in the 21 Parganas, Hidgelee and Midnapore on ordinary wages, but without adhering, at the commencement, to the strict exaction of work to be done for the day's wages. He also directed that all people asking for work should be employed in this manner, without making any exception for women and children.

In the marine department too, active measures were taken from the very day of the storm to save life and property and to mitigate the effects of the disaster. On the evening of 5 October, as soon as the abatement of the gale rendered communication possible, the Celerity and Koladyne were held in readiness and started on the following morning, one to render aid to distressed vessels and the other in search of Sir William Peel with her flats, having on board the 12th Native Infantry proceeding to Bhutan.

The Cyclone of 1867

The cyclone of November 1867 was a major tropical cyclone in Bengal that swept over the swampy Sundarbans and its adjacent areas, annihilated Port Canning and proved Piddington's prophecy to be true. It proved to be a vicious tropical cyclone, popularly known as the cyclone of 1867, and hit Kolkata on the evening of 1 November and Canning on the following morning, on 2 November. It damaged huts and livestock and killed several lives inland. The study of the storm of 1867 demonstrates the prospects of human settlers of the fragile environment of deltaic lower Bengal and, in turn, reveals how catastrophes prevented societal development and economic growth therein.

This discourse, to be more specific, shall seek to unveil how the fragile environment of the deltaic lower Bengal imposed a barrier to its economic growth and collective development. The geo-morphological settings and fragile environment of the region also heightened its vulnerability to climatic onslaughts of a catastrophic nature. Iftekhar Iqbal, in his pioneering work *The Bengal Delta*,[14] explains the role played by calamities in creating hindrance for economic growth and social development in this delta. Ranjan Chakrabarti, another leading scholar arguing on the same lines, explicated that there was no steady settlement in the region. The settlers often moved elsewhere, abandoning everything there, while calamities befell these parts and damaged their livelihoods. There are innumerable evidences of incidents like floods and storm surges destroying several villages and compelling the inhabitants to move to other places. Every year, the rivers of the Bengal, specifically those in the lower deltas, flooded the adjoining villages during monsoon. River bank erosion due to storm surge was one of the chief reasons that led to the desertification of villages and caused salty water to inundate arable lands and wipe out fecundity.

Literally, the deltaic Bengal is denoted as an extensive tract of cultivated and forest-covered realm, composed of alluvial and transported

---

[14] Iftekhar Iqbal, *The Bengal Delta: Ecology, State and Social Change, 1840–1943* (London: Palgrave, 2010).

silt brought down by the Ganges and Brahmaputra rivers and their tributaries. The water sweepings of two basins almost cover a total area of 432,480 mi^2. The delta is intersected from north to south by several broad rivers and numerous creeks running into one another and proliferating the region with saltwater, especially in the areas near the sea. This tract of land, in form resembling the Greek letter Delta, occupies approximately 28,080 mi^2 of superficial area, which is double the area of the delta of the Nile, measuring from west to east, or from the right bank of the Hooghly River opposite to the Sagar tripod on the southwest point of Sagar Island to Chittagong (presently in Bangladesh). This delta is also referred to as the Gangetic delta or the Ganges–Brahmaputra delta. It is 270 miles in width, presenting to the Bay of Bengal a series of low, flat mud banks, covered at high water and dry at low water. A few miles further from the low water lie the mangrove swamps sprawled everywhere. Inland trees appear a little further to that, and finally, cultivation makes its presence felt, the nearest cultivation in the central portion of the delta being 47 miles from sea. In the sea front of the delta, there are nine principal openings having a head stream, that is, having water flowing direct from the Ganges or from the Meghna or the Brahmaputra. Beside these large rivers, there are numerous openings having no head stream, being mere salt water tidal estuaries. These openings or headless rivers are of the deepest kinds as no silt or deposit is poured into them from the higher lands.[15] This delta has a large coastline and vast stretches of coastal wetlands, estuaries, bays, backwater, lagoons and mangrove swamps. This is the country of the Sundarbans, a tidal wetland, the largest mangrove forest and the only mangrove tiger land in the world.[16] The Sundarbans forms the lower part of the Ganges delta, and it is intersected from north to south by estuaries of the river. This delta is a unique natural zone and boasts of a unique history. The geologists have labelled it as a complex sedimentary system comprising a multitude of depositional environments. The entire delta can sometimes change location through large-scale avulsions to build separate sub-delta complexes.

Once upon a time, the Gangetic delta was covered almost entirely by the Sundarbans. A large portion of this delta was uninhabited or sparsely populated. In the medieval texts, the entire region stretching from the eastern shores of the Hooghly River in the west to Chittagong

---

[15] *The Calcutta Review* (March 1859, Vol. 32): 1–2.
[16] Chakrabarti, 'Local People and the Global Tiger', 75–76.

in the east has been referred to as *Bhati*.[17] In other words, it has been defined as a tract of the tidal country. Forest clearance was incepted by the colonial government. In the late-19th century, the Sundarbans area was demarcated by the Dampier-Hodges line. It is an imaginary line named after the surveyors who had surveyed the region.

It is believed that at one time, the Sundarbans was far more extensively inhabited and cultivated than at present, and this might have been possibly due to the shifting of the mainstream of the Ganges from Bhagirathi to Padma. Thus, the decline in the supply of freshwater from the north might have rendered the tract less fit for human habitation. Another plausible reason of depopulation of this tract may be considered in the predatory incursions of Magh pirates and Portuguese buccaneers in the early part of the 18th century.

Some erratic descriptions of this cyclone are found in several colonial records and elsewhere, there being no systematic study of natural calamities at the time, although some observatories had already been established by meteorologists. Meteorologists like Blanford conducted systematic observations of the climate. They endorsed the establishment of observatories in the region. One such observatory was established at Sagar Island, on the mouth of the Ganges River. A cyclone is not an unknown thing to the settlers of deltaic Bengal. Every year, these cataclysmic storms hit inlands and cause heavy damage. The most notable storms in our recorded history are the 1737 cyclone, the 1864 cyclone, the 1867 cyclone and, most recently, the Aila 2009. The cyclone of November 1867 was not as violent as the likes of 1737 and 1864. It was moderate in character, yet we shall bring it over to the discussion table because of the impact it created. This storm not only wreaked havoc on Port Canning but also eliminated any possibility of future development and economic growth in the region. The destruction of Port Canning led to huge financial losses that the colonial government could never make up for. The cyclone of 1867 serves as an interesting lesson to scholars, exposing how intensely the people of the lowland deltas were vulnerable to nature. They could understand the consequence of the tropical cyclones on these deltaic islands of the Sundarbans. Several scientists and meteorologists observed why tropical cyclones often turn more severe as they sweep over the lowland Gangetic delta. Henry Piddington was the earliest one who studied and also observed the tropical cyclones on the Indian Ocean from close quarters. The lowland Gangetic delta lies to the east and southeast of Kolkata (previously Calcutta).

---

[17] Ibid.

Impact of the Cyclone of 1867

As far as the recorded history is concerned, the cyclone of October 1864 is considered the most violent of its kind due to the incalculable loss of life and property it caused. In 3 years' time, the storm made a return, in November 1867, and even though the force of the wind was no less violent, there was no storm wave in the Hooghly River. Consequently, the magnitude of damage inflicted was much less in Kolkata. The intensity of the cyclone of November 1867 was moderate, yet it registered an immense loss in the countryside. Unfortunately, the loss was not measured accurately at that time. Erratic descriptions of the cyclone were penned by contemporary authors like W. W. Hunter, C. E. Buckland and L. S. S. O'Malley among others. It is noteworthy that the cyclone of 1867 did precisely what Piddington had predicted earlier. In 1853, Piddington was concerned about the vulnerability of a new port that was proposed for the Matla River as a viable alternative for Port Kolkata. He presaged the dangers relating to Port Canning on the bank of the Matla River, explaining how storm surges could inundate it. However, his advice was ignored, and Port Canning was built on the Matla. On the morning of 2 November 1867 (9 years after Piddington's death), a cyclone produced a storm surge that did just what Piddington had predicted, passing 'over the town with fearful violence'. At the same time, and ironically so, a storm surge in the Hooghly River did no damage to the Port of Kolkata. Five years later, Port Canning was abandoned. Amitav Ghosh sketches a fine description of the cyclone and the destruction of Port Canning in his celebrated novel *The Hungry Tide*.

In 1864–1866, it had been proposed that Port Canning be built on Matla River as a subsidiary port to Kolkata. Subsequently, a railway line of 28 miles was constructed to connect the two points between Kolkata and Port Canning. Such a measure was deemed indispensable due to the surging traffic in Hooghly River for the growing mercantile in Kolkata. Besides, the necessity of providing for safe storage of the imports of kerosene and mineral oils was also being strongly felt, something that led to the reconsideration of the Matla project. It was also proposed that a ship canal should take off from that river and debouch into the Hooghly near the Kidderpur dockyard, within the limits of the Port of Kolkata. Thus, an alternative waterway would be supplied for the commercial benefit of the capital. Kolkata would no longer be dependent on the shifting channels of the Hooghly, and Port Canning would afford a place of storage for mineral oils whose increasing import had become a source of threat to the crowded shipping in the Kolkata Port, notwithstanding the precautions adopted to safeguard against explosive materials. The expense of the proposed scheme was estimated to run into a massive figure.[18]

Indications of the approaching disturbance were observed early on 1 November. Shortly after dark, the weather turned threatening, and the gale gradually began to gain strength until it attained its maximum force in Kolkata between the hours of 1:30 and 3:30 AM. Rain fell in torrents, inundating the city entirely, and hostile winds tore away the doors and windows of domestic and commercial buildings. The effects of the storm were most disastrous in Port Canning, where the gale was accompanied by a storm wave 5 ft high, the water of which passed over the town with fearful violence. The station house, goods sheds and the railway hotel were all blown off, and the Port Canning Company's store hulk, *Hashemy,* was carried a great distance away from the railway jetty. The freshwater tanks were salted by the storm wave. At Canning, the total number of casualties reported was 90. About 500 heads of cattle were destroyed.[19] The calamity in some other portions of 24 Parganas (then undivided) was equally severe. The storm traversed the entire countryside, stretching nearly due east from Kolkata to Bashirhat on the Ichamati river. Along this line, innumerable villages were blown away, and the resulting destruction was accompanied by heavy loss of life. The more populous places to suffer severely included names like Baruipur, Diamond Harbour, Atharabanka, Basirhat, Gobardanga and Satkhira (in Bangladesh). The storm was severely felt in Jessore and Nadia, and as far as in Dacca and Backergunge.[20]

It was reported in the *Press* and in the *Arghus* that

a storm-wave, reaching up to five and a half feet in height, passed over Port Canning. The larger part of the ballast of the rail was carried away as far as Bursa, which was three miles away. The station and goods' shed were blown down. Only the front cylinders of the railway jetty were left standing. Two wooden jetties were gone. The sea had broken into the dock through the neglected part of the embankment of the Bydiadurree. Mr. and Mrs. Hamilton and their grown-up son were buried in the ruins of the station, and it was considered impossible to

[18] W. W. Hunter, *The Imperial Gazetteer of India*, vol. III, 2nd ed. (London Trubner & Company, 1885), 261–262.

[19] C. E. Buckland, *Bengal Under the Lieutenant-Governors; Being A Narrative of the Principal Events and Public Measures During Their Periods of Office, from 1854 to 1898*, Vol. 1 (Calcutta: K. Bose, 1901), 407.

[20] Ibid.

look for their remains at the time due to paucity of labour force. Five natives were reportedly killed in the station, but no other European was known to have been killed by the time of publication of the report. Two Chinamen and one mistry were washed away, and it was believed that a number of other people had drowned without a trace. Every native hut was destroyed, and the people were starving for want of rice and water. People in huge numbers were leaving for Kolkata, and several from the out-stations were flocking into Canning. The Port Canning Company had ordered 200 maunds of rice to be sent to the sufferers, but want of water is what the natives were at present suffering from more particularly.[21]

One major consequence of the storm wave was the salting of all of the freshwater tanks. However, it was from the river that the worst news was received; there, the destruction of life and property was the most disastrous. The whole length of the Kolkata shore, down to the India General Steam Navigation Company's yards, was strewn with wrecks of country boats and cargo boats, and the loss of life from these vessels was enormous.[22]

The cyclone that swept over Kolkata on 1 November 1867 was only marginally less violent and less destructive than that of 5 October 1864. Fortunately, there was no storm wave here on this occasion. The vortex seems to have formed in the north of the bay, and while passing over eastward of Kolkata, the particular force of the wind operated from the north and the northwest. The consequences were, therefore, not as disastrous as they were during the 1864 cyclone, but the force of the wind was such that destruction in the city and the suburbs, due entirely to this fact, was greater than it was on the last occasion. The shipping had sustained considerable damage, but the wind blowing from the northwest at its greatest fury only drove many of the vessels onshore instead of making them drift along or across the river in dangerous confusion, and the flood-tide coming in just then seems to have saved them.[23]

The cyclone had its origin apparently at some point in the northwest portion of Bay of Bengal and the centre of it was ascertained to have passed through east of Sagar Island, from the mouth of the Matla over

---

[21] *Press, Disastrous Cyclone at Calcutta*, XII, issue 1612, 8 January 1868, p. 2, http://paperspast.natlib.govt.nz/cgi-bin/paperspast?a=d&d=CHP18680108.2.18
[22] Ibid.
[23] *The Argus, Melbourne, Vic. 1848–1957*, Wednesday, 18 December 1867, http://trove.nla.gov.au/newspaper/article/5786140

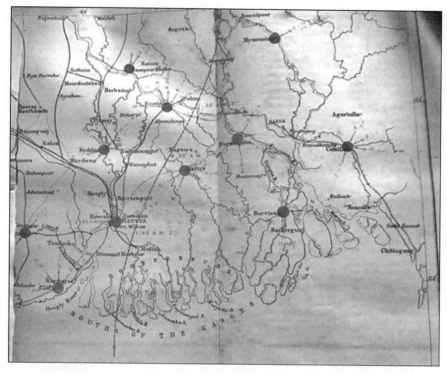

Track of the Cyclone Across the Delta of the Ganges in 1867

Source: West Bengal State Archive, *General Proceedings of the Lieutenant Governor of Bengal* (Calcutta, 1868) vol. 122, October, Kolkata.
Note: The track of the cyclone is marked by circles and dashed line.
Disclaimer: The figure is for representation purpose only.

Port Canning and Bashirhat and thence in a north–northeast direction to the east of Kumrakhali and the west of Sirajganj in Bangladesh.

The cyclone seems to have passed right over the mouth of the river in the northeastern direction and then moved off due east, as a consequence of which Port Canning suffered severely. A storm wave amplified the destruction there further, and the works, thereby, of both the railway and the Port Canning Companies underwent extensive damage. The entire countryside lying between the Hooghly and the Matla rivers, the Sundarbans and the south-eastern portions of the latter suffered gravely. Crops had been destroyed to an incalculable degree, villages got levelled to the ground and the cataclysmic storm, inarguably, occasioned a great loss of life. The effects of the storm seem to have been felt till as far as Kolkata and the suburban regions of Dacca, Jessore and Chittagong. In Kolkata, it became evident that the distress was considerable. The number of lives lost in the city and suburbs was 1,016, and the number of houses and huts ravaged stood at a little more than 29,000.

Aila in 2009

Natural disasters like earthquakes, droughts and cyclones have held their reputation of being the uncontrollable problems of mankind in the world. The damage to property, loss of life and devastation of flora and fauna by natural hazards are also significant problems of several countries. The increase in the number of storms or natural disasters is due to the phenomenon of global warming. Several types of storms like tropical cyclones, thunderstorms, hurricanes and tornados are causing unparalleled devastation of the environment. The issue of climatic change has now turned into a burning problem for the whole world. Scarcity of water, increased frequency of floods, growing temperature and occurrences of cyclones are the major issues in today's world. Cyclones' frequency has increased all over the world due to rapid change in the global climate. The intensity of the tropical cyclone, however, is variable over the world.

In 2009, the severe Aila washed away the dwellings of thousands of people. It robbed them of whatever little stock of food they had, leaving them eventually without even drinking water. Desperate people were compelled to travel for miles in search of drinking water. The beautiful islands of the 'Sundarbans' had turned into a 'torture zone' by the climatic disaster within a few hours. Every living being—man, animal and plant—succumbed or remained helpless in the face of nature's vengeance. They could not figure out how to survive against the menace of this great and calamitous cyclone. This is not a one-off incident but the real picture of the natural calamities of cyclones, droughts and floods all over the world.

On 22 May 2009, the monsoon current advanced towards the southeastern part of the Bay of Bengal. The period of summer monsoon's onset was almost over in India. NASA issued a warning about Cyclone Aila and cautioned against the probable, and alarming, consequences. The name of storm, 'Aila', was designated by the Indian Meteorological Department. The low pressure intensified into a depression after about 30h, and the Indian Meteorological Department (IMD) fixed its location at 16.5°N and 88°E at 0600 UTC of 23 May 2009. Thereafter, the IMD and experts, after observations of Doppler Radar at Kolkata, acquired the intensity of a deep depression at 0300 UTC of 24 May, a cyclone storm at 1200 UTC of 24 May and a severe cyclonic storm at 0600 UTC of 25 May which crossed the coast near Diamond Harbour. The system was named Aila.[24] The storm moved northwards, which is climatologically over the same region in south-eastern Bay of Bengal. The special feature of the cyclonic storm of Aila sent strong winds and rain over the whole of southern West Bengal, about 80 km inland from the coastal area.

The storm surge associated with the cyclone was about 2 m over the Sundarbans and about 3 m over the adjoining Bangladesh. The astronomical tide of landfall was between 4 and 5 m. The storm surge led to a total sea level elevation exceeding 6 m and was the prime cause of the loss of human lives in both India and Bangladesh.[25] The telling impact of Aila, the storm and the rainfall, was felt over the whole of West Bengal, Odisha, Sikkim and Nepal.

The distribution of wind pressure of Aila on 25 May was 120–140 km/h on the world's largest delta, the Sundarbans. On the morning of the day Aila struck, clouds had obscured the entire sky, and the fulcrum of the storm lay about 300 km south of the city over the Bay of Bengal. The storm struck at mid-day, accompanied with heavy rain and wind at 60–90 km/h, in a rampaging manner. The impact of the storm was narrowing down at the Sundarbans and Sagar Island, which was 150 km from the city of Kolkata, with a diameter of 350 km. The Kolkata Meteorological Centre, Alipore Director G. C. Debnath declared that: 'Aila made its landfall near Sagar Island around 2pm, with a wind speed of 120 km ph.'[26] At about 4 PM Aila was moving towards the northerly direction, and it ferociously hit the whole southern coastal Bengal including regions of north and south 24 Parganas, Midnapore, Hooghly, Howrah and Kolkata. After the first day (Monday), the director of the regional meteorological centre at Alipore, G. C. Debnath, said that: 'the cyclone is beyond danger now, it is on the wane and moving in a northern direction'.[27] The cyclone came as close as 15 km to the city of Kolkata. However, it could not hit the city with full strength and only had a peripheral impact. It never could match the speed of

---

[24] B. K. Basu and K. Bhagyalakshmi, *Forecast of the Track and Intensity of the Tropical Cyclone AILA Over the Bay of Bengal by the Global Spectral Atmospheric Model Varsha,* Current Science, Vol. 99, No. 6, 25 September 2010 (Bangalore: Flosolver Unite CSIR, National Aerospace Laboratories, 2010), 765.

[25] Ibid, 766.

[26] *Telegraph*, Calcutta, 26 May 2009, https://m.telegraphindia.com/states/west-bengal/cyclone-aila-to-bring-heavy-rain/cid/1265193

[27] Ibid.

wind greater than 120 km/h and the diameter of 250–350 km that it had acquired when it ran through the Sundarbans and Sagar Island in the coast of south Bengal.

The great cyclone, Aila, devastated the whole coastal region of southern Bengal. Nearly 100 people lost their lives and 500,000 houses got demolished in southern Bengal. The Indian Red Cross Society responded with relief measures as early as possible by arranging for drinking water and foods and other materials.[28] The damage impact assessment was carried out by government of West Bengal and United Nation Development Programme (UNDP). Aila damaged life and property in copious numbers, but it also registered long-term detrimental effects on the flora and fauna of the coastal region of south Bengal. People were reminded of the great Kolkata Cyclone of 1864 in which 60,000 people had perished and which had almost obliterated the entire southern Bengal.

The Sundarbans National Park and the forest-dwelling people of the Sundarbans were worse affected by Cyclone Aila. Countless trees were uprooted in the whole southern Bengal region, and nearly 2,000 in Kolkata city only. One lakh people were affected by Aila in southern Bengal. The public transport system collapsed, and several flights got suspended for five hours at the Netaji Subhash Chandra Bose International Airport in Kolkata. In the coastal regions, villagers and fishermen are meant to receive prior notice under early warning system from the government. However, it was at the coastal villages that the greatest number of people suffered and the damage to property and agricultural production was most extensive. The cyclone of October 1864 had caused incalculable damage in the southern region of the district of 24 Parganas. A stormy wave 11 ft high rushed over the Diamond Harbour subdivision and affected a huge loss of life measuring up to nearly 12,000 people. The floods in 1900 caused widespread damage to the rice crops, especially in the ill-drained area between Kolkata and Diamond Harbour.[29] However, the magnitude of Aila's devastation surpassed all previous records in the history of cyclones in India.

Cyclone Reaches Odisha

India is surrounded by oceans from three sides. It is dreadfully prone to cyclones. Thus, cyclones have an impact on the whole of India, even though the east coast is slightly more exposed to cyclonic interventions

---

[28] Information Bulletin, International Federation of Red Cross and Red Crescent Societies, 29 May 2009.

[29] *Imperial Gazetteer of India*, Vol. i, Bengal, (Delhi: Usha,1984), 356.

than the west coast. Moreover, the humans and non-human organisms living in the coastal areas collectively shoulder the extra risk of meteorological and seismic hazards originating from the seas. Tropical cyclones represent the most influential and vicious of all oceanic perils. Odisha is located on the eastern coast of India. The state has a 480 km–long coastline, with a considerably high population mass in the coastal areas. This is a place highly vulnerable to cyclones. From early times, Odisha has had a long history of cyclones. It is mostly during October–November that cyclones hit Odisha. Hathigumpha inscriptions have documented the cyclone that devastated Kalinganagari and inform about the city's subsequent repair by Kharavela. Throughout the 19th century, cyclones lashed Odisha on several occasions. The major cyclones to hit Odisha before Independence were those on the dates 22 September 1885, 31 October 1931 and 16 October 1942. After Independence, the deadliest cyclones to have hit Odisha arrived on 29 October 1971, 25 October 1999 and 12 October 2013. This area is extremely well developed due to the prolific soil of the coastal area, well-developed irrigation and healthy communication system. It is socio-economically and culturally very well off too. However, cyclonic disorder keeps creating plenty of problems, and the state suffers economic turmoil on a frequent basis.

On 29 October 1971, the 1971 Cyclone hit Odisha at midnight. Its speed rose up to 175 km/h, and it plundered on over 8,214 mi^2 across Cuttack, Balasore, Puri, Mayurbhanj, Keonjhar and Dhenkanal. The wind had destroyed crops, paddy fields and human and non-human individuals. Approximately 10,000 people died in the cyclone. Cuttack was the worst sufferer as 520,438 houses got ruined and 33.04 lakh people suffered from this cyclone alone. 6,065 km^2 of cultivated area was affected. High tidal waves and the devastating gale heavily damaged coastal Odisha within minutes.[30]

Super cyclone wind speed usually exceeds 200 km per hour while encountering the core area. The 1999 Orissa Super Cyclone formulated in the Bay of Bengal near Andaman–Nicobar Islands on 25 October and finally arrived at Paradeep on 29 October in the morning. The speed of the wind was approximately 300 km/h.[31] From 29 October to 1 November, cataclysmic winds kept lashing the entire coastal

---

[30] Kishor C. Samal, 'Facing Sudden Impact (Experience of Orissa Super Cyclone of 1999)', *Man & Development*, March 2006, admin.indiaenvironmentportal.org.in/files/Orissa%20super%20cyclone.pdf

[31] K. K. Khatua and R. N. Dash, *Management of Super Cyclone and Flood in Orissa*, www.indiaenvironmentportal.org.in/.../management%20of%20super%20cylone%20i

area of Odisha. The constant rainfall and depression at the Bay of Bengal made the situation dreadful. Jagatsinghpur, Balasore, Bhadrak, Kendrapada, Puri and Ganjam districts were severely affected from this tropical cyclone.

Due to the tremendous rains, 1.89 crore people were affected and 10,000 people lost their lives. The loss of 4.45 lakh cattle and 75 per cent trees took a heavy toll on the flora and fauna of the region.[32] Cyclonic winds completely disrupted linkage of cable connection, broadcast towers, poles, lines, supply of electricity, supply of water, etc. The super cyclone destroyed roads, bridges, official and non-official build-ings, schools, colleges and almost every edifice that stood in its way. It goes without saying that the super cyclone caused colossal health hazards. The list of casualties bore testimony to the merciless nature of the October 1999 cyclone. Erasama block of Jagatsinghpur district cre-ated a path-breaking record when it came to death tolls. Several people were grievously injured, crushed or wounded under the falling trees and the crumbling buildings. The local people were traumatized and were given treatment by experts from the psychological and mental nervousness fields.

The state government tried to revive the socio-economic condition of the suffering people. The government announced a Disaster Management Policy that was aimed at mitigating the agony of the locals. Odisha's chief minister formulated a State Level Natural Calamity Committee, a Village Level Task Force Committee at district level and block level at Gram Panchayat level. Later on, the Odisha government formed the Odisha State Disaster Management Authority (OSDMA) and also formulated five units of Odisha Disaster Rapid Action Force (ODRAF). The government adopted the National Cyclone Risk Mitigation Project (NCRMP) to con-trol and reduce the risk of tropical cyclones.

The Very Severe Cyclone Storm 'Phailin' originated at the South China Sea and marched towards the low pressure area of Tenasserim coast on 6 October 2013. The wind moved on towards Andaman Sea on 7 October and then strengthened into a deep depression on the morning of 9 October. It struck the coast of Odisha on 12 October 2013, accompanied with a gale of very high speed and heavy rains. Cyclone Phailin lashed the coast of Odisha near Gopalpur in Ganjam district, affecting about 13.2 million people in 171 blocks across 18 districts of state. The wind's velocity climbed up to 220 km/hr, and it brought

barna Mishra and Dipika Kar, *Cyclonic Hazards in Odisha and Its* lisha.gov.in/e-magazine/Orissareview/2016/Jan/engpdf/38-42.pdf heavy rainfall that caused substantial demolition in the districts of Ganjam, Puri, Khurdha and the Chilika Lake. Forty-four people died, 256,633 homes got destroyed and 13 million lives got affected on the whole. About 1,292,967 hectares of land space involving agriculture, horticulture, domestic animals, trees, and fishing villages suffered grievously due to heavy rain and flood. In particular, the *kutcha* and semi-*pucca* houses bore the brunt of high-speed winds and associated rainfall. Communication link, telecommunication, power supply and water supply were entirely dislocated due to this natural disaster. Due to incessant and heavy rains, the Baitarani, Budhabalanga, Rusikulya, Subarnarekha and Jalaka rivers overflowed and affected Mayurbhanj, Balasore, Bhadrak, Keonjhar, Jajpur and Ganjam districts enormously.[33]

Cyclone or disaster is a natural phenomenon, and even though we cannot alter its route, through awareness, proper mitigation strategy and proper disaster management policy, we can certainly tame down the vulnerability of the situation and the impact of the storm. The government of Odisha, therefore, took steps to control and reduce the number of deaths and loss to property. The path, intensity and magnitude of the cyclone were constantly tracked by the OSDMA. More than 500 buildings were identified for shelter and people were displaced from the high alert zone. Flood Shelter Management and Maintenance committees were to work appropriately. The government of Odisha cancelled the *Dussehra* holiday. Many non-governmental organizations (NGOs) leapt into action to carry out rescue operations. The management of Phailin serves as evidence to mankind that the impact of a natural hazard can be checked and the damage can be controlled if the right steps are taken at the proper time and in the most fitting way.[34]

Cyclone Hits Andhra Pradesh

The coastline enjoys roughly 1,000 km of Andhra Pradesh. Studies by National Climatic Data Center (NCDC) of the 1996 storm trajectory reveal that the coast of Andhra Pradesh is the most cyclone-prone region in India.[35] Every year, on several occasions, the coastal region

---

[33] *INDIA Cyclone* Phailin *in Odisha October 2013: Rapid Damage* and *Needs Assessment Report,* December 2013, ncrmp.gov.in/wp-content/uploads/2014/03/Odisha-Phailin-report-Final.pdf

[34] Ibid.

[35] Greg O'Hare, 'Hurricane 07B in the Godavari Delta, Andhra Pradesh, India: Vulnerability, Mitigation and the Spatial Impact', *The Geographical Journal* 167, no. 1 (March, 2001): 26.

of Andhra Pradesh is affected by natural hazards like floods or storms. In the 100 years between 1877 and 1976, the coast of Andhra Pradesh withstood assaults from 39 severe storms, mostly during the autumn and winter months of October–December.

After the rainy season ended in South India during November 1977, a tropical cyclone took birth on the southern coast of Andhra Pradesh. The wind pressure nosedived in the southwest bay on 13 November 1977 and moved westward, heralding a cyclonic storm on 15 November in the south central Bay of Bengal. On 16 November, it moved south-west and took a curve in the south-western direction. It was between 17 November morning and 18 November that it gradually moved eastward, and it hit the coastline of Andhra Pradesh on 19 November. Then, on 20 November, it crossed Andhra Pradesh.[36] The cyclone caused heavy rain and wind and boasted of a diameter ranging beyond 60 km. The storm moved with a speed of 11 knots from the south to the southeast on the affected region.

The heaviest devastation from the cyclone occurred on 19 November 1977. The intensity of the storm had magnified, and the wind speed hovered between 225 and 250 km/h. The 1,000 km dimension hurricane crashed on southern Andhra Pradesh, mainly in the Machilipatnam region, killing over 10,000 people.[37] Rain at landfall point stretched for about 30 mi from the northern distributaries of Krishna River. The storm was equally strong at Palkayatippa, coast of Sorlagondi and Hamsaladevi in the northern distributaries region.[38] The seawater also spread out with the storm over the coastal region in Andhra Pradesh. Everything got swept away due to the massive wind pressure and rains in the coastal belt.

The torrentially stormy winds hit the coastal region of Andhra Pradesh, wiping off, almost completely, the 60 villages that sat there. The inhabitants, who were mostly fishermen and farmers, were severely affected by this great cyclone. The most heavily affected region was Krishna district in Andhra Pradesh. It was a nightmarish experience for people as the storm surge occurred, along with a tidal wave, on the night of 19 November 1977. About 8,000 died in Krishna District and 2,000 others elsewhere in the state. However, the effects of this cyclone

---

[36] I. Subbaramayya, R. Ramanadham, and N. Subba Rao, 'The November of 1977 Andhra Pradesh Cyclone and the Associated Storm Surge', 45A, no. 4. Indian National Science Academy (15 January 1979), 294.

[37] O'Hare, 'Hurricane 07B in the Godavari Delta, Andhra Pradesh, India', 27.

[38] Subbaramayya, Ramanadham, and Subba Rao, 'The November of 1977 Andhra Pradesh Cyclone', 300.

were hardly the most destructive on records in South Asia (the 1970 East Bengal cyclone killed about 500,000).[39] Overall, Andhra Pradesh's nine coastal districts, with a cumulative area of 92,906 km, were the ones most affected by the tropical cyclone. The agricultural lands and small industries were highly affected, especially those situated in the coastal areas. Agriculture suffered due to the stormy winds and from floods that spread throughout the area. People lost property and live-stock across the delta.

The Andhra government sent medical help and drinking water after the outbreak of epidemics. People fell prey to cholera and other water-borne diseases. The Members of the Legislative Assembly estimated that nearly 50,000 people had died due to the cyclone at Andhra Pradesh.[40] The government delayed reaching the affected areas with food and drinking water. The cyclone affected an air force station at Suryalanka, a small town near Bapatla. The state government did not arrange for any credible relief measures and evacuated poor people and fishermen from the coastal belt.[41] Those people had barely escaped the wrath of the cyclone, but till November, no government aid had been sent for the distressed people stationed at Kodur, Jayapuram and Challapalli. A few local mill owners distributed some rice to the villagers. People lived in abysmal situations due to insufficient food or drinking water. The relief materials were not appropriately disbursed in the cyclone-affected areas.

The growth in population and increased wealth of industrial goods has affected the environment of coastal region in India. In Andhra Pradesh, an increasing number of people have continuously inhabited the coastal area. Massive destruction of forest is carried out every day on the costal belt of almost every region in India. Rapid economic establishment too polluted the environment in numerous ways. Interestingly, and perhaps fittingly, the cyclones of 1977 and 1990 hit the same areas and with the same intensity.

Hudhud hit Visakhapatnam on 12 October 2014. Cyclone Hudhud was one of the first episodes in current history wherein a cyclone of such strength had landed on an urban city. A severe cyclonic storm originated somewhere over the Tenasserim coast and North Andaman Sea on the

---

[39] Stephen P. Cohen and C. V. Raghavula Paul, *The Andrah Cyclone of 1977: Individual and Institutional Responses to Mass Death* (New Delhi, 1980, review by Greenough), *The Journal of Asiatic Studies* 40, no. 4 (August, 1981): 815–816.

[40] C. Venkata Krishna, 'Politics of Cyclone Relief', *Economic and Political Weekly* 12, no. 49 (3 December 1977): 2002.

[41] Ibid.

morning of 6 October 2014; on 7 October, the storm blew over North Andaman Sea in the morning. Then, it shifted towards the northwestern direction on the morning of 8 October. Subsequently, it emerged out into the Bay of Bengal. It intensified into a severe cyclonic storm on the morning of 9 October and turned into a very severe cyclonic storm on the afternoon of 10 October. It continued to gain strength as it moved towards the northwest and reached Andhra Pradesh coast in the early morning of 12 October with a 180 km/h speed. Then, heavy rainfall lashed north Andhra Pradesh and the adjoining districts of the south Odisha coast. Floods occurred at several places in the state. Hudhud seemed relentless, and it affected Visakhapatnam very badly.[42]

The Cyclone Hudhud caused widespread destruction in the affected districts where a heavy number of trees got uprooted, roads and private and official buildings caved in and electricity and telecommunication lines got snapped. About 9.2 million people in over 7,285 villages in four coastal districts were affected, leading to 61 human casualties. The government of Andhra Pradesh had taken some heartening steps after the cyclonic disaster. 222,000 people were vacated immediately from the high alert zone. 310 relief camps and 1,688 medical camps were set up, and about 2.9 million food packets and 6.5 million water packets were distributed in the following days. Local self-governments, the National Disaster Response Force (NDRF), the Indian Army and the Navy put in strong efforts to gain control over the situation. About 112,850 houses had suffered damage in the coastal areas of Vishakhapatnam alone. More than 752,540 domestic animals, agriculture, horticulture, livestock, fisheries and industries had suffered in a major way.[43]

Cyclone Lashes Tamil Nadu

Tamil Nadu has a long history of tropical cyclones. Throughout the year, Tamil Nadu combats a series of cyclonic storms of varying intensity that cause depressions and floods. The coastal areas of Tamil Nadu suffer the maximum number of cyclones, especially the areas of Chengalpattu, Chennai, Pudukkottai, Ramanathapuram, Tirunelveli and Kanyakumari. Pondicherry is also affected by cyclones on a frequent basis.

The cyclonic storm Fanoos, 2005, had formed over the Bay of Bengal between 5 December and 10 December. Instruments at the weather

---

[42] 'Cyclone Hudhud', *Strategies and Lessons for Preparing Better & Strengthening Risk Resilience in Coastal Regions of India*. National Disaster Management Authority, August 2015

[43] Ibid.

department recorded a Central Sea Level Pressure (CSLP) of 984 hPa and high wind speed of 130 knots. The storm had originated over the Gulf of Burma. On 5 December, a low-pressure region was observed over the southeast bay at 0300 UTC, and the low-pressure system slowly shifted towards the northwest on 6 December at 0300 UTC. It gradually moved towards the northwest on 7 December. On 8 December at 0300 UTC, this cyclonic low-pressure system moved towards the southwest and intensified into a severe cyclonic storm. The coastal areas of Tamil Nadu and coastal Andhra Pradesh faced a severe rainfall on 8 December. Several rivers of Tamil Nadu began to overflow and caused floods.[44] Pondicherry and Chennai, Tiruvallur and Kanchipuram, Villupuram, Cuddalore, Tiruvarur, Thanjavur and Nagapattinam districts suffered heavily from the atrocious gale. About 100,000 people had to be shifted from coastal settlements. Fifty-one coastal villages fell under the Red alert zone. Consequently, 15 medical teams worked indefatigably, tending incessantly to the suffering people.

According to the IMD, the Cyclone Nisha, 2008, passed over the southwest of Bay of Bengal, shifted towards the northwest and landed at 0530 IST on 27 November 2008 near Tamil Nadu and Pondicherry coast, and on 28 November, the depression found its way into the interiors of Tamil Nadu. Very heavy rainfall lashed the state during the next 24 hours. More than 800,000 people got affected, and about 100,000 people had to be displaced from Tamil Nadu and Pondicherry due to this natural calamity. Almost 89 people lost their lives in Tamil Nadu. Agriculture and crops were heavily destroyed, and roads and buildings suffered severe damage. Relief camps were formed at several districts and food and cash were being distributed. The Government of India had formed a team to work towards alleviation of sufferings of human beings.

A severe cyclone, Jal, in 2010 originated in the Bay of Bengal between the 4 and 8 November 2010. Its minimum CSLP was 988 hPa and maximum wind speed (MSW) was 60 knots. The low pressure formed at 1200 UTC on 2 November over south Bay of Bengal had turned into a depression over southeast Bay of Bengal by 4 November. It moved in a west–northwest track and intensified into a deep depression over southeast Bay of Bengal on 5 November. After that, it moved towards the west and west–northwest in the form of a severe cyclonic storm and blew over southeast Bay of Bengal on 6 November. The wind shifted

---

[44] S. Ramalingeswara Rao, K. Muni Krishna, and O. S. R. U. Bhanu Kumar, *Study of Tropical Cyclone 'Fanoos' Using MM5 Model—A Case Study* (Vienna: Natural Hazards and Earth System Sciences, 2009).

towards northwest and made a landfall at the Chennai coast on 7 November. More than 70,000 people had to be transferred to secure places, and 54 people died in this incident.[45]

Cyclone Nilam, 2012, was another prominent storm that passed close to Hyderabad between 30 October 2012 and 3 November 2012. A depression had formed over southeast and adjacent Bay of Bengal in the formative stage. It moved westward and strengthened into the cyclonic storm Nilam, which moved towards northwest, blowing 480 km away from Hyderabad on 2 November 2012 and subsequently dissolving over Rayalaseema. Almost 150,000 people had to be relocated from the danger zone and sheltered at secure places.

In Tamil Nadu, a cyclone named Madi took birth on 30 November 2013 with the lowest pressure (mbar) of 986 hPa. It intensified gradually, and on 7 December, it turned into a deep depression. By 8 December, it began rotating in the shape of a very severe cyclonic gale. But the storm diluted later and made a landfall near Vedaranyam, Tamil Nadu as a mere depression. The damage caused due to Madi was mild and manageable.

Conclusion

Cyclone or natural disaster is a natural phenomenon. We certainly cannot alter its course or avoid its occurrence, but awareness, proper mitigation strategy and proper disaster management policy can help check the grim situation somewhat. It must also be remembered that the east coast is more in danger of cyclonic assaults than the west coast, but that should not make the authorities stationed at the west coast any complacent. India has a coastline of 7516.6 km touching 13 states and union territories. It lies between the Eastern Ghats and the Bay of Bengal and expands from the Ganga delta to Kanyakumari. Every year, heavy losses are faced by people in the coastal areas who also suffer huge losses of their livestock. Beaten hard by these natural forces, countless humans and non-human agencies migrate from one place to another. Consequently, human settlements and settled economies have shifted over the decades. Coastal areas of India are highly vulnerable, bearing plenty of risks. Presently, Government of India has taken some crucial steps to keep a leash on the terrible situation.

---

[45] C. V. Srinivas et al., *Real-Time Prediction of a Severe Cyclone 'Jal' over Bay of Bengal Using a High-resolution Mesoscale Model WRF (ARW)*. https://cdac.in/index.aspx?id=pdf_10.1007_s11069-012-0364-5

Climatic Change and Its Impact on Northeast India

Sajal Nag

Introduction

Northeast India is known as nature's gift to India. It is mountainous, is thickly forested, has massive rivers, is nourished by heavy rainfall, has a diverse wildlife and is inhabited by a number of mountain dwellers called tribes who cherished environmentalist ethos. Yet, environmental history in northeast India has yet to take off. The region has been experiencing environmental depletion, which was a result of colonial policies, exploitation of its ecological and mineral resources, large-scale transborder immigration and settlement of people, establishment of plantation industry through deforestation, dependence of dairy industry on grazing and so on. Invisible to public eye, there are signs that would spell doom for the future of the region. The rainfall has seen a decline in Cherrapunji—world's wettest place; there have been regular massive dust storms in Guwahati, massive deforestation in all the states despite the ban by Supreme Court, monsoon seasons have changed, there have been massive floods due to melting of glaciers at the origins of the rivers, spells of drought despite the rains, climatologists predict more drought and desiccation of the region, unseasonal storms in

Manipur, dying of rivers and water bodies and decline of river crops. All these have a massive impact on the crop production of the region affecting the food security. There is an urgency that the historical process that led to the environmental degradation is investigated so that measures could be taken to prevent further devastation of the environment of the region. The chapter details the indications corroborated by the findings of the climatologists and environmentalists to depict the environmental scenario in Northeast India.

In the 21st century, because of global warming, an environmental concern has become the focus of all nations and communities. But 100 years ago, this very relationship between man and nature, now more holistically called 'the environment', was very differently premised. Since the heydays of the industrial revolution and the emergence of capitalism as systemic appropriation of resources for development, the face of the world has changed and continues to do so. The 'blame game' and 'responsibility sharing' that is being played out between nations of the world, developed and developing, over protection and exploitation of resources have raised and brought forward the conflicting and contentious histories of resource sharing into focus.

Admittedly, environment and politics have shared a determining relationship in defining policies, protection and usage. We have looked at continuities and change and marked the advent of colonialism and imperialism as a real watershed. But the relationship between people/communities and environment has always been tenuous and based on understanding and tolerance and also aggression. It is also based on our notions of civilization and progress. Environmental history, therefore, has moved out of forests, rivers and wildlife and began to cover the study of climate, agriculture and economic practices of the people. The growing anxieties of the scientific community about ozone layer depletion have also become a concern of the environmentalists. It has led historians to trace the historical roots of the crisis in the man–environment relations. Indeed, due to our obsession with political history, we know precious little about the impact of European colonialism on environment, ramifications of liberalization and globalization of the post-colonial economies. In fact, no aspect of human life has been left untouched by the devastation brought about on our environment. There is no water in the river. Even if there is, it is polluted with intoxicants, seas and oceans have become the dumping ground of nuclear and such wastes, streams blocked, rains reduced, forest covers depleted, wildlife dwindled, concrete jungles replaced green fields and natural water-bodies, desertification of landscapes happened. It had its own impact on human life as well. Drought, flood, dust storm, landslide, water shortage, agricultural decline and food crisis, starvation and epidemic followed. The Earth and its inhabitants are currently in its most devastating man-made crisis for survival. Environmental history has emerged from this crisis. Its objective is to not only provide a narrative of the past but also understand that what has happened in the past is linked inextricably to its present and future. Attention should be drawn to the gathering of the ominous signs of environmental catastrophe that loomed imminent on Southeast Asia, with special reference to Northeast India. It is in this backdrop, this chapter proposes to deliberate on the global challenges to environment and relate them to the North Eastern Region (NER).

Northeast India is called nature's gift to India. It is mountainous, thickly forested, nourished by massive rainfall, has massive rivers, has a diverse wildlife inhabited by a number of forest dwellers called tribes who cherish environmentalist ethos. Yet, environmental history in Northeast India has yet to take off. The region has been experiencing environmental depletion, which is a result of colonial policies, exploitation of its ecological and mineral resources, large-scale transborder immigration and settlement of people, establishment of plantation industry through deforestation, dependence of dairy industry on grazing and so on. There is an urgency that the historical process that led to the environmental degrdation is investigated so that measures could be taken to prevent further devastation of the environment of the region.

Ominous Signs

The first ominous signs of the impact of global climatic change on Northeast India were the long dry spells over the region even during monsoon period. The entire Northeast, climatically, falls within the high rainfall zone. Drought has been virtually unknown to the region. Rather, it was the devastating floods and inundation that were characteristic of the region. Ironically, in the Copenhagen conference in 2009, it was Assam's flood that was discussed as part of the discussion of the impact of climate change over South Asia, at a time when the region was actually going through spells of drought.[1] In fact, in the year 2008, Assam was declared by the State as 'drought affected'. In the same year, however, there was flood surprisingly in the month of October when monsoon was already over. The irregularity and irrational behaviour of the monsoon were beginning to be evident from

---

[1] See report on the Copenhagen Conference, 2009.

the turn of the century. The city of Guwahati has been experiencing massive dust storms regularly during March–April every year for the past 3 years; the intensity of these dust storms has been increasing every year. The dust storms were so severe that they brought life to a standstill. Massive dust covers reduced visibility even within the range of few meters. They stopped pedestrians on the way; vehicular traffic came to a halt and air traffic was disrupted for almost a week. Schools were declared shut for days and life was halted periodically during such storm. Such dust storm was characteristic of only a desert area, not a hilly rainfall area. The people of Assam now have begun to expect it every year around March–April.

Similarly, the highest rainfall spot of the world, Cherrapunji (locally known as Sohra), was experiencing spells of dry seasons frequently. Climatologists had already been discussing and monitoring the rainfall. They observed that the average rainfall decline was not much, though there were severe dry spells in some years. Deficit of rainfall coupled with massive potable water had become a problem of the people of Cherrapunji, who were used to living in a high rainfall zone. The acuteness of the problem was understood when Cherrapunji was declared to be no longer the recipient of highest rainfall and a nearby village Mawsynram was declared to be that spot. Soon after that shifted to a place in South America. Cherrapunji is now battling to not only come to terms with the lost glory but also manage its drinking water problem.[2]

Near Cherrapunji, there is another hill station called Jatinga, which is known for strange bird behaviour. By the end of the monsoon, around October–November every year, birds flying in massive numbers at night would be attracted to the flame of the torch that villagers used to light, whereupon they were caught and killed by the villagers. Jatinga, therefore, came to be known as place of suicidal birds, where tourists visited to observe the phenomenon and ornithologists visited to study the phenomenon. It was believed that these birds were migratory birds, which used to be confused by the lit torches as dawn and flew into the burning flames only to be burnt or hurt. But for the past several years, despite the best efforts of the government and people to attract the birds, birds have not been visiting Jatinga. It is believed that due to the change in the climate, the birds have changed their migratory routes or have perished.

---

[2] For details, see Sajal Nag, *Rain, Rain, Come Again: History of Rainfall, Deforestation and Water Scarcity in Cherrapunji, the Rainiest spot in the Globe* (Guwahati: ICHR, 2008).

The small northeastern state of Manipur is ecologically diverse and rich. The plains of the state are surrounded by hills, while they are dotted with rivers and natural lakes. The small natural lakes called *pat* are an amazing ecological gift of the nature to Manipur playing a significant role in the livelihood practices of people.[3] There are about 155 *pats* or patches of wetlands covering over 2.37 per cent of the state's entire geographical area. The largest of them is known as the Loktak, which includes four wetlands such as Sona pat, Laphu pat, Thaunamcha pat and Utra pat. Loktak is the largest fresh water lake in northeastern India. The lake also includes unique Keibul Lamjao floating park, spreading over an area of 24,672 ha, containing some endangered animal and aquatic species. Most of them are on the verge of extinction and fast disappearing. Meanwhile, another threat has emerged in Manipur in recent times. It has been observed that for some time, hurricane-like strong tropical winds lash out Manipur quite regularly. This storm-like phenomenon is presumed to have been originated from somewhere in the Middle Eastern (Arab) countries to reach Manipur in between April–May, every year from 2008. This has uprooted standing crops in hundreds of hectares besides destroying houses in past few years. In contrast, floods have become a regular occurrence during October–November, when the monsoon have long gone. It is a clear sign of climate change, palpably observed even by common people not just the experts and climatologists.

It is already established by the scientific community that global warming and climate change have resulted in the melting of glaciers in the Himalayas, which are retreating at an average rate of 15 m per year. This is in accordance with the rapid warming recorded at the Himalayan climate stations since the 1970s.[4] Gangotri glacier, the head stream of river Ganga, the life stream of entire North India, has been receding at an alarming rate of 28 m per year. It could have devastating consequences. As the climate gets warmer, the glaciers are likely to melt at a much faster rate, increasing the water flows in the rivers during summer and inundating widespread area along the banks. This would be a regular phenomenon initially for few decades. But as the glaciers dry up, the flow would reduce, progressively leading to the drying up of the river and resulting in acute water crisis. The scientific community has already warned about the consequence as widespread

---

[3] Sobhapati Samom, 'Dying Wetands of Manipur', *North East Sun*, 16–31 January 2011, 8–11.

[4] M. K. Chakma, 'Environmental Thwart will Wreck North East', *Look East*, Kolkata, October 2010, 12–13.

water scarcity due to decrease of glacial contribution in the other river basins like Indus and Brahmaputra river systems known as Yarlung Jhangbo in Tibet, China and some its tributaries like the Subansiri and the Jia Bharali. This could be compounded by the accompanying alarming phenomenon of declining rainfall of 11 mm per decade in this high rainfall region. At this stage, an effort to relate such predictions of the scientific community with some of the recent cyclic events of natural calamity in this region seems to be a meaningful exercise. The case of immense draught in Assam in the years 2005 and 2006 may be mentioned here as a reference point. It had created havoc in the life of agricultural community, as more than 75 per cent of the 26 million people of the state of Assam are associated with agriculture for their livelihood. The IPCC (International Panel on Climate Change) Report of 2007 also recognized it as a signature of climatic change, as rainfall in the region has been observed to be nearly 40 per cent below normal. [5] In other states of the region too there was 30–40 per cent short of normal rainfall except in Mizoram. Apart from the incidence of draught, the region also witnessed the incidence of devastating flash floods resulting from cloudbursts in recent times. It may be mentioned that, in 2004, there were two unwarranted flash floods in Goalpara and Sonitpur districts of Assam, resulting in huge devastation, which were reportedly caused by cloudbursts of unprecedented intensity not known in the region's history. These floods in 2004 resulted in the death of scores of people. In 2008 too, there were similar flash floods in the Lakhimpur district of Assam, resulting in the swelling of rivers like Ranganadi, Singra, Dikrong and Kakoi. The wrath of nature caused the death of about 20 people and inundating more than 50 villages, leading to the displacement of 10,000 people. The cause of the flood was traced to the cloudbursts and sudden downpour in the hills of Arunachal Pradesh, which bordered these Assam districts. In this context, it is important to remind that the scientific community already predicted that with climatic change, new and numerous glacial lakes could be formed in Nepal, Bhutan and Tibet Himalayas, which would in turn increase the possibility of glacial outbursts and consequent unprecedented inundation. Along with floods, the incident of landslides in the upland river courses in the Himalayan region may also cause formation of landslide dams. This could result in more frequent flash floods in the downstream with greater devastating power, which would be caused by the outburst of such landslides dams in the days ahead.

_____

[5] *Look East*, 'Report on the Regional Consultation on Combating Climate Change in the North Eastern and Lower Himalayan Regions of India', *Look East*, October 2010, 16–18.

Invisible Terminator

This has now been confirmed that the Northeast is heading for major spells of drought. A new study analysing the summer monsoon rainfall in the region as well as in the rest of the country beginning from 2000 has shown that the probability of drought-like situation in Northeast India was 54 per cent, whereas it was only 27 per cent in the traditionally arid zones of Kutch, Saurashtra in Gujarat and desert areas of Rajasthan.[6] The report said 'this is a surprise because the north has been considered a region of rainfall abundance'.[7] The climatic record shows that the NER of India, which is historically the wettest region of the country, has experienced spells of drought more frequently than even the arid and rainfall short region of western India in the past one and a half decade. The finding also cautioned that this trend has serious implications for crop productivity in the region. The research seems to support the contention of another study conducted at the Space Application Centre, Ahmedabad by Parida and Bankim Chandra Oinam of the National Institute of Technology in Imphal, which detected a sharper decrease in the monsoon rainfall in the NER compared to the rest of India, which itself has been experiencing declining rainfall. The study had analysed the rainfall patterns and measure of soil moisture in Assam and Meghalaya, contrasting it with Kutch, Saurashtra in Gujarat and Rajasthan during the period between 2000 and 2014 and came out with the startling revelation that Assam and Meghalaya have actually experienced drought in 8 of the 15 years of study, while the western region did so only for 4 years. The researchers, however, could not confirm whether such experiences were related to the ongoing global phenomenon of climate change, but the correlation seems to be quite obvious.

Droughts are not really visible to the city and urban dwellers. Only the farmers and food growers see this, and the government agencies and meteorological agencies monitor and record them. In some tribal areas like Northeast, where dominant form of cultivation is swidden, it is often ignored. But perpetual drought not only halts food production for the years of drought but also dehydrates and desiccates farming land

---

[6] Bikash Ranjan Parida and Bankim Chandra Oinam, 'Unprecedented Drought in North East India Compared to Western India', *Current Science* 109, no. 11 (December 2015): 2121–2126.

Also see a newspaper report of study in *The Telegraph*, 'Study Rings Drought Alarm for Northeast', *The Telegraph*, Kolkata, 13 December 2015, 6.

[7] Bikash Ranjan Parida, Author of the Study in Climate change in Shiv Nadar University, quoted in *The Telegraph*, 'Study Rings Drought Alarm', 6.

permanently. Therefore it is an invisible threat, unknown to the middle and upper classes, which are not much bothered about the price rise and food shortage. Some people are not even aware that their area is undergoing, or has undergone, spells of drought, as it is sometimes subtle and slow. But for the general populace and policymakers, succeeding droughts are invisible threats looming to aggravate the agricultural prospects of the country. Drought is a hydro-meteorological natural hazard and often catastrophic in nature causing widespread impact on the society. It is defined as 'a period of abnormality dry whether sufficiently prolonged for the lack of water to cause serious hydrological imbalance in the affected area.'[8] Droughts therefore could be a massive threat to a country, which has a growing population, leading to increased demands for food, water and land. The global climatologists have provided a list of drought spells that have affected South Asia during 2000–2004, impacting over 462 million people. The list shows that the spell had impacted Western India (Gujarat and Rajasthan), Sindh and Baluchistan in Pakistan and regions in Iran and Afghanistan most severely. [9] The report shows that due to the drought spells during the period of 1980–2014, more than 832 million South Asians have been compelled to abandon their habitats.[10] The Emergency Events Database (EM-DAT)[11] of the period reported several such droughts in India, which went unnoticed by the people in the rest of the country and tackled locally. These years were 1982, 1987, 1993, 1996, 2000, 2002 and 2009, affecting more than 751 million people. This is particularly important as events of drought generally occur in India every 3 years in Western India (Gujarat and Rajasthan) and once in every 15 years in Northeast India (Assam and Meghalaya).

If we check the records, it could be seen that drought was experienced in Northeast India in places such as Bongaigaon, Cachar, Dhubri, Goalpara, Golaghat, Hailakandi, Jorhat, Kamrup, Karbi Anglong, Kokrajhar, Lakhimpur, Morigaon, Nagaon, Nalbari, Sivasagar, Sonitpur and several districts of Meghalaya consecutively during 2005 and 2006, even though these areas fall under the humid region classified as 'rare

---

[8] Parida and Oinam, 'Unprecedented Drought in North East India'.

[9] P. S. Thenkani, N. Gamage, and V. Smakhin, 'The Use of Remote Sensing Date for Drought Assessment and Monitoring in South West Asia', IWMI Research Report 85 (Colombo: IWMI, 2004), 25, cited in Parida and Oinam, 'Unprecedented Drought in North East India'.

[10] *EM-DAT: The OFDA/CRED International Disaster Database* (Brussels, Belgium: Universitie cathalique de Louvain), www.emdat.be cited in Parida and Oinam, 'Unprecedented Drought in North East India'.

[11] Ibid.

drought event zone' and its traditional frequency was once in 15 years. Following 2009, however, all the seven states of the region had experienced severe spells of drought. Assam, for example, was subjected to drought in all its 10–14 districts, which lasted for three consecutive years beginning 2009. It suggested that drought has become more frequent in recent decades.[12] There was a deficiency of almost 9 per cent rainfalls during *kharif* season in 2014, impacting 12–14 districts of the state. The shortfall affected not just the crop production but also its prized agro industry—tea. Such drought spells appear to affect people more than other hydro-meteorological natural hazards that India experiences.

The above-mentioned study is significant as it was one of pioneering attempts. It was based on the correlation between rainfall departure data compiled for two decades with that of agricultural production over western India and Northeast India. Such comparison itself was unthinkable until recently, as the two regions provide complete climatic contrasts. A meteorology-based drought index known as crop moisture index was used to detect elements of drought in Gujarat. As far as Northeast India is concerned, Assam was considered for analysis, as it was witnessing unprecedented drought-like situation during 2005–2006 and again in 2009–2011. Although underplayed by the Assam Government, it caused havoc on agricultural and horticultural crops of the state. It is the Southwest Monsoon that comprises 80 per cent of the rainfall amount in Northeast India. Therefore, rainfall departure data of the south west monsoon (June–September) and as it travelled to Assam was chosen for analysis. Assam was selected because it has a humid climate, is surrounded by hills and the massive Brahmaputra river flows from east to west. There are 27 districts in the state where paddy is the main food crop, requiring wet field and regular feeds of rainwater. The crop is also cultivated in all the three seasons—summer, winter and autumn. Besides paddy, the tea crop also requires stipulated regular feeds of rain. There are other crops like Jute and pulses. Annual flood inundation is common in the state on account of its geographical setting, high intensity rainfall and a network of connected water bodies. The study found that Assam had received about 30 per cent less rainfall than normal in the year 2006, as a result of which the paddy harvest too was less, highlighting the correlation between the two. The traditionally high yield districts such as Dhubri, Nalbari and Jorhat were the most affected. However, even after a shortfall of rains, the harvest was higher than it should have been. This is due to the

---

[12] Ibid.

fact that even during drought years, the amount of rainfall received in these high rain zones is quite high. That is the reason the impact of drought in Eastern and Western zones is varied. In traditionally high rainfall regions like Assam, a short fall was likely to have less adverse effects than an arid region like Gujarat and Rajasthan. The study also recorded that the seasonal Rainfall Departure Data and the Long-Term Average Rainfall data for Assam and Meghalaya showed that there was not a single year when there was excess rainfall, though for 10 years, the states received normal rainfall (1997–2000, 2003–2004, 2007–2008, 2012 and 2014). The same states' experienced departure rainfall was deficient for 8 years (2001–2002, 2005–2006, 2009–2011 and 2013). The years 2009 to 2011 were successive drought years for the same sites. Therefore, within these 18 years, 8 years were meteorological drought years, signifying a probability of drought as much as 44 per cent. The drought years of 2002, 2006 and 2009 were associated with impact of El Nino. During the decade 2004–2014, 27 per cent cases of drought were observed in Western India against 54 per cent in the NER, which suggested the impact of global climate change. The analysis confirmed that the effect of El Nino causing drought was relatively moderate (40–50% probability) in the recent decade, and most of the drought incidences were related to rainfall shortage during southwest monsoon.

Besides the studied states of Assam and Meghalaya, there were widespread drought in other states of Northeast India such as Manipur, Mizoram, Tripura and Arunachal Pradesh in 2009. Since most of these states are dependent on imported rice, the impact on their crop production was invisible to the people. But as 84 per cent of the cultivated area is rice producing, any rainfall deficiency could lead to complete loss of rice crop. In the absence of irrigation facilities, such drought scenario could threaten the complete collapse of paddy production. Assam is the only state which has semblance of irrigation, but that too is a merely 25 per cent against the irrigation potential of 66 per cent. The impacts of climate change may therefore intensify the vulnerability of south west monsoon rainfall. The report stated 'Since Industrial revolution, atmospheric concentration of greenhouse gases, particularly CO_2 has increased significantly. The annual mean temperatures are expected to further increase by 3–5* in NER'.[13] There is high confidence that projected rising temperature, and the resultant warming could lead to

---

[13] R. K. Chaturvedi et al., 'Multi-model Climate Change Projections for India Under Representative Concentration Pathways', *Current Science* 103 (2012): 791–802 cited in Parida and Oinam, 'Unprecedented Drought in North East India'.

more drought and desertification. IPCC[14] reported decreasing trends in annual rainfall observed across the NER. Change in temperature, owing to warming-induced summer season rainfall variability, may cause warming-induced drought, with severe impacts on agriculture and food security.[15]

The NER has long been classified as a zone of high rainfall with a subtropical and humid climate. The scientists say the drought pattern they have observed may reflect an increasing variability—the erratic behaviour—of the monsoon predicted to occur under the influence of global warming. A temperature rise is associated with global warming, which could lead to warming-induced drought and also adversely impact crop yields. In 2014, Markand Oza and C. K. Kishtwal at the Space Application Centre had analysed century-long rainfall pattern across the country and observed that the rainfall decrease is twofold steeper in the Northeast than in the rest of the country: 'the rate of decrease is steeper towards the east'.[16]

There is an official confirmation to the situation. Union Minister of DoNER (Development of North Eastern Region), Jitendra Singh stated in the Parliament on 16 December 2015 that a study predicted an overall warming, increase in precipitation with variable water yield, change in the composition of the forests, spread of Malaria in new areas and threats of its transmission for longer duration. Addressing the Lok Sabha, Singh said that nearly 2°C increase in temperature has been observed in the North East, severely affecting the environment as well as disrupting the lifestyle of the people. Quoting the Indian Network of Climate Change Assessment (INCCA) report, the minister said

the Report projects a rise in temperature in the North Eastern Region (NER) in the range of 1.8°C to 2.1°C and an increase in the mean rainfall in the order of 0.3 per cent to 3 per cent in 2030s. Projected increase of nighttime temperature may lead to decrease in the production of rice and may affect the nutritional health of the population.

---

[14] M. L. Parry et al., eds., *Climate Change 2007: Impacts, Adaptation and Vulnerability*. Contribution of Working Group II to the Fourth Assessment Report of the Intergovernmental Panel on Climate Change (Cambridge: Cambridge University Press, 2007), 976 cited in Parida and Oinam, 'Unprecedented Drought in North East India'.

[15] Parida and Oinam, 'Unprecedented Drought in North East India'.

[16] Oza and Kishtwal quoted in *The Telegraph* 'Study Rings Drought Alarm', 6.

The study has been conducted by the Indian Network of Climate Change Assessment (INCCA) to assess the impact of climate change on four key sectors of the Indian economy—agriculture, water, natural ecosystems and biodiversity. In addition, researchers observed the impact over four regions, where climate change is most sensitive in the NER. Further, human activities have vastly affected the environment. Heavy deforestation and increase precipitation events have led to soil erosion, which further risks landslides that affect agriculture (especially tea plantation) apart from killing people and disrupting lifestyle. Singh said that the government formulated the National Action Plan on Climate Change (NAPCC) in June 2008 to deal with climate change-related issues. He said that 32 states and Union territories have prepared the State Action Plan on Climate Change (SAPCC), consistent with objectives of NAPCC and incorporating State-specific vulnerabilities, adaptation needs and other priorities. 'SAPCC will be implemented by the State plans, central schemes and other sources of funding. A thematic scheme on 'Climate Change Action Programme (CCAP) with an outlay of ₹290 crores was launched during the Twelfth Five Year Plan to address the issues related to climate change', he stated. He further explained that NAPCC basically focuses on eight mainstream areas such as solar energy, enhanced energy efficiency, sustainable habitat, water, sustaining Himalayan eco systems, green India, sustainable agriculture and strategic knowledge for climate change.[17]

The maximum temperature in Guwahati was 2°C above normal in June 2009, 2–5°C above normal in July and 3–6°C above normal in September. In August, the maximum temperature was below normal. A similar pattern was observed throughout the past 3 years in the region. There is equal truant monsoon causing deficit in the rainfall (Table 12.1).

Traditional subsistence economies and access and availability of water was directly impacted by such climatic changes. Cherrapunji of Meghalaya, once world's wettest place, is increasingly facing water shortage. Umiam Lake is facing water shortage due to limited rainfall. The trend of floods in Assam and Meghalaya has become increasingly unpredictable and severe in impact. Climatologists have confirmed steady decrease in rainfall in the region. Mizoram witnessed increasing dry spells and many springs and streams are drying up with large-scale landslides. Natural wetlands were shrinking in many parts of the region. *Dipor Bil* in Guwahati and *Chatla Hawar* in Cachar are glaring examples.

---

[17] *Eastern Chronicle*, 'North East India to be Adversely Affected by Climate Change: Study', *Eastern Chronicle*, Silchar, 19 December 2015, 2.

State	Actual Rainfall (mm)	Normal Rainfall (mm)	Percentage of Departure
Nagaland	681.8	344.1	49
Meghalaya	3,148.0	5,585.7	44
Arunachal Pradesh	1,248.9	1,834.9	32
Manipur	615.9	839.3	27
Mizoram	1,086.6	1,345.1	19
Assam	1,180.3	1,434.1	18
Tripura	1,348.2	1,476.6	9

TABLE 12.1 *Rainfall Deficit in Northeastern States in 2009*

Source: *The Telegraph*, Northeast Edition, Guwahati, 10 October 2009.

In Manipur, the year 2007 witnessed two devastating floods, first one at the onset of spring and the second one at the end of summer, both leading to crisis in food production. Interestingly, the year 2009 was marked by drought, with rains coming almost at the end of the monsoon. Already floods had marred the state twice in the year 2010. One, in June and the other in September–October 2009. Salt water intrusions in freshwater supplies caused by higher water levels of Bay of Bengal and the contamination and reduction of groundwater, extinction of endangered species of plants and animals will also be some of the impacts on Northeast.

Manmade Disasters in the Making

As one travels from Shillong to Silchar along the course of river Luva, one can notice a fantastic phenomenon. The river water is muddy brown during monsoon and then turns to green as the rainy season weakens and swimming pool blue during winter. It is so beautiful that one feels like taking a deep into the water. But when one goes near the water, the villagers will warn you not to touch the water. It is poisonous. One can then notice that there are no fish in the river, not even an insect. In fact, no living organism can live in the water because the water has become acidic due to limestone quarrying in the nearby hills and open cast coal mining. The gravity of the situation is realized only when the Dimasa Student Union complained to the National Green Tribunal about the impact of coal mining in Jaintia hills on the rivers. As result of the poisoning of the river water, a number of villages such as Borkhat, Natbor, Kwator, Dem Lakang,

Pdeng Wah Khynriam, Kharkhana, Pasadwar, Lumpyngngad, Kamsing, Jalia Khala, Sangkhat and Tongseng, Sakhri, Sunappyrdi, Shymplong, Lejri, Bosara, Kuliang and some of the villages downstream of the river Myntdu and Lukha—two of the three dead rivers of Jaintia Hil—have been completely devastated. The tribals inhabiting these villages lived along the polluted rivers, who lived off the water of the river by fishing, drinking, boating and so on. But as a result of mining in Khliehriat, Ladrymbai, Rymbai, Sutnga, Wapung Lumchnong, Narpuh and even Mynthning and Semmasi, these people have been forced to leave their ancient habitat and migrate elsewhere. It was based on the complaint of two organizations from Dima Hasao, who live downstream of the river Kupli, that the National Green Tribunal ordered a complete ban of rat-hole mining and the immediate halt to transportation of coal from Meghalaya. There is ample evidence of how Acid Mine Deposit (AMD) from coal mining areas has affected the lives of the people in the villages downstream. For so long, the villages, which are pre-cariously located on steep hills and very close to the rivers, earn their livelihood from betel nuts and betel (pan) leaf plantation and fishing. But for people downstream of Lukha, their worst nightmare began in February 2007, when the river turned blue and killed every living being in the water. And the people downstream of the river Myntdu still remember with great sorrow the summer of 1984, when the water from uphill laced with poison killed hundreds and thousands of fishes of all shapes and sizes. The incident did not attract media attention because the villages were inaccessible then, but since then, life has never been the same for the people who live in these areas. If one visits the area, one can even see the tell-tale signs of the AMD on the banks of these rivers, as the rocks, sands and pebbles on the entire stretch of the rivers have a rusty colour. Even if one takes a handful of sand from the river, one can see tiny coal particles mixed with sand when one opens one's palm. Pollution of the river is due to coal mining and evidences that can be seen even by the naked eyes all over the place.

The people in these villages used to have a very close relationship with the rivers; they fish, bathe and wash in the rivers, and they know all the fishes by their names. For them Myntdu, Lukha and Kupli are not just rivers, they are part of their lives but all that is gone now. They have not only lost their livelihoods to mining; in the process, part of their culture also gradually faded away with the dead rivers. Even the river Kupli, on which there is a huge dam which supplies most of the electricity to the region, is having problems with coal par-ticles and AMD in the water producing electricity. The North Eastern Electric Power Corporation (NEEPCO) is struggling to clean the water before processing. The problem is with the pollution of rivers and the government should instead come up with strategies on how it plans to reclaim the dead rivers, particularly Kupli. The Meghalaya State Pollution Control Board report 2007–2008 on Lukha shows the problem faced by NEEPCO on the pollution of Kupli and the negative impacts of coal mining. Rat-hole mining of coal has also attracted international media from Al-Jazeera to NBC and international print media from New York Times to Christian Monitor have done stories on mining in Jaintia hills.

The situation has now taken a more serious turn with the discovery that the water supplied to the city of Shillong by Public Health Engineering Department of the Government of Meghalaya too is acidic, and hence unfit for human consumption. Over the suspicion that the water supplied to the dwellers of shilling city is drawn from some of the rivers which are polluted by the acidic dust resulted from coal mining in the area, the KHNAM (Ka Hynewtrep National Awakening Movement) had got the water tested by the Pasteur Institute of shilling, which confirmed that the water supplied to the residents of Shillong is indeed acidic. This has sent a panic signal to the people. The Pasteur Institute confirmed the acidity report saying 'we labeled the sample with a number and source of the sample is recorded to be from the clear water storage from 4.1/2 mile, Upper Shillong where the pH level is found to be 5.7 which is slightly acidic'.[18] The KHNAM too reiterated that the water samples, which were collected from the Greater Shillong Water Supply Scheme located at Upper Shillong, were found acidic from tests. A cornered state government came out with a public notification that the allegations were not true and water was indeed fit for human consumption. It stated that the source of Greater Shillong Water Supply Project is the water impounded by the Dam constructed across the River Umiew at Mawphlang. Along the banks of the river which originates at Shillong Peak and its tributary river Umtyngngar, the government notification asserted, there is no coal mining activity which possibly could pollute the river water, though there are stone and sand quarrying activities. The project is equipped with a laboratory manned 24 h a day, where the parameters of incoming raw water and outgoing treated water are monitored at regular intervals and found pH level of the Umiew River within permissible limits most of the time. Although the pH value of the incoming water was 6.5 (above permissible limit) during the period between 1 January 2016 and 15 January

---

[18] *Shillong Times*, 'Pasteur Institute Confirms Acidity Claim by KHNAM', *Shillong Times*, 18 January 2016, 1.

2016, as per government records, the pH value of the treated water was within permissible limits. It also asserted that acid level of the water was regularly monitored and hence the Shillongites need not fear.[19] What the public noticed was agreed upon by the officials that the incoming water, that is, the Umiew river water indeed had high pH value (6.5) and it failed to explain how it became acidic if there were no coal mining activity along its banks.

Deforestation and Loss of Green Cover: The Aggravator

Although climate change are a global phenomenon and has global reasons, Ozone layer depletion, are responsible for it, local reasons are no less important. Although climate change is a global phenomenon caused by global reasons such as ozone layer depletion, local reasons are equally responsible for the impact it had on the regions. For example, during 2007, 2008 and 2009, there have been regular sand storms in Assam, mainly Guwahati, during February and March. It is strange that a city that has the mighty Brahmaputra running through it has dust storms of such intensity. In 2009, it was so bad that it was like a thick fog in the middle of the day and nothing was visible within a distance of 12 feet because of the dust. Flights had to be cancelled continuously for 1 full week. It was reported that the dust storm was generated from surrounding hills of Guwahati, mainly the Khasi hills, which were completely denuded of its green cover. Without the trees, the dry grass cover was further exposed to sunlight and forest fire. *Jhumming* practices made it worse by burning the dry forests. As a result, the dry soil cover of the hills was dustified and blown away by February winds, which are strong in the region, generating the dust storm. The Northeast has a substantial part of India's remaining forests. According to some estimates, somewhere around one-third of India's forest resources is to be found in the region. The official figures speak of forest cover of 80 per cent of the total geographical area. But there is an alarming rate of forest loss estimated to be about 8 per cent annually. The Brundland Commission says worldwide we lose about 11 million acres yearly. The Northeast Indian situation is of equal alarm.

The NER is not only undulating and terrain trodden with a spread over of all types of rock from sedimentary to metamorphic, it also has objectionable land gradient at many places. Hence, it is absolutely necessary to preserve its top soil cover at any cost. The Cherrapunji region

---

[19] *Shillong Times*, 'Public Notification noCE/PHE/TB:188/2015-16-4, dated 16 Jan 2016' *Shillong Times*, 18 January 2016, 1.

has already been termed as wet desert. The hilly part of the region would in no way be able to protect or preserve its top soil under the impact of mega rainfall, unless there is adequate green coverage in the concerned areas. Hence, deforestation of the region would be synonymous with desertification as is evident from Tables 12.2–12.5.

TABLE 12.2 *Distribution of Recorded Forest Area in the NER as per State Forest Report 2003 (Area in km²)*

State	Reserved Forest Cover	Protected Forest Cover	Unclassed Forest	Total Forest Area
Arunachal Pradesh	10,178	9,535	31,826	51,540
Assam	18,060	–	8,958	27,018
Manipur	1,467	4,171	11,780	17,418
Meghalaya	1,112	12	8,372	9,496
Mizoram	7,909	3,568	5,240	16,717
Nagaland	308	508	7,813	8,629
Tripura	5,452	389	–	5,841
All India	399,919	238,434	136,387	774,740

Source: Basic Statistic (Shillong: NEC, 2008).

TABLE 12.3 *Loss of Forest Cover in 2003 Assessment Compared to 2001 (Area in sq. km)*

State	Loss Due to Shifting Cultivation	Loss Due to Other Reasons	Total	Gain Due to Natural Regeneration and Other Reasons	Net Change (Loss or Gain)
Arunachal Pradesh	925	256	1,181	155	−26
Assam	609	2,086	2,695	2,807	112
Manipur	855	108	963	1,256	293
Meghalaya	684	71	755	2,010	1,255
Mizoram	687	900	1,587	2,523	936
Nagaland	1,332	57	1,389	1,653	264
Sikkim	–	–	–	69	69
Tripura	384	1	385	1,413	1,028
All India	5,476	3,479	8,955	12,886	3,931

Source: Basic Statistic (Shillong: NEC, 2008).

TABLE 12.4 Changes in Forest Cover in Northeast India During 1990s (Area in km²)

States	1990–1991	1993–1995	1995–1997	1997–1999	Net Gain (+)/ Loss (–)
Arunachal Pradesh	−96	−40	−19	+245	+90
Assam	−243	−447	−237	−136	−1063
Manipur	−64	−63	−140	−34	−301
Meghalaya	−106	−55	−57	−24	−242
Mizoram	−156	−121	−199	−437	−757
Nagaland	+27	−57	−70	−57	−157
Tripura	+3	0	+8	+199	+210
Total	−635	−783	−316	−278	−2220

Source: Zahid Hussein, ed., *Environmental Issues of North East India* (New Delhi, Regency, 2003), 199.

TABLE 12.5 Land Cover Changes Around Sohra (Cherrapunji, from 1910 to 2002)

Land Cover	1910 km²	1910 %	1966 km²	1966 %	2002 km²	2002 %	Annual Rates of Change (%) 1910–1966	Annual Rates of Change (%) 1966–2002
Forest	6.46	12.12	3.80	7.13	2.63	4.92	−0.09	−0.06
Grassland	45.49	85.37	46.94	88.08	45.53	85.44	0.05	−0.07
Agriculture	0.16	0.30	0.00	0.00	–	–	−0.01	–
Built-up area	1.18	2.21	2.32	4.36	4.55	8.54	0.04	0.12
Quarry	–	–	0.23	0.43	0.58	1.10	–	0.02

Source: H. J. Siemlieh, *Environmental Conditions Over the Southern Parts of Meghalaya Plateau*. Paper presented in a Seminar on Environmental History and Politics in North East India, Assam University, Sichar, 16 and 17 February 2010.

Hence, arresting deforestation and spreading plantation and other agrarian activities in the possible deforested parts of the region are two essential most fundamental propositions to be realized in practice at all cost in the NER to save the region, particularly the hilly region. The deforestation issue took a critical turn and the apex court of the country had to intervene.

TABLE 12.6 *Receding Forest Cover in the Northeast as Recorded in 2003*

States	Geographic Area	Recorded Forest Area	Percentage of Forest Area	Forest Cover	Percentage of Forest Cover
Arunachal Pradesh	83,743	51,540	61.55	68,019	81.22
Assam	78,438	27,018	34.45	27,826	35.48
Manipur	22,327	17,418	78.01	27,826	77.12
Meghalaya	22,429	9,496	42.34	16,839	75.08
Mizoram	21,081	16,717	79.30	18,430	87.42
Nagaland	16,579	8,629	52.05	13,609	82.09
Sikkim	7,096	5,841	82.31	3,262	45.97
Tripura	10,486	6,293	60.01	8,093	77.18
All India	3,287,263	774,740	23.57	678,333	20.64

Source: Basic Statistic (Shillong: NEC, 2008).

In Nagaland, out of the total land areas of 1,657,900 ha, forest occupied an area of approximately 862,930 acres. The forest cover, as per forest survey of India for the year 2003, was 82.09 per cent. In 1998, it was 85.43 per cent. In 5 years, there was a decrease of 3 per cent of dense forest.[20] Both Nagaland and Meghalaya administration could do nothing about the decreasing forest cover, as more than 90 per cent land was not under its jurisdiction. Because of scheduled area provisions, Meghalaya state has control only over 4 per cent of its forest land and Nagaland only 11 per cent. At the same time, to improve the situation, the forest cover needs to be soon increased to over 60 per cent, which seems an impossibility. The receding forest cover in the Northeast as recorded in 2003 is given in Table 12.6.

The Supreme Court of India issued an interim order on 12 December 1996. The Judicial intervention surely helped in conserving the biodiversity and forest cover in the region. Ultimately, the Supreme Court disposed of the writ petition by passing an order on 15 January 1998. The judgement clearly states that felling of trees will be controlled by the government and local requirements will be met through conservation and maintenance of environment and ecology. But this is not

---

[20] S. Victor Babu, 'Ecology, Nagas and Development', in *Scheduled Tribes of North East India and Development*, ed. Th, R. Tiba (Delhi: B. R. Publishers, 2010), 123–129.

TABLE 12.7	Shifting Cultivation in Northeast Region (up to 2007)			
States	Annual Area Under Shifting Cultivation (Sq. km)	Fallow Period (Years)	Minimum Area Under Shifting Cultivation One Time or the Other (Sq. km)	No. of Families Practicing Shifting Cultivation
Arunachal Pradesh	700	3–10	2,100	54,000
Assam	696	2–10	1,392	58,000
Manipur	900	4–7	3,600	70,000
Meghalaya	530	5–7	2,650	52,290
Mizoram	630	3–4	1,890	50,000
Nagaland	190	5–8	1,913	116,046
Tripura	223	5–9	1,115	43,000

Source: Basic Statistic (Shillong: NEC, 2008).

enough as a research comment: more accountability of forest and environment department is essential.

There is the consistent threat to forest from the *jhum* (swidden cultivation) or shifting cultivation, which is widely practised all over North East India (Tables 12.6 and 12.7). Despite efforts from the respective state governments, *jhum*s are still the most practised agricultural pursuit in the region. The effect of this practice in depletion of forests is all but visible. Miles after miles of hills look barren, dry and bereft of any vegetation at all.

According to an expert committee recommendation,

All the state in NER should raise forest protection force for conservation of forests. The demand and supply gap of forests produce has to be narrowed down through alternative sources of non conventional energy as a substitute of fuel wood. ...the shifting cultivation has to be checked though terracing and semi *tangua* system...local people have to be conceived to grow bamboo which grows very quickly and can be sued by handicraft artisans similar to China.[21]

In fact, 61 species out of the 127 species of bamboo are available in India and most of them are indigenous to Northeast. According to

---

[21] *The Telegraph*, 'Climate Alert for Cachar Tea', *The Telegraph*, Guwahati, 7 July 2016, 4.

experts, the world has identified bamboo as the material for the future. Germany is doing research to find ways to extract fuel from bamboo, while China and Japan are trying to utilize bamboo as a source of charcoal. The reduction in soil erosion through afforestation/plantation/ vegetation, in turn, would reduce siltation in the rivers down below in the valley areas, thereby diminishing this disastrous impact of flood in the region in a sustained manner.

Impact on Crop Pattern

The changes in the climatic cycle are already visible to the people of Northeast India. It has come to the notice of the farming community and agriculturists that climatic cycles do not follow the earlier pattern and as such defies predictability, which is an integral part of monsoon dependent agriculture. It is for everyone to see that rainfall has become erratic, and flash floods and droughts have become frequent in the region. Such erratic climate adversely affects the agriculture, making people vulnerable to climatic conditions. The sole industry in the region is tea. Established by the Europeans in the early 19th century, the industry grew by leaps and bounds during the colonial period and survived to be the only profit-making industry in the region having a global market. A huge manpower is employed in the sector, who are dependent on the industry. But the sector is now facing grave danger from climate change. A working group on climate change has studied the impact of climatic change in the tea plantation and have come up with a warning that tea production could be hit very badly by rising temperature in the coming decades, as it is known that tea plants require cool climate, hilly terrains and tea shadows to grow. But the rising temperature and regular flooding could adversely affect its growth, threatening the sustainability of the industry. The warning was issued in a climate suitability map, a long-term future scenario grid for tea from 2020 to 2100, prepared by the Jorhat based Tea Research Association (TRA) that used global and regional circulation models. The Working group of the Food and Agriculture Organization's Inter-governmental Group on Tea published the map, which shows the effects of climate change at its 22nd meeting in Kenya during 25–27 May2016. The FAO brought out a booklet, which outlines climate change adaption strategies in India, Kenya and Sri Lanka. The report authored by R. M. Bhagat, coordinator for the working group and deputy director of the tea association stated 'it has been observed that temperature-wise, Cachar will be the most vulnerable while the rest of Assam will be moderately suitable, while precipitation-wise the south bank of Brahmaputra has more drought vulnerability and Cachar is the most flood-vulnerable'.[22] The report states that the rate of temperature increase will be faster after 2080. While the average annual maximum temperature has a decreasing trend till 2080, sharp increasing trends will be observed after that, particularly in the southern and middle parts of Assam. Assam's annual temperature is likely to increase, especially in Cachar, where it may reach up to 36°C. Cachar district of Assam has 104 tea gardens, which produced 49.03 million kg of tea in 2014–2015. In 2015–2016, it declined to 47.64 million kg. The production suffered due to adverse climate. Erosion is another major concern, and there are several tea gardens where large areas have been eroded. 'Over time these changes are expected to have implications on tea resulting in some traditional areas becoming unsuitable for cultivation. Producers will have to make considerable changes to their existing practices in order to continue to meet the global tea demand and quality requirement.'[23] It recommended that high-resolution models were required for better understanding of the vulnerability of tea growing areas in the Northeast.[24]

People in Northeast India have been experiencing the impact of these changes. Here winters have shortened, there is decrease of rainfall, increase in heat waves, rise in temperatures and decrease of migratory birds. The deficit in rainfall and increasing temperature have been immensely noticeable in the region for past few years.

Climate change has slowly begun to impact people's lives. It has attacked the food security of people. Unseasonal rains with great wind speeds, especially at a time of ripening of rice and other crops followed by long spells of dry weather when it should be raining, have devastated farmers. They can no longer depend on weather. Sensing the change in climate, and in an attempt to adapt to this changing climate, the farmers have stopped growing traditional indigenous crops because they do not yield as much as they used to. So under the auspices of Agricultural department, they have now begun growing more exotic crops in controlled conditions. But whether this coping mechanism affects biodiversity is a study not yet conducted. In most areas, the cropping patterns were rice cultivation twice in a year: Sali, variety of rice in the monsoon and Boro in the winter. But due to the change in rainfall, Sali is washed out in flood and Boro which is a dry weather crop is affected by rain in the winters.

---

[22] Ibid.
[23] Ibid.
[24] Ibid.

In Meghalaya, for instance, strawberries have become the horticulture crop of choice because they have a ready market and grow well in some of the warmer areas of the state. Another favourite crop is Jatropa—the biodiesel crop which is supposed to augment fuel needs of the country. Using fertile lands for this crop could seriously imperil the state's food security. But this shift from food crops to horticultural crops also means that the state now has to depend on neighbouring states even for the normal vegetables that it used to produce for its own use and even for export in the past. Meghalaya grew potato, cabbage, cauliflower, beans and peas besides other vegetables. Now farmers in large parts of the state complain that the pea plantation has been badly hit by sudden thunder storm, which came at a time when the plants were flowering and required a month of sunny weather with light rains. Strong gales destroyed the flowers and there was very little crop. In the plains of Meghalaya, farmers have shifted to tomato cultivation beside many other hybrid vegetables. However, thankfully, they continue to grow the traditional crop of ginger and turmeric and it is hoped they do not shift from this yet. However, everything is not hunky-dory with the farmers. The Northeast supports 63 per cent of the country's green cover. But it is slowly depleting because of mining and other commercial activities. All minerals are located under virgin forests. But the Ministry of Environment and Forests continues to clear mining licences without setting guidelines for the miners. So the rivers of Jaintia hills have been poisoned from effluents such as sulphuric acid draining out of coal mines reducing the pH content of water to 3 per cent and 3.7 per cent, making it highly acidic for human consumption. Traces of arsenic have also been already found in the water of the area. The shift to alternative crops leading to large-scale depletion of forests has another dimension. The state sponsored support to cash crop production. The Rashtriya Krishi Vigyan Yojana (RKVY) excluded forestry, wildlife and plantations from the list of agro-industries depriving North East India to benefit from the government schmes of aid and encouragment for some of its most valuable pursuits like tea, coffee, and bamboo that are natural part of the ecology of the region (Table 12.8). So the inclusion of plantation with the RKVY as a special incentive to the region would increase the area coverage under agriculture, and that in turn would not only be a direct boost to the NER states for enhancement of plantation but would also increase the overall allocation RKVY for the NER states.

Conclusion

The Northeast has been turbulent since the time of Indian independence. Strong movements for sovereignty and autonomy rocked the

TABLE 12.8	Area Under Plantation in North Eastern Region (Area in ha)			
States	Area Under Tea in 2002	Area Under Rubber in 2002–2003	Area Under Coffee in 2003–2004	Total Area
Arunachal Pradesh	2,250	372	1,009.00	3,631.00
Assam	270,163	13,208	2,093.70	285,464.70
Manipur	950	1,708	102.00	2,760.00
Meghalaya	370	4,586	2,053.50	7,009.50
Nagaland	1,270	2,087	3,418.00	6,775.00
Tripura	6,700	28,853	1,267.85	36,820.85
Mizoram	400	696	1,006.50	2,102.50
Sikkim	300	–	–	300.00
Total Area	282,403	51,510	10,950.55	344,863.55

Source: Basic Statistic (Shillong: NEC, 2008).

region for last 70 years. Violent autonomy movements, ethnic conflicts, anti-state movements, inter-tribal and tribal–non-tribal conflicts coupled with prolonged period of martial rule by the State had virtually destabilized the region. Unlike the rest of India, the people of Northeast have very little experience of a peaceful, normal life. While the people of the region were grappling with these political problems and still wondering how to deal with issues of citizenship, statehood, democracy, there has been a silent invasion of nature. However secluded and insular life the people of the region might have led, they could not escape the impact of global climate change. The region has experienced decline in rainfall, increase in temperature, reduction of green cover, drying up of rivers and streams, dehydration of lands, acidicization of drinking water and endangering of food security without people even noticing them. Human greed has aggravated the situation further. Lands have been dug up to their core to extract coal, limestone, dust emanating from such digging poisoned the river water, aquatic organisms including fish have all died, trees felled, birds and animals hunted down, rivers are being damned and poisonous minerals like uranium are sought to be mined jeopardising the future of its own people. All these amount to only one thing: slow but total annihilation. We are facing a huge terminator in our midst, destroying its way through without we even noticing its presence.

About the Editor and Contributors

Editor

Ranjan Chakrabarti is the Vice Chancellor of Vidyasagar University, West Bengal. Professor Chakrabarti has taught history at Jadavpur University, Kolkata, and Visva-Bharati university, Santiniketan, West Bengal. A former Fulbright visiting professor at Brown University, recipient of the prestigious Charles Wallace Fellowship at the School of Oriental and African Studies, University of London, and Alexander O. Vietor Memorial Fellowship at Brown University, Professor Chakrabarti is an acclaimed historian with a keen interest in environmental history and related areas, including the history of science and technology.

Professor Chakrabarti's major publications include *A History of the Modern World: An Outline* (2012), *Terror, Crime and Punishment* (2010), *Situating Environmental History* (2007), *Does Environmental History Matter?* (2006), *Random Notes on Modern Indian History* (2006, 2008), *Space and Power in History* (2001), *Political Economy and Protest* (1997) and a coedited volume *Natural Resources, Sustainability and Humanity* (2012).

About the Contributors

M. Amirthalingam is an environmental researcher and education officer at CPR Environmental Education Centre, Chennai. He has a PhD in botany and environmental history from the University of

Madras. He is a Google Scholar, editor and co-editor of books. He has published many research articles in journals, magazines and proceedings. Dr Amirthalingam is the project coordinator of the ICHR Special Project 'Environmental History of India'. He is a project investigator of sacred groves of Tamil Nadu and their Management and All India Coordinator of Project on the Ecosystem Services provided by sacred groves in inland plains of Tamil Nadu at research centre in Chennai.

Michel Danino is a scholar of Indian civilization, author of *The Lost River: On the Trail of the Sarasvati* (2010) and *Indian Culture and India's Future* (2011). In 2015–2018, he was a member of the Indian Council of Historical Research (ICHR); he is a member of the Indian National Commission for History of Science and visiting professor at IIT Gandhinagar, where he assists its Archaeological Sciences Centre.

A. S. Gaur is a principal technical officer at CSIR-National Institute of Oceanography. He did his PhD on Maritime Archaeology of Gujarat Coast from Tamil University, Tanjavur (1999). He has been working at the Marine Archaeology Centre of the National Institute of Oceanography, Goa, since 1988. He has authored a book, co-authored three books and edited three books. Over 150 research papers have been published by him in the national and international scientific and archaeological journals.

Mili Ghose obtained MA in history from Jadavpur University. She worked as a research assistant in the ICHR special project on environmental history of India. She worked as a research fellow at Maulana Abul Kalam Azad Institute of Asian Studies (MAKAIAS) until April 2016 and has been a UGC project fellow at Jadavpur University since 2006. She has contributed as many as 20 entries on different historical places and personalities to the *Dictionary of Historical Places: Bengal, 1757–1947* (2013) and *Dictionary of Historical Personalities: Bengal, 1757–1947* (forthcoming), apart from important editorial work and overall planning of the said projects.

Nanditha Krishna is a historian, an environmentalist and a writer based in Chennai. She holds PhD in ancient Indian culture from University of Mumbai. She has been a professor and PhD research advisor at CPR Institute of Indological Research, affiliated to the University of Madras. She is the president of the C. P. Ramaswami Aiyar Foundation and founder-director of its many constituent bodies. Dr Krishna is the author of several articles and books, including *Hinduism and Nature, Sacred Plants of India* and *Sacred Animals of India*, and has documented and edited the *Ecological Traditions* of India series. She has been a member of the Indian Council of Historical Studies.

Mayank Kumar teaches history at Satyawati College (Evening), University of Delhi. His area of research is environmental history of medieval India. He has several articles published in reputed journals such as *Conservation & Society* (2005), *Studies in History* (2008, 2016), *Medieval History Journal* (2013) and *Pratiman* (2016). Dr Kumar has published a monograph *Monsoon Ecologies: Irrigation, Agriculture and Settlement Patterns in Rajasthan during the Pre-Colonial Period*. Recently, he has co-edited a volume *Revisiting the History of Medieval Rajasthan: Essays for Professor Dilbagh Singh* (2017). He was associated with Decision Centre for Desert City, Arizona State University, as a Fulbright fellow. He was a fellow at Nehru Memorial Museum and Library before availing UGC Research Award.

Nirmal Kumar Mahato is an assistant professor of history at the University of Gour Banga, India. Previously, he taught at the Department of History and Ethnography, Mizoram University. He is the author of *Sorrow Songs of Woods: Adivasi–Nature Relationship in the Anthropocene in Manbhum* (forthcoming).

Sajal Nag is a professor of modern and contemporary history at Assam University, Silchar, India. Earlier he was a Netaji Subhash Chandra Bose Distinguished Chair Professor of social sciences, Presidency University, Kolkata. He is the author of *The Uprising: Colonial State, Christian Missionaries and the Anti-Slavery Movement in North East India* (2016), *Beleaguered Nation: Making and Unmaking of the Assamese Nationality* (2016) and *Playing with Nature: Essays on Environmental History and Politics with special Reference to North East India,* 2 volumes (2016). He has co-authored *Bridging State and Nation: Politics of Peace in Nagaland and Mizoram* with Rita Manchanda and Tapan Bose (SAGE, 2015).

Anantanarayanan Raman is a professor of agricultural ecology and sustainable agriculture at Charles Sturt University, Orange Campus, New South Wales, Australia. He has been teaching for more than four decades in both India and Australia. He has published extensively in the fields of ecological physiology of plant-feeding insects, agricultural ecology and sustainable land management as evidenced in approximately 350 papers in internationally reputed professional journals and 12 research books published by leading publishers of the world. Passionately, he has been pursuing the science history—especially medical history—of colonial Madras city and the presidency. Touching on various aspects of Madras' science history, he has published 50 odd papers in *Current Science* (Bangalore), *Indian Journal of History of Science* (New Delhi), *Indian Journal of Natural Products & Resources* (New Delhi), *Archives of Natural History* (Edinburgh), *Oriental Insects* (London), *Indian Journal of Cancer* (New Delhi), *Indian Journal of Dermatology, Venereology and Leprology* (Kolkata), *The National Medical Journal of India* (New Delhi), *Insects* (London) and *Archives of Natural History* (Edinburgh).

Kakoli Sinha Ray is an associate professor of history, Lady Brabourne College, Kolkata. Dr Ray obtained her PhD degree from Jadavpur University in 2017. She specializes in environmental history with a focus on the woodlands and wildlife of India. She has completed two UGC-sponsored minor research projects titled 'Shikar, Ecological Changes and Notions of Conservation in the Raj 1850–1947' (2010) and 'Breaking Barriers and Escaping Conventionalities: Memsahibs and Shikar in Colonial India' (2017). Dr Ray has published many articles on the forests and wildlife of India and has presented papers on the same in India and abroad.

Gopa Samanta is a professor of geography, The University of Burdwan, West Bengal. Dr Samanta has worked in a number of funded research projects on small city urban phenomena with a particular focus on water. Her co-authored book *Dancing with the River: People and Life on the Chars of South Asia* was published in 2013. She is engaged in researching water in cities with a special focus on the small cities of eastern India.

Index